FEARING THE WORST

WOODROW WILSON CENTER SERIES

FEARING THE WORST

HOW KOREA TRANSFORMED

the

COLD WAR

————

SAMUEL F. WELLS JR.

Columbia University Press
New York

Columbia University Press
Publishers Since 1893
New York   Chichester, West Sussex
cup.columbia.edu

Library of Congress Cataloging-in-Publication Data
Names: Wells, Samuel F., Jr., author.
Title: Fearing the worst : how Korea transformed the Cold War / Samuel F. Wells, Jr.
Other titles: How Korea transformed the Cold War
Description: New York : Columbia University Press, [2020] | Series: Woodrow
Wilson Center Series | Includes bibliographical references and index.
Identifiers: LCCN 2019028614 (print) | LCCN 2019028615 (e-book) |
ISBN 9780231192743 (cloth) | ISBN 9780231549943 (e-book)
Subjects: LCSH: World politics—1945–1955. | World politics—1955–1965. |
Cold War. | Korean War, 1950–1953—Influence. | Korea—Strategic aspects. |
United States—Military policy. | United States—Military relations—Soviet
Union. | Soviet Union—Military relations—United States.
Classification: LCC D843 .W434 2020 (print) | LCC D843 (e-book) |
DDC 951.904/21—dc23
LC record available at https://lccn.loc.gov/2019028614
LC e-book record available at https://lccn.loc.gov/2019028615

Columbia University Press books are printed on permanent
and durable acid-free paper.
Printed in the United States of America

Cover design: Noah Arlow
Cover images: (*Top, from the left*) Mao Zedong (AP Photo), Joseph Stalin
(National Archives), Harry S Truman (White House Archives),
Kim Il-Sung (National Archives); (*Bottom*) Battle of Chosin Reservoir
(U.S. Marine Corps Archives)

FOR SHERRILL BROWN WELLS,
FOR FIFTY YEARS MY SCHOLARLY
COMPANION, MY GUIDE AND
INSPIRATION, AND THE LOVE
OF MY LIFE

It was the Korean War and not World War II that made us
a world military-political power.

CONTENTS

ACKNOWLEDGMENTS

Over the years that I have worked on this book, I have benefited from great assistance and support. First and foremost, I want to express my deep appreciation to my graduate doctor/father, the late Professor Ernest R. May of Harvard University, who introduced me to the arts of using history to analyze issues of current public policy and specifically to the multinational study of security problems. In addition to my graduate training, he brought me into the study of the "Soviet-American Strategic Arms Competition" and later into the five-nation Nuclear History Program. The late Dr. Alfred Goldberg, chief historian of the Office of the Secretary of Defense, was of great assistance in managing a complex strategic arms study, especially in gaining access to closely held government records and bringing in retired senior officials to explain to baffled young professors how the Pentagon budget process actually worked in the early 1950s. I am also indebted to my collaborators on the political decisions part of the study, Samuel R. Williamson Jr. and Steven L. Rearden, for their valuable assistance and thorough critiques of my drafts.

In my many years at the Woodrow Wilson International Center for Scholars, I have received exemplary support from a series of directors, starting with James H. Billington, and including more recently Lee H. Hamilton and Jane Harman. Former congresswoman Harman has provided special leadership in expanding the Center's outreach and in increasing joint activities with South Korea through the work of the History and Public Policy Program. My work on this project also owes a great deal to my colleagues Robert Litwak, Christian Ostermann, and my long-serving executive assistant Jane Mutnick. The staff of the Center's library—Janet Spikes, Michelle Kamalich, and Katherine Wahler—have been of immense assistance in obtaining books, articles, and documents from the Library of Congress and other repositories and databases. The Wilson Center Press director, Joseph Brinley, provided sound advice at early stages of this project, and editor Shannon Granville gave me significant assistance in refining my draft chapters. The current managing editor and business manager of Wilson Center Books, Alfred Imhoff and Suzanne Napper, have been highly efficient and supportive in preparing and producing the final manuscript.

A series of excellent student interns recruited by coordinator Krishna Aniel have been of exceptional assistance in research for my project. I could not have produced this book without their energy, language skills, and attention to detail. In order of succession they have been: Anastasia Voskresenskaya, Tamara Polyakova, Alexey Katukov, Joy Neumeyer, Evgeniya Khilji, Yong Kwon, Maria Whittle, Alex Urban, Fan Zhang, Thomas Pennington, Ryan Ricks, Sung Kim, Christie Lee, Ying Chen, Paul Mercandetti, Saule Dairabayeva, Kayla Orta, John Indergaard, Jintong Han, Brian Federov, and Jeffrey Nocton.

The staff at Columbia University Press have been outstanding in all phases of the production and presentation of the book. Special thanks go to Stephen Wesley, Christian Winting, and Kathryn Jorge for their excellent assistance and patience.

INTRODUCTION

This book shows that the Cold War shaped the development of the international system after World War II and demonstrates how this strategic confrontation between two superpowers flowed from the Korean War. The book examines the competition between the United States and the Soviet Union, each superpower's relations with its allies, and the roles of technology, intelligence, and domestic politics in the decisions of the key nations. More than any other volume, it analyzes all the major participants involved in the important turning points in the drama as the reader is taken from Washington to London, Paris, and Bonn, as well as to Moscow, Beijing, Pyongyang, and Seoul.

This study concentrates on the ways in which military and political events in Asia, Europe, and the United States interacted to militarize and escalate the Cold War. The Korean War and the manner in which American leaders interpreted Soviet and Chinese motives were the main catalysts for the transformation of US policy. The book analyzes the key decision points, using newly available documents and memoirs, and it features profiles of the principal policymakers in each area. It makes special use of materials from archives and previously restricted published works in Russia, China, and North Korea that have become accessible in recent years. These materials provide valuable insights into the reasons behind choices made by leaders in the communist countries to add to the well-researched records on the Western side.

The book focuses on the factors that produced the first major escalation of the Soviet-American strategic arms competition. It covers combat operations, American domestic politics, Soviet and Chinese policies in Korea, the transformation of NATO, Soviet and US intelligence, and biographies of leading figures such as Stalin, Mao, Kim Il-sung, Truman, Acheson, Marshall, and Kennan. It also includes profiles of lesser known but central figures including Joe McCarthy, Paul Nitze, Douglas MacArthur, Peng Dehuai, Matthew Ridgway, Robert Lovett, Andrei Tupolev, Curtis LeMay, Igor Kurchatov, and Walter Bedell Smith.

The book's title—*Fearing the Worst: How Korea Transformed the Cold War*—highlights the major aspect of my interpretation. The United States reluctantly funded massive increases in nuclear weapons, strategic bombers, and nuclear submarines because the leaders of the Truman administration concluded that Stalin was prepared to start World War III to advance his interests in Asia and Europe. In the absence of any reliable intelligence on Soviet or Chinese decisionmaking, the key people in the administration accepted the worst case as a real possibility. And they used this possibility to persuade a budget-conscious president and congress to support large increases in defense spending. What they did not know was that Stalin was consistently working to avoid war with the United States, that Mao was not a puppet of Moscow but had his own ambitious agenda in Asia, and that Kim Il-sung had convinced Stalin that he could produce a low-cost victory in Korea that would give the Soviet Union warm-water ports and a reliable client state strategically positioned to influence Japan and the states of Southeast Asia.

A parallel theme is that Soviet leaders began projects by early 1943 to build nuclear weapons and long-range bombers capable of reaching the United States. These efforts sharply accelerated in early 1946 and consumed significant scarce resources in struggling to overcome technological deficiencies and raw material shortages. In addition to providing the vast majority of weapons, ammunition, and supplies for North Korean and Chinese forces in the war, Moscow spent billions of rubles and immense human resources on strategic weapons programs. Although American intelligence specialists and policymakers were aware of these programs, they did not know they began as early as they did and underestimated

Soviet progress on nuclear weapons while overestimating the capabilities of the bombers produced. In fact, the ambitions and the defense programs advanced by Soviet leaders easily matched the worst case presented to justify the Truman administration's response to the Korean conflict.

In the years after 1989, significant new evidence of Soviet and Chinese defense plans, expenditures, and intelligence operations became available to Western researchers. Scholars such as David Holloway, N. S. Simonov, L. D. Riabeva, Evgeniy Bajanov, and Natalia Bajanova showed the surprising degree of investment and progress on nuclear weapons. L. I. Kerber and Yu. A. Ostapenko explained the intense drive to develop a long-range bomber. The historians Chen Jian, Shen Zhihua, Yafeng Xia, and Shu Guang Zhang explained how Mao Zedong decided by early July 1950 that the new People's Republic of China should fight the United States in Korea to advance its effort to lead communist revolution in Asia. In analyzing the new evidence presented by these scholars, I determined that I had to revise my interpretations on US policy decisions to reflect the fact that the threat facing Truman and his advisers was greater than I had concluded from Western records. That is what led me to the conclusion that the threat posed by the North Korean attack and the Chinese intervention, both fully supported by the Soviet Union, was *the worst case.*

Much of my professional career has focused on the study of strategy and nuclear weapons in the Cold War. My introduction to the archival study of these issues came as a member of the Executive Group which designed and supervised a large classified study for Secretary of Defense James R. Schlesinger on "The Soviet-American Strategic Arms Competition." For this project, I coauthored a special study, "High-Level Political Decisions on US Strategic Arms, 1945–1974." Work on this project convinced me that in order to understand defense policy, it was essential to master the budget process. Public documents on national strategy are largely aspirational without full information on final spending levels. It is the budget passed by Congress and signed by the president that determines force structure and weapons acquisition which in turn drives decisions on actual strategy and tactics.

An even broader perspective on nuclear policy came from being a member of the Executive Committee of a five-nation Nuclear History

Program involving former nuclear policymakers and scholars from Great Britain, France, Germany, Italy, and the United States. This program began in 1990 and operated for ten years, producing over two dozen books and monographs.

My work in the Defense Department led to a fellowship at the Woodrow Wilson International Center for Scholars in Washington, where in 1977 I was asked to create the Program on International Security Studies to explore many of the same issues in contemporary terms with a group of invited American and international scholars and officials. When the Soviet Union collapsed in 1991, a group of US scholars and I created the Cold War International History Project at the Wilson Center to investigate the documents becoming available from archives in Moscow and Central and Eastern Europe. This project collected thousands of documents from former communist governments and established the Digital Archive on the Wilson Center's website. This archive makes the documents available to the public in translated form. Unfortunately, I have to report that the valuable archives in both Russia and China have recently been closed to scholars.

I have also profited from involvement with the North Korea International Documentation Project and the Nuclear Proliferation International History Project at the Wilson Center. Both these projects have sponsored conferences and scholars in residence at the Center and have produced books from their research. In recent years, we have especially benefited from scholarly exchanges with the University of North Korean Studies in Seoul and East China Normal University in Shanghai, in addition to the Center's scholarly programs on Russia and China.

Taken together, these projects have provided opportunities for the discussion of research findings with a wide range of US and foreign officials and scholars. The documents and studies from these scholars are cited in my notes, and the interpretations advanced in my book have benefited from many interviews and debates with scholars and officials in Europe, Russia, China, and Korea. These experiences since the end of the Cold War have enabled me to analyze decisions and policies from both the communist and the Western sides to create a more complete integrated narrative. The recent information and insights from the communist side in particular have led me to revise my interpretations on a number of points.

PART I
The War

1

STALIN ENDORSES WAR IN ASIA

Joseph Stalin made a fateful decision in late January 1950. He agreed to provide limited support to a North Korean invasion of South Korea, with the conviction that this initiative would strengthen the Soviet Union's position in Asia at very little risk. The Soviet Union was recovering from the devastation of World War II and had consolidated its control over the important states of Central and Eastern Europe. The communists had just won a lengthy civil war in China, and Mao Zedong was in Moscow at this time to negotiate a treaty of alliance and economic assistance. A Soviet-sponsored regime had established firm control in North Korea, while South Korea was riven with factional disputes and intrigue against the central government. In the United States, the administration of President Harry Truman was increasingly unpopular and under attack for poor management of the economy and foreign affairs. The president and secretary of state had recently announced a new strategy for East Asia that involved withdrawing from Taiwan and South Korea.

The Soviet leader was also keenly aware that the legacies of the Great Patriotic War contained very substantial vulnerabilities. The war had caused at least 25 million deaths, including about 9 million in military action and the rest as a result of German occupation and Soviet purges. A minimum of 2 million deaths occurred in the interior controlled by the communist government. Most of these individuals died in poor conditions in Soviet labor camps; many died in deportations of the Volga Germans and Chechens, who were accused of collaboration with the Nazis; and at least 800,000 died in the three-year siege of Leningrad. Many cities west of Moscow and at least 70,000 villages and towns were destroyed, many in the scorched earth retreat ordered by Stalin. By the end of the war, the Soviet economy had lost 20 percent of its population and 25 to 33 percent of its physical wealth.[1]

Still, the effects of the war were not all negative. Much of Soviet industry in the west was dismantled as the Nazis advanced and moved to the Urals, to be reassembled under brutal conditions. The vital sectors of defense industry remained in the interior after the war—to be developed into closed, secret cities removed from all maps. These changes made defense industries more efficient by being concentrated and closer to their essential raw materials. They were also better protected from land invasion. The Soviet leaders completely reformed defense production processes during the war. They devised new methods to mass-produce rifles, artillery, tanks, and support vehicles in simple, sturdy designs. By the later stages of the war, the Soviet economy outproduced that of Germany in weapons, ammunition, and equipment. The five-year plan published in 1946 emphasized rebuilding heavy industry, including large allocations for defense. Consumer items, housing, and food supplies remained inadequate as late as the early 1950s.[2]

THE DICTATOR

By 1945, Stalin had gained full control of both the Communist Party and state power through a political system that operated on intrigue, intimidation, and terror. Starting in 1934, with the murder of Sergei Kirov, he gradually centralized authority for himself and a small group of party protégés as he eliminated his potential rivals step by step. In addition to having senior party officials tried and executed, he ordered purges of senior military leaders, which removed the most capable and experienced generals and admirals on the eve of war with Germany.[3] In her memoirs, Stalin's daughter, Svetlana Alliluyeva, describes how, after her mother's suicide in 1932, Stalin became increasingly isolated and suspicious of everyone. Specially chosen members of the secret police managed the household, cared for the children, and provided security. All his food was specially grown on a closed farm or imported, and each element was tested and certified by doctors as free of poison.[4] During the war, Stalin went to the front only once, when preparations were under way for the Smolensk offensive in August 1943.[5]

Beyond his appetite for power and his brutal methods of ruling, Stalin had more human qualities. His personality included a lighter side, although his dark inner core occasionally showed itself. Numerous observers commented on Stalin's capacity for playacting. One of his closest colleagues, Anastas Mikoyan—an original Bolshevik who remained in the inner circle through all the purges—said in his memoirs that "when in his opinion it was necessary, Stalin could be the complete master of himself, knew how to receive people and converse with them so as to cast an excellent, pleasant impression of himself. This applies to both Soviet people and, especially, foreigners." The Yugoslav communist Milovan Djilas, who visited the Soviet leader many times, said it was "impossible to separate" Stalin's role playing from his actual views. The diplomat Oleg Troyanovsky, who as a child first knew Stalin and later served as his translator, declared that the wily dictator "used his born abilities for acting as a means of achieving his political goals."[6]

Stalin loved movies, and he had his minister of cinematography build a collection of the leader's favorite adventure films with lavish amounts of blood and gore. Most of the movies were in English without subtitles, and neither Stalin nor his film master knew English, so the minister would memorize the plot and make up dialogue to accompany the film. According to Nikita Khrushchev, who attended many dinners and film sessions, Stalin would occasionally correct the minister's dialogue or provide his own "translation." Mikoyan describes one evening when the group was watching one of Stalin's favorites. The plot revolved around a criminal gang hired by the king of England to go to India and bring back treasure. The gang leader organized his men, and after several mishaps they found their gold, diamonds, and rubies. The leader decided he wanted to keep a large share for himself, so he had the rest of his crew killed. Stalin, Mikoyan reports, "was enchanted. 'Well done! How smart to do it that way!'" On another evening, the group watched a film about Ivan the Terrible, the tsar with whom Stalin most closely identified. Ivan is best known for unifying Russia by eliminating many of the higher nobility, or boyars, to win control of their land and power. "Stalin said that Ivan the Terrible didn't kill enough boyars," Mikoyan says, and "that he should have killed them all" in order to consolidate power earlier. These evenings could not have been fully enjoyable for the guests, for, as Mikoyan recalls, "No one could ever feel completely at ease with Stalin."[7]

After the war, Stalin worked less frequently in the Kremlin but stayed for long periods in one of his dachas outside the city or in the south on the Black Sea. He devoted less time to government and party affairs and spent long hours alone reading and listening to classical music. Both Troyanovsky and Vyacheslav Molotov note in their memoirs that Stalin loved to read, and he was devoted to "thick literary journals. . . . The only literature Stalin considered to be especially valuable was that which would . . . strengthen the reader's thoughts and emotions . . . [and] be useful to build socialism," remarks Troyanovsky. The Soviet leader also spent long periods listening to music. He received all the records available in Moscow, and after listening to each of them, he would rate them as good, acceptable, bad, or garbage. He would put the records in the first two categories in a jukebox given to him at the end of the war by the Americans and listen to them over and over.[8]

Increasingly, in the late 1940s, the isolated dictator revealed severe but humorous obsessions. His frequent companion Mikoyan comments: "In his last years, Stalin would from time to time display capricious stubbornness, stemming from, as it seems, his limitless power." One particularly striking episode involved Stalin's love of bananas. One day at his dacha, he tasted bananas that were not fully ripe. He asked Mikoyan why they tasted funny, and the loyal Armenian replied that it must be the result of a mistake in the controls that allowed a bunch to be shipped too early. Stalin immediately blamed Mikhail Menshikov, the minister of international trade, for doing a "bad job as minister." He demanded that the guilty party be found; but not waiting for a reply, he called Mikoyan at six the next morning with orders to fire Menshikov and fix the supply controls. When Kumykin, the chosen successor, was told of his appointment, he begged Mikoyan: "Don't do this to me, please, don't destroy me!" Apparently, a big promotion to minister was not always welcomed when it involved working directly for the Big Boss.[9]

A small group of Politburo members often did business casually over drunken, late dinners at Stalin's dacha. Both Khrushchev and Djilas describe these evenings in graphic detail. The dinners would sometimes begin as late as 10 P.M. and last for six hours, with an abundance of liquor, many toasts, and meats prepared in the Georgian style. Along with a few items of business, Stalin would organize games during the meal, usually drinking games involving music and dancing. "Stalin found it entertaining to watch the people around him get themselves into embarrassing and even disgraceful situations," Khrushchev reports. During one summer vacation by the Black Sea, the Hungarian dictator Matyas Rakosi irritated Stalin by intruding on his holiday and then made it worse by complaining that everyone at dinner was drunk. The next night, the Soviet leader responded by forcing so much wine on the Hungarian that Khrushchev feared he "would drink himself to death." The next morning, Khrushchev recalls, "Stalin was in a good mood all day and joked, 'You see what sort of a state I got him into?'" By 1948, Djilas declares that as the dinners increased in decadence, Stalin and his guests discussed less and less business.[10]

STALINIST CONTROL: THE LAST PHASE

Recognizing his physical decline, Stalin had already begun to reduce his daily responsibilities. On February 26, 1947, in explaining to the plenum of the Central Committee why he was giving up his prized post as minister of the armed forces, he declared: "I am very overworked, especially as, since the end of the war, I have had to immerse myself in civilian affairs. . . . Comrades, I am very overworked and ask that you do not oppose this. My age, too, has taken its toll." N. V. Novikov, a diplomat who had not seen Stalin since the end of the war, remarked in April 1947 that the ruler had become "an old, very tired old man." At this point, Stalin was sixty-eight years old.[11]

Under Stalin's direction, a resolution of the Council of Ministers on February 8, 1947, to some extent rationalized the relationship of the government ministries with the Communist Party. On paper, the division of authority was clear. The Council of Ministers controlled the economy, while the Politburo managed all political affairs, including government appointments, defense, foreign affairs, and internal security. But the defining feature of the new structure was that Stalin, who for the first time since the start of the war held no position in government, could define any issue he wanted as "political." Although the Council of Ministers was run by committees and with routine bureaucratic procedures, the Politburo operated completely on the basis of the dictator's personal decisions regarding membership, agendas, and the location and frequency of meetings.[12]

Complicating matters further was the shift, after Svetlana's first marriage in 1944, in Stalin's working hours to a nighttime schedule, with most Politburo business done over dinner and movies at his dacha. This meant that the key ruling group of six to eight members of the Politburo had to work at their regular duties during the day, try to steal an afternoon nap, and then remain available for a late-night summons until 4 or 5 A.M. When decisions were made at these night meetings, the resolutions would be circulated by courier to those Politburo members who had not been invited for them to sign. This tied them in a form of collective responsibility to decisions in which they had no part. Djilas, who attended at least two of these sessions, records that "a significant part of Soviet policy was shaped at these dinners. . . . It resembled a patriarchal family with a crotchety head who made his kinsfolk apprehensive."[13]

Some aspects of Stalin's earlier system of intimidation continued in his last years. In the winter of 1948–49, the Soviet leader orchestrated attacks on his two longest-serving Politburo colleagues, Molotov and Mikoyan. The charges were manufactured, and both men had experienced Stalin's brutality before. Yet the punishment, especially for Molotov, was painful and personal. Molotov's official mistake, in October 1948, was making changes in the draft Constitution of the German Democratic Republic (East Germany), which Stalin disliked and rejected. But his real offenses were being seen by many in the Communist Party as Stalin's logical successor and the fact that his wife, Polina Zhemchuzhina, had been a close and supportive friend of Stalin's wife, Nadezhda Alliluyeva, who had committed suicide in 1932. At Stalin's instigation, charges were brought against Zhemchuzhina, leading to her dismissal from a senior party position in 1939. Years later, it was her misfortune to have her name connected with the leaders of the Jewish Anti-Fascist Committee when, in the fall of 1948, they became the object of a vicious investigation by the security service. Stalin ordered Molotov to divorce his wife; and after he did so, the dictator had her expelled from the party, arrested, and finally sentenced to a labor camp. On March 4, 1949, Molotov was dismissed as foreign minister and later assigned to a third-tier job in the Bureau of Metallurgy and Geology. For his part, Mikoyan was asked by Stalin if he was not ready to move on from being minister of foreign trade, and he agreed to be replaced, thereby avoiding any investigation and charges.[14]

Stalin designed these humiliations, according to the leading scholars of the Soviet ruling group, to discipline colleagues of long standing and also to send a message to all other party and government officials. But unlike his purges of the late 1930s, Stalin tempered the punishment of these two senior colleagues. Although dismissed as ministers, both Molotov and Mikoyan "remained highly influential members of the Politburo," and they soon resumed many of the most important duties at their former ministries. Furthermore, the details of the attacks and punishments were restricted to a small group of senior party members.[15]

The Leningrad and Gosplan affairs represented a more serious episode in Soviet governance than the earlier chastising of two senior members of the Politburo. But they stemmed from the same cause—Stalin's boundless suspicions—and served the same purpose: to demonstrate the despot's unlimited power. The linked affairs began with the discovery in January 1949 of an all-Russian trade fair in Leningrad that had not been authorized by the Council of Ministers. Investigators produced evidence of a network of patronage among Leningrad party leaders, which demonstrated autonomous tendencies that prosecutors could use to charge them with being an antiparty group. Tied to the Leningrad group was Politburo member Nikolai A. Voznesensky, the head of Gosplan, which was the economic planning agency responsible for coordinating the economy's various sectors. When Stalin discovered that Voznesensky was not only a close associate of the Leningrad group but also had altered parts of the central economic plan and covered up the changes, he ordered a full inquiry.

The results of this inquiry were predictable. Stalin had placed a target on Voznesensky's back, and his Politburo rivals, Minister of the Interior Lavrenti Beria and Central Committee Secretary Georgi Malenkov, were quick to encourage their friends in the security service to dig up damning evidence. In August, five senior Leningrad officials—including Aleksei Kuznetsov, a secretary of the Central Committee—were arrested. Later, investigators discovered that secret Gosplan documents were missing, resulting in Voznesensky's arrest in October. After a year's torture and interrogation, the Leningrad Five and Voznesensky were tried in secret, found guilty, and executed on October 1, 1950. Altogether 204 officials, including a Politburo member (Voznesensky) and a secretary of the Central Committee (Kuznetsov), were sentenced to death or exiled to the gulag in these two linked affairs.[16]

In reasserting his authority over both party and government in a widely known manner, Stalin accomplished three tasks that he deemed important. He reorganized and revitalized Gosplan under new leadership. In executing two very senior officials, he demonstrated to anyone in doubt that he "still had the power and the will, over a decade after the Great Terror, to have high-level political leaders killed off." And he established complete control over the security service by eliminating Kuznetsov, who was the patron and protector of the minister of state security, Viktor Abakumov.[17]

After 1950, Stalin increasingly relied on the state security services to enforce his domination of all important aspects of Soviet life. "Always a central pillar of the dictatorship, Stalin's direct control of the secret police assumed particular importance in the leader's old age," contend Yoram Gorlizki and Oleg Khlevniuk, the leading authorities on the ruler's last years. "Although quite willing to excuse himself from secondary commitments, Stalin would not let the direction of the security services out of his clutches for a moment."[18] Agents from the security services produced, and often fabricated, evidence of violations, and then they organized prosecutions in the frequent purges of party and government agencies. They devoted special attention to the top leaders, including members of the powerful ruling group. The Ministry of State Security provided 24-hour guards and protection for all senior officials that involved drivers and special cars, the operation of a secure telephone system, delivery and decoding of memos and telegrams, inspection of food supplies, and provision of household staff. State security agents also managed additional forms of surveillance at Stalin's direction, such as the hidden microphones installed in the homes of Molotov and Mikoyan in 1950. To maintain his personal control, Stalin frequently changed top personnel in the security services. After Abakumov's protector Kuznetsov was eliminated in the Leningrad affair, for example, Stalin placed new deputies in the Ministry of State Security. When evidence surfaced that Abakumov was responsible for obstructing investigations into terrorist groups, he and several loyal deputies were removed and prosecuted. They were replaced by party officials who were fully aware that they owed their new posts to Stalin himself.[19]

As the Leningrad affair moved to its harsh conclusion, Stalin began to restructure the Politburo to provide new members to balance Beria and Malenkov, who were clearly the strongest members of the middle generation. The old Bolsheviks Molotov and Mikoyan remained in the ruling group, but with reduced influence. Due to his association with the Leningrad faction, Aleksei Kosygin was marginalized while remaining on the Politburo. Stalin created an opening to bring Khrushchev back from his period of exile from Moscow, when he had served as party chief in Ukraine. As a full member of the Politburo since 1939, Khrushchev became a secretary of the Central Committee and leader of the party in Moscow. He was a good counterweight to Beria and Malenkov, and soon joined them as a member of the ruling group. The final addition to the inner circle was Nikolai Bulganin, who had performed well after his big promotion in 1947 to replace Stalin as minister of armed forces.

The following year, he became a full member of the Politburo, and in April 1950 Stalin made him first deputy chair of the Council of Ministers, designated to chair meetings of the top committee and the full presidium of the council in Stalin's absence. For Stalin's purposes, Bulganin was an ideal first deputy. He was "an experienced, obedient, and harmless administrator." He had no agenda of his own, and he would not be considered as Stalin's successor.[20]

By July 1950, the restructured ruling group of the Politburo was complete, and it would remain in this form until the spring of 1952. The group consisted of seven senior officials, often referred to as the septet, including three longtime members and four from a later generation of party leaders. Molotov, Mikoyan, and Lazar Kaganovich represented the "old guard," and the younger members were Beria, Malenkov, Khrushchev, and Bulganin. At this stage in the dictator's life, the Politburo was an informal group that had no regular meetings and no agendas or minutes. Gorlizki and Khlevniuk, the leading specialists on Stalin's system of governance, declare that

> Politburo decisions could be taken in Stalin's office or at his dacha, in the company of the Foreign Minister or without him, by a small cabal or by Stalin alone. What lent coherence to Politburo decisions was the fact that all, at one stage or another, received Stalin's personal blessing. Stalin determined not only the content of Politburo decisions but the procedures by which these decisions were made and enacted. Stalin's approval was the glue that held the informal system of Politburo decision making together. The members of the ruling group had learned an important lesson from the Leningrad affair. They understood that their leader's arbitrary and unpredictable actions could be triggered by reports of conflict or violations of party rules, and they kept their rivalries in check and pursued a form of collective leadership without open conflict in order not to spark another purge that could sweep any of them away.[21]

Stalin's methods of centralizing power, along with his declining strength and physical isolation, meant that he frequently lacked the information and analysis necessary for making sound decisions. His top lieutenants were very hesitant to report problems or failures. The most crucial tasks often went to those of proven loyalty, but Stalin frequently moved top assistants to other posts to prevent them from becoming too powerful. Top advisers often screened information and negotiated recommendations with one another before putting problems before their leader. A final limitation on Stalin's capacity to make good decisions was the fact that he had no foreign language beyond a bit of German and little knowledge of foreign cultures or political systems.[22]

The process for making policy decisions in the Soviet Union was dysfunctional during the critical period from 1948 to 1950. The supreme leader was failing physically and mentally. He would lash out at his top officials in a capricious manner at any moment. The members of the ruling group were bruised from prior attacks and afraid of taking initiatives for fear of being purged. There were increasing signs of unrest among Soviet citizens long deprived of adequate food, housing, and personal security. Dissent was also rising in the states of Central and Eastern Europe, which provided the Soviet Union with a significant barrier against another invasion from the West. The major question in international affairs was how the Soviet leadership would respond to these challenges.

FOREIGN POLICY PRIORITIES

Stalin's foremost objective in foreign policy was to maintain control of Central and Eastern Europe in order to prevent a military threat from the Western powers, especially a revived Germany. In the summer of 1947, the United States' offer of economic assistance for reconstruction to all the European countries, including the Soviet Union, posed a challenge to Moscow's domination of its eastern neighbors. US secretary of state George C. Marshall proposed the aid program, which would become known as the Marshall Plan, in a commencement speech at Harvard University on June 5. The US State Department invited the European governments to develop a comprehensive program with specific recommendations to respond to Marshall's proposal. The British and French foreign ministers arranged a meeting in Paris in late June, and they invited the Soviet Union to join them in starting to develop a request. Molotov joined the meeting, bringing a delegation of a hundred officials with him. But the Soviet foreign minister's interest soon dissolved when he discovered that, at US insistence, the British and French would include capitalist elements in the proposal for assistance and that aid to the Western occupation zones of Germany was a central goal of the plan. Stalin himself became outraged when the Polish and Czech governments expressed strong interest in joining the Marshall Plan. In early July, the Soviet leader ordered the Central and Eastern European governments not to participate in the US program. As Klement Gottwald, the communist leader of Czechoslovakia, explained to his government, "the Soviet Union would regard our participation as a break in the front of the Slav states and as an act specifically aimed against the USSR."[23]

The fall of 1947 saw a further hardening of Soviet policy toward the West. Security police and censors increased pressure on dissidents and intellectuals to obey the official line, and government and party bureaucrats launched a propaganda campaign against the Marshall Plan, which reached a new extreme by comparing Truman to Hitler. In September, Moscow created the Communist Information Bureau (the Cominform) to coordinate the activities of all the European communist parties, both in the East and West. The new organization was headed by Andrei Zhdanov, a member of the Soviet Politburo ruling group and a protégé of Stalin. At its initial meeting, the Cominform leadership directed the French and Italian communist parties to stage a series of violent strikes to destabilize their governments and disrupt the arrival of Marshall Plan assistance.[24]

Stalin's attention soon shifted to a series of independent actions by the communist leader of Yugoslavia, Josip Broz Tito. Among the transgressions of this Balkan strongman were support for the communist revolt against the Greek government and the movement of troops into Albania to prevent Greek attacks across the border in the hope of later creating a Yugoslav-Albanian confederation. Stalin summoned top Yugoslav officials, including Djilas, to Moscow for talks, and he let them know in no uncertain terms that he was displeased with these initiatives. When Tito chose to defy the Soviet demand for the control of Balkan policy, Stalin had Yugoslavia expelled from the Cominform in June 1948. "Stalin had a gift," argues William Taubman, "for turning allies (whether Yugoslavs or Americans) into enemies."[25]

The split with the strong-willed Tito had a lasting effect on Stalin. He became determined to eliminate other Central and Eastern European leaders who showed Titoist tendencies. In March 1948, the communist leaders in Czechoslovakia staged a coup and gained full control of their government. Moscow then initiated purges of communist leaders to impose Stalinist policies in Poland, Bulgaria, Czechoslovakia, and Hungary. One scholar estimates that one-fourth of the party membership in Central and Eastern European states was purged.[26]

With Central and Eastern European governments under firm control, Stalin concentrated his energy on Germany. His policy objective was to reunify Germany after the occupation ended and to keep it demilitarized and tied as closely as possible to Moscow. Under Allied occupation, the three Western powers and the Soviet Union each had zones of occupation in both the country and in Berlin, which lay 110 miles deep inside the Soviet zone. Soviet leaders were already concerned about increasing evidence of Western resolve. Support from Washington, mainly from the newly formed Central Intelligence Agency, helped the Christian Democrats defeat the Communist Party in hard-fought elections in Italy in March 1948. In the same month, five Western nations (Britain, France, Belgium, the Netherlands, and Luxembourg) signed a defensive alliance called the Brussels Pact to calm fears, especially in France, that Soviet threats might force a US withdrawal from Europe. The Truman administration pledged to support this agreement and helped sponsor what became the bipartisan Vandenberg Resolution in the US Senate, which endorsed such regional security treaties.

The three Western powers occupying Germany were also well advanced in negotiating currency reform to link their zones as a key step toward creating a separate West German government. After the Soviets encouraged a communist coup in Prague and restricted Western rail access to Berlin in March, the Western powers moved ahead with currency reform, and on June 18 they announced their plan to introduce the new deutsche mark in the three Western zones. The Soviets responded immediately by declaring that all zones in Berlin would use a new Soviet currency. On June 23, the Western powers extended the use of the deutsche mark to their zones in Berlin; the next day, the Soviet Union blocked all land and water access to Berlin and cut off electricity to the Western zones.[27]

The Western response to the Berlin Blockade was not what Stalin wanted or expected. Instead of seeking negotiations, the United States and Great Britain launched a massive airlift to resupply their sectors of the city. For more than ten months, the airlift kept over 2 million Berlin occupants supplied with food and fuel, with an average of 130 planes making 250 daily round trips to Tempelhof Airfield in Berlin. Finally acknowledging defeat, the Soviet Union lifted the blockade on May 12, 1949. US officials had misread Stalin's intentions, thinking he wanted to push Western forces out of Berlin, and ultimately out of Germany. But the Soviet leader sought negotiations and concessions from the West on the future status of Germany. Talks were held, and the Soviet negotiators waxed first warm and then cold when the West proved unyielding.

Meanwhile, the Cominform, working through the French Communist Party, launched a peace offensive to undermine support for an alliance and then turned to an attack on nationalism, calling for a pledge to never fight against the Soviet Union on behalf of British and American imperialism. Both efforts failed and only added to the suspicion and anxiety created by the Berlin Blockade. In April 1949, the nations of Western Europe joined the United States and Canada in forming the North Atlantic Treaty Organization (NATO). The next month, the Western powers took another major step in their grand strategy for defending Europe. The Federal Republic of Germany (West Germany) was created with the promulgation of its Basic Law on May 23. Elections for the Bundestag were held in August, and the new legislature elected Konrad Adenauer as chancellor by a single vote in September. Stalin's policy of threats and intimidation had failed. His two main goals in Germany—a unified country and prevention of a Western alliance that included the

United States—were thwarted, and West Germany was well on its way to becoming a central partner in NATO, the West's transatlantic alliance.[28]

The spring and summer of 1949 delivered some reversals for Stalin's postwar strategy. The use of Marshall Plan aid to suppress attempts by national communist parties to destabilize Western Europe, the failure of the Berlin Blockade, the creation of the Brussels Pact and NATO, and the founding of a separate West German state were all serious blows to Moscow's goals in Europe. But there were some rays of hope, and they began to shine more brightly by the fall of 1949. Two positive developments resulted from Soviet initiatives. Soviet scientists successfully tested the country's first atomic bomb on August 29, 1949, and President Truman announced this event to the world on September 23. The other welcome accomplishment was the establishment of control over Central and Eastern European states, including the formation of the German Democratic Republic in October. Two other beneficial results flowed from actions outside Soviet control. The Chinese Communists declared victory in their civil war and established the People's Republic of China on October 1, 1949. The remaining gift to the Soviet leadership was the Truman administration's announcement in January 1950 of a new security policy for Asia. The president and Secretary of State Dean Acheson, who were under attack by the Republicans in Congress for the loss of China and for harboring communists in US government positions, declared a consolidated security perimeter for Asia that excluded South Korea and Taiwan from areas of designated vital interest.[29]

NEGOTIATING WITH MAO ZEDONG

While his attention was focused mainly on Europe, Stalin also had to deal with emerging challenges in Asia. The Communist victory over Nationalist forces in the Chinese Civil War came as an unwelcome surprise to Stalin, who had significant interests invested in continued Nationalist rule. In 1945, at the Yalta Conference, he had exacted large concessions in China from Franklin Roosevelt and Winston Churchill, and he had then pressured the Nationalist leader Jiang Jieshi to sign a treaty endorsing these privileges—including control of Outer Mongolia, special rights in Manchuria, a naval base in Lushun, a harbor in Dalian, and control of a railroad linking Siberia to these ports. The Soviet leader wanted to retain these concessions, and he had maintained formal diplomatic relations with the Nationalist government even after it had to evacuate its capital in Nanking in April. When the Chinese Communists were on the edge of victory in the summer of 1949, Stalin still retained his low opinion of their leader, Mao Zedong, and of Mao's peasant-based guerrilla strategy. He wanted to bring a Communist China into the Soviet Bloc, but he sought to keep Mao in a supplicant's position. He treated him coolly, never greeting him with the warm collegial phrases that he used for the Communist Party leaders of France and Italy. He never issued a grand proclamation saluting the victory of the Chinese Communist Party. The founding of the People's Republic of China was announced on October 3 on the front page of *Pravda*, the first time the Communist victory had appeared on page 1.[30]

Shortly after his victory, Mao arranged a trip to Moscow to negotiate an alliance with the Soviet Union and win commitments for economic assistance. He arrived, on his first visit outside China, on December 16, 1949 (see figure 1.1). He came with high hopes, and he would remain in the Soviet Union for two months. He was the victorious leader of the most populous member state of the communist world, and he owed the least of any party chief to Stalin for his success. Although he was aware of Stalin's brutal, imperious character, he was not prepared for the harsh greeting he received. He was welcomed by Molotov, a Politburo member and first vice premier, and the reception for his delegation was held, "not in the Great Hall of the Kremlin, but in the old Metropole Hotel, the usual place for entertaining visiting minor capitalist dignitaries."[31]

Mao was even more irritated by the early substantive exchanges between Beijing and Moscow. Although, in his telegram proposing a visit to Moscow, the Chinese leader had clearly indicated his desire to revise the 1945 Sino-Soviet Treaty, Stalin refused to discuss the subject in their first two rounds of talks, contending that the Yalta agreements with the West made it undesirable, and possibly dangerous, to change

FIGURE 1.1 A celebration of Stalin's seventieth birthday, on December 21, 1949, at the Bolshoi Theater. Mao Zedong is on the Soviet leader's right, and Nikita Khrushchev is on his left.

Source: Russian State Archive of Social and Political History.

the treaty with China. Angry and frustrated, Mao sulked in his dacha for eight days, until Stalin sent Molotov and Mikoyan, another vice premier and Politburo member, to say that the Soviet leadership had agreed to negotiate a new treaty. Soviet officials worked for three weeks developing twelve draft agreements that met the approval of the Central Committee. On January 22, 1950, the key points were presented to Mao and to his newly arrived chief negotiator and diplomat, Zhou Enlai. The new Soviet proposals repackaged the elements from the 1945 treaty but offered few concessions to the Chinese.[32]

As Zhou analyzed the issues and the political environment, the Chinese approach to the negotiations changed dramatically. On January 26, the

Chinese submitted a draft agreement on all the concessions contained in the 1945 treaty. This audacious proposal shocked the Soviet negotiators because it completely restructured the negotiations. Under Zhou's guidance, the Chinese proposed that the Soviet Union give up its lease on the Lushun naval base, its rights in Dalian, and all its rights to the railroad connection from Siberia, effective with the conclusion of a peace treaty with Japan, or by the end of 1952 in any event. Zhou sweetened the new initiative with an unrequested concession. Although Mao had previously agreed that the status of Mongolia would not be discussed, the Chinese now proposed to recognize the independence of Outer Mongolia, thus ensuring continued heavy Soviet influence. A copy of the agreement in the Soviet archives shows that "Stalin struck out almost every word of the Chinese document." But tempers cooled, and on January 28 the Soviets returned a slightly revised draft accepting virtually all the Chinese proposals. Essentially, the Chinese won most of their negotiating objectives by linking the concession on Mongolia to the abolition of the 1945 treaty and incorporating this exchange in the new Sino-Soviet Treaty of Friendship, Alliance, and Mutual Assistance, which was signed on February 14, 1950.[33]

In his abrupt reversal, Stalin decided, for three diverse reasons, to abandon his goals in Northeast China and accept the Chinese proposal. The unexpected offer of a secure buffer in Mongolia would solve one of his principal Asian concerns. He was also aware of a growing campaign by American and British officials to lure the Chinese Communist government into strategic ties with the West, and he wanted to end the possibility of an Asian Tito by cementing an alliance with Mao. The final and most important factor in the Soviet dictator's decision was his conception of a new policy for Korea. If properly planned and executed, he saw a way to gain his goal of warm-water ports in East Asia, have a dependent ally in control of the Korean Peninsula, and build a bulwark against future influence of a revived Japan on the Asian mainland.[34]

The new leader of North Korea, Kim Il-sung, was eager to unify his country. He had made many requests for Soviet support for an invasion of South Korea before Stalin announced at the end of January 1950 that he was willing to begin discussions of an offensive. Kim would not have understood why Stalin changed his mind, and the Soviet leader was not in the habit of explaining his decisions to anyone, especially not to a young foreign protégé. Kim had fought Japanese forces in Korea and Manchuria as a young guerrilla commander in a Chinese unit. After the Soviet Union entered the war against Japan in August 1945, he returned to Korea with the Soviet occupation forces, wearing the uniform of a captain in the Red Army. With the sponsorship of the Soviet political commissar Colonel-General Terentii Shtykov, Kim advanced rapidly to become prime minister of the Democratic People's Republic of Korea (North Korea) when it was founded in September 1948.[35] Only thirty-six years old, the brash leader launched a series of requests, starting in March 1949 with a proposal to Stalin and other Soviet officials for approval to attack the south. Each appeal was rejected on the grounds that North Korea was not militarily prepared, the Chinese Communists were still engaged in a civil war, and US troops remained in South Korea. Then, on January 17, at a luncheon hosted by the North Korean foreign minister, Kim pleaded with now–Soviet ambassador Terentii Shtykov to help arrange a trip to Moscow to discuss an invasion of the south with Stalin. The Soviet dictator replied on January 30, directing Shtykov to tell Kim that

> I understand the dissatisfaction of Comrade Kim, but he must understand that such a large matter in regard to South Korea such as he wants to undertake needs large preparation. The matter must be organized so that there would not be too great a risk. If he wants to discuss this matter with me, then I will always be ready to receive him and discuss with him. Transmit all this to Kim Il-sung and tell him that I am ready to help him in this matter.[36]

Stalin's breathtaking reversal of Asian policy reflected his newfound confidence, stemming from breaking America's atomic monopoly. His difficult negotiations with Mao and Zhou forced him to realize that the new Chinese government would not be easy to manipulate, whereas his political commissar in Korea had carefully groomed a new leader for North Korea who should prove to be much easier to control. Knowing that he was taking some risk in this policy shift, Stalin would seek to limit his vulnerability through shrewd negotiations with Kim Il-sung.

2

KIM IL-SUNG PLANS AN ATTACK

Around midnight on August 10–11, 1945, during a late night planning session for the end of the war in the Pacific, US assistant secretary of war John J. McCloy asked Colonel Charles H. Bonesteel and Major Dean Rusk to withdraw to another office and draft a proposal for the division of the Korean Peninsula between the Soviet Union and the United States. They had 30 minutes to develop a response and only a small-scale wall map of the Far East to work with. Bonesteel pointed out that the 38th Parallel passed north of the historic capital of Seoul and divided the territory almost evenly. Although not discussed, the southern half of the country, which was destined to become the US zone of occupation, also contained two-thirds of the population, a majority of the light industry, and the most productive agricultural lands. The recommendation of the two officers to divide Korea at the 38th Parallel became US policy. Soviet leaders were not consulted.[1]

As the war ended, Korea was in chaos. Although it had not been a zone of combat, it had suffered deprivation, dislocation, and exploitation as a result of the war. After a millennium of independent existence, Korea had become a Japanese colony in 1910, and it had served as a source of manpower and war production for the Japanese military campaigns in Manchuria and China. Between 1935 and 1945, millions of Koreans—probably 20 percent of the population of 25 million—were forcibly moved from their homes to work in factories, mines, and construction sites in Manchuria, Japan, and northern Korea. Some 200,000 males were conscripted to fight in the Japanese army, and at least 50,000 young females were forced to serve the needs of the troops as "comfort women." In 1945, 2.5 million Koreans were working in Japan. After the Japanese surrender on August 14, 1945, most of these displaced Koreans returned to their towns and villages, and roughly 30,000 political and economic prisoners were released by the Japanese in southern Korea.[2]

INSTABILITY IN THE SOUTH

The abrupt ending of the war forced the American units selected to occupy southern Korea to take several weeks to reorganize before moving to their new assignment. The advance party arrived at the port of Inchon on September 8 and traveled to Seoul to accept the Japanese surrender. It took US troops another month to occupy the cities and towns of the south, and civil affairs teams did not arrive to set up local government offices until the end of October. Meanwhile, aspiring Korean leaders eager for independence proclaimed the Korean People's Republic in Seoul on September 6, and hundreds of people's committees took over management of towns and factories across the south. The activists involved with the People's Republic and the associated people's committees wanted to replace the large landowners and wealthy businessmen who had collaborated with the Japanese in managing the country as a colony. These groups contained a number of members with leftist views, and they would soon clash with US forces when they began to replace the people's committees with more established and conservative officials.[3]

In reaction to the leadership and program of the People's Republic, another Seoul political faction came together to form the Korean Democratic Party. This group included leaders with strong patriotic credentials, while some members had maintained close wartime relationships with the Japanese. Many of the leaders had been educated at top Western or Japanese universities and had held high executive positions in business and education. Many were committed Christians who had endured punishment or prison for their faith. After he returned from thirty-four years of exile in the United States, Syngman Rhee would associate himself with the Korean Democratic Party. The two parties shared the vision of building a new, nationalistic Korea with a strong central government. The top leaders of both parties had authoritarian instincts, and none were Jeffersonian democrats. The main differences between the two were over personalities and their attitude toward concentrated wealth. On the latter issue, the Korean Democratic Party was the more traditionally conservative one.[4]

US policy for Korea, especially as reflected by the State Department, favored a Soviet-American trusteeship over the whole country during a period of occupation, to be followed in several years by elections for an independent Korean government. The two occupying powers created a version of trusteeship in early 1946 as the Joint Commission, but this body was doomed from the start because neither power would accept the operating conditions for Korean institutions that the other proposed. Meanwhile, events in the two zones of occupation were proceeding toward separate governments. In the north, the chosen representatives of the Soviet commander were gradually consolidating power in the police and security services; in the south, the US commander, Lieutenant General John R. Hodge, made a series of decisions that formed the basis for an autonomous government. In the autumn of 1945, Hodge and his colleagues set up the Korean National Police (which included many holdovers from Japanese colonial rule), began the formation of an army, and brought Rhee from Hawaii to assume a leading role in Korean politics. "By early 1946," the Korean specialist Bruce Cumings asserts, "Korea was effectively divided and the two regimes, and the two leaders (Rhee and Kim Il-sung) who founded the respective Korean states in 1948 were effectively in place."[5]

As chronic Soviet-American confrontation hardened into Cold War, the Truman administration adopted the policy of containment. The president announced the basic elements of the new policy in a speech before a joint session of Congress on March 12, 1947. In what became known as the Truman Doctrine, he offered economic and military assistance to

Greece and Turkey as well as to other states "resisting attempted subjugation by armed minorities or by outside pressures." Adding weight to the new doctrine was the Marshall Plan of economic aid to reconstruct Europe announced in Secretary of State George C. Marshall's speech at the Harvard University commencement on June 5, 1947. Conflicts with leftist groups came earlier for the American occupation forces in Korea than in Europe. Faced with revolts in southwestern Korea involving leftist members of people's committees and other opponents of the occupation, General Hodge increasingly backed conservative leaders and supported firm responses to the uprising by the Korean National Police. In effect, the adoption of containment in Washington basically endorsed the antileftist policies that US occupation forces had developed in Korea during 1945 and 1946. In coming months, South Korea informally became part of the Marshall Plan assistance program, had a military advisory group, received support from the United Nations, and hosted one of the largest and most active US embassies.[6]

By early 1947, South Korean politics was a cauldron of factional disputes and violent anti-occupation protests. Rhee, brought back by the Americans as a potential conciliator between the emerging factions, had soon allied himself with the bankers and landowners of the Korean Democratic Party and worked tirelessly for an early end to the occupation and the election of a separate government. In September, a strike by more than 8,000 railroad workers in the port city of Pusan ignited widespread revolts throughout the southern provinces, with students and peasants soon joining the protests. Some members of the Korean Communist Party, along with members of the people's committees, worked to coordinate the rebellions, but their degree of influence is disputed. Strong evidence indicates that most of the peasants and village demonstrators were motivated by local grievances against landlords and the police. In any event, US military officials accepted the arguments advanced by the business leaders and police that the revolts were the work of communists directed from North Korea, and American troops assisted the national and local police in suppressing the uprisings by the end of the year. The results included about 200 policemen and perhaps 1,000 rioters killed, extensive property damage, and a shaken US commander who wanted to hand over control of the south to Korean leaders as soon as possible.[7]

During this political and social unrest, in May 1948 US officials organized and held elections for a national legislature, with the endorsement and assistance of representatives from the United Nations. Voting was conducted under the restrictive laws established by the Japanese colonial administration, which limited the ballot to landowners and taxpayers in the larger towns, with elders voting for all the members of their villages. The members of the new legislature selected Rhee as their chairman and drafted a constitution. The assembly then overwhelmingly elected Rhee as the first president of the Republic of Korea, and he took office on August 15, 1948.[8]

As the new government was being formed, revolts and demonstrations continued in South Korea, and they even grew to a level that has led many specialists on the region to conclude that a Korean civil war existed by October 1948. The most violent and destructive clashes occurred on Cheju Island, a beautiful, autonomous province about 50 miles off the southwestern tip of the Korean Peninsula. Since late 1945, people's committees had ruled this island of some 300,000 population, most of whom were farmers and fishermen with little education. In April 1947, the US occupation commander appointed a new governor with conservative views, and he used the constabulary, the police, and paramilitary youth groups to break up the control of the people's committees in the towns and villages. Widespread insurgencies broke out in April 1948 and lasted for more than a year. The rioters were protesting against greedy landlords, corrupt police and youth militia, and the elections being held to create a new South Korean government that would exercise authority over the island. Although the actual degree of communist control of the uprisings is in dispute, it is a well-established fact that the people overwhelmingly wanted to continue self-rule and opposed being governed from Seoul. When the new government came into office, President Rhee moved to assert more national control over Cheju Island, sending additional army and police forces to suppress what he called a communist uprising. As with the revolts on the mainland a year earlier, US occupation leaders accepted this interpretation and sent military units to advise and support the central government forces. The costs of the Cheju insurgency included 80,000 killed, 40,000 who fled to Japan, and the destruction of more than half the island's 400 villages.[9]

Other violent conflicts threatened the authority and stability of the new South Korean government well into 1950. A revolt related to the Cheju uprisings began in October 1948 in the southeastern port city of Yosu. This incident started with the refusal of parts of two army regiments to embark on a counterinsurgency mission to Cheju Island, and their harsh repression by government forces advised and assisted by US units. The unrest spread to other provinces and received extensive international press coverage before being quelled by the spring of 1950. At the same time, throughout 1949, there were probes and attacks between North Korean and South Korean forces along the 38th Parallel. Leaders on each side wanted to attack the other and unify the nation under one government. Especially heavy fighting developed on the Ongjing Peninsula northwest of Seoul in August 1949, resulting in a complete defeat of the South Korean forces. Altogether, more than 100,000 Koreans were killed in the southern part of the new state before the Korean War began.[10]

Confronted with endless factional disputes and frequent uprisings, the Truman administration concluded that events in South Korea were beyond American control and that the Korean Peninsula was not a vital interest for US security policy in Asia. To prevent a major attack on North Korea, the United States withheld all heavy weapons from South Korean forces, including artillery, tanks, and combat aircraft. Washington also withdrew its occupation troops by the end of June 1949, leaving only a lightly armed advisory group of about 500 officers and men. When these actions did not deter aggressive South Korean commanders from initiating most of the clashes along the border during 1949, US officials made it absolutely clear to Rhee that in case of war, no American military support would be considered unless South Korea were attacked without provocation. In approving National Security Council Report 48/2 on December 30, 1949, President Truman endorsed these policies and also confirmed the end of any assistance to noncommunist forces in China or on the island of Formosa.[11]

Meanwhile, in the northern part of the Korean Peninsula, a similar process of consolidation was going on, although for an unusual set of reasons and with considerably less violence.

THE FORMATION OF "THE SUPREME LEADER"

Kim Il-sung returned to Korea with units of the newly victorious Soviet Army on September 19, 1945. Only thirty-three years old and wearing the uniform of a Red Army captain, Kim had just been appointed deputy commandant of Pyongyang. Beyond the sixty other partisans who had fought against the Japanese and came with him to Korea, he knew no one in his new city and had no political organization. However, by February 1946, Kim became head of the new North Korean Provisional People's Committee, and he began implementing a broad program of communist reforms. The personal experience and local circumstances that combined to propel him to the leadership of the new government make a fascinating story.[12]

The man history knows as Kim Il-sung was born Kim Seongju in 1912 in a small village near Pyongyang. His father was a part-time teacher and Christian activist, and his grandfather served as a Protestant minister. In about 1917, Kim's father became involved with an anti-Japanese nationalist group and may have been imprisoned for his opposition activities. Two years later, the family moved to Manchuria, and young Kim attended a Chinese school and learned Mandarin. He returned to Korea in 1923 to attend a school run by his grandfather, but he returned to Manchuria after two years. His father died in 1926, when Kim was fourteen years old. The following year, he entered a Chinese middle school in Jilin, where he was heavily influenced by an ardent Marxist teacher who introduced him to the writings of Lenin and Marx. In 1928, Kim took part in a protest against a proposed Japanese railroad, and police records listed him as a member of the Joseon Communist Youth League. His anti-Japanese activities soon led to his arrest the next year and a sentence of several months in jail. From the fragmentary records that can be verified, we know that by the age of seventeen years, he was a member of communist anticolonial groups, was fluent in Chinese, and was ready to leave school and make his way in the chaotic region bridging Korea and Manchuria.[13]

Soon after his release from prison, Kim made an important political move, from a Korean nationalist faction to the Seoul-Shanghai section of the Joseon Communist Party. His new affiliation would, in future years, position him to win the crucial support of the Soviet officials who would occupy northern Korea. To cement his new relationship, he joined a communist guerrilla unit in Jilin and began active operations when the Japanese invaded Manchuria in September 1931. After Japanese troops defeated his group, the survivors were ordered to join the Chinese Communist Party. Moving to a Chinese guerrilla unit, Kim soon won command of a small force in April 1932, rose rapidly, and became commander of an undersized division. When several Korean leaders were accused of being Japanese spies and were executed, Kim overcame the rumors against him and retained the confidence of the Chinese leadership in Manchuria. In June 1937, Kim led a force of 200 guerrillas into Korea to attack a police station in the small town of Bocheonbo and a nearby timber camp, killing several Japanese police, capturing nine soldiers, and seizing a number of weapons. Although the number of casualties and the amount of damage were relatively modest, reports of the bold guerrilla leader's exploits circulated across Korea and drew the attention of the Japanese military command. After the Japanese launched a concerted offensive against the guerrillas in Manchuria, Kim withdrew his entire force across the Amur River into the Soviet Union in September 1940. Two years later, Soviet officials created a new brigade, including Kim's Chinese-led unit as well as a contingent of Nanai soldiers from the Soviet Maritime Province. Starting in August 1942, Kim served as a captain in the 88th Independent Brigade of the Red Army.[14]

Contrary to North Korea's official history, Kim's return to Korea was less than auspicious. After the defeat of Germany in May 1945, the commander of the 88th Independent Brigade divided his force into Chinese and Korean units to prepare for the liberation of their respective countries from the Japanese. According to the Korean specialist Charles

Armstrong, "the Korean group chose Kim as their leader in the summer of 1945 over older and more experienced partisans," as a result of "his combination of luck, political maneuvering, and force of personality." Kim arrived in Pyongyang on September 19, 1945, with sixty of his guerrilla veterans, but his unit had not been part of the invading force and arrived over a month after Soviet forces began their occupation of Korea. The Soviet occupation authorities named Kim deputy commandant of Pyongyang, yet he was not (contrary to US and South Korean contention) Moscow's handpicked strongman for north Korea. Indeed, the Soviet Union had no plan to create a friendly communist state in north Korea, and the ill-prepared occupation force developed policies on an ad hoc basis. In general, they followed patterns applied in Central and Eastern Europe of working with local leaders in coalition governments; but in Korea, they allowed people's committees to exercise authority in local affairs for the remainder of 1945. Kim took advantage of this fluid situation and his reputation as a bold guerrilla leader to help the Soviet officials establish control in the Pyongyang area in the face of rigid resistance by local Korean nationalists, who pushed for early independence. By the end of October 1945, Kim had emerged as the preferred Korean leader for Soviet commanders.[15]

Over the next three years, Kim worked to consolidate his power and to extend central authority over the diverse range of people's committees across north Korea. On October 14, 1945, Kim addressed a crowd of some 70,000 gathered in Pyongyang to welcome the young guerrilla leader back to his homeland. With the Red Army commanders behind him, Kim was introduced by the popular nationalist leader Cho Mansik and took advantage of the opportunity to present himself as a rising leader from a new generation ready to remake Korea. Kim and Cho cooperated for a time, and Kim's support grew as more communists returned from China and the Soviet Union. On December 17, Kim became head of the northern section of the Korean Communist Party. Coalition politics ended in January 1946, and Kim became the sole recognized leader in Soviet-occupied Korea when Cho Mansik was removed from his position as head of the Council of People's Committees and placed under house arrest for refusing to accept the trusteeship imposed on Korea at the Moscow Conference of Foreign Ministers the previous month. The new leader's position was formalized when representatives of the people's committees, political parties, and social organizations held a conference to consider the creation of a provisional central government. On February 8, 1946, the conference voted unanimously to create a central administration and named Kim chairman of the North Korean Provisional People's Committee.[16]

In addition to his war experience, ambition, and malleability, Kim's relationship with two key Soviet officials played a large role in his rapid rise to power. Colonel-General Terentii F. Shtykov was the senior Communist Party official who served as political commissar of the Far Eastern Front. From 1945 to 1948, he was—in the judgment of Andrei Lankov—"the real supreme ruler of North Korea." Shtykov was the protégé and son-in-law of Andrei Zhdanov, second secretary of the Soviet Communist Party and for a time after 1945 considered the likely successor to Stalin. Shtykov met Kim during the latter's exile in the Soviet Far East and was frequently in Pyongyang starting in September 1945, until he moved there permanently the following February. Shtykov provided the critical link for the young captain between Pyongyang and Zhdanov and Stalin in Moscow. In some ways more important to Kim in everyday operations was Colonel Alexandre M. Ignatiev, the official responsible for civil administration and shaping North Korean politics. "Colonel Ignatiev was the key person," contends Kim's biographer Dae-Sook Suh, "who maneuvered Kim Il Sung into power, sustained him there, and supported him in the North." When Soviet military forces withdrew from North Korea at the end of 1948, Shtykov became the Soviet ambassador in Pyongyang and Ignatiev joined the embassy as his political adviser.[17]

As the head of the network of people's committees and with the backing of the Soviet occupation leadership, Kim moved quickly to expand his personal authority and to create a separate state. He launched significant reforms, including nationalizing heavy industry and redistributing agricultural land. A parallel effort began to promote a cult of personality for the young leader. A new university was named for Kim in July 1946; and by the next month, songs and poems about his guerrilla heroics against the Japanese were being widely publicized. These activities received support from a new network of local police recruited from the peasantry and supervised by Kim's partisans. With support from occupation officials, Kim and the Koreans who had returned from the Soviet Union established a small security force and an officer's training academy in late 1945, and by February 1948 the Korean People's Army (KPA) was authorized by the People's Assembly. Soviet forces helped Kim neutralize the only armed group that could challenge his authority. When about 2,000 Korean soldiers returned from Yenan, China, Kim and his security troops met them at the Yalu River border and disarmed them before they were allowed to enter North Korea. In preparation for the withdrawal of Soviet occupation forces, the North Korean government was founded on September 9, 1948, roughly a month after the announcement of the formation of South Korea. Kim was named prime minister of the new government, and—with the support of the Soviet Koreans, many workers and peasants, and the remaining Soviet military and diplomatic officials—he had firm control of the government.[18]

Winning leadership of the Communist Party proved to be a more difficult task. By early 1946, Kim faced serious competition for authority over the Communists in Korea. Established Communist leaders already existed in Seoul, and they were soon joined by Korean commanders from Northeast China who had fought with Mao Zedong in Yenan. Under the guidance of Colonel Ignatiev, Kim organized the separation of the North Korean Communist Party from the umbrella party in Seoul. Then he negotiated a coalition with the New Democratic Party, a group based on the Yenan communist faction, creating the Workers' Party of North Korea in August 1946. Kim Tu-bong of the Yenan group was named chairman, with Kim Il-sung as one of two vice chairmen. After separate governments were formed in North Korea and South Korea, many Communists from the south moved to North Korea to avoid arrest. After lengthy political maneuvering and some degree of coercion, the northern and southern communist parties merged in June 1949 as the Workers' Party of Korea. Kim Il-sung became chairman, and only at this time was he finally in control of both the government and the ruling party of North Korea.[19]

PREPARATION FOR WAR

As Kim Il-sung expanded his authority over the North Korean government and party, he used attacks along the border from the south as justification for increased aid from Moscow. Soviet ambassador Shtykov
reported numerous incursions by South Korean police in January and
February 1949 and emphasized the urgent need for the shipment of
arms promised to the northern army and police. In March, Kim led a
delegation to Moscow to request naval vessels and a credit of 200 million rubles for economic development. In a meeting on March 5, Stalin
questioned Kim about the border fighting and showed his strong desire
to avoid war in the near future when he declared: "The 38th Parallel
should be peaceful. It is important." The clashes at the border intensified
in May and were especially heavy on the Ongjin Peninsula in August,
when South Korean forces suffered a serious defeat. Tensions along the
parallel diminished after September, when the South Korean government turned its attention to a campaign to suppress guerrillas operating
widely through the central and eastern provinces. The brutal counterinsurgency effort lasted until the spring of 1950 and succeeded in breaking
up the guerrilla threat on the mainland and on Cheju Island, at the cost
of at least 100,000 lives. In the process, the campaign removed one of the
principal weapons Kim Il-sung counted upon in overthrowing the Rhee
government: a massive revolt in the south (see figure 2.1).[20]

Throughout 1949, Kim continued to strengthen the KPA. As early as
1947, Kim provided active support to the Chinese Communists in Manchuria by sending tens of thousands to fight as volunteers, supplying
food and weapons, and hosting Chinese units in North Korea for periods of reorganization and resupply. During the last phase of the Chinese
Civil War, between 100,000 and 150,000 Koreans gained combat experience and made important connections that would prove valuable in
coming months. In addition, the KPA trained new recruits to expand its
forces in North Korea; starting in June 1949, Moscow began transferring
large quantities of weapons from small arms to tanks and fighter aircraft
to North Korea, a process that would sharply increase after April 1950.

FIGURE 2.1 Kim Il-sung, premier of North Korea and soon to be named supreme commander of the Korean People's Army, announcing the outbreak of the Korean War to his country, June 25, 1950.

Source: AP Images.

During 1949, these volunteers began to return to North Korea with their weapons and experience with the unique Chinese forms of tactics and leadership. The Chinese Communist victory and the establishment of the People's Republic of China in October 1949 marked the start of a new era for communism in Asia. This advance, together with the successful Soviet atomic test in August of that year, emboldened Kim Il-sung to use the growing power of his partners to press harder for the support needed to attack the south and unify Korea under his leadership.[21]

At this point, as Stalin was concluding difficult negotiations with Mao Zedong, Stalin decided to revise his Asian policy and support Kim Il-sung's proposal to attack the south. On January 30, 1950, he invited the North Korean leader to visit him to discuss preparations for war.

An optimistic Kim arrived in Moscow with a sizable delegation on March 30. They stayed in the Soviet capital for over three weeks, and Kim held three substantive meetings with Stalin. The North Korean leader made a strong case that the United States would not intervene. He contended that his forces would launch a surprise attack that would capture Seoul and win the war in three days; a force of 200,000 communists would rise against the South Korean regime to support the KPA; and China, victorious in its civil war and now allied with Moscow, would help if difficulties arose. Stalin accepted Kim's arguments but said that due to challenges in Europe, the Soviet Union would not become involved in the war beyond providing supplies and military assistance in planning the attack. All preparations were to be completed by midsummer of 1950. The Soviet leader insisted that Kim consult Mao to get his approval and support as a condition of Moscow's assistance. In a blunt reiteration of this requirement, Stalin declared to Kim, according to M. S. Kapitsa, the Soviet diplomat in charge of Korean affairs: "If you should get kicked in the teeth, I shall not lift a finger. You have to ask Mao for all the help."[22]

As preparations for war continued, Kim made the critical trip to Beijing to win Mao's support for the attack. The North Korean leader and a small group of colleagues were in the Chinese capital from May 13 to 16 and met with Mao and Zhou Enlai on the evening of their arrival. Kim reported on his discussions with Stalin, emphasizing the changes in the international situation that had led the Soviet leader to endorse his plan for attacking the south. He added that he was asking now for Mao's approval, but not his assistance. Mao replied that he needed to have Stalin verify what Kim had reported. That same evening, the Soviet ambassador in Beijing cabled Mao's request, adding in conclusion: "The Chinese comrades request a speedy answer." The next day, Stalin's deceptively general reply arrived, saying only that "in the conversation with Korean comrades, Philippov [Stalin's pseudonym] and his friends expressed an opinion that due to the changed international situation, they agree with the proposals of Koreans to commence unification. With this, it was agreed that the final decision on the issue must be made jointly by Chinese and Korean comrades. In case Chinese comrades disagree, the decision must be postponed until [there could be] a new discussion. Korean comrades can inform you about details of the conversation."[23]

Over the next two days, Mao and Kim and their top advisers discussed the proposed attack on South Korea. Kim described in very general terms his plan of attack. Mao replied that he had wanted to liberate Taiwan before dealing with Korean unification, but Stalin's approval of moving first in Korea had changed his mind. The Chinese leader asked what Kim thought about the possibility of Japanese or American intervention, and Kim responded that neither was at all likely. Declaring that US involvement would be a very serious event, Mao said China would be prepared to intervene in Korea with at least three armies if the Americans entered the war and crossed the 38th Parallel. Kim thanked Mao for his offer of support but assured him it would not be necessary. On May 15, at a dinner in honor of Kim, the Korean leader reported to Soviet ambassador N. V. Roshchin in Mao's presence: "Our negotiations with comrade Mao Zedong went very smoothly. Comrade Mao Zedong completely approved the plan of the liberation. He supported what had been agreed upon in Moscow with comrade Stalin."[24]

In endorsing and supporting Kim's plan for an attack on South Korea, Stalin proceeded in a cautious manner. By committing the Soviet Union to provide only supplies and limited air support, he ensured that his nation would not become directly involved in the conflict if the attempt at forced unification went badly for North Korean forces. Conversely, Mao accepted quite casually his role as the emergency reserve force if disaster struck the North Korean invaders. Although he did check Kim's version of Stalin's endorsement of the attack, he did not probe further when he received the Soviet leader's very general statement of what he had approved. Nor did he question Kim's sketchy description of his plan of attack. At Stalin's insistence, Mao agreed to give Kim a blank check to cash if he got into trouble. This gamble was the price he paid for the tough treaty negotiations he had successfully pursued during his January–February visit to Moscow.

Given the uncertainties facing him, Kim was making a bigger bet than Mao. His plan of attack relied heavily on a large uprising in the south and on the Truman administration refusing to intervene. Although the

North Korean armed forces were superior to their South Korean rivals in weapons and combat experience, they still confronted significant challenges. The KPA had to integrate many poorly trained recruits with a large number of veterans returning from the Chinese Civil War. The troops had many different types of small arms requiring a wide variety of ammunition. The army had inadequate ground transportation to support rapid movement of forces or to supply units fighting deep into South Korean territory. And complicating all preparations, the government and army had less than three months from Kim's visit with Stalin to the planned invasion.[25]

3

TRUMAN CONSOLIDATES
US COMMITMENTS

I n the fall of 1949, Harry Truman found his once-promising administration dealing with a mountain of problems. In September, he
learned that the United States had lost its valuable monopoly of
atomic weapons when a US Air Force reconnaissance plane brought
back filters containing radioactive particles from a successful Soviet
atomic test. On October 7, the Soviet Union created the German Democratic Republic (East Germany) out of its occupation zone, thus cementing a dividing line between contending political blocs in Europe. Earlier
that same week, Mao Zedong and his comrades celebrated their victory
in the Chinese Civil War by creating the People's Republic of China.
The two major communist powers soon announced common purpose
by signing a treaty of alliance and mutual assistance in Moscow on
February 14, 1950. Events at home magnified these challenges for the
administration. Early in February, police arrested the British physicist
Klaus Fuchs for conducting atomic espionage while working on the
Manhattan Project during the war. Senator Joseph R. McCarthy (R-WI)
exploited these developments by attacking the Truman administration
for protecting communists in the government in a speech in Wheeling,
West Virginia, on February 9.[1]

The president and his cabinet were poorly positioned to deal with
these issues. The economy had fallen into recession in the spring of

1949, and by midyear Truman had decided to withdraw his proposed tax increase and to balance the budget by cutting defense spending. When an interagency committee reviewed the proposed cuts for the fiscal year 1951 budget in September, the main objections came from the State Department. The State Department's representatives fought to retain assistance funds for Japan and South Korea as well as provide military and economic aid to countries in Southeast Asia and the Middle East. At the same time, Great Britain faced a balance-of-payments crisis, and despite a 30 percent devaluation of the pound sterling in September, US officials were convinced Britain would require continued aid from Washington beyond 1952. The president and his advisers in the White House found themselves torn between their top two priorities: maintaining a strong national security posture, and balancing the budget.[2]

Things turned even more negative when reporters and Senate investigators exposed a series of gifts and special favors to members and friends of the administration, which created what the journalist Robert Donovan calls "an aura of scandal." Although the items involved were relatively minor, the series of exposés diminished Truman's capacity to lead and tarnished his reputation. In this atmosphere, a coalition of Republicans and conservative Democrats collaborated to block every item of the president's Fair Deal domestic legislative program, except for a bill to fund an expansion of low-income housing.[3]

THE UNINTENDED PRESIDENT

In June 1944, Harry Truman expected to continue serving as a US senator from Missouri until he retired to his hometown of Independence. The next month, on the eve of the Democratic National Convention, he was as surprised as anyone when President Franklin D. Roosevelt selected him to be his vice presidential running mate in the race for his fourth term for the White House. Taking account of the strong support of national party leaders and organized labor for the Missouri senator, Roosevelt chose Truman because of his loyalty to the Democratic Party and New Deal legislation, his solid Midwestern values, and his strong performance as the chairman of the Senate Special Committee to Investigate the National Defense Program. But after the Democratic ticket was elected, Truman served as vice president for only eighty-eight days before Roosevelt died suddenly and the former Missouri county commissioner became president on April 12, 1945.[4]

Although he came from a farming family of modest means and had only a high school education, Truman was a buoyant, self-confident politician who remained unpretentious and secure in who he was. He dressed neatly in double-breasted suits and wore a large Masonic ring on his left hand. Sixty years old, he kept in good physical condition with brisk morning walks. A devoted family man, he preferred dining privately with his wife Bess and daughter Margaret to Washington dinner parties. For relaxation, he enjoyed playing poker and telling stories with friends, always with a glass of bourbon and water at hand. He took special pleasure in playing the piano for visitors and in reading widely in history. He had the high respect of his colleagues and staff, and he responded with deep loyalty to them, even on occasions when they had served him poorly. But, if crossed, he could show intense anger and deliver scathing criticism. He was noted for making hard, sometimes impetuous decisions, and for being ready to live with the consequences.[5]

Truman's experience before becoming vice president left him well prepared to deal with domestic issues. He spent his early years on a farm, and, after working at several odd jobs, after he finished high school he returned to the farm to work with his father. When the United States entered World War I in 1917, Truman joined the Missouri Army National Guard, received officer training, and served in combat in France as an artillery battery commander. He remained in the National Guard after the war, became active in veterans' affairs, and he always showed great respect for the courage of soldiers and their noncommissioned officers. After an unsuccessful two-year venture running a men's clothing store in Kansas City, he became involved in local politics and won the support of Tom Pendergast, the boss of the local Democratic machine, who helped him win election in 1922 as a county commissioner. He failed in his bid for reelection in 1924, but two years later, with strong backing from the Pendergast organization, he was elected head of the board of the county's commissioners. During two terms as head of the local government, he implemented a ten-year plan that revitalized the Kansas City region with a program of public works, including a prominent new county court building. When he expressed interest in running for governor or Congress, Pendergast discouraged him and supported others. Only when four other potential candidates for the US Senate declined to run did the boss turn to Truman in 1934. He was not disappointed, as Truman defeated two representatives in the Democratic primary and then won over the Republican incumbent by 20 percent.[6]

In the US Senate, Truman loyally supported the president's legislative program without becoming a New Deal ideologue. In 1940, he won a difficult primary against two significant political figures and narrowly beat his Republican opponent in the general election by 2 percent. When he returned to Washington for his second term, he became increasingly concerned that the huge defense appropriation of over $10 billion passed the previous year was being spent wastefully and without adequate opportunities for small business owners to win federal contracts. His speeches and lobbying led to the creation of a special committee, called the Truman Committee, to investigate the war mobilization program. This committee's work brought national attention to Truman, including a cover story in *Time* in March 1943 and a spot on *Look*'s list of the ten most valuable officials in Washington in May 1944. His new prominence was a key factor in Roosevelt's choice of the Missouri senator as his vice presidential candidate; but during the three months he served in his new position, he had very little contact with the president. He had no role in the Yalta Conference in February 1945, and he was not informed about the project to develop an atomic bomb.[7]

It is deeply ironic that Truman, who had no experience in foreign affairs, found that international crises dominated his first four years as president. His initial test came after only three months in office, when he had to attend the Potsdam Conference and negotiate with Stalin and Churchill over the occupation of Germany; reparations; Polish boundaries; and the status of the former Nazi allies Italy, Hungary, Bulgaria, and Romania. Churchill and Stalin had led their nations' mobilization and strategy throughout the war and had negotiated with one another on numerous occasions. Truman was the new boy without experience either in his job as president or in international affairs. His task was further complicated when, at the start of the conference, Stalin proposed that Truman, as the only head of state and government, chair the proceedings. The conference stretched for seventeen days, beginning on July 17, 1945.

Negotiations were difficult, but Truman held his own. His hand was strengthened by the news received the day before the meetings began that the long-anticipated atomic test at Alamogordo, New Mexico, had been highly successful. Truman came to the conference with a desire to continue cooperation with the Soviet Union. He liked Stalin, who put on an effective show of cordiality and even humor on social occasions while remaining businesslike but unyielding on reparations and control of the countries of Central and Eastern Europe. From the American perspective, the negotiations achieved some progress on the terms of German occupation, and Truman easily won Stalin's pledge to enter the war against Japan at an early date. But on other issues, the Soviet position prevailed, or the failure to reach agreement was papered over by promises to continue discussing the topics in the Council of Ministers. In the last week of the conference, at the end of a plenary session, Truman casually informed Stalin that the United States had a new weapon of great destructive power, which he hoped would end the war. The Soviet dictator showed no surprise and asked no questions. He simply said that this was good news and wished the United States a positive result from the new weapon.[8]

Truman's hopes for a degree of continued cooperation with Moscow began to evaporate soon after the surrender of Japan on August 14. Almost immediately, problems developed in allocating scarce resources in the occupation of Germany, and Washington officials saw increasing evidence that Moscow would not honor their pledge at Yalta to hold free elections in Central and Eastern Europe. In February 1946, George F. Kennan, the senior American diplomat in Moscow, sent his famous "long telegram" to the State Department explaining the motives behind Soviet international policy as "a totalitarian regime bent on expansion."

He called for a steady, consistent policy of containment of Soviet power. In Central and Eastern Europe, communists began to take over power from coalition governments, and Soviet pressure threatened the stability of Iran along with Greece and Turkey. By the spring of 1946, key US officials saw the Soviet Union as the primary enemy and the source of many problems in Europe and the Middle East. By the autumn, this attitude had become a general consensus, and the Cold War had started.[9]

When the Soviet Union continued to threaten Greece and Turkey, and the British announced that they could not continue to provide economic and military support to these governments, Washington took the bold step of announcing on March 12, 1947, what became known as the Truman Doctrine. In this major speech, the president declared that the United States would "support free peoples who are resisting attempted subjugation by armed minorities or by outside pressures" and requested $400 million in economic and military assistance. Congress approved the appropriation by large majorities on May 15. This unprecedented peacetime commitment was soon followed by the Marshall Plan to stimulate European economic recovery and encourage regional cooperation and by support from the administration and the Senate for the Brussels Pact, a defensive alliance of Britain, France, and the Benelux states (Belgium, the Netherlands, and Luxembourg). When Soviet pressure on the three Western occupation zones of Berlin led in June 1948 to the blockade of all land access to the city, the United States responded with a massive airlift to provide the former German capital with food and supplies. By the late summer of 1948, Truman had launched a very promising series of programs to respond to Soviet challenges in Europe and the Middle East, but he faced daunting odds in his battle for reelection at home.[10]

When the president began his formal campaign on Labor Day, his prospects for reelection appeared bleak. The party conventions had met, and Truman survived an attempt to dump him from the head of the ticket. But the Democratic activists had split with the liberal Progressive Party, nominating former secretary of commerce Henry A. Wallace for president, while a conservative southern faction backed Governor Strom Thurmond of South Carolina on the States' Rights Democratic

Party, or "Dixiecrat," ticket. Making matters worse, most political analysts thought the president's main opponent—the Republican nominee, Governor Thomas E. Dewey of New York—was an overwhelming favorite to win. At the end of August, a study of daily newspaper editors found 65 percent prepared to endorse Dewey but only 15 percent for Truman. The prominent pollster George Gallup questioned why the Republicans wanted to pay for any advertising when the "results are a foregone conclusion." Another well-regarded expert, Elmo Roper, published no more presidential polling results after September because he was convinced that Dewey "is almost as good as elected."[11]

Truman went on the attack, with his focus on the Republican majorities in both houses of Congress. He called Congress back for a special session on inflation and economic issues in late July, and he used some of the messages he had refined on a "nonpartisan" tour of the country by train in June. In a speech to a joint session of Congress, the president called on Congress to act promptly on some of the pledges made in the Republican platform as well as some economic measures, such as controls on inflation and relief for the housing shortage. When Congress passed only two ineffective bills restoring limits on consumer credit and easing the terms of federally issued mortgages, Truman denounced them as advancing the interests of the privileged elite. He then sharpened his charges against the "do-nothing" Eightieth Congress. Toward the end of the campaign, in late October, the president delivered a scathing attack on the Republican candidate and Congress. Comparing Dewey, in Robert Donovan's words, with "the front man for fascist elements that might destroy democracy in the United States," he quoted Dewey saying that "the Eightieth Congress delivered as no other Congress ever did for the future of this country." Then he charged: "Well, I'll say it delivered. It delivered for the private power lobby. It delivered for the big oil company lobby. It delivered for the railroad lobby. It delivered for the real estate lobby. . . . Republican leaders stand ready to deliver to big business more and more control over the resources of this nation and the rights of the American people." (See figure 3.1.)

Still, on the eve of the election, virtually all political columnists and experts predicted a Dewey victory. The final Gallop poll gave the

FIGURE 3.1 On his whistle-stop reelection campaign, President Harry S Truman receives a Navajo rug from Chief Joe Deerfoot in Gallup, New Mexico, June 15, 1948.

Source: Truman Library.

Republican nominee a 5 percent lead. In the final days, Truman intercepted his special counsel Clark Clifford with a copy of *Newsweek* headlining a survey of fifty leading journalists, all of whom believed that the president would be soundly defeated. After quickly perusing the story, Truman declared, "I know every one of these fifty fellows, and not one of them has enough sense to pound sand into a rathole." As Election Day approached, the underdog president remained confident and feisty.[12]

To almost everyone's surprise, Harry Truman won a resounding victory in the Electoral College, where he received 303 votes to 189 for Dewey, 39 for Thurmond, and none for Wallace. But the election was much closer than the Electoral College margin made it appear. Only 51 percent of eligible voters cast their ballots, and many overconfident Republicans stayed at home. In the popular vote, due to defections for Thurmond and Wallace, Truman received only 49 percent, while Dewey got 45 percent. Analyses showed that the shift of a small number of votes in three states—Ohio, Illinois, and California—would have delivered victory to Dewey. Truman had been able to hold together enough of Roosevelt's New Deal coalition to win despite the loss of southern Democrats and northern progressives. The pollsters missed the shift of the farm vote to Truman in the last days of the campaign, and the Midwest and West carried the election for the president. Adding to the sweet presidential victory, the Democrats won control of both houses of Congress. Yet omens of conflict with Congress remained because the members of the Republican minority felt they had been denied a victory that was rightfully theirs.[13]

INTERNATIONAL AND FINANCIAL CHALLENGES

As the euphoria from his upset electoral victory began to subside, Truman faced hard choices at the start of his second term. He had committed the United States to globally containing Soviet communism, and at the same time he wanted to keep a balanced budget while introducing a new legislative program. His priorities required him to keep a tight ceiling on defense spending of no more than $15 billion per year. The chiefs of the military services pressed for expanding spending limits for fiscal year (FY) 1950, and in an attempt to justify an increase beyond the president's ceiling, Secretary of Defense James V. Forrestal called for a new assessment of policy toward the Soviet Union. The hawkish defense secretary hoped that the communist threat would persuade the president to loosen the purse strings. Soon after the election the National Security Council (NSC) completed the study Forrestal had wanted, and NSC Report 20/4 was discussed by the council and approved by the president on November 24, 1948. The report declared that the goal of

US policy was to prevent the Soviet Union from dominating Eurasia by reducing "the power and influence of the USSR to limits which no longer constitute a threat to the peace, national independence and stability of the world family of nations." The study provided no details on priorities, tactics to be pursued, or prospects for splits within international communism. The rhetoric of NSC 20/4 could have provided the basis for a decision to increase defense spending above the president's limit. But when Forrestal submitted two proposals for the FY 1950 defense budget—one totaling $14.4 billion within the ceiling; and a second, which he personally recommended, for $16.9 billion—Truman immediately chose the lower one. The fact was that the president was firmly committed to a balanced budget and paid close attention to budgetary details but had little interest in the basic elements of national security policy. Evaluating these decisions, Melvyn Leffler concludes: "So at one and the same time Truman vetoed Forrestal's budget and sanctioned NSC 20/4, perpetuating the gap between means and ends. In the future, this gap would not only beleaguer his foreign policy but would also play into the hands of his domestic opponents, whose bile was mounting as they licked their wounds from their 1948 defeat."[14]

When Dean Acheson returned to office in January 1949 as secretary of state for Truman's second term, he once again faced urgent problems in Western Europe. Acheson and almost all other senior diplomatic and military leaders agreed that the security and stability of Western Europe was the top priority in US international policy. In one of his first appearances before Congress, the new secretary declared to the House Committee on Foreign Affairs that "Western Europe is the keystone of the world." Administration officials were pleased that, with the aid and guidance of the Marshall Plan, European economies were reviving—but the challenges now lay in the security area, as reflected in the continuing Soviet blockade of Berlin. Acheson and his top advisers saw Germany as the cornerstone of a stable Western Europe, and they realized that the three Western zones of Berlin needed to be integrated into Atlantic institutions before occupation ended. The challenge in achieving this goal hinged on persuading the French to move beyond their deep-seated security anxieties about a revived German threat. As the Berlin airlift continued through the winter of 1948 and the following spring, negotiations advanced to create a defensive alliance that would link the United States and Canada with the members of the Brussels Pact. At a later stage, US officials expected to include the West German government in this alliance.

In his negotiations, Acheson was especially delighted to find that French foreign minister Robert Schuman shared his views about the need to reconcile with Germany and integrate the Western zones of Berlin into democratic institutions. To help the French minister convince his colleagues to support an Atlantic Alliance and an independent West German government, Acheson made two major concessions to France: including its neighbor Italy in the Alliance (a step that Truman initially opposed) and pressing Congress to pass a military assistance program to help build up the French and European armed forces. Later, Acheson declared that having Schuman as his negotiating partner was "one of the greatest strokes of luck that has come along in a long time."[15]

As the talks about forming a Western Alliance advanced, American diplomats noticed signals from Moscow that appeared to express interest in negotiations to end the Berlin Blockade. When talks began, it quickly became clear that the Soviet Union wanted to make a deal to lift the blockade in exchange for stopping, or at least delaying, the creation of the West German government. US officials contended that the Allied counterblockade of trade with the Soviet zone was both economically and politically more costly to Moscow than the Soviet blockade was to the Western powers, and they persuaded the British and French governments to join in insisting on the termination of the Soviet blockade first without linking it to the future status of Germany. The Western nations also moved ahead to sign the North Atlantic Treaty on April 4, and continued talks to create the West German government. The Soviet Union ended its blockade on May 12. The German parliamentary council representing the three Western occupation zones approved the Basic Law on May 8; and after ratification by the state parliaments, it went into effect on May 23.

After the elections, the Federal Republic of Germany was established on September 21, with Konrad Adenauer as chancellor. Upon ratification of the North Atlantic Treaty, President Truman submitted legislation to Congress for the Mutual Defense Assistance Program; and after heated debates, this bill passed. On October 6, the president signed the act authorizing $1.3 billion in military aid to Allied and friendly nations. By mid–October 1949, US policy for Western Europe had made great strides. The defensive Alliance had been established, the new West German state had been created, Marshall Plan aid was stimulating more European cooperation and economic recovery, and a new military assistance program had been approved to strengthen European defenses.[16]

SHAPING A NEW ASIAN POLICY

In Asia, the Truman administration faced a much less promising situation than it had in Europe. The Nationalist government in China was on the brink of collapse when Dean Acheson returned to government as secretary of state. Earlier, General George C. Marshall had made a thirteen-month mission to China to evaluate the situation and urge reforms on Jiang Jieshi. When he arrived in China on December 20, 1945, Marshall found reason for hope. But as his discussions and negotiations continued, he became very irritated by Jiang's resistance to his recommendations and the Nationalist generals' growing corruption and military incompetence. These trends continued to deteriorate while Marshall served as secretary of state from 1947 to 1949. By early 1949, his successor and all the Asian specialists in the State Department concurred that the Nationalists were destined for defeat. However, because of increasing pressure from the loud and well-funded China lobby reinforced by anticommunist activists, the administration had to continue pursuing a policy of declared support for the Nationalist government while limiting aid as much as possible within the terms of congressional legislation. Acheson and his advisers on China even considered a wedge strategy that would offer support to the Chinese Communists in the hope of attracting them away from a highly dependent relationship with the Soviet Union. But fear of more intense congressional attacks and a

fundamental opposition to communist ideology prevented the administration from any serious pursuit of this promising policy option.[17]

As the Nationalists' collapse became obvious to everyone, the State
Department labored intensely to compile a justification of its policy
for China. This massive study, known as *The China White Paper*, was
released on August 5, 1949. Through four hundred pages of narrative
and six hundred pages of documents, the report argued that the demise
of the Nationalist government was due to Chinese mistakes and corruption, and nothing the United States did or could have done would have
prevented this defeat. *The China White Paper* had very little influence on
public opinion, but Acheson's letter accompanying the report provided
ammunition for his critics. In two key sentences, he abandoned his earlier thoughts about using Chinese nationalism to resist Soviet influence
and declared: "The heart of China is in Communist hands. The Communist leaders have forsworn their Chinese heritage and have publicly
announced their subservience to a foreign power, Russia." The failure
of the Nationalist government would bind the enemies of the Truman
administration more closely to one another, and the China lobby would
charge the State Department and the president with treason in abandon-
ing its hero, Jiang Jieshi.[18]

While policymakers in Washington sharply reduced the priority
they placed on China, their hopes shifted to Japan. Within the broad
objective of denying further expansion of communist control in the Far
East, the central pillar was to tie revived Japanese industrial power to the
United States. Officials ranging from George Kennan to senior analysts
at the CIA and General Douglas MacArthur, the Supreme Commander
for Allied Forces in Tokyo, agreed that Japan was the key to strategic
control in Asia. MacArthur's occupation forces, with help from economic and civil affairs specialists at the State and Defense departments,
worked to reconstruct Japanese industry, control a festering communist movement, and find sources of raw materials and food to lessen
Japanese dependence on US assistance.[19]

A central element of the Japan-centric policy was to prevent the spread
of communist influence in Southeast Asia, a vital source of raw materials and a potential consumer of Japanese manufactured exports. All the

nations of Southeast Asia, except Thailand, had been European colonies before the Japanese invasion and brutal occupation, and in the late 1940s each nation contained a nationalist movement that included a significant number of communists. As it had in China, the State Department shaped its policies for these countries to reduce communist influence, even when it involved ignoring the interests of noncommunist nationalists who appeared on their way to achieving independence. In Vietnam, the United States aided France in establishing a nominally independent noncommunist government, with Paris retaining control of military and foreign policy. The victory of the communists in China, along with the significant overseas Chinese populations throughout Southeast Asia, further complicated policymaking for Washington.[20]

Early in 1949, US officials became embroiled in a debate over the security of South Korea. The NSC had decided in April of the previous year to withdraw all combat troops by the end of 1948. When that date arrived, the State Department argued for and won the retention of a reinforced regiment of 8,000 troops. In the review of this decision, a CIA memorandum argued for the continued presence of the regiment, emphasizing in a prescient forecast that the removal of all combat troops from Korea "would probably in time be followed by an invasion, timed to coincide with Communist-led South Korean revolts." The army staff, supported by General MacArthur, opposed this recommendation and contended that the South Korean forces were adequate to defend against a North Korean invasion and there was no evidence of Chinese or Soviet support for an attack.

The Truman administration's basic assessment held that the greatest threats to South Korean security were rampant inflation, corruption, and political infighting. Key officials did not fear a North Korean invasion; but they did fear South Korean president Syngman Rhee diverting attention from his internal problems by attacking the north and begging for US assistance to help him succeed. Despite pleas and lobbying from Rhee for a larger army with heavy weapons and a public US pledge to defend South Korea, the administration decided to withdraw all combat troops by the end of June. They would be replaced by an advisory group of 500 soldiers to complete training of the defensively armed

South Korean army. The main US support would be assistance to strengthen the economy. These policies were codified in NSC Report 8/2, which was approved by the president on March 22. The US occupation of South Korea ended on June 29, 1949, with the withdrawal of all remaining combat forces.[21]

BUDGET PRESSURES FORCE
REDUCED COMMITMENTS

A strong factor behind Truman's decisions to limit commitments to the Chinese Nationalists and South Korea was a sharp downturn in the economy in the spring of 1949. In April, the director of the Bureau of the Budget, Frank Pace, reported to the president that the recession would produce federal deficits of $4 billion to $8 billion per year for the next four years if current spending levels were maintained. After further analysis, the president informed all agencies and departments that cuts in their budgets were likely, and he told the secretary of defense that his new spending ceiling for FY 1951 would be $13 billion, with reductions in expenditures also to be applied to the current budget. In the Pentagon, the military service chiefs had been fighting among themselves since January to reduce their budget requests to meet a $15 billion ceiling, so this presidential directive came as especially unwelcome news. But the president had named Louis Johnson as secretary of defense in March, with a mandate to reduce expenditures, and Congress was considering draft legislation to give the secretary extensive new authority to shape the department's budget. As a result, the service chiefs did not openly protest the new lower ceiling, but all senior officers realized that funds for equipment and operations would be very tight for the next few years.[22]

Truman felt confident that he could reduce military spending without endangering national security on the basis of recent intelligence analyses, which had concluded that the Soviet Union was not likely to initiate war with the United States for at least several years as it rebuilt its industry and strengthened its armed forces. Although Moscow had significantly increased its military spending in 1948, its forces were mainly equipped for a land war in Europe. The Soviet Air Force had no substantial, long-range bomber wings, and it was only capable of providing tactical support for ground forces. The navy was focused mainly on submarines, but these were poorly constructed, easy to detect underwater, and manned by inexperienced crews. More seriously, US intelligence specialists pointed out serious limitations in the Soviet Union's industry and infrastructure. Its petroleum and machine-tool sectors were inadequate to support a modern arms industry, and its electronic and other technology sectors were seriously inferior to those in the West. As long as the United States retained a superior long-range offensive capability, a stronger industrial base, and a monopoly of atomic weapons, Truman and his advisers believed the nation would remain secure.[23]

Before the spending cuts were implemented and in advance of the public announcement of new policy priorities for East Asia, Secretary of Defense Louis Johnson challenged the State Department's disengagement from the Chinese Nationalists. Sharing many of the views of the China lobby, Johnson had for some time been publicly critical of the administration's China policy. As a means of reopening the policy debate, he asked the NSC staff to draft a "comprehensive plan" to contain communism in Asia. As the bureaucratic battle over the language of the new paper developed, the defense secretary and the Joint Chiefs of Staff shifted their goal to gaining control of part of the Mutual Defense Assistance Program (MDAP) to support the Chinese Nationalists, most of whom had retreated to the island of Formosa, in their continued opposition to the Communists on the mainland and at sea. The funds sought by the Defense Department were contained in Section 303 of the MDAP Act, which authorized the president to use, at his discretion, $75 million for the purposes of the act in the "general area of China." This section, creating what came to be known as "303 funds," had been added to the bill largely devoted to military assistance for Europe as a concession to Senator William Knowland, a leading figure in the China lobby, to win his support and that of his colleagues for the overall bill.

The president and the State Department had no intention of using the 303 funds for the defense of Formosa or for covert actions on the

Chinese mainland. But the Defense Department made a concerted push to have the NSC paper, designated as NSC Report 48, authorize use of most of the 303 funds for a program of overt and covert activities to resist the Communists' consolidation of control in China. When this effort was defeated, the Joint Chiefs shifted their approach in December and, using the support of General MacArthur, called for the 303 funds to be largely used for the protection of Formosa. The State Department succeeded in blocking this gambit as well, with the result that NSC 48/2 was a general restatement of policies for China, Korea, trade in the region, and aid to Southeast Asia. The important new dimension of the document was the commitment to assist the nations of the region in strengthening their internal security to resist the spread of communism. This commitment, together with the availability of the 303 funds, laid the foundation for the extension of containment to Asia. President Truman, in an unusual appearance, attended the NSC meeting that discussed the policy document and signed NSC 48/2 on December 30, 1949.[24]

Unfortunately for Truman and the State Department, the approval of NSC 48/2 may have temporarily settled the debate within the administration over aid to the Nationalists and the defense of Formosa, but this decision only intensified the attacks on these issues from the China lobby and many Republican leaders. Strident proposals from Senator Robert A. Taft and former president Herbert Hoover to use the US Navy to protect Formosa from a Communist takeover came with endorsements from the usual supporters of the Nationalist government. In response to the Republican attacks and misrepresentations, President Truman issued a press release on January 5, 1950, stating that the United States was honoring commitments made with its World War II Allies at the conferences in Cairo and Potsdam to return Formosa to China. And, he continued, "the United States Government will not pursue a course which will lead to involvement in the civil conflict in China. Similarly, the United States Government will not provide military aid or advice to the Chinese forces on Formosa."[25]

Amid continuing criticism in the press and at congressional hearings, Acheson delivered a comprehensive public defense of the administration's new Asian policies at a National Press Club luncheon on January 12. In what became the most controversial portion of his remarks, the secretary of state drew a defensive perimeter in the Western Pacific that ran from the Aleutian Islands through Japan and Okinawa to the Philippines. It notably did not include Formosa or South Korea. He placed his comments on the defensive perimeter in the context of the desire of the peoples of Asia to maintain their recently found freedom from colonialism and foreign domination. Within the region, he argued, the United States had "direct responsibility" for the military security of Japan and "the same thing to a lesser degree" in South Korea. If an attack should occur outside the stated perimeter, the resistance of the populace would attract assistance from the civilized world under the terms of the United Nations Charter. The exclusion of Formosa and South Korea was not highlighted in press reports at the time because it was already widely known. Only the South Korean ambassador made a special comment in expressing the appreciation of President Syngman Rhee and the Korean National Assembly for Acheson's support of their country. It is worth noting that General Douglas MacArthur had described the defense perimeter in exactly the same terms in a March 1949 speech, which had attracted no negative comments from the friends of Nationalist China and South Korea. Acheson's defense perimeter speech became highly controversial only after the North Korean attack, when Republicans asserted that the secretary had given a green light for the Communists to invade South Korea.[26]

The Republican charges about the impact of Acheson's speech on Soviet policy were well wide of the mark. At the time of the National Press Club speech, Stalin and Mao were in the midst of negotiating a treaty of alliance and economic assistance. They quickly learned of the speech, and Stalin's reaction was to arrange parallel Soviet and Chinese rebuttals of Acheson's implication that the Soviet Union was pursuing imperialistic policies in dominating the Chinese Communists. In any event, the Soviet leadership surely knew of the shift in US policy for Asia before the public statements of Truman and Acheson because of the work of its spy network, which was led by Guy Burgess in the Far Eastern Department of the Foreign Office in London, and by Kim Philby, who was the representative of the Secret Intelligence Service (later MI6) in the British Embassy in Washington. For their part, the Chinese had carefully analyzed American policy and capabilities and concluded that the United States was too weak militarily to take action to defend Formosa or South Korea for at least five years.[27]

At a time of political challenges in Europe, rising communist power in Asia, and recession at home, the Truman administration adjusted its Asian policy to clarify commitments and avoid encouraging further conflict in China and possible offensive action by South Korea. It did so in the context of demonstrating its priority to reconstruct and defend Western Europe and rebuild economic strength at home. Each of these decisions would soon confront severe tests.

4

JOSEPH McCARTHY SELLS THE POLITICS OF FEAR

I n the early days of 1950, the Truman administration had made reasonable policy decisions about the major problems confronting the
country. It had restrained spending, limited commitments in Asia,
and put institutions in place to maintain security in Europe. In response
to the newly discovered Soviet atomic weapons capability, the president
was nearing a decision to accelerate development of a thermonuclear
weapon and approve a review of national security policy in light of the
growing Soviet threat and the communist control of China. Yet by the
end of March, a firestorm of charges that the administration was soft on
communism threatened its ability to implement any of its policies.

In addition to the Soviet atomic test and the "loss" of China to the
communists, a series of unwelcome events fueled the attacks. Within
a few weeks, Alger Hiss, a senior State Department official, was found
guilty of perjury and sentenced to five years in prison; Klaus Fuchs,
a British scientist, was arrested for espionage during his work on the
wartime Manhattan Project; and Judith Coplon, a Justice Department
employee, was convicted of passing secrets to a Soviet agent. And in
early February, a relatively unknown US senator launched a series of
sensational charges of treason against a large number of State Department officials.

THE INITIAL CHARGES

On February 9, 1950, Joseph McCarthy, a first-term Republican senator from Wisconsin, delivered a speech before the Ohio County Women's Republican Club in Wheeling, West Virginia. This was the first of several stops on a speaking tour for the Republican Party to celebrate Lincoln Day. The senator arrived with notes for two different speeches: one on housing, the other on the threat of communism. The sponsor of the evening event urged him to use the second speech. Before dinner, McCarthy reorganized the notes that a Washington journalist had collected from recent anticommunist speeches and articles. After dinner, the senator spoke from notes—he had no text, and his notes have not survived, with the result that differing reports exist of what he said that evening. Describing the development of the Cold War after 1945, he highlighted the conflicts in morality and ideology between Russia's "communist atheism" and the Christian West. America had suffered losses, he asserted, not due to outside aggression but "because of the traitorous actions" of those who have benefited from the best homes and education and held the top government jobs. This behavior was "glaringly true in the State Department." Explaining that he lacked the time to name all those identified as members of the Communist Party or participants in a spy ring, he mentioned several by name and then declared: "I have here in my hand a list of 205 . . . a list of names that were made known to the Secretary of State and who nevertheless are still working and shaping the policy of the State Department."[1]

As he continued westward on his speaking tour, McCarthy showed his lack of preparation and discipline when, in successive statements, he gave varying numbers of disloyal diplomats and changed the nature of their transgressions. At the Denver airport, he announced to reporters that he had a list of "207 bad risks"; in Salt Lake City, he charged that he had the names of 57 "card-carrying members of the Communist Party"; in Reno, he sent a telegram to President Truman demanding the release of the State Department's loyalty files or else face the prospect of the Democratic Party being identified as "the bedfellow of international communism." Back in Washington, and under some pressure to reconcile his conflicting statements, on February 20 he made a long, rambling speech on the floor of the Senate. During his remarks, he said he did not think he used the number 205 in Wheeling, and he went on to give examples of questionable activities taken from the files of 81 suspected State Department employees. When challenged by Democratic senators, McCarthy restated his charges in less serious terms and said he would release specific names only in executive session.[2]

We now know that the Wisconsin senator had no new list but was selecting items from a list of 108 individuals whose State Department loyalty files were examined in 1947 by members of the staff of the House Appropriations Committee investigating the department's loyalty program. Some of the 108 people listed were simply applicants for State Department positions; and at the time the list was drawn up, only 57 were actually working in the department. The files were raw data, and the number 57 was meaningless. The anticommunist fervor that McCarthy exploited originated, argues Robert Donovan, "as a result of Dewey's loss to Truman and the almost simultaneous crumbling of . . . [Nationalist China]. Those events, colored by the Hiss case, stripped the Republican right wing and its friends of decent restraint in political conduct, opened the doors of demagoguery, and generally strengthened the orientation of the Republican Party toward the anticommunist issue as a means of returning to power. It was in that part of the garden that McCarthy's roots sank at a time when the senator was seeking an issue on which to win reelection himself in 1952."[3]

TAIL-GUNNER JOE

Joe McCarthy was a most unlikely politician to lend his name to the anticommunist movement that shook the Truman administration to its foundations. Born in 1908 into a modest farm family, he left school at fourteen and started a poultry farm, which failed when he was incapacitated by influenza. He managed a grocery store and then finished his high school courses in a single year before going to Marquette University, where by 1935 he had received bachelor's and law degrees. After working as a lawyer and running unsuccessfully for district attorney as a Democrat, he moved to the Republican Party and ran in 1939 for a seat as a circuit court judge. In an energetic campaign, he misrepresented the age of his opponent, a sixty-six-year-old judge with extensive time on the bench, as too old for the job, saying that he was seventy-three, or on occasion eighty-nine. He won a surprising victory, and as a judge he worked hard to clear up a backlog of cases, often cutting corners on due process.[4]

When the United States entered World War II, McCarthy joined the US Marine Corps as a second lieutenant and served as an intelligence officer with a dive-bomber squadron in the Pacific. His judicial post would have exempted him from military service, but he reportedly entered the marines in the hope of enhancing his prospects as a candidate for higher political office. His military duties mainly involved analyzing intelligence reports and briefing pilots before their bombing missions. Wanting more action, he volunteered as a tail-gunner on twelve observation flights. This became the basis for his nickname "Tail-Gunner Joe." As he would also do later in life, McCarthy substantially embellished his war record when describing it during his political campaigns. He claimed that he had enlisted as a "buck private" and worked his way up to become a commissioned officer. He expanded his twelve volunteer flights to the thirty-two combat missions required to qualify for the Distinguished Flying Cross, an award he received in 1952. And he forged a letter of commendation from his commanding officer, which he said had been countersigned by the chief of naval operations, Admiral Chester W. Nimitz.[5]

In relaunching his political career, McCarthy continued his pattern of ethical and legal misdeeds. While on active duty with the marines, he campaigned for the Republican nomination to the US Senate in 1944 using profits from investments in the stock market on which he had not paid taxes. He resigned from the military five months before the Pacific war ended in order to run unopposed for his judgeship; and once on the bench, he quickly began to organize his primary campaign for the

Republican Senate nomination in 1946. He saw an opportunity to defeat three-term senator Robert M. La Follette Jr., who had entered the Senate as a Republican but left to create the Wisconsin Progressive Party in 1934. After the experiences of the New Deal and the world war, support for the Progressive Party was dissolving, so La Follette decided to run for the Republican nomination. McCarthy sensed that many Republican voters would resent their former opponent trying to return to the party. The circuit court judge ran an aggressive campaign presenting himself as a war hero with the slogan "Congress Needs a Tail-Gunner." He falsely charged that, while "Tail-Gunner Joe" had been serving his country in the Pacific, La Follette had not enlisted in the war and, staying in Washington, had made large profits from wartime investments. In fact, La Follette was forty-six years old when Pearl Harbor was attacked and thus over the age limit for military service, and he had not made any significant profits from investments during the war. Initially holding a large lead in the polls, La Follette stayed in Washington to win passage of an important piece of legislation and did not campaign effectively to answer his opponent's charges. When the polls closed, McCarthy had scored a narrow primary victory of 5,400 votes out of 410,000 cast. He then went on to post an easy win over his Democratic opponent in the general election. In both his 1946 campaign efforts, he was in violation of the state Constitution because he refused to resign from his nonpartisan judicial post while running for elective office.[6]

When he entered the Senate, McCarthy brought an undistinguished and somewhat sleazy background. He also knew very little about communism and showed little interest in it as a political issue. In his first three years in Washington, he made occasional references to the issue of communism and to the problem of communist influence in government; but this was only a minor theme in his extensive and often disorganized presentations in the Senate and in public appearances. His unimpressive record during his first term consisted mainly of supporting random issues urged upon him by lobbyists or vocal constituents. He opposed price controls on sugar to assist a Pepsi-Cola executive, gained favor with realtors by arguing against public housing, and won support among right-wing German American constituents by calling for the commutation of death sentences for Nazi SS troops who massacred unarmed civilians and American prisoners of war in 1944 at Malmédy, Belgium.

Not long after his defense of the Nazi massacre, the reporters covering the Senate voted McCarthy "the worst US senator" of the current body. He offended his Senate colleagues with his disruptive behavior and unsubstantiated assertions, and in 1949 he lost his most important committee assignment, on the Banking and Currency Committee, when the chairman-designate told the majority leader that he would not accept this important post if McCarthy remained on the committee. Back in Wisconsin, criticism of the senator spread on the basis of reports in the Madison *Capital-Times* of his ethical and legal lapses in past campaigns and in Washington. A reporter for the paper filed a lawsuit claiming that McCarthy had violated state law and the bar association's code of ethics by running for the Senate while holding a judicial post. McCarthy needed a galvanizing issue for his reelection campaign in 1952, and in Wheeling he found one.[7]

THE CHINA LOBBY AND THE HISS CASE

Since 1945, the small but fiercely committed group that made up the China lobby had been gathering arguments to attack Truman's Asian policies. Like many conservative Republicans since the Spanish-American War brought the Philippine Islands under US control, the lobby's members believed America's future lay in Asia. They were strong supporters of the generations of American missionaries who had spread Christianity in China and Korea. And during World War II, many of them had criticized Roosevelt's strategy of placing priority on a victory in Europe first. As a result, they became known in the media as "Asia-firsters," and they were strong supporters of Jiang Jieshi and his stylish, Wellesley-educated wife. Almost all the members of this group had opposed every aspect of the New Deal and had supported the investigations of communist influence in the federal government that had begun in 1938 with the creation of the House Un-American Activities Committee (HUAC).

The leading American figure in this lobbying group was Alfred Kohlberg, a wealthy importer of Chinese lace and a frequent contributor to the group's dedicated publication *The China Monthly: The Truth about China*. The lobby made repeated charges about Roosevelt's "Yalta betrayal" of Nationalist China for agreeing to the Soviet Union's gaining significant concessions in ports, railroads, and economic monopolies in Manchuria and Outer Mongolia. As the Nationalists' fortunes declined after 1947, Kohlberg and others asserted that the cause was "treason" in Washington, not incompetence in China. The China lobby's activities and positions were strongly backed by Henry R. Luce in his publications *Time*, *Life*, and *Fortune*, as well as by *Collier's*, the *Saturday Evening Post*, *Reader's Digest*, and *US News & World Report*. Much of the lobby's political direction and funding came from wealthy Chinese in the United States, many of whom were relatives of Madame Jiang or close political and financial partners of her husband. They provided material for articles, books, and congressional testimony, along with gaining contracts for military and economic projects in China with the help of American contacts.[8]

Before 1948, the main political activities of the China lobby focused on normal diplomatic methods of winning economic and military assistance. In his campaign against Truman, Governor Thomas E. Dewey pledged that he would reverse the Democratic administration's policy and help the Nationalist government fight communism by providing military assistance and much greater financial aid. After meeting with Dewey, Vice President Chen Li-fu told the Chinese press that the Republican candidate was sure to win and would provide much more assistance to China when he took office. After Dewey was defeated, the China lobby had to expand its activities and launch full-scale attacks on the Truman administration. Madame Jiang came to the United States and held numerous strategy sessions with groups of supporters in the home of her brother-in-law in Riverdale, New York, and in the homes of loyal Nationalist supporters and embassy officials in Washington. In pursuing this effort, the lobby called upon its friends in Congress to help bring pressure on the administration for expanded aid to the Nationalists.

Among the lobby's key supporters on Capitol Hill were the Republican senators Owen Brewster of Maine, Styles Bridges of New Hampshire, Harry P. Cain of Washington, Homer Ferguson of Michigan, Bourke Hickenlooper of Iowa, William F. Knowland of California, Joseph R. McCarthy of Wisconsin, and H. Alexander Smith of New Jersey, along with the Democratic senators James O. Eastland of Mississippi and Pat McCarran of Nevada. Prominent Republican representatives who helped the Nationalist cause were O. K. Armstrong of Missouri, Walter H. Judd of Minnesota, Joseph W. Martin of Massachusetts, Lawrence K. Smith of Wisconsin, and John M. Vorys of Ohio. After the Communist victory in China and the publication of the State Department's *China White Paper*, the lobby's congressional bloc of supporters would concentrate on charging the administration with betrayal and treason in Asia and were primed to join McCarthy in his attacks on disloyal communists in government.[9]

Unfortunately for the Truman administration, the indictment of Alger Hiss for perjury on December 15, 1948, added fuel to the fire for those seeking to prove treason and disloyalty in the federal government. Hiss had served as a midlevel official in the State Department for ten years starting in 1936 and had been a key participant in designing the United Nations. He had attended the Yalta Conference with President Franklin D. Roosevelt and served as the secretary-general of the San Francisco conference that drafted the UN Charter in 1945. Coming from a Baltimore family of modest means, Hiss had been an excellent student at Johns Hopkins University and Harvard Law School and had clerked for Supreme Court Justice Oliver Wendell Holmes. He left the State Department in 1946 to become president of the Carnegie Endowment for International Peace. But Hiss's highly respectable career received a sharp jolt when Whittaker Chambers, a former communist who left the party after Stalin's purges to become a fervent anticommunist, testified before HUAC on August 3, 1948, that he and Hiss had belonged to a secret group within the Communist Party of the United States.[10]

Hiss went before the same committee and flatly denied the charges by Chambers, demanding that Chambers repeat them in a public forum where his statements could be challenged in court. Chambers, a senior editor at *Time*, appeared on the national radio show *Meet the Press* and again called Hiss a communist. Hiss filed a libel suit against Chambers, who escalated the conflict by asserting that in his communist activities, Hiss had committed espionage. In deposition proceedings preceding the trial, Chambers presented copies of State Department documents that he claimed Hiss had copied and passed to him. Because the Chambers documents showed dramatic evidence of espionage, the lawyers for both sides agreed to turn them over both to the judge in the libel suit and to the Justice Department. Officials of the Justice Department provided copies of the documents to a grand jury already impaneled in New York to investigate communist espionage in the government. After hearing testimony from a number of witnesses, the grand jury indicted Hiss on two counts of perjury. He could not be prosecuted for espionage because the statute of limitations for that crime had expired. Although Chambers admitted previously lying under oath several times, he cooperated fully with the prosecution and was not charged. Hiss's trial lasted five weeks and ended with a hung jury. The prosecution initiated a second trial, in which Hiss was convicted of two counts of perjury by an eight-to-four vote. On January 25, 1950, the federal judge sentenced the former diplomat to two concurrent terms of five years in prison.[11]

The Hiss case produced intense debates between liberals and conservatives that still continue today. The available literature includes at least two dozen books and scores of articles and opinion pieces. Significant new evidence appeared in the 1990s, after the collapse of the Soviet Union, when limited access to Soviet archives, including those of the KGB, disclosed many details of the Soviet espionage networks in the United States. In addition, the National Security Agency released the decoded transcripts of a number of intercepted messages between Moscow and its spy handlers in the United States, known as the Venona transcripts. Until his death in 1996, Hiss maintained his innocence. In a detailed rebuttal of the prosecutor's case, Hiss argued that the documents used as the key evidence against him had been forged. Among the findings from recent evidence are that both the prosecution and defense legal teams in the Hiss trials engaged in misconduct; that the crucial documents were likely forged by US Army Counterintelligence; that J. Edgar Hoover, the director of the Federal Bureau of Investigation (FBI), had ordered an illegal wiretap on Hiss's telephone, had him and his wife followed for over two years, and shared much of the material collected with both Representative Richard M. Nixon (the most active member of HUAC) and Senator Joseph McCarthy; and finally, that the KGB records strongly point to Hiss as a spy for Moscow. The best conclusion comes from one of the leading historians working on the Hiss case and its impact, Allen Weinstein, who argues on the issue of Hiss as a Soviet spy that the evidence "remains persuasive but not conclusive." On the question of the Hiss trials, Weinstein declares: "Although arguments will persist in the court of public opinion, the body of available evidence proves that Hiss perjured himself when describing his secret dealings with Chambers, so that the jurors in his second trial made no mistake in finding Alger Hiss guilty as charged."[12]

For McCarthy, the conviction of Hiss was a godsend. Just as he was preparing his Wheeling speech, the public learned that a highly placed State Department official from a good background had been found guilty of perjury and disloyalty and was probably also guilty of espionage for the Soviet Union. The accusations made at Wheeling fell on receptive ears, and as McCarthy gained wider public attention, the senator from Wisconsin modified and expanded his charges to link them with the older, more respected anticommunist movement in the Republican Party. As he broadened his attacks, he would use material provided by Alfred Kohlberg, Walter Judd, Patrick Hurley, Richard Nixon, and General Douglas MacArthur to accuse the Truman administration of treason in the "betrayal" of the Nationalists and the "loss" of China.[13]

Several issues reached a peak of public awareness at the same time to allow this unknown Midwestern senator in search of an issue for reelection to become the poster child for a powerful anticommunist movement in the United States. Within six months, Americans learned of the Soviet atomic test, the Chinese Communist victory, the Klaus Fuchs arrest, and the conviction of Alger Hiss. The disorganized and inept response of the administration and the Democrats in Congress to McCarthy's charges kept the spotlight on him.

THE ADMINISTRATION'S RESPONSE
AND THE TYDINGS COMMITTEE

Truman had established the line of defense against the initial charges that Hiss and others were communists in the federal government who were protected by the administration. After the testimony by Chambers to this effect before HUAC in August 1948, a reporter had asked the president on August 5 if the emphasis placed by Congress on "the spy scare" was a "'red herring' to divert public attention from inflation." The president replied by stating administration policy that denied committees of Congress access to personnel and loyalty review files and said that the FBI already knew everything that the hearings had discovered. He declared that the committee was "undermining public confidence in the Government" and added a phrase that would prove damaging in future months, saying the hearings "are simply a 'red herring' to keep from doing what they ought to do."[14]

After McCarthy and other Republican speakers repeated similar charges early in 1950, the State Department took the lead in replying and singled out the Wisconsin senator as its principal target. The day after the Wheeling speech, State Department press officer Lincoln White declared that no communists were on the department payroll and that if any should be discovered, they would be fired immediately. The following day, John Peurifoy—who was the deputy undersecretary of state responsible for security, including the mandated Loyalty Review Boards—sent McCarthy a telegram asking him to submit the list of 205 employees he had charged with disloyalty. On February 13, Peurifoy told reporters that loyalty reviews had not disclosed any communists in the State Department and added that the Wisconsin senator had not responded to his request for the list. At a press conference three days later, Truman hoped to put the McCarthy charges to rest when he asserted that there "was not a word of truth in what the senator said."[15]

McCarthy was not deterred. On February 20, he launched into a restatement of his accusations on the floor of the Senate. In a six-hour marathon, he reported disloyal or suspicious actions by eighty-one State

Department officials who he claimed were either members of the Communist Party or committed to its principles. Democratic senators challenged his numbers and demanded names; but their ripostes seldom hit the mark, and McCarthy only moved on to another case. Although the charges failed to demonstrate that the State Department was infested with communists, the evening's debate showed the Republicans united in support of their Wisconsin colleague while the Democrats were disorganized and singularly ineffective in rebuttal. The two sides did agree to support a Republican proposal to have the Senate Foreign Relations Committee investigate each of McCarthy's allegations about current employees of the State Department suspected of disloyalty to the United States. A version of Senate Resolution 231, amended to include former employees, was approved by the Senate on February 22.[16]

Tom Connally, the chairman of the Senate Foreign Relations Committee, persuaded Senator Millard Tydings of Maryland to chair a subcommittee to investigate McCarthy's charges. A conservative Democrat with twenty-four years' service in the Senate, Tydings was chairman of the Military Affairs Committee and an acknowledged expert on foreign policy and defense issues. Joining him on the subcommittee were the Democrats Brien McMahon of Connecticut and Theodore F. Green of Rhode Island, who were both strong supporters of the administration. The subcommittee's two Republicans were Henry Cabot Lodge Jr. of Massachusetts, a leading internationalist in the party and the grandson and namesake of Woodrow Wilson's nemesis in the battle over the Versailles Treaty and the League of Nations, and Bourke B. Hickenlooper of Iowa, one of the most conservative and isolationist members of the Senate and a natural McCarthy ally. The Democrats were poorly prepared to deal with an adversary as pugnacious, deceptive, and irresponsible as McCarthy. They believed that a full examination of his accusations in open hearings would show them to be baseless. The executive branch had no coordinated strategy. White House officials were complacent and assumed the problem could be easily managed. Although the State Department was concerned and anxious to disprove the charges, its procedures were too ponderous and reactive to deal with McCarthy's constantly shifting points of attack. The Democratic chairman did not establish a solid foundation for the investigation. He began hearings a scant two weeks after the resolution passed; he did not insist on a list of names or any hard evidence from McCarthy before starting open proceedings; and the subcommittee hired a staff only during the first week of hearings.[17]

The Republicans prepared for the hearings with high expectations. Public opinion in the country had shifted as the shocking events of the last six months had unfolded. Many who normally paid little attention to international affairs showed increasing concern about Chinese and Soviet successes along with subversion in Washington. The conviction of Hiss for perjury in late January was followed by Judith Coplon's guilty verdict for espionage on March 7, the day before the Tydings Committee's hearings began. Equally important, Republicans in Congress were united behind anticommunism as the potential winning issue in the forthcoming midterm elections, and they were willing to use McCarthy as their assault dog. Senator John Bricker of Ohio captured the sentiment of his fellow Republicans when he declared: "Joe, you're a dirty son of a bitch, but there are times when you've got to have a son of a bitch around, and this is one of them." His Ohio colleague, Senator Robert A. Taft, shared this feeling. The leader of the Republicans' isolationist wing privately supported McCarthy and defended him against Democratic attacks, but resisted making this an official party position. Well before the hearings began, the Republicans launched a concerted attack on the administration to force the release to the committee of the State Department's loyalty files on the suspected employees. They were confident that if the files became available, the committee would be able to find damaging evidence; if, conversely, the files were kept confidential, they would charge the administration with covering up subversion and espionage.[18]

When the Tydings Committee began hearings on March 8, the Democratic members frequently interrupted and challenged Senator McCarthy and showed their intention to disrupt and discredit his charges. They underestimated the resourcefulness of their opponent, for the Wisconsin senator jumped from one case to another, moved beyond his stated eighty-one suspects, and introduced nine additional persons, some with no affiliation with the State Department or the federal government. Among these added cases were Dorothy Kenyon, a New York lawyer and former judge with no connection to the State Department; Owen Lattimore, an Asian specialist at Johns Hopkins University; the China specialist John Stewart Service, who had previously been investigated and attacked by Nixon and McCarthy for sharing classified State Department documents with the left-wing journal *Amerasia*; and Ambassador-at-Large Phillip C. Jessup, a senior diplomatic troubleshooter for Secretary Acheson.[19]

Inspired by McCarthy, other Republican senators and representatives launched fierce attacks on Acheson as a security risk for protecting disloyal subordinates and presiding over the unprecedented "degradation" of the State Department. The president came to Acheson's defense. In an attempt to persuade Senator Styles Bridges of New Hampshire not to deliver a further attack, Truman wrote: "The communists have never had as much help from all the so-called disloyal people as they have had from the indefensible attacks on Mr. Acheson." The former secretary of state and FDR's secretary of war, Henry L. Stimson, aimed the sharpest Republican criticism at McCarthy in a letter to the *New York Times* on March 27, 1950, when he charged that the Wisconsin senator was injuring the innocent and was embarrassing America overseas with his wild accusations. For the respected Republican icon, it was "quite clear that the real motive of the accuser in this case is to cast discredit upon the Secretary of State of the United States. This man is not trying to get rid of known Communists in the State Department; he is hoping against hope that he will find some." Stimson pointed out the "extraordinary responsibility" vested in the position and argued that the secretary should be exempt from "the ordinary trials of politics. The man who seeks to gain political advantage from personal attack on a Secretary of State is a man who seeks political advantage from damage to his country." The highly respected elder statesman concluded by calling for the "stern rebuke" of such "noisy antics" and for the "outspoken support of the distinguished public servants against whom they are directed."[20]

Political discourse in Washington had deteriorated to such an extent by the end of March that the "stern rebuke" of Stimson had little effect. Bridges went ahead with the speech the president had attempted to stifle;

and in response, Truman let loose at a press conference on March 30, asserting that McCarthy was "the greatest asset the Kremlin has" and going on to castigate senators Bridges and Wherry as McCarthy's partners in obstruction. When Senator Taft complained that the president had "slandered" the Wisconsin senator, Truman shot back: "Do you think that is possible?"[21] (See figure 4.1.)

At the end of March, McCarthy revived his stalled campaign by introducing sensational charges against Lattimore, a favorite target of the China lobby. One of the nation's top experts on China and Central Asia, Lattimore was the director of the Walter Hines Page School of International Relations at Johns Hopkins University. In the 1930s—as editor of *Pacific Affairs*, the journal of the Institute of Pacific Relations—Lattimore had written articles and published the work of others favorable to the Soviet Union and the Asian communist movements. He was associated

FIGURE 4.1 Senator Joseph McCarthy (*left*) consults with Roy Cohn, his clever but equally unprincipled chief counsel, at an early session of the Army-McCarthy hearings, April 26, 1954.

Source: AP Images.

with FDR's policies on Asia and the Soviet Union and had been Roosevelt's appointed adviser to Jiang Jieshi for eighteen months during the war. Subsequently, while teaching at Johns Hopkins and writing extensively on Asia, he had served as a consultant to the State Department and the United Nations on several occasions. His published views favorable to Soviet policies and his sharp criticism of the corrupt regime of Jiang and the Nationalists made him a sworn enemy of the China lobby and the anticommunist activists.[22]

For much of April, McCarthy and the witnesses he chose attacked Lattimore before the Tydings Committee. In executive session, the Wisconsin senator declared that the China specialist was "the top Soviet espionage agent in the United States." After the spying charge leaked and Drew Pearson published a column about McCarthy's bombshell, the Democrats responded strongly to the leak and challenged the accusation. In open session, McCarthy then modified his claim and asserted that Lattimore was a sympathizer with Stalin and Soviet policies and had been "the architect" of the Asian policies that abandoned Jiang. Much of the information for McCarthy's sustained attacks came from Kohlberg or from secret FBI interviews with Soviet defectors and material that the FBI had been collecting on Lattimore since 1942. McCarthy also made extensive use of testimony from Louis F. Budenz, now a stalwart anticommunist who had for years been the editor of the *Daily Worker*, the main publication of the Communist Party of the United States. Budenz testified that Lattimore was not a Soviet agent but was an undercover communist who gave valuable support to Soviet policies as an agent of influence. Lattimore returned from Afghanistan, where he was working as a consultant to the United Nations, to refute the charges against him. He testified before the committee that he had never committed espionage nor was he procommunist. But in the face of aggressive questioning, his memory of meetings with suspected communists and their publications fifteen years before was poor, and his appearance was generally unimpressive.[23]

As the testimony against Lattimore continued through April, Democratic leaders grew concerned. Contrary to their expectations, McCarthy's charges could not be put to rest, and polls showed that a significant number of respondents believed his accusations were true. Tydings and other Democrats, including Acheson, pressed the president to reverse his policy of keeping the loyalty files confidential. They believed the files would show that McCarthy had no real evidence of disloyalty and subversion. On May 4, Truman finally relented and made the eighty-one files available to members of the committee, to be read in the Cabinet Room of the White House under strict conditions—no notes could be taken from the room, and no committee staff members were to be present. Committee members spent much of May and June reading through the thick loyalty files. This proved to be hard and unrewarding work, and the senators had other obligations on Capitol Hill and in their home states. In the end, they gave up the task, with Senator Lodge finishing twelve files and Senator Hickenlooper only nine. The Republicans sought to introduce other issues before the committee, such as the State Department reports discussed in *Amerasia* five years earlier and homosexuals in government as security risks. But these topics gained no traction with the media or the public. Then, on June 25, news reached Washington of the North Korean invasion of South Korea, and attention shifted to more urgent matters of how the United States should respond to overt communist aggression.[24]

The Tydings Committee came to an inconclusive end. No communists were unveiled; McCarthy's charges were not completely refuted. Over Republican objections, the Democratic majority on the committee wrote a report and released it on to the public on July 17. When the report came before the full Senate Foreign Relations Committee, it could not win approval and was sent to the Senate without recommendation. After heated debate and three votes, the Senate decided along strict party lines to accept and print the report. The majority report rejected all of McCarthy's charges as baseless or outdated and found that none of the accused had been disloyal or subversive, although it criticized Lattimore, Service, and Kenyon for indiscretion and poor judgment. The majority authors accused McCarthy of deceiving the Senate and of perpetrating "a fraud and a hoax." In a blunt conclusion, they declared that McCarthy's barrage of innuendo and direct accusations was "perhaps the most nefarious campaign of half-truths and untruth in the history of the Republic." Not to be outdone rhetorically, Senator William E. Jenner of Indiana attacked Tydings as a "trained seal" for the administration who had directed "the most scandalous and brazen whitewash of treasonable conspiracy in our history." The Senate traditions of courtesy and decorum had completely evaporated under the heat of McCarthyism.[25]

The Tydings Committee's hearings constituted the most important chapter in the surge of McCarthyism before the outbreak of war in Korea. Scholars generally agree that the committee's majority did not achieve its political objective of dismissing McCarthy's charges of disloyalty and subversion within the Truman administration. Robert Donovan declares that the "investigation produced one of the greatest backfires Washington has ever heard." The most comprehensive scholar of McCarthyism, Richard Fried, concludes that "as an attempt to adjust a shifting political balance, the Tydings committee investigation had failed." The Democrats clearly made several mistakes in setting up the hearings. They were too complacent that they could easily show McCarthy's accusations to be baseless and false. This led them to delay in appointing a staff until the hearings were under way. More seriously, they began the hearings without establishing that there was any evidence behind the Wisconsin senator's charges—despite the fact that the day after Senate Resolution 231 was passed, reporters had identified the 1947 origin of the poorly prepared "list" of 205 disloyal State Department employees, which raised serious questions about its validity. The majority compounded these errors by agreeing to open hearings and by allowing McCarthy to bring up additional cases and broaden the focus with additional charges and altered testimony. Yet McCarthy did not prove that the State Department employed any communists, and all those he named were subsequently cleared by further security reviews. The most balanced evaluation comes from Lattimore's biographer, Robert Newman, who argues: "The Tydings report was not a thorough investigation of the loyalty and security of State Department employees as a whole; it was a reasonable examination of the evidence about the ten individuals publicly accused by McCarthy. All of them, especially Lattimore, were found to be loyal Americans. The report was essentially accurate. Only with the recent opening of FBI files has it been clear how accurate it was."[26]

THE IMPACT OF McCARTHYISM

The steady stream of attacks on the Truman administration by McCarthy and his Republican colleagues through the spring of 1950 created an environment of suspicion and guilt by association. Officials in the government felt besieged and reacted defensively. When North Korean forces attacked in late June, "the United States had become so ideologically mobilized," Ellen Schrecker contends, "that there was no debate about the Soviet Union's responsibility. Though the invasion was actually the culmination of a festering civil war, most American policymakers and ordinary citizens assumed that Stalin was testing the nation's resolve." The war shifted the focus to the administration's Asian policies and forced unwelcome decisions on Truman and Acheson. Vicious attacks on Asian policy and again on Lattimore were revived early in 1951, when Senator Patrick A. McCarran, a conservative Democrat from Nevada and a fierce critic of Truman, began hearings by the Senate Internal Security Subcommittee on the operations of the Institute of Pacific Relations. In the meantime, Senator Tydings lost his race for reelection in November 1950, in large part due to his attempt to defend the administration against McCarthy's accusations.[27]

For his part, the Wisconsin senator continued to revise and restate his attacks on the administration's Asian policies, Acheson, the State Department, the conduct of the war in Korea, and General George C. Marshall, who had been pressed to return to government as the secretary of defense. McCarthy would win reelection in 1952, along with the victory of Dwight D. Eisenhower for president and Republicans taking control of both houses of Congress. With the Republican Party back in power after twenty years of Democratic rule, McCarthy became less useful to his colleagues. His excessive and abusive behavior became an embarrassment when he launched a disorganized series of televised hearings to attack the US Army. His true nature was unmasked in 1954 by a shrewd Boston lawyer, Joseph Nye Welch, who was serving as special counsel for the army, and by two episodes of Edward R. Murrow's documentary television series *See It Now*.[28]

McCarthy found an unstable political situation in 1950 and exploited it in an outrageous, unprincipled manner. He did not create the circumstances that allowed him to flourish. The times "were ripe for a quintessential demagogue to carry the communist issue to its ultimate extremity," argues Fried. "That man, Joseph McCarthy, gave his name to the era. However, it is important to note that anxieties of the Cold War . . . would guarantee that this period—with or without McCarthy—would be a grim one."[29]

The winter and spring of 1950 saw many critical events unfold. The *New Yorker* writer Richard Rovere makes the important point that during these tumultuous days, the Tydings Committee, representing one-third of the membership of the Senate Foreign Relations Committee, and a large number of the administration's senior officials were forced by circumstance "to sit and listen for days and weeks and months on end to a poolroom politician grandly seized with an urge to glory, . . . reciting facts that were not facts about State Department employees who were not State Department employees."[30]

In examining the origins of the Truman administration's decision to launch a major buildup of strategic forces to confront the Soviet Union, it is a critical fact that the major review of US national security policy that produced National Security Council Report 68 and the decision to intervene in Korea were made in an atmosphere of hysteria over communist threats at home and abroad.

5

PAUL NITZE SOUNDS THE TOCSIN

As Paul Nitze assumed the duties of director of the State Department's Policy Planning Staff in January 1950, important debates raged within the administration and Congress over changes in national security strategy to meet an expanding Soviet threat (see figure 5.1). Without any comprehensive plan, several significant steps had already been taken. Surprising technological advances from the Sandstone tests in the spring of 1948 enabled scientists at the Atomic Energy Commission (AEC) to design weapons with yields of up to 75 percent greater explosive power while using less scarce fissionable material. In the coming months, this would generate increased weapons production with various models for tactical battlefield use along with larger strategic bombs of up to 50 kilotons, or four times the power of the Hiroshima bomb. Soon after taking office as secretary of defense in March 1949, Louis Johnson canceled the US Navy's prized supercarrier and allocated the funds for long-range bombers. In May, Lieutenant General Curtis E. LeMay, the hard-charging commander of the Strategic Air Command, won approval from the president to cancel several midrange bomber programs in order to expand production of the new intercontinental B-36 bomber. With the economy in recession, in July President Truman announced a cut of $2 billion in the defense budget for fiscal year (FY) 1951, which led to more intense rivalry for resources

FIGURE 5.1 Paul H. Nitze, the director of the State Department's Policy Planning Staff and principal author of National Security Council Report 68, would remain a prominent advocate of a strong policy against the Soviet threat throughout the Cold War.

Source: Wikimedia.

among the military services. In October, not long after the announcement of the Soviet atomic test, the president authorized a significant increase in the production of fissionable material for nuclear weapons. Together, these decisions moved the United States well along the road to adopting an atomic strategy based on an expanded stockpile of nuclear weapons and a force of intercontinental bombers.[1]

THE HYDROGEN BOMB DECISION

During the fall of 1949, the most fateful debate revolved around the question of whether the United States should attempt to create a thermonuclear weapon. Popularly known as the hydrogen bomb, or H-bomb, such a weapon would explode as the result of a fusion reaction and was estimated to have explosive power 100 times greater than the fission bomb used on Hiroshima. After extensive discussions, the leading scientists agreed that the feasibility of the superbomb (often called simply "the super" by nuclear specialists) could probably be demonstrated within three years without major interruption of the production of current and improved types of fission weapons. But they disagreed fundamentally on the political and ethical aspects of building the hydrogen weapon; and on November 9, 1949, the AEC's members reflected this division in a three-to-two recommendation against developing the super at that time. Members of the congressional Joint Committee on Atomic Energy and defense leaders, both civilian and military, strongly opposed this recommendation and launched efforts to win Truman's endorsement of immediate development of the hydrogen bomb. Senator Brien McMahon (D-CT), the joint committee's chairman, expressed the views of the H-bomb's proponents when he declared, in a long letter to the president, that "if we let Russia get the super first, catastrophe becomes all but certain—whereas, if we get it first, there exists a chance of saving ourselves."[2]

Public concern and press reports about this battle within the administration forced Truman to make an early decision. On November 18, he directed a special committee of the National Security Council (NSC) to make a thorough review of the superbomb issue, including political and military as well as technical factors. This group consisted of the secretary of defense, the secretary of state, and AEC chairman David E. Lilienthal. Johnson favored, but Lilienthal opposed, rapid development of the new weapon. Left as the swing vote, Acheson found his views increasingly shaped by arguments that the Soviets would build a hydrogen bomb regardless of US action and that sole Russian possession of the new weapon would severely damage America's military and political position. He was able to minimize the impact of his decision to support accelerated development of the super and to offer some comfort to his friend Lilienthal by adopting Nitze's proposal to separate the decisions for development and production and sponsor a full-scale review of US strategic programs "in the light of the USSR's probable fission bomb capability and its possible thermonuclear bomb capability." According to the Nitze compromise, the government would begin a priority study of the bomb's feasibility at the same time as it conducted a major review of strategic policy. Any decision about production of the H-bomb would be made only after its feasibility was proven and could be informed by the conclusions of the policy review.[3]

The special committee reported to the president on January 31, 1950, that it favored accelerated development of all forms of atomic weapons, including the hydrogen bomb, and that it proposed a major review of US strategic programs. Truman accepted both recommendations, and the White House released a terse announcement about continued weapons development that afternoon. At the same time, without publicity, the president directed the strategic review that would result in NSC Report 68.[4]

OPPOSITION TO AN ATOMIC STRATEGY

The hydrogen bomb debate marked the final stage in forging a consensus among national security policymakers in favor of an atomic strategy. This rough set of plans and assumptions had not developed through any careful study of US national interests and capabilities as compared with those of the most likely enemy. Rather, it had grown by accretion in response to various economic, political, and technical developments in the United States and to Soviet actions in Europe and Asia since 1948. An atomic strategy had gained a powerful supporter by July 1949, when Senator McMahon wrote Louis Johnson that America's first line of defense had become strategic bombing with nuclear weapons and argued that the country could not have too many atomic bombs. The terms of advocacy for the superbomb used by prominent scientists such as Ernest Lawrence, Edward Teller, and Luis Alvarez advanced the case within the government. The chairman of the Joint Chiefs of Staff, General Omar Bradley, publicly endorsed the atomic strategy when he commented in the *Saturday Evening Post* that the atomic bomb will be "our principal initial offensive weapon in any future war."[5]

However, opposition remained within the government to relying on nuclear weapons as the principal means of national defense. In October, J. Robert Oppenheimer, chairman of the AEC's General Advisory Committee and chairman of the Institute for Advanced Study in Princeton, complained to James Conant, his friend and colleague on the advisory committee, that the superbomb "appears to have caught the imagination, both of congressional and of military people, as *the answer* to the problem posed by the Russian advance" (emphasis in the original). Though admitting that "it would be folly to oppose exploration of this weapon," Oppenheimer still feared the consequences of accepting it "as the way to save the country and the peace." On October 30, Oppenheimer and Conant led the General Advisory Committee to make a unanimous recommendation against development of the hydrogen bomb. Lilienthal welcomed their conclusion and wanted to join a presidential renunciation of the superbomb with a new plan for international control of weapons of mass destruction.[6]

George F. Kennan, counselor of the State Department starting in October 1949, launched a broad attack on the atomic strategy.[7] In a long report on the "International Control of Atomic Energy" completed on January 20, 1950, and submitted "as a personal paper" to the secretary, Kennan assessed the problems of international control of atomic energy and the development of the hydrogen bomb within the broad context of American strategic plans. He declared that "the crucial question is: Are we to rely upon weapons of mass destruction as an integral and vitally important component of our military strength, which we would expect to employ deliberately, immediately, and unhesitatingly in the event that we become involved in a military conflict with the Soviet Union? Or are we to retain such weapons in our national arsenal only as a deterrent to the use of similar weapons against ourselves or our Allies and as a possible means of retaliation in case they are used?"

Kennan proceeded from two important assumptions: that "no basic change in the nature of the regime in power in Russia can be brought about . . . by anything short of a major upheaval . . . ;" and that, "barring some system of international control and prohibition of atomic weapons, . . . *some* weapons of mass destruction must be retained in the national arsenal for purposes of deterrence and retaliation" (emphasis in the original).[8]

Kennan's analysis showed that two courses were open. If American leaders were not willing to alter their strategic plans and abandon their "reliance on 'first use' of weapons of mass destruction in a future war, then we should not move closer than we are today to international control." If, however, military planners renounced the first use of atomic weapons, the nation would need to entirely reorient its strategy. Necessary steps would include completely revising military plans and capabilities to strengthen conventional forces, gaining NATO approval for this shift, adopting a different position on international control, and making a serious attempt to win prohibition of nuclear weapons.[9]

The counselor expressed a clear preference for the second alternative, which involved a reorientation of American strategy. Although structuring his paper as an argument against first use and primary reliance on atomic weapons, his basic desire to abolish nuclear weapons was apparent. Such weapons, he said, could never achieve the goals of a democratic society, and "the absence of international agreement outlawing the weapons of mass destruction . . . [would only] encourage the belief that somehow or other results decisive for the purposes of democracy can be expected to flow from the question of who obtains the ultimate superiority in the atomic weapons race." Kennan exposed the fallacy of this belief, and he went on to counter the assertion that nuclear weapons differed only in degree of destruction and horror from many conventional weapons. He pointed out the inhumane and imprecise nature of atomic weapons, which did not "spare the unarmed and helpless non-combatant . . . as well as the combatant prepared to lay down his arms." After acknowledging that, if attacked with atomic weapons, the United States should retaliate in kind, he restated his case for control and ideally for prohibition.[10]

Although Kennan had worked on this paper for three months, and had poured much of his soul into it, he admitted that the chances of his proposed course of action being adopted were very slight. Nevertheless, in case an agreement on international control were to be sought, he offered guidelines on how to first approach the Atlantic Pact nations and then the Soviet Union. Concluding his argument with a plea for clear thinking about national goals, he declared that, in a time of rapid and dangerous international change, "there is only one thing a nation can do which can have any really solid and dependable value, and that is to see that the initial lines of policy are as close as possible to the principles dictated by its traditions and its nature, and that where it is necessary to depart from these lines, people are aware that this *is* a departure and understand why it is necessary. For this reason, there is value in a clean and straight beginning, even though the road ahead may be tortuous and perhaps impassable" (emphasis in the original).[11]

Kennan's expectation that his arguments would be rejected proved correct. Other policymakers did not accept his view of the Soviet Union as an ambitious but relatively cautious and insecure nation. As John Lewis Gaddis argues in his superb biography, Kennan's memorandum "was of little use in shaping immediate policy. He had become prophetic but no longer relevant." No one was willing to make additional concessions to win an agreement with the Soviets for international control of atomic energy. But his eloquent paper did make several small gains. It helped persuade senior Defense Department officials of the necessity for a thorough review of national objectives and strategic programs, including the use policy for atomic weapons. In addition, he won Nitze's support for giving serious consideration to a policy restricting the employment of atomic weapons to retaliation for prior use by an enemy.[12]

The opponents of an atomic strategy failed in their attempt to reduce the degree of dependence on nuclear weapons. Soon, two of their most forceful advocates would leave the government—Lilienthal in February, Kennan in June. Their failure (and the almost certain success of atomic strategy) flowed from the interaction of two seemingly contradictory factors: increasing concern about the Soviet threat, and the constraints imposed on defense programs by the president's view of the economy.

TRUMAN'S DEFENSE BUDGET CEILING

The president and his principal advisers in the White House and the Bureau of the Budget believed that national security depended equally on a "sound economy" and a powerful air force. Truman had categorically stated in his 1948 campaign that the economy could not afford defense spending in excess of $15 billion a year; and in July 1949, under pressure from a recession, he had cut this ceiling by an additional $2 billion. Expert opinion held that military expenditures were an economic drain rather than a stimulus; and, guided by this economic thinking, political and business leaders sought ways to revive growth. As Representative George H. Mahon (D-TX), the chairman of the Defense Appropriations Subcommittee, told the House, "Nothing would please a potential enemy better than to have us bankrupt our country and destroy our economy by maintaining over a period of years complete readiness for armed conflict." The president brought Louis Johnson in as secretary of defense to enforce economy on the defense establishment. Nurturing his ambitions to be the Democratic Party's nominee for the White House in 1952, the new defense chief saw a potential platform in the reduction of military spending and improved management.[13]

Despite his commitment to the air force and its deterrent mission, Truman refused to alter his limits for the defense budget for FY 1950. Representative Carl Vinson (D-GA), the new chairman of the House Armed Services Committee, led a successful battle to reduce appropriations for the navy and the army in order to add $800 million for long-range bombers and an additional ten groups for the air force. The first Soviet atomic blast had shocked the United States only two months earlier. Yet, in signing the appropriations bill on October 29, 1949, the president declared that he would not spend the additional funds and would keep the air force at forty-eight groups. At this point, Truman's commitment to budgetary imperatives still prevailed over the Soviet threat.[14]

For the officials assigned to assess US strategic programs in light of growing Soviet nuclear power, the salient practical reality was the president's defense budget ceiling. With most of this group convinced that their job was to make the case for an expanded defense effort, everyone realized that their target audience consisted of a single individual: Harry Truman.

THE MAKING OF A PRUDENT HAWK

The task before the group drafting the strategic assessment was clear; and the time was short. Nitze would be the central person shaping the substance of the study, and his preparation for this challenge was not that of a traditional Foreign Service officer. Nitze was the grandson of German immigrants who settled in Baltimore after the Civil War, and he spent his formative years on the South Side of Chicago, where his father was chairman of the Department of Romance Languages and Literature at the University of Chicago for thirty years. With his family, he traveled in Europe many summers, and in 1914 he was in Austria and Germany when World War I broke out. In Munich, he witnessed firsthand German soldiers marching off to war through crowds filled with "patriotic enthusiasm." After finishing University High School at the age of fifteen, he spent two years at Hotchkiss before enrolling at Harvard. In Cambridge, he became a serious student only in his senior year, when he concentrated on economics and won summa cum laude for his senior thesis.[15]

Graduating in 1928, Nitze chose a career in business and spent his first year in low-level jobs, including an eight-month tour of Europe evaluating investment opportunities in Germany. His tightly reasoned, negative report on German prospects won the attention of Clarence Dillon, head of the investment banking firm Dillon, Read, and Company. Convinced that the United States was on the eve of a sharp depression, Dillon closed down his national network of offices and terminated four thousand employees. But the prominent banker was so impressed with the young Nitze that, even in the midst of downsizing, he offered him a position with the fifty-person core group remaining on Wall Street. Nitze began work at Dillon, Read only days before the Black Tuesday crash in October 1929. His next eleven years would be spent as an investment banker, with all but one year at Dillon, Read. During this period, he married Phyllis Pratt, who was the daughter of John Teele Pratt, a prominent lawyer and Standard Oil heir, and of Ruth Baker Pratt, a Republican congresswoman from the Silk Stocking District of Manhattan. The young banker made sound investments; and with his wife's inheritance, Nitze and his family were financially independent when World War II began.[16]

As war spread across Europe in the summer of 1940, Nitze came to Washington to be an assistant to his friend and mentor James Forrestal. Currently president of Dillon, Read, Forrestal was called to Washington to be one of six special assistants to Franklin Roosevelt as he worked to improve relations with the business community in anticipation of expanding military production to provide assistance to Great Britain and France in their desperate battle against Nazi Germany. After the Japanese attack on Pearl Harbor, Nitze became head of the Office of Metals and Minerals in the Board of Economic Warfare, which in 1943 was restructured as the Foreign Economic Administration, where the banker was director of overseas procurement. As the result of a conflict with the head of this administration, Nitze resigned in the fall of 1944 and immediately was named a director of the newly formed US Strategic Bombing Survey. With his knowledge of Germany and his command of the language, he led a team into the country closely following Allied combat units. Their mission was to evaluate the effectiveness of Allied bombing and to develop recommendations on how best to use air bombardment to end the war with Japan. The team concluded that the concentrated effort to destroy end products such as ball-bearing plants and airframe factories had not been effective. Instead, targeting basic industries such as oil, gas, and chemicals and destroying transportation networks had proved much more damaging to overall German war production.[17]

In early September, Nitze arrived in Japan with a new team and an expanded mission. In addition to assessing the effectiveness of the bombing campaign, the group was to evaluate the effects of the atomic bombs on political will and war production, along with how Japan decided to surrender. The president also asked for recommendations on postwar reorganization of the armed forces and the role of air power. The members of the survey team found a higher level of destruction in Japan than in Germany because of saturation bombing with incendiary weapons on buildings constructed largely of wood. They reported that the atomic bombs used on Hiroshima and Nagasaki had devastating effect on those cities but did not seriously interrupt war production. As the principal author of the final report, Nitze concluded that the Japanese economy was so severely damaged that surrender would likely have come by November 1945 without the use of atomic weapons or an invasion.[18]

The experience of leading the strategic bombing survey was a significant turning point in Nitze's career, argues the historian Steven Rearden. It provided Nitze's first immersion in the complexities of modern warfare and the great destructive power of new weapons. In his report, the new strategic analyst called for the integration of economic, scientific, and military evidence in defense planning. He made the case for a vigorous program of research and development of weapons, greatly improved intelligence, and a unified Defense Department with clear missions for the services based on modern weapons technology. He also strongly urged the strengthening of America's defense capabilities in order to deter any potential aggressor. In many ways, Nitze's final report on the Pacific war can be seen "as the forerunner of NSC 68." The bombing survey also demonstrated many of the qualities that would characterize Nitze's entire career. He showed a keen intelligence, rigorous analytical skills, a willingness to question both authority and conventional wisdom, great organizational ability, unusual physical and mental endurance, and passionate advocacy for his convictions.[19]

In late 1946, Nitze joined the State Department as deputy director of the Office of International Trade Policy. He quickly became an important player in his new bureaucracy when he helped design the economic and military aid program for Greece and Turkey, which represented the substance behind the Truman Doctrine of March 1947. Later, he took a central role during the last half of 1947 in developing the complex economic and mutual assistance programs under the Marshall Plan. Given his mastery of the program's details and his ability to testify effectively before sometimes hostile members of Congress, he was a major witness in making the case for passage of the appropriations bill by the legislative branch. After Truman's reelection, Nitze became deputy assistant secretary of state for economic affairs and had his first experience negotiating with a high-level Soviet delegation over German and Austrian issues. He worked closely with the new secretary of state, Dean Acheson; but despite apparent success, their proposals for an Austrian peace settlement were rejected by Moscow at the last moment and would not be resolved until 1955, when new Soviet leadership was in place.[20]

Nitze became deputy director of the State Department's Policy Planning Staff in the summer of 1949. Realizing that US policies in the Cold War were hardening in a manner he opposed, Kennan soon announced his intention to retire, moved into the conference room, and allowed Nitze to take his office and direct the activities of the small planning staff for the remainder of the year. Acheson had proposed Nitze for his new job to improve communication with the Defense Department and add economic expertise to the office. The new deputy's views on nuclear weapons were also a factor in the decision. As the debate over the H-bomb revealed, Nitze's conviction that the United States had to rely on nuclear weapons of the most advanced types as a key part of its defense strategy had won Acheson's support. In contrast, Kennan's idealistic argument for international control and a reduced strategic role for nuclear weapons had little support in the administration after the successful Soviet atomic test. Two issues dominated Nitze's work in the fall of 1949: whether to pursue development of a thermonuclear weapon, and how to respond to the victory of the Communists in China. After arranging detailed interviews with the leading nuclear specialists, he concluded that Soviet scientists were most likely also working on an H-bomb and that the United States could not allow itself to fall behind in the development of powerful new weapons. This argument carried the day with the NSC's special committee and, most important, with President Truman. Because Nitze had formally become director of the planning staff on January 1, 1950, his next task was to direct the strategic review that was a component of the final H-bomb decision.[21]

DRAFTING NSC 68

Like most government studies, NSC Report 68 was drafted hastily in response to an immediate need. The president issued the formal directive for this review on January 31, 1950, and the completed study circulated on March 30 to the assistant secretaries of state and other top officials for their reactions. In his directive, Truman announced his decision to proceed with the development of the hydrogen bomb, and he instructed secretaries Acheson and Johnson "to undertake a reexamination of our objectives in peace and war and of the effect of these objectives on strategic plans, in the light of the probable fission bomb capability and possible thermonuclear bomb capability of the Soviet Union."[22]

While the members of the State-Defense Policy Review Group collected data and shaped their thoughts, an increasing sense of threat from the Soviet Union developed in Washington and around the country. Nitze reported that at the secretary's staff meeting on February 2, he had been asked about the danger of war, and he "had replied that it seemed considerably greater than last fall." After some discussion within the Policy Planning Staff, Nitze directed John Paton Davies Jr. to write a paper on the probability of war with the Soviet Union "in the immediate future." In the meantime, Nitze himself completed a study on "Recent Soviet Moves," in which he argued that "the USSR had already committed itself to the defeat of the United States," but pointed out that recent events do not indicate "that Moscow is preparing to launch in the near future an all-out military attack on the West. They do, however, suggest a greater willingness than in the past to undertake a course of action, including a possible use of force in local areas, which might lead to an accidental outbreak of general military conflict. Thus the chance of war through miscalculation is increased." The planning staff director identified the primary areas of Soviet interest as establishing firm control in China and improving the communist positions in Indochina, Korea, Berlin, and Austria; and he concluded that "the USSR considers this a favorable and necessary moment for increased political pressure, and, when feasible, taking aggressive political action against all or most soft spots in its periphery."[23]

During these weeks, Acheson publicly voiced many critical comments on Soviet conduct. In his major address to the National Press Club on January 12, the secretary described communism as "the spearhead of Russian imperialism" and asserted that the Soviet attempt to annex "the four northern provinces of China is the single most significant, most important fact, in the relation of any foreign power with Asia." On February 8, he spoke at a press conference of the way in which "situations of weakness" in Europe and Asia provided "an irresistible invitation for the Soviet Government to fish in those troubled waters." He discussed the range of tensions with the Soviet Union before the Advertising Council at the White House on February 16 and at the University of California at Berkeley on March 16, and in the earlier speech he bluntly declared that "the only way to deal with the Soviet Union, we have found from hard experience, is to create situations of strength. Wherever the Soviet detects weakness or disunity—and it is quick to detect them—it exploits them to the full."[24]

The authors of NSC 68 also saw new and higher estimates of the Soviet threat emanating from the Defense Department and the CIA. On January 31, on behalf of the Joint Chiefs of Staff, Lieutenant General Alfred M. Gruenther forwarded a study prepared collectively by the three services titled "The Need of Defense Measures Against Increasing Threat of Atomic Attack Against the Continental United States." The paper, to be presented to the NSC on February 1, examined the possible effect of dropping sixteen atomic bombs on major American targets. In his cover letter, Gruenther declared that "Friday, 23 September 1949, when the President announced that we had evidence of an atomic explosion in the USSR, is to us as historic a date as Pearl Harbor or Hiroshima, for it has posed us with the possibility that the atomic bomb, which ended World War II, and which we now believe is produced by the Soviet, might in the future be used against us in a new type of a Pearl Harbor attack of infinitely greater magnitude than that of 1941."

From an analysis of the latest intelligence estimates, he concluded that the Soviets would have a stockpile of 10 to 20 atomic bombs by mid-1950, and 70 to 135 by mid-1953. The CIA, on February 10, released a report on a similar topic, forecasting a Soviet stockpile of 100 Nagasaki-type

bombs by 1953 and 200 by the end of 1955. In a highly qualified statement, the agency estimated that a strike with 200 atomic weapons delivered on prescribed targets "might prove decisive in knocking the United
States out of a war," but it could not suggest how many bombs would be
required for 200 to get through successfully. It did contend that possession of the atomic bomb would lead the Soviets to more venture-
some conduct when they felt they could take the United States out of a
war totally, declaring that "the critical date for a possible all-out Soviet
atomic attack on the United States would not be earlier than 1956–57."[25]

These projections of increased Soviet capabilities had a particularly
strong impact on the defense members of the review group. On the basis
of a critique of the CIA report by two of his senior military officers,
Robert LeBaron reported to Secretary Johnson on February 20 that,
given "these assumptions, the Soviet A-Bomb and H-Bomb capabilities
are much higher than that contained in the latest CIA estimate." In a few
days, Najeeb Halaby wrote the secretary of defense that within the last
year, the Soviet Union had improved its position relative to the United
States in ten categories. When the Allies joined NATO, he declared, "they
risked their necks for US leadership, assistance and strength based primarily on the atomic monopoly. . . . They now wonder if they shouldn't
slow down their collaboration with the United States 'in its struggle against the USSR' and assume a more neutral position." This well-
coordinated series of inputs led Louis Johnson on February 24 to propose to the president an "all-out program" for the hydrogen bomb. Less
vigorous action, he argued, would endanger national security.[26]

Before leaving for a long tour of Latin America, Kennan attempted to
deflate the growing consensus about an escalating Soviet menace. "There
is little justification," he asserted, "for the impression that the 'cold war,'
by virtue of events outside of our control, has suddenly taken some drastic turn to our disadvantage." He pointed out that both the collapse of
China and the Soviet atomic capability had long been anticipated and
did not alter in any fundamental way the international position of the
United States. "And insofar as we feel ourselves in any heightened trouble at the present moment, that feeling is largely of our own making." The
main thrust of the Soviet challenge was on the ideological and societal

levels, and Kennan argued that the policies of political containment and domestic revitalization remained valid and should be continued. "In the military sphere," he declared, "we should act at once to get rid of our present dependence, in our war plans, on the atomic weapon." To meet its defense requirements, the United States should probably move toward "a state of semi-mobilization, involving some form of compulsory military service and drastic measures to reduce the exorbitant costs of national defense."[27]

Those policymakers who did not want to hear Kennan's plea for patience and subtlety received good reason to follow their own hard line in a survey of public attitudes about stronger diplomatic action. The results of this study of media and public opinion, analyzed during the first week of March, showed that most Americans were "prepared for a period of protracted tension in East–West relations" and endorsed a more vigorous policy toward the Soviet Union without being willing to increase government spending significantly. Further evidence to support this view came from the assistant secretary of state for public affairs, Edward Barrett, who reported that his talks with congressmen in recent days indicated their mail reflected an "increasing public pressure, which could become dangerous, for some sort of bold action.[28]

This evaluation of public opinion reached the State-Defense Policy Review Group just as it was testing its draft report on a series of elder statesmen and experts. Of the six outside consultants, only two— J. Robert Oppenheimer and James Conant—voiced significant disagreement with any part of the study. In coming months, these two distinguished scientists would join with other prominent national leaders to form the Committee on the Present Danger. In his meeting with the group, Oppenheimer accepted the need for an increased defense effort, and he strongly endorsed an ambitious program to explain the facts of the current international situation to the public. However, at the same time, he called for a marked reduction in government secrecy regarding technical information and argued for a shift away from "complete dependence on the atomic bomb." Conant, the president of Harvard University, complained that parts of the study set American sights "much too high." He particularly opposed the objectives of "restoring freedom to victims of the Kremlin" and "bringing about a change in the Soviet system. . . . For the next 20 years our objective should be," he proposed, "to live on tolerable terms with the Soviet Union and its satellites while avoiding a war." Expressing "great skepticism on the effectiveness of air bombing," he suggested "cutting back on strategic air power and putting more emphasis on land forces and tactical air power. He believed we would be better off if we had one million more men under arms rather than more air power."[29]

By far the strongest endorsement of the review group's work came from Robert Lovett, who would be appointed deputy secretary of defense within six months. He agreed entirely with the basic conclusion that American military strength needed to be increased, emphasizing that this required "giving the facts to the public." He declared: "We must realize that we are now in a mortal conflict; that we are now in a war worse than any we have ever experienced. Just because there is not much shooting as yet does not mean that we are in a cold war. It is not a cold war; it is a hot war. The only difference between this and previous wars is that death comes more slowly and in a different fashion."

To deal with this threat, Lovett called for a marked increase in the quality of intelligence facilities, for coordination of the Cold War effort by a group headed by a recognized leader of cabinet rank, and for an increased propaganda program—and also that "we should use every method of economic warfare which could possibly throw the enemy off schedule or off balance. This would have a good psychological effect both in our camp and in the camp of the enemy. In other words, the efforts of a 'Department of Dirty Tricks' should be commensurate with that of all other agencies." This respected investment banker contended that the additional expenditures needed for defense could benefit the American economy, and he urged that the program of challenging the Soviets not wait for completion of the military buildup but begin right away.[30]

By March 30, the review group had completed its study and was ready to seek the reaction of senior officials in the State and Defense departments. In a preliminary meeting with Acheson and the authors, Louis Johnson denounced the whole effort as a conspiracy of the military and the State Department to increase defense spending. Despite his vow to stop the entire review, the defense secretary proved unable to block or redirect the study. Nitze had created a cohesive study team and had established his personal dominance within it. He had started the review from a solid bureaucratic position, because his view about a stronger policy toward the Soviet Union and development of the hydrogen bomb had already won Acheson's endorsement and in the process had led to the selection of Nitze to replace Kennan as director of the Policy Planning Staff. The State Department's representatives on the review group were either his subordinates in policy planning or others, like Gordon Arneson, who shared his attitudes toward the Soviets. The senior Defense Department member, Major General James H. Burns, basically agreed with his colleagues from State on the need for increased conventional forces and continued development of the atomic strike force. In order to avoid a direct clash with Johnson, Burns and the other members of the group agreed to avoid discussion of specific defense increases and their budgetary implications. Privately, most members of the group agreed that the buildup they contemplated would require defense expenditures of about $40 billion a year for several years.[31]

NSC 68 moved smoothly along toward consideration by the NSC. To the surprise of Acheson and others, Johnson promptly circulated the study to his senior officials, and on April 11 he forwarded it to the president with his endorsement. The product of the Nitze group's labors was scheduled for discussion by the NSC on April 20.[32]

THE MESSAGE: SUBSTANCE AND TONE

NSC 68 opens with the assertion that the traditional balance of power that has allowed independent states to prevent the hegemony of a single nation is endangered. The results of World War II have left the Soviet Union and the United States as the only two major powers. However, "the Soviet Union, unlike previous aspirants to hegemony, is animated by a new fanatic faith, antithetical to our own, and seeks to impose its absolute authority over the rest of the world." As the only powerful opponent of Soviet domination, the United States is "the principal enemy whose integrity and vitality must be subverted or destroyed by one means or another if the Kremlin is to achieve its fundamental design."[33]

In "the realm of ideas and values," the study contends, "there is a basic conflict between the idea of freedom under a government of laws, and the idea of slavery under the grim oligarchy of the Kremlin." The idea of freedom has a corrosive effect on a slave society, and knowing this Stalin insists on absolute control within the Soviet Union and throughout the communist world. "The assault on free institutions is worldwide now; and in the context of the present polarization of power, a defeat of free institutions anywhere is a defeat everywhere."[34]

Examining the objectives of the United States in this threatening situation, the policy review group declares that the basic containment goals of NSC Report 20/4, of November 23, 1948, remain valid. But changing international conditions require additions and changes of emphasis: "Coupled with the probable fission bomb capability and possible thermonuclear bomb capability of the Soviet Union, the intensifying struggle requires us to face the fact that we can expect no lasting abatement of the crisis unless and until a change occurs in the nature of the Soviet system." This demand for a change in the nature of the Soviet system represents the most notable new element stated in the national security objectives of NSC 68.[35]

With regard to the means used to reach an objective, the argument of the review group reflects an even greater departure from previous norms. The United States, the authors declare, must take whatever action is necessary to protect its basic values: "The integrity of our system will not be jeopardized by any measures, covert or overt, violent or non-violent, which serve the purposes of frustrating the Kremlin design, nor does the necessity for conducting ourselves so as to affirm our values in actions as well as words forbid such measures, provided only they are appropriately calculated to that end and are not so excessive or misdirected as to make us enemies of the people instead of the evil men who have enslaved them." Within this rhetoric, lie the seeds of justification for many subsequent actions against the global communist movement.[36]

In estimating Soviet intentions and capabilities, the review group states that Kremlin policy toward the United States is "animated by a peculiarly virulent blend of hatred and fear" and that "the Kremlin is inescapably militant." With regard to military capabilities, the Joint Chiefs of Staff estimate that if a major war developed during 1950, the Soviet Union could overrun Western Europe, with the possible exceptions of the Iberian and Scandinavian peninsulas; drive toward the oil lands of the Near and Middle East; consolidate gains in the Far East; launch air attacks against the United Kingdom and air and sea attacks against Western lines of communication in the Atlantic and Pacific oceans; and make atomic attacks against selected targets in the United States and Canada. The agreed-on intelligence estimates predict a Soviet stockpile of fission weapons of 10 to 20 by mid-1950, 45 to 90 by mid-1952, and 200 by mid-1954. The intelligence experts further predict that by mid-1954, the Soviets would have the capability to deliver 100 atomic weapons on targets in the United States (assuming that 50 percent of those launched would reach their targets). There is also good evidence to indicate that the Soviets will be working to develop a thermonuclear bomb and will at the same time be improving their defenses against an air attack.[37]

Soviet theory and practice show, the authors contend, that the Kremlin proceeds by subversion and infiltration to undermine all the basic institutions of our society: "At the same time, the Soviet Union is seeking to create overwhelming military force, in order to back up infiltration with intimidation." The Soviet possession of atomic weapons increases the chances of a surprise attack and of a more ruthless prosecution of the Cold War against us; "it also puts a premium on piecemeal aggression against others, counting on our unwillingness to engage in atomic war unless we are directly attacked."[38]

The authors present their most important arguments in their section titled "Atomic Armaments." This part of the study contains the review group's responses to critics of the atomic strategy—most notably Kennan—joined with the case for a buildup in both nuclear and conventional weapons. The United States, they argue, now has atomic superiority. But this advantage will disappear by 1954, when the Soviets will

attain the capability to inflict serious damage on the American homeland by surprise nuclear attack.[39]

The review group then proceeds to reject each of the proposed
alternatives to or modifications of the atomic strategy. In opposing the
elimination of nuclear weapons, a pledge that the United States would
never be the first to use such weapons, and comprehensive international control, these planners reveal the pattern of assumptions about
Soviet behavior that had effectively doomed all of Kennan's suggestions
and led to his retirement. In a curiously circular logic, they contend
that if the Soviet Union develops the atomic force by 1954 that we now
estimate, "it is hardly conceivable that, if war comes, the Soviet leaders
would refrain from the use of atomic weapons unless they felt fully
confident of attaining their objectives by other means." After discussing the need in negotiations with the Soviets always to assume "the
absence of good faith," they then conclude with the negative estimate
that "it is impossible to hope that an effective plan for international
control can be negotiated unless and until the Kremlin's design has
been frustrated to a point at which a genuine and drastic change in
Soviet policies has taken place."[40]

In its final analytical section, the review group advances four "possible courses of action" open to the United States. These include continuation of current policies and programs, isolation, preventive war,
and a rapid buildup "of the political, economic, and military strength
of the free world." After an extended discussion, each of the first three is
rejected. The authors argue that a continuation of current policies would
only lead to further deterioration of America's relative military position
as the Soviet nuclear arsenal develops. Isolation is even less acceptable,
because it "would in the end condemn us to capitulate or to fight alone
and on the defensive, with drastically limited offensive and retaliatory
capabilities in comparison with the Soviet Union." If Americans, in a
desperate attempt to correct the strategic balance, came "to favor a surprise attack on the Soviet Union," it is not likely that Russia "would wait
for such an attack before launching one of its own." War, the third alternative, holds few if any advantages for the United States. Even a massive
atomic attack against the Soviets, the planners contend, "would not force

or induce the Kremlin to capitulate, and . . . [it] would still be able to use the forces under its control to dominate most or all of Eurasia."[41]

For the review group, a broadly based and rapid buildup was the only course of action "which is consistent with progress toward achieving our fundamental purpose." This includes expanded political, economic, and military programs. The immediate goals "are a renewed initiative in the Cold War and a situation to which the Kremlin would find it expedient to accommodate itself, first by relaxing tensions and pressures and then by gradual withdrawal." The United States should generate the will and the means to resist and win the cooperation of its Allies in this process: "At the same time, we should take dynamic steps to reduce the power and influence of the Kremlin inside the Soviet Union and other areas under its control. The objective would be the establishment of friendly regimes not under Kremlin domination. Such action is essential to engage the Kremlin's attention, keep it off balance and force an increased expenditure of Soviet resources in counteraction. In other words, it would be the current Soviet Cold War techniques used against the Soviet Union."

A program of this nature will be demanding and costly, but half measures would be even more expensive because they would not prevent war: "Budgetary considerations will need to be subordinated to the stark fact that our very independence as a nation may be at stake."[42]

The implementation of this rapid buildup would require a "substantial increase in expenditures for military purposes" and the improvement of programs for internal security, intelligence, and civilian defense. This shift in priorities will necessitate increased taxes and the reduction of federal expenditures for "purposes other than defense and foreign assistance." The study also calls for the "intensification of affirmative and timely measures and operations by covert means in the fields of economic warfare and political and psychological warfare with a view to fomenting and supporting unrest and revolt in selected strategic satellite countries." The success of this program depends upon winning broad bipartisan support in Congress and among the public. For the budget-conscious White House, the authors recall the lesson from World War II "that the American economy, when it operates at a level approaching full efficiency can provide enormous resources for purposes other than civilian consumption while simultaneously providing a high standard of living." After restating in less specific terms the case for the buildup, the review group concludes: "The whole success of the proposed program hangs ultimately on recognition by this Government, the American people, and all free peoples, that the Cold War is in fact a real war in which the survival of the free world is at stake."[43]

RESPONSE TO THE CALL

Among the senior State Department officials asked for reactions to NSC 68, most approved the proposal for a stronger and more active response to the Soviet Union; but many raised significant points of criticism. George Perkins of the European Affairs Office and his deputy, Llewellyn E. Thompson Jr., agreed with the conclusions of the study but felt they were not supported by adequate analysis. Edward W. Barrett of the Public Affairs Office declared that "the whole paper seems to me to point to a gigantic armament race, a huge buildup of conventional arms that quickly become obsolescent." Willard L. Thorp, assistant secretary for economic affairs, disagreed strongly with the study's contention that the Soviets were closing the gap in economic strength and advanced figures to show that the United States invested twice as much as the Soviet Union in 1949 and that America had a defense budget of $16.2 billion, compared with $9 billion for the Russians.[44]

The most interesting and most negative State Department response came from Charles Bohlen, who objected to the contention that

> the fundamental design of the Kremlin is the domination of the world. If by this is meant this is the chief purpose and, as it were, the raison d'être of the Kremlin, this carries the implication that all other considerations are subordinate to this major purpose and that great risks would be run for the sake of its achievement. It tends, therefore, to oversimplify the problem and, in my opinion, leads inevitably to the conclusion that war is inevitable. . . . I think that the thought would be more

accurate if it were to the effect that the fundamental design of those who control the USSR is (a) the maintenance of their regime in the Soviet Union, and (b) its extension throughout the world to the degree that is possible without serious risk to the internal regime.

Bohlen went on to question the deterrent value of America's nuclear arsenal and to oppose both the current atomic strategy and a proposed massive buildup of conventional arms. Instead, he wanted a clear distinction drawn between the military requirements for a cold war and those needed for a hot war and called for the integration of European forces into a defensive strategy based on new weapons against tanks, bombers, and submarines balanced with an effective strategic bomber force.[45]

The most striking aspect of these reactions is the large number of senior officials who declared that the conclusions of NSC 68 could be implemented without a significant increase in spending. Among the diplomats, Llewellyn Thompson expressed the belief that a thorough study of current programs and future needs would show "that no very great increase in our present rate of expenditure would be called for, but rather a better allocation of resources and a unified national policy." Perkins and Barrett voiced their agreement. Bohlen called for a massive program of research and development for high-quality defensive weapons and strategic bombers "in order to avoid kicking off a full-scale rearmament program."[46]

PRESIDENTIAL SKEPTICISM

Harry Truman received NSC 68 on April 11; and after reading it, he referred it to the NSC the following day. Requesting that the members devote special attention to the nature of the programs involved in the study's recommendations and their cost, he said: "Because of the effect of these Conclusions upon the budgetary and economic situation, it is my desire that the Economic Cooperation Administrator, the Director of the Bureau of the Budget and the Chairman, Council of Economic

Advisers participate in the consideration of this Report by the Council, in addition to the regular participation of the Secretary of the Treasury."

When the NSC met on April 20, it discussed the report and decided to establish an ad hoc committee to respond to the president's request for details on programs and costs. The committee included representatives of the agencies with specific economic responsibilities, and clearly the budgetary implications of the study were foremost in the president's mind.[47]

Before the outbreak of the Korean War, the Ad Hoc Committee on NSC 68 had met about eight times but had not completed its work. It had agreed on the broad outlines of the programs required and had set August 1 as a date for having "rough general plans and estimates" in hand. At a meeting on May 12, the committee members agreed that, even if contained within its present boundaries, the Soviet Union posed a threat to the United States "of increasing gravity." There was "general agreement on the serious risks of war involved in proceeding with more aggressive political, economic, and psychological measures in the absence of any adequate military shield."[48]

The main work of the committee involved estimating the costs of essential programs. By May 22, Frank Whitehouse of the Munitions Board could report tentative agreement on proposals for economic and military assistance, civil defense, propaganda, and covert activities which, taken together, required an increase from $5.2 billion in FY 1951 to $7.5 billion in FY 1955. Most elements of this evaluation depended on the magnitude of the military increases, and no final figures would be available before July. But Johnson's directive to senior defense officials on May 25 indicated that he did not anticipate a massive increase in military spending. The Joint Chiefs of Staff followed the defense secretary's guidance, and their proposals to implement the study were very close to those they had made unsuccessfully in 1948 for about $26 billion a year for FYs 1951–55, far below the cost of the massive buildup Nitze had in mind. This fiscal restraint was challenged by the National Security Resources Board, which called on May 29 for the expenditure of $11 billion on civil defense and $4.5 billion on additional strategic stockpile items from FY 1951 through FY 1955. Within a week, however, opponents of a spending binge led by the undersecretary of state,

James Webb, moved to head off excessive requests such as that from the National Security Resources Board.[49]

The start of hostilities in Korea prevented the completion of cost estimates, but the basic programs of NSC 68 won formal approval. At a meeting on September 29, the NSC "adopted the Conclusions of NSC 68 as a statement of policy to be followed over the next four or five years, and agreed that the implementing programs will be put into effect as rapidly as feasible, with the understanding that the specific nature and estimated costs of these programs will be decided as they are more firmly developed." The following day, President Truman approved this action and directed the implementation of the study's conclusions "by all appropriate executive departments and agencies of the US government."[50]

ASSESSMENT

NSC 68 essentially represents a call for increased effort and a tougher stand against the Soviet Union. In an interview decades later, the China specialist John Paton Davies described the study as "highly schematic, it was a counter to the Communist Manifesto." NSC 68 is not a dramatic departure, for it restates at length the established objectives of American policy as set forth in NSC 20/4 of November 1948. But its tone is more hostile and more urgent that the earlier study, and it contains the new goal of changing the nature of the Soviet system through political pressure backed by economic, psychological, propaganda, and covert activities. It identifies the mission of the United States as exercising active leadership of the free world in a global conflict with the Soviet Union that proceeds on political, military, and ideological levels. This study also reflects the need for a major effort at educating the America's people and its Allies about the need for greater exertion and sacrifice in the Cold War.[51]

Years later, Acheson contended in his memoirs that the purpose of NSC 68 "was to so bludgeon the mass mind of 'top government' that not only could the President make a decision but that the decision could be carried out." Yet even viewed as a call to action, NSC 68 is an amazingly incomplete and amateurish study. The authors overdraw the monolithic and evil nature of the communist bloc. They overlook many nations in the "free world" that have no democratic or responsible government. The review group also draws large and significant conclusions (e.g., the impossibility of international control of atomic energy) from broad assumptions about Soviet behavior and from vague estimates of economic and technological capabilities (e.g., the contention that the Soviets are catching up with the United States in military strength). The concluding analysis of courses of action is sophomoric, in posing four alternatives—which include two straw options (isolation and war), one unacceptable choice (continuation of current policies), and the obviously desired solution (a rapid political, economic, and military buildup). Most serious, the authors deliberately avoided including specific recommendations for program expansion or estimates of cost, despite their belief that vastly increased expenditures would be necessary.[52]

The Korean War provided the necessary impetus for the adoption of the programs implicit in NSC 68. If war had not intervened, there is strong evidence that no major increase in defense spending would have won the administration's approval. The number and position of people who either opposed increased spending or assumed it was not necessary is very impressive, as are the critical comments on proposed programs made in the Ad Hoc Committee by representatives of the Bureau of the Budget, the Treasury, and the Council of Economic Advisers. Most important, Truman certainly would not have accepted a large increase in spending without an overwhelming case being made. If peace had continued under basically similar conditions through 1950, it is likely that the cost of NSC 68 programs would not have exceeded $3 billion annually. What NSC 68 did accomplish was to start senior officials thinking about an increasing Soviet threat and how to respond to it. The real significance of NSC 68 was its timing—the tocsin sounded just before the fire.

6

NORTH KOREA DRIVES SOUTH

I n earlier chapters, we have examined how Kim Il-sung won Stalin's approval for an invasion of the south and how the Soviet leader then shifted the burden of support in case of a military disaster to Mao Zedong. In this series of maneuvers, Kim was the driving force for an attack, while Stalin was the enabler and ultimate decisionmaker who shrewdly manipulated Mao into pledging to provide emergency rescue services.

Kim had a compelling vision of a unified Korea. As he argued in his meetings with Stalin and Mao, the Democratic People's Republic of Korea (North Korea) was "the only true representative of Korean national independence," whereas the Republic of Korea (South Korea) was "an illegitimate client state of the United States." Now was the time to attack, because the north was strong and had large revolutionary cadres in the south that would rise to support the revolution. This was also the ideal opportunity to push "American imperialism" off the peninsula, before the south rearmed and Japan revived and recreated its military strength. The fact that the Truman administration had withdrawn US combat troops from South Korea the previous year and was known to be consolidating its commitments in East Asia was another important factor in the Soviet and Chinese leaders' calculus.[1]

THE FORMATION OF A REVOLUTIONARY ARMY

The Korean People's Army (KPA) emerged from the public security component of the North Korean Provisional People's Committee starting in September 1946. This central group organized people's committees in every city and village in the north, and the carefully selected members of these local bodies provided the basic political and economic guidance for the nascent North Korean state. The local committees identified loyal residents for recruitment into the security forces. The instructions for the local committees were to concentrate on male workers and peasants between eighteen and twenty-five years of age who were mentally and physically fit. The central government's ability to create mass mobilization down to the village level "far exceeded anything accomplished earlier in Korean history," contends Charles Armstrong. The KPA was formally created on February 8, 1948. The leaders of this young army were Kim Il-sung's closest comrades from his days fighting the Japanese in Manchuria, and they included Ch'oe Yonggon, Kim Ch'aek, Kim Il, and Kang Kon. This group would remain at the core of North Korea's leadership, forming a "guerrilla band state"—an illuminating description coined by Wada Haruki, the leading Japanese specialist on North Korea's formative years.[2]

From the start of the occupation, Soviet officers played a key role in training North Korean security forces. They established the Pyongyang Academy as a military training school with instructors from the sizable group of Soviet Koreans, devoted Korean Communists who had been trained as political commissars and staff officers in Moscow. Before the Red Army combat troops withdrew at the end of 1948, several thousand Koreans went to the Soviet Union for education in various fields including military affairs. This process was formalized for military staff officers by mid-1948. Also at this time, all officers who had served in the Japanese military were removed from the KPA. In South Korea, by contrast, the army was led almost entirely by men who had served in the Imperial Japanese Army, a point often emphasized by North Korean propaganda.

With the departure of their combat troops, Soviet advisers remained with the KPA, working as far down in the ranks as battalion level.[3]

The Chinese Communist Party (CCP) also made significant contributions to the preparation of North Korea for combat. When the civil war broke into full-scale conflict on multiple fronts in June 1946, the Nationalists cut off the lines of communication and supply of the main Communist forces with their units in Northeast China. With encouragement from the Soviets, North Korea offered support to the Communists by allowing them to use the region south of the Yalu River as a rear area to care for their sick and wounded, to transfer supplies and ammunition between north and south Manchuria via North Korean railroads and ports, and to purchase war materials from North Korea. "Without the assistance of the North Korean Communists, CCP forces in southern Manchuria could have been totally destroyed by the" Nationalists, contends Chen Jian. Support with war material and transportation from North Korea "dramatically strengthened the CCP's strategic position in China's civil war." Indeed, Mao and his colleagues would later use this critical aid "to justify their decision to send Chinese troops" to join North Korea in fighting American forces.[4]

When a Communist victory was in sight, the Chinese leaders agreed to return Korean units with their arms to Pyongyang's control. Between September 1949 and June 1950, over 47,000 Korean combat veterans returned to form the core of the North Korean invasion force. At the time of the attack, over half the KPA force had battle experience in China, including a substantial proportion of their officers. These combat hardened veterans gave the North Korean forces a considerable advantage over their South Korean opponents.[5]

Despite the extensive cooperation between Chinese and North Korean communist leaders, Kim Il-sung did not want to become dependent on Mao. After all, his own political training and sponsorship on the road to power in Pyongyang had come from Soviet officials with Stalin's blessing. He also relied heavily on the Soviet Koreans for management of the army and the security forces, which formed the foundation of his control of state institutions. Scholars of North Korean politics in this period are in broad agreement that the Korean Communist Party was sharply divided in mid-1950 between a southern faction headed by Pak Hon-yong; a Chinese section led by Pak Il-yu, Kim Ung, and Mu Chong; and a central group headed by Kim Il-sung and including the Soviet Koreans. Kim Il-sung's basic identity was as a Korean nationalist. As Chen Jian argues, "Kim needed Beijing's support, but he would not totally rely on Chinese goodwill." The same can be said for full reliance on Moscow.[6]

The KPA's expansion and rearmament began as early as December 1946, when the first contingent of Soviet occupation troops withdrew, leaving their arms for the local security force. Other arms transfers occurred in the summers of the next two years, and a large cache was left when the remaining Soviet combat troops withdrew at the end of 1948. A major increase in military strength began at the end of April 1949, when Kim wrote Stalin asking for arms and ammunition for new artillery and tank units that were being formed. The negotiations over the types and numbers of weapons were concluded in an agreement of June 4, and the promised goods soon began moving into North Korea. Among the items provided by the Soviet Union were 98 propeller-driven aircraft of World War II vintage, 87 tanks, 57 armored personnel carriers, 102 self-propelled guns, numerous small arms, landing craft, torpedo boats, and a range of communications equipment. In return for this vast trove of weapons, the Soviet Union required North Korea to pay with exports of rice and other food items and various types of metals.[7]

In sending arms to Pyongyang in mid-1949, Moscow's main concern was an attack from South Korea soon after US combat troops withdrew in June. Ambassador Terentii Shtykov reported frequently to Stalin about the lack of North Korean defenses against the repeated invasion threats from Syngman Rhee. Stalin consistently urged Shtykov to prevent North Korean troops from starting skirmishes with South Korean forces across the 38th Parallel. When, in September 1949, Kim expressed a desire to attack South Korean units in the Ongjin Peninsula west of Seoul, the Soviet ambassador and his military staff strongly opposed this provocation and reported it to Moscow. The foreign minister took this report before the Politburo, and the leadership declared on September 24 that North Korea was not ready for war and had many preparatory steps to complete before any attack. Only a month later, Moscow thought Shtykov might be encouraging Kim to probe South Korean defenses. This time, Stalin personally sent a strong cable to his ambassador on October 30, rebuking him "for provoking [the] North Koreans to start local offensive operations against South Koreans." He added: "Such provocations are very dangerous for our interests and can induce the adversary to launch a big war. Your actions are totally irresponsible." Shtykov immediately defended his actions and claimed he had done nothing to encourage North Korean attacks. Stalin remained concerned about premature North Korean offensives and restated the leadership's strict rules in another cable three weeks later. Throughout 1949, Stalin made every effort to avoid war in Korea.[8]

At the same time that Moscow was repeatedly urging restraint, Kim Il-sung was continuing to build up his military forces. Late in December 1949, Kim requested through Ambassador Shtykov large quantities of small arms and ammunition in order to equip new units to be formed in the next few months. He proposed to pay for these weapons with a shipment of rare and nonferrous metals. These items arrived in North Korea early in 1950. Even before Kim arrived in Moscow to discuss Stalin's cable of January 30 offering to help prepare an invasion of the south, the Soviet leader dispatched a large military training mission to North Korea. Starting in February, this contingent traveled to Pyongyang. The group included 150 officers and men commanded by Lieutenant General Nikolai A. Vasiliyev, a decorated armor commander from the battles of Stalingrad and Kursk. This unit brought the total number of Soviet advisers in North Korea to at least 1,000. After Kim's three-week visit to Moscow in March and April, a wide variety of arms began to flow to North Korea in large quantities.[9]

As the KPA trained new units and helped them adapt to recently arrived weapons, senior officers with their Soviet advisers drafted a plan of attack. The basic objectives of the plan were strikingly audacious: capture Seoul and break the will of the South Korean government in four days; join a guerrilla force in the center of the country estimated to be 200,000 strong; and celebrate complete victory and unification in Pusan on August 15—Korean Independence Day. Kim was determined to launch the attack before the end of June, when the summer rainy season would begin. In April, the plan based on these objectives was flatly rejected by General Vasiliyev and his senior colleagues as incomplete and inflexible in case of unanticipated circumstances. Veterans of the fierce battles against Nazi Germany then drafted a more complex plan by mid-May and had it translated into Korean.[10]

The elements of the approved plan for Operation Preemptive Strike started with a political diversion. Kim called for the convening of an all-Korean conference sponsored by the Democratic Front for the Unification of the Fatherland, expecting that Rhee would immediately reject this proposal. North Korean propaganda officials would then issue reports of South Korean troop movements and an attack against northern forces on the Ongjin Peninsula. The KPA would next launch its offensive under the guise of a counterattack. The initial North Korean attack would be on the Ongjin Peninsula, to be followed later on the first day by an invasion through Kaesong. The main assault would come a bit later on a corridor leading directly to Seoul, and this would be supported by a force attacking further to the east, which, after breaking through defenses, would turn to the west and occupy territory south of Seoul to prevent reinforcement from the center of South Korea. The central premise remained that with the capture of Seoul within a week or less, the Rhee government and the South Korean army would collapse, and the only other task would be cleaning up pockets of resistance on the route to Pusan.[11]

One might reasonably ask why the invasion's planners would not see the contradiction in presenting as a counterattack an invasion code-named Operation Preemptive Strike. The answer is simple: Only a very small group knew that an invasion was planned for late June, and even fewer knew its code name. The preliminary orders for the assault force to move into position went out on June 8, and final operational orders went to corps and division commanders on June 15. The political diversion went as planned, with a prompt rejection from Seoul, and the North Korean propaganda machine moved into action. But reports that the invasion preparations had leaked to the South Koreans forced a change in the attack schedule on June 21. Instead of a phased attack on day one, all KPA assault units would attack at the same time, at 4 A.M. on Sunday, June 25. Stalin was notified of this last-minute change, and on June 21 he replied: "We agree with Kim Il-sung's idea for an immediate advance along the whole front line."[12]

ORDERS OF BATTLE

On the eve of two years of border skirmishes becoming a full-scale civil war, it is useful to evaluate the respective armed forces of the two combatants. We will forgo the full detail of what military planners call an order of battle and concentrate on a series of telling comparisons and imbalances. Almost all these comparisons show an advantage for North Korea. The KPA had a force of 150,000 troops, plus 34,000 local constabulary police; South Korea had an army of 95,000, of which at least one-third were in training or support duties at the outbreak of war. North Korea had a clear advantage in combat experience, with three divisions recently returned from serving with the People's Liberation Army (PLA) in China. Pyongyang's forces also benefited from having at least fifty Soviet Korean generals, many with World War II experience, as well as ten generals who had served with the PLA in China. By contrast, four of eight South Korean divisions spent the first half of 1950 patrolling in the center of the country in a pacification program to suppress insurgents. In motivation and loyalty, the North had a further advantage. Kim and his colleagues had purged the KPA of officers and senior noncommissioned officers who had served with the Japanese, and a program of mass mobilization down to the village level had been in effect in North Korea since the middle of 1946. The months of counterinsurgency in the South had left many of South Korean forces dispirited and with poor motivation, while the best of their senior officers had served with the Japanese and were not fully trusted by Rhee.[13]

Beyond the size and quality of its forces, North Korea had a significant advantage in training and armament. In addition to the instruction by about 1,000 Soviet advisers, the KPA benefited greatly from the return

of at least 47,000 ethnic Korean "volunteers" from the Chinese Communist forces. The North had a sizable armored force built around 151 T-34
tanks and an artillery component of 176 SU-76 self-propelled guns and
a large number of 122-millimeter howitzers. To provide close air support, North Korea had 130 fighters and fighter-bombers of World War II
vintage. In comparison, South Korea had no effective combat aircraft
and no tanks or antitank mines, and none of its guns could penetrate
the frontal or turret armor of the T-34 tanks. The South was also inferior
in the number of artillery pieces (it had 91 105-millimeter howitzers)
and in their maximum range. The South Korean Army's 105-millimeter
howitzers had a range of 8,000 yards, while the three types of KPA guns
had ranges from 14,000 to 22,000 yards, which meant they could destroy
the South's artillery before it became a threat to KPA forces. On command-
and-control questions, the North had a clear advantage. The top three
officials in control of defense, industry, and the army were Kim's closest colleagues from fighting in Manchuria, while in South Korea the
defense and army leadership were fractious and even the top generals
were suspected of being more loyal to the US Korean Military Assistance Group (KMAG) than to Rhee. The most serious weakness of the
North Korean military was its logistical capacity. If the invasion did not
crush the will of the South Korean government and destroy most of its
top forces in capturing Seoul quickly, the North would have great difficulty in providing supplies and transportation for a conflict of several
months. "Much like the German Schlieffen Plan of 1914," argues Allan
Millett, "the North Koreans planned for a short war since it was the only
war they could win."[14]

In all these hasty preparations, one important partner was kept in the
dark: Mao Zedong. The CCP leader was in Moscow negotiating a treaty
of alliance and support for two full weeks after Stalin decided to assist
Kim in his often-proposed invasion, but the Soviet dictator did not mention his changed policy to Mao. Stalin and Kim kept Mao out of all planning for the war, even as the People's Republic of China returned three
divisions of Korean soldiers to Pyongyang's control. Mao was given no
date for the attack and did not know the details of Soviet arms shipments
to North Korea, because they all arrived by sea. Mao had no embassy in

Pyongyang, only a small economic mission that learned nothing of the war preparations. While Mao was absorbed in domestic issues, including land reform and a massive demobilization of the PLA, he had pledged to provide reserve forces if problems arose. In any normal alliance, he would have been kept informed. As it was, the head of the Chinese economic mission in North Korea was on vacation when the invasion occurred, and Mao received a briefing from a Korean officer two days after the war began. After this meeting, Mao complained to his adviser and Russian translator, Shi Zhe, that "they are our next-door neighbors, but they did not consult with us about the outbreak of the war. They did not come to tell us until now." This failure to share important information gives an insight into Kim's determination to control everything himself. The stakes were very high for Kim. If his plan succeeded in unifying Korea, he would become the unquestioned leader of the country and would win considerable autonomy from his patrons in Moscow and Beijing. But if his plan failed, there would be serious consequences. In either outcome, this behavior toward Mao portended even greater rivalry and suspicion between the three communist rulers in coming years.[15]

THE ATTACK

After making last-minute adjustments to the battle plan, seven KPA divisions launched simultaneous attacks along five corridors on June 25, 1950. At 4 A.M. on a rain-swept Sunday, the invasion caught South Korean forces completely by surprise. Backed by 151 tanks, 130 aircraft, and a sizable array of artillery, the KPA advanced steadily in the early hours of the assault. Behind the attacking force were three reserve divisions with additional armored units. Given their training, combat experience, and armaments—plus the important element of surprise—the KPA should have moved swiftly to open the three corridors to Seoul and the Han River bridges. But due to cautious leadership, a fear of mistakes, and a misuse of tanks and artillery, the army managed to capture Seoul in four days and then ground to a halt.[16] (See figure 6.1.)

FIGURE 6.1 Kim Il-sung addresses a political conference in front of a portrait of his patron, Joseph Stalin, October 1953.

Source: US National Archives.

A substantial portion of the credit for the North Korean success should be attributed to the poor preparation, inadequate armament, and inept leadership of the South Korean forces. Part of this was due to the surprise attack. The two divisions defending two of the corridors to Seoul were at partial strength—half the troops had leave for a long weekend, and many of their officers were in Seoul for the Saturday opening of a new officers club. The responsibility for insufficient armaments lay with the United States, which had refused repeated requests for tanks, heavy artillery, and combat aircraft as a means of preventing Rhee from attacking the North, as he frequently threatened to do. The greatest responsibility for an inadequate defense falls upon President Rhee, the defense minister, the army chief of staff, and the division commanders. Among these officials, the most serious mistakes are attributable to General Chae Pyong-duk, a former Japanese ordnance officer now serving as the South Korean Army's chief of staff. Although a genial person, General Chae was known to the US KMAG as someone who was unwilling to stand up to the president's shifting whims and as somewhat deficient in energy and judgment. When the divisions guarding the approaches to Seoul were overwhelmed, Chae hastily ordered parts of four other divisions to join them, thereby losing the opportunity to forge an integrated defense of the capital or a coordinated counterattack. Yet even with these limitations, the South Korean forces achieved some success. The most significant was a naval victory, when a destroyer sank an armed North Korean freighter carrying 600 commandos on a mission to block the port at Pusan. The notable achievement on the ground was the successful defense of Hongchon by the South Korean Sixth Division, which was well positioned and fought off two KPA divisions.[17]

As the North Korean forces moved steadily toward Seoul, the acting commander of the KMAG relayed reports from his advisory teams with the four South Korean divisions deployed near the border. US ambassador John J. Muccio made his first report to the State Department at 9:30 A.M., describing the attack as "an all-out offensive against the Republic of Korea." A similar report went from the military attaché to General MacArthur's Far East Command headquarters in Tokyo. After receiving further details on the military situation, MacArthur sent a radiogram to the Joint Chiefs of Staff calling for aid to South Korea. Privately, he told a Republican newspaper editor that this act of "inexcusable, unprovoked aggression" had to be confronted and expressed the belief that American opinion would persuade the president to intervene. Responding to an urgent request from the ambassador in Seoul, MacArthur ordered shipments of weapons and ammunition be sent to South Korea as quickly as possible. He made this commitment on June 25, a full day before it would be approved by the Joint Chiefs and the president. Rhee, in a state of panic, called MacArthur at 3 A.M. on June 26, only to be told by an aide that the general did not receive calls outside office hours. When the seventy-six-year-old president exploded in anger and anxiety, MacArthur came on the line to reassure him that ammunition, F-51 fighter-bombers, 105- and 155-millimeter howitzers, and antitank rockets were on their way.[18]

Meanwhile in Seoul, Ambassador Muccio and his staff implemented their emergency plan to evacuate American dependents and civilians. The initial group of 700 sailed from Inchon for Japan on the evening of June 26. Within the South Korean government, top officials debated whether to abandon Seoul and establish a line of defense south of the Han River. General Chae overruled strong arguments for a coordinated defense south of the river and ordered disorganized units to join a defense north of the capital. The North Korean advance soon overwhelmed this poorly conceived plan, and emergency arrangements were made to evacuate the capital. During these debates and decisions, President Rhee was paralyzed with fear and missed several key meetings. On Tuesday, June 27, the president and his cabinet abandoned the capital on a special train at 4 A.M., moving to the central city of Taejon to set up a temporary government. In a confused withdrawal, military engineers blew up the bridges over the Han River between 2 and 4 A.M. on Wednesday, June 28, stranding many troops, supplies, and civilians in the city. Over the next two days, a makeshift flotilla of ferries and private boats evacuated some remaining troops along with tanks, ammunition, artillery, and communication equipment. By June 29, Seoul was in the control of North Korean forces, except for a few isolated pockets of resistance.[19]

The capture of Seoul did not produce the results Kim had forecast to his Soviet partners and his own colleagues. The South Korean government, though severely shaken, did not collapse. The ROK army was battered and disorganized, but it had survived and would be reconstituted. There was no uprising of Communist supporters to clinch the North Korean victory. To make matters worse, and to almost everyone's surprise, the Truman administration made a quick decision to intervene in support of South Korea. On the evening of June 25, the president ordered the use of US air and naval forces to protect the evacuation of American personnel. The next evening, he expanded this order to authorize these forces to attack North Korean units operating below the 38th Parallel. By the 27th, US Air Force planes were in action over South Korea, which would have a significant effect in blunting the KPA advance. Adding to this litany of bad news for Pyongyang, the United Nations Security Council voted on June 25 to condemn the North Korean aggression and demand that its forces withdraw. And on June 27, the UN Security Council called on all members to assist South Korea in repelling the armed attack and restoring peace in the region.[20]

7

TRUMAN REVERSES POLICY

I n the days before North Korean divisions attacked across the 38th Parallel, United States and South Korean officials had no sense of an imminent conflict. Tension along the border had been much higher in 1949. A small US intelligence unit in Seoul reported accurately on the buildup of Soviet arms and trainers in North Korea, the evacuation of civilians from the border region, and the expansion of the Korean People's Army with new conscripts and veterans from the Chinese Civil War. But no one on General MacArthur's staff in Tokyo or in Washington put this information together and argued that an invasion was probable. The CIA's last prewar estimate for Korea—on June 19, 1950—showed that the North Korean forces had improved their capability for an invasion, yet the estimate stopped short of predicting the likelihood or the timing of an attack.[1]

The principal concerns of General of the Army Douglas MacArthur were rebuilding Japan into a democratic partner of the United States and a bulwark against the expansion of Soviet Communism and strengthening the defense of Formosa (Taiwan) to protect his good friend Jiang Jieshi. After the withdrawal of US combat troops from South Korea in June 1949, that country was no longer under the authority of MacArthur's Far East Command. Although his highly loyal intelligence chief, Major General Charles A. Willoughby, did collect reports from the intelligence unit in Seoul and forward them to Washington, MacArthur did not read them. As Allan Millett argues, "The defense of South Korea was not a MacArthur priority."[2]

The main news reports on the Far East in the week before the invasion concerned the visit of two delegations from Washington. A group led by John Foster Dulles, special adviser to the secretary of state for negotiation of a peace treaty with Japan, was in Seoul from June 18 to 21. The top Republican foreign policy specialist was in South Korea to reassure Syngman Rhee of the United States' continued support. During his visit, he addressed the National Assembly and made a trip to inspect the border fortifications at the 38th Parallel on June 19. At the same time another delegation—led by the secretary of defense, Louis Johnson, and the chairman of the Joint Chiefs of Staff, General Omar Bradley—was in Tokyo June 18–20 to discuss with MacArthur the implications of a peace treaty with Japan on defense strategy for Asia. Their talks focused on retaining military and naval bases in Japan and the defense of Formosa. While in Tokyo, Major General Willoughby briefed the visitors on recent intelligence reports but gave no indication of impending troubles. A concerned citizen reading a major US newspaper the week before the invasion would have gathered no sense of tension or looming conflict at any level in Korea.[3]

Meanwhile, in Washington June was another intense political month with no foreboding of war in Korea. The Tydings Committee investigating Senator McCarthy's charges of communist influence and disloyalty in the State Department was in its third month of hearings. On June 15, drawing inappropriately on testimony given in an executive session, McCarthy made additional accusations in a speech before the National Editorial Association in Groton, Connecticut. The Wisconsin senator asserted that the deputy undersecretary of state, John Peurifoy, had arranged a "secret 'payoff'" for a witness in exchange for favorable testimony. Both Peurifoy and the witness categorically denied these charges. Other comments about the Tydings Committee's work came from Senator Henry Cabot Lodge Jr., who told reporters that, after reviewing "a representative cross section" of the loyalty files of eighty-one accused State Department employees, he found the files incomplete and inadequate either to prove or disprove McCarthy's accusations. The new assistant secretary of state for Far Eastern affairs, Dean Rusk, testified on June 20 before an executive session of the House Foreign Affairs Committee that "our goal . . . is to assist the South Koreans to establish a security force which can deal with domestic disorders, armed bands coming across the 38th Parallel, and force the opposition to make the choice to fight a major war as the price for taking over southern Korea. We see no present indication that the people across the border have any intention of fighting a major war for that purpose."[4]

In attempting to reduce international commitments and limit defense spending, the Truman administration was dangerously vulnerable before its political opponents if it lost any more territory to the communists. The president had often told his cabinet members and senior officials to recommend the policies that were right for the nation and leave the politics to him. He had undertaken extensive obligations under the Truman Doctrine, the Marshall Plan, and the North Atlantic Treaty. However, if a foreign adversary challenged any of these commitments, both the current levels of the armed forces and the budgets for economic and military assistance were inadequate. While pledging support for the Republic of Korea, the administration had pulled out its combat troops, even as the Soviets armed and trained the North Korean Army. The president had denied repeated requests from Syngman Rhee for tanks, heavy artillery, and combat aircraft, and General MacArthur's forces in Japan were below half strength of their authorized numbers. The Republicans and many others blamed Truman for losing China to the communists. Further complicating the administration's future policy choices, the Republican Party had adopted McCarthy's virulent charges and would support them as long as they proved useful. Anticommunism was rampaging, and bipartisanship was dead. The cocky Missouri politician would soon find the political and military buck landing squarely in his lap.

A QUIET WEEKEND INTERRUPTED

On a hot summer afternoon, Harry Truman arrived at his home in Independence, Missouri, for a 48-hour visit with his wife and daughter and a welcome respite from the political battles of Washington. It was Saturday, June 24, and on his flight to the Midwest the president had stopped in Baltimore to dedicate Friendship International Airport. Unknown to him, as he flew from Baltimore to Kansas City, war erupted on the other side of the international dateline, as North Korean forces poured across the 38th Parallel. Questions of foreign policy were far from Truman's mind as he looked forward to relaxation and home-cooked meals, and to making arrangements to put a new roof on the family farmhouse a few miles away in Grandview.[5]

After dinner with his wife Bess, his daughter Margaret, and Bess's mother, they chatted about family and local news on the screened-in porch. They had just gone inside when, at 9:20 P.M., Dean Acheson called from Washington with the news of the North Korean invasion. The secretary of state reported that it was not yet clear how serious the crisis was; but to be prudent, he recommended calling for an emergency session of the United Nations Security Council. Truman endorsed this proposal and was prepared to return to Washington that night, until Acheson convinced him to wait until the next day when more details of the conflict would be known. The secretary made sure that the news of taking the issue before the UN would be in the Sunday morning papers along with the announcement of the outbreak of war.[6]

On Sunday, Truman went about his normal routine of a morning walk and a trip to his farm in Grandview to complete plans for the new roof on the farmhouse and to inspect a new milking machine. Meanwhile, officials in Washington analyzed reports from overseas that gave more details of the fighting. Ambassador John J. Muccio cabled that South Korean forces needed an urgent shipment of ammunition from US supplies in Japan, and a few hours later reported that four North Korean fighters had attacked Kimpo Airport near Seoul. He repeated his earlier plea for sending fighter aircraft for the defense of South Korean troops and civilians, declaring that the outcome "of hostilities may depend largely on whether US will or will not give adequate air assistance." General Willoughby reported to the army's chief of staff that Seoul and the US Embassy were threatened and that General MacArthur, in response to the ambassador's request, had ordered the evacuation of American dependents and civilians to begin the next day under air and naval protection by US forces from Japan.[7]

Further reports contended that the Soviet Union was obviously behind the North Korean invasion and called for prompt US action in a rapidly deteriorating situation. The counselor of the US Embassy in Moscow, Walworth Barbour, argued that the attack was a "clear-cut Soviet challenge . . . [to] our leadership of [the] free world" and the defeat of South Korea would seriously unsettle relations with Japan and Southeast Asia. He called on the United States to defend South Korean independence "by all means at our disposal, including military help." From Tokyo, John Foster Dulles and John Allison, the senior State Department officer managing Northeast Asian affairs who was accompanying Dulles, jointly urged Acheson to support a strong response including force if necessary because a North Korean victory "would start [a] disastrous chain of events leading most probably to world war." MacArthur reported on a worsening situation in Korea, and Ambassador Muccio described a late-night meeting in which President Rhee appeared under "great strain" and spoke in incomplete and disorganized sentences.[8]

Late Sunday morning, senior State Department and Defense Department officials gathered to develop recommendations to present to the president when he returned to Washington. They reached an early consensus that it was very important to take a strong stand against what all saw as a challenge initiated by the Soviet Union. The State Department's representatives proposed recommendations for the president to consider, and the military officials accepted them. Taken together, these proposals called for American intervention to defend South Korea, if possible, under a UN mandate. Acheson called the president midmorning after he had returned home from the farm. The secretary said the president should return to Washington as soon as possible. Truman, with Margaret's help, made preparations for a rapid departure. After a quick lunch, the presidential party drove to the airport, leaving two White House staff members behind in their haste.[9]

INCREMENTAL INTERVENTION

While Truman was traveling back to Washington, the UN Security Council met and passed a resolution designating the North Korean invasion "a breach of the peace" and calling for North Korea to cease hostilities and withdraw to the 38th Parallel. The council called on all members to give "every assistance to the United Nations in the execution of this resolution." The resolution passed unanimously, with Yugoslavia abstaining and with the Soviet ambassador absent as a protest of the council not accepting the People's Republic of China (PRC) as the representative of China in place of the Nationalist government. Also, during the afternoon, the State Department's Office of Intelligence Research sent a report to senior officials analyzing the implications of a communist victory in Korea. In its evaluation of Soviet motives, it asserted that "the North Korean Government is completely under Kremlin control and there is no possibility that the North Koreans acted without prior instruction from Moscow. The move against South Korea must therefore be considered a Soviet move." In assessing the implications for the rest of Asia, the analysts argued that the domination of Korea by the Soviets would be most severe for Japan, which would be intimidated, and it "would strengthen [the] existing widespread desire for neutrality." There would also be negative impact on the ability of Formosa and Southeast Asia to resist communist influence. A failure of the United States to protect South Korea would have a strong effect on Western Europe, where US Allies would question American will and power. The damage would produce a special degree of alarm in Germany, and the authors forecast that "Germans in all Zones will inevitably consider the possibility of the East German paramilitary police playing in Germany the same 'unifying' role the Soviet has assigned to its North Korean forces." The strong message of this intelligence estimate was that the cost of US inaction would be extremely high around the world.[10]

The president arrived at Washington's National Airport shortly after 7 P.M., where he was met by Acheson, Louis Johnson, and James Webb. On the ride to his temporary residence in Blair House (the White House was undergoing renovation), Truman declared: "By God, I am going to let them have it!" The president's attitude foretold the course of decisions to be taken over the next three days. On short notice the president had arranged for dinner to be served at Blair House for a working session with his top diplomatic and military advisers. During drinks before dinner, Secretary of Defense Johnson asked General Bradley to read a memorandum they had been given by General MacArthur in Tokyo emphasizing the high strategic value of Formosa and the importance of defending it. Acheson saw Johnson's initiative as an attempt to refocus the forthcoming discussion on broader issues of Asian security and away from Korea, which he deemed unimportant. Before others could jump in, Truman cut off the exchange and said they should postpone substantive discussions until they met privately, after dinner was finished and the table had been cleared.[11]

Serious discussion began after dinner, when the president asked Acheson to report on recent news from Korea and present the recommendations for policy decisions developed earlier in the day. The group generally agreed with the recommendations, and General Bradley supported taking a firm stand in Korea and Formosa and justified this in part by emphasizing that he felt the Soviet Union was not prepared to engage in general war. The chairman of the Joint Chiefs of Staff contended that the conflict in Korea "offered as good an occasion for action in drawing a line as anywhere else." He added that he was not in favor of sending American ground forces to Korea, and he was joined in this opinion by Secretary of the Army Frank Pace and Louis Johnson. The president asked the chief of staff of the air force, General Hoyt Vandenberg, if the United States could destroy all Soviet air bases in the Far East if necessary, and the general replied that it could be done but might require the use of atomic bombs. Truman then announced his decisions:

- MacArthur to ship such arms, ammunition, and supplies to South Korea as requested by the ambassador in Seoul;
- MacArthur to send a survey team to Korea to evaluate the military situation;

- The US Seventh Fleet to head north from the Philippines toward the Formosa Strait and await orders on its mission;
- The US Air Force to develop plans to destroy Soviet air bases in the Far East but take no action until ordered; and
- Top officials of the State Department and Defense Department to study "the next probable place in which Soviet action might take place."

In conclusion, the president directed air and naval forces to protect the evacuation of American dependents from the Inchon-Kimpo-Seoul area. During their discussion of actions to be taken, both Acheson and Johnson strongly urged the president to give careful, precise instructions to General MacArthur and not leave him room to exercise his discretion. Truman knew this was good advice, but he understood that it might not always be easy to implement. As the group relaxed over a nightcap, the president said to John D. Hickerson, assistant secretary of state for United Nations affairs: "Jack, in the final analysis I did this for the United Nations. . . . It was our idea and in this first big test we just couldn't let them down." The United States had taken the initial steps to commit air and naval forces to action in Korea. The commitment could have ended with the evacuation of American civilians. But the context and tone of the discussion at Blair House on the night of June 25 indicated that all present were prepared to take additional steps to defend South Korea if they were needed.[12]

By midmorning on Monday, June 26, a report from Seoul raised questions for the hopes of the previous evening at Blair House. Ambassador Muccio described a situation of "rapid deterioration and disintegration," saying that he had begun evacuation of embassy personnel to the south of the country. As this news reached senior officials, Harry Truman made his first formal statement on the Korean conflict. Without describing the decisions that had been made, he endorsed the action of the UN Security Council and declared that the United States "will vigorously support the effort of the Council to terminate this serious breach of the peace." The president concluded with a portentous statement: "Willful disregard of the obligation to keep the peace cannot be tolerated by nations that support the United Nations Charter."[13]

That same morning, Truman explained his thinking about the crisis to George Elsey, a member of his administrative staff. In response to Elsey's comment that the next communist move could be an invasion of Formosa, the president said he was much more concerned with the Middle East because of Stalin's need for oil. He then drew a comparison with the crisis over Greece in 1947, saying: "Korea is the Greece of the Far East. If we are tough enough now, if we stand up to them, like we did in Greece three years ago, they won't take any next steps. But if we just stand by, they'll move into Iran and they'll take over the whole Middle East. There is no telling what they'll do if we don't put up a fight now."[14]

Truman's analysis may appear simplistic and uninformed on Soviet capabilities as well as Middle East realities. Yet consider that Charles E. Bohlen, one of the top American experts on Soviet politics and Stalin's strategic thinking, arrived at the same conclusions about the nature of Soviet policy and how the United States should respond to the North Korean invasion. Bohlen, then the minister at the US Embassy in Paris, cabled a personal message on June 26 to his fellow Kremlinologist, George Kennan, who had delayed his planned leave of absence to stay in his post as counselor of the State Department to deal with issues concerning Korea and Soviet policy. Bohlen's immediate goal was to argue against a proposal from the department to make a direct appeal to the Soviet Union to help end hostilities in Korea. He contended that such a step would hand "a distinct tactical advantage" to the Soviets by allowing them to use the promise of diplomacy to delay or possibly defeat US and UN action in Korea and also remove the Kremlin leaders' appearance of noninvolvement, which could allow them at a later date to pressure the North Koreans to back down without losing face. Bohlen then went on to give the context of his analysis of Soviet policy, saying that this appeared to him as

a very clear case of typical Stalin methods, whereby he initiates action not formally and directly involving the Soviet Union which he can and will press to the full if only weakness is encountered while leaving himself a way out without too direct loss of Soviet face if he considers the risks were becoming too great. . . .

This is the clearest case of direct defiance of the United States, plus for the first time overt violation of a frontier that has occurred since the end of the war, and you may be sure that all Europeans, to say nothing of the Asiatics, are watching to see what the United States will do. It is a situation requiring the maximum firmness, and even a willingness to take major risks, in order to convince the Kremlin that we mean business without, however, forcing them publicly into a position from which there can be no retreat.[15]

Subsequent events would show that Bohlen's assessment and his policy recommendation were astute and that the president had, by a different route, come to make the appropriate decisions.

As the afternoon of June 26 progressed, reports told of the disintegration of the defenses north of Seoul, and General MacArthur cabled that "complete collapse is imminent." A cable from Ambassador Muccio said that President Rhee and most of his cabinet had left Seoul for a new location in the south. Acheson called the president just before 7:30 P.M. to propose another Blair House meeting. Truman agreed, and the same group gathered at 9 P.M. When General Vandenberg opened the discussion by reporting that US pilots had shot down a Soviet-made YAK-3 fighter over Kimpo Airfield, the president said he hoped this would not be the last one. Acheson then proposed the commitment of air and naval forces for the full support of the South Korean Army. Truman approved—with the limitation that, for the present, no US forces should be engaged in combat above the 38th Parallel. Then the secretary of state moved to reverse a carefully developed policy toward Formosa by proposing that the Seventh Fleet be positioned in the Formosa Strait to prevent either the Communists or the Nationalists from attacking the other across the strait. The president approved this fateful decision, which once again engaged the United States in the tangles of the Chinese Civil War.[16]

Other decisions made that evening expanded American commitments in other parts of the region and started consideration of possible deeper involvement in Korea. Acheson proposed increasing the number of US forces at bases in the Philippines and speeding up promised aid to the government, as well as expanding aid and sending a military mission to the French in Indochina. Truman approved these recommendations. The president also enthusiastically endorsed a new draft resolution to the UN Security Council expanding the requests to members for assistance to South Korea. He said he had tried to prevent this type of crisis for five years: "Now the situation is here and we must do what we can to meet it. . . . He repeated we must do everything we can for the Korean situation—'for the United Nations.'" When discussion turned to the continued deterioration of South Korean defenses, General Bradley declared that if US ground forces had to be committed, it would be necessary to mobilize the National Guard in order to meet other obligations. General J. Lawton Collins, chief of staff of the US Army, agreed. The president asked the Joint Chiefs of Staff to consider the issue of mobilization for a few days, adding "I don't want to go to war."[17]

On Tuesday, June 27, the president informed the congressional leadership—and, several hours later, the public—about the decisions to order air and naval forces into combat in support of South Korea. He used fairly general terms in describing what forces had been committed, but he specified the steps taken to defend Formosa, the Philippines, and Indochina. Without naming the Soviet Union, his statement issued to the public said that "the attack upon Korea makes it plain beyond all doubt that Communism has passed beyond the use of subversion to conquer independent nations and will now use armed invasion and war." Later in the day, the UN Security Council passed a resolution introduced by the United States recommending action by all members to "furnish such assistance to the Republic of Korea as may be necessary to repel the armed attack and to restore international peace and security in the area." Later, in the autumn, the last, seemingly innocuous, phrase of this resolution would become the basis for significantly expanding the US mission in Korea. For the time being, no questions were raised, and reaction from Congress and the public showed widespread approval. New York governor Thomas Dewey, the Republican presidential candidate who had been defeated by Truman in 1948 and still the titular head of the party, telegraphed the president to express full support for his decisions, which were "necessary to the security of our country and the free world." The *New York Herald Tribune*, the leading Republican newspaper in the East, praised Truman in an unusual front-page editorial, declaring: "The President has acted—and spoken—with a magnificent courage and terse decision."[18]

THE RELUCTANT FINAL STEP

With his additional authority, General MacArthur used all available aircraft, including B-29 heavy bombers from Guam, to stem the North Korean advance. This proved insufficient. The survey group from Tokyo, led by Brigadier General John H. Church, evaluated the situation and radioed MacArthur on June 28 that the use of American ground troops would be essential to stop the North Koreans and drive them back to the 38th Parallel. In Washington, the National Security Council (NSC) met in the afternoon of June 28 with the Joint Chiefs of Staff in attendance. Secretary Acheson expressed concern that if the Korean conflict dragged on, the administration would face a serious decision. The president responded that he "did not intend to back out" unless a more severe threat arose at another point. The secretary of the air force, Thomas K. Finletter, showing a map of air bases in North Korea, asserted that air attacks could not be fully effective unless they could strike the bases and fuel depots north of the border. Truman acknowledged that such targets might be necessary in the future, but he was not yet ready to approve them. Acheson said he hoped that American forces would not cross the 38th Parallel, and Truman reaffirmed that this was his decision. At the secretary of state's suggestion, the president asked the Joint Chiefs of Staff to review all forces available in the Far East in case they might be needed. Later that day, in assigning this task to the Joint Strategic Survey Committee, Rear Admiral Arthur C. Davis, director of the Joint Chiefs, commented that the Joint Chiefs "do *not* want to commit troops."[19]

A more pessimistic assessment came from General of the Army Dwight D. Eisenhower, now serving as president of Columbia University.

On June 28, he came to Washington to meet with a group of senior army generals, most of whom had worked for him during the war in Europe. After receiving the latest reports from Korea, Eisenhower drew a number of cogent conclusions: The conflict created the chance to strengthen the armed forces for future years of testing by the communists; the administration should build up European defenses with two additional US divisions; any significant assistance to South Korea would need to include ground troops, which would require general mobilization; no geographical limits should be placed on American operations in Korea; the Joint Chiefs should study possible uses of atomic weapons in Korea; and MacArthur should be kept on a tight leash to limit his tendency to fight his own private war. Returning to these Pentagon discussions two days later, Eisenhower recorded in his diary his serious concern that President Truman did not fully understand he was entering a major war and that the army leadership had not explained to him how demanding this intervention would be.[20]

On Thursday, June 29, General MacArthur made a daring personal inspection of the front lines in Korea. As his plane was en route to Korea with some of his staff and several reporters, the commander in chief for the Far East ordered strikes on air bases north of the 38th Parallel. He took this step on his own initiative almost 24 hours before it would be authorized by the chairman of the Joint Chiefs of Staff. In the meantime, the Joint Chiefs completed a new set of orders for MacArthur, which pulled together previous directives and added new elements authorizing him to conduct operations north of the 38th Parallel if he believed his mission could not be achieved otherwise. To allow the air force to operate from Korean fields closer to their targets, Secretary Johnson added authority to use ground and naval forces to protect the airfield and port at Pusan. He then asked the president to call another meeting of the NSC to consider the draft orders.[21]

Truman met with reporters just before another session with his senior advisers. After summarizing recent developments in Korea, he took questions. Saying he did not know if the army had sent tanks or artillery to Korea, he declared emphatically: "We are not at war." He described the North Koreans as "a bunch of bandits," and he accepted a reporter's term that this was "a police action under the United Nations." The president and other senior officials would continue through the summer to use this phrase to present American involvement in Korea as a limited effort.[22]

The NSC met in the late afternoon of June 29. As Johnson began reading the draft orders for MacArthur, Truman broke in to declare that he wanted no implication that the United States was "planning to go to war with Russia under present circumstances." He insisted that he wanted "to take every step necessary to push the North Koreans back behind the 38th Parallel" and that American actions were "designed to keep the peace in Korea and to restore the border." The president accepted the need to use some ground forces to protect the bases around the Pusan beachhead. But he wanted any attacks above the 38th Parallel to be limited to air bases, fuel and ammunition depots, troop columns, and other "purely military targets." Acheson agreed that the air force should not "be hampered in its tasks by staying rigidly below the 38th Parallel" and that, in any event, most valuable targets were close to the border. He went on to add that he thought it unlikely that the Soviets would intervene directly; but they might "utilize the Chinese Communists." The secretary pointed out a recent statement by PRC premier Zhou Enlai calling the stationing of the US Seventh Fleet in the Formosa Strait an act of "armed aggression against Chinese territory." He suggested that this might be a step toward justifying a future Chinese intervention in Korea. This prescient statement deserved further investigation, but it would receive none.[23]

General MacArthur returned to Tokyo the same evening and wrote a caustic description of the lack of discipline, combat effectiveness, and leadership of the South Korean forces, concluding with a call for the prompt commitment of US ground forces. He asserted: "The Korean army is entirely incapable of counter action and there is grave danger of a further breakthrough. If the enemy advance continues much further, it will seriously threaten the fall of the Republic. The only assurance for the holding of the present line, and the ability to later regain the lost ground, is through the introduction of US ground combat forces into the Korean battle area."

MacArthur ended his message with the request for authority to move a regimental combat team quickly to reinforce the central front and follow soon with two divisions "for an early counteroffensive." For unknown reasons, however, MacArthur did not send this important message for almost 12 hours. His thunderbolt arrived at the Pentagon shortly after midnight on June 30.[24]

General Collins, the army's chief of staff, received the message at 1:30 A.M. and knew immediately that it would force the decision that all Washington had hoped to avoid. Two hours later, he had a secure teletype conference with General MacArthur. He told the Far East commander that the president would need to decide on his request to send a regimental combat team into battle; but, while waiting for a decision, the team could move to Pusan under the previous authority to defend the airfield and port facilities. MacArthur replied brusquely that the proposal "does not give sufficient latitude for efficient operation . . . a clear-cut decision without delay is imperative." Collins reported this exchange to the army secretary, Frank Pace, who called Truman at 5 A.M. The president was already up and getting ready for his morning walk; and after hearing the request from Tokyo, he gave immediate approval to commit the regimental combat team to help stem the North Korean advance—but he wanted to confer with his advisers before committing the two additional divisions.[25]

The president met with his national security team at 9:30 A.M. After explaining his decision to commit a regimental combat team to the battle in Korea, he described Jiang Jieshi's offer to send 33,000 Nationalist troops to join the United Nations forces and said he was in favor of accepting this assistance. Acheson opposed using the forces from Formosa, fearing it would provoke PRC intervention in Korea, and the military chiefs objected because the Nationalist force would require arms, supplies, and transportation, which were badly needed by the American troops being organized for commitment to the defense of South Korea. Confronted with these substantial arguments, the president changed his mind and announced he would refuse Jiang's offer. To everyone's surprise, Truman then proposed giving MacArthur more resources than he had requested. Instead of the two divisions that the Joint Chiefs of Staff had recommended, the president said he would authorize the Far East commander to commit as needed all the forces under his command—then four divisions. He also accepted a proposal by the chief of naval operations, Admiral Forrest P. Sherman, to set up a naval blockade of North Korea. All those attending approved these decisions, and the meeting adjourned after half an hour. Later that day, the president explained the new commitments to congressional leaders and at the same time informed the public with a press release. Although the specific details of troop commitments were not mentioned, members of Congress, the press, and the public understood that US troops were headed into ground combat. The response was overwhelmingly positive. By 3 A.M., July 1, in Tokyo, the regimental combat team was on its way to Korea.[26]

STABILIZING THE PUSAN PERIMETER

For the troops arriving in Korea, July and August were among the most difficult months faced by American forces since the early battles in North Africa during World War II. The attacking divisions of the Korean People's Army (KPA) were built around seasoned fighters from the Chinese Civil War, backed by Russian-supplied tanks and artillery. In contrast, the Americans coming from Japan were in poor physical condition, inadequately armed, untrained for combat, and short of tanks and artillery. The replacements sent to fill slots for the wounded and bring units up to full strength were even less prepared for combat. Units sent to the front were made up of groups that had never worked together. Allan Millett describes the forces coming from occupation duty in Japan thus: "The Eighth Army was an army of strangers."[27]

The experience of the first regimental combat team to engage in the ground war foreshadowed the fate of other units coming from Japan during July and August. The army infantry team—known as Task Force Smith, after its commander, Lieutenant Colonel Charles B. Smith—consisted of 540 officers and enlisted men, including a battery of six 105-millimeter howitzers. They traveled by train and trucks to a defensive position north of Osan on the main road from Seoul to Pusan, and they dug in on July 4 to block the KPA's 4th Division moving south. The next day, the unit was hit by an artillery barrage, which was followed by an advancing column of thirty-two tanks and supporting infantry. The light weapons of the American force could not even slow down the tanks, which knocked out most of the howitzers and kept moving toward Osan. The North Korean infantry then overwhelmed Task Force Smith, killing and wounding many and causing the rest to flee for their lives, leaving mortars and machine guns behind. In its first day of combat, Colonel Smith's unit lost 40 percent of its men and all its weapons except small arms.[28]

As July progressed, other elements of the Army's 24th Division arrived in Korea to join the battle. Put together from different posts in Japan, this division had no coherence and was poorly armed and short of ammunition and effective antitank weapons. Given the desperate military situation, units of the division went to the front as soon as they arrived. The results were predictably disastrous. In its first week of action, parts of the division reported 1,500 men missing. Basically, the 24th Division lost two infantry regiments before its components had all arrived in the battle area. Further complicating the American defensive effort was a massive stream of refugees moving ahead of the invading force, clogging roads and masking the infiltration of ununiformed KPA troops, who got behind US lines and attacked command centers and supply depots. Even the engagement of two additional American divisions could not stem the North Korean advance. Finally, General Walton Walker, commander of all US forces in Korea, selected a more defensible line running from the Naktong River in the west to the sea in the east and including the city of Taegu and the port of Pusan. This area, which was roughly 100 miles long and 50 miles wide, became known as the Pusan Perimeter, and Walker ordered his forces to hold it at all costs (see figure 7.1).[29]

The period from early August to mid-September saw the arrival in Korea of many additional US troops and more heavy weapons. By early September, the Eighth Army and South Korean forces outnumbered the KPA surrounding the Pusan Perimeter by 142,000 to 80,000 in troops and by 5 to 1 in tanks. The combined American–South Korean force included 82,000 troops of the South Korean Army—reformed, expanded

FIGURE 7.1 US soldiers man a machine gun emplacement outside Taejon overlooking an important route of withdrawal to consolidate forces in the Pusan Perimeter on August 8, 1950.

Source: US Army photograph, Truman Library.

with new recruits and leadership, and ready to fight for their lives. The North Koreans made successive bold attacks against the Pusan defenses on three fronts in a major attempt to push the United Nations forces into the sea. The Allied army under General Walker beat back each assault, with heavy loss of North Korean lives and weapons. By mid-September, the KPA withdrew to its earlier positions, and was exhausted and short of ammunition and food. With the stalwart defense by a reinforced Eighth Army and a revitalized South Korean force, the Pusan Perimeter was stabilized. Meanwhile, MacArthur's promised strategic counteroffensive was being prepared by newly arrived elements of the Seventh Fleet and the First Marine Division.[30] Figure 7.2 shows the general front line for United Nations forces as the war progressed during 1950 and 1951.

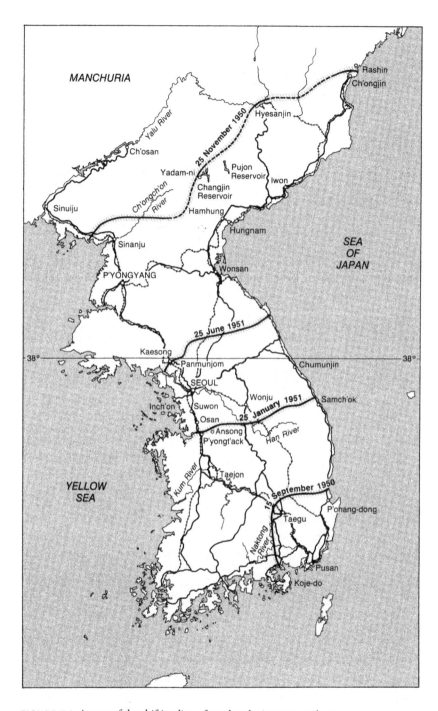

FIGURE 7.2 A map of the shifting line of combat during 1950 and 1951.

Source: Reprinted with permission from Doris M. Condit,
The Test of War, 1950–1953: History of the Office of the Secretary of Defense, vol. II
(Washington, D.C.: Historical Office of the Office of the Secretary of Defense, 1988), 79.

AN INEVITABLE REVERSAL

Strictly speaking, nothing in human affairs is inevitable. Yet given the personalities involved and the political environment, the series of decisions leading to intervention in force in Korea was as close to inevitable as any event gets. The Truman administration devoted months to shaping policies to build up Europe, implement political containment of Soviet expansionism, reduce obligations in Asia (especially to the Chinese Nationalists and South Koreans), and maintain limits on defense spending in order to support a Fair Deal reform agenda at home. The president's domestic program was blocked by steady Republican opposition and a lack of enthusiasm among Southern Democrats, and McCarthyism damaged the administration's reputation for sound foreign policy management in Asia and for eliminating communist influences in the federal government. Limited intelligence capabilities left Washington officials uninformed about the machinations among the communist powers—including Mao's contentious negotiations with Stalin, Kim's incessant pleas for support to invade South Korea, and Stalin's decision to endorse the invasion and demand that Mao provide backup for the North Koreans.

When North Korea attacked, Truman and all his advisers agreed that the United States should intervene to help South Korea repel the invaders. Everyone sought to limit American involvement to air and naval forces. The president and all senior officials assumed that the invasion was initiated by the Soviet Union as a test of American will to resist communist expansion in an area that the administration had declared to be of no strategic importance. During the first week of the crisis, every few hours brought ever darker news of defeats before a much more powerful army than US military specialists had estimated. The inadequacy of South Korea's defenses and American occupation forces in Japan, which could clearly be attributed to administration policies, left the entire national security team vulnerable to political attacks. Reports reached Washington daily of nervous Allies in Europe, Japan, and the Philippines anxious about the value of US pledges of protection. Many officials, including the president, thought of the lessons they drew from the 1938 Munich crisis when appeasement did not constrain an aggressive Nazi Germany.

Given this chain of events, the Truman administration was unified in deciding that it was essential to confront communist aggression and not lose South Korea. On this basis, US ground forces were committed. General MacArthur confidently advised the Pentagon that he could stop the invaders and regain the 38th Parallel with two divisions of American troops. When this force was overwhelmed, additional units had to be organized and sent from the United States to prevent defeat.

The public endorsed the president's decision. A Gallup poll showed that 65 percent of respondents approved intervention in Korea, although the fact that 57 percent believed this meant that the United States was already in another world war raises the question of how well they understood the situation. The poll also contained a warning for the Democrats, in a finding that 50 percent believed American defenses were weak and by a 3-to-1 margin blamed this on the president and his party. As the historian Robert Dallek argues, although Truman did not want to acknowledge that Republican pressure influenced him to stand up to the communist challenge, he did "understand that another setback in the Cold War could decisively cripple his capacity to govern." The chief executive therefore did what he thought was necessary to protect the nation and his presidency.[31]

But in this decision process, Harry Truman made what his biographer Robert Donovan calls "a costly mistake." He led the country into what had already become a larger war without congressional approval. Dean Acheson pressed the president several times to explain to Congress his reasons for committing American forces in Korea and argued that a congressional joint resolution endorsing his action would be a very prudent step. But Truman had convinced himself that he had the constitutional authority to commit US forces, and he still deluded himself that it could be a brief conflict. The failure to obtain approval from Congress when almost all its members and a large majority of the public endorsed his decisions would create problems for the administration later in the war and would set a dangerous precedent for future chief executives.[32]

8

DOUGLAS MacARTHUR GAMBLES AND WINS

By early September, it was clear that the South Korean army had gained strength and the will to fight, American forces were growing in numbers and combat skills, and the Pusan Perimeter would be held. As plans developed for an early amphibious attack, new units needed to be formed and equipped; contracts had to be issued for supplies, vehicles, and weapons; and a more efficient policy process had to be put in place. Also, congressional authorization and appropriations were necessary for many of these steps to begin.

ORGANIZING FOR WAR

As Dwight Eisenhower had shrewdly observed on June 28, Harry Truman did not at this point recognize that he was entering a major war. But he did understand that he needed to be personally more engaged in policy deliberations and that he should expand the White House staff. He began to regularly attend the meetings of the National Security Council (NSC), and he met frequently with General Omar Bradley, the chairman of the Joint Chiefs of Staff. He requested that W. Averell Harriman, then in Paris as ambassador at large to the Marshall Plan countries, return to serve as a special assistant to coordinate policy decisions among the executive branch's departments. In contemporary terms, Harriman would function as the president's national security adviser. Harriman, a wealthy New Yorker who was a former ambassador to the Soviet Union and was well connected to major figures in the administration, was a significant new force in the policy process. He joined the important NSC meeting on June 28 and was a strong voice for intervention in Korea.[1]

The president also took steps to improve coordination between departments and within agencies. To expand collection of intelligence and improve analysis, he appointed Lieutenant General Walter Bedell Smith the director of the CIA. He named N. Gordon Dean as chairman of the Atomic Energy Commission to improve decisionmaking and to accelerate the production of fissile material for the nuclear weapons program. And most important, he forced Louis Johnson to resign as secretary of defense in order to bring in General George C. Marshall, a personal hero of Truman's. Known as the organizer of victory in World War II, Marshall was a towering figure who would bring order to the rivalry among the services and vastly improve coordination with Dean Acheson, who had worked well with the general when he served as secretary of state. Marshall assumed office on September 21 and brought in the able banker Robert A. Lovett as deputy secretary. Having worked closely with Marshall as his undersecretary at the State Department, Lovett's new responsibility would be to run the department's daily operations, leaving the secretary free to concentrate on policy issues. Soon, the new national security team set an example for interagency cooperation, with regular meetings of Marshall, Acheson, Lovett, and Bradley in the map room of the Joint Chiefs of Staff.[2]

Two other areas showed signs of problems that would pose political threats to the administration in future months. The first was in Congress. The president could be confident that congressional Republicans would support his taking a stand against the North Korean attack and would likely be enthusiastic about his positioning a naval force to protect Formosa. But it was also highly probable that they would use every opportunity to attack the administration's earlier policies toward South

Korea and Formosa and insist on congressional approval for any military intervention. Truman informed members of Congress of his decisions on Korea on June 27 and 30, and on each occasion a Republican senator pointedly asked why authorization from Congress had not been requested before engaging US military forces. The replies, in essence, were that this was an emergency and that it was a police action, not a war. The nation's foremost isolationist, Senator Robert Taft, posed a clear warning for the administration in a sharp speech in the Senate on June 28, charging "a complete usurpation by the president of authority to use the armed forces of the country." Acknowledging that the United States had obligations under the United Nations Charter, he concluded that, even in light of this treaty, "there is no authority to use armed force in support of the United Nations in the absence of some previous action by Congress dealing with the subject and outlining the general circumstances and the amount of force that can be used."[3]

Government lawyers and diplomats developed responses arguing that executive authority justified the president's actions. Secretary Acheson proposed that the president appear before a joint session of Congress to explain the situation in Korea and present his decisions as those of the commander in chief. If Congress chose to pass a resolution of approval on its own initiative, that would be helpful but not essential. But the president declined to accept this advice. Racing to prevent defeat in Korea, and aware of the widespread expressions of approval from congressional leaders and the public, Truman remained firm in his conviction that all his decisions were being properly made under his authority as commander in chief. His first message to Congress on the Korean crisis came on July 19 and asked not for approval of his decisions but for legislation to prosecute the conflict and for supplemental appropriations. The administration would be attacked for pursuing a war without congressional approval as the conflict dragged on; but there is every reason to agree with Alonzo Hamby that resolutions of congressional approval in July 1950 would not have muted or prevented such attacks from the desperate Republican opposition in future months.[4]

The second brooding problem for the administration was with General Douglas MacArthur. From his experience as an artillery captain in France during World War I, and later as a senator chairing investigations into military contracting and profiteering, Truman had developed a hearty distaste for the self-important behavior of generals and admirals. Early in his presidency, he expressed his dislike of MacArthur in a June 17, 1945, memorandum. He called the hero of the Pacific War "Mr. Prima Donna, Brass Hat, Five Star MacArthur. He's worse than the Cabots and the Lodges—they at least talked with one another before they told God what to do. Mac tells God right off. It is a very great pity we have to have stuffed Shirts like that in key positions." During the early days of the Korean War, the president criticized MacArthur in the presence of his staff. Eben Ayers, the assistant White House press secretary, wrote in his diary that the president believes "that MacArthur is a supreme egotist, who regarded himself as something of a god."[5]

During the early weeks of the Korean conflict, senior officials in Washington had no problems with MacArthur's actions; but at the end of July, there was a serious disagreement over Formosa. Before the war broke out, the general had proposed that he travel to Formosa to conduct a survey of what was needed to defend the island from a communist invasion. When Acheson strongly objected, the trip was delayed. After the Seventh Fleet was stationed in the Formosa Strait to neutralize the island, MacArthur's command authority was extended to include the defense of Formosa. In late July, the Joint Chiefs of Staff grew concerned over reports of growing concentrations of troops and ships on the mainland, in apparent preparation for an amphibious assault on the last remaining Nationalist Chinese sanctuary. On July 29, the Far East commander informed the Joint Chiefs of Staff that he would travel to Formosa on July 31 with some of his staff for the proposed survey of defense requirements. MacArthur flew to Taipei with his air force and naval commanders, thirteen other senior officers, and a group of reporters on two C-54s. They held two days of meetings with Jiang Jieshi and his military staff and issued statements for the press before returning to Tokyo. MacArthur's comments emphasized the military nature of the talks and declared that "arrangements have been completed for effective coordination" between American and Chinese

Nationalist forces to defend the island. Jiang's statements hinted at new cooperative efforts "to fight communist aggression."[6]

Although MacArthur was within his authority as theater commander to visit a threatened area newly assigned to his region of responsibility, the way this trip was managed appeared designed to challenge the authority of the president, who had clearly restated his policy of no commitments to Jiang. The reporters who were on the trip filed stories about the cordial talks between the Nationalist leader and the American commander, and a State Department representative in Taipei erroneously reported that MacArthur had ordered three F-80 jet fighter squadrons to Formosa. As these reports circulated, Truman and Acheson were furious about this trip that had taken them by surprise and about MacArthur's refusal to report to Acheson what had been discussed in Taipei. The general told the senior political adviser attached to his command, William Sebald, "that he had no intention of providing details" to the secretary of state of "talks [that] were purely military in nature" and done under "his sole responsibility" as Far East commander. Continuing his contentious response, MacArthur waited a week to send a bland report of the trip to the secretary of defense. Meanwhile, the president had dispatched his top assistant, Harriman, to Tokyo to restate the administration's policies on relations with Jiang and Formosa. After explaining to the general that he must not allow the Nationalist leader to involve the United States in a war with the People's Republic of China (PRC), he reported to Truman that MacArthur "accepted the President's position and will act accordingly, but without full conviction."[7]

Before the fallout from MacArthur's Formosa visit had fully dissipated, another incident related to the island added to the hard feelings between the general and the president. One of the State Department's main activities in the hectic summer of 1950 was to win the support of as many United Nations members as possible for the enforcement of the resolutions on the Korean conflict. When the president ordered the Seventh Fleet to neutralize Formosa, Zhou Enlai, the PRC's foreign minister, protested to the UN secretary-general on August 24 that the US action was an act of aggression against the PRC, which claimed the island as its territory. Great Britain, an important US ally, and India, an influential neutral country, had recognized the PRC as the government of China, and both were anxious that MacArthur's support for Jiang could possibly involve the United States in a war with Communist China. The US ambassador to the United Nations, Warren Austin, sent a letter to members of the Security Council on August 25 assuring them that the United States had no plans for military bases or any special role on Formosa. To the great dismay of administration officials, that same evening the Associated Press put out a story that General MacArthur had released an advance copy of a dramatic statement on Formosa to be read to the annual convention of the Veterans of Foreign Wars in Chicago on August 28. In this message, MacArthur presented Formosa as a key strategic location of great importance to the United States, strongly implying a desire for military bases on the island.[8]

The message from the Far East commander contradicted US policy on several critical points and completely undercut the pledge made in Ambassador Austin's letter. Truman was livid at this act of insubordination by MacArthur, who had recently been cautioned by both Harriman and the Joint Chiefs of Staff about the limits on US involvement with the Nationalists on Formosa. The president read a copy of the general's statement to a meeting of his national security advisers on August 26 and demanded that the secretary of defense direct MacArthur to withdraw his message. When Johnson hesitated, and then sought to soften and evade this clear instruction, Truman telephoned him and dictated the message he wanted sent in writing to MacArthur: "The President of the United States directs that you withdraw your message . . . because various features with respect to Formosa are in conflict with the policy of the United States and its position in the United Nations."[9]

This episode showed how reluctant Johnson and the Joint Chiefs were to discipline MacArthur. Truman soon fired Johnson, and after considering replacing MacArthur as Far East commander, he decided against it because of the political firestorm it would have created. From this point on, the White House kept a close eye on the activities of "Mr. Prima Donna" in Tokyo.[10]

EXPANDING THE DEFENSE BUDGET

In the early weeks of the Korean War, the administration and the military services were slow to understand the extent of the problems faced in Korea. They hoped the "police action" would be brief and would not require a significant war effort by the United States. They expected the South Korean forces to perform better than they did and for few American resources to be needed. As the chairman of the Joint Chiefs of Staff, General Bradley, later said: "The first few days, we did not know just how good these North Koreans were, and it was some time before we could get a good picture." Because of these optimistic expectations and American forces' low state of combat readiness, the administration was unable to respond promptly when urgent requests for more troops and supplies came from Tokyo.[11]

When the war broke out, Congress had not acted on the fiscal year 1951 defense budget. The president had requested a total of $13 billion for defense to support a US Army of 630,000 men in 10 understrength divisions; a US Navy of 239 combat ships; two US Marine divisions at 36 percent strength, for a US Navy-Marine force of 461,000; and a US Air Force of 48 groups (later designated as wings) and 416,000 men. Total military manpower was 1.5 million. Congress did authorize the expenditure of fiscal year (FY) 1951 funds in advance of approval of the appropriation. With requests from General MacArthur coming in every few days pleading for more troops, the Joint Chiefs and the president approved three force additions by July 19, raising total authorized manpower to 2.1 million, an increase of 41 percent in two weeks. This would provide for an 11-division US Army, a US Navy of 282 combat ships and 12 carrier air groups, a two-division US Marine Corps with increased strength levels, and a US Air Force of 58 wings.[12]

With funds being rapidly spent to support a significant increase in the armed forces, Congress finally passed the FY 1951 defense budget for $13.3 billion, and the president promptly signed it on September 6. While the annual budget was being finalized, Congress was also reviewing the administration's request for the first supplemental defense appropriation submitted on July 24. This proposal had been held to $10.5 billion because Johnson wanted to limit spending in the hope that the fighting in Korea would end quickly. The chairman of the military appropriations subcommittee, Representative George H. Mahon (D-TX), sharply questioned Johnson, the service secretaries, and the Joint Chiefs about whether this amount was sufficient and if they believed that the United States was facing the start of World War III. The defense officials replied that under present circumstances, this was their best estimate of costs—but General Bradley added that if the conflict went badly, they might "have to come back later and ask for more." At the urging of Congress, the administration asked for an additional $1.2 billion for army and navy construction and for naval aviation. Together, the FY 1951 budget and the supplemental request totaled $25 billion. As the historian Doris Condit points out, while the first supplemental funded the troops being sent to Korea, "it was in fact a stopgap measure formulated in response to an emergency situation without being closely related to larger national security considerations. In the summer of 1950, US policymakers still sought an appropriate response to what they perceived as the Soviet challenge without wreaking havoc on the US economy."[13]

When the fighting in Korea had been under way for a month, Truman decided it was time to formulate national security requirements for the next five years. On July 27, he directed the NSC to develop the programs needed to implement the recommendations of NSC Report 68. On August 19, the budget office of the Office of the Secretary of Defense sent to the White House the estimated costs of the force recommendations from the Joint Chiefs of Staff for FYs 1951–55 at $150 billion. The members of the NSC's staff and the working group for NSC 68 felt these estimates were insufficient and asked for revisions. On September 1, the Joint Chiefs responded with "dramatically expanded" force goals for mid-1954, which were estimated to cost $214 billion. After further reworking by the Joint Chiefs and the military service secretaries, on September 12 Johnson submitted a program for $260 billion to the president.[14]

Common sense, integrity, and decades of experience took charge of the defense planning process when George C. Marshall became secretary of defense on September 21. After examining the military programs submitted by his predecessor, the former army chief of staff concluded that the costs were so high they would damage the economy and, more seriously, that the public would not support such sustained levels of defense spending. He asked Major General (Retired) James H. Burns, his assistant for foreign military affairs and military assistance, to review the proposal. Burns shared the secretary's concerns, and two weeks after the successful Inchon assault, he advised Marshall to ask the NSC staff to revise the five-year program under a limit of $200 billion, not including the expenses for Korea. At an NSC meeting on September 29, the president proposed approving NSC 68 as policy for the next four to five years, while working out the details of funding as the programs were more fully developed. This recommendation was adopted, and on September 30 Truman signed NSC 68/2 as policy. Deputy secretary of defense Robert Lovett and Office of the Secretary of Defense comptroller Wilfred J. McNeil and their staffs reviewed the military programs over the next month, paying special attention to guidance given by Marshall on October 17 to base their military expansion on a long-term political and economic basis that would be supported by Congress and the public. By November 1, McNeil produced a new estimate for NSC 68 programs for five years, including $131 billion for the military services— plus funds for nuclear weapons, military assistance, and unanticipated contingencies—for a total of $191 billion. This unprecedented sum was approved as the basic budget for NSC 68 programs.[15]

MacARTHUR'S BOLD STRIKE

As early as mid-July, MacArthur had his mind set on an audacious amphibious landing at Inchon, to be followed by a drive to recapture Seoul. This strike was scheduled for mid-September (the only time when the tides were adequate for such an operation) and was designed to sever the North Korean supply lines and destroy the invasion force in the south.

From the start, the plan to launch an early assault on Inchon faced immense obstacles. The US and South Korean forces were in steady retreat before attacks from the Korean People's Army (KPA) and would not stabilize a defense for another six weeks. The administration was still debating what level of mobilization to achieve, and troops and equipment could only move slowly to Korea. Even before a defensive perimeter was established, MacArthur sought to hold out the best forces for the Inchon operation. The most serious problem was that Inchon represented one of the most difficult sites for an amphibious operation in its physical environment and in its natural defensive positions. No small additional point was the fact that the officer chosen as commander of the invading force, Major General Edward M. Almond, had no experience in amphibious operations. Further complicating the preparations was the absence from the planning group of representatives from the two key subordinate commanders: one—Vice Admiral Arthur D. Struble, commanding officer of the Seventh Fleet—controlling the naval forces to transport, launch air and naval gunfire to soften the target, and provide air cover for the landing force; and the other—Rear Admiral James H. Doyle—commanding the amphibious task force. Finally, key units of the invading force, such as the First Marine Division, had not been brought up to combat strength and equipped; and after this was completed, they would need at least two weeks to travel to the war zone from the US West Coast.[16]

Although some Pentagon officials knew as early as July 23 of MacArthur's intention to mount an operation to land behind North Korean lines, they were unaware of the landing site or the target date and knew none of the detailed plans for what was designated Operation Chromite. As these plans took shape, the senior officers in the navy and marine corps who were assigned to make the assault realized the huge difficulty of landing at Inchon. They began to search for an alternative site and developed a strong case for a beach further south, at Posung-myon, with access to roads leading to Seoul 34 miles to the north. The debate over Inchon as the appropriate landing site reached a critical phase on August 23, when a delegation of top military officers came to MacArthur's Tokyo headquarters to evaluate the plans. The principal attendees were Army Chief of Staff General J. Lawton Collins, Chief of Naval Operations Admiral Forrest P. Sherman, and Vice Chief of Naval Operations and Commander in Chief Pacific Admiral Arthur W. Radford. Although the First Marine Division had been selected to lead the amphibious assault, the division commander, Major General O. P. Smith, and the commander, Fleet Marine Force Pacific, Lieutenant General Lemuel C. Shepherd Jr., and his important operations officer, Colonel Victor H. Krulak, were excluded from the conference by General Almond in his capacity as MacArthur's chief of staff. This critical decision removed the most forceful advocates for the Posung-myon site from the debate.[17]

When the conference opened, MacArthur asked Admiral Doyle to speak first to present the naval dimensions of the landing and supply operations, knowing that he would bring up many of the problems of Inchon as a site. Doyle and his staff described in detail the long list of challenges at Inchon: a long, narrow entry channel that could be easily mined; superb defensive positions on islands along the channel; lengthy mudflats that would entrap landing ships, except for short periods at record high tides; the lack of actual beaches, which would force all ships to unload at a high seawall; and the vulnerability of supply ships, which had to unload in a receding tide and wait for the next high tide to withdraw. The demands of the tides meant that the principal island defenses had to be attacked during the morning high tide but the main assault force of two Marine regiments could not land until the next high tide, at twilight 12 hours later. At the end of the naval briefing, Admiral Doyle concluded by saying that, if asked for his opinion, "the best I can say is that Inchon is not impossible."[18]

After brief discussion of a landing site at Kunsan, far south of Inchon, MacArthur took the floor, and for 45 minutes he delivered what Allan Millett calls his "greatest soliloquy." Speaking without notes, he pointed out that the great majority of KPA forces were concentrated around the Pusan Perimeter. Their supply lines were long, and they were completely unprepared for an enveloping attack deep to their rear. Kunsan would be too close to their lines and would be ineffective. Only a hard, deep strike at Inchon would cut off the KPA's supplies and equipment, capture Seoul, and entrap them between the assault force and the Eighth Army at Pusan. Such a maneuver could save 100,000 lives, crush the invading force, and win the war. The hero of the Pacific War compared his plan with Wolfe's classic surprise landing at an impossible site and capture of Quebec from Montcalm in 1759. He acknowledged Admiral Doyle's list of problems but said they could be overcome. Believing Admiral Sherman was the essential one to persuade, MacArthur asserted: "The amphibious landing is the most powerful tool we have. To employ it properly, we must strike hard and deep!" He even suggested that perhaps he had more confidence in the navy than they had in themselves, adding that "the Navy has never let me down in the past, and it will not let me down this time." The general concluded his oration by declaring "I realize that Inchon is a 5,000 to 1 gamble, but I am used to taking such odds. . . . [dropping his voice] We shall land at Inchon and I shall crush them!"[19]

His audience was mesmerized. Reflecting later on this performance, Admiral Doyle asserted: "If MacArthur had gone on the stage, you would never have heard of John Barrymore." Although some would remain unconvinced, none would effectively challenge MacArthur's choice. The die was cast for Inchon.[20]

MacARTHUR'S AURA

For anyone not versed in US military history, it would be reasonable to ask why MacArthur was retained as the commander in chief of United Nations Forces when he did not support many of the Truman administration's policies, showed open disrespect for the president and secretary of state, and treated the members of the Joint Chiefs of Staff as clerks and supply officers. The short answer is that MacArthur was a living legend, the man who had orchestrated victory in the Pacific War, brought independence to the Philippines, and managed the reform and reconstruction of Japan. Yet these accomplishments do not fully explain his influence and virtually unchallenged authority.

MacArthur's power had many dimensions. Within the US military, he was the most senior officer, the only five-star general on active duty. In a culture structured on seniority and rank, he had more years of service and outranked all his nominal superiors. He had been an officer twelve years longer than Omar Bradley, the chairman of the Joint Chiefs of Staff; and he had served fourteen years longer than J. Lawton Collins, the army chief of staff. Indeed, MacArthur had been army chief of staff in 1930. His authority within the military establishment did not rest only on rank and seniority. As Robert Debs Heinl Jr. declares, "MacArthur was a strategist without peer—no theoretician either, but a proven, fighting practitioner of war at all levels of command." Although he was seventy years old in 1950, with reduced energy and mobility, no one in Washington—civilian or military—was eager to question his judgment or military recommendations.[21]

On a personal level, MacArthur followed an unusual lifestyle for a man who was both in charge of the reform and governance of Japan and commander of all US forces in the Far East theater. He and his family lived in the large walled compound at the American Embassy, along with a number of his aides and household staff. He had the same daily routine every day of the year. He worked at home for an hour or more after breakfast, reading reports and answering correspondence; he arrived at the office at about 10:30 A.M. and worked until 2 P.M.; he returned home for lunch and a nap; and he went back to the office for work from 4 P.M. until 8 or 10 in the evening. He made no attempt to maintain personal contact with Japanese citizens or his own soldiers and sailors. Between 1945 and 1950, he visited no Japanese city or town and made no appearances at US bases around the country. He entertained visiting dignitaries from the US mainland and Allied representatives at luncheons, where he would frequently expound at length on a topic he found of interest. In the evenings, he had dinner with his wife Jean, and he watched a movie of his choice with her and members of his personal staff. Jean MacArthur was a dedicated wife, and by all accounts a vivacious, charming hostess. Twenty years younger than her husband, she often represented him at diplomatic and Japanese ceremonial occasions, accompanied by the general's longtime aide, Colonel Sidney L. Huff.

The MacArthurs had a son, Arthur, who was twelve in 1950 and was cared for mainly by a Chinese nurse and an English tutor.[22]

Despite his cloistered life, MacArthur had a strong, positive impact on almost everyone who worked with him or met him at his frequent luncheons. His most prominent biographer, D. Clayton James, did massive research for his three-volume study, including interviews with 180 senior officers and civilian officials. He contends that those who knew MacArthur best generally agreed on central aspects of his character and personality. They declared that "MacArthur was the most complicated person they had ever met, and they knew of no one who fully understood him and of only a few who were genuinely close to him." They agreed there were large differences between his public reputation and the man they knew. He combined many contradictory attributes. "He was intensely conscious of himself as a 'man of destiny,' but he refused to fire incompetent staff members, shifted blame for blunders to others, and fretted over his tenure and his image." Known for his dramatic role-playing for most of his career, he developed this "to a high art in Tokyo." Many felt his most effective role "was still that of the chivalrous officer-aristocrat."[23]

In discharging his official duties, MacArthur relied on a small group of loyal staff officers to protect his consistent routine, make most noncritical decisions, and avoid surprises. He preferred reading reports in private, he limited meetings to essential issues, and had no telephone in his office. Most decisions and requests were channeled through his chief of staff, Major General Edward M. (Ned) Almond. A master of administrative organization and detail, Almond's promising career stalled in World War II when he received the unwelcome command of two poorly performing African American infantry divisions assigned to the Italian front. When he joined the headquarters staff at the Far East Command, Almond worked hard to make himself essential to MacArthur, and in 1949 became his chief of staff. Based on extensive research, including oral history interviews with many senior officers who served under him in Korea, Millett describes Almond's style as a commander in harsh terms: "impulsive, given to ignoring expert advice and the chain of command, a tyrant with his staff, a searcher for errors and omissions, a bully

of subordinates." These corrosive qualities would become highly important when Almond became commander of the invading force at Inchon.[24]

Even closer to MacArthur than Almond was Major General Charles
A. Willoughby, chief of intelligence (G-2) for the Far East Command.
Willoughby had joined MacArthur in the Philippines in 1940 and served
as his head of intelligence throughout the Pacific War. He was one of
only two generals who had evacuated Bataan with MacArthur in 1942,
and still remained with him in Tokyo. Born in Germany as Adolph C.
Weidenbach to a minor nobleman and an American mother, Willoughby
had immigrated to America at the age of eighteen and joined the US
Army. When he became a commissioned officer in 1916, he changed
his name to Charles A. Willoughby (his mother's maiden name). From
long experience, Willoughby knew that his boss did not like to receive
bad news. Accordingly, in the spring of 1950, when he was receiving
reports on the rapid buildup of the North Korean army, he softened the
messages in his summaries for MacArthur of the intelligence coming
from his agents in Korea but sent the full reports to the army staff in
the Pentagon, where they were largely ignored as pleas for more arms
for the Rhee government. Within MacArthur's staff, an intense rivalry
and mutual dislike developed between Almond and Willoughby as they
competed for their commander's attention.[25]

The other staff officer in Tokyo who was part of what was known in
the army as the "Bataan gang" was Brigadier General Courtney Whitney, who managed public relations and Japanese civil affairs. Led by
these three generals, the staff members of the Far East Command dedicated themselves to support MacArthur's vision of how he wanted the
occupation and reconstruction of Japan to proceed. When war broke out
in Korea, much of the stable staff routine would be disrupted by a series
of defeats and greatly increased pressures.[26]

Given his long years of military service and the demands of being
overall commander of a new war, MacArthur's health soon became an
issue for the president and other officials in Washington. Early in August
1950, Truman sent a trusted personal friend, Major General Frank E.
Lowe, to serve as the president's liaison with MacArthur's headquarters.
One of Lowe's confidential assignments was to evaluate MacArthur's

health and his ability to handle the stress of wartime command. In reporting to the president, Lowe said the general was "hale and hearty," describing him as in good physical shape and mentally very sharp. Other visitors, including his personal physicians, confirmed this general assessment, although some pointed out signs of deafness and digestive disorders. MacArthur was noted for pacing back and forth for long periods while thinking or talking through a problem. One of his physicians, a neurosurgeon, noted clear signs of Parkinson's disease, and reported that the general masked the tremors by keeping his hands busy with his pipe or with gestures when talking. Everyone who commented on his health and appearance noted that he looked twenty years younger than he was and was mentally alert and persuasive.[27]

As preparations for Inchon advanced, MacArthur seemed poised between either a dramatic victory or a humiliating defeat. Some of the conditions that had fostered his past successes had disappeared. His biographer, James, identifies three important changes that significantly altered the environment for MacArthur in 1948. The MacArthur for President effort in the Republican primaries drew very little popular support and died quietly. It became painfully clear that the general's destiny was not in electoral politics. More serious for his military activities was the departure from Tokyo of Lieutenant General Robert L. Eichelberger, who was his main confidant from the Pacific War and the only person in his immediate circle who would challenge his judgments on important issues. Increasingly, James argues, "after Eichelberger's exit MacArthur's channels of information narrowed and his sources of fresh, objective thinking declined." The third change was a shift in US policy for Japan with the adoption in October 1948 of NSC Report 13/2, which called for a turn from reform to economic revival and significantly reduced MacArthur's authority and staff. In the extension of Cold War containment to East Asia, Japan was to become the anchor of US strategic interests. In the future, most policy decisions would be made in Washington.[28]

Two additional factors would ultimately constrain MacArthur's future freedom of action. After Truman's election as president in his own right in November 1948, the administration was dominated by men who were dedicated to protecting US interests in Europe above all else—a group known to MacArthur and his Republican friends as "Europe-firsters." This meant that the general had no strong advocate in either civilian or military circles if events in the region turned sour. Finally, MacArthur lost what every commander values most: good luck. "MacArthur's fortune had been incredibly good at timely moments in the past," declares James. "But the main difference between the MacArthur of old and the general during his final half year in Tokyo was that his luck finally ran out."[29]

OPERATION CHROMITE

An amphibious assault against a defended landing site presents the most severe challenges of any combat operation. To be successful, the attacking force must have excellent intelligence on the sea and land conditions of the site; close coordination of naval, air, and ground components; well-trained cohesive military units that know how to manage the problems encountered in a landing; and experienced resourceful commanders. At Inchon, none of these conditions were fully met.

Preparations for the landing faced many problems up to the final day. When chosen on July 20 to be the lead invasion unit, the First Marine Division was at 15 percent of its combat strength. A reinforced regiment of the division, formed as the First Marine Brigade of 6,500 men, was already at sea on the way to join in the defense of South Korea. The division staff had only three weeks to add another 12,000 troops by cannibalizing other combat units, mobilizing reserves, and borrowing from training centers and diplomatic posts. The newly reorganized division arrived in Japan at the end of August and in early September. Their component brigade was withdrawn from heavy fighting on September 5 and sailed from Pusan on the 13th to join the division at Inchon, after adding 3,000 troops of the South Korean Marine Corps. The other main assault unit—the Army's Seventh Infantry Division, which was based in Japan—was in much worse condition than the marines. Many of its officers and men had been sent to the front to fill out the understrength Eighth Army, which bore most of the fighting for the first three months of the war. The Seventh Infantry Division was rebuilt with transfers from other occupation units, new arrivals from the United States, and a large group of 8,300 South Korean conscripts who had no training and no English.[30]

Unlike most previous amphibious landings, Operation Chromite had no time for rehearsals of any type. In a short period, the marine and navy logisticians had to prepare and load 71,000 troops, 25,000 tons of equipment and supplies, and 6,000 vehicles, including 250 tanks. Navy planners had to organize over 230 ships from the United States and six Allied navies for arrival in the target area in a precise order and prepared for combat. Complicating this accelerated schedule was the arrival a few days apart of two typhoons. The first hit Japan during the loading period. With another larger storm approaching close to the sailing date, the naval commanders persuaded MacArthur to put the armada to sea a day or two early to avoid the worst of the major typhoon. Topping off this litany of problems was the high probability that the invading force had lost the important advantage of surprise. Not only had the Chinese informed Kim Il-sung that their analysis showed that MacArthur was very likely to make an amphibious assault on Inchon but also, in September, US counterintelligence had discovered a communist spy ring in Japan that had detailed knowledge of preparations for the attack. Indeed, among the Western press corps in Tokyo, the invasion was often referred to as Operation Common Knowledge.[31]

Symptomatic of the haste with which the whole operation was organized was the fact that the assault began before the Joint Chiefs of Staff had approved it in concept. After delays and debate in Washington, the Joint Chiefs finally gave authorization for the operation to MacArthur on September 8. In fact, daily air assaults on the Inchon area began on September 4, and the slowest ships of the assault force sailed from Yokohama the next day. To make sure that no changes could be made to his plan, the impatient Far East commander delayed sending his detailed operations plan, so the first marines went ashore at Inchon before the briefing officer from Tokyo had finished answering questions about the plan from the Joint Chiefs.[32]

MacArthur's massive ego further complicated the landing operation. Contrary to doctrine and all precedents, the Far East commander insisted on being present on the amphibious command ship during the assault. To make matters worse, he brought with him six other generals, his retinue of aides, and some twenty favorite reporters, adding to the crowded conditions on the ship and diverting the attention of the tactical commanders from their direction of the landing. The top general and his party boarded the USS *Mount McKinley* just as a major typhoon approached Japan. For the assembled newsmen, the general himself led a detailed and highly optimistic briefing on the plans for the attack on Inchon and how it fitted into his larger strategy for reversing the course of the war and defeating the North Koreans. During the night, MacArthur—who had a history of fainting spells before big battles and was susceptible to seasickness—became violently ill. His aides tried to comfort him and eventually persuaded him to have a large glass of Scotch (he normally drank only wine). Soon, he was fast asleep. On the morning of September 14, the chastened commander awoke feeling much better, enjoyed a hearty breakfast, and went on deck to observe the start of the naval bombardment preceding the landing.[33] (See figure 8.1.)

Despite the obstacles of landing at Inchon and the haste in preparing the invasion force, Operation Chromite went smoothly. After heavy bombardment by naval gunfire and air strikes, a marine battalion landing on the morning high tide captured Walmi-do, the key island defending the long channel to Inchon Harbor. Two regiments of the First Marine Division went ashore against minimal resistance on the evening high tide, and by midnight they had occupied the high ground behind the city of Inchon. The 2,500 North Korean troops did not defend the seawall, which was the marines' most vulnerable point; nor had they sowed the stock of tethered mines that had arrived from the Soviet Union on September 2. On D-Day, the Marines suffered 21 dead and 174 wounded. The North Korean defenders were all killed, taken prisoner, or in flight. On the first day, amphibious units landed 13,000 troops with their equipment, and nineteen transports docked or anchored to unload.[34]

Against all the odds, the Inchon-Seoul attack justified MacArthur's supreme confidence. In large part, this was attributable to the excellent

FIGURE 8.1 After seasickness during a stormy voyage, General Douglas MacArthur observes the Inchon landing with his public relations chief, Brigadier General Courtney Whitney (*left*), and the commander of the X Corps, Major General Edward M. Almond (*right*), September 15, 1950.

Source: US Army photo, National Archives.

performance of the navy and marine forces that led the assault. But North Korean strategic and tactical mistakes also made a significant contribution to the outcome. Kim Il-sung did not heed Chinese and Soviet warnings to bolster Inchon's defenses. Kim and his commanders did not mine the channel leading to Inchon, and they did not defend the seawall. Reflecting his confidence, MacArthur personally supervised the operation from the amphibious command ship USS *Mount McKinley*. This was the first time to date when a US unified commander had accompanied a major assault force. The general ensured that Congress and the American people would know about the risks and successes of the landing by inviting eighty-six correspondents to join the amphibious task force, including such prominent figures as Joseph Alsop, Bill Blair, Homer Bigart, Keyes Beech, Marguerite Higgins, and Carl Mydans. The reporters for the wire services and the major radio and television networks were aboard the command ship and received tours of the operations rooms by Admiral Doyle and a strategic briefing by the Far East commander himself. As an expression of GI humor for the people back home, troops had painted "Truman's Police Force" on the side of some landing craft.[35]

The operation's main objective was to capture Seoul and sever the main North Korean supply route to the south. After the marines had secured the city of Inchon and moved on to capture the vital Kimpo Airfield on September 18, the Seventh Infantry Division landed and fought its way south of the marines to cut the highway and rail routes to Pusan. The marines moved steadily toward Seoul and, with elements of the Seventh Division, completed the conquest of the capital by September 29. On that day, General MacArthur and assorted dignitaries flew in from Tokyo to meet President Rhee and the members of his cabinet, who had flown from Pusan. In a brief ceremony, the proud general returned control of the capital city to the South Korean president. US forces lost 3,500 men (2,450 were marines); North Korea lost 14,000 casualties and 7,000 prisoners. Overall, during the month of September, including the Eighth Army's offensive to break out of the Pusan Perimeter, the KPA suffered 200,000 casualties and lost 130,000 prisoners, many of whom were new recruits with little training. Despite the risks taken both before and after the landing, US forces had won an epic victory. Hungry to move beyond their defeats, the American leaders exulted in their success and believed that they had crushed the KPA. But their vision of total victory would soon lead to decisions that sowed the seeds of disaster. The army's chief of staff, General J. Lawton Collins, later evaluated the mind-set of senior military leaders: "The success of Inchon was so great, and the subsequent prestige of General MacArthur was so overpowering, that the [Joint] Chiefs hesitated thereafter to question later plans and decisions of the general, which should have been challenged. . . . Inchon marked the peak of the extraordinary career of one of America's most brilliant soldiers. From then on, he seemed to march like a Greek hero of old to an unkind and inexorable fate."[36]

A FATEFUL DECISION: CROSSING THE 38TH PARALLEL

As early as July, long before the Inchon assault was planned, some senior State Department officials began to advocate unifying Korea under the friendly government of Syngman Rhee. On July 1, John Allison, director of the Office of Northeast Asian Affairs, wrote to his boss, Assistant Secretary Dean Rusk, urging him to prevent a proposed statement by the president that the United States would not advance beyond the 38th Parallel. He contended: "I personally feel that if we can, . . . we should continue right up to the Manchurian and Siberian border, and call for a UN-sponsored election for all of Korea. Any action on our part now which would inhibit such action in the future would . . . be most unwise." Rusk wrote on the memorandum "Agree, DR."[37]

Other officials, including the president, were more cautious. A draft memorandum by the Policy Planning Staff three weeks later pointed out the possibility of a wider war with the Soviet Union or the PRC if UN forces approached their borders in an attempt to unify Korea under a government they did not control. The policy staff concluded that any unification of Korea could occur only if North Korean forces disintegrated, the Soviet Union and China did not intervene, and the UN Security Council passed another resolution authorizing the creation of a unified Korea. Secretary Acheson and President Truman wanted to delay any policy decision until they saw a successful US counteroffensive at Inchon and had a better sense of Soviet and Chinese intentions. When asked at a news conference on July 13 if US forces would move north of the 38th Parallel, Truman responded: "I will make that decision when it becomes necessary to do it."[38]

US leaders in Washington failed to appreciate how aggressive their policies on Taiwan and Korea looked to Mao Zedong and his Politburo colleagues in Beijing. American civilian and military officials presented their decision to station the Seventh Fleet in the Taiwan Strait as "neutralizing" Taiwan. The United States also sent military assistance and a military mission to strengthen Jiang Jieshi's defenses. Acheson and his Asian and Soviet specialists in the State Department consistently described the PRC as the agent or puppet of Moscow. Yet we now know that Chinese leaders were deeply troubled by these actions, which they saw as Washington again siding with the Nationalists in the civil war. They were increasingly anxious about increased Nationalist military power, the successful defense of the Pusan Perimeter, and US bombing near their border with North Korea.[39]

As the summer unfolded, US officials thought more positively about the advantages of unifying Korea. Three weeks after the war began, Truman asked the NSC to prepare a report on what policy the United States should pursue "after the North Korean forces have been driven back to the 38th Parallel." A draft memorandum from the Defense Department on July 31 analyzed the political and military situation, and argued that the Korean conflict "provides the United States and the free world with the opportunity to displace part of the Soviet orbit." The unification of Korea by UN forces could break up the Soviet "strategic complex" in the Far East, provide contacts and trade with Manchuria, and reassure Japan. "The significance in Asia of the unification of Korea . . . would be incalculable." A State Department draft memorandum of August 21 repeated much of the same analysis but, fearful that an immediate attempt to unify Korea would "cause the Soviet Union to commit either its own forces or those of Communist China or both with the consequent danger of global war," recommended a more cautious diplomatic process that ensured full UN backing for any effort at unification.[40]

Meanwhile, at the United Nations, the Soviet ambassador ended his boycott and returned on August 1 to begin his scheduled term as president of the Security Council. Soviet diplomats were more conciliatory than in the recent past, and they spoke of a cease-fire and supervised elections leading to a unified Korea. Washington officials took their behavior as a signal that Stalin wanted to avoid any confrontation over Korea. This perception fueled increased interest in pursuing the current military advantage to unify Korea. After further debate between defense and diplomatic representatives, on September 11 the president approved NSC Report 81/1, which with significant conditions approved MacArthur's advance across the 38th Parallel. The report specified that the UN commander would likely be authorized to cross the 38th Parallel "for the purpose of destroying the North Korean forces, provided that at the time of such operations there has been no entry into North Korea by major Soviet or Communist Chinese forces, no announcement of intended entry, nor a threat to counter our operations militarily in North Korea." MacArthur was directed to avoid military action along the Soviet and Chinese borders and to use South Korean units close to those boundaries. He was cautioned that final approval would be determined by the political and military situation at the time, and before advancing into North Korea he should obtain the express authorization of the president. The NSC report stated the objective of UN forces as establishing the independence and unification of Korea, and it called for detailed preparations to win the approval of UN members before unification was achieved.[41]

The brilliant success of the Inchon assault and the capture of Seoul two weeks later produced such a surge of optimism in Washington that the limitations spelled out in NSC 81/1 faded from official memory. The president, pundits, and world leaders praised MacArthur as a strategic genius. A consensus formed in Congress and among the public to take advantage of a great victory to finish the task. When a false report circulated in the press that South Korean troops would halt at the 38th Parallel to regroup, Republicans in Congress demanded that the president authorize crossing the border and destroying the enemy's armed forces. The fact that midterm congressional elections were only weeks away reinforced the administration's desire to take full advantage of the rout of the KPA created by Inchon. Recalling those days when he served as de facto national security adviser, Averell Harriman said that the pressures to cross the parallel were intense. "It would have taken a superhuman effort to say no," he declared. "Psychologically, it was almost impossible not to go ahead and complete the job."[42]

On September 27, the Joint Chiefs of Staff sent its directive to General MacArthur, setting out the terms for his operations north of the 38th Parallel. In guidance approved by Secretary of Defense Marshall and the president, the chiefs authorized military operations including airborne and amphibious landings for the purpose of destroying the armed forces of North Korea. The conditions placed on military activities by NSC 81/1 were quoted in full, with the added stipulation that the commander "make special efforts to determine whether there is a Chinese Communist or Soviet threat to the attainment of your objective, which will be reported to JCS [Joint Chiefs of Staff] as a matter of urgency." To allay the State Department's anxieties about the desires of MacArthur and Syngman Rhee to expand South Korean administrative jurisdiction over the whole of North Korea, the directive insisted that South Korean authority was to be restored only in South Korea and that the political status of North Korea must wait for UN action.[43]

Marshall agreed with MacArthur and the Joint Chiefs of Staff on the need to exploit the UN forces' current military advantage. Aware that Allied members of the UN wanted to avoid a vote on whether to authorize crossing the 38th Parallel, the secretary of defense sent an urgent radio message to MacArthur on September 29 directing him to make no public statement about the border, adding that "we want you to feel unhampered tactically and strategically to proceed north of the 38th Parallel." MacArthur happily accepted this personal green light from Marshall, and he replied: "Unless and until the enemy capitulates, I regard all of Korea open for our military operations." The UN commander would later argue that this message from Marshall freed him from the restrictions of the September 27 directive from the Joint Chiefs of Staff. In the meantime, President Rhee—fearing that Washington would delay, waiting for UN approval—ordered South Korean troops to cross the 38th Parallel on October 1. In stretching directives to and beyond their limits, MacArthur and Rhee sowed the seeds of future disaster.[44]

9

MAO ZEDONG INTERVENES MASSIVELY

When the founding of the People's Republic of China (PRC) was celebrated on October 1, 1949, the leaders of the Chinese Communist Party (CCP) knew that they faced huge problems. The Nationalist government of Jiang Jieshi had collapsed suddenly, and the Communist forces took over large parts of the country in which they had little support. The CCP had developed its revolutionary structure and programs as a peasant-based movement in Northeast China. The party had no organization and few adherents in the Eastern and Central regions, and virtually none in the Northwest or south of the Yantgze River. A clear majority of the cities were actually anticommunist. Greatly complicating the task of creating an integrated political system was the size of the country. As a comparison, John K. Fairbank, the dean of China studies in the United States citing demographic data for 1982, declares that "a billion or so Europeans in Europe and the Americas live divided into some fifty separate and sovereign states, while more than a billion Chinese live in only one state." A further constraint was the fact that China, even in the cities, was a series of small communities with a tradition of cultural but not political nationalism. The mechanisms did not exist for mass mobilization. In order to revive a prostrate economy and win political support in the newly liberated areas, the CCP needed to develop both new programs and techniques for disseminating them quickly.[1]

MAKING THE NEW CHINA

The CCP's Central Committee designed a strategy called the Common Program to create "the new China." A United Front government containing the nominally democratic parties representing the bourgeoisie, intellectuals, and urban workers joined the dominant CCP to implement this program. The goal of the United Front was to begin with a broad coalition of groups working to achieve a limited agenda, which created only a small number of opponents. Indeed, the new government allocated eleven of twenty-four ministerial posts to members of the democratic parties. On June 6, 1950, Mao Zedong explained his approach to a plenary session of the Central Committee:

> We should rally the petty bourgeoisie and the national bourgeoisie under the leadership of the working class and on the basis of the worker–peasant alliance. The national bourgeoisie will eventually cease to exist, but at this stage we should rally them around us and not push them away. We should struggle against them on the one hand and unite with them on the other. We should make this clear to the cadres and show by facts that it is right and necessary to unite with the national bourgeoisie, the democratic parties, democratic personages and intellectuals. Many of them were our enemies before, but now that they have broken with the enemy camp and come over to our side, we should unite with all these people, who can be more or less united with. It is in the interest of the working people to unite with them. We need to adopt these tactics now.

Later in his remarks, Mao concluded: "In short, we must not hit out in all directions. It is undesirable to hit out in all directions and cause nationwide tension. We must definitely not make too many enemies, we must make concessions and relax the tension a little in some quarters and concentrate our attack in one direction."[2]

Even within the limited agenda of the Common Program, not all changes were to be applied in every region. For example, land reform was essential to end the conditions comparable to serfdom endured by the poor peasants who made up roughly 80 percent of the population. These reforms had been completed in the North and Northeast regions, which had been under Communist control for almost two decades. The new government approved a land reform decree in June 1950 but delayed in applying it to the newly liberated areas in order to limit dissent and opposition from the rich peasants and to maintain agricultural production at a high level. Another policy that differentiated among the parts of the country was military rule. For administrative purposes, China was divided into six large regions. The two regions where military tasks such as suppressing bandits and counterrevolutionaries and imposing land reform were completed—North China and the Northeast—were administered by people's governments. The other four, largely covering the newly liberated areas, had military governments. As reforms were carried out and stability was established, control shifted from military to civilian administrations.[3]

Having led a peasant revolution, Mao and his colleagues now shifted their focus to the cities. The CCP members from the countryside who had fought the civil war lacked the skills to manage the administration and businesses in urban areas. The solution was to arrest a few top Nationalist leaders and powerbrokers while keeping most workers and managers in their jobs. To develop loyal party members who could manage the cities, the CCP recruited educated urban youth who could be trained in the doctrine and discipline of the party and promoted as their reliability was proven. This combination of old and new workers and managers labored to win the support of city residents by improving the economy, controlling inflation, and fighting corruption. These policies achieved considerable success in reviving the economy and reducing inflation by 1952. The urban population, which had suffered during the previous two decades of Nationalist misrule, developed strong support for the new Communist government.[4]

From late 1949 into the spring of 1950, Chinese security policies evolved toward a more assertive role in the Asia-Pacific region. After the Soviet atomic test, the CCP's suppression of many Nationalist opponents, and the treaty with Moscow, Chinese leaders saw their strategic position grow significantly stronger. Once it completed the unification of its territory with the capture of Taiwan, Beijing planned to be the leader of Asian revolution in supporting communist movements in Vietnam and Korea. Although the United States was reducing its commitments in Asia and did not appear likely to attack China in the near term, America remained the world's strongest power and continued to provide aid to the Nationalists on Taiwan while refusing to recognize the Communist-led United Front as the legitimate government of China. Officials in Beijing believed that, ultimately, the PRC would have a major confrontation with the United States, and they began to prepare for this eventuality.[5]

The first step was to restructure its military forces for possible conflicts in the region. Planning for reform of the military began in the fall of 1949, and the Central Committee approved the final version in April 1950. According to a detailed report by Nie Rongzhen, the acting chief of staff of the People's Liberation Army (PLA), the comprehensive plan sought to achieve several important objectives. It would reduce the size of the army from its peak strength of 5.7 million men to cut costs and also remove Nationalist soldiers who had been forced into service when captured and whose loyalty to the new government was questionable. The savings from a reduced army would allow a buildup of the air force and navy, which was essential for the capture of Taiwan and for protection against American threats from the air and sea. Finally, the new land force would be reorganized to create a mobile central reserve to deal with "any crisis situation caused by the Americans in Taiwan, the Korean Peninsula, or Indochina."[6]

The Communist leadership planned two other major reform movements before the Korean War broke out, but it delayed their implementation until China entered the war. The delay was initially part of the calculated design of the Common Program to avoid creating too many enemies at the start of the new government. After the war began and the United States quickly intervened by sending ground forces to Korea and stationing the Seventh Fleet in the Taiwan Strait, the Central Committee decided to use the patriotic campaign begun in the summer of 1950 to persuade the population that strong measures were necessary to create national unity and rid the country of spies and counterrevolutionaries. The coordinated effort of political mobilization was initially presented as "defending the homeland and safeguarding the country," and with the war it expanded into the "Great Movement to Resist America and Assist Korea." Under these banners, the party began an extensive program of land reform in the newly incorporated rural areas and soon followed in early 1951 with successive movements in urban areas to suppress counterrevolutionaries, eliminate corrupt cadres, break up the national bourgeoisie, and remove opposition intellectuals. There is strong evidence that the party used the Korean War as an opportunity to implement patriotic campaigns to eliminate opponents and increase political mobilization for the regime. Together with wartime sacrifices, these Communist reforms created great suffering, intimidated many who may have remained ambivalent about the new regime, and cost the lives of thousands of real and imagined enemies.[7]

Beyond the mainland, Mao's concept of "continuous revolution" drove the policies of the New China toward Taiwan, Indochina, and Korea. Mao repeatedly lectured party leaders on the need for successive waves of revolutionary activism to purge Chinese society of "all the feudal oppression of thousands of years and the imperialist oppression of a hundred years." The chairman believed this revolutionary mission for China should naturally extend to its relations with its neighbors in the region, and he welcomed the division of labor suggested by Stalin during the Chinese leader's Moscow visit that China should assume responsibility for spreading socialist revolution in Asia.[8]

The top priority was completing the civil war by capturing Taiwan. The CCP leadership began planning to "liberate" the strategically important island as early as June 1949. After negotiations with Moscow, Soviet air and naval aid began to arrive in September to satisfy the essential military requirement of creating an adequate amphibious capability to defeat the Nationalists. Mao set a tentative date for the Taiwan attack in the summer of 1950, but serious setbacks occurred the previous fall, when attempts to capture two small offshore islands were soundly rejected. In late October, the Nationalists handed the PLA its worst defeat of the entire civil war on the island of Jinmen (Quemoy), when 10,000

Communist troops were killed or captured. Evaluating their defeats, the CCP leadership concluded that American-supplied airplanes and warships gave the Nationalists decisive control of the approaches to the islands. A successful campaign against the offshore islands and ultimately the capture of Taiwan would require greatly increased Soviet aid for air and naval forces. As Chen Jian argues, this reassessment of their strategic position led the Communist leaders to harden their conviction that "the United States was their primary enemy."[9]

By the spring of 1950, China's strategic situation had changed significantly. The Truman administration had announced in January that its Asian defense perimeter did not include Taiwan or South Korea. China concluded a major treaty of alliance and mutual assistance with the Soviet Union in February. And in May, Beijing learned that Stalin had approved a North Korean invasion of the south, which would delay Soviet supplies to China for an invasion of Taiwan. At this point, Mao and his colleagues again reluctantly postponed the attack on Taiwan for another year.[10]

As the Taiwan campaign faced delay, the PRC offered substantial assistance to the Vietnamese Communists in their fight for independence against France. The president of the fledgling Democratic Republic of Vietnam (North Vietnam), Ho Chi Minh, had ties to the Chinese Communists going back to the 1920s. He spoke fluent Chinese and had fought with the Communist forces against the Japanese in the 1940s. After the CCP's victory in the civil war, the two communist parties worked to strengthen cooperation. The PRC extended diplomatic recognition to North Vietnam in mid-January 1950, and after Stalin passed the responsibility for aiding the Vietnamese to Beijing plans developed quickly for PLA advisers to assess the Vietnamese needs and train their forces. The advisory group received training in May and moved to Vietnam a few weeks later. At the same time the Truman administration, concerned about the spread of communism in Indochina, began a program of military advice and assistance to the French forces in Vietnam, with the first aid shipments arriving in June 1950. Before war began in Korea, the United States and the PRC had committed advisers and military assistance to opposing sides in Vietnam.[11]

The final area of Chinese Communist regional engagement, and the most complex, was Korea. Chapter 6 discussed the extensive assistance provided by the North Koreans to the PLA in its civil war with the Nationalists. This included providing over 47,000 ethnic Koreans as combat troops; giving massive supplies to the PLA; and allowing North Korean territory to serve as a sanctuary for military units, food and equipment, and the transportation of men and material around Nationalist forces. The government of Kim Il-sung provided critical support to the CCP during its most difficult days, and leaders in Beijing were well aware of their debt to Pyongyang. As partial repayment, the Chinese returned these 47,000 combat veterans of Korean origin with their weapons between the fall of 1949 and the following spring. These troops would form the elite units of the Korean People's Army invasion force in June 1950.[12]

Yet the debt from the Chinese Civil War and the close connections between the CCP and the Korean party posed problems for Kim Il-sung. Although he himself had been a member of the Chinese party at one time and fought with them against the Japanese, he was a fervent Korean nationalist and was a leader trying to consolidate his own power. Recent research shows a significant degree of factional struggle for power in Pyongyang on the eve of the war. Kim's main rivals were Koreans with very strong ties to the CCP and a group headed by Pak Hon-yong, which had originally been based in Seoul. Kim's aversion to dependence on Beijing also reflected the historic resistance of all Koreans to their long dominance by Chinese rulers. This desire to be fully in control of the effort to unify Korea explains Kim's late visit in May 1950 to explain his invasion plans to Mao and his refusal to share the date or any details of his plan of attack with Chinese leaders. The ambivalent nature of this relationship would only deepen when Kim had to plead with Mao for assistance during the war.[13]

Although Chinese activities regarding Taiwan, Vietnam, and Korea were dealt with separately by officials in Washington, leaders in Beijing felt they were closely connected. As Zhou Enlai later explained, these policies were elements of "the concept of confronting the United States on three fronts."[14]

PREPARATIONS FOR WAR

The North Korean invasion took Chinese leaders by surprise because Kim Il-sung had given them no indication of when he would attack. The initial reactions from Beijing were sharp criticism of the US decision to move the Seventh Fleet into the Taiwan Strait. On June 28, before the central government council, Mao declared that US intervention in Taiwan had shown that Truman's statement of January 5 about nonintervention in Chinese internal affairs was merely "a pack of lies." That same day, Zhou Enlai denounced the new stationing of the American fleet as "a violent invasion of Chinese territory." In practical terms, the government indefinitely postponed the planned attack on Taiwan. This verbal assault showed that Chinese officials took a very different view of the movement of the US fleet from the widespread assumption in Washington that the Truman administration had acted to prevent the Nationalists from attacking the mainland in a vain attempt to revive the civil war and regain active American involvement.[15]

When the United States committed ground troops to defend South Korea and succeeded in winning a United Nations mandate for its operations, Chinese leaders took steps to prepare for more direct challenges. At Mao's request, Zhou organized two conferences on July 7 and 10 with members of the Central Military Commission and senior PLA officers to consider responses to the US intervention in Korea and how to carry out the chairman's decision to create a defensive force on the Chinese–Korean border. The conference participants recommended sending three armies of the PLA's best troops to Northeast China to join forces in the region to form the Northeast Border Defense Army. The Standing Committee of the Politburo promptly ordered these recommendations to be implemented, and by the end of July the troops had arrived on the Korean border to form a force of 260,000.[16]

The decisions of Chinese leaders in the first three weeks after the North Korean invasion are central to understanding why the PRC intervened in the war. Research by Chinese scholars since the end of the Cold War has produced convincing evidence that Mao was the sole driver of these decisions. He determined that the United States was China's principal threat and called for the deployment of a significant defense force on the Korean border. Planners and logistics managers of the PLA, pushed at every step by Zhou, arranged new methods of supply and funding for the new border army and stockpiled weapons, ammunition, and food during July and August. The most important conclusion to draw from these actions is that by mid-July, Mao had decided that a confrontation between China and the United States was inevitable and that Korea was the likely venue. The unanswered questions for the chairman were how long it would take to persuade his Politburo colleagues to support his analysis and when the clash would occur.[17]

During August, the war prospects became clearer for Chinese leaders. As the North Korean attack stalled before the defensive perimeter established by the US and South Korean forces around Pusan, General MacArthur made a highly publicized visit to Taiwan to coordinate defense policies with Jiang Jieshi. This trip and the exaggerated reports from the journalists accompanying the UN commander increased concern among Chinese officials about Washington's aggressive intentions. On August 4, Mao met with the Politburo to analyze the Korean conflict. He argued that China had to prepare for intervention, saying, "If the US imperialists win, they will be complacent and pose a threat for us. We cannot but help Korea in the form of volunteers. We should of course choose a good time, and we have to be prepared." The next day, Mao instructed Gao Gang, commander and political commissar of the Northeast Region, to convene a meeting of senior officers to organize preparations for operations in Korea.[18]

On August 13, Gao Gang chaired a conference attended by several senior officers from Beijing and the army and division commanders of the Northeast Border Defense Army. After hearing the instructions from the Politburo, the participants discussed the goals and significance of the war effort. They concluded that the PLA should not wait for the Americans to take over all of Korea and then attack China, but should "take the initiative, assisting the Korean People's Army to wipe out the enemy and defend ourselves." The experienced commanders then analyzed the strategy and tactics necessary to overcome the large US advantages in firepower and mobility. They agreed that the PLA should avoid frontal attacks and concentrate instead on penetrating weak points between units, often at night, in order to get behind the front lines and destroy transportation and communication centers before attacking the fortified positions from the rear. Some commanders were concerned about the need for political indoctrination and mobilization of troops who had most recently been working on farming and reconstruction projects. One army corps reported that only about 50 percent of its soldiers were motivated to fight in Korea, while 40 percent were passive and 10 percent opposed to fighting. The participants concluded that they could not complete adequate preparations for combat by the end of August as Mao had directed. Gao Gang then requested an extension of the deadline to the end of September, and Mao accepted this new date. By August 18, a month before MacArthur's landing at Inchon, the Chinese Politburo and the commanders of the Northeast Border Defense Army were committed to being prepared for intervention by the end of September.[19]

As the combat units hastened their training, the PLA General Staff closely analyzed the likely course of fighting in Korea. On August 23, the Operations Bureau held a meeting to forecast the next moves of US forces. The session was chaired by Lei Yingfu, Zhou's military secretary, who also served as vice director of the bureau. Convinced that the North Korean offensive was unable to break through the Pusan Perimeter defenses, the participants took special note that General MacArthur had held two fresh divisions in Japan, that these troops were training for amphibious operations, and that the Far East Command was assembling warships and landing craft from around the Pacific. They were very familiar with MacArthur's series of successful amphibious assaults during the war against Japan; and based on these factors, the group concluded that US forces would soon make a major landing at one of five Korean ports with the most probable and the most damaging option being Inchon. Lei immediately presented this analysis to Zhou that evening, and the premier informed Mao right away. The chairman asked Lei to join them and questioned him in great detail about the staff's discussions. Convinced by their reasoning, Mao then asked about MacArthur's personality. Lei replied that as a commander, the American general was noted for his arrogance and stubbornness. Impressed and pleased, Mao declared: "Fine! Fine! The more arrogant and more stubborn he is, the better. An arrogant enemy is easy to defeat."[20]

Anxious about the possibility of a major American breakthrough in Korea, Mao ordered his staff and the Northeast Border Defense Army to move more rapidly in their preparations. He informed Kim Il-sung and Stalin of his General Staff's analysis and the likelihood of a landing at Inchon. Although the Chinese leader urged him to improve defenses at the port, Kim took no action on the warning from Beijing. Zhou chaired an important meeting of the Central Military Commission on August 26, opening the session by setting a broad context for the proposed intervention. The conflict in Korea, he said, was much more important than an issue "concerning a brother country." It was "an important international issue" that could change the course of communist competition with the Western imperialists. "If Korea wins the victory," he argued, "we will find an easier solution for our Taiwan issue." The premier then stated the mission when he declared: "Korea is equipped with the basic capabilities to fight a protracted war. But it seems the task of annihilating the American troops one by one in the last phase certainly will fall to us." He went on to discuss in detail how each service of the PLA should improve itself for the clash with the United States. The participants determined that much work needed to be done to prepare the air force and airborne and tank units for war. At a subsequent meeting of the commission five days later, the members decided to increase the Northeast Border Defense Army to eleven armies totaling 700,000 troops. They also directed each military region to contribute units for a reserve and moved part of that reserve force close to the Northeast region.[21]

Mao was convinced of the need to intervene, but he realized that many of his senior colleagues had deep reservations about this major commitment. And in order to win the support of the wider CCP membership and the public, the chairman understood that he had to make a convincing case that Chinese security was threatened by American aggression in Korea. In addressing the central government council on September 5, he used arguments that he would repeat many times during the month in his effort to win broad endorsement for intervention as a necessary step to defend Chinese interests and advance the revolution. An important element in his campaign was to persuade the public that China could stand up to American power. He argued that, though the United States had a strong economy and produced large amounts of steel, it was conducting an unjust war against Asian people and had little popular support at home. He pointed out the heavy American commitment to Europe, its long supply lines to Korea, and the low combat readiness of US forces. Against this enemy, China had many advantages. Its populace was greatly superior in numbers, bravery, and unity, and its soldiers had recent combat experience and were highly motivated. He concluded that China could win this struggle and end the attempt to revive Western imperialism in Asia. As training of the forces progressed and additional supplies arrived from the Soviet Union, Mao continued to build a consensus of the leadership and the public behind his plan.[22]

Other factors complicated an early commitment of Chinese volunteers to Korea. Before Beijing could send military forces into Korea, Kim Il-sung had to request their assistance. Not only did Kim not inform Chinese leaders of the timing of his attack; he also had all the arms shipments from the Soviet Union arrive by sea to keep Chinese intelligence from learning the extent of his buildup for war. After the conflict began, Kim continued to refuse to share information with Chinese officials. When, in early August, the Central Committee of the CCP ordered Deng Hua, the new commander of the Thirteenth Army Corps in the Northeast, to go to Korea to evaluate the war situation, Kim denied him permission to enter the country. In addition, beyond asking the PLA to move a reserve force to the Northeast, Stalin had not requested any Chinese assistance for the war effort. Pyongyang would not ask for help from the Chinese until its army faced defeat after Inchon. In the meantime, Mao could only concentrate on preparations for intervention.[23]

THE CHAIRMAN

Who was this person preparing so feverishly to intervene in a conflict he had no role in starting and about which he had been given little information? Who was Mao Zedong, and how had he accumulated such authority within the new PRC?

The man who would become the leader of the world's most populous nation was born in 1893 in the southern province of Hunan into a relatively wealthy family. Mao was the eldest surviving son, and two younger brothers rounded out the family. Two sons had died before Mao's birth, and two daughters later died as infants. His father was a stern, frugal farmer who could be coarse and cruel toward his family. By the time Mao was ten years old, his father had bought additional land and become a rich peasant who hired others to help him tend his crops and purchased grain from smaller farmers to sell at higher prices in the winter. Having only two years of schooling, the father wanted Mao to be educated in the Confucian classics so that he could help advance the family business and represent his father in court proceedings. Mao's mother was often abused by her husband and provided the warm support that her sons needed in their harsh family environment.[24]

As a child, Mao grew up in a village characterized by hard work, poverty, and violence. Beyond the great majority of peasants who labored every day to scratch out a subsistence livelihood was a rural underclass of day workers, beggars, and thieves who composed roughly 10 percent of the population. This roving mass of unemployed poor frequently formed bandit gangs that robbed more well-to-do peasants and staged insurrections against the local authorities. Provincial leaders regularly put down these uprisings with brutal force, including public executions staged as spectacles and object lessons for the populace. A voracious reader, the young Mao devoured numerous historical novels about rebellions involving warriors, knights, and bandit chieftains. In their excellent biography of Mao, Alexander Pantsov and Steven Levine contend that "already in early childhood, under the influence of his despotic father, incendiary literature, and his surroundings, he concluded that open rebellion was the only way to defend one's rights. If you remained humble and obedient, you would be beaten over and over again."[25]

At his local school, Mao was an intense but willful student. He excelled in the subjects that interested him but disliked Confucian philosophy, science, mathematics, and English. After leaving school at thirteen, he read widely at home before moving to a more rigorous middle school three years later. The following year, 1911, he moved again to a school in Changsha, the lively provincial capital of Hunan. There, he experienced life in a big city for the first time and continued to excel in his favorite subjects, social science and literature. He was especially strong in writing. "He wrote quickly as if sparks were flying from his writing brush. His class compositions were posted as examples on the walls of the school. He could read two or three times faster than anyone else," his fellow student Xiao San later wrote. In 1913, he met Professor Yang Changji, who would have a great influence on the future leader. Yang had studied in Japan, Scotland, and Germany, and he had specialized in Chinese and Western philosophy and ethics. The professor emphasized to his students China's need for strong personalities who would focus their energies on achieving large goals. Using the work of the German philosopher Friedrich Paulsen, Yang argued that a great person could rise above normal morality to achieve major objectives. The principle of "the end justifies the means" played a large role in shaping Mao's personal philosophy. This proud son of Hunan saw himself destined for glory.[26]

During his years in Changsha, Mao experimented widely with ideas and schools. For a time, he changed schools monthly before leaving studies structured by professors to read and write on his own at the public library for eighteen months. During this independent study, he became very concerned about the domination of China by foreign governments and companies operating in large concessions, organized initially by the British and French and joined later by the Americans and the Germans. When Japan took advantage of the terms of its alliance with Great Britain to declare war on Germany in 1914 and seized German concessions in China, Mao and many young Chinese reacted strongly on nationalist grounds against the prospect of Japanese domination of their homeland. In April 1918, Mao and some school friends formed a society to reform academic studies and advance self-improvement. This idealistic group grew to seventy-five members and soon expanded its goals to seek reform of China and the world beyond. Many of the society's members would become leaders in the communist movement in later years. In subsequent discussions with the journalist Edgar Snow, Mao would recall that "at this time, my mind was a curious mixture of ideas of liberalism, democratic reformism, and Utopian Socialism. . . . I was definitely anti-militarist and anti-imperialist."[27]

As World War I was grinding to its conclusion, Mao continued to search for a compelling concept to fuel his desire for political activism. Starting in August 1918, he spent seven months in Beijing working as an assistant to the librarian of Peking University. There, among a group of professors and politically active students, he became acquainted with the principles of anarchism and communism. But it was nationalism, not either of his new political theories, that drove him to launch his first significant political organization. The decision of the Paris Peace Conference in 1919 to award the German concessions to Japan rather than returning them to China angered Mao. Returning to Changsha, he recruited friends and activists to develop a boycott of Japanese products in their region. After some initial success, the boycott was broken up by armed groups led by a local warlord. Mao found his efforts at local reform stifled by a modest show of force and the apathy of his fellow students and citizens.[28]

The success of the Bolshevik revolution in Russia provided the catalyst to force Mao to choose a new course for his political ambitions and abandon his dreams of liberal or anarchist paths to power. The ease with which his boycott had been suppressed convinced him that China could be reformed only by a strong centralized party with the capacity and willingness to use force. The Bolsheviks provided the model, and by November 1920 Mao decided Bolshevism would be his approach. "It was not the romance of universal equality that enticed him to embrace communism," argue Pantsov and Levine. "What attracted him was the apologia for violence, the triumph of will, and the celebration of power." Mao now began organizing Communist cells in Changsha in coordination with friends in Beijing and Shanghai. By the summer of 1921, there were six cells operating in Chinese cities, and the arrival of a new representative of the Comintern from Moscow sparked the creation of a national party. Mao was among the founding members when representatives from the six cells gathered in Shanghai in July 1921 to create the Chinese Communist Party.[29]

For much of the 1920s, the CCP remained under the firm control of the Comintern, and funds from Moscow provided almost all the party's income. The Comintern put pressure on the small CCP to join the Kuomintang (KMT), the Nationalist party. When party leaders resisted, Moscow threatened to cut off their funding and expel them from the international communist movement. The Chinese party had to give in and join the Nationalists, thereby creating the United Front. A CCP congress in June 1923 elected Mao to its five-man Central Bureau and named him secretary of the Central Executive Committee. The party at this time claimed 420 members. Soon after the congress, Mao joined the KMT and cooperated fully with its legendary Nationalist leader Sun Yatsen, who had led the overthrow of the Qing Dynasty and founded the Republic of China in 1912. After Sun's death in 1925, a series of intrigues dominated the United Front, and the next year Jiang Jieshi emerged as a strong man and forced Mao and his Communist colleagues out of the joint party leadership. In April 1927, Jiang consolidated his control of the KMT and reversed the policy of the United Front. The CCP was removed from the party, and Jiang had thousands killed as he suppressed his left-wing opponents.[30]

In these turbulent times, Mao was virtually alone among Communist leaders in concluding that the CCP would need to develop its own military force in order to succeed in ruling China. He proceeded to create a Red Army from the available underclass of bandits, beggars, and soldiers, including many who belonged to secret societies. He developed his unusual array of guerrilla tactics in the mountains and successfully evaded three of Jiang's campaigns to destroy the Communist forces. The Soviet policy of providing support to both the Nationalists and the Communists always favored the KMT. Stalin and his colleagues saw the KMT as the strongest political group in China, and they viewed Mao as too independent-minded to be a loyal client of Moscow. On several occasions, Comintern officials removed Mao from the top CCP leadership, replacing him with Zhou and others. Mao was fortunate to be out of power when Jiang's forces imposed a costly defeat on the Communists. As a result of mistakes leading to this serious loss, Zhou was demoted and Mao regained a leadership position. At this point in 1934, to avoid complete defeat, the Red Army began the Long March from the south of China to the northwest. The remnants of the Communist force numbered 86,000 men when the Long March started. But after traversing 6,000 miles, battles, disease, and desertions left only 5,000 when they reached Shaanxi Province in the north in October 1935.[31]

After the Long March, Mao benefited from the military defeat of Zhang Guotao, who was his main rival for leadership. The Japanese attack on northern China in 1937 also served Mao's interests because it forced Jiang to return to the United Front with the CCP in order to combat the larger existential threat from an imperialistic Japan, which had already taken over Korea and Manchuria. During the long war against Tokyo's forces, Mao gained control of his party's leadership and expanded the strength of the Red Army. At the defeat of Japan, the Communist forces were stronger than those of the KMT. By the end of August 1945, Mao had consolidated all the power of the CCP for himself. His colleagues in the party leadership had elected him chairman of the Central Committee, the Politburo, the Secretariat, and the Military Council of the Central Committee. And his collected writings were enshrined as party doctrine in the new party Constitution.[32]

Almost immediately after the Japanese surrender in September 1945, clashes resumed between the Nationalists and the Communists. A full-scale civil war erupted in June 1946. Although Stalin did fund and support the CCP, he did not fully trust Mao and maintained some support and advice for Jiang. At the same time the United States, which had fought as an ally of the KMT during the war, continued to support Jiang and even airlifted Nationalist units to the Northeast to allow them to accept the surrender of Japanese forces in the cities. When, in November 1946, Zhou and some other CCP and Soviet officials advised joining the Jiang-sponsored National Assembly, Mao refused to collaborate again with the KMT. He recalled Zhou from negotiations and explained his views in a long session with his chief deputy, Lui Shaoqi, and Zhou. The chairman contended that the world was now in a sustained struggle between American imperialism and Soviet revolution and that the CCP must in this situation stand with the Soviet Union and oppose Jiang. Mao predicted, according to the historian Odd Arne Westad, that even though it would take at least a year before the Communist forces could go on the offensive against the KMT, "it would be a long war, but in the end the CCP would win."[33]

The civil war ground on for over three years. Initially, the KMT was able to take control of about 80 percent of the country and worked to revive the economy and maintain order after almost a decade of war. Militarily, the Nationalists drove the Red Army back into a small section of northern China. But the economy did not improve, and corruption and high inflation soon began to turn the public against the KMT. Factionalism and venality among the Nationalist leadership cost political support, and by mid-1947 military incompetence and corruption in combat, along with problems in the delivery of supplies and weapons, weakened the performance of the military. In February and March 1948, the CCP forces in Manchuria under Lin Biao's strong direction destroyed many of the best KMT units and set the stage for gaining control of the industrial heartland of northern China. The Red Army continued its success through the summer and fall as it moved from the north into central China. At the same time, the economic and political institutions of the KMT lost urban support as efforts to reform the financial system failed. Throughout the military operations of 1948 and early 1949, Mao demonstrated audacious strategic analysis and shrewd judgment as he directed his commanders in detailed telegrams on a daily basis. As Westad describes it, "Over the past months, Mao's status in his party had taken on godlike proportions. The victories in the Northeast . . . were ascribed to Mao's military genius."[34]

With his army disorganized and in retreat, Jiang staged a false resignation in January 1949 and had his vice president, now named acting president, circulate an appeal for negotiations with the CCP and mediation by the major powers. To Mao's surprise and anger, Stalin wanted to accept the invitation to mediate and cabled a draft response for the chairman to use in reply. In a remarkably bold step, Mao rejected the Soviet dictator's instructions and had the brass to dictate a suggested reply for Stalin saying the Soviet Union could not agree to mediate because of its commitment to "the principle of nonintervention in other countries' internal affairs." Despite the Kremlin's adoption of his proposal, Mao remained suspicious of Stalin's motives and believed he would have been pleased to see a stalemated civil war lead to a partitioned China.[35]

Mao saw the foundations of the Nationalist regime crumbling, and he wanted to press his advantage to win a quick and complete victory. For him, Moscow's interference was an attempt to thwart his final offensive, and in later years he would cite this as an early example of Stalin's duplicity. Without any foreign mediation, Mao agreed to peace negotiations with the KMT while he repositioned his armies for attacks against both central China and the south. The Red Army entered Beijing at the end of January 1949 against minimal resistance, and the Communists began to organize it as China's new capital. Representatives of the CCP leadership persuaded some KMT army and navy commanders and even some peace negotiators to defect, and Mao then presented a virtual ultimatum to surrender to the acting Nationalist president. When he refused, the PLA crossed the Yangzi River and captured the Nationalist capital Nanjing on April 23. In late May, Communist forces marched into the abandoned commercial center of the country, Shanghai, after it had been looted by Jiang as he fled to Taiwan. The CCP leadership celebrated the founding of the PRC on October 1, 1949, in a massive event in Beijing with Mao making his first and only speech from the top of the Tiananmen Gate.[36]

Like many revolutionary leaders, Mao's personal life transcended the normal morality of his day and followed the teachings of Friedrich Paulsen, whose works he had studied as a teenager in Changsha. In his drive to achieve greatness for China and for himself, Mao acted as if all personal choices should be made to satisfy his immediate needs. His relations with his family showed the familiar self-centered personality and capacity for brutality evident in his political and military activities. His sexual desires were immense. He was married four times and abandoned three of his wives. He left his second wife, Yang Kaihui, with two sons when he fled from an attempt to capture him. She was later executed when she refused to denounce him in return for her freedom. His third wife, He Zizhen, was devoured by jealousy over his sexual adventures with young actresses and dancers and spent many years in a mental hospital. His final wife was the famous actress Jiang Qing, known later during the Cultural Revolution as the infamous Madame Mao. She developed a more effective survival strategy by serving Mao as "not only a passionate lover but also an exacting secretary and housekeeper. She looked after his health and daily regimen, his schedule of visitors, his clothes, diet, and walks." She even "steered young girls to him" and concentrated on maintaining her power in the household, contend Pantsov and Levine. A few years later, when Mao had lost sexual interest in Jiang Qing, the Red Army organized a special entertainment group of young women whose "major function was to provide bed mates for Mao," according to Chang and Halliday. "Apart from singers and dancers, nurses and maids were handpicked for Mao's villas to provide a pool of women from whom he could choose whoever he wanted to have sex with."[37]

In addition to his sexual requirements, Mao spared no expense on his security and food. The chairman "treated the funds of the state as his own," and he had more than fifty elaborate villas built in choice locations over the course of his twenty-seven-year rule. All were built with high security features: bombproof, nuclear shelters in some, and identical warehouse style of one-story design due to his fear of being trapped on the second floor. All had heated swimming pools for his favorite form of exercise. Security was carried to an extreme in his travel arrangements. He kept trains, planes, and ships at his disposal and never gave advance notice of his travel plans. At some villas, he had a railroad spur built up to the front door so he could reduce the risk of assassination. He "frequently slept in his train parked at military airports, ready to make a quick getaway by train or plane in case of emergency." He loved to eat the best food available. His favorite items were grown in the ideal locations and shipped to him from all parts of China. The meals were prepared by a special house-keeper, who tasted each dish for poison. The chairman had ample cash for any personal needs. Everyone had to buy his books, and the royalties were placed in a private account of more than 2 million yuan. For comparison, his staff had an annual average income of four hundred yuan. "Mao was the only millionaire created in Mao's China."[38] (See figure 9.1.)

When he arrived in Beijing in January 1949, Mao was fifty-six years old and in poor health. After twenty-five years of hard living, frequently on the move while engaged in guerrilla warfare and party intrigues, he was overweight and suffered from insomnia and frequent colds. Most

FIGURE 9.1 Mao Zedong writing while on one of his special armored trains used extensively for security reasons, circa 1954.

Source: National Archives.

seriously, he had been affected for years by angioneurosis, a disorder of the blood vessels that caused headaches, sweating, dizziness, and neuropathy in his joints and extremities. His daily routine did not help. He continued to work 15 hours a day, laboring through the night with meetings and writing into the morning. He slept until two or three in the afternoon. Worst of all, he smoked three packs of cigarettes a day. During his visit to Moscow in January 1950, Soviet doctors diagnosed him as suffering from arteriosclerosis and emphysema and also a serious skin rash and widespread dental cavities. They learned that he never brushed his teeth but relied only on rinsing his mouth with green tea. The advice from the physicians was to stop smoking, have regular massages and walks, and take vitamin B1 and injections of Pantokrin, a remedy made from Siberian stag antlers. They reported that there was no known medical treatment for angioneurosis.[39]

Despite his health problems and his chaotic personal life, Mao demonstrated the leadership qualities that won him the preeminent position in the ruling party and the government of the new PRC. He showed great vision in his belief that China was ripe for revolution and that, if effectively led, a peasant movement could achieve this goal. He was pragmatic in his refinement of a guerrilla strategy to defeat a better-armed and -supplied Nationalist army. Pragmatism was also central to his adoption of the United Front policy, first with the KMT and later with bourgeois parties in the PRC's early days. His ultimate pragmatism was to ally himself and the CCP closely with the Soviet Union and, despite numerous slights and broken promises, to praise Stalin's leadership and design for Communism in China. Mao's expressions of fealty to the Soviet dictator reflected in no small measure his capacity as a great actor. As Andrei Orlov, the Soviet physician assigned to attend Mao in China, reported to Stalin, Mao "is able to conceal his feelings, and play the role that is his; he talks about this with intimates . . . and laughingly asks whether he has pulled it off well."[40]

"Mao's unchallenged authority was the linchpin of the entire edifice of elite stability" in the early years of Communist Party rule, contends Frederick Teiwes. The chairman maintained his control through a collective leadership, whereby very able senior party members exercised significant authority in their areas of expertise. "Unlike Stalin, Mao did not set his colleagues at each other's throats. . . . Instead, the ranking members of the ruling elite were men of talent and major figures in the history of the CCP in their own right." Mao took the lead in the areas of agriculture, advancing socialist revolution, and foreign policy. Zhou was the leader in administration, and he shared authority in foreign policy and military affairs with Mao. Others shaped policy in economics, an area about which Mao openly admitted his lack of knowledge. Teiwes, who carefully analyzed Mao's leadership role in the period 1949–57, argues that Mao overrode opposition from his senior colleagues and persuaded them to endorse his view on only three occasions in these years. The first and in many ways the case that set the path for the others came in October 1950 with the commitment to enter the war in Korea.[41]

THE DECISION TO INTERVENE

The Inchon landing soon changed the course of the war and forced significant policy adjustments in the three communist capitals. In Beijing, party leaders realized that Chinese troops would no longer have the role of turning a stalemate into victory, but they would now bear the brunt of the fighting and be primarily responsible for preventing the conquest of North Korea by United Nations forces. To improve their access to timely information, the Central Military Commission on September 17 ordered five experienced intelligence officers to proceed immediately to Korea. They arrived in Pyongyang on September 20, and with personal introductions from Kim Il-sung they departed for different sectors of the front to learn as much as possible about the course of the war. At the same time, Mao wrote to Gao Gang: "It seems that we have no other alternative but to send troops there. You must lose no time in making preparations."[42]

The crisis created by MacArthur's Inchon assault found Stalin on vacation on the Black Sea. Although dependent on news sent from Moscow, the Soviet leader still made a shrewd assessment of the situation. He understood that he had to urge Kim Il-sung to withdraw several divisions from the Pusan Perimeter to prevent their envelopment by UN forces, and he had to persuade the Chinese to intervene. Both tasks were addressed on September 16, when he wrote to Kim, directing him to pull four divisions back to form a defensive shield to the northeast of Seoul, and cabled Mao to ask if Chinese forces in the northeast were able to intervene to help the Korean People's Army. It soon became obvious that the North Koreans did not follow Stalin's firm advice when M. V. Zakharov, the leader's personal emissary in Pyongyang, wrote on September 26 to say that the military situation was desperate, with heavy losses, poor command, and a severe lack of supplies and fuel. Recent evidence shows that Stalin resisted early Chinese offers to intervene in support of a failing North Korean invasion. He opposed Chinese proposals to send military advisers and supplies in July and October and overruled Kim Il-sung's request for Chinese intervention in mid-September. Only after UN forces captured Seoul and were preparing to cross the 38th Parallel did the Soviet leader ask Mao for immediate assistance on October 1.[43]

In Pyongyang, the imminent prospect of defeat produced an urgent search for foreign assistance and a revival of factional rivalry within the Communist leadership. Two senior party officials, one from the Chinese section of the Korean Workers' Party and the other from the southern section, traveled to Andong to plead with the commanders of the Northeast Border Defense Army to intervene. The Chinese military leaders agreed to forward their appeal to Beijing and pledged to be ready to help if the request was approved. On September 29, Kim Il-sung and Park Hon-yong, vice premier and foreign minister as well as leader of the southern wing of the party, wrote to Stalin to ask for Moscow's military assistance and, if that were not possible, for the Soviet leader to help "in the creation of international volunteer units in China and in other people's democracies." Kim also sent Park to Beijing with a direct appeal to Mao for troops. He arrived on the evening of October 1, and he immediately presented the request to Mao and Zhou. In the requests to both Stalin and Mao, Kim was careful to associate his factional rivals with the pleas for help.[44]

In his Black Sea dacha, Stalin was also busy on October 1 working to place the responsibility for rescuing the North Korean regime firmly on the Chinese. He directed Kim Il-sung to prepare for a sustained battle north of the 38th Parallel by organizing reserve forces and simultaneously starting a guerrilla struggle in the south. On the issue of military assistance, the Soviet leader stated that "we consider a more acceptable form of assistance to be assistance by people's volunteers. On this question, we must consult first with the Chinese comrades." Earlier, Stalin had asked Mao if China could provide troops to help North Korea but got no answer. He wrote again on October 1, saying directly that, if possible to respond in this emergency, "you should send at once five or six divisions to the 38th Parallel" to allow the Koreans to organize a defense under your screen. He added that these volunteers would "of course . . . be commanded by the Chinese."[45]

Mao took initial steps toward intervention in Korea on October 2, but serious opposition from his senior colleagues caused him to hesitate. He ordered Gao Gang to return to Beijing for consultations and directed Deng Hua to complete preparations with the Northeast Border Defense Army and be ready for combat on short notice. The chairman then personally wrote a telegram to Stalin stating that the PRC would send twelve divisions of volunteers to Korea and had another twenty-four divisions as a reserve in the Northeast region. Recent research has shown that this telegram was never sent. Shen Zhihua argues persuasively that Mao withheld this message as a result of strong objections voiced by members of the secretariat of the Central Committee, including several of the party's most illustrious commanders from the civil war led by Lin Biao. When the participants could not agree to support Mao's proposal to intervene, they agreed to have a second meeting of the enlarged Politburo on October 4.[46]

Later that evening, Mao conveyed a second, temporizing message to Stalin. This message was contained in a telegram from the Soviet ambassador in Beijing, N. V. Roshchin, to Stalin, and Mao probably delivered it orally because no written copy with a notation of when it was sent has been found in Chinese archives. Mao said that Chinese leaders had planned to move several divisions into Korea when US forces crossed the 38th Parallel. But having analyzed this carefully, "we now consider that such action may entail extremely serious consequences." He mentioned that the Chinese troops were poorly equipped, and if they were facing defeat, "the Soviet Union can also be dragged into war." The chairman's basic message was: "Many comrades in the . . . [Central Committee] judge that it is necessary to show caution here." He added, in conclusion, that this was a preliminary message, and another meeting was scheduled with wider participation to make a final decision on the issue.[47]

At the enlarged Politburo meeting on October 4, Mao included the regular members based in Beijing as well as Gao Gang from the Northeast Region and Peng Dehuai, the commander of the Northwest Military Region. Also attending were the commanders of the navy, air force, armored and artillery forces, and railway engineer corps. The discussion was heated during the long meeting and failed to reach a consensus. Indeed, there is good evidence that a majority of the participants opposed intervention at that time and preferred to wait until it could not be avoided. Among the objections raised: the people and troops were exhausted from decades of war, some areas of China were not yet liberated or reformed, and economic reconstruction should remain the top priority. Lin Biao made a strong case against early intervention on military grounds. The PLA's weapons were worn out and greatly inferior to those of the US forces, he argued, and China lacked the air force and navy necessary to oppose the Americans on a peninsula like Korea. He contended that the PRC should concentrate on building up its naval, air, and artillery power and should in the meantime support the North Koreans in a guerrilla war.[48]

After hearing this range of opposing views, Mao made a powerful appeal for prompt intervention. Emphasizing America as the main threat to the Chinese revolution, he argued that if US troops occupied all of Korea, they would next move to strengthen their positions in Taiwan, Indochina, and the Philippines. China would then be encircled and at some future point could face a war on two or three fronts. He pointed out the weaknesses of the American military position in the terms he had used since August. And he added that Chinese forces would receive massive arms shipments from the Soviet Union and would have Soviet air force defense of Chinese cities and possibly air support for the troops in Korea. Political and economic reconstruction could not continue, he contended, with an American threat to Chinese heavy industry and electric power plants in the Northeast and with the expense of maintaining a large army in the border region until the United States chose to attack. Finally, he asserted that "it feels sad to stand by with folded hands and watch your neighbor [suffering from] a national crisis." When this plea did not win the desired approval, the chairman called for another session the following day.[49]

The next afternoon, October 5, Mao continued his campaign to win the support of his colleagues on the Politburo. In advance, he sought the backing of one of the top commanders from the civil war, Peng Dehuai. Delayed by weather in arriving at the previous session, Peng had reached the meeting in time to hear Mao's comprehensive argument for intervention. He wrestled with the elements of the chairman's case through the night and was finally persuaded that it was correct. The next morning, Mao summoned Peng to an early meeting and asked if he thought intervention was justified. On learning that the commander agreed with his proposal, Mao expressed great relief and then asked if Peng would serve as commander of the volunteer force in Korea. Peng replied that he would accept. At the Politburo meeting, Peng announced his strong support of Mao's policy: "It is necessary to dispatch troops to aid Korea. Even if [China] is devastated [by US forces] in war, it would only mean that our liberation war lasted a few years longer. Should its troops be poised on the bank of the Yalu River and Taiwan, the US will be able to find a pretext to invade us at any time."

Peng's statement persuaded a majority of the members to back the proposal for intervention, although some, like Lin Biao, remained opposed. At the end of the meeting, Mao told Peng he had ten days to prepare and set October 15 as the date for intervention. On October 8, Mao gave the directions for the first elements to move into Korea on the 15th and appointed Peng as commander and political commissar of the volunteers and Gao Gang as commander of all logistical services.[50]

During the extended Politburo debates in Beijing, Stalin continued to pressure China to send troops to Korea as soon as possible. He argued that China would have strong backing from the Soviet Union and made the ultimate point that it would be easier to confront the Americans now than at a later date when they were stronger. The Soviet leader contended: "China will be involved in the war. At the same time, because the Soviet Union and China have a treaty of mutual assistance and alliance, the Soviet Union will also be involved in the war. Are we afraid of this? In my opinion we are not, because we are joined together. We shall be more powerful than the United States and Great Britain. . . . If war cannot be avoided, then let it come now, not several years later when Japanese militarism will recover and become an ally of the United States."

After the Chinese decided to intervene, Mao wrote Stalin on October 7 saying that the PRC would send nine divisions to Korea, but they would not depart until after a delegation from Beijing came to Moscow for a discussion of cooperation in the war.[51]

Mao purposely left his plan to intervene in general terms in an attempt to get firm commitments from Stalin on arms shipments and air support. Zhou left for Moscow on October 8, and then traveled with Politburo member and vice premier Nikolai Bulganin to meet the Soviet chief at his Black Sea dacha. At a meeting on October 11, Stalin said that, though no Soviet troops could be engaged in the battle in Korea, he strongly supported China sending its forces, which he promised to arm and equip. Zhou responded by citing a range of difficulties that complicated China's effort to send its volunteers into Korea. The Soviet leader reacted to this surprising news by saying that it would then be necessary for Kim Il-sung to withdraw his forces to China in order to reorganize and resupply them for future battles. At some point in their long discussion, Soviet leaders informed Zhou that their aid would take time to be delivered and the air support to protect Chinese cities would not be available for another two and a half months. Disappointed by the Soviet failure to honor its pledge of a joint war effort, Zhou persuaded Stalin to send a telegram with him to Mao and the Central Committee explaining the status of their negotiations.[52]

The Stalin-Zhou telegram caused anxious reconsideration of plans when it reached Chinese leaders on October 12. Mao quickly cabled Peng Dehuai and Gao Gang that the order to intervene on the 15th "should not be carried out for the time being," and he instructed them to come immediately to Beijing for consultations. A hastily called meeting of the Politburo assembled on October 13. When they learned of the limitations on Soviet aid, and especially on air support, the members were angry and felt betrayed. Peng threatened to resign as commander of the volunteers. Mao took over the meeting, emphasizing that the Soviet Union would provide massive amounts of arms and supplies and that its air support would be available by the end of the year. On balance, the chairman argued, it was in Chinese interests to enter the war and fight on Korean territory as soon as possible. After more discussion, the members agreed with this reasoning, and Mao telegraphed Zhou that "the comrades of the Politburo . . . are still convinced that dispatching our troops to Korea would be beneficial to us. In the first phase of the war, we may concentrate on fighting the [South Korean] puppet army, which our troops are quite capable of coping with."[53]

Following the Chinese Politburo's decision on October 12, a flurry of activity occurred in Beijing and Moscow as messages crossed one another and plans were canceled and reinstated. Immediately after the Politburo session, Mao telegraphed Zhou in Moscow to remain there for several days to try to win firm commitments from the Soviets to lease rather than buy the arms and equipment needed by the volunteers and get a pledge for Soviet air units to provide cover in Korea as well as protecting Chinese cities. Mao also made detailed plans for the intervention in Korea, including doubling the size of the initial force to 260,000 troops and setting the date to start crossing the Yalu River as October 19.[54]

Meanwhile, before learning of the Chinese decision to enter Korea, Stalin cabled Kim Il-sung on October 12, saying: "The Chinese have again refused to send troops. Because of this you must evacuate Korea and retreat in the northern direction in the shortest possible period." As the North Korean leadership debated how to react to the Soviet directive, Stalin cabled again on the 13th with the new information on China's plan to intervene, and he told Kim "to postpone temporarily evacuation and retreat of Korean troops to the north." In Moscow, Zhou continued to negotiate with Soviet officials about arms and air support. On Mao's instructions, Zhou had posed a number of questions to Stalin, who remained at his Black Sea retreat. The negotiators came to an agreement on October 14, when the Soviet representatives pledged to provide the arms and equipment on credit and to send sixteen regiments of fighter jets to protect Chinese cities and reserve forces. But Stalin flatly rejected Zhou's most important request. In a telephone call to the first deputy premier, Vyacheslav Molotov, he refused to allow Soviet air support of the Chinese volunteers in Korea.[55]

Chinese leaders learned the results of Zhou's negotiations on October 17, and again they reviewed their decision to intervene in light of the Soviet refusal to provide air support for the volunteers. Mao restated the date for the first units to cross into Korea as October 19 and recalled Peng and Gao to Beijing for a conference. On October 18, Zhou reported to the Central Committee on his meetings in Moscow, and Peng briefed the members on the preparations for intervention. Mao stated the group's decision at the end: "Now the enemy is besieging Pyongyang. In a few more days, the enemy will reach the Yalu River. No matter what enormous difficulties we have, we cannot change again the plan for the volunteers to cross the river to aid Korea." The formal order to intervene in Korea was issued that evening, and the advance force crossed the Yalu into Korea during the night of October 19.[56]

THREE SCORPIONS

China's intervention in Korea transformed the war and much of the course of the Cold War. It saved North Korea from total defeat and the unification of Korea under Syngman Rhee. It generated two decades of Sino-American animosity and tension. And it sparked a major defense buildup in the United States, which in turn caused the Soviet Union to devote even more resources to its nuclear weapons and long-range bomber programs than the regime had planned to invest.

In order to understand the Truman administration's decision to expand its strategic weapons and intelligence capabilities by a factor of four, we must appreciate how and why the Chinese intervened in Korea and how few of the maneuvers that lay behind the decision to enter the war were known in Washington. Only then will we have the context within which to judge the assumptions about communist bloc unity and the magnitude of the threat that shaped the US strategic buildup.

Relations among the three communist autocrats were marked by suspicion, deceit, and manipulation. We have seen in earlier chapters how Stalin decided during difficult negotiations with Mao to shift his policy on Korea and endorse an invasion of the south by Kim Il-sung. He did not inform Mao of this change of policy, but had Kim do so in May, when preparations for an attack were well advanced. Even then, neither Stalin nor Kim gave the Chinese any information on the timing and strategy of the attack. As a result, Mao was diverted from his top priority of capturing Taiwan and pulled step by step into approving the North Korean invasion and, more seriously, serving as the backup if the war went badly.

Mao, for his part, decided in July that China's security interests and the consolidation of the Communist regime's power required the PRC to intervene if North Korea faced a stalemate or defeat in the conflict. He worked for two months preparing to intervene if necessary and persuading his colleagues on the Central Committee of the wisdom of this course. After Inchon, when Stalin pressed hard for Chinese help for North Korea, Mao was coy about his ability to win the support of the leadership and people and sought commitments of extensive financial and military aid if he were successful in his campaign of persuasion. This campaign shows Mao to be "perpetually enigmatic" in his behavior toward his colleagues and foreign leaders.[57] During the frenzied first part of October, with the UN forces advancing rapidly toward the Yalu and Stalin ordering Kim to withdraw his forces into China's Northeast region, the chairman faced the unwelcome prospect of US attacks on Korean forces in China and potential Soviet intervention in Chinese territory to help hold the line. Ultimately, Mao had no acceptable choice but to intervene in order to obtain the arms and supplies he needed, to prove to Moscow that he was a loyal ally, and to protect China's security interests against its principal enemy, the United States.

Kim Il-sung's motives and decisions were more transparent and self-interested, but he still was a willing accomplice in Stalin's manipulation of Mao. Also, he added his own devious behavior in refusing to share information on the course of the war or to allow PLA commanders to go to the front to evaluate the status of the conflict when Chinese intervention was desperately needed.

In China's twisting route to war in Korea, the three communist leaders behaved like scorpions circling one another. Within this menacing trio, Joseph Stalin was clearly the biggest and baddest of the group.

10

PENG DEHUAI AND MATTHEW RIDGWAY FIGHT TO A STALEMATE

O nce the decision to intervene was made, the commander of the Chinese People's Volunteers (CPV), Peng Dehuai, had to move his units as quickly as possible into position to block the drive of United Nations forces to occupy all of North Korea. Peng worked against immense constraints. Training for his troops had been short; units had never fought together; and none of the officers and men had ever confronted the firepower that US forces could deliver on the ground and from the air. The Chinese units had little artillery support and no air cover. The infantry had a wide range of small arms requiring an equally diverse supply of ammunition. The armies had few trucks to move troops and supplies, which meant that the infantry walked and often had only two or three days of food, which each soldier carried. Still, the volunteer force had some advantages. They had a significant superiority in the number of troops, ample reserves just across the border, and only limited concern for casualties. Although their lack of vehicles restricted their mobility, it meant they could move through the mountains and not be limited to Korea's very poor road system as the Americans were. Given these conditions, it is not surprising that with maximum effort it took the CPV advance force of 260,000 men two weeks to enter Korea and take up positions in the mountains northeast of Pyongyang.[1]

In their planning for Korea in mid-August, the senior commanders of the Northeast Border Defense Army developed the strategy and tactics they would use against the United Nations forces. Their initial objective was to stop the advance of the Americans and their Allies. Then the CPV would focus its attacks on the South Korean units to destroy them as an effective fighting force. They would next attempt to inflict so many casualties on US units that they would withdraw to Japan. In a version of what today would be described as asymmetrical warfare, the Chinese leaders used the disadvantages of the weak to attack the stronger power. They would avoid frontal attacks and would search for weak spots in defenses and the areas between units to attack and penetrate to the enemy's rear to destroy command centers and artillery and capture valuable arms, ammunition, radios, and food. Most attacks would come at night, and infantry would advance to within 20 yards before firing. These tactics always emphasized stealth and deception, and most movements were on foot. If successful in getting behind enemy front lines, the CPV would set up ambushes and "firesacks" to attack retreating units in vulnerable locations such as narrow valleys and approaches to bridges.[2]

THE VOLUNTEERS ATTACK

The first Chinese offensive began on October 25 and sought to ambush a South Korean army corps advancing rapidly toward the Yalu River. Before the trap was fully set, initial contact occurred when a South Korean unit ran into a Chinese patrol that morning. The fighting expanded the next day and continued until November 5, with four South Korean regiments destroyed and a unit of the US Eighth Army taking significant losses. The war changed dramatically on October 26, argues Allan Millett, "but only the Chinese knew it." This was because General Charles Willoughby, MacArthur's loyal intelligence chief, and CIA analysts questioned whether the Chinese force was of significant size, and the CIA even contended that the attacking unit was composed of Manchurian Koreans attached to the Korean People's Army. Those

Americans who had experience with the People's Liberation Army from the civil war—including marine battalion commanders and the Eighth Army intelligence chief—knew they were up against Chinese regulars and correctly argued with minimal effect in Tokyo and Washington that this was a large new force. All US analysts were surprised and perplexed when the Chinese force broke contact and fell back to defensive positions on November 6. In fact, Peng Dehuai knew his troops were exhausted and poorly armed, and he wanted to wait for other units to join his force and for arms from the Soviet Union to arrive before he launched a major offensive.

Peng faced more problems than insufficient troops and inadequate arms. From the start, he had serious conflicts with Kim Il-sung and his generals over who was in overall command. Stalin and Mao had agreed that the Chinese were dominant in the management of the war, but Kim resisted giving up control. "Peng felt that the North Korean commanders were amateurs" and made many fatal mistakes, contend Zhihua Shen and Yafeng Xia. Disputes quickly arose over unity of command, strategy and tactics, allocation of supplies, control of the railroads, and treatment of deserters and captured prisoners.[3]

Although American officials struggled to understand what new opponent they faced in Korea, two additional problems complicated their analysis. On November 1, MiG-15 jet fighters with Soviet pilots appeared over the Yalu River and attacked US bombers and their fighter escorts. During a week of skirmishes, no US aircraft were lost; but it was clear that the Soviet jets posed a serious challenge to continued bombing of targets near the border. The MiG-15 proved to be faster, more maneuverable, and more heavily armed than the American F-80 and F-84 and was easily capable of eliminating the B-29 bomber threat. In response, the Far East Air Force commanders requested authority to attack the Soviet air bases in Northeast China and asked for more capable fighter squadrons of F-84E and F-86A aircraft. MacArthur approved these requests and added an order for heavy bombing of cities near the Yalu border. Senior officials in Washington were shocked at the implications of widening the war by attacking Soviet bases within China. After emergency consultations, the Joint Chiefs of Staff with the president's clear endorsement ordered the raids to be canceled only hours before they were scheduled to launch.[4]

The second issue affected both air and ground operations in Korea. The first two weeks of November saw ferocious storms hit Korea, with temperatures plummeting. By November 16, the temperature had dropped below freezing and would remain there for weeks. The cold, rain, and snow affected all personnel and equipment in the combat areas, and each activity required four times as much effort and time as before the freeze.[5]

Confronted with a new situation, the administration began a strategic review of the war on November 5 that lasted until the 21st. At this point, none of the intelligence services could deny that a Chinese force had entered the war, but they continued to underestimate its size and mission. The CIA, State Department, and MacArthur's intelligence staff in Tokyo all agreed that the best estimates of Chinese troop strength in Korea were between 30,000 (CIA) and 98,000 (General Willoughby). A new National Intelligence Estimate (NIE)—a joint effort of the CIA, State Department, and the military services intelligence staffs—stated that if Chinese territory were attacked, Beijing would probably intervene with its 700,000-man reserve force from Manchuria. But the analysts contended that the likely Chinese objective was a limited buffer zone south of the Yalu, which they would attempt to hold with their present force. They added that there was no evidence of expanded Soviet involvement beyond the air cover at the Yalu border.[6] During the review, policy recommendations ranged from the State Department's proposal to accept a buffer zone and seek negotiations with Beijing to the Joint Chiefs of Staff's support for leaving MacArthur's instructions as they were—that is, to conduct limited probes to assess Chinese objectives and follow with a larger offensive to destroy enemy armed forces if possible. Dwight Eisenhower, serving as a consultant to the joint chiefs, expressed sympathy for the president in his diary entry for November 6: "And poor HST [Harry S. Truman], a fine man, who in the middle of a stormy lake, knows nothing of swimming." After several exchanges of views, the senior officials essentially adopted the Joint Chiefs of Staff's recommendation when Acheson sided with the Pentagon. The guidance for MacArthur was to continue preparations for an offensive, keep US forces 10 to 25 miles south of the border, and avoid bombing in Manchuria. When none of his top advisers expressed concern that UN forces could face a serious defeat, Truman approved this recommendation.[7]

In mid-November, both Chinese and American commanders prepared for major offensives. While Washington conducted its strategic review and MacArthur organized his troops for what he predicted would be a "home-by-Christmas" drive to the Yalu, the Chinese added 150,000 men to Peng Dehuai's initial force. Because the new units traveled by night and rested in the woods during daylight, UN reconnaissance flights and ground patrols did not discover this significant reinforcement of the CPV armies. Douglas MacArthur still did not believe that Beijing had made a serious intervention, because he told Ambassador John Muccio on November 17 that "no more than 30,000 Chinese could have been infiltrated into North Korea." In fact, at that time the CPV force numbered 388,000. Peng Dehuai's strategy was after initial contact to withdraw his troops into the mountains and allow the UN units to spread out and advance into a trap. With US and South Korean troops in the lead, Allied units moved steadily toward the border, and a lead patrol of Americans reached the Yalu on November 21. On the night of the 25th, the Chinese struck in strength. Surprised by the size of the attacking force and its ability to move behind Allied lines without detection, UN units were driven back with large losses. The US Eighth Army in the west withdrew below the 38th Parallel, while the US and South Korean units in the east evacuated by ship from North Korean ports.[8]

The second Chinese offensive lasted until December 24, and while it pushed almost all Allied forces out of North Korea, it proved very costly. The CPV lost one-third of its total force in three weeks of fighting, with severe frostbite causing as many casualties as combat. The UN command lost 50,000 casualties (killed, wounded, and frostbitten). The most costly loss for the United States was the death of the Eighth Army commander, Lieutenant General Walton H. Walker, who was killed in an accident on December 23 when his vehicle was hit head-on by a truck driven by a South Korean soldier who crossed the line in chaotic traffic. The new Eighth Army commander was Lieutenant General Matthew B. Ridgway, who had been slated to replace Walker in the spring of 1951.[9]

DEVELOPING A NEW US STRATEGY

The strength of the Chinese offensive and Beijing's willingness to absorb a large number of casualties forced an urgent reassessment of strategy in Washington. Starting with a National Security Council meeting on November 28, discussions and analyses at all levels of government ran through most of December. From the beginning, senior officials agreed that—if at all possible militarily—the United States must regroup and keep fighting in Korea, that a general war with China should be avoided, that a cease-fire around the 38th Parallel would be acceptable, but that it should not be discussed until the United States had improved its military situation and could negotiate from a position of strength. These early policy objectives found support in a CIA memorandum of December 2, which argued that the Soviet Union was the source of the Chinese intervention and its main supplier with "the minimal purpose" of making the UN effort in Korea "untenable." The agency concluded with the ominous statement that "the USSR is prepared to accept, and may be seeking to precipitate, a general war between the United States and China, despite the inherent risk of global war." By December 3, the administration had agreed on its policy goals. The United States would resume its military effort to improve its situation on the battlefield before considering a cease-fire; officials believed the Soviet Union would not go to war to protect China; and American resources had to be reserved for the top priority of defending Europe, which meant that MacArthur would have to fight the war without a large addition of troops.[10]

The next day, a British delegation led by Prime Minister Clement Attlee arrived in Washington determined to challenge virtually every element of the recently achieved policy consensus. Concerned about the overall course of US policy in Asia and by Truman's statement to the press that the administration was considering all options for dealing with the Chinese intervention including the use of nuclear weapons, the British proposed an early cease-fire in Korea and negotiations with the People's Republic of China (PRC) that would cover recognition of the communist government as the sole legitimate government of China, a peace treaty with Japan, and the admission of the PRC to the United Nations. Responding to the prime minister's suggestion that the Allies might be able to negotiate successfully with Beijing, Secretary Acheson asserted that we have "to bear in mind that the central enemy is not the Chinese but the Soviet Union. All the inspiration for the present action comes from there." Somewhat later, he added: "The Chinese Communists were not looking at the matter [the war] as Chinese but as communists who are subservient to Moscow. All they do is based on the Moscow pattern, and they are better pupils even than the Eastern European satellites." With regard to seeking an immediate cease-fire, Truman made it clear that he intended to continue the war. In an early session, the president declared: "If we abandon Korea the South Koreans would all be murdered. . . . He did not like to go into a situation such as this and then to admit that we were licked. He would rather fight it to a finish. . . . He wanted to make it perfectly plain here that we do not desert our friends when the going is rough."[11]

As the discussions moved to the conduct of the war, the United Kingdom's senior military representatives sharply criticized MacArthur's performance and proposed a shared command. After General Bradley flatly stated that "a war could not be run by a committee," the president added in firm tones that the United States would stay in Korea, that MacArthur was doing a fine job in difficult circumstances, and that as commander in chief he ran the war and General MacArthur followed his orders. The president attempted to reassure the prime minister and his delegation that he had no intention of using nuclear weapons but would not declare a no-use policy and that he recognized the need to negotiate with the PRC at some point but not right away. In six meetings during December 4–8, the Americans calmed British anxieties over nuclear weapons use and the prospect of a general war with China and restored a measure of solidarity to the "special relationship" with London while rejecting most of the closest ally's specific proposals.[12]

If Anglo-American leaders had any doubts about the need to respond in force to the Chinese attack while continuing to build up Europe's defenses, a message in the CIA's daily briefing of December 7 should have put those doubts to rest. The agency reported that Zhou

Enlai had declared to the East German ambassador in Beijing that "a third world war is inevitable as long as neither UN nor Chinese forces are willing to leave Korea. Zhou said that China has therefore made itself ready for World War III." The massive Chinese intervention and the report of Zhou's comment made a vivid impression on Harry Truman, who recorded in his diary for December 9: "It looks like World War III is here."[13]

At the UN, a flurry of initiatives for a cease-fire and disengagement from the representatives of India, Canada, Iran, and the secretary-general all failed to win the approval of the PRC. Zhou Enlai bluntly rejected all these UN proposals on December 22, declaring them illegal because the PRC was denied China's seat in the international organization and comparing the latest proposal for a three-man committee to negotiate a cease-fire with a "formula" advocated by George C. Marshall in 1946 when he attempted to arrange a peace agreement in the Chinese Civil War. In undiplomatic language, the Chinese premier asserted: "No, the old trick of General Marshall will not work again in the United Nations."[14]

Meanwhile, in Washington senior officials studied what conditions in a cease-fire agreement would be acceptable and not place UN forces at a military disadvantage. By late December, the president and secretaries Acheson and Marshall agreed that while China had the forces available to drive the United States out of Korea, they would direct MacArthur to fight as effectively as possible to exact heavy losses on the CPV without sacrificing a large proportion of UN forces in the hope of persuading Beijing to accept a cease-fire on reasonable terms. If these measures failed, the officials acknowledged that evacuation of the forces from Korea might be necessary. With the president's approval, the Joint Chiefs of Staff sent these directions to the Far East commander on December 29. In conclusion, they invited MacArthur to send his views on what circumstances would force an evacuation.[15]

The new instructions from the Joint Chiefs reached MacArthur when he was in a trough of despair. He immediately drafted a response posing a choice for the administration between four forms of increased pressure on the PRC and the huge troop losses involved in an attempt to hold a position in Korea. In a message on December 30, he advocated a blockade of the Chinese coastline, naval and air attacks on China's war industries, adding Chinese Nationalist troops to the coalition in Korea, and supporting Nationalist military operations against the mainland of China. The Joint Chiefs of Staff studied each of these proposals in detail; and after considerable debate, it endorsed the first three, with significant conditions, in a January 12 memorandum to Marshall. The president wrote a personal letter to the Far East commander on January 13 emphasizing the importance of continuing the battle in Korea as long as possible, but pointing out that an expanded war could bring the Soviet Union into active support of the PRC before the US military buildup was completed. He also insisted that it was essential to maintain the support of America's Allies in any new measures undertaken. The administration made no change in MacArthur's guidance while General Collins and General Vandenberg went to Tokyo and to the battlefront to get a first-hand evaluation of the status of UN forces.[16]

THE PEASANT MARSHAL

The commanders of the opposing sides in Korea were as starkly different as the countries they represented. Peng Dehuai was a top general in the revolutionary Red Army and played an important role as Mao's colleague in building the armed forces. Like many of the leaders of the Chinese Communist Party (CCP), he came from a family of peasant farmers in rural Hunan Province. After his mother's death, he left school early to help the family survive; and following two years of poor harvests, his father had to sell most of his land. At the age of twelve years, Peng left home to work long hours in a coal mine and later as a construction worker on a large dam project. Four years later, when the dam was finished, he joined the army of a warlord as a private at sixteen. On several occasions, he became involved in protests against wealthy landlords and merchants who exploited the poor in the villages. By 1921, he was commissioned a second lieutenant but soon decided to leave the warlord's army to join the Kuomintang (KMT). He took leave to attend the Hunan Provincial Military Academy. After graduation, his unit joined KMT forces under Jiang Jieshi, and Peng became a major with command of a battalion.[17]

Disillusioned by the KMT's corruption and focus on urban elites instead of the problems of the rural poor, Peng joined the Communist Party in 1928. Sparked by the unfair arrest of a fellow officer, he soon led a segment of the Hunan Army to revolt against reactionary rule and liberate the town of Pingjiang. His units then joined the Red Army, and in the next decade he led his forces in many battles against groups affiliated with the KMT. He saved Mao from encirclement and capture and fought other engagements with mixed results. In recognition of his success, he was named in 1931 to the Central Military Commission and the Central Executive Committee of the Jiangxi Soviet, his first political leadership position in the Communist Party. In 1934, a large force led by Jiang Jieshi surrounded the Red Army and almost destroyed it, but a small contingent broke through and began the Long March to Shaanxi in north central China arriving in October 1935. For his work in rebuilding the army and consolidating a new base, Peng was promoted to vice commander of all Chinese Communist forces in 1937. He was recognized as a strong leader who won the loyal support of his soldiers by often joining them on the front lines.[18]

In July 1937, a clash between Chinese and Japanese troops at the Marco Polo Bridge outside Beijing initiated formal war and led to the creation of a Chinese United Front between the Kuomintang and the Red Army to fight the invaders. As a general in the unified command Peng wanted to engage fully in the anti-Japanese conflict, while Mao argued for a token effort with more attention to developing support in the countryside for a later continuation of the civil war. Peng's position won the debate within the leadership, and he conducted extensive operations against the Japanese including a broad series of attacks against communication and logistic networks in the late summer of 1940. His operations were generally successful but proved costly, with heavy casualties. Over a year later, after several defeats drove Peng back to the communist base in Yan'an, Mao forced him to undergo political indoctrination for forty days, admitting failures and engaging in self-criticism. Only by completely accepting Mao's leadership did Peng retain his military position, but he deeply resented Mao's vicious treatment because the chairman had supported his offensive operations and praised him at the time.[19]

With the end of World War II, the civil war resumed in China. Peng was again on good terms with Mao; and at a party conference in June 1945, he was named vice chairman of the Military Commission, a member of the Central Committee, and, most important, a member of the Politburo. Early the next year, the Red Army was reorganized as the People's Liberation Army, and Peng was named commander of the Northwest Field Army of 175,000 troops. Despite the fact that he was assigned to defend the area around the communist capital in Yan'an, Peng's forces had the least effective armament of all the People's Liberation Army units. On several occasions, the KMT attacked Yan'an with its best forces, and at least twice Peng saved Mao and the leadership from capture. Living off the land and using captured weapons and supplies, Peng gradually won control of much of central and northwestern China. In the process, he added defeated units, composed largely of mercenary troops, to his own expanding army. With the creation of the People's Republic of China in October 1949, Peng became chairman of the Northwest China Military and Administrative Commission and commander in chief and political commissar of Xinjiang Province.[20]

Having analyzed Peng's account as well as the works of many other generals and military specialists, Jurgen Domes declares that Peng's record as a combat commander up to 1949 was "a mixed one. Of twenty-nine major battles which he personally directed, fifteen were victories and fourteen resulted in defeat for his units. . . . In particular, Peng had difficulties holding his own when confronted by enemy commanders who were either moderately or exceptionally good strategists." Overall, over twenty-one years of steady warfare, Peng's performance indicates "that he was extremely brave, a good campaigner and tactician, but at best a fair if not a mediocre strategist."[21]

A central theme in Peng's military career was his relationship with Mao Zedong. In November 1935, Mao became chairman of the Military Commission, and until his death he would remain undisputed leader of the party. There was still a collective leadership under the Politburo, and

Mao did not formally become chairman of the party until 1943. In an excellent essay on the Mao–Peng relationship, the distinguished China scholar Frederick Teiwes argues that, though there were heated arguments, the two men basically cooperated on military affairs. Peng was junior to Mao in age, party membership, and standing within the party. As the party struggled to survive in a civil war and long conflict with Japan, there were disagreements over basic priorities and also military tactics and strategy.[22]

Adding to the pressures of the situation were the contrasting personalities of the two military leaders. Peng focused primarily on military operations and, lacking political sophistication, often accepted the leadership's views on political issues. "But if Peng was uncertain on political matters," declares Teiwes, "throughout he forcefully expressed his military opinions whether they clashed with Mao's or anyone else's view." His outspoken nature and "his crude and ill-tempered manner alienated many within the leadership." Even after Mao became the undisputed leader, Peng acted as his equal and did not hesitate to challenge him on military issues or make occasional criticisms of the chairman's luxurious lifestyle.[23]

For his part, Mao had a massive ego and saw himself as an intellectual, a grand strategist, and a master of political manipulation. He also had "an explosive temper" and did not easily accept challenges to his authority. These qualities foretold a tempestuous relationship. "Other leaders," reports Teiwes, "sometimes privately referred to the Party Chairman and his outspoken general as 'two bad tempered mules from Hunan.'"[24] (See figure 10.1.)

Surprisingly, the relationship remained essentially cooperative but testy through 1958. "Mao's faith in Peng was clearly indicated by the tasks the chairman entrusted to him," argues Teiwes, "the defence of Mao and other central leaders when Yan'an came under [KMT] attack in 1947, the Chinese war effort in Korea and, finally, overall responsibility for national defence." Disagreements over strategy and tactics in the Korean War and any responsibility Peng might have had for the death of Mao's eldest son during the conflict "do not appear to have been major issues," says Teiwes. Mao directed general strategy for the war, while Zhou Enlai

FIGURE 10.1 Marshal Peng Dehuai commanded the People's Volunteer Army in Korea, and in September 1954 he became the first defense minister of the People's Republic of China.

Source: US National Archives.

managed relations with the Soviet and North Korean governments and Peng commanded military operations in Korea. The general's *Memoirs* give a mainly cooperative account of his communications with Mao during the conflict.[25]

Unfortunately, the tensions in the relationship would explode at the Lushan Conference in 1959, when Peng sharply criticized the harsh measures imposed on the rural poor by Mao's Great Leap Forward. By then, the chairman had become increasingly authoritarian and reacted strongly to any real or perceived challenge to his power. He removed Peng as minister of defense, had him purged from all party positions, and later turned him over to the Red Guards for interrogation. For the next fifteen years, Peng suffered over 130 brutal interrogation sessions involving many forms of torture. He died a broken but defiant soldier in November 1974.[26]

THE PARATROOP GENERAL

Matthew B. Ridgway was a professional soldier like Peng Dehuai, but he had a positive career path without the privation and political turmoil endured by his Chinese opponent. Ridgway came from a line of soldiers, and his father attended West Point and retired as a colonel with a specialty in artillery. Matthew also graduated from West Point, where he was an average student finishing in the middle of the class of 1917. He sought an assignment in the artillery like his father, but those appointments went to other cadets with higher class standing. Given a position in the infantry, he determined to work hard and make the best of his specialty. Despite attempts to get into a combat unit in France, Ridgway spent World War I patrolling the Mexican border and teaching Spanish at West Point.[27]

After normal tours of duty at army schools and overseas assignments in China, Nicaragua, and the Philippines, Ridgway achieved a career breakthrough in the late 1930s, when he came to the attention of Brigadier General George Marshall. As assistant chief of staff of an army corps during maneuvers, Ridgway impressed Marshall, who was commanding a brigade in the same exercise, with his leadership and aggressive tactics. Noting his intensity and long hours, the general complimented Ridgway on his performance and offered a friendly word of caution. He urged the young major to take proper care of his "human machine" so that he did not "burn out a fuse" that could not be quickly replaced. Marshall's advice went for naught as Ridgway continued to be a deeply serious, driven soldier who did not drink, smoke, party, or even tell off-color jokes.[28]

When war broke out in Europe, Marshall, now army chief of staff, needed to strengthen his staff quickly. He remembered the hard-charging major from recent maneuvers and summoned him to Washington to join the War Plans Division. In this position, Ridgway worked for two and a half years under Dwight D. Eisenhower developing detailed plans for contingencies in the Western Hemisphere and in Europe. Early in 1942, Ridgway was promoted to brigadier general and became assistant division commander of the 82nd Infantry Division in the process of being reconstituted. His division commander, Major General Omar Bradley, delegated all aspects of training the new recruits to Ridgway. The new general took to the task with "dedication, zeal and intensity." Colleagues noted that he showed "a pronounced talent for getting men to pull together and for inculcating unit pride. . . . He was out front all day, exhorting, cajoling, teaching." Ridgway made it a point of personal pride to memorize the name of every officer with the rank of major and above in his division without name tags or coaching by an aide.[29]

After a few months, Bradley was reassigned to build another division, and Ridgway became commander of the 82nd Division and was promoted to major general. The army leadership chose the 82nd to be one of the first units to be converted to an airborne division trained to attack behind enemy front lines using gliders and parachutes. Ridgway was selected to lead this complicated process of experimentation and training because he was "intelligent, dynamic, and flexible," according to the commander of army ground forces, Lieutenant General Leslie J. McNair. Ridgway became one of the first senior officers to qualify with the parachute and ride in a glider during exercises and in combat. With only about a third of its training completed, the general and the 82nd Division joined the US forces in Tunisia to prepare for the airborne operations involved in the invasion of Sicily.[30]

The attack on Sicily—launched the night of July 10, 1943—was the first large-scale Allied airborne operation. It proved to be a costly learning experience. Due to strong winds, limited training in night parachute jumps, transport pilots untrained in night navigation, and friendly fire on descending troops, the airborne soldiers were widely dispersed and suffered heavy casualties. The two reinforced regiments involved in the air attack were dropped on successive nights because of limited available aircraft. Both groups were hit by friendly fire, mainly from ships involved in the amphibious landing. Both were scattered, with many landing 60 miles from their designated landing zones. The other units of the division with Ridgway and his staff landed across the beach. Despite these immense problems and sizable casualties, the 82nd Division regrouped its survivors and achieved remarkable success in disrupting enemy responses by cutting communication wires and blocking two counterattacking forces. Five days after the initial landing, Ridgway reported to his commander, Lieutenant General George S. Patton, that of the more than 5,300 men who jumped onto the island, he had tactical control of only 3,883. The other 1,424 were dead, wounded, or missing.[31]

After gathering what remained of his battered division, Ridgway led the 82nd in attacking effectively up the west side of the island against light Italian resistance. The airborne unit worked smoothly with Patton's US Seventh Army. Meanwhile, a British airborne division fought with the Eighth Army under General Sir Bernard Montgomery up the east coast against stubborn but outnumbered German forces. In the Sicily campaign, Ridgway established his reputation as an aggressive commander by leading his troops from the front. When his advanced unit hesitated as it first came under fire, the general went forward to urge his men on. "Every phase of the advance," records the division historian, "was led in person by General Ridgway, who kept himself in personal touch with the reconnaissance elements, the point, and the advance guard command." His equally aggressive commander, Patton, exclaimed to his staff: "That damned Ridgway has got his CP [command post] up where his outposts ought to be. Tell him to get it back." One of his regimental commanders, Colonel James M. Gavin, described Ridgway's leadership style best: "He was a *great* combat commander. Lots of courage. He was right up front every minute. Hard as flint and full of intensity, almost grinding his teeth with intensity; so much so, I thought: that man's going to have a heart attack before it's over."[32]

During this operation, Ridgway also became known as a demanding taskmaster when he relieved and replaced several regimental and battalion commanders for not leading their units with the desired level of offensive effort. After Montgomery's force became bogged down by stout German defense and was unable to capture the main prize of occupying Messina, Patton's army was ordered to move across the north of the island and take the principal city closest to the Italian mainland. The Americans were pleased to seize this opportunity and took Messina on the thirty-ninth day of the campaign—but not in time to prevent the efficient evacuation of about 40,000 German and 70,000 Italian troops and 17 tons of supplies.[33]

Sicily was always a prelude to invading the Italian Peninsula and capturing Rome, hopefully knocking the Italians out of the war in the process. The Allies were already pulling troops out of the Mediterranean to prepare for their invasion of France in the late spring of 1944. Planning for the invasion of the mainland was severely constrained by a short timetable (less than a month), and the strict limit on troops available (the Allies had the same number of men as the German defenders, not the three-to-one advantage normally required for an amphibious assault against a defended beach). Further complicating the operation were the use of Montgomery's Eighth Army for an attack on the toe of Italy's boot in Calabria to move up the east coast, where there were no objectives of great strategic value and Eisenhower's frequently changing choices for landing sites and the units to be used. Contributing to Eisenhower's difficulties were shifting Italian government positions on surrendering as the Allies invaded and ultimately, when Italy did surrender, the German takeover of Italy including the defense of Rome. For Ridgway and the 82nd Airborne Division, the lessons learned in Sicily about the need for sustained coordinated training of paratroops and flight crews would not be applied in the next attack.[34]

Ridgway's division made vital but limited contributions to the Italian campaign, and its efforts came at the last possible moment. In the days before the invasion at Salerno, the 82nd division was assigned three highly risky missions, all of which were canceled partly due to Ridgway's strong protests against these "harebrained" schemes. When Lieutenant General Mark W. Clark's US Fifth Army landed on the beaches near Salerno, the troops faced withering artillery fire and air strikes. The German generals had correctly calculated that after Montgomery landed his force far to the south, the main attack would come at Salerno, and they had prepared powerful defenses. The Germans brought in additional divisions; and by the fourth day, the battered Allied troops were close to being pushed into the sea. Clark urgently ordered Ridgway to bring as many of the 82nd Division from Sicily as he could transport that night. Within seven hours, Ridgway and his officers had 1,300 paratroopers boarding C-47s to jump onto the narrow beachhead. Another 2,000 men of the 82nd jumped into the Allied zone the next night. Along with the heavy fire from US and British warships offshore, the paratroopers provided critical assistance in beating back a German counterattack and sealing the rescue of the Allied invading force. By September 18, the Germans began to withdraw toward Naples.[35]

The 82nd Division played a leading role in the breakout from Salerno and the drive on Naples. When strong German resistance blocked the Fifth Army's advance toward Naples, Clark called on the 82nd to help battle through the Sorrento Mountains. The division accomplished this assignment with great effort, fighting on foot over pathways through the rugged terrain above the coast. After the engagement, Ridgway received a strong endorsement of his leadership from a young captain commanding a parachute company who later stated: "I thought there was no way General Ridgway could be a better division commander. He was most respected but not feared. We welcomed his visits. He never talked down to us, but spoke as though we were on his level. . . . He gained the respect of my people by pointing out mistakes in a gentlemanly, but firm, manner and he therefore secured instant compliance."

The troops then earned some easier duty as the occupation force for Naples, the major port city of the south that the retreating Germans had systematically destroyed. Part of Ridgway's division had their occupation duty interrupted when Allied forces became stalled by a heavy German defense on the Volturo River south of Rome. Two battalions were detached to help cross the river, and they proved valuable in completing this hazardous mission. In mid-November, Ridgway withdrew his division to embark for Northern Ireland in preparation for the Normandy invasion.[36]

Planning and training for the landing in Normandy (code-named Overlord) were chaotic and competitive. This would be the big show, and every senior officer wanted a leading role in the drama. Ridgway pushed hard and repeatedly for a major airborne component. Eisenhower had always been dubious about the value of airborne operations, and the errors and heavy losses in the Sicily landings confirmed his views. But with the strong support of Marshall and Bradley, who would command US ground operations, Ridgway eventually won approval for two airborne divisions to participate in Overlord. The divisions were Ridgway's 82nd and the 101st, commanded by new Brigadier General Maxwell D. Taylor. These airborne divisions were assigned to land by parachute and glider on the Cotentin Peninsula jutting between the English Channel and the Atlantic Ocean. Their mission was to seal off the peninsula from German counterattacks to allow Bradley's US First Army to capture the major port of Cherbourg for use as the main supply entry point for the first phase of the attack on France.[37]

Years later, in an interview with Clay Blair, Ridgway's personal aide de camp, Captain Arthur G. Kroos, incisively described the general's style of command:

It was a very demanding, but interesting, job. Ridgway was hard to talk to—little small talk, never any letdown in discipline. No warm spirits. Everything was business—war business. He was always very courteous and seldom raised his voice—at least not to me. When he did raise his voice to someone, boy, he was dead from that time on.

I held him in awe. He was very brilliant and intense. Intense all the time. I think he slept that way. I never saw him cross his legs. Unbelievable! He sat up straight—no slouching—and no matter how soft his chair might be, the goddamned chair stiffened when he sat in it. He was very determined. He knew what he wanted and wouldn't tolerate anything that was not right up to perfection. When things were not to his liking, his expression told you everything. . . .

He would walk in a room and he would create a presence by being in that room. He didn't have to say anything. Just the way he walked, the way he looked. When his eyes would go over a room, everyone was instantly drawn to him, just like that. He didn't have to say a word. But when he spoke, he had a commanding voice. He was just a remarkable person—determined to get what he wanted and absolutely fearless.[38]

On D-Day, the 82nd Airborne Division suffered another widely dispersed and nearly disastrous landing. Despite this tragic start, the division's achievements in thirty-three days of intense combat "became the stuff of instant legend," declares Blair. "Its record in Normandy may well have been the most remarkable of any division in Army history." Surrounded quickly by a much larger experienced German force, Ridgway's men defended themselves for 36 hours with no tanks and only a handful of light artillery pieces. Once joined by an American regiment from Utah Beach, the 82nd assumed the offensive and accomplished all its missions in an amazingly short time. "It was the kind of performance generals dream about but seldom achieve," says Blair. "Under Ridgway and [Assistant Division Commander Brigadier General James M.] Gavin's frontline, personal leadership, most of the paratroopers—and ultimately most of the gliderists—had performed magnificently." This success came at a high cost. Of the 12,000 members of the 82nd who landed in Normandy, 46 percent were casualties, including 1,282 killed, and 50 percent of the battalion commanders were casualties. Ridgway took these heavy losses personally. He wrote the families of all the dead and missing soldiers his condolences, and he also wrote the loved ones of his staff to assure them that they were safe and to praise their superb performance in the initial engagement in France.[39]

Among the many words of praise that Ridgway received was a message from his immediate superior in Normandy, Major General J. Lawton Collins, who awarded him a Distinguished Service Cross and said: "The battle across the Merderet River . . . was one of the toughest operations during the campaign and called for the highest order of valor . . . [and] to the 82nd Division must go credit for having broken the back of German resistance in the Cherbourg Peninsula." More important to Ridgway was the attitude of his paratroopers. "They had been awed by his unflinching courage," records Blair, "his coolness and clearheadedness, his nearly flawless leadership in tight corners, and when it was done, his compassion for those who had fallen. Gavin, who did not lightly bestow praise, wrote: 'His great courage, integrity, and aggressiveness in combat all made a lasting impression on everyone in the division.'"[40]

Impressed by the general success of large airborne operations in Normandy, Allied leaders expanded airborne forces in August 1944 by creating the First Allied Airborne Army, which was composed of a British-led corps and a US corps. Eisenhower chose Ridgway to command the 18th Airborne Corps, which included three divisions—the 82nd, the 101st, and the new 17th. The first major operation for this force was an ambitious attack on the strategic city of Arnhem, a key gateway from Holland over the Rhine River into Germany. The assault against Arnhem, code-named Market Garden, was the first to utilize a full airborne corps of three divisions made up of paratroopers and glider-borne infantry and artillery under British command. Despite successful operations by the two American divisions deployed, the overall mission failed. Arnhem was expertly defended by the Germans, with heavy Allied losses. The costly defeat had many contributing factors: a flawed plan of attack, inadequate resupply and reinforcement, strong German resistance, and overly cautious British leadership of an airborne division and an advancing infantry corps.[41]

When present during the fighting, Ridgway was furious about the British lack of aggressive offense, but he was not in command. After analyzing all aspects of the operation, Blair contends that if Ridgway had been in command, he would have corrected the mistakes in the plan and during combat "he certainly would not have tolerated the slow, cautious advance of the British 30 Corps. Rather than a disaster, Market [Garden] might well have been a smashing triumph, with incalculable gains for the Allies." Max Hastings, the highly respected British military analyst, agrees, saying: "Many even among the British would have been happier to see command of Market Garden in the hands of the capable and combat-experienced American airborne commander Matthew Ridgway."[42]

Having blocked the Allied offensive at Arnhem, Hitler launched a massive attack through the Ardennes forest on December 16, 1944, with the goal of breaking through to capture Antwerp. German armored forces made significant advances in what is known as the Battle of the Bulge, but they were stopped short of their objective. Early on, on the 18th, Ridgway was ordered to move his corps from Reims in France to northern Belgium to strengthen weak points in Bradley's front. When he arrived at his new CP, the situation was chaotic. "While others around him grew ever more frantic and disorganized, he became increasingly cool, deliberate, and methodical. . . . The more dire the threat, the calmer he appeared to be," asserts Blair. "In the bulge, he would become a rock to which many senior commanders would cling."[43]

Bradley and Ridgway quickly developed a plan to counterattack after the German offensive stalled. Patton would attack from the south and Ridgway from the north to cut off the German forces at the neck of the bulge. Eisenhower derailed this plan when he decided to shift two US armies, including Ridgway's corps, to Montgomery's command. The British field marshal then replaced Ridgway's offensive with a more cautious plan of his own. Compared with the comments of several panicked senior officers, Max Hastings describes as "striking" Ridgway's exhortation to his unit commanders on Christmas Eve: "The situation is normal and completely satisfactory. The enemy has thrown in all his mobile reserves, and this is his last major offensive effort in this war. This Corps will halt that effort; then attack and smash him." Within the limits assigned, the airborne general went to the front and personally urged each battalion commander to be more aggressive. In the process, he relieved several generals as well as company and platoon commanders who had lost the will to fight.[44]

The active defense by the American units played a central role in stopping the German offensive on December 26. Ridgway's immediate superior, Major General Courtney Hodges, awarded him a Bronze Star for heroism and said in his letter of commendation: "Your tactical ability, inspirational leadership and personal courage won the respect of all who observed your actions as you moved among the forward elements of your command, always appearing at the critical spot at the time when your presence was most needed." In this intense battle, Ridgway learned a lesson that would prove critical later in Korea. He found that, "in time of battle, when victory hangs in the balance, it is necessary to put down any sign of weakness, indecision, lack of aggressiveness, or panic, whether the man wears stars on his shoulder or chevrons on his sleeve, for one frightened soldier can infect his whole unit." Such individuals had to be relieved immediately and removed from the front for the welfare of the troops they commanded as well as the outcome of the unit's mission.[45]

When the German offensive ended, Bradley advanced plans for an attack to pin enemy forces inside the bulge. Ridgway, still attached to Montgomery's army group, enthusiastically endorsed the concept, only to have Montgomery again insist on delay and a continued defensive posture. "Eisenhower, Bradley, and the American corps commanders, . . [including Ridgway] were furious at Montgomery's delays and indecisions," reports Blair. Ike ordered an offensive to begin January 1. Monty, finding reasons to delay for two more days, began the attack on January 3, after the Germans had time to prepare defenses. After making two changes in his headquarters staff, Ridgway remained at the front during the month of hard fighting through deep snow. He and his new deputy corps commander each visited half their battalion commanders each day, consulted about any changes needed, and switched battalions the next day. By the end of January, the bulge was eliminated. Several hundred German troops were captured, but most of them withdrew across the Rhine. In the Battle of the Bulge, the three American airborne divisions suffered an estimated 10,000 combat casualties and another 5,000 lost due to frostbite, trench foot, or illness. Overall American casualties in all units during the battle were 80,987.[46]

Ridgway's forecast on Christmas Eve proved correct. The Germans exhausted their offensive capacity in the bulge, with two powerful Panzer divisions destroyed and much of their fuel reserves consumed. Starting in late March, Ridgway's corps spearheaded the drive across the Rhine with British forces and later joined Bradley's army group to help clear the Ruhr of surrounded German units. In mopping up the Ruhr pocket, Ridgway showed a more humane side of his character. His four divisions cut a swath through the pocket, splitting it in two. The German commander, Field Marshal Walter Model, was urged by his chief of staff to surrender. Constrained by his code of honor and his pledge to Hitler never to surrender, Model refused. Meanwhile, Ridgway sent a surrender demand to the German commander, which he rejected. Ridgway tried again appealing to Model to make an "honorable capitulation," arguing: "In light of a soldier's honor, for the reputation of the German Officer Corps, for the sake of your nation's future, lay down your arms at once. The German lives you save are sorely needed to restore your people to their proper place in society. The German cities you will preserve are irreplaceable necessities for your people's welfare." Again, Model refused; but he chose to dissolve his command to allow each soldier to fend for himself. Then he walked into the woods and committed suicide. Almost all the German troops surrendered, creating a flood of prisoners. Expecting 125,000, the Americans collected 317,000 prisoners and "liberated 200,000 slave laborers and 5,639 Allied prisoners of war." Ridgway received high praise from Bradley, who recommended his promotion to lieutenant general. Eisenhower cabled Marshall that Ridgway was "one of the finest soldiers this war has produced" and warmly endorsed his promotion.[47]

In the Allies' final push into Germany, Bradley's three armies reached the "stop line" at the Elbe River well ahead of Montgomery's slow-moving army group. Eisenhower persuaded the proud field marshal to accept American assistance and assigned Ridgway's airborne corps to join and speed up the British march to close off Denmark from the Soviet advance. Eager to be part of the final offensive, Ridgway responded enthusiastically, "surely breaking all records for speed and efficiency," contends Blair. He organized his corps and moved it 250 miles to the Elbe, forced a river crossing under heavy German artillery barrages, and advanced another 60 miles to the Baltic Sea—all in eleven days. In the process, his units accepted 359,796 prisoners, including 50 generals, most eager to surrender to Americans instead of Soviets. Responding to this accomplishment, Bradley called it "remarkable"; while Marshall, always measured in his praise, declared it to be "sensational."[48]

The two generals who directed the fighting in the final two and a half years of the Korean War—Peng and Ridgway—shared some characteristics. Both were professional soldiers who related well to their troops and often led combat at the front lines. Both demonstrated great personal courage and a willingness to take risks to get what they wanted. Both tried to avoid involvement in politics; and when forced to engage with political issues, both performed less effectively in the political arena than in the military.

Yet their experience and strong points were quite different. Peng had little formal education, was unsophisticated, and was a self-taught soldier. His record showed him to be a good tactician in guerrilla warfare but a mediocre strategist when opposed by an accomplished enemy commander. Ridgway had an elite military education, from West Point through the Army Command and General Staff College and the Army War College. He served in the War Plans Department for over two years. During World War II, he had extensive experience as a commander in large-scale military operations, was an excellent tactician, and created much of the training program, doctrine, and strategy for airborne forces. His wartime record showed him to be a very good strategist for both airborne and infantry missions.

The command situations in Korea also differed greatly for the two leaders. Peng had a massive army, but his troops were poorly trained and badly equipped. They were frequently short of ammunition and food. They had few heavy weapons and no air support over the battle zones. Ridgway assumed command of a force limited in size and low on motivation and morale. Compared with their opponents, United Nations units had better weapons, large numbers of artillery and tanks, and virtually unchallenged control of the air.

Furthermore, the leaders had different relationships with their top political authorities. Peng had to accept strategic direction and frequent tactical interventions from Chairman Mao. Ridgway had a free hand within the limits of his force structure and bombing guidelines. His nominal military superior, General Douglas MacArthur, gave him freedom to operate as he saw fit in Korea. His civilian superior, George C. Marshall, had been his patron in the US Army and was now secretary of defense. And Marshall basically set policy with the nearly total support of the secretary of state and the president.

RIDGWAY REVIVES THE OFFENSIVE SPIRIT

With MacArthur fulminating against the orders to keep fighting with his present troop level and with continued restrictions on bombing beyond the Yalu border, Peng Dehuai launched his third offensive. The

Chinese commander had argued for postponing the next offensive until spring. But Mao demanded more early victories, and Stalin urged him on with promises of more arms. The offensive began on December 31, with a CPV force of 400,000 and 75,000 from reformed and equipped Korean People's Army divisions. The UN had only 270,000 troops in a weakened and dispirited state to confront the attackers. The communist armies pushed UN forces out of Seoul, Inchon, and Kimpo airfield to below the Han River. To the intense irritation of the new commander, Lieutenant General Matthew Ridgway, the UN units did not maintain contact with the enemy or counterattack as he had ordered. After nine days, Peng halted his attack and placed his forces in defensive positions to reorganize and prepare for what he expected to be a final offensive to end the war scheduled for mid-March.[49]

Disappointed by the poor performance of his forces, Ridgway began an emergency campaign to rebuild the combat potential of the Eighth Army and instill an aggressive fighting spirit. He replaced the commanders of several divisions and one army corps; he delivered a personal inspirational speech to every battalion and lectured commanders on the need to be aggressive and well coordinated with other units; he integrated half the South Korean divisions into US Army corps, where they had solid artillery and armor support; and he improved logistics to provide more hot meals and weapons that worked in the bitter cold weather. By mid-January, Ridgway was ready to give a demonstration of how he wanted the Eighth Army to fight. Picking a battle-tested regiment led by an officer known to be a warrior, the new commander ordered a probe of Chinese defenses starting on January 15. The reconnaissance-in-force moved up the west coast of Korea and efficiently eliminated the limited resistance it encountered. Ten days later, UN forces followed with a division-sized assault to try to reach the Han River. Meeting stiff resistance, Operation Thunderbolt still advanced 10 to 12 miles and showed new cohesion and spirit in battle. These two operations set a new standard for UN forces; and even if they did not reach the Han River, Ridgway's successful offensives generated optimism in Tokyo and Washington about the ability of the Allies to hold their ground in Korea.[50]

The improved military situation shaped the administration's action on MacArthur's proposals for an expanded war against China. The encouraging report from the front by General Collins and General Vandenberg on January 19, 1951, helped guide the discussion. The State and Defense departments' representatives on the National Security Council staff insisted that any new measures against the PRC would need to win the support of Allies in the UN coalition, an outcome they knew to be virtually impossible to obtain. When the National Security Council met on this set of proposals on January 24, the members postponed any action and called for further study. General Marshall would later state that the administration considered it "inadvisable" to endorse these measures, "in view of the radical change in the situation which had given rise to them." With the decision to resist the pressure to expand the war as MacArthur demanded, the Truman administration made a clear choice for a limited war in Korea. MacArthur's prestige and credibility were seriously damaged by his performance in the November offensive and his subsequent distress and panic. As his principal biographer contends, "the mid-January exposure of MacArthur's false dilemma marked the beginning of the end of his military career."[51]

RIDGWAY BLOCKS THE CHINESE ADVANCE

As the Chinese armies replaced their dead and wounded and reorganized for the next offensive, Ridgway continued his pressure and probes toward the Han River Valley. The UN attacks disrupted CPV preparations but led Peng Dehuai to reshape his next move to concentrate on South Korean forces rather than the more aggressive US units. Peng had argued strongly for delaying the offensive until mid-March, but Mao overruled him and insisted on attacking to push the UN lines further south. The fourth Chinese offensive began on the night of February 11 and focused its attack on two South Korean divisions supported by US artillery and tank units. In three separate engagements, the UN forces prevailed in two, holding their lines of battle and exacting 53,000 CPV casualties while taking many less themselves. In order to protect the integrity of his force, Peng decided that he had to stop his offensive after nine days to begin a mobile defense while waiting for reinforcements. UN forces continued to push north, recaptured Seoul by March 15, and moved up to the 39th Parallel to establish a sound defensive line. The Chinese offensive had suffered a serious defeat. Under Ridgway's strong direction, UN forces had developed the solution for defeating a larger CPV army by using carefully prepared defensive positions, superior artillery, tank, and air support, and aggressive leadership.[52] (See figure 10.2.)

Ridgway's success had unexpected consequences for both the conduct of the war and for Douglas MacArthur. It allowed both the general and leaders in Washington to think again about the ultimate goals of the

FIGURE 10.2 Lieutenant General Matthew Ridgway, commander of United Nations Forces in Korea (*left*), with Major General Charles Palmer, commander of the First Cavalry Division, in Chunchon, Korea, March 25, 1951.

Source: US Army photograph, National Archives.

war. Basking in the progress on the battlefield, the Far East commander happily took credit for victories large and small. He also restated prior comments about the need for more troops and fewer limits on air and naval strikes. On March 20, he responded to a request from the House of Representatives' minority leader, Representative Joseph W. Martin Jr. (R-MA), for his views on using Chinese Nationalist troops to expand the war. MacArthur replied that he had without success tried to convince administration leaders that Asia was the main focus of the battle against communism and if the war was lost in Asia, "the fall of Europe is inevitable." He concluded with a phrase that would echo for years in American politics: "There is no substitute for victory."[53]

In Washington, senior officials concentrated on preparing the political ground for a diplomatic initiative to explore negotiations for settling the war at the UN. When MacArthur heard of these preparations, he issued a press statement on March 24 declaring that "Red China" was in a weak position and should either negotiate a peace settlement or face an expanded war. Allied diplomats immediately expressed concern over the prospect of a wider war, and Truman was furious at MacArthur's usurpation of presidential authority over foreign affairs. After Representative Martin entered MacArthur's "no substitute for victory" letter into the *Congressional Record* on April 5, the president decided that the general had to be removed. It took a few days for Truman to persuade all his senior advisers, the Joint Chiefs of Staff, and the Democratic congressional leadership of the wisdom of his decision. Rumors of MacArthur's impending dismissal circulated around Tokyo, and the Pentagon forced a premature announcement of the decision and the appointment of Matthew Ridgway to all four of MacArthur's commands at 1 A.M. on April 11. Truman based his decision on strong evidence that MacArthur had repeatedly challenged his authority as commander in chief. As he wrote to a friend, "I think everyone who stops to think will understand that there can't be two policy makers at the head of a Government. I fear very much that our Far Eastern General had decided that he was a big enough 'Proconsul' to tell the Government at home what to do."[54]

While Washington prepared for Senate hearings on MacArthur's conduct of the war and Truman's decision to relieve him, Peng Dehuai put the final touches on his plan for a fifth offensive, which would involve the largest attacking force and the most intense combat of the war. The CPV used 548,000 frontline troops in the initial phase of the offensive with another 503,000 available in Korea as reserves. Before the ground attacks began, the US Air Force eliminated eight airfields that the Chinese were racing to complete as bases for ninety additional MiG-15s that Moscow had supplied. This left air superiority over the battlefield completely to UN forces because the Soviets still refused to allow their fighter units to operate south of the Yalu River Valley. The Chinese launched the first phase of their fifth offensive on April 22, and it continued for seven days of ferocious combat. The large CPV force drove United Nations units below the 38th Parallel to just north of the Han River. With a stout defense, Ridgway's troops were able to hold Seoul and exact 30,000 Chinese and North Korean casualties while losing only 4,000 Allied men. After both sides regrouped and resupplied, Peng initiated a second phase of his spring offensive on May 16, focusing his attack on a South Korean corps positioned between two American divisions. The Chinese were at a disadvantage in this assault, because while they used fresh troops from their reserve, the new units were inexperienced and had never faced the firepower that US forces could deploy. Using a mobile defense and massive artillery fire, the UN coalition stopped the larger army and imposed 70,000 to 80,000 casualties in a week of fighting.[55]

Ridgway deserves the high praise he received for reversing the fortunes of a dispirited United Nations force. The military analyst Thomas Ricks describes his greatest achievement: "The Joint Chiefs wanted to abandon Korea in a Dunkirk-type operation, while General Douglas MacArthur advocated a broad war against Communist China. Ridgway offered an alternative: better leadership. He relieved one general heading a corps, five of six division commanders, and 14 of 19 regimental leaders. Within three months, he had badly mauled the Chinese and pushed them back over the 38th Parallel, saving South Korea."[56]

Taking advantage of the serious Chinese defeat, Ridgway and Van Fleet immediately began a counteroffensive to try to reach well into North Korea. On May 23, they had the whole Allied force attack across the peninsula and drove the disorganized CPV units back toward

Pyongyang. With a restored military advantage, the UN forces dug in at a sound defensive position after June 10 and prepared to hold their lines. The Chinese lost 100,000 men and 12,000 prisoners, versus the UN's loss of 40,000. By the end of June, each side realized that it could not defeat the other, but the military commanders did not know how to stop the fighting. Political leaders in Washington and Beijing had already begun to work on how this could be accomplished.[57]

THE TORTURED TRAIL TO AN ARMISTICE

Efforts to initiate talks on a cease-fire took time and additional UN successes before they began. The US State Department had signaled to Moscow and Beijing through back channels several times after January that Washington was interested in talking about ending the fighting. Only after the costly first phase of the fifth Chinese offensive did the communists respond. On May 3, a junior diplomat in the Soviet delegation to the UN mentioned to an American counterpart that his government might be open to discuss a cease-fire in Korea. The State Department decided to ask George F. Kennan, its most experienced Soviet expert, to explore this issue with Moscow's ambassador to the UN, Yacov Malik. Kennan was an excellent choice because his knowledge of Soviet politics and culture was unmatched and he was on leave from the department at Princeton's Institute for Advanced Study, and thus any statement he made could be plausibly denied as unauthorized. But Kennan also brought political baggage. He was known to have opposed the decision to unify Korea by force, and he had recently leveled sharp criticism at MacArthur's testimony before the Senate in an interview with a prominent columnist, Stewart Alsop. Kennan met with Malik on May 31, and again on June 5, and he came away with the message that Moscow wanted a peaceful solution in Korea but would not participate in any talks itself. Kennan found this cautious position sufficiently positive that he recommended strongly that Acheson pursue it. The secretary accepted this recommendation and made it clear through statements on background to newsmen and in open testimony to a Senate committee that the United States was interested in pursuing a cease-fire.[58]

Officials in Washington waited for a further response from Moscow or Beijing as the three communist chiefs exchanged views on when and where talks should be held and how they would be conducted. On June 23, Ambassador Malik provided a signal that Moscow endorsed cease-fire negotiations and suggested that the 38th Parallel be the dividing line and that troops should withdraw to create a neutral zone between the opposing forces. In the meantime, representatives of the State Department and Defense Department had worked out the initial UN negotiating position. The talks would focus only on the military issues involved in a Korean cease-fire; there would be no discussion of future relations with China, Taiwan, or Japan. The negotiators for the UN side would be led by the Far East commander, General Ridgway. A cease-fire would leave troops in place; military leaders preferred their current positions to a withdrawal to the 38th Parallel. This policy assumed that fighting would continue until an agreement was signed. An agreement would include provisions for a demilitarized zone that would be 20 miles wide. And an exchange of prisoners of war (POWs) would be arranged on a one-to-one basis. With these elements approved by Acheson and Marshall and by the president, General Ridgway made a radio broadcast on June 30 inviting the communist military leaders to propose a time and place to discuss a cease-fire. Peng Dehuai and Kim Il-sung replied the following day, proposing Kaesong as a site for talks. After a further exchange, July 10 was agreed for the first meeting.[59]

The truce talks ran intermittently for two years. Frequent breaks in the sessions occurred when one side or the other sharply disagreed with its opponent's negotiating demands. When the UN negotiators realized that Kaesong was serving as a propaganda site for the communists, they insisted on moving to a location between the opposing forces and eventually settled on Panmunjom. Fighting continued during the talks, with ground actions limited in their objectives. The UN command carried out numerous heavy bombing and incendiary raids on railroads, supply depots, and cities in North Korea to prevent a buildup of supplies and personnel for a revived offensive. Casualties continued to mount, and when the communists began a series of attacks to improve their position just before the armistice was signed, they lost over 108,000 troops, compared with 53,000 for the UN.[60]

Two issues dominated the cease-fire negotiations. The first was the location of the truce line. After many months of delay, the Chinese and North Korean delegation surprised the UN team by reversing their position and accepting the battle line when an agreement was signed. The parties agreed to the terms on implementing a truce line on November 27, nearly five months after the talks began. The most difficult issue of the terms for return of prisoners took another eighteen months. The basic problem was the United States' insistence on the voluntary return of prisoners, which meant that any POW who did not wish to return to the country he was fighting for when captured would not be forced to go back. The UN command held many more prisoners (132,000) than the communists (11,400), and the UN military leaders knew that many of the soldiers they held had been forced into service by the Chinese and North Koreans and did not want to be returned to harsh treatment or execution by those governments. When a survey of prisoners' wishes showed that only a little more than half of the UN prisoners wanted to return, the communists challenged the result and walked out of the negotiations. Months passed without progress, and the two sides exchanged accusations in an effort to gain some advantage. The United States charged the communists with harsh treatment of POWs—including beatings, starvation, brainwashing, and executions—and the communists in return accused the United States of using germ warfare to debilitate their populations.

Recently declassified documents show that Chinese and North Korean leaders clashed over armistice terms. Mao won a debate over accepting the current line of battle as the armistice line. Kim then sought a cease-fire and was willing to accept a partial repatriation of POWs, but Mao insisted on continuing the conflict in order to get all prisoners returned, to receive more Soviet military aid, and to solidify Chinese leadership of the Asian revolution. By early 1953, the Chinese had achieved most of their objectives and were willing to seek a cease-fire.[61]

Changes at the top of the governments in Washington and Moscow eventually broke the deadlock at Panmunjom. In November 1952, Dwight D. Eisenhower won a resounding victory as president, in part due to his pledge to end the war in Korea. He made an early trip to the battlefront to survey conditions personally; and after his inauguration, he directed the Joint Chiefs of Staff to develop plans for additional pressure on the communist side, including the use of nuclear weapons, if they continued to block a negotiated truce. The Eisenhower administration encouraged discussion in the media about the possible use of nuclear weapons and also sent diplomatic signals through neutral ambassadors. However, contrary to some arguments at the time and since, it was the death of Stalin on March 5, 1953, that led to the end of combat in Korea, not nuclear threats which circulated the following May. On March 19, the Soviet Council of Ministers adopted a resolution calling for prompt agreement to an armistice. And on March 30, Zhou Enlai announced that the communists would accept voluntary repatriation of prisoners.[62]

Negotiators settled all but a few details of the prisoner repatriation issue by June 8—but one major obstacle remained. Syngman Rhee had strongly opposed all attempts to stop the fighting and accept a truce at roughly the 38th Parallel, and the South Korean public fully supported him. When the armistice was being finalized, Rhee, in an attempt to torpedo its signing, ordered the release of 27,000 North Korean prisoners on June 18. American and Allied military and civilian leaders were furious, and they denounced Rhee's actions in the harshest terms. The Eisenhower administration put intense pressure on the South Korean president to pledge not to further obstruct the armistice, and the aged autocrat was finally won over by the promise of a security treaty with the United States and significant aid for reconstruction. For their part, after routine complaints about the prisoner release, the communist leaders indicated their willingness to accept the agreement. On July 27, 1953, the chief negotiators finally signed the armistice. President Eisenhower and Secretary of State John Foster Dulles were justly proud of their termination of a highly unpopular, stalemated war. They could not know how crucial the death of Stalin was to this outcome. But they did understand that only a Republican president with strong military credentials could have concluded such an agreement and successfully sold it to the new Republican Congress and to the American people.[63]

AN ASSESSMENT

North Korea initiated the war and would have won with relative ease if the United States had not reversed its stated policy and intervened to protect South Korea. The communist regime in the north survived with Kim Il-sung as its leader; and to solidify his control, he organized a purge of his rivals from the South Korean Communist Party, including the vice chairman of the party in the north, who also served as his vice premier, Pak Hon-yong. The costs of the war were extremely high. The cities and industries were in rubble; the population was battered and hungry. In estimated military losses, the Korean People's Army suffered 215,000 to 350,000 killed, 303,000 wounded, and 120,000 missing or in prison. Civilian casualties of all types were estimated to be 1,550,000.[64]

South Korea was also physically devastated and had high human losses, but it retained its independence, with Syngman Rhee as its increasingly autocratic leader. The country would endure a difficult period of high corruption as it rebuilt. Aid for reconstruction and reviving the army continued to come from Washington. South Korean military losses were 137,899 killed and 450,742 wounded, while civilian casualties of all types were 990,968.

The United States preserved the independence of South Korea and showed that it would use force to stem communist aggression in a country not viewed as being of high strategic importance. After receiving adequate troops and equipment and appointing strong leadership, American forces could have driven the Chinese and North Koreans off the peninsula. But the Truman administration determined that the military and diplomatic costs would be too high, and chose a limited war, leaving a still-simmering conflict between the two Koreas. In the process, the United States also prevented the annexation of Taiwan by the PRC and earned continuing hostility and suspicion from Beijing. The war raised questions of judgment among America's Allies about the administration's continued support for Douglas MacArthur as United Nations commander for months after his disastrous strategic miscalculations. Korea also encouraged doubts among potential Asian antagonists about the strength of the American public's resolve when confronted with inconclusive foreign conflicts. The United States' losses in the war were significant but were far less than those of the other three major combatants. American troops counted 36,574 killed and 103,284 wounded.

The PRC fought the world's strongest superpower to a deadlock and used the war to solidify the control and legitimacy of its communist government. But Mao Zedong could not fulfill his pledge to drive the American imperialists off the Korean Peninsula. The conflict demonstrated that the strategy that had won the civil war was inadequate to overcome the firepower and mobility of the US forces. Mao did succeed in showing that China was a revived military power that would fight for its interests, and he removed the prospect of an early US attack on the communist regime. After the war, the Soviet Union provided generous aid to build industrial and infrastructure projects across China. The CPV's estimated losses included 152,000 killed, 383,500 wounded, and 450,000 hospitalized. However, US military sources consider these totals low and estimate Chinese losses as 400,000 killed and 486,000 wounded. It should also be noted that the Soviet Union lost 282 killed, mainly while providing air cover over the Yalu River Valley.

During the period of Chinese leadership of the war effort, "Moscow agreed with Beijing on all major issues," contend Shen and Xia. The PRC dominated decisions relating to the war and in the process humiliated Kim, who developed "a bitter grudge against Beijing." Chinese military leaders "were often contemptuous of the command and fighting abilities of the North Koreans." However, contrary to some interpretations, "Mao never thought of deposing Kim Il-sung" and never interfered in North Korean domestic affairs.[65]

"Ironically," argues Henry Kissinger, "the biggest loser in the Korean War was Stalin." Despite his authorizing the attack and providing virtually all the weapons and supplies, the Soviet leader saw North Korea defeated and devastated, with Beijing replacing Moscow as the major influence in postwar North Korea. Having coerced China to intervene, Stalin found that his rearmament and training of the People's Liberation Army resulted in encouraging Mao to act more independently. With the end of the war, "Soviet relations with China deteriorated, caused in no small part by the opaqueness with which Stalin had encouraged Kim Il-sung's adventure, the brutality with which he had pressed China toward intervention, and, above all, the grudging manner of Soviet support, all of which was in the form of repayable loans. Within a decade, the Soviet Union would become China's principal adversary."[66]

Although major combat operations stopped in July 1953, frequent clashes still occur between the opposing Korean armed forces. The United States today maintains 29,300 troops in South Korea, but in recent months it has built a new base complex and pulled its forces back about 40 miles south of Seoul. Washington plans to keep forces in South Korea until the political situation on the peninsula becomes more stable.[67]

The most important outcome of the Korean War was a huge escalation of the strategic arms competition between the United States and the Soviet Union. Based on estimates of the threat to American interests from the Soviet Union and China that were viewed as possibly leading to World War III, the United States launched an unprecedented buildup of its military forces, which transformed the Cold War. For the first time in its history, the United States maintained a large standing army in peacetime supported by a massive defense budget and important industrial interests concentrated on keeping military spending at a high level. The Soviet Union had been improving its armed forces after 1945; but faced with the US expansion of armaments and bases, leaders in Moscow devoted more resources to their military than planned.

The remainder of the book focuses on how this increase in military forces developed in the United States and the Soviet Union. Those who would like further information on the conduct of the war in Korea should see the literature cited in the note appended here.[68]

PART II
The Transformation

11

GEORGE C. MARSHALL AND ROBERT LOVETT GUIDE A US BUILDUP

The Chinese intervention in Korea on October 19, 1950, completely altered the course of the conflict and substantially transformed the Cold War between Moscow and Washington. But due to poor American intelligence and effective Chinese deception, US officials did not fully understand the significance of events for another month. As discussed in the previous chapter, analysts sifted through reports for two weeks before agreeing that the fresh troops in Korea were Chinese; and even then, they seriously underestimated the numbers and mission of the new force. By mid-November, a consensus developed among civilian and military leaders that the Chinese intervention was limited in size (probably under 100,000 troops) and had the objective of establishing and holding a buffer zone south of the Yalu River border. Senior officials in Washington agreed on two points: The Soviet Union ordered and controlled the new Chinese action, and the United States should avoid a general war with the People's Republic of China.

In preparing new directions for the coalition commander, some State Department officials recommended ceasing the United Nations' offensive operations, withdrawing to a defensive position across the waist of the Korean Peninsula, and proposing negotiations to end the fighting. At a November 21 meeting in the Pentagon, the Joint Chiefs of Staff and General Marshall proposed endorsing MacArthur's plan for a full offensive to destroy opposition forces. The defense officials argued that proposing a cease-fire at this point was conceding the conflict before the enemy's real strength and intentions were clear. The attendees adopted the Defense Department's recommendation for a full offensive when Secretary Acheson accepted the arguments advanced by General Marshall.[1]

MacArthur's offensive began on November 24 and quickly encountered serious difficulty. Peng Dehuai's second offensive, bolstered by an undetected addition of 150,000 troops and better intelligence, struck on the same day and exploited the extended supply lines of the UN forces and the huge vulnerability created by MacArthur's leaving a gap between his X Corps advancing up the east coast and the Eighth Army moving up the west coast. By November 28, both UN units were confronting the prospect of complete defeat. They withdrew as best they could from the approaches to the Yalu border, and they were able to regroup with large losses of men and equipment some days later only when they were below the 38th Parallel. At this point, MacArthur's judgments on strategy no longer dominated decisions in Washington, and new approaches would be shaped by the new secretary of defense and his deputy.[2]

THE GENERAL AND THE BANKER

When George C. Marshall and Robert A. Lovett assumed leadership of the Department of Defense in September 1950, they already had an unusually close working relationship. It would serve them and the country well in the demanding days ahead. Their close relationship was all the more surprising because they came from quite different backgrounds and training. Marshall's family was of moderate means before it lost much of its money in poor investments. Desiring a military career, George chose to attend Virginia Military Institute and did not seek an appointment to West Point because of his limited knowledge of mathematics. At the institute, he learned self-control, discipline, and how to manage men. With hard work and leadership, he was named first captain of the corps of cadets in his third year. He faced long odds in gaining a commission in the army, which was small and dominated by West Point graduates. He demonstrated ambition and audacity in sneaking into the Oval Office with a man who had an appointment and pleading his case before President William McKinley. He succeeded in being named a candidate for examination, passed the exam, and was commissioned as a second lieutenant on February 2, 1901.[3]

Marshall's early years in the army provided assignments that prepared him well for future advancement. After tours of duty in the Philippines, the Oklahoma Territory, and Texas, he spent ten years in army schools and in staff work, where he learned all aspects of war planning and tactics. He also grew increasingly concerned about the rigidity and impracticality of officers' training. When the United States entered World War I in 1917, Marshall joined the first units going to France. He served on the staff of General John J. Pershing, the overall commander of American forces, and distinguished himself as a specialist in tactics and logistics who excelled at improvising solutions to unanticipated problems. After the armistice, Marshall became Pershing's aide, including during his service as army chief of staff. In this position, which he held for more than five years, the young major learned a great deal about how the military engaged with leaders in politics and business.

Leaving Washington, Marshall commanded a regiment in China for three years, and in 1927 he began a five-year assignment as assistant commandant and head of the academic department at the Infantry School in Fort Benning, Georgia. In this training post, he completely revised the curriculum to emphasize principles of leadership and command in wartime conditions of chaos and uncertainty. He taught pragmatic responses to battlefield situations and insisted, according to his biographer, Forrest Pogue, "that the only orders worth giving were those that could be prepared and delivered in time and readily understood by troops not long removed from civilian life in the confusion and unreadiness of the first days of war." During these years, Marshall identified the brightest and most promising combat commanders among his students and kept in touch with them. They would form the core of the senior commanders he chose in World War II.[4]

Various assignments in the 1930s rounded out Marshall's preparation for higher duty. Experience gained in contact with politicians and the public convinced him that the country would not support a large standing army. Any major external threat would need to be met with a rapidly mobilized force of volunteers, draftees, and National Guard members. Three years of service as liaison with the Illinois National Guard showed what type of training would be required to make these civilian soldiers into an effective combat unit. He also learned that American manufacturing companies would require significant time and money to convert to military production, and he became a strong advocate for advanced planning for industrial conversion in times of international crisis. Contact with the senior officials of the War Department showed the new brigadier general (as of October 1936) that the army staff structure was rigid and unresponsive to new circumstances because of its iron rule of seniority and the self-serving autonomy of the various bureaus. These insights—along with his commitment to pragmatic, flexible training and tactics—would guide him in all his future public service.[5]

Marshall moved into national prominence when he was appointed deputy chief of staff of the army in October 1938. War clouds were gathering in Europe, and the new arrival soon found himself in disagreement with the president. Within his first month on the job, Marshall attended a White House meeting on the rapid expansion of military airplane production to meet Franklin Roosevelt's desire to sell tens of thousands of American built warplanes to Britain and France. As the requirements for this industrial crash project were discussed, Marshall was the only one who argued against the president's program. He felt strongly that there should be a significant buildup of US ground and air forces along with any aid to Britain and France. And he contended that even with a large number of planes going to Europe, the United States should train pilots and mechanics and produce munitions for the airplanes. The decision went against the outspoken brigadier general, and many of those present thought this incident might ruin his career. But it did not. Roosevelt named Marshall army chief of staff in April 1939, and he took office as a four-star general on September 1, the day Germany invaded Poland, starting World War II.[6]

Marshall's relationship with President Roosevelt and his fellow flag offi-cers reflects several important aspects of his personality and his approach to his demanding job. He was acutely aware that his promotion to four-star rank over many more senior generals could generate jealousy and resistance, and he carefully protected his independence from compro-mising deals with colleagues and superiors and would not allow personal relationships to determine his decisions on assignments and promotions. His strict professional demeanor resulted in testy initial relations with the president, who operated in a free-wheeling manner with little regard for lines of authority or legal limitations and who believed he could charm anyone into doing his bidding. Throughout his wartime service, Marshall restricted his contact with the president and worked mostly through the trusted White House aide Harry Hopkins. He called Roosevelt directly on only the most important issues and avoided all possible social con-tacts. His first visit to the president's Hyde Park estate was to help Mrs. Roosevelt arrange the president's funeral in April 1945.

Marshall later recalled that, at his first meeting over expanded air-plane production for European partners, the president had called him "George." He told an interviewer that this incident "rather irritated me because I didn't know him on that basis. . . . I wasn't very enthusiastic over such a misrepresentation of our intimacy." At a later meeting, the chief of staff asked the president to call him "General Marshall" when others were present. Believing the United States would soon be involved in the European war, Marshall had reservations about the president's policy process, finding him "undisciplined" and often not making "clear-cut" decisions. But the president's firm response to the Japanese attack on Pearl Harbor changed Marshall's opinion. For his part, Roos-evelt had misgivings about his new army chief, fearing that he was too rigid and would not always be a cooperative partner. However, by the end of 1943, he had gained full confidence in Marshall and would later withdraw his promise to assign him as commander of the Normandy invasion, telling the general that "he would not be able to sleep at night if he was out of the country."[7]

The years before the United States entered World War II were highly challenging for Marshall. He later stated that he and his staff had to work on "a wartime basis with all the difficulty and irritating limitations of peacetime procedures." Their efforts were complicated by the attitude among the public and the Congress that the war in Europe was not an issue for America and the belief that their country was protected by oceans to the east and west and friendly neighbors to the north and south. Marshall concentrated his energies on expanding the army, reforming the promotion system to reward leadership ability rather than seniority, and increasing weapons production capability. Obtaining adequate weapons and supplies proved the biggest problem for Marshall, and this would continue throughout the war years. Initially, the issues revolved around expanding production capacity when Congress would not appropriate the funds for purchases. Later, the conflict between providing airplanes and supplies to Britain and France and building up US forces demanded sustained attention. In preparing the army for a likely war when Congress was still heavily influenced by its isolationist members, Marshall became the administration's strongest advocate for greater defense appropriations and fewer restrictions on their use.[8]

After the United States was pulled into the war, Marshall's agenda changed dramatically. No longer did he labor to obtain resources for the army or face resistance to his plans for internal reform. His challenges became choosing the leaders for a rapidly expanding army, improving staff efficiency, allocating troops and supplies for wars in Europe and Asia, and creating time to develop and implement overall strategic plans. Just three weeks after Pearl Harbor, Marshall had to play a major role advising the president during a lengthy conference in Washington with Prime Minister Winston Churchill and his chiefs of staff. This critical planning session for the new Allies, code-named Arcadia, showed how unprepared the Americans were for global war compared with the British leaders, who had already been toughened by over two years of battle against overwhelming odds.

Marshall realized that he had to cooperate fully with the British while avoiding being used to provide the troops, weapons, and supplies to conduct a strategy developed in London to protect the United Kingdom's imperial interests in the Middle East and South Asia. The Arcadia conference established the role of the combined Anglo-American chiefs of staff, based in Washington, to plan and coordinate the war effort. To manage this unprecedented joint enterprise, Marshall selected the secretary of the Joint Board, Brigadier General Walter Bedell Smith, as the secretary of the Combined Chiefs of Staff, convinced that he was exactly the "lean and hungry type . . . needed for a ruthlessly efficient office." Marshall reluctantly agreed to postpone an early invasion of France for a less difficult attack in North Africa to be launched in November 1942. He fully agreed with the "Europe First strategy," but he continued to advocate an early attack on German forces on the European continent.[9]

At the same time that he was preparing the army for combat in North Africa and the Pacific, Marshall directed a major reorganization of the service to delegate much of his authority and improve efficiency. In his immediate headquarters staff, he sharply reduced the number of officers who had direct access to the chief of staff from sixty to six. All reports, requests, and appointments for those without direct access had to go through Brigadier General Smith. The numerous bureaus, agencies, and commands were restructured to function under three basic commands: ground forces, air forces, and service forces. The most dramatic change came with the rapid expansion of the Army Air Forces in size, mission, and autonomy. The heightened activity in this area brought Marshall into frequent contact with Robert A. Lovett, a War Department civilian who would later become his alter ego in the postwar State Department and Defense Department.[10]

Marshall and Lovett came from different social and career experiences but would work together like "identical twins," according to Marshall's biographer. Marshall spent his youth in small towns in the upper Middle West, while Lovett grew up in Houston, Manhattan, and Long Island. Marshall was fifteen years older and had lived a strict military life, whereas Lovett was a banker, organized amateur theatricals, and was tapped for Skull and Bones at Yale. Lovett's father was chief counsel to the railroad magnate E. H. Harriman, and upon his death succeeded him as chairman of the Union Pacific and Southern Railroad. The Lovetts and Harrimans socialized together frequently, and Bob often played with Averell and his siblings. At the Hill School outside Philadelphia, Lovett was the top student academically and cofounded the Shakespeare Club.

The school history describes him as displaying "exuberance, infectious humor, and an often stinging wit." Lovett continued as a serious student at Yale while combining his academic work with participation in the drama society and in the exclusive literary Elizabethan Club. But in 1916, the war in Europe seized his attention, and with a dozen friends he founded the Yale Unit of the Naval Reserve Flying Corps. This group fought with the British in France and distinguished itself on repeated bombing raids of German facilities. By the end of the war, Lovett was acting wing commander of a bomber group and was awarded the Navy Cross. He would remain a lifelong advocate of air power as a strategic asset.[11]

During the interwar years, Lovett established the foundation of his fortune and refined his analytical skills as an investment banker. For a decade, until 1930, he worked for his father-in-law at Brown Brothers, and the firm then merged to form Brown Brothers Harriman, uniting Lovett with his childhood friend, Averell Harriman. Many of the partners in each firm were members of Skull and Bones. In the new firm, Lovett managed international currency and lending operations and worked closely with European companies. He quickly became expert at analyzing financial statements and evaluating the economic prospects of borrowers. Unlike many "numbers men," he was also a consensus builder with colleagues and clients. "By nature and breeding, Lovett was tactful, suave, and smooth," contend two shrewd observers; "he excelled at bringing people together, calming controversies with his congenial wit, resolving problems in a collegial way." He worked smoothly with his more prominent partner, Averell Harriman, because he refused to be put off by Harriman's "imperious" behavior and was normally deferential and conciliatory.[12]

Returning from Europe in May 1940, as France was collapsing before the Nazi Blitzkrieg, Lovett expressed deep concern about America's lack of military preparedness. During the fall, he made a tour of US airplane manufacturers on both coasts and wrote a report arguing that the construction methods of the factories were inadequate to meet the government's needs. He called for the US administration to play a larger role in directing the companies to adopt the mass production techniques of the automobile industry. James Forrestal, a neighbor and friend of Lovett's and undersecretary of the navy, showed this report to Secretary of War Henry L. Stimson, who recruited Lovett for his staff and early in 1941 named him assistant secretary of war for air. In his new position, Lovett became a powerful advocate for an expanded mission for air power in defense operations. He pushed through his concept of restructuring airplane manufacturing to achieve a vast increase in fighter and bomber production. He also persuaded senior War Department officials, including Marshall, of the larger role that strategic bombing could play in combat, clearing the way for the Army Air Forces to advance beyond its traditional mission of support for ground forces.

Most important, he made a bargain with Marshall to help restrain pressure from Congress and air power supporters for an independent air force in exchange for granting a large measure of autonomy during the war. In Lovett's mind, this was both politically and practically desirable because it gave the Army Air Forces time to develop the leadership and doctrine needed for a separate branch of the military. During his War Department years, Lovett learned important skills in cultivating the press and media and in winning congressional support for administration programs. He became one of the most effective advocates for defense appropriations, with his "practice of disarming questions with surprisingly candid responses and reams of factual material." In both private and in public, Lovett "was incisive and persuasive," argue Isaacson and Thomas. "He managed at once to seem shy yet commanding, polished yet never condescending. His humor and warmth, sprinkled with light profanity, could be disarming, but he had a demanding and forceful intellect."[13]

By the fall of 1945, when Lovett left Washington to return to Brown Brothers Harriman, he had acquired "immense influence." Isaacson and Thomas contend that "more than any of his colleagues, he had come to be regarded by those within the Wall Street and Washington Establishment as a touchstone of things safe and sound. Because of the respect others had for his impeccable credentials and motives, he imparted a seal of approval upon people and policies he supported."

He frequently traveled to Washington to advise Acheson, Harriman, and at times the president. Lovett had become "the reliable focal point for a group of bankers, lawyers, journalists, and public officials who viewed themselves as the backbone of a nonpartisan foreign policy elite."[14]

When, as the new secretary of state early in 1947, General Marshall needed to find a replacement for Dean Acheson as his top deputy, it was entirely natural for him to choose Lovett as the next undersecretary. It proved to be an excellent choice, and the two men worked almost as one through the crises of the next two years. The new appointment was also very timely. "With the pronouncement of the Truman Doctrine and the Marshall Plan, the task became to implement these grand gestures," declare Isaacson and Thomas. "The transformation of America's global role took Acheson's force to create it, but Lovett's tact to sell it." Lovett was of great assistance in shaping the terms of European requests for Marshall Plan assistance and in persuading Congress to support the approved programs.

Lovett played a key role in shaping policies for the Berlin airlift during Marshall's absences due to medical problems and a lengthy trip to Latin America. And he carefully cultivated Senator Arthur Vandenberg, Republican chairman of the Senate Foreign Relations Committee, to win his backing for the European alliance that was established by the North Atlantic Treaty. Marshall and Lovett developed a remarkably close working relationship. Lovett later said that "I was his alter ego. We worked together like brothers." Pogue adds: "They did not need to have long talks about policy because they normally reacted the same way to issues and problems. In his State Department post, . . . Lovett worked so harmoniously with Marshall that it is difficult to separate their thinking and their actions." The general was very pleased to have this banker managing his affairs.[15]

REVIEW OF US POLICY

The dramatic reversal created by the Chinese intervention forced Washington officials to launch an urgent strategic evaluation of the war beginning on November 28. After studying reports from the front and

MacArthur's headquarters in Tokyo, senior officials of the State and Defense departments gathered at the Pentagon on December 1, joined by CIA director General Walter Bedell Smith and the president's top adviser on national security, W. Averell Harriman. Acheson opened the meeting with a discussion of what should be done if the UN offensive failed. He reported that American Allies at the United Nations were in a "virtual state of panic, . . . complaining that the United States leadership has failed, and [saying] the present difficulties are the fault of General MacArthur's action." Mentioning the possibility of a cease-fire, he declared: "In any event, we must do something in Korea, and we must do something to counter the rapid resurgence of neutralism in Germany."

The secretary of state then asked for suggestions from the military, and General Bradley said it was not clear at that time whether US forces could stop the Chinese advance and establish a line of defense. General Marshall added that it would be very difficult to create such a line and went on to raise the possibility of attacks from the Chinese air force against Allied forces and air bases. The military officers all agreed that even if the Chinese resorted to air strikes, any US response should be limited in order not to provoke the intervention of Soviet air power. General Bedell Smith of the CIA stated that a new estimate of Soviet actions would be completed in a few days, and it would contend that Moscow's "first purpose is to defeat European rearmament." The Russians, he said, would be pleased to "bleed us to death in Asia while defeating the armament effort in Europe." Deputy Secretary of Defense Lovett summarized the discussion, saying that he found "a consensus on two points: first, that Korea is not a decisive area for us; and second, that, while the loss of Korea might jeopardize Japan and perhaps bring about its eventual loss, Western Europe was our prime concern and we would rather see that result than lose in Western Europe." When Acheson again raised the desirability of a cease-fire, General Marshall responded flatly that "the acceptance of the cease-fire would represent a great weakness on our part."[16]

The situation in Korea had clarified somewhat by December 3. MacArthur reported that the X Corps was fighting its way back to the port of Hungnam for evacuation by sea and the Eighth Army was withdrawing to the area north of Seoul. He insisted that this "entirely new war" required large ground reinforcements and new operational directions for the struggle against "an entirely new power of great military strength." At a wide-ranging meeting at the Pentagon on December 3, the civilian and military principals discussed at length the problems involved in seeking a cease-fire. In light of growing interest in such an agreement among American Allies and neutrals and the likelihood that the People's Republic of China (PRC), at Soviet direction, would insist on unacceptable conditions, they concluded that a cease-fire was not desirable at that time. During discussion of the problems of establishing beachheads for the two major UN units without a cease-fire, Acheson interjected a telling statement about the current situation: "The great trouble is that we are fighting the wrong nation. We are fighting the second team, whereas the real enemy is the Soviet Union." The following day, George Kennan presented to Acheson and his senior staff some thoughts on how Moscow would react to a United States proposal for negotiations. He believed the Russians would view this as an appeal for peace and would seek to extract as many concessions as possible. He concluded that "now was the poorest time possible for any negotiations with the Russians. He said that if there were validity to the theory that negotiations should be from a condition of strength, this was clearly a very bad time for an approach to the Russians."[17]

The imminent arrival in Washington of a British delegation led by Prime Minister Clement Attlee forced the Truman administration to end its lengthy canvas of possible policy choices and reach conclusions. Acheson had learned from preparatory meetings with the British ambassador, Sir Oliver Franks, that London's main concerns were the conduct of the war, a wrongheaded US policy toward communist China, and the president's comments about the possible use of atomic weapons in Korea. Believing that defeat in Korea was likely, the British wanted early negotiations with China that would end the fighting, and give US recognition of the PRC as the legitimate government of China with a permanent seat on the UN Security Council, the right to rule Formosa, and a role in negotiating a peace treaty with Japan. If these goals could be gained, the Foreign Office thought that a wedge could be driven between Beijing and Moscow.[18]

The Anglo-American talks stretched over six sessions in five days, December 4–8. Although the Americans listened to the British proposals, they were firm and united in presenting different views on almost all points. Truman led the way, declaring that the real enemy was the Soviet Union while the PRC was its willing agent. He repeatedly emphasized that Korea was a test of the West's will to resist direct communist military aggression. If this challenge were met successfully in Asia, European security would be strengthened. Part of the discussion dealt with strengthening the defenses of Europe, and Acheson pointedly remarked that the American public and Congress would be reluctant to invest in building up Europe if its Allies limited their commitment in Asia. The president asserted that he would continue to fight in Korea, with or without Allies, adding for emphasis that "we do not desert our friends when the going is rough." When Prime Minister Attlee and his military colleagues attacked General MacArthur's conduct of the war, Truman came to his commander's defense, saying that the UN had asked him to establish a unified command, that he had done so, and that MacArthur had followed his orders. Acheson and Marshall added important points of policy: The United States opposed a cease-fire at the present time and would not engage in early negotiations with the PRC. When the military situation improved, the administration would consider a cease-fire, but it opposed negotiations on any broader issues such as Formosa or recognition of the Beijing government.

The Americans satisfied some of the British policy concerns. The president declared that only he could authorize the use of nuclear weapons, that he had no intention of doing so in Korea, and would in any case consult with the British prime minister before any such decision might be made in the future. Acheson assured the visiting delegation that the United States had abandoned its goal of unifying Korea and would accept at the right time a cease-fire at the 38th Parallel. He also stated that the United States would not engage in a general war with China. British anxieties were eased further by a report on December 8 from General J. Lawton Collins, who had returned the day before from a visit with MacArthur in Tokyo and the commanders in Korea. The army chief of staff said that the withdrawal of US forces was proceeding in

FIGURE 11.1 President Harry Truman's closest national security advisers, Secretary of State Dean Acheson (*left*) and Secretary of Defense George Marshall (*right*), welcome him back to Washington on December 26, 1950, from spending the Christmas holidays in Independence, Missouri.

Source: Truman Library.

an orderly manner, and they would be able to reorganize and continue to fight. Replacement weapons and troops were on the way to Korea, and he was confident that the United Nations coalition could maintain its air and naval superiority. Overall, the Anglo-American discussions strengthened British confidence and resolve, and they confirmed the strategic concepts that would guide the Truman administration for the remainder of the war.[19] (See figure 11.1.)

Beyond the agreement with the British on strategic concepts for Korea, the administration still had to resolve a difficult situation in the immediate conduct of the war. Truman, and probably other senior officials, remained acutely aware of the report about Zhou Enlai's comment that had produced the president's diary entry of December 9: "It looks like World War III is here." The Chinese launched a third offensive on December 31 and succeeded in pushing UN forces out of Inchon and Seoul to below the Han River. Claiming that he might have to evacuate all coalition units from Korea if his needs were not met, MacArthur continued to press for more ground troops, a wider air and naval war against the PRC, and new instructions for dealing with the major Chinese challenge. For several days in mid-January 1951, a debate raged in Washington over the terms of guidance for the Far East commander. The central issue was how to hold South Korea against the combined Chinese–North Korean offensive without provoking general war with China and the Soviet Union and without compromising the buildup of European defenses.

On January 12, the president held a long meeting with his advisers to discuss a draft from the Joint Chiefs of Staff on how to resolve this complex problem. The Joint Chiefs recommended continuing to resist the enemy forces with the present UN troop level. They recognized that the massive Chinese intervention might force the evacuation of UN units to Japan and, given the priority assigned to Japan as the anchor of US Asian strategy, they emphasized that "an overriding consideration" should be "the preservation of the combat effectiveness of our forces." They also called for the strengthening of defenses in Japan, Formosa, Indochina, and the Philippines through the provision of weapons and training by military advisers.[20]

The following day, Truman sent a message as guidance for MacArthur, providing a broad diplomatic context for making every effort to continue "successful resistance in Korea." He emphasized the importance of firm US opposition to communist aggression as an example to nations of the free world to mobilize them "to meet the worldwide threat which the Soviet Union now poses." An effective defense of Korea would also "deflate the dangerously exaggerated political and military prestige of Communist China," honor America's commitment to South Korea, underline the urgency of a significant strengthening of Western European defenses, and support the important UN effort in collective security. The president clearly stated that if an evacuation became necessary, he wanted it to be obvious to all that "that course is forced upon us by military necessity." He closed with a bold statement of his top priority: "In reaching a final decision about Korea, I shall have to give constant thought to the main threat from the Soviet Union and to the need for a rapid expansion of our Armed Forces to meet this great danger."[21]

Within days after the president's new guidance reached Tokyo, General Ridgway launched limited counterattacks against Chinese forces that showed a new aggressive spirit in coalition units. The rapid UN recovery after the communist offensive caught Peng Dehuai by surprise because his forces were resting and reorganizing for a major spring attack. And in Washington, this modest success after a series of bitter defeats during the fall and early winter created a newly hopeful atmosphere. As Allan Millett concludes: "the Truman administration by mid-February had staked out its fundamental position on the Korean war: continue to fight and seek a negotiated settlement that would ensure the security of South Korea but not bring on a wider war outside Korea with China and the USSR."[22]

FUNDING THE US BUILDUP

Long before they had decided the diplomatic and military strategies for responding to the Chinese intervention in Korea, administration officials were working to determine what additional forces were needed and what it would cost to meet the Soviet-sponsored global threat. As discussed above, on September 27 Congress had passed the fiscal year 1951 defense appropriation of $13.3 billion plus the first supplemental defense appropriation of $11.7 billion, for a total of $25 billion. Preparations for a second supplemental appropriation had begun on September 13, as Secretary of Defense Louis Johnson was leaving office. Early estimates of the cost of the necessary increase in forces and equipment were about $20 billion, and these additions would in some cases meet the 1954 goals set in National Security Council (NSC) Report 68 before the war broke out.

With the military success that followed the Inchon landing, pressure began to build among Pentagon civilians, led by Deputy Secretary Lovett, for a reduction of the increases advocated by the military services. From his first days as secretary of defense, when the NSC was discussing the programs to be funded under NSC 68 in late September, General Marshall had emphasized the need to structure the defense buildup in such a way that the industrial base would be developed to support an increase in military manpower over the long haul. The historian Doris Condit describes his firm conviction: "He wanted US expansion efforts under NSC 68 predicated not on anxieties of the moment but on a long-term politically and militarily feasible basis, one that Congress and the public would continue to support."[23]

In mid-November, debates continued over the amount to be requested for the second supplemental defense appropriation. The Joint Chiefs of Staff, with a few minor changes, continued to argue for $20 billion as the amount necessary to support the goals set forth in NSC 68. The chiefs received support for their recommendation from Paul Nitze, the principal author of NSC 68, who now expressed concern about the effect of a potential Chinese intervention. General Marshall and Deputy Secretary Lovett acknowledged the possibility of an expanded war in Korea, but on balance they were more committed than the military leaders and Nitze to holding down costs. The Bureau of the Budget agreed with Marshall and Lovett, and, after reworking the Joint Chiefs' numbers, proposed an estimate of $10.9 billion. No sooner had this proposal been circulated than news reached Washington of Peng Dehuai's second offensive. When this powerful attack "caused MacArthur's forces to begin a massive retreat," Condit declares, "there was an equally massive retreat on budget cutting in Washington."[24]

From this point on, the administration moved quickly to complete the request to Congress for the second supplemental appropriation. A series of meetings at the Pentagon produced an addition to the draft proposal of $5.9 billion for weapons, facilities, and an expanded production base. On November 30, Lovett sent a request to the Bureau of the Budget for an appropriation of $16.8 billion. This amount covered essentially all the elements proposed by the Joint Chiefs earlier in November. The Bureau of the Budget and the president approved the request at once, and the president sent it to Congress the next day. In his letter of transmittal,

Truman stated that the requested appropriation of an additional $16.8 billion would make a total defense appropriation for fiscal year (FY) 1951 of $41.8 billion. He asked, in addition, for an appropriation of $1.05 billion for the Atomic Energy Commission for increased production of fissionable material and the manufacture of additional atomic weapons. The president pointed out America's "long history of friendship for the Chinese people and support for Chinese independence," and said that the PRC had no reason to attack UN forces. "The only explanation," he declared, "is that these Chinese have been misled or forced into their reckless attack—an act which can only bring tragedy to themselves—to further the imperialist designs of the Soviet Union."[25]

As Congress considered the president's request for additional funding, the public gave strong support to the expanded war effort. In an editorial on December 16, the New York Times declared that Truman's radio address of the previous evening, together with his scheduled proclamation of a national emergency, "will be remembered as the point at which the Administration and the country for the first time marched forward together in a solid front." Focusing responsibility for the new crisis entirely on Moscow, the Times praised Truman for accepting "the challenge of Russia in this battle of production." Even before the full-scale Chinese intervention, when MacArthur's drive to unify Korea appeared on the verge of success, the New York Times called on October 29 for "hard and bitter sacrifices," including increased taxes to strengthen the nation's defenses. The editorial argued: "It is better to win a cold war than to have even the most sweeping victories in a hot war."

At this point, there was widespread popular support for stronger defense forces to confront Russian and Chinese aggression. The results of Gallup polls taken in November and December showed 81 percent believed Russia was seeking to become "the ruling power of the world"; 51 percent were willing to pay more taxes (and 26 percent were ready to borrow) to support the defense buildup; 50 percent approved doubling the size of the armed forces and 33 percent thought the target of 3 million men was too low; when asked what mistakes the administration had made in Asian policy, 18 percent mentioned poor military preparation while only 9 percent said intervention in Korea was a mistake;

and 81 percent believed "the Chinese entered the fighting in Korea on orders from Russia."[26]

But not all prominent Americans agreed. Senator Robert A. Taft Jr., a leading isolationist, expressed cautious criticism. In an early January speech, he argued that the president violated US laws and the Constitution in sending troops to Korea without congressional approval, but went on to say once the troops were engaged in combat, they should be supported. In a contradictory conclusion, he declared: "The threat of communism is real. . . . America must be the leader in the battle to prevent the spread of communism and preserve the liberty of the world. . . . Operations on the continents of Europe and Asia, if any, should be undertaken only with the greatest care and under careful limitation. We must not so extend ourselves as to threaten economic collapse or inflation for a productive and free America is the last bastion of liberty."

Former president Herbert Hoover made a speech in early February sharply attacking Truman's proposed budget for FY 1952. He was especially concerned that such large defense expenditures would wreck the American economy. "The whole Korean tragedy," he said, "is developing proof that the way to punish aggression is from the air and sea and not by land armies." The administration's proposed defense program would place an "unbearable strain on our economic system." He concluded that "my personal conviction is that we should not create land armies for expeditions into the quicksands of either Europe or China. I do not want to even start on the road to another Korea." Denouncing the president's "unconstitutional military fiasco in Korea," the *Chicago Tribune* asserted that "the bill which Mr. Truman presents . . . [in his budget request] is a bill to American taxpayers to buy arms for Britain so that Britain can continue its wasteful socialism. . . . The goal is not the preservation of America, but the preservation of Europe." The *Tribune* closed with the declaration: "Instead of considering his budget, Congress should be considering his impeachment."

The prominent columnist Walter Lippmann complained about the lack of any middle policy option between global policeman and fortress America. He foresaw the United States facing a stark choice: "There is indeed a rising tide of isolationism in this country. It could carry with it a withdrawal that could take us very far, perhaps as far as Mr. Joseph P. Kennedy proposes—that is to say, to the positions we occupied in 1939. If this happens, it will be because the people have been taught by the Administration and its spokesmen that there is nothing between globalism of the Truman Doctrine and the isolationism of Mr. Kennedy." Lippmann also called for a new doctrine based on air power and sea power combined with a diplomacy matched to their strengths and limitations. Only such a policy can prevent the slide to isolationism.[27]

CONGRESSIONAL ACTION

Before examining how Congress responded to the president's spending requests, it is useful to explain several points on the functioning of the budget process in the early 1950s. For all federal agencies and departments, the fiscal (budget) year began July 1 and ran until June 30 of the next year. At any one time, officials dealt with three budgets in different stages of the process. For example, when the Korean War broke out in June 1950, the Department of Defense was completing expenditures under the FY 1950 budget, it was defending the FY 1951 budget before Congress, and it had begun working on the FY 1952 budget the previous January. As we have seen, the demands of war caused both a sharp increase in emergency expenses and a decision to launch a much larger defense buildup under NSC 68 than had been anticipated. This required several revisions of the FY 1951 budget to produce requests for four supplemental appropriations (only three of which dealt with funds for defense) and a total reworking of the FY 1952 initial projections.

In thinking about the enormity of the planning process, one must remember that the budget and finance staff at the Pentagon was small and had no computers. The staff members worked with typewriters and adding machines. For Congress, the situation was even worse. The pertinent committees had only a few staff members, whose expertise was mainly political, not budgetary or accounting. Given these limitations and the need for quick action in wartime, members of Congress essentially had to accept the Pentagon's justification for force levels, weapons procurement, and unit costs. They could change the amount of the appropriation and let Defense Department officials adjust numbers within a new ceiling, but they had neither the time nor the expertise to analyze the specific items within the request.

Congress has a complex system for dealing with budget requests from the president. All action on funding begins in the House of Representatives. Both the Senate and the House have authorizing committees and appropriating committees. For defense spending, the Committee on Armed Services must authorize expenditures, while the Committee on Appropriations will approve appropriation of funds. Then both House and Senate members must vote to approve the same agreed-on appropriation bill before it becomes law with the president's signature. Detailed discussions of federal budgets will mention funds authorized and those appropriated. For a large project such as a new battleship or bomber, authorizations are normally for two to four years, whereas appropriations are voted annually. Because authorizations can be modified or canceled, this study, when possible, uses figures for appropriations that are the most accurate single measure of government expenditures.

Funding for defense during the first year of the Korean War was especially chaotic because of the dual requirements of meeting the costs of the war and implementing the long-term buildup plus the shifting assumptions about the nature of the Korean conflict. When the first and second supplemental requests were developed, everyone in the administration assumed it would be a short war lasting at most a year. After Inchon, General MacArthur often talked of having the troops home by Christmas. But when the Chinese intervened in full force, it became obvious that the war would last longer. The request for the fourth supplemental appropriation was a response to this shift. Even more important than the Chinese entry in shaping the FY 1952 budget request was the decision to accelerate completion of the NSC 68 programs scheduled for 1954 by the end of June 1952. Through all the changes imposed on the budget process in 1950–51, the priority remained on completing the long-term buildup. Only in June 1951, when combat lines stabilized and

an armistice became an active consideration, did defense budget preparations resume a somewhat normal procedure.[28]

Upon receipt of the president's request of December 1 for the second supplemental appropriation, Congress acted with uncharacteristic
speed. Representative George H. Mahon (D-TX), chairman of the House
Subcommittee on Defense Appropriations, began hearings within an
hour of receiving the official papers. The lead witness was General Marshall, who after brief remarks asked that the chairman of the Joint Chiefs
of Staff, General Omar Bradley, review for the committee the military
situation in what he described as a crisis extending across "the entire
world." After Bradley's testimony, Mahon asked Marshall and each member of the Joint Chiefs if the amount requested was adequate to meet
this serious threat. Marshall and his service colleagues asserted that the
requested amount was what they needed at that time. Although known
as an advocate of budget stringency, Mahon clearly wanted to make sure
that the military got all the money it needed, and he pressed the secretary again to see if more funds were required. Marshall reminded the
committee of his experience with periods of military expansion going
back to problems in World War I, when an appropriation for military
aircraft far exceeded the production capability and led to significant
waste of funds. He then restated his long-standing principle of developing an adequate industrial production base before expanding the force
size and training new recruits.[29]

After three weeks of testimony from Defense Department officials and
settling minor differences between the House and Senate bills, Congress
passed the second supplemental appropriation of $16.8 billion for the
Defense Department and the president signed it into law on January 6,
1951. Because this budget request was developed before the Chinese intervention, it was inadequate for longer-term requirements when passed. A
fourth supplemental was formulated in parallel with the FY 1952 defense
budget, and this bill provided an additional $6.4 billion for defense. It
was signed by Truman on May 31, 1951. The total defense appropriation
for FY 1951 thus came to $48.2 billion. It more than doubled the size of
the armed forces from 1.5 million to 3.3 million men. This huge increase
expanded the US Army from 10 to 18 divisions, the US Navy from 237
to 342 major combat ships, the US Marine Corps from 2 divisions at

TABLE 11.1 Increases in US Defense Spending, 1950–53

Fiscal Year	Budget or Force Level	
	Budget (Not Including Military or Foreign Aid)	Manpower Strength (Actual, on June 30)
1950	$13.1 billion	1.5 million
1951	$48.2 billion (including 3 supplementals)	3.3 million
1952	$60.4 billion (including supplemental and deficiency)	3.6 million
1953	$47 billion (including supplemental and deficiency)	3.5 million

	Force Level (Actual, on June 30)			
	Army*	Navy**	Marine Corps*	Air Force***
1950	10	237	2	48
1951	18	342	2 + 1 RCT	72
1952	20	400	3	80
1953	20	401	3	83

* divisions (RCT = regimental combat team)
** major combat ships
*** groups

Source: Compiled by the author from data in *The Test of War, 1950–1953: History of the Office of the Secretary of Defense*, vol. II, by Doris M. Condit (Washington, D.C.: Historical Office of the Office of the Secretary of Defense, 1988), 224–84 passim.

36 percent strength to full strength plus a new regimental combat team, and the US Air Force from 48 to 72 wings. See table 11.1 for the details.[30]

THE FISCAL YEAR 1952 DEFENSE BUDGET

The Chinese intervention and the basic decisions made by the Truman administration in November and December 1950 changed the military requirements for the next budget year so completely that all previous work had to be thrown out. In January, the service planners began from a new start to develop their recommendations for FY 1952. After weeks of intense work, the service chiefs submitted a combined request for $82 billion in February. Marshall and Lovett found this amount to be far beyond what was needed and could be obtained from Congress, and they referred it to an internal committee for revision. When the services resisted any significant reductions, a team from the offices of the comptroller of the Defense Department and the Bureau of the Budget responded in early April with a proposal for a defense budget of $49.3 billion. After renewed appeals from the services, Deputy Secretary Lovett agreed to restore about $7 billion to the draft and submitted a final request for $56.3 billion. With minor revisions by the Bureau of the Budget, the president requested $56.2 billion from Congress on April 30, 1951.[31]

When the House first began to consider the president's request in early May, members expressed concern that the amount sought might not be adequate. In response, Lovett argued that the request would be sufficient if the conflict in Korea did not expand into general war. Over the next few weeks, some members of each house complained that the explanations for this massive amount were unclear and impossible to analyze. Representative Clarence J. Brown Sr. (R-OH) spoke for many who were perplexed by the budget bill when he said that he and many colleagues did not "know whether or not the appropriation items contained in this bill are actually needed, or whether these proposed expenditures are adequately justified." The chairman of the Senate Defense Appropriations Subcommittee, Joseph C. O'Mahoney (D-WY), candidly explained that the members of both subcommittees did not want "to substitute their civilian judgment for the military judgment of the men who, in the democratic process, . . . [were] charged with the responsibility for handling . . . military affairs."[32]

Only in July did General Marshall testify before the House in support of the budget request. By then, the atmosphere had changed due to criticism of the administration's handling of the war, which had attracted widespread publicity during the congressional hearings on the firing of General MacArthur. Even more important in shifting the opinion of members was the sudden Soviet signal in late June that Moscow would support early armistice negotiations in Korea. On this occasion, sub-committee chairman George Mahon reversed his position from when he had questioned Lovett ten weeks earlier and asked Marshall whether the defense request should not be cut. With all the conviction he could convey, "the Organizer of Victory" in World War II rejected the idea of making a significant change in a long-range program "every time the Kremlin decides on some new front." He defended the budget as a responsible policy to build up American strength and support European rearmament, whether or not the conflict in Korea ended. The House ultimately reduced the request by only $1.5 billion. When the bill reached the Senate, the armistice negotiations had deadlocked and the fighting continued. Attitudes shifted again. The Senate restored some funds and responded to continued air force lobbying that cuts in its budget prevented meeting the approved strength of ninety-five wings.

The Senate persuaded the House to adopt an additional $5 billion, mainly for Air Force contracts to expand production capacity for electronics and jet engines, shortages of which were slowing aircraft completion. The final bill provided appropriations of $55.5 billion, plus $5 billion obligation authority for aircraft, of which only $0.5 billion could be spent in FY 1952. The president signed the compromise bill on October 18, 1951. The total authorization for defense for FY 1952 was $60.4 billion. This represented the largest military budget approved since 1945.[33]

DEFENSE SPENDING SLOWS IN FISCAL YEAR 1953

Well before the defense appropriation for FY 1952 was passed and signed into law, the debates over the next year's budget had begun. The prospect for continuing the pace of the military buildup steadily diminished after the fall of 1951. Some months later, Truman would describe the FY 1953 budget process as his "biggest headache." He faced a conflict between responding to a growing Soviet capability in atomic weapons and long-range bombers and a strong feeling in Congress that high defense spending threatened to undermine the strength of the American economy. Each of the military services wanted to increase its forces to meet the requirements of "the year of maximum danger" now advanced to mid-1952, while many in Congress and the public felt the defense establishment had been wasteful in using its recent funding. The debates over what amount should be spent and which forces and equipment funded played out against the backdrop of a Korean conflict with mounting casualties and seemingly endless armistice negotiations.[34]

While the military planners developed their force requirements in June and July 1951, intelligence and policymaking officials worked on a review of the status of national security programs approved under NSC Report 68/4. The result of this review would be designated NSC 114 and would replace NSC 68 as the statement of basic national security policy. The point of departure for the new policy was an updated estimate of the Soviet threat to mid-1952, as set forth in National Intelligence Estimate (NIE) 25 on August 2. The NIE opened with a bold description of Soviet intent: "We believe that the ultimate Soviet objective is a Communist world dominated by the USSR and that the Kremlin believes its vital interests can be assured over the long run only by the elimination of all governments it cannot control. This objective probably reflects a Kremlin conviction that peaceful coexistence of the USSR and its empire on the one hand, and the US and its Allies on the other, is impossible and that an armed conflict between them is eventually inevitable."

The NIE went on to state that the "principal immediate Soviet objectives" were to split the Western Alliance; block Western, German, and Japanese rearmament; and stop the creation of a network of US overseas bases. With regard to military capabilities, the analysts contended that Soviet ground forces could overrun Europe and the Middle East "within a relatively short period," and the air force could support these land campaigns and at the same time attempt "a strategic air offensive" against the United Kingdom and North America. In a concluding paragraph, which the State Department director of intelligence described as the subject of "great struggle," the NIE's authors said that they cannot make "a precise forecast" of the likelihood "that the Kremlin will deliberately precipitate or provoke general war" with the United States. But they state that "the

USSR has the capability to launch general war and may decide to precip-itate general war. Moreover, the international situation is so tense that at any time some issue might develop to a point beyond control."[35]

Because threat estimates were used to justify the level of the US response, it is important to note that the leading Soviet expert in the State Department was critical of the arguments of NIE 25, which were included in an early draft of NSC 114. Charles Bohlen arrived in Wash-ington from Paris in July to assume his duties as counselor of the State Department, a senior position that involved serving as the personal troubleshooter for the secretary. He wrote to Paul Nitze on July 28 with reactions to the NSC 114 draft, which the planning staff director had been writing with colleagues at the NSC. His main criticism, Bohlen said, "is the presentation of the Soviet Union as a mechanical chess player engaged in the execution of a design fully prepared in advance with the ultimate goal of world domination." Although there is "a serious and continuing risk of war" in the current situation, there is no Soviet grand design. He reminded the principal author of NSC 68 that he—and most Soviet specialists, including George Kennan—never thought the Korean War was part of a new departure in Soviet policy that indicated an acceptance of "the grave risk of precipitating global war. . . . Most evidence . . . [indicates] that the Russians made a gross miscalculation in Korea and did not anticipate any such risk." Bohlen also questioned the assertion that Soviet military strength has increased since April 1950 compared with that of the United States and requested to see the evi-dence for this argument. On the issue of nuclear weapons, he asked, if the balance of atomic power is the controlling factor in Soviet decisions as the NSC 68 series contends, "how can Korea be regarded as a willing-ness . . . to court general war," when the Soviet Union remains behind the United States in nuclear development. Bohlen requested a meeting with Nitze before he left for Europe; but despite these strong objections, few changes appeared in the final version of NSC 114.[36]

In an NSC meeting on August 8, the members discussed and endorsed the revised NSC 114/1, and the president approved the conclusions the following day. The survey of the world situation closely followed NIE 25 in showing Soviet advantages increasing since NSC 68 was written. With regard to nuclear capabilities, the review "now estimated that the USSR will have in mid-1953 the atomic stockpile formerly estimated for mid-1954. The date when a surprise attack on the United States might yield decisive results is correspondingly advanced." In US military programs, the authors found results falling behind goals and called for increased effort, especially in the production of weapons with a long lead time. The policy statement concluded that US national security faced greater peril than was forecast when NSC 68/4 programs were developed: "It now appears that the United States and its Allies are already in a period of acute danger which will continue until they achieve a position of strength adequate to support the objectives defined in NSC 68."[37]

NSC 114/1 represented a modest evolution of the estimated threat and recommended continuing the buildup set forth in NSC 68/4. The elements in this program were heavily concentrated on meeting the challenge from the Soviet Union. China, North Korea, and the Central and Eastern European allies were treated as satellites under the complete control and direction of Moscow. The policy statement did not reflect the fact that Chinese volunteers entered the war, stopped and reversed the UN advance, and fought the coalition to a standstill at the 38th Parallel. It merely stated: "The Chinese Communist regime has considerable military capabilities at its disposal, has undertaken military action in the Soviet interest, and thus far, at least, has made progress in consolidating its control in China." The authors did acknowledge that "North Korean and Chinese Communist forces, with Soviet logistical and technical support, have demonstrated a military capability greater than had been previously estimated." They then contended that "Communist forces must therefore be credited with the ability to overrun East and Southeast Asia, and threaten the security of the [US] off-shore island defense line." Finally, the new national security policy minimized any problems that might diminish Soviet control of its Asian satellites. There was no hint of the possibility of exploiting friction between the Soviets and the Chinese. It contended that the war has posed "increasingly serious economic difficulties" for the PRC, but these do not threaten its stability. It referred to "rumors of mutual dissatisfaction" between Moscow and Beijing, but found "no firm evidence to substantiate these rumors." With regard to the impact of the Chinese military effort in Korea, "there is as yet no firm indication that the Chinese Communist regime has been jeopardized or that Soviet influence over the regime has been reduced."[38]

Meanwhile, during August and September, the armed services had been engaged in a heated debate over force levels for the remainder of FY 1952 and for the budget proposals for FY 1953. Although each of the services needed more men and equipment to meet the goals set in NSC 114, the central issue was the aggressive campaign by the air force to increase from 95 combat wings to 138. The cost of the proposed air force expansion was so high that it drove the army and navy chiefs to cooperate in an effort to block the ambitions of the newest military service. Robert Lovett, who had managed the budget process in the Pentagon since his arrival, replaced General Marshall as defense secretary on September 17, 1951. When the services could not reach an agreed-on recommendation, Lovett created a panel of weapons specialists and directed them to answer questions about the projected time when weapons under development would become available. The panel reported promptly that tactical atomic weapons could be ready by mid-1953 but would not replace the need for strategic bombers; that two types of guided missiles with atomic warheads would be available by mid-1953, and two more within another year; and that, based on these expectations, they recommended a reduction in the air force request for heavy bombers. Under pressure from the service secretaries, the Joint Chiefs of Staff submitted recommendations for somewhat reduced force levels for FY 1953 on September 26, including a proposal for the air force to expand to 126 combat wings. Lovett sent these recommendations to the president, and Truman approved them—for budget planning purposes only—on October 5.[39] (See figure 11.2.)

The administration confronted more difficult problems in reaching agreement on the defense budget request for Congress. The basic contradiction was that the force levels necessary to meet the agreed-on threat from the Soviet Union were much more expensive than Congress would fund. Pentagon officials were working on the military requirements for an update of NSC 114/1 at the same time as they prepared the

FIGURE 11.2 President Truman with Secretary of Defense Robert Lovett, circa 1952.

Source: Truman Library.

budget recommendations for FY 1953. The Joint Chiefs of Staff reported on October 11 that these projected forces for the next FY would cost $64.2 billion. Under pressure to reduce spending by his comptroller and the Office of Defense Mobilization, Lovett sharply cut this amount to $45 billion as a planning figure for the NSC study. On the minds of the policymakers as they debated these issues was the October 3 announcement by the White House of the second Soviet atomic test, soon followed by news of a third successful detonation. The draft of NSC 114/2 that was circulated on October 12 forecasted increasing Soviet military strength over the next several years. It projected that the Soviets could be able to strike the United States by mid-1953 with a force of long-range bombers able to destroy American retaliatory capabilities, whereas NATO would not be able to defend Western Europe against an attack for at least four years. Even though the force levels proposed in NSC 114/2 did not meet the threat assessment given earlier in the draft, the members of the NSC were more concerned with holding down the cost than with logical consistency. Based upon the NSC's recommendation, on October 18 the president directed the Defense Department to prepare a detailed budget for FY 1953 using $45 billion as a rough objective. The services continued to argue for higher spending limits and submitted a request for $71 billion. After unsuccessful attempts to get further cuts, Lovett sent a budget proposal to the Bureau of the Budget for $51.9 billion that reduced force levels below the Joint Chiefs' recommendations and included no funds for combat operations in Korea. The president feared that such a level of defense spending could wreck the American economy and urged further cuts. After several rounds of negotiations with Budget Bureau officials, Lovett agreed to request $49 billion for the Defense Department. On January 21, 1952, Truman asked Congress for $48.6 billion in defense spending authority for the next FY.[40]

Faced with another anticipated budget deficit, Congress refused to approve Truman's request for additional taxes and chose instead to cut the defense budget. After reductions in the Appropriations Committee, the full House made additional cuts to vote a defense bill of $43.9 billion. Even worse from the administration's perspective, an amendment introduced by Representative Howard W. Smith (D-VA) limited total expenditures for all defense purposes to $46 billion in FY 1953. Lovett fought this rigid limit and explained to the Senate that such a restriction would force the cancellation of at least $6 billion in contracts for long-range items that had been appropriated in the previous year's budget. He graphically compared the effect of the Smith amendment, as Condit says, "to amputating an arm to save the cost of a coat sleeve." The Senate voted to remove the Smith amendment and approved a bill of $44.1 billion. The two houses finally agreed on $44.3 billion in new obligation authority, and Truman signed the bill on July 10, 1952. With additions for prior year deficiency and a small supplemental appropriation, total defense appropriations for FY 1953 came to $47 billion.[41]

In the difficult budget process for FY 1953, Congress cut the president's request by about 10 percent. Although the force goals remained those specified in NSC 114/2, the administration succumbed to budget concerns and agreed to stretch out the time for completing the agreed-on force levels. In the appropriation battle among the services, the army was the big loser and the air force was the main winner, receiving nearly 44 percent of the FY 1953 funds. The combination of budget pressure and frustration with the land war in Korea had persuaded Congress and the reluctant administration to resume a fundamental shift in US strategy—begun in 1949 and delayed during the war in Korea—toward a clear priority for air power focused on the delivery of strategic nuclear weapons.

12

DEAN ACHESON LEADS THE DEFENSE OF EUROPE

The North Korean attack in June 1950 shocked officials in Washington and forced fresh thinking on many issues, especially those related to military spending. The decision to intervene brought sharp increases in defense budgets and force structure. But some priorities remained the same. The main strategic objective was to prevent the expansion of Soviet power, and the key element of policy in achieving this goal was to help Western Europe become strong economically and militarily. The instruments to be used already existed, as a result of initiatives taken by the administration in the previous two years: economic assistance through the Marshall Plan to revive economies and encourage European economic and political integration, and a defensive alliance through a strong NATO.

Some successes had been achieved through these path-breaking policies. American assistance had averted economic collapse in Britain and France and helped stimulate recovery in the smaller countries. The German economy had begun to revive, and the three Western occupation zones had merged to form the Federal Republic of Germany (West Germany). The North Atlantic Treaty had been signed in April 1949, and a basic organizational structure was established and elementary strategic planning begun. A program of military aid, the Mutual Defense Assistance Program (MDAP), was approved in October 1949, and negotiations with each Alliance member for aid packages were completed in the early months of 1950.

However, significant problems remained and were exacerbated by fears of wider Soviet aggression after the outbreak of war in Korea. European economic recovery was slow, and governments could not allocate new funds to improve their weak military forces. Washington officials were concerned over possible neutralism in Europe and, worst of all, the prospect of a weak German government being susceptible to a deal with Moscow of pledging neutrality in exchange for unification with the eastern provinces. Within NATO, there were tensions and reservations. Britain wanted to avoid being part of an integrated European economy and sought to place its fortunes in a close relationship with the United States and the members of the Commonwealth. France, in turn, resented being excluded from Anglo-American dominance in NATO, and the smaller countries objected to being left out of the Alliance's decisionmaking process.

EUROPE FIRST

Ever since its victory over Spain in 1898 established the United States as a world power, Washington's principal strategic interest had remained Europe. Playing vital roles in two world wars deepened this commitment. Indeed, in World War II the American strategy dictated a strong priority for providing vastly more manpower and resources to the European theater than to the conflict in the Pacific. Beyond shared culture and political institutions, Europe had provided successive waves of immigrants to the United States and represented the largest region for American trade and investment. Much of American foreign policy after 1945 focused on the recovery and security of Europe, including the Truman Doctrine, the Marshall Plan, and MDAP. Soon after taking office as secretary of state, Dean Acheson testified before the House of Representatives' Committee on Foreign Affairs that reviving the European economies was the administration's first priority, because Western Europe "is the keystone of the world." Prosperity in Europe, he declared, would advance US security by expanding international trade, resisting communist expansion, and limiting nationalist uprisings. Following Acheson before the House committee, Averell Harriman, the coordinator of European assistance, went further to assert that American aid and support sought to bind a united Western Europe to the United States and reduce the chances of neutralism on the continent.[1]

When war erupted in Korea on June 25, 1950, officials in Washington immediately shifted their attention to the Far East. Europe would continue as the government's main priority, but the United States had first to stave off defeat in Korea. Strategic planners saw the Korean conflict as a test of American will to defend a country that had been publicly placed outside the US defense perimeter in Asia. They also believed that Moscow would not be prepared for war in Europe for several more years. This allowed a gradual buildup of European defense forces. The initial appropriation for MDAP, signed by the president on October 6, 1949, allocated over 75 percent of the funds to the European members of NATO ($1 billion out of $1.3 billion). Due to congressional opposition to any "giveaways," the sum of $1 billion was all that could be obtained for Europe, but it remained pitifully small to help rebuild the military forces of the ten Allied nations.

The actual supply of equipment and the start of training were slow, for two principal reasons. The United States had very limited quantities of excess usable weapons to send and few troops to assign to training. And a cumbersome bureaucracy was created to survey the defense needs of each nation, negotiate detailed defense plans, agree on what equipment was needed, and coordinate military aid with ongoing economic assistance under the country teams of the Economic Cooperation Administration. France was arguably the member state most in need of defense support. The agreement to implement MDAP in France was signed on January 27, 1950, and the US military assistance team began operating in Paris the following May. The growth of the military aid program was destined to continue at a modest pace when, on June 1, the president requested an appropriation of only $1.2 billion for fiscal year 1951. By June 1950, only a small amount of equipment had been delivered, and some training programs had begun. This would change dramatically within months, as the budget for MDAP increased fourfold.[2]

THE GERMAN PROBLEM AND FRANCE

For American policymakers, the central problem in Europe was how to create a stable, prosperous West Germany tied to Western institutions. Washington officials were acutely aware that the punitive settlement after World War I had created the seeds of anger and resentment that led to the Nazi takeover and World War II. This postwar period was different. The Germans had been totally defeated and had surrendered unconditionally, and the country was now divided and occupied. By 1950, the division had solidified, with the three Western zones merged into the Federal Republic of Germany (West Germany, or the FRG) with an elected government led by the Christian Democratic politician Konrad Adenauer, while the Soviet zone had become the German Democratic Republic (East Germany, or the GDR), led by the Soviet-chosen Walter Ulbricht. The former capital Berlin was divided, and the Western zone was surrounded by the GDR and isolated from the FRG. Berlin technically remained under four-power occupation, but most West German laws were adopted for West Berlin residents, who were legally citizens of West Germany. The Western occupying powers continued to exercise broad powers of review over the actions of the FRG government through a three-member Allied High Commission, which resided in the Hotel Petersberg, located near the capital, Bonn, on a prominent mountain overlooking the Rhine River.[3]

The top American in Germany was John J. McCloy, a senior Wall Street lawyer who had served during the war as assistant secretary of war and later as president of the World Bank. Raised in a German American family and having extensive legal experience in prewar Germany, McCloy was the ideal US representative to lead the transition from occupation to partnership with West Germany. Basically a consensus builder, the Republican internationalist was pragmatic in his approach to his huge task, but he had the capacity to be direct and tough when necessary. Understanding the bureaucratic competition for authority over German policy, McCloy negotiated with Truman to be named both high commissioner and administrator of the Economic Cooperation

Administration, reporting directly to the president. The new American proconsul began his service in Germany as military governor in July 1949, and he moved to the High Commission when that body was established the following September.[4]

McCloy quickly grasped the problems and opportunities in the fluid political and economic conditions of West Germany. At a Paris meeting of US ambassadors in Europe in late October, he reported on a range of critical issues facing the new government, including a stagnant economy, high unemployment, a large number of refugees from the East, and the loss of its natural source of grain and food from East Germany. The people of West Germany were deeply pessimistic about the division of their country and concerned about the vulnerability and high costs of supporting West Berlin. Adenauer, he was pleased to say, strongly favored the integration of West Germany into Western Europe, but he would insist on equal treatment and full acceptance by France. With regard to the United Kingdom, the chancellor was very critical of the Labour government's resistance to any form of integration with the continent and its frequent proposals for socialist solutions to German problems, which would in practice favor his political opponents, the Social Democrats. A few months later, McCloy and his advisers found that the fundamental economic problems had not improved, despite an increase in productivity to prewar levels. Unemployment stood at over 12 percent, with a large proportion being refugees, and there were severe shortages of investment capital and housing. "Most American officials," according to the historian Thomas Schwartz, "doubted whether . . . [West Germany] could achieve 'viability' by 1952, the cutoff date for Marshall Plan assistance."[5]

If Germany was the central problem facing US policymakers, France posed the most complex array of issues. Its economy was performing poorly, with inadequate capital and frequent disruptions by communist-led strikes. Having lost three wars with Germany in the past seventy-five years, its population was defeatist and fractured by suspicions of widespread collaboration with the Nazis and the French Vichy government, fears that would not begin to be openly discussed for another thirty-five years. French coalition governments were unstable and often collapsed before shifting parliamentary alignments. Between 1948 and 1952, the nation had ten different coalition administrations. Although many French leaders recognized the need to reconcile with Germany, they still viewed each issue in zero-sum terms. Every German advance was a loss for France.

London's surprise 30 percent devaluation of the pound sterling on September 18, 1949, sparked a three-way crisis. France followed, with a 22.5 percent devaluation of the franc. Not wanting to let its exports lose out to cheaper British goods, the German government, after long debate, decided on a 25 percent devaluation of the deutsche mark. French officials would not accept a German devaluation larger than their own, and threatened to block it in the High Commission. Paris also demanded that Germany drop its dual pricing for coal. German coal for domestic use was priced 30 to 40 percent less than coal that was exported. France depended on German coal for much of its steel production and wanted to end this disadvantage. After active negotiations by McCloy and Acheson, a compromise was reached, under which Germany would devalue the mark by 20 percent and would lower the export price of coal by 20 percent. This episode illustrates the intimate connections between French and German domestic issues, the fragility of French politics, and the central role played by Washington in managing policies and feelings.[6]

When Dean Acheson returned to the US government as secretary of state, he recognized that Germany was the principal problem in Europe but had no plan for dealing with the issues involved. He believed that France was the key nation for generating the revival of Europe and understood that French security needs had to be satisfied in order to achieve Franco-German reconciliation. His first task was to resolve the remaining issues delaying completion of the North Atlantic treaty, and he firmly believed that this Alliance would go a long way toward providing the necessary security for France. While these negotiations were under way, he appointed a committee headed by George Kennan, head of policy planning, to analyze all aspects of Germany's place in Europe and develop options for consideration by the National Security Council. After two months of investigation and debate—and a critical convergence of views between General Lucius Clay, the US military governor in

Germany, and the French foreign minister, Robert Schuman—the Kennan committee proposed the creation of a West German government for the three Western zones and a civilian High Commission supervising the new government under a more flexible occupation law.

These proposals, called the Washington Agreements on Germany, were adopted by the three Western governments on April 8, 1949, four days after the signing of the North Atlantic Treaty. A meeting of the four-power Council of Foreign Ministers in Paris in May and June showed that the Soviet Union was strongly opposed to giving up any control over its zone in eastern Germany. This rigid response to the plans of the new Western Allies to grant more self-government to Germany convinced Acheson that the United States had to concentrate on integrating West Germany into Europe and that German reunification would have to wait until a later day.[7]

In dealing with the web of issues between France and Germany, Acheson came to rely heavily on the close relationship he developed with Schuman. A veteran Christian Democratic politician with close ties to the Rhineland, Schuman had served as prime minister in 1947–48 and would be foreign minister from 1948 to 1952. In the revolving coalition governments of the Fourth Republic, he was the foremost advocate of reconciliation with Germany within a supranational European community. The nature of the Acheson–Schuman collaboration was illuminated in a conversation they had during the session of the United Nations General Assembly in New York on September 26, 1949. Acheson had asked the foreign minister to meet him so that he might clarify the US position on a proposed resolution of the German currency devaluation issue and also resolve a misunderstanding about the American commitment to Europe. The secretary explained what McCloy was doing to develop a solution to the German devaluation, and Schuman agreed to help advance this proposal with his government.

Then Acheson raised the issue of a mistaken report to Paris by Henri Bonnet, the French ambassador in Washington, who claimed that the British and American governments had agreed to a form of close cooperation that would reduce US engagement with the continental Allies. Schuman interrupted him to say that this was clearly an incorrect report and went on to restate his understanding of Washington's policy as being "that the future of Western Europe depended upon the establishment of understanding between the French and the Germans; that this could only be brought about by the French, and only as fast as the French were prepared to go; and that, therefore, the role of the US and UK in this matter was to advise and to assist the French and not put them in the position of being forced reluctantly to accept American or UK ideas." The French minister added that "misunderstandings often arose when he was absent from Paris. He said that he deeply appreciated the close and confidential relations which existed between" them, and he assured the secretary that he would immediately raise any doubts or questions he had in the future.[8]

In the coming months, Acheson continued to push for a revived Germany within an integrated Europe, but progress was neither quick nor steady. In preparing for the Paris meeting of US ambassadors in Europe in late October, the secretary cabled a message setting out several themes for discussion. He emphasized the pressing need for closer integration of the Western world, although he acknowledged that the United States and the British Commonwealth had limits on their ability to merge sovereign powers with continental Europe. He hoped that the English-speaking nations could take some steps of closer association now and consider others at a later date. His central point was the strong imperative for early integration in Western Europe to stimulate economic revival and pull West Germany into European institutions while the "character of [the new state] and of its relations to its neighbors is rapidly being molded." Acheson restated the points he had earlier made to Schuman: "The key to progress towards integration is in French hands. In my opinion France needs, in the interests of her own future, to take the initiative promptly and decisively if the character of Western Germany is to be one permitting healthy development in Western Europe. Even with the closest possible relationship of the US and the UK to the continent, France and France alone can take the decisive leadership in integrating Western Germany into Western Europe."[9]

Participants in the Paris conference agreed with the goal of early integration, but their comments focused on the obstacles to reaching that objective. The US Economic Cooperation Administration's head, Averell Harriman, voiced sharp criticism of British actions in resisting any steps toward integration with the continent, most recently their opposition to proposals that would strengthen the powers of the Organization for European Economic Cooperation, an agency established to advance the Marshall Plan's goal of economic integration. British policies, he said, posed a big problem for Paris, because "French fears of being left alone on the Continent are insidious and dangerous." Lewis Douglas, the ambassador in London, agreed, but he added that Washington's options for influencing British policies were quite limited. The ambassador in Paris, David K. E. Bruce, spoke in detail about the well-founded French belief that British participation was essential for successful European integration and also for containing German power. He argued that Acheson's cable was "unrealistic in urging that France alone can take the lead in bringing about the reintegration of Germany into Western Europe." He contended that a desirable outcome could only be attained with the "full backing of the US and of the UK," including binding security arrangements. In the end, there was general agreement with Ambassador Bruce's position and acceptance of the need to develop a list of actions the British government should be persuaded to adopt.[10]

By the early months of 1950, the recovery in Europe remained stalled, despite large infusions of Marshall Plan assistance and the start of the military aid program. Britain had a serious balance-of-payments problem, even after its 30 percent devaluation of the pound. France and the Benelux countries would need economic and political assistance beyond the scheduled end of Marshall Plan aid in 1952. The American effort to stimulate early steps toward European integration had foundered as each nation struggled to improve living conditions for its own population. Beyond Western Europe, Moscow and Beijing had signed an important economic and security alliance; a communist revolt grew stronger in French Indochina; and skirmishes increased in frequency and intensity between the two Koreas. In Washington, officials felt they were losing the initiative to the Soviet Union and needed to develop creative policies to deal with the interaction of British detachment, stirrings of German recovery, and French fears of German revival breeding thoughts of neutralism. Making this challenge even more complicated were the conviction for perjury of former State Department official Alger Hiss, the start of Senator Joseph McCarthy's attack on communists in the State Department, and continued denunciation of the administration for the "loss" of China.[11]

THE SUPREME COUNSELOR

At the center of this tangled web of issues stood Dean Acheson. In the legal tradition of Elihu Root and Henry Stimson, and enriched by lessons drawn from the social and economic disruption caused by World War I and the Great Depression, the new secretary of state was well prepared for the challenges he would face. The fifty-five-year-old lawyer brought a rigorously logical approach to his work, along with a sharp wit and a social conscience stimulated by brilliant mentors who guided his thinking on legal and political issues. From his experience with Franklin Roosevelt's New Deal, he believed in a strong federal government that could help solve problems created by the Industrial Revolution, which had been based on the unrestricted power of money and property. Acheson was an elitist who felt that the gifted few should develop programs to help ordinary people improve their condition in life. This viewpoint, along with his strict code of loyalty and integrity, led him to be contemptuous of most politicians, who made their careers through compromise and favoritism toward their wealthy supporters. These attitudes would pose problems in his future dealings with Congress and the public. When attacked by opposition politicians and media, Acheson relied on the strong support of his wife and family and on a stoicism based on high self-confidence.[12]

The son of an Anglican priest who became the Episcopal bishop of Connecticut and a Canadian mother who was the granddaughter of a prosperous Toronto distiller, Acheson grew up in Middletown, Connecticut, with a younger sister and brother. Like many bright young men in New England, he attended Groton, Yale College, and Harvard

Law School. At Yale, he was a member of a fraternity and was known especially for his love of parties and pranks. Despite his criticism of the college curriculum for its emphasis on the memorization of unimportant facts, he was elected to Phi Beta Kappa and was tapped for the secret society Scroll and Key. In his second year of law school, he found his greatest challenge and inspiration to date in the teaching and personal philosophy of Felix Frankfurter. He became intensely engaged with the young professor's approach to the social uses of the law and was selected for the law review while finishing fifth in his class. While at Harvard, he roomed with the songwriter Cole Porter, who entered law school but soon moved to the faculty of music. After his second year at law school, Acheson married Alice Stanley, whom he had met when his sister brought her Wellesley College roommate home for the weekend. Alice was a lively and steadying influence on her husband, and, while raising their son and two daughters, she became a professional painter and an avid gardener at their Maryland farm.[13]

On Frankfurter's strong recommendation, Supreme Court Justice Louis Brandeis appointed Acheson as his clerk and retained him for two terms of arduous but highly rewarding apprenticeship at the highest level of the legal profession. While working with the liberal Justice Brandeis, the young clerk had frequent contact with Justice Oliver Wendell Holmes Jr., who was already a legend for his brilliant opinions, which often created new pragmatic approaches to the law. His close association with Brandeis and Holmes reinforced Acheson's tendency toward elitism and a sense of mission that led him to judge others sternly by the high standards he set for himself. After his clerkship, he joined the rising new Washington law firm of Covington & Burling, where he quickly won a high reputation for arguing international legal cases before the US Court of Appeals.[14]

Before being named secretary of state, Acheson had received broad and valuable experience in the federal government. Early in the Roosevelt administration, he was appointed undersecretary of the treasury. But after only a few months, his service ended abruptly, when he was forced to resign because of his strong objection to the president's plan to inflate the dollar by setting a below-market price for gold.

As he resumed his law practice, Acheson learned to appreciate that he had acted hastily and without appropriate respect for the much wider range of issues before the chief executive. This lesson would serve him well in his future relations with cabinet members and presidents. In time, Roosevelt understood that he also had acted precipitously in demanding the young lawyer's resignation. When the war in Europe began increasingly to involve US interests, the president brought Acheson back into the administration in January 1941 as assistant secretary of state for economic affairs. In his new post, Acheson implemented many of the policies that aided Great Britain through the Lend-Lease program and coordinated with Britain and the Netherlands to impose an oil embargo to restrict Japanese aggression in Southeast Asia and China. He also served as head of the State Department's delegation to the Bretton Woods Conference, which created the postwar international economic institutions, including the International Monetary Fund, the World Bank, and the General Agreement on Tariffs and Trade. In late 1944, he was appointed assistant secretary of state for congressional relations, and to his surprise he enjoyed working with the members of Congress to pass a number of important bills, including the Tariff Agreement Act, the Bretton Woods Agreement, and the United Nations Charter.[15]

When the war ended, Acheson resigned as planned to return to his law firm, only to be called several days later by the new secretary of state, James F. Byrnes, who offered him the post of undersecretary of state. As the State Department's second-ranking official, he often served as acting secretary when Byrnes and his successor, General George C. Marshall, were out of the country for international meetings. In this capacity, he played a large role in shaping the Acheson-Lilienthal Plan for the international control of atomic energy, developing the Truman Doctrine for aid to Greece and Turkey, and drafting the Marshall Plan for the economic recovery of Europe. Acheson's service in the State Department taught him how to push analysis and decisions through a largely reactive and ineffective bureaucracy. And especially during his period as undersecretary, from August 1945 to June 1947, he accomplished a great deal in developing postwar international institutions, establishing the policy of containment of the Soviet Union, and fostering European economic

revival. He resumed his law practice with a solid reputation for achievement and a wide circle of international contacts, especially in Europe.[16]

When he returned to the State Department to assume the top position,
Acheson was as well qualified to direct American foreign policy as any
of his predecessors since the nation became a world power at the turn
of the century. He was a confirmed Anglophile with a deep respect for
the British policy of maintaining a balance of power in Europe through
the nineteenth century. He was well versed in economics and an expert
on Europe. His view of Soviet policy had hardened since he left office as
undersecretary. He now felt that negotiations were fruitless and that the
United States should lead the West in resisting Moscow's constant probing. He believed this approach would require stronger military power
to accompany the political and economic measures already under way.
His main liability was his limited knowledge of Asia, especially his lack
of understanding of the wide support among the Chinese population
for the Communist Party's nationalist opposition to Western influence,
which extended to a willingness to fight to eliminate Western involvement in Asian affairs. The incoming secretary brought a distinguished
presence to his highly visible role. Always well tailored, with a prominent
mustache and formidable eyebrows, he looked more like a senior British
barrister or diplomat than most drab American officials. His son David
later wrote that the mustache was "his father's 'chief vanity,' regularly
treated with 'Pinaud's mustache wax' to secure its 'ends against gravity.' "
Although he sometimes appeared haughty and could deliver stinging
criticism, he also showed kindness to colleagues and an expansive, even
earthy, sense of humor. At lengthy UN meetings and international conferences, he appeared to be taking notes on ministers' speeches but often
was in fact composing limericks making fun of their pompous phrases.[17]

An additional advantage for Acheson was his strong relationship with
Harry Truman. Although the president and the secretary came from
very different backgrounds, both were powerful personalities whose
strengths complemented each other. Truman needed an authoritative
secretary of state, and Acheson needed a chief executive with a wide
political base and sound judgment. Facilitating this relationship was
the fact that both men were enthusiastic, loved a good joke, and had

a mischievous streak. They worked very well together; but given their different paths of career development, they did not relax together. Truman preferred to unwind over a game of poker with political cronies and an ample supply of bourbon, while Acheson would choose to attend a musical or an opera with lawyers or writers from Georgetown. The president did his homework by carefully reading all the sometimes lengthy memos and drafts that the secretary sent him. He generally accepted Acheson's recommendations; but on occasion, when he felt strongly about an issue, he insisted on a different course. Acheson also proved to be highly accomplished in persuading Truman to accept his views. As James E. Webb, a Truman confidant who served as undersecretary of state, later observed, "Acheson respected Truman's judgment, but he studied Truman carefully in terms of how he could meet Truman's political needs and requirements and still preserve his own standard as to what should be done in the international field."[18]

THE SCHUMAN PLAN

As the spring of 1950 unfolded, Acheson's careful cultivation of European leaders such as Robert Schuman, Ernest Bevin, and Konrad Adenauer began to pay dividends with the development of a major initiative to integrate the economies of continental Europe. For almost a year, the American secretary had worked to persuade the European nations to move beyond restrictive national economic programs to create a large market with easy currency conversions that would be built around French-led reconciliation with Germany. With great effort, he had persuaded the Labour government in Britain that it could pursue an economic agenda focused on close relations with the Commonwealth and the United States independent of continental integration, but that it would not take steps to obstruct the increased coordination of continental economies.[19]

The concept for what became the Schuman Plan was developed by Jean Monnet, the French economic planner and "unconventional statesman," while he was on a walking vacation in the Alps in March 1950. Concerned about the growing pessimism in France over the nation's slow economic recovery when faced with the revival of the more powerful German economy, Monnet conceived a proposal to pool the coal and steel resources and industries of the two countries as a way to harness the German revival to that of France while creating institutions that would prevent future war and help relieve French anxieties. On returning to Paris, he worked out the details of his proposal with a team of economists and lawyers, and he presented it to Schuman at the end of April. The foreign minister immediately realized that Monnet had produced the initiative he had been seeking. In addition to advancing Franco-German reconciliation through European integration, this plan also responded to the urgings of Acheson, McCloy, and Marshall Plan officials for France to take steps to anchor Germany in Western European institutions. Knowing that this bold proposal would meet resistance from some ministers, industrialists, and even officials in his own ministry, Schuman presented it confidentially to Acheson and Adenauer before sharing it with the cabinet. After initially fearing that the plan would create "the damnedest cartel I have ever heard in my life," Acheson quickly understood the tremendous potential that it held and gave it his full support. In Bonn, the German chancellor also responded very positively. With the endorsements of Acheson and Adenauer, Schuman won the approval of the French cabinet and announced the plan before a crowded audience at the Quai d'Orsay on May 9. It would take two years of intense negotiations with industrialists, unions, and political leaders in six nations before the treaty creating the European Coal and Steel Community would be approved. But an immense step had been taken toward creating what would become the European Union.[20]

While the Europeans debated the details of the Schuman Plan, American officials moved ahead with other policies to expand European cooperation. Led by Averell Harriman, Marshall Plan representatives successfully completed long negotiations with Britain over currency requirements and commonwealth needs to conclude a European Payments Union that would liberalize trade across Western Europe, including the United Kingdom. The US Defense Department worked on a range of programs to strengthen European defenses, including design-ing new weapons, stationing more US troops in Europe, and increasing coordination with the French military. Early war plans in 1948 and 1949 had concluded that Western forces could not stop a Soviet invasion at the Rhine River, even with the use of atomic weapons against tanks and large troop concentrations. The best they could hope for was to try to hold Soviet armies at the Pyrenees. After a yearlong buildup of troops and equipment, along with strategic bombing of Soviet industries and military targets, the Allies would begin to liberate Western Europe. Realizing that European leaders would never accept such a strategy, the planners began to argue within the military establishment for German rearmament as an essential part of stronger European defenses.

But when the Joint Chiefs of Staff began to advocate the creation of a German federal police force as a step toward broader rearmament in May 1950, Truman flatly refused, saying that these proposals were "decidedly militaristic and in my opinion not realistic with present con-ditions." In a separate memorandum to Acheson, he went further in crit-icizing the British military for encouraging German officials to support the police structure as a route to rearmament. In advocating arming Germany, he declared that "the British are doing everything possible to break up Western European unity. . . . France would immediately get a severe case of jitters if the subject is ever seriously considered." With these firm instructions, Acheson put an end to discussion of rearming the Germans through the first weeks of war in Korea.[21]

When war broke out, Washington's efforts concentrated on getting forces into battle to stop the North Korean advance. Almost all US offi-cials and political leaders thought the Soviet Union was responsible for the invasion and that the attack was a test of American will. They also expected the conflict to be brief, with a likely victory for the UN coalition. As poorly prepared troops retreated during the last half of July toward what would become the Pusan Perimeter, questions arose in Congress and among Allied governments about the United States' capacity to avoid defeat. Anxiety over their own security quickly sur-faced within European governments. In giving his assessment of the situation to the cabinet on July 14, Acheson said "the feeling in Europe is changing from one of elation that the United States has come into the Korean crisis to petrified fright. . . . Our intentions are not doubted, but . . . [our] capabilities are doubted." Concern was most acute in Germany, where Adenauer contended before the High Commission on July 12 that if the Allies did not take actions "to convince the Germans that some opportunity will be afforded them to defend their country in the event of an emergency," they might reconsider their relationship with Moscow.[22]

THE PUSH FOR GERMAN REARMAMENT

In late July, multiple pressures to strengthen European defenses confronted administration officials. The Germans pleaded urgently for some ability to defend themselves; the French called for more American troops to be based in Europe as a necessary step to support their increased defense effort; and US representatives at NATO headquarters argued that a significant commitment of American ground units to Europe was essential to prevent stalling the Alliance's buildup. A number of senior officials began to think positively about German rearmament. Central among this group were High Commissioner McCloy in Bonn and Colonel Henry Byroade, head of the State Department's Office of German Affairs. With indications that the French were willing to consider a European defense force that included German units, they convinced Acheson to present this concept to the president. The secretary raised the possibility of a European army including German forces under NATO command on July 31, and Truman approved studying the idea.

Important leaders in Congress and public sentiment also favored arming Germany. The Gallup poll showed a marked shift from 34 percent endorsing German rearmament in May before the North Korean attack to 71 percent in August. By mid-August, the State Department sent a plan to the Pentagon for review proposing continuation of Marshall Plan aid to Europe linked to assigning four to six additional divisions to Europe to be under NATO with a US supreme commander. Acheson and his colleagues assumed that the American ground troops would be sent to Europe and that the Europeans would take steps to increase their defense forces before the issue of German rearmament was raised. The Joint Chiefs of Staff rejected this timing and insisted that, in light of the possibility of a Soviet attack in Europe, German rearmament had to proceed at the same time as additional US forces were transferred to the continent. After a long discussion with General Bradley on August 30, Acheson accepted the Joint Chiefs' position that German rearmament had to be part of a "single package" for sending more troops to Europe. The president remained unconvinced.[23]

As preparations advanced in the State Department for over two weeks of intense negotiations with the British and French followed by a session of the North Atlantic Council, Chancellor Adenauer and Republicans in Congress pressed for a decision to arm West Germany. Although Acheson agreed with each element of the single package, he still felt that the Allies needed more time to be persuaded to accept German rearmament. Truman helped clarify the US commitment to the continent when, on September 9, he announced that additional American ground combat units would be sent to join NATO. Acheson's position gained more strength on September 12, when he learned that the president had demanded the resignation of Louis Johnson as secretary of defense and that George C. Marshall would be his successor.

Meetings of the Big Three (Bevin, Schuman, and Acheson) began in New York on September 12 and continued for two additional days. Acheson was very assertive in proposing the single package of more US troops and financial aid to Europe, an American commander for NATO, and rearming Germany. He insisted that any adequate European defense had to begin at the eastern border of West Germany and had to include West German troops. If the Allies did not accept this package, he declared that Congress would be inclined to cancel funds for MDAP. Although McCloy leaked the outline of the single package to the press before the European ministers arrived in New York, the French delegation referred to the Acheson proposal as the "bomb in the Waldorf" (alluding to the Waldorf-Astoria Hotel, where the meetings were held).

Schuman strongly opposed rearming Germany in any fashion, asserting that neither French politicians nor the public was ready for this step. Bevin was hesitant, but he eventually accepted the secretary's package, with some conditions. As Acheson wrote Truman, the principal Allies were prepared "to accept what we offered" [more American troops and aid and a supreme commander] but not "what we asked" [arming the Germans as part of the bargain].[24]

Starting September 22, the full North Atlantic Council of twelve members continued the negotiations. The Netherlands and Belgium led the smaller states in accepting the US package, but the French would not budge. Eventually, Acheson accepted what he could get. The United States split the package proposal and agreed to send more troops and nominate an American as Supreme Allied Commander Europe (SACEUR)—assumed by all to be Dwight D. Eisenhower—and all accepted the statement that in some manner Germany would participate in the defense of Western Europe. As concessions to Adenauer, the Allies agreed to allow the creation of a small West German police force, to lessen some occupation restrictions, and to announce that NATO guarantees extended to defending West Germany if it were attacked. On the important issue of German rearmament, Acheson made no concrete progress, but he did tie West Germany closer to the alliance and win a commitment from France to include Germany in Western defenses in some way in future years.[25]

Before the New York meeting of the North Atlantic Council, French leaders had begun work on a plan to wrap German rearmament within a European army in a way that would protect and advance the negotiations for the Schuman Plan. The inspiration for this initiative came again from Jean Monnet, who wrote his friend Prime Minister René Pleven on September 3 urging him to take the lead in transforming the debate on the defense of Europe. With more details from Monnet, the prime minister endorsed the concept of adding a defense component to the Schuman Plan. Building on the idea of a European army advanced earlier by McCloy, the essence of the new proposal was to create an integrated European defense force of about 100,000 men composed of small national units and including German troops. The army would be commanded by a European general reporting to a European defense minister who would be responsible to a European political assembly. There would be no division-sized German units and no German military staff, and the European army would not be under NATO. To this plan, Pleven added provisions that the European defense force would not be created until the Schuman Plan for coal and steel production was implemented, along with its political and judicial institutions. What became known as the Pleven Plan was introduced in the French National Assembly on October 24 and won approval by a margin of 343–220.[26]

During the fall of 1950, a frenzy of meetings and negotiations occupied officials in the Allied capitals. From the start, Beisner argues, Acheson saw the Pleven Plan as "a blueprint for delay, French preeminence, and permanent German inferiority." Marshall, who only two days after being sworn in as secretary of defense on September 21 had used his immense prestige to win approval of a list of concessions to Germany from the members of the North Atlantic Council, referred to the French plan as a "miasmic cloud." The British were even more caustic in their reactions. But leaders in Washington and London realized by mid-November that they could likely win more from the French by attempting to compromise than by flat opposition. Working with McCloy and the American ambassadors in Paris and London, Charles M. Spofford, the deputy US representative to NATO and chair of the Council of Deputies, advanced a compromise proposal that offered new US divisions and a US commander to NATO in exchange for French acceptance of the principle of German rearmament and the inclusion of German regimental combat teams (units roughly half the size of a division) in NATO.

On November 29, Acheson sent a strong personal message to Schuman highlighting the "dangerous drift in German opinion" and urging the French minister to work with the Germans and other European Allies to accept the Spofford proposal to link "the free nations of Europe more closely together in the spirit so well represented by the Schuman Plan." He reaffirmed the US commitment to European integration and declared that "the broad framework of the Atlantic Community is an essential part of the free world structure, whether it be from the point of view of global security or of permanently ending the threat of German domination." After negotiating the details, Acheson sent a final proposal to Schuman on December 7 that included an added commitment for the United States to support the Pleven Plan's efforts to create the institutions of a European army. Under pressure from both Washington and London, the French government accepted the Spofford Plan the next day.[27]

The negotiations over the Pleven Plan and the development of the Spofford Plan came at a time of high crisis for the Truman administration. The Chinese had launched their massive second offensive in Korea on November 24. UN forces were in disorganized retreat and were taking large losses. General MacArthur was demanding more combat troops and the authority to bomb targets in China. Pentagon officials began a weeks-long strategic evaluation of the war on November 28. European governments were in a panic over the possibility of a Soviet attack in the West. And a delegation from London led by Prime Minister Clement Attlee descended on Washington from December 4 through 8 for urgent talks on the Korean conflict, China policy, the Soviet threat, the possible use of atomic weapons, and the defense of Europe.

Acheson and his colleagues soon learned that careful consideration had to be given to German political interests as well as to the French. A complex approach was needed because when the leaders of Adenauer's center-right coalition realized how valuable a German military contribution would be in the crisis environment created by the Chinese intervention in Korea and Soviet threats over possible German rearmament, they increased their demands for an end to occupation and significant steps toward political and economic equality with the nations of Western Europe. Both Adenauer and the leader of the opposition, Kurt Schumacher—head of the Social Democratic Party (Sozialdemokratische Partei Deutschlands)—strongly criticized the Spofford Plan. The chancellor complained that the proposal would use German soldiers as "cannon fodder," and Schumacher now claimed to support rearmament but did so with such unacceptable conditions that he effectively opposed rearming. American officials were furious. Acheson told the cabinet on December 8 that, in order to deflate the German sense of self-importance, he planned to put the rearmament issue "on ice" and let the Germans "stew for a time."[28]

While Washington concentrated on the visit of the British delegation, McCloy sent Acheson his thoughts on a three-part plan that could
ease French security concerns, produce a European army with German
participation, and make progress toward German equality. The first
step was to implement the Schuman Plan, which was essential for the
French to consider rearmament of their longtime enemy. Next would
be to modify the Pleven Plan with the help of the new NATO supreme
commander to make it more workable in military terms. McCloy believed
participation in a Western European army under European control would
appeal to the Germans' strong support for European integration. Finally,
he would end the Western powers' occupation through a package of contractual agreements that would, step by step, restore German equality.
The necessary catalyst for these elements to succeed was strong, flexible
American leadership. McCloy's elaborate plan was an outline of what
would be the ultimate solution; but it would take many twists and turns
before it would win approval in May 1952.[29]

Acceptance of the Spofford Plan by France and Britain cleared the
way for a successful meeting of the North Atlantic Council in Brussels
on December 18–19. The council approved detailed recommendations
from the Defense Committee on German participation in a European
force within NATO and restructuring the Alliance's command and
headquarters. These actions represented an endorsement of the Spofford Plan. The members also requested President Truman to name General Eisenhower as SACEUR, which he promptly did on December 18.
The council created two sets of negotiations to complete implementation of these decisions. The High Commission and West German leaders were to meet at the Petersberg Hotel to propose how German units
would be trained and organized for inclusion in NATO and other steps
to expand the authority of the Bonn government. A second negotiating
track would meet in Paris to work out the details of creating a European
army, as proposed in the Pleven Plan. Acheson urged each member government to immediately place the units designated for NATO under
Eisenhower's command and move to expand their forces as quickly as
possible. Under firm American leadership, the North Atlantic Council had created the structure for an integrated force within a defensive

FIGURE 12.1 President Truman discusses the recent meetings with NATO foreign and defense ministers in Brussels with Secretary of State Dean Acheson, December 21, 1950.

Source: Photograph by Abbie Rowe, US National Park Service, Truman Library.

alliance and placed an experienced and highly respected commander in charge. The members had also, as Beisner points out, "clearly agreed to . . . [place] the priority . . . [on] military over economic and political issues."[30] (See figure 12.1.)

The decisions made in Brussels resolved NATO's structure and command, but they only delayed the issues of Germany's role and the purpose of a European army. The harsh fact was that the two sets of negotiations approved by the council predictably pulled in different directions. The interest of the participants at the Petersberg, led by the British and American commissioners, was to develop a way to place a European army with German units within NATO and under SACEUR's command. In these discussions, Adenauer and his colleagues would continue to press for restoration of German sovereignty and an equal military role. In contrast, the negotiations in Paris under French leadership would push for a European army to be under full European control, with a mission to cooperate with NATO while remaining outside the Alliance.[31]

By late December, military necessity drove decisionmaking in Washington, while domestic politics dominated thinking in Bonn, Paris, and London. As it became clear to German leaders that under American pressure all NATO members except France endorsed the need for German rearmament, Adenauer and his ministers expanded their demands for an end to occupation restrictions and full military participation. The French government faced multiple urgent problems. The leaders feared being abandoned by the United States, whose forces were being driven back in Korea by a massive Chinese intervention; having Germany rearm before France could both develop superior strength in Europe and fight an expanding war in Indochina; and failing to win any continental commitment from Britain, which was financially weak and struggling to protect its interests in Asia and Africa. Further complicating matters, the Soviet Union began to exploit the divisions within NATO by calling for the negotiation of a peace treaty with Germany to end the occupation and unify East and West Germany with a commitment that the united nation would not rearm. These combined pressures would ultimately persuade Acheson that the United States could not force German rearmament on an unwilling France and risk a German resurgence that would alarm other European Allies. The process of bringing the French around to support German rearmament within NATO would explore many dead-end routes and require long negotiating sessions before being resolved.[32]

THE GREAT DEBATE

While diverging negotiations dragged on in Germany and France during the early months of 1951, an intense debate raged in the United States over sending additional divisions to Europe. Although the plan to increase

American troop strength had been widely discussed since September, Truman's announcement on December 19 that he would send more divisions to augment NATO sparked strong reaction. The real driver of the debate lay in the Republicans' conviction that their victories in the midterm congressional elections had given them a mandate to participate in decisions on overseas troop deployments. Although the Republicans had not won a majority in the Senate, they had cut the Democratic majority from 54–42 to 49–47 and had in the process defeated several strong supporters of administration foreign policy, including Democratic leaders Scott Lucas of Illinois and Millard Tydings of Maryland. As Ronald Caridi describes the clash: "On the surface, the issue concerned which branch of the government should have the final say on sending troops to Europe, but on a more profound level was the question of whether or not the United States should adopt a policy of neoisolationism."[33]

The debate began in earnest with a national radio broadcast of a speech by former president Herbert Hoover on December 20. Concerned about the impact of high defense costs on the economy and irritated by the unwillingness of the Europeans to pay for their own security, Hoover declared that "no more American men and materiel should be sent to Europe until the free peoples of that continent had turned their territories into an impregnable fortress." Instead of continuing economic and military aid to Europe, the former president called for building up the air force and navy, concentrating on the defense of the Western Hemisphere, and relying on atomic weapons to defend American interests. He strongly opposed having US ground troops stationed in Europe.[34]

Just back from the NATO meeting in Brussels, Acheson decided to respond to Hoover's arguments at a press conference on December 22 before the country's attention was diverted by the Christmas break. He charged that the former president's proposal to withdraw to the Western Hemisphere was an invitation to the Soviet Union to take over all of Europe. If this effort were to be successful, Moscow would control economic and military resources far greater than those available to Washington. Even Hoover's military strategy was flawed because US bombers could only reach Soviet targets from the vital bases in Western Europe. The secretary rejected "any policy of sitting quivering in a storm cellar waiting for whatever fate others may wish to propose for us." He then reaffirmed America's policy as working with its free Allies in a collective effort to build and maintain peace and security in Europe and Asia.[35]

The debate on defense commitments in Europe intensified when Robert A. Taft of Ohio took the floor of the Senate on January 5, 1951, to deliver a lengthy speech. Having been reelected by a large margin the previous November, Taft commanded wide attention as a leading conservative who was already the favorite of Republican state chairmen as the party's presidential nominee in 1952. In a nuanced manner, the prominent senator endorsed many of the points made several weeks earlier by Hoover. He was concerned about Truman's plan to send as many as ten divisions of combat troops to Europe. Although he accepted the obligations of NATO and could consider a modest-sized force in Europe, he feared that such a large deployment would provoke the Soviets, strain the American budget, and encourage the Europeans to depend on Washington instead of strengthening their own defenses. He argued that the United States should not attempt to match the Soviet Union in ground troops, its strongest asset. Instead, America should strengthen its air and naval forces and encourage the Europeans to provide their own ground units. Restating his main point, the Ohio senator declared: "Operations on the continents of Europe and Asia, if any, should be undertaken only with the greatest care and under careful limitation." Taft concluded by charging that Truman's plans for Europe were provocative and unconstitutional because the president needed congressional authorization to send troops overseas in peacetime.[36]

The debate in Congress would continue for another three months, until it was resolved in early April 1951. On January 8, Senator Kenneth Wherry (R-NE), one of Acheson's bitterest opponents, introduced a resolution stating that it was the sense of the Senate that no ground troops should be deployed in Europe until the Congress approved. This explicit limitation on the authority of the president would be the principal issue of the debate, although numerous arguments and proposals would range far beyond it. The discussions dominated press coverage on many days in this period, and public figures outside the government took stands on the issues. Republicans were clearly the largest component of the opposition to sending more troops to Europe, but they were joined by some conservative Democrats like Senator Walter George and a few liberal Democrats such as Senator Paul Douglas. Conversely, prominent Republican internationalists like John Foster Dulles, Thomas E. Dewey, Harold Stassen, Senator Henry Cabot Lodge Jr., and Senator William Knowland backed the administration's position.[37]

In joint hearings, the Senate Foreign Relations Committee and Armed Services Committee heard nearly fifty witnesses, ranging from senior military officials to Eisenhower to Marshall to Bradley to ordinary citizens. Before the formal hearings, the recently installed SACEUR, General Eisenhower, met with the committees to report on his findings after a tour of Allied capitals. When he returned from Europe, the top NATO commander had told the president and the cabinet that he felt the United States should assign ten to twelve divisions to an Allied force that would ultimately reach fifty-sixty divisions. But in his executive session with the senators on February 1, Eisenhower carefully avoided saying how many divisions he would recommend, while urging the members not to set any limitations on troop numbers. In his testimony, the general emphasized the close ties between the United States and Europe, the importance of Europe for American security, and the urgent Allied need for US equipment. He also declared that the Soviet Union could be deterred from attacking by the force that NATO was assembling. Among the reasons for Eisenhower's refusal to specify how many divisions he wanted was his knowledge that on January 29, the Joint Chiefs of Staff had recommended sending four divisions to Europe and Truman had approved this number and directed that it be kept secret for a time.[38]

Secretary of Defense George Marshall was the first witness to testify when the formal hearings began on February 15. He opened his prepared remarks with a review of the strong support provided by the Senate for strengthening the economic and military capabilities of Western Europe since 1948. Emphasizing that a strong North Atlantic community was a key element protecting the United States, he declared that the current challenge was building up military strength in order to deter a clear and growing Soviet threat. Pointing out that the Europeans would provide the bulk of Alliance ground forces, he said that the United States should make a significant contribution to ground units while supplying the largest component of air and naval power. In light of "the great amount of discussion which has been centered on the subject of ground forces," he stated that with "the express permission of the president," he could say that the administration planned to send four divisions of ground troops to Europe to join the two divisions already there as occupation forces. He added that these six divisions would serve as a strong core of the Allied force and would, along with US leadership and equipment, encourage the Europeans to strengthen their own defenses. Stressing that the present situation in Europe was "far more delicate and more dangerous" than building the coalition in the recent world war, he declared: "The most important, the greatest factor, in the creation of military strength for Western Europe in my opinion is to build up morale—of the will to defend—the determination to fight if that be necessary." When asked if six divisions would be sufficient, he said they were adequate for deterrence under present conditions and acknowledged that the real problem for the army would be, given the demands of the conflict in Korea, recruiting enough troops for four new divisions. In conclusion, he urged the senators to place no limits on the number of troops to be assigned to Europe and to give the administration flexibility with regard to both America's Allies and possible opponents.[39]

After General Marshall's testimony the next day came another big gun, Secretary of State Dean Acheson. Responding to one of the main arguments of the Hoover-Taft opposition, he stated boldly that the administration had no thought of trying to match Soviet ground strength in Europe. The purpose of American strategy was to deter Soviet aggression in any form. Regarding the opponents' call for reliance on atomic weapons and air power, Acheson contended that it would be a drastic error to wait until Europe was attacked before the United States responded. Such a policy would risk losing Europe to intimidation, subversion, and other means of "indirect aggression." He emphasized that the American lead in air power and atomic weapons would continue to decline over time. He declared that "the best use we can make of our present advantage in retaliatory air power is to move ahead under this protective shield to build the balanced collective forces in

Western Europe that will continue to deter aggression after our atomic advantage has been diminished." The objections to the administration strategy for Europe were based, he insisted, on unrealistic fears and exaggerated threats. He told the members that a more limited, balanced force in Europe could respond to and deter the most likely threat—which was aggression by satellite forces, as had happened in Korea. In response to the argument that the United States should wait until Europe had rearmed before sending more troops, Acheson declared that the need to strengthen deterrence was "immediate. . . . Our Allies are building their forces now; the time for our own contribution is now. If each of the North Atlantic nations should wait to appraise its partners' efforts before determining its own, the result would be as disastrous as it would be obvious." Addressing a question about the president's authority to deploy troops, the secretary assured the committees that Article 2, Section 2, of the US Constitution gave the president full authority as commander in chief of the armed forces to deploy them as he found necessary to protect the nation.[40]

As the hearings ground ahead until the middle of March, opposition to the administration strategy gradually ebbed. Two factors were largely responsible. General Marshall's statement that the administration planned to send only four divisions (about 80,000 troops) to Europe eased the fears of those like Senator Taft who had spoken about the prospect of deploying 2 million US troops to Europe. The other reassuring development was the steady success of US forces in Korea, as General Matthew Ridgway fought his way back to the 38th Parallel.[41]

After heated debate, Senator John L. McClellan (D-AR) proposed a face-saving amendment to the Wherry resolution, which stated that no more than four divisions should be sent to Europe "without further congressional approval." This amendment passed 49–43 on April 2. Two days later, the Senate passed the resolution as amended, 69–21. More than half the Senate Republicans, including Senator Taft, voted in favor of the measure, which approved in principle the deployment of four divisions to Europe as well as the appointment of General Dwight Eisenhower as SACEUR. This resolution expressed the will of the Senate but did not carry the force of law.[42]

The Great Debate concluded with a two-thirds majority of the Senate endorsing the administration's European policy while insisting that Congress should be consulted on major overseas commitments. In many ways, this episode marked the last charge of neoisolationism, or what is more precisely described as a policy of minimal security involvement in Europe and first priority to Asia. But this political battle was not the end of heated opposition to the Truman administration, which would reach fever pitch within days after the firing of General Douglas MacArthur.

ACHESON PUSHES FOR EUROPEAN
DEFENSE COOPERATION

While defending administration policies during the Great Debate and the MacArthur hearings, Dean Acheson tried several approaches to win French approval of German participation in a European defense force. From the early weeks of 1951, two sets of negotiations were under way on creating a European army. Acheson placed primary emphasis on the talks at the Petersberg Hotel outside Bonn among representatives of the high commissioners and West Germany, which he expected to propose early armament of German units that would be part of NATO. The United States was not a direct participant in the negotiations in Paris designed to create an integrated European force, and the secretary's view was that the European Defence Community (EDC) talks would be a long-range project, one which could be fused with NATO at a later date.

The Petersberg group concluded its work in June with a plan for twelve German divisions with tanks, artillery, and tactical air units to be part of NATO. This proposal reflected the views of the German and US governments; but for the French, it gave Germany too much military strength and did not provide Paris with adequate control over the force. The French government flatly rejected the Petersberg plan, leaving an undefined EDC as the only option. The French political elite had many reasons to feel to feel vulnerable and angry. Anxious about the rapid German resurgence, which had strong American support, both the leaders and the public became increasingly nationalistic and anti-American under Washington's pressure to modernize the economy, expand the military, accept US interference in budget allocations, and provide infrastructure for a new Allied headquarters outside Paris. These attitudes dominated the June parliamentary elections, in which the centrist parties that supported the EDC suffered large losses, and it took René Pleven almost two months to form another government.[43]

Acheson needed a new concept that could bridge Franco-German differences. As it happened, his two top representatives in Europe, John McCloy in Bonn and David Bruce in Paris, had formulated a program that strengthened European defenses and satisfied both German desires for equal rights and French security needs. Their proposal required giving full US support to the EDC, using General Eisenhower to help make a European force militarily effective while including German units, and negotiating contractual agreements to restore most elements of German sovereignty. McCloy arranged for Eisenhower to meet Jean Monnet; and over a long lunch on June 21, the French originator of both the Schuman Plan and Pleven Plan persuaded the new SACEUR that a hasty push for German units in NATO would create deep French resentment and lead to a crisis in the Alliance. The fundamental issue, Monnet argued, was political, and the solution was to emphasize European unity in defense to match the recently approved economic integration of the European Coal and Steel Community. (See figure 12.2.)

Eisenhower wrote Marshall on July 18, with a personal copy to Acheson, saying he was fully convinced that a European army was the way to resolve the Franco-German deadlock. He also requested their approval to serve as an observer at the EDC negotiations, which the French wanted, and promised to do everything possible to support a prompt resolution of the outstanding issues. Ambassador Bruce followed the next day, with a long message to Acheson arguing the same case. This coordinated effort persuaded the secretary of state and helped remove doubts about the EDC held by Marshall, the Joint Chiefs of Staff, and the president. A proposal developed by the State Department to implement this program was approved by senior Defense Department officials. Acheson presented it to the president on July 30, and he

FIGURE 12.2 President Truman with his strong national security team of (*from the left*) Dean Acheson, Averell Harriman, and George Marshall, July 13, 1951.

Source: Photograph by Abbie Rowe, US National Park Service, Truman Library.

approved it that day. It was subsequently circulated to the members of the National Security Council (NSC) and, when approved, was designated NSC Report 115. After another ten months of negotiating with Allies, the three occupying powers signed the contractual agreements with West Germany on May 26, while West Germany, France, Italy, and the Benelux governments signed the EDC Treaty on May 27, 1952. The US Senate approved the contractual agreements on July 1, 1952.[44]

Despite Acheson's tenacious backing and the fact that American assistance was funding much of the European defense buildup, support for the EDC among the key continental governments began to wane. Economic recovery was stalled in the face of high social costs, increased military spending, and inflation. In addition to these problems, France was engaged in a full-scale war in Indochina. At a February 1952 North

Atlantic Council meeting in Lisbon, Acheson succeeded in winning commitments for higher force levels from the Allies; but as domestic demands increased, the governments soon ignored these pledges. As the United States pressed for German rearmament and the Bonn government became enthusiastic about the EDC, French officials increasingly focused on fears of resurgent German military power.

While the Korean War armistice negotiations dragged on, European leaders became less concerned with the Soviet threat. This attitude reached a peak with Stalin's death, which soon was followed by the signing of the armistice in Korea in July 1953. After months of debate, the French National Assembly defeated both the EDC Treaty and the contractual agreements with Germany on August 30, 1954, by a vote of 319–264. With the Eisenhower administration now in office in Washington, the United States negotiated with its NATO Allies and set the stage for signing an agreement between the three occupying powers and Germany in October 1954 to end the occupation of West Germany. Later that month, West Germany was invited to join the Alliance, and on May 9, 1955, West Germany formally entered NATO, ten years after the end of World War II in Europe.[45]

AN ASSESSMENT

Acheson's goal of adding German forces to Western defenses was finally accomplished three years after he left office. His steady pressure for German rearmament in the end may have been counterproductive because it led to the reopening of old French wounds suffered in three defeats at German hands. However, in his defense, his consistent efforts to remove occupation restrictions and his support for Adenauer's policies undoubtedly helped contain and reduce neutralist opinion in Germany and in the process tied West Germany to the West. It is also very likely that French security anxieties over a rearmed Germany would not have subsided as long as the best French military units were being overwhelmed in Indochina. It is clear that French insecurity diminished with the end of the war at the Geneva Conference in July 1954. Another factor in reducing French security concerns is worth noting. In the last half of 1953, the US Army deployed its first tactical nuclear weapons in Germany; and by the end of the year, twenty atomic-capable, 8-inch howitzers were operational in the US European Command. This significant step reduced the need for large numbers of German conventional forces and gave NATO a distinct advantage over Soviet armored forces in Central and Eastern Europe.[46]

Despite delays and resistance, Dean Acheson richly deserves to be known as "the defender of Europe." He helped design and implement the Marshall Plan, pushed the North Atlantic Treaty to completion, and organized the transformation of NATO into a functioning, integrated Alliance. In achieving these results, he had unmatched support from the Europeanists in the State Department; from his icon, George Marshall, and his very able deputy, Robert Lovett, at the Defense Department; and from the president's de facto national security adviser Averell Harriman. A superb trio of ambassadors—David Bruce, John McCloy, and Lewis Douglas—advised and advanced his programs in Europe. Another trio of leaders in Europe—Robert Schuman, Jean Monnet, and Konrad Adenauer—shared their vision of a unified Western Europe with him and helped create key elements of his plan. Equally important were the consistent support and encouragement of President Harry Truman.

Under Acheson's leadership, the structure of the North Atlantic Alliance became operational in the early 1950s. The major governments built the command structure of the integrated Alliance, and the Allies unanimously chose Dwight Eisenhower as the first SACEUR. A significant buildup of European defense forces began with a large program of US military assistance, and the Truman administration contributed four additional divisions to the Alliance. The members established a logistical network and communication infrastructure. By 1952, the US Air Force had completed building seven principal air bases in the United Kingdom, four in France, six in Germany, and several more in French Morocco. In February 1952, NATO extended its defensive capacity to the southern flank, when Greece and Turkey joined the Alliance. The United States supported the independence of Yugoslavia, which had split from the Soviet Bloc in 1948, by providing military assistance; and in 1953, with Washington's backing, Belgrade signed a five-year treaty of friendship and cooperation with Greece and Turkey. In September 1953, after years of military aid and negotiations about defense cooperation, the United States signed an executive agreement with Spain to build air and naval bases in exchange for military and economic aid. These important facilities greatly increased America's ability to control the Mediterranean and to project military forces into the Middle East if necessary.[47]

Dean Acheson played the leading role in building a strong, prosperous, and united Western Europe that frustrated any Soviet effort to divide and dominate the whole continent. He established Europe as the top priority for US security and economic policy, and he accomplished this while defeating the challenge of the Asia-first movement at home and the North Korean and Chinese assault in Asia. These policies put in place by Truman and Acheson would continue throughout the Cold War and into the twenty-first century.

13

ANDREI TUPOLEV CREATES A STRATEGIC BOMBER FORCE

At the conclusion of World War II, the Soviet Union had a sizable but largely obsolete air force. Given the conditions under which the aircraft industry had worked, only a Herculean effort had produced the airplanes that the nation possessed. With the sudden initial strikes of the German invasion in June 1941, the Luftwaffe had eliminated more than 4,000 Soviet aircraft before they could get off the ground. "It is well that we have destroyed the Russian Air Force in the very beginning," Hitler boasted on July 4. "The Russians will not be able to recover it." However, with immense sacrifice, Soviet workers produced 137,000 airplanes during the war; and of these, 108,000 were military aircraft. Due to the deep penetration of German forces, 94 percent of the aircraft design bureaus and construction plants had to be evacuated far to the east and rebuilt under primitive conditions. A worker from a Moscow plant transported to Kuibyshev (now Samara) described his working environment: "The evacuated workers and specialists had to unload equipment and do construction jobs. There was no automated way to lift and transport cargo, and everything was done with the help of crowbars, rollers, and sheets of steel, on which the machines were loaded, and then tens of people would harness themselves and drag the equipment from the railroad to its prescribed destination. . . . We worked twelve hours a day, and often did not leave the workshop for several days on end."[1]

During the war, the Soviets concentrated on building large numbers of basic aircraft for tactical support of ground operations. They had to use plywood for much airframe construction and were far behind other countries in developing electronics, radar, light alloys, high-horsepower engines and superchargers, and jet aircraft. In a report to Stalin on his service's postwar needs, Air Marshall A. A. Novikov, the commander of the air force, declared that "the USA emerged from the war with a powerful strategic aviation and a tactical aviation weaker than ours. . . . Moreover, the USA is considerably ahead of us, and also England, in equipping aircraft with more sophisticated aircraft navigation instruments, sights, radar, communications, and fire control systems." He urged that new construction should focus on strategic bombers: "Daytime strategic (but not nighttime) aviation should be recreated so that it comprises no less than 20 percent of the total composition of the military's air forces."[2]

Stalin was well aware of the need for long-range bombers. He had begun a project to build an atomic weapon in late 1942, and he lacked an aircraft capable of delivering it against the United States. Informed by his espionage network of American efforts to build an atomic bomb as well as the construction of the B-29 to deliver it, the Soviet leader had requested B-29s through the Lend-Lease program. US officials had quickly rejected at least three requests, and Stalin realized that he had to build his own delivery vehicle.[3]

ANDREI N. TUPOLEV

When Stalin decided to build a strategic bomber, the obvious choice for chief designer was Andrei Nikolaevich Tupolev. Having designed and built heavy bombers and airplanes that set world records for long-range flights, Tupolev had an enviable international reputation in the rapidly developing field of aeronautical design and engineering. Before examining his efforts to meet Stalin's demands, it is useful to understand his earlier challenges and accomplishments.

Tupolev was born on a small farm in Tver Province about 125 miles north of Moscow on November 10, 1888, the sixth of seven children, and he grew up in a comfortable environment typical of minor gentry in the countryside. His father worked as a village notary in addition to farming, and his mother had graduated from the gymnasium and spoke French and German. The parents placed a high value on education and sent all their children to the Tver gymnasium, despite the strain of the school fees on their finances. At school, Andrei took special interest in physics and mathematics and was fortunate to have a science teacher who worked with him on experiments in mechanics, optics, and electricity. This early fascination with science led him in 1908 to enter the Imperial Moscow Technical Institute, where he became a student and soon a disciple of N. Y. Zhukovskiy, a distinguished scientist and engineer who became known as "the father of Russian aviation."[4]

In Moscow, Tupolev excelled in the classroom and the laboratory, and by 1910 he was Zhukovskiy's top assistant. His participation in student uprisings led to an interruption of his studies when he was arrested by the Tsarist Police in March 1911 and expelled from school for a year. His father died shortly after his arrest, and Tupolev returned to operate the farm during his period of suspension while studying aeronautics and the works of radical authors at night. Returning to school, he completed his degree with distinction while working as an engineer in two different ministries. When the Bolshevik Revolution came in 1917, Tupolev joined Professor Zhukovskiy and other top students in pledging support to the new communist government. During the fall of 1918, while working with his professor and several colleagues in a design bureau by day, the group devoted their nights to developing a proposal for a new institute that would teach and apply all the disciplines involved in aerodynamics and hydrodynamics. Eager for prompt approval of their plan, Tupolev bypassed the bureaucracy and directly approached the head of the scientific department of the Supreme Council of the National Economy, who was a close associate of V. I. Lenin. Impressed with the proposal and the audacity of its proponents, on December 1, 1918, the Bolshevik leader authorized the creation of the Central Aero-Hydrodynamics Institute (TsAGI) and allocated working space and personnel to assist the founders. Zhukovskiy was the head of the new institute, and Tupolev soon became his top deputy and chief of the design bureau. Following Zhukovskiy's teachings, Tupolev was one of the earliest design engineers in the Soviet Union to incorporate theoretical calculations in the design and construction of aircraft. The TsAGI became one of the leading aviation centers in the world, and today it remains the top aeronautical institute in Russia.[5]

In the 1920s, the Soviet aviation industry faced great obstacles. Four years of civil war had seen the closure of many factories due the shortage of workers and materials along with the emigration of numerous skilled engineers and designers like Igor Sikorsky. A significant number of factory owners, rejecting Bolshevik ideas, closed their businesses and moved to the West.[6]

Despite these difficulties, Tupolev made important progress in airplane design and construction. In 1923, he held the initial flight test of his first airplane: a small, single-engine monoplane made of fabric and wood, which was designated the ANT-1 after the chief designer's initials. While building this airplane with handmade wooden parts, Tupolev was developing an aluminum alloy invented in Germany to use as the skin of an all-metal airplane. This plane, the ANT-2, first flew in May 1924. Asked by the government to design a bomber, Tupolev and his colleagues worked feverishly to create this much larger, more complex aircraft. By November 1925, they had built a twin-engine all-metal monoplane with a crew of six and a range of 1,000 miles, called the TB-1 (ANT-4). A series of test flights confirmed the airplane's performance and reliability. "With the construction of the TB-1," asserts Tupolev's engineer colleague and biographer L. L. Kerber, "the USSR seized primacy in airplane construction and 37-year-old Tupolev became one of the world's greatest aircraft designers." Eager for recognition of the Soviet Union's aeronautical accomplishments, Stalin ordered a demonstration flight to the United States. In 1929, a TB-1 flew from Moscow across Siberia to New York, where it was received with great acclaim by aviation specialists and the press.[7]

The Tupolev bureau produced more innovative aircraft in the next eight years. To satisfy the air force's desire for a larger bomber with greater range, the chief designer and his engineers expanded the basic concepts of the TB-1, and by 1932 had produced a new four-engine bomber with a range of 1,900 miles. This simple, reliable aircraft was built in massive numbers and developed in passenger and cargo models. The TB-3 was used in conflicts in Mongolia, the Winter War with Finland, the annexation of Poland and Bessarabia, and the war against Germany. Between 1929 and 1934, the design team built thirteen test airplanes, including a giant passenger plane for eighty-five and seaplanes as well as torpedo boats. In 1930, Tupolev was named chief designer of the main aviation administration, and in the subsequent years he received several high awards, including the highest honor, the Order of Lenin. In 1933, he was elected an associate member of the USSR Academy of Sciences.[8]

The next big challenge for the bureau was to design an airplane to set a distance record for continuous flight. Work began in 1931, and after many test prototypes and modifications, including several failures and accidents, in July 1937 the ANT-25 flew from Moscow to San Jacinto, California, near the Mexican border. This grueling flight set a new world record of 6,292 miles in a little over 62 hours. This achievement won widespread accolades from American military and aviation officials and from the government and public in the Soviet Union. The three crewmen and the designers, especially Tupolev, were highly praised.[9]

Tupolev's character and personality were essential to his survival and success in the chaos of the early Soviet Union. Equally critical were his brilliant but practical mind and his country's desperate need for a new aviation industry. The young engineer possessed vision in solving technical problems in ways that moved his aircraft to a higher level of performance; and once his analysis was complete, he held firmly to his convictions. An excellent example was his conclusion, after examining pieces of the metal skin of a downed German Zeppelin, that the future of aviation lay in all-metal aircraft. He tenaciously fought the entire aviation bureaucracy to win permission to develop aluminum alloy for his next airplane, the ANT-2. He worked in a collegial manner with groups of engineers and specialists in developing concepts for new aircraft designs and welcomed their ideas as the process advanced. But he could be quite authoritarian and unyielding once he made up his mind.

Like many creative leaders, he disliked dealing with bureaucrats; yet, when necessary, he could persuade the key people to approve his projects and provide the necessary workers and equipment. After new aircraft had been tested and approved, he would continue to improve them by seeking feedback from workers in assembly plants and from pilots who flew his aircraft.

While working as a medical orderly during the civil war, Tupolev had met a nurse, Yulenka Zheltikova, and they were married in 1922. Yulenka was very musical and entertained their friends by playing the piano and singing. She brought artists and writers into their home and created a warm environment for Andrei. They soon had a daughter and a son, and Tupolev became a devoted family man to balance his obsession with aeronautics. He especially enjoyed ice skating and fishing with family and friends. But his rewarding life of professional success and a loving family was abruptly interrupted by unfathomable actions of the Soviet state.[10]

On October 21, 1937, three months after being celebrated for setting the world record for continuous flight distance, Tupolev was arrested by three agents of the NKVD, who came to his house at 11 P.M., searched every room, and took him away to the infamous Lubyanka Prison. He was later charged with allegedly selling plans for a new fighter to Germany. His arrest was part of Stalin's Great Purge, which was at its peak between 1936 and 1938. The initial targets were senior Communist Party leaders who were accused of Trotskyite or opposition views, and a second wave included senior military officers, most of whom were also party members. Tupolev's arrest was part of a third wave of attacks on technical specialists and intellectuals. At Lubyanka, he was kept standing for hours of questioning about his alleged espionage, but he was not otherwise tortured. He was later transferred to Bolshevo Prison, where he was required to write down the names of aviation specialists already in prison. He knew some who had been arrested before him, but was unsure of those arrested later. "After thinking things over," he later recounted, "I decided to list everyone I knew. After all, they really couldn't have imprisoned the entire aviation industry, could they? This seemed to be a rational approach, and I wrote out a list of about 200 men. It turned out that, with rare exceptions, all of them were already behind bars."[11]

Tupolev later learned from his colleagues what had happened. Many aeronautical engineers and designers were arrested and sent to various prison labor camps. Leonid L. Kerber was assigned to a camp near Arkhangelsk in the north to cut trees; Sergei P. Korolyov, the future leader of the Soviet space program, was sent to a harsh camp in Kolyma in northeast Siberia to dig for gold with a pick. A group of second-rate designers and engineers were moved to Tupolev's old bureau, but after some months they had produced no workable designs. This ultimately would reflect badly on NKVD head Lavrenti Beria, who had been in charge of arresting the more qualified specialists, so Beria negotiated with the Aviation Ministry for the NKVD to assume control over it. With Stalin's approval, Beria then moved Tupolev and his chosen colleagues back to their old buildings, which were made into a relatively comfortable prison workshop. After Tupolev's death, his colleagues learned that many of the false accusations in his NKVD file had come from two of the foremost aircraft designers, who at the time were Tupolev's jealous younger competitors, Sergei V. Il'yushin and Alexander S. Yakovlev. When asked years later why distinguished designers like Tupolev and Korolyov were imprisoned, the old Bolshevik Vyacheslav Molotov said: "They all talked too much. . . . They didn't support us. People like Tupolev could become dangerous enemies. . . . For a while they were our enemies, and more time was necessary to bring them closer to Soviet power. Tupolev is from a certain category of the intelligentsia which the Soviet state needed very much, but in their souls they are against us."[12]

In the TsAGI compound, which Tupolev had initially organized and directed, the NKVD set up four design bureaus to be staffed primarily by prisoners. An NKVD colonel commanded the overall compound, while a major directed each bureau with Tupolev and three senior colleagues as "deputies." About 150 designers, engineers, and specialists were transferred from their prisons to Tupolev's bureau and were assisted by several hundred free workers. The prisoners slept on cots in old conference rooms, had hot meals and polite guards, worked on aircraft projects during the day, and had time for reading and exercise on the roof at night. Their living conditions were greatly improved over the labor camps, where many prisoners died from exhaustion, injury, or disease. After some months, the prisoners could have supervised visits from their wives and family members, but they still lived in a prison environment where, periodically, a colleague would be taken away without explanation and not seen again. For Tupolev personally, this was a serious hardship and humiliation. He had to take orders from an uneducated policeman, and his wife was also in prison, with her mother taking care of the children. Tupolev had no income to help with the children's care and education, and the children and grandparents lived in a single room, often without heat.[13]

Having to work at a high level of performance under such harsh conditions posed a severe test for Tupolev's character and leadership. Two examples from many stand out. At a point before his team was fully formed, Tupolev was ordered to report on the concept for his dive bomber Tu-2 to Beria at Lubyanka Prison. After listening to the description of the airplane's specifications and capabilities, Beria responded with an outrageous alternative: Instead of a two-engine ground support dive bomber, the security chief said he had Stalin's approval to build a different airplane. He called for a high-altitude, long-range, four-engine dive bomber, which would be called the PB-4. Tupolev returned to his small band of senior engineers "as mad as a thousand devils." He said he feared that Beria had already persuaded Stalin to change to a completely unworkable concept, adding, "I know Stalin a little: He doesn't like to change his decisions." Tupolev told his colleagues that they had to take the proposal seriously and do the weight and lift calculations to show that the plane was not workable with the materials and engines available. With these calculations in hand, he wrote a response for Beria, arguing that a proven high-altitude, long-range, four-engine bomber was already built—the ANT-42—and that it only needed to be put into production; a dive bomber had to be a small, highly maneuverable aircraft in order to evade defensive batteries; and he could guarantee the performance of the Tu-2 dive bomber, whereas the calculations showed the proposed PB-4 to be unworkable.[14]

A month later, Beria summoned Tupolev to report on his research. After explaining his analysis and conclusions, Tupolev later told his colleagues that "Beria [was] openly angry" and looked at me spitefully."

The designer wondered what Stalin had said to Beria, and after a long pause, the security chief said that he and his advisers would look at Tupolev's report. For several days, Tupolev "sat in a solitary cell, worried about my fate." When he was finally called back, Beria declared: "Comrade Stalin and I went over the materials once again and made a decision: Make the airplane with twin engines, and quickly." And then, asserting his authority, he demanded that the Tu-2's speed be increased from 600 to 700 kilometers per hour, its range from 2,000 to 3,000 kilometers, and its load capacity from 3 to 4 tons. This decision was a cause for celebration within the design team. Years later, in recounting the episode, Tupolev mused, "Recalling his [Beria's] malicious look, I'm inclined to believe that he would have sacrificed us without a moment's hesitation, and what would our fate have been?"[15]

Another incident demonstrated Tupolev's strong personality and willingness to take risks. At some point in late 1940, when the Nazi-Soviet Pact was still being honored, the Germans gave several of their top combat aircraft to the Soviets for examination and test flights. Tupolev and a team of engineers were taken to inspect the airplanes in detail and learn what they could about the technology. One of the aircraft was the Messerschmitt Bf-110, a twin-engine fighter bomber that had performed with great success in the German attacks on Poland and France. This was the airplane built from plans that Tupolev had allegedly sold to the Germans. With the inspection completed, the group was taken to the air force mess hall for lunch, and the prisoners, accompanied by one of their minders, an NKVD major, were directed to the generals' private dining room. The three generals who were seated there all knew Tupolev, welcomed him enthusiastically, and began asking about the engineers' evaluations of the German aircraft. One of the generals, P. A. Losyukov, had been head of an air force commission that inspected an early prototype of the Tu-2 and had given it a very positive assessment. During a general conversation, Tupolev said to Losyukov, "Well, Prokhar Alekseyevich, I was honored: I examined the Messerschmitt Bf-110, and saw 'my' airplane." The room went silent. Everyone knew that Tupolev had challenged the validity of the charges against him. The lunch ended shortly, and "Losyukov went up to Tupolev and shook his hand warmly."

As Kerber the biographer reflected on it, this "unexpected meeting" was "a signpost of the times. They saw, they were horrified, but they remained silent." In the end, "sincerity had the upper hand."[16]

IN PRISON AND DURING THE GREAT PATRIOTIC WAR

During his time in the prison design bureau, or *sharaga*, Tupolev's main assignment was to build a high-performance, twin-engine dive bomber superior to the German Junkers Ju-88. This aircraft began as Project 103, and would eventually be designated the Tu-2. With the concept for the airplane completed, Tupolev had to spend several months fending off Beria's misguided attempt to shift the project in a completely infeasible direction. Only then could the fabrication of parts and construction begin. Despite the frustrations and delays of building an airplane under the scrutiny of guards who saw every change from the blueprints as attempted sabotage, Tupolev's team members and their shop workers had the first airplane ready for flight testing in the fall of 1940. The flight tests went well, but the military insisted on several changes that added weight and required significant redesign. With signs that war with Germany might break out soon, Tupolev pressed his colleagues to work harder than normal on the changes. The new version was completed in the spring of 1941, and on its initial flight an engine caught fire. The investigation that followed produced demands for a change to heavier, air-cooled engines, which required another redesign.[17] Before the second revised design was finished, the Germans attacked on June 22, 1941.

Events changed quickly for the design bureau. Tupolev was freed from prison in July, and in August the entire team and its equipment, including the partially assembled airplane, were evacuated to Omsk—some 900 miles east of Moscow and just north of the border with Kazakhstan. At the new site, the team members assembled their equipment in a partially built factory and had to build a new plant for production of the aircraft. Gradually, groups of prisoners were freed by seniority and could join their families, who had also been evacuated to Omsk. Working long hours, the team completed the prototype, tested it successfully, and put it into mass production in September 1941. The Tu-2 entered combat in March 1942 and became one of the mainstays of the Red Army's drive across Eastern Europe to Berlin. With modifications from combat experience, over 2,200 Tu-2s were built until it went out of production in 1948.

After Soviet forces had stopped the German assault at Stalingrad and taken the offensive, Tupolev's bureau moved back to Moscow in the summer of 1943 and worked on a range of projects that focused on improving the production of weapons for combat. Overall, during the war Tupolev and his colleagues completed ten types of aircraft and torpedo boats, including the highly effective Tu-2. The military historian Steven Zaloga contends that the Tu-2 "was far superior to any twin-engine bomber in Soviet or German service. The design was so good that in 1943 Tupolev was awarded the Stalin Prize and a cash bonus of $25,000. Stalin reportedly apologized to Tupolev for his rough treatment in prison," and personally assigned the designation Tu-2 to the airplane.[18]

In September 1943, aviation industry officials directed Tupolev to design a strategic bomber with a range of 6,000 kilometers and a bomb capacity of 10 tons. Designated Project 64, this airplane was developed as a delivery vehicle for an atomic bomb, although no one was told this at the time. Beria, who headed the supersecret atomic bomb project begun at the end of 1942, was also assigned to supervise Project 64. As he worked on the requirements for this large, complex airplane, Tupolev realized that he needed new forms of controls that would enable precise navigation and bombing, secure communications from a high altitude, and automated gunnery. He had heard of American advances in the new scientific field of cybernetics, the study of communications and automated controls based on mathematics. Before he could explore how this new field could be applied to his airplane design work, the chief ideologist of the Soviet Communist Party, fearing that this new science would undermine acceptance of dialectical materialism as the basis for the Marxist-Leninist worldview, declared it a "pseudoscience" and banned it from Soviet writings and projects.

Despite his recent imprisonment on charges of espionage, which would not be lifted until 1956, Tupolev worked persistently to identify senior specialists and Communist Party officials who would understand the need to adopt automated control systems in order to build an efficient strategic bomber. His effort involved significant risk, but he continued his campaign for three years, until the Politburo approved the creation of the Academic Council on Cybernetics within the Presidium of the Academy of Sciences. He was now free to work on automated control systems and basic computers. During his long struggle to win approval, he would often recite to his closest colleagues a list of all the top scientists and their achievements while denouncing the phony scientists like Trofin Lysenko and his tricks of agronomy. "After finishing this long tirade, he would laugh," reports Kerber. Then he would declare: " 'You know, it is really amazing. All the leaders of our group are non–Party members, and they haven't disgraced the Motherland!' "[19]

Tupolev's problems finding adequate control systems and electronics within Soviet industry showed how domestic research had not kept up with Western innovation. Stalin blamed his outdated aviation industry on its leadership, and he removed the air force commander, Air Marshal A. A. Novikov, and the people's commissar of the aviation industry, A. I. Shakhurin. The two wartime leaders of Soviet aviation were sent to labor camps, and their achievements were expunged from the records. After working on the bomber design for nineteen months, Tupolev won approval of the blueprints for Project 64 in April 1945. But he still faced significant problems in manufacturing the controls and engines he would need to meet the specified performance requirements. When Beria explained these difficulties to Stalin, they decided to choose another route to gaining a long-range bomber that could deliver an atomic bomb.[20]

REVERSE-ENGINEERING THE B-29

On June 5, 1945, Stalin summoned Tupolev and his deputy, Aleksandr A. Arkhangelskiy, to the Kremlin. Assuming that the chief wanted a briefing on Project 64, the two engineers took with them a colorful album describing the projected flight performance of the new bomber. But Stalin had a different agenda. He quickly declared, as Arkhangelskiy reported, "Comrade Tupolev, you will be copying B-29." The new project received the highest state authority, and Beria had the power to redirect resources and manufacturing priorities in all industries. The massive effort to construct the B-4, as the Soviet copy was designated, would ultimately involve 64 design bureaus and research institutes and 900 factories in the development and production processes. Although Tupolev requested three years for the project, Stalin granted only two years and directed that the B-4 be ready to participate in the air show in the summer of 1947.[21]

This course was possible as a result of the exigencies of America's war against Japan and Soviet chicanery. Although Washington had rejected Soviet requests for B-29s through the Lend-Lease program, Stalin gained possession of three operable Superfortresses and the parts from a fourth that had crashed in a Siberian forest. When US pilots were unable to return to their bases after raids on Japan, they would land around Vladivostok, with Soviet permission. The Soviet Union was an ally of the United States in the war against Germany, but it remained neutral in the conflict against Japan. As a result, it was obligated to detain the aircraft and crews of those planes operating against Japan. When Moscow joined the war against Japan in August 1945, Soviet leaders refused to return the US aircraft. With the white stars painted red, the three B-29s were flown to the Moscow area, where one was disassembled to make blueprints for copies, one was used for training flights, and the third was kept in reserve.[22]

Initially, Tupolev believed it would be relatively easy to copy the basic airframe of the B-29, but he realized it would be a serious problem to replicate the equipment and armament. The aircraft industry would have difficulty creating the electronics, plastics, metals, and radios that were needed. As he inspected the first airplane while it was being disassembled, he was especially baffled by the "millions of wires" that connected the gunsights, navigation controls, and computers. Puzzling over how to copy this web of wiring, he "became extremely agitated," Kerber recounts. And the wiring and equipment were not his only problems. The aluminum skin of the American airplane was one-sixteenth of an inch thick, but because Soviet mills used machinery with metric measurements, this thickness—1.5875 millimeters—could not be duplicated.

After much debate, the engineers decided to vary the thickness of the skin from 0.8 to 1.8 millimeters depending on the strength required for each section to avoid increasing the weight of the airplane and thus reducing its speed and range.[23]

Stalin's order had specifically stated that the B-29 was to be copied exactly in all details, except for the conversion to metric measurement. This led to some absurd and other dangerous results. Although Soviet pilots were not allowed to smoke on duty, workers installed ashtrays in the cockpit and sealed them shut. More seriously, they copied precisely the Identification Friend or Foe system, which would have resulted in the Soviet bombers being identified as foes by Soviet fighters. This was discovered in tests and was corrected before friendly fire episodes occurred. In a few cases, senior officials approved changes from the B-29 equipment. Soviet machine guns were installed, and a superior, ultra-high-frequency radio system was used. Looking back at this process, Tupolev concluded that it would have been much easier to build a new airplane than to copy one made in a different system.[24]

With pressure from the Kremlin to produce a strategic bomber quickly, Tupolev and his colleagues developed several innovations in the production process. Working under the authority given to Beria, the chief designer created a network of senior officials in each ministry to be "personally responsible for producing and delivering the new equipment." These "horizontal relationships" eliminated much of the inefficiency in the aviation industry and greatly expedited the complex process of replicating the B-29. As parts became available, two factories assembled twenty prototype aircraft for testing. The first flight test of the B-4 came on May 19, 1947, only twenty months after the project began. Three of the new bombers appeared in the annual air show on August 3, 1947, along with a passenger version that contained parts and engines from the B-29 that had crashed in Siberia. Continued flight tests of the initial twenty airplanes exposed several problems, including fires and engine failures, that required modification before mass production began.[25]

Years later, Petr Dement'yev, the first deputy minister of the aviation industry, described how the bomber had been approved and named.

One evening after the testing was complete, Stalin directed Dement'yev and his minister, Mikhail Khrunichev, to bring the test report to his dacha. Displeased with the lengthy period of testing, "Stalin was clearly not in a good mood," Dement'yev recalled. "After looking through several pages of the report, he pushed it aside and said 'Late by one year exactly.'" The disgruntled dictator invited the two officials to dinner, which took place in absolute silence. When he was finished eating, Stalin stood up, took the report, and left without saying a word. After a long wait, Stalin's security chief appeared and said that the leader had signed the document and they could return to Moscow in one of Stalin's cars. On the trip back to the city, the driver took a circuitous route, and when the car entered Lubyanka Square, the two officials felt that this might be their final destination. But the car continued on to their ministry, and the two shaken officials went quickly to their office and opened the package. They were greatly relieved to discover that the report had been approved and signed by Stalin, who had crossed out "B-4" and written in blue pencil "Tu-4." Despite his intimidating reception of the report, Stalin was very pleased with Tupolev's work and rewarded him with a second Stalin Prize. Tupolev's colleagues expressed their approval and relief with a joke claiming that he had won his award for a conversion calculation, changing the measurements from inches to millimeters.[26]

The Tu-4 represented a major technological advance for Soviet aviation. But its strategic value was relatively short-lived due to the rapid development of jet fighters and bombers in the United States. The new bomber went into service in the air force in May 1949; and when its serial production stopped in 1952, three plants had completed 847 aircraft. They included long-range bombers and reconnaissance aircraft as well as transport and passenger versions. Eighteen Tu-4As were modified to deliver the newly developed atomic bomb. This mission soon ended with the entry into service of the turbojet-powered Tu-16 in 1954. The Tu-4 posed a serious threat to American bases in Europe and the Pacific, but no real threat to the continental United States under normal use. Due to its limited range of 1,700 nautical miles on a round trip from the airbase at Anadyr in Siberia, it could not reach northern Washington State. It could attack targets in the western United States on a one-way mission, but its chances of being intercepted on a 10-hour flight by American jet fighters were very high. Despite efforts to develop aerial refueling starting in 1948, the air force achieved this capability only in 1952, when the Tu-4's strategic utility had dropped sharply.[27]

The successful reverse engineering of the B-29 had two lasting results, which to a degree offset one another. The process of manufacturing the Tu-4 substantially modernized the Soviet aviation industry. The design teams solved a number of their problems with airframe construction and automated controls. However, the new Soviet capability to strike the western United States on one-way missions stimulated American officials to take the problem of air defense seriously and thus to start construction of a radar-warning network and fighter bases to protect the lower forty-eight states.

THE QUEST FOR INTERCONTINENTAL RANGE

From the 1930s forward, Tupolev always worked on multiple airplane projects simultaneously. He focused on the overall design concepts and calculations and on solving new technological problems. Normally, the air force and occasionally Stalin himself would direct Tupolev to design an airplane for a specific mission, such as a two-engine dive bomber for combat support. From among the hundreds of specialists in his bureau, he would assign teams to work on engines, airframes, or communication and navigation systems. While an airplane was being flight-tested—or later, after it was in service with the air force—he would keep improving the design to correct problems or improve performance with a new engine or tail configuration. In the late 1940s, he designed several advanced models of his two top military aircraft: the medium-range bomber, Tu-2; and the larger, long-range bomber, Tu-4. Starting in early 1950, he began to combine features of the two types to create a medium-range bomber that would take advantage of new turbojet engines and incorporate swept-wing concepts. This plane would become the Tu-16. First flight-tested in April 1952, it had a maximum speed of 590 miles per hour, a range of 4,000 miles, and a load capacity of over 3 tons. More than 1,500 airplanes in almost fifty versions were built before production stopped in 1961. The Tu-16 was the first Soviet airplane to drop a hydrogen bomb, and it was used extensively in the conflict in Afghanistan in the 1980s.[28]

As the Tu-16 was being designed, Tupolev was already at work on a new model in the Tu-4 long-range bomber family. Less than a month after the successful test of an atomic bomb, on September 16, 1949, the government ordered Tupolev to design and construct a four-engine bomber incorporating the latest piston engines, which would be able to deliver a 5-ton load with a range of 7,500 miles. In addition to more powerful engines, the most significant changes over earlier models were increased wing length and area and a much larger fuel capacity. The initial flight test came ahead of schedule in January 1951, when the Tu-85 successfully met the government's performance requirements, showing that it was capable of delivering an atomic bomb on a US target and returning to base. The new bomber flew in the annual air show in July with Stalin's aviator son Vasili on board.[29]

Serial production of the Tu-85 had begun in March; but due to developments in the Korean War, it was abruptly stopped in November. The reason for this change was the experience gained in the battles over North Korea between Soviet MiG-15s and American B-29s. The result was reported to Stalin by the commander in chief of the Soviet Air Force, Air Marshal Pavel Zhigarev, who wrote: "In five dogfights against numerically superior enemy aircraft, the MiG-15 shot down ten American B-29 aircraft and one F-80 aircraft, and suffered no losses." He concluded that the Tu-4, based on the B-29, and the new Tu-85 were both highly vulnerable to new jet interceptors. Stalin took his advice and canceled the Tu-85. It is ironic that the ten-year Soviet effort to build a strategic bomber that could attack the United States was finally achieved only to be rendered obsolete by the rapid advance in jet interceptor engines. The quest now turned to designing a jet-powered strategic bomber.[30]

Aware of the reason for the cancellation of the Tu-85, Tupolev continued to investigate other engine designs. He explored the performance of turboprop and turbojet engines and a possible combination of the two. He concluded that turbojet engines were inferior to turboprops, while the latter were at the limit of their development and could not reach a sufficient speed to evade much lighter jet interceptors. Tupolev then wrote Stalin that his analysis of different turbojet engines showed that to reach a minimum range of 11,000 kilometers (6,820 miles), the aircraft would need to be too gigantic to fly. The dictator was not pleased with this report. He asked the aviation minister, Khrunichev, if the Tu-16, which had just completed successful flight tests, could be enlarged and with two added engines be able to reach intercontinental range. When this question was put to him, Tupolev was indignant and said he would not design such an unworkable airplane. He declared that the Tu-85 was an effective strategic bomber and could achieve greater speed when better engine technology was developed.[31]

Informed of Tupolev's refusal, Stalin asked him to explain his reasons in person. The meeting, as reported by Leonid Kerber, did not go well:

Stalin was gloomy. "Why, Comrade Tupolev, are you refusing to carry out the government's assignment and build an intercontinental jet bomber which we need greatly?" Stalin asked.

I explained that, according to our very careful calculations with existing engines it was impossible to do this, because fuel consumption was too great.

Stalin approached the table, opened a folder, removed a sheet of paper, looked it over, and put it back. "Well, there is another designer who is trying to create such an airplane. So why is it working for him, Comrade Tupolev, but not for you? That is strange!"

After waiting a bit, evidently to assess my reaction, although I was silent, he continued: "I think that we are capable of creating working conditions that are no worse for this designer than for you. That is what we will do, in all probability."

And he dismissed me with a nod of his head. I understood that he had remained extremely dissatisfied.[32]

Tupolev's bold competitor was Vladimir Miasishchev. A designer of modest achievements, fourteen years younger than Tupolev, Miasishchev had worked in the Tupolev design bureau and was in the gulag at the same time but was given his own bureau. He had been an active designer for almost a decade, but none of his aircraft had been accepted for production. "Miasishchev too often made rosy-eyed assessments of upcoming propulsion technologies and designed his aircraft around new power plants that were not yet proven," contends Steven Zaloga. "His lack of realism proved to be a fatal flaw in most of his designs." In 1946, Miasishchev lost his design bureau and was assigned to teach at the Moscow Aviation Institute. He returned in February 1951 to a concept he had worked on just after the war and submitted a proposal for a strategic bomber with four turbojet engines, a range of 7,500 miles, and a load of 5 tons. These were the very specifications the government wanted to fulfill, and it was his proposal that Stalin had mentioned to Tupolev. On March 24, the Aviation Ministry authorized Miasishchev to establish a design bureau and build the intercontinental bomber that would be designated the M-4. The ministry assigned most of his institute students and some specialists from other bureaus to work with Miasishchev, and within weeks he had 1,500 engineers and workers in his bureau.[33]

Miasishchev and his team created an elegant, streamlined design for the M-4. It had swept wings, and the engines were built into the wings rather than hanging as pods below them. The first test flight came in January 1953, and it revealed multiple problems that required correction. The modified version of the bomber had rigorous tests from May through July 1954 and performed well—except for its range. The problem again was with the turbojet engines, which were very heavy and consumed fuel at a high rate. As a result, its maximum range was 6,000 miles—enough to reach targets in the western United States, but not sufficient to return to base. Eager to have a long-range jet bomber, however, the Soviet leadership put the M-4 into production despite its inadequate range. The new bomber appeared in the 1954 May Day parade, and it greatly impressed Western military attachés when a squadron of ten M-4s flew in the air show of July 1954.

Based on reports from US attachés and other intelligence, the CIA estimated in 1957 that the Soviet Union would have 400 to 600 heavy bombers by 1960. The designers improved the M-4 by 1957 with more powerful engines and in-flight refueling capability, which enabled it to achieve a range of 9,000 miles with two in-flight refuelings. It had finally fulfilled the original air force specifications, yet serious problems remained with the airplane. Of the thirty-five M-4s produced, six crashed and the rest were mainly used for in-flight refueling of other aircraft. In the meantime, Tupolev had been working to overcome problems with a new design that could fill the need for a reliable intercontinental bomber (see figure 13.1).[34]

FIGURE 13.1 Andrei N. Tupolev, the Soviet airplane designer, with a model of the Tu-95, his most successful long-range bomber, October 11, 1969.

BUILDING THE TU-95

Even though Stalin had accepted Miasishchev's plan for a turbojet bomber, Tupolev continued to analyze the government's basic specifications for a strategic bomber. Convinced that the available turbojet engines could not achieve intercontinental range, he carefully examined the performance of recently created turboprop engines, which are a jet turbine driving a conventional propeller. The NK-6 engine developed by N. D. Kuznetsov was promising but not powerful enough. Because the government had demanded rapid progress on the new bomber, Kuznetsov and his propulsion team designed a radical solution. As described by Kerber, their proposal was as follows: "Two NK-6 engines would be installed in each of the four engine nacelles on the first experimental airplane. Each engine in the pair would use common reduction gearing to drive not a single common propeller, but two coaxial, counterrotating propellers with a slightly smaller diameter." For the airframe, Tupolev modified the Tu-85 plans to accommodate greater range and load and incorporated a swept-wing design, which had been successful in the Tu-16.

With the design completed, Tupolev submitted his proposal for a new turboprop bomber to the Aviation Ministry. Because the creation of an intercontinental bomber was so critical to government plans, and because some aviation specialists shared Tupolev's analysis of the limitations of the M-4 turbojets' engines, the Council of Ministers approved Tupolev's strategic bomber project on July 11, 1951. The first prototype of the Tu-95 was completed in the fall of 1952 and had its initial test flight in November. This flight and others went well under various conditions, but a tragic crash in the spring of 1953 showed that the new engine had a serious defect.[35]

During a flight on May 11, 1953, the pilot reported a fire in engine number three and declared that he had ordered the crew to bail out. Four of the eleven crew members, including the pilot and the chief engineer, died in the crash. An examination of the damaged engine revealed that the reduction gear pinion, which transmitted the engine output to the propellers, had been made of metal that was too weak. It broke, and fragments started an oil leak, which caused the fire that engulfed the wing. Further investigation found that the manufacturing plant had used the wrong type of metal for the pinion. With the bomber being a high strategic priority, Stalin had once again placed its construction under Beria's supervision. The security chief called in the lead test engineer, an old Communist Party member, and said: "Help us figure this out. A strange bunch has gathered around Tupolev. The surnames alone tell you something: Yeger, Stoman, Minkner, Kerber, Val'ter, Saukke. . . . A nest of Germans and Jews. And notice: not a single Communist. Perhaps that is the explanation for the disaster?" He ordered his party comrade to keep a close eye on his team and write down everything that looked suspicious. According to Kerber, the test engineer reported this conversation to Tupolev and the senior members of the bureau, and thereafter ignored Beria's instructions. But the burden of NKVD suspicion weighed on the team. It took Tupolev two months to win approval of the report on the cause of the crash. Only then could the members get back to fully concentrating on building a new prototype with a significantly stronger reduction gear pinion.[36]

After the crash report was accepted, the Tu-95 went through over four years of modifications and tests before it was accepted into service by the air force. Much of the attention focused on the safety and performance of the engines, and every component of the airplane was thoroughly checked and changed if necessary. The next flight test came in February 1955, and it was generally successful. Tests by the manufacturers and by a government commission led to more refinements until August 1956. Flight tests showed good handling and performance, but the availability of a more powerful engine caused further delay as new turboprops were installed and tested. Finally, in August 1957, the new version—designated Tu-95M—successfully completed its flight tests. It achieved a top speed of 562 miles per hour and a range of 8,200 miles, thereby satisfying the government's performance requirements. The next month, the approved Tu-95M was accepted into service. A nuclear-capable model of the new bomber was created in a few months. It had a heated and air-conditioned bomb bay; an antiflash, white-painted fuselage and underwing surfaces; and a cockpit transparency visor. These new versions were designated Tu-95A and Tu-95MA. Other models were developed for special missions, such as antisubmarine warfare and long-range reconnaissance. Production of the Tu-95 continued until 1959 and totaled 175 aircraft of all types.[37]

"The USSR now had a first-rate strategic bomber able to deliver nuclear weapons," conclude the aviation historians Yefim Gordon and Vladimir Rigmant. "For forty years it served as the basis for bombers, long-range reconnaissance aircraft, over-the-horizon targeting aircraft and a whole series of missile carriers." From a Western perspective, the remarkable aspect of building the Tu-95 is that it could be accomplished under constant police supervision and suspicion and with inferior technology in electronics, computers, and metallurgy. The success of Tupolev's bureau is a tribute to his vision, pragmatism, and mental toughness—as well as his leadership in a treacherous bureaucratic environment. His engineer colleagues and their support staff also deserve high praise for their professionalism and loyalty.[38]

In Washington, intelligence officials continued to forecast a large Soviet strategic bomber threat by mid-1959. On April 18, 1956, CIA director Allen Dulles testified in executive session before the Subcommittee of the Air Force of the Senate Armed Services Committee, chaired by Senator Stuart Symington (D-MO). He described in detail the combined estimate of the military services and the CIA, saying: "Currently, we estimate that Soviet long-range aviation has at its disposal more than 1,000 bombers." He contended that "the Soviets are psychologically capable of undertaking one-way missions if required," adding that "inflight refueling is well within Soviet capabilities." In an off-the-record section not contained in the executive session text but available in an earlier draft of April 13, he estimated that by mid-1959, the Soviet long-range bomber fleet would contain 700 Tu-16s, 400 M-4s, and 300 Tu-95s. American analysts clearly had no knowledge of the problems facing the M-4 and the Tu-95 or how few bombers the Soviet air force actually possessed. Although the Tu-95 had excellent range and was very reliable once problems with its engines were resolved, it was relatively slow, at 560 miles per hour. And for an attack from long range against the United States, the Tu-95 would need to fly at a considerably reduced cruising speed to conserve fuel.[39]

Ironically, as a result of its exaggerated estimates of the Soviet bomber threat, the United States developed substantial air defenses by the time the Soviet Union had an operational force of reliable Tu-95s in the late 1950s. American jet interceptors had supersonic speed and were armed with missiles that could strike from outside the range of the bombers' defensive cannon. The Eisenhower administration had established a network of early warning radar towers across Canada and the northern United States, stationed fighter squadrons along likely flight paths, and deployed surface-to-air missiles around key cities. At the cost of billions of dollars, the United States had created an air defense system to neutralize Andrei Tupolev's outdated bomber force.[40]

14

CURTIS LeMAY BUILDS THE STRATEGIC AIR COMMAND

As had been the practice after all American wars, once peace returned in 1945, the Truman administration implemented a rapid and disorganized demobilization. Over the protests of some senior officers, the civilian leadership paid little attention to the retention in the military services of a minimum core of skilled officers and senior enlisted men. This was especially the case in the Army Air Forces (AAF), which dropped sharply—from 2,253,000 men in August 1945 to 303,000 in May 1947. This reduction in force was reflected in the decline from 218 combat-ready groups to only 2 by March 1946. Although the United States would not be firmly committed to an atomic strategy until Truman's decision to build the H-bomb in January 1950, the AAF planned for such a strategy starting in 1946, and shaped its organization to implement an atomic war plan. Based on a study proposing an "atomic strike force" as the principal element of the air force, the new AAF chief of staff, General Carl Spaatz, ordered a reorganization of the forces in March 1946, including the Strategic Air Command (SAC) as the largest of the three combat commands. At the same time, proponents of air power had been working to win independence for the air force. This was accomplished with the signing of the National Security Act on July 26, 1947, which created three executive departments for the army, navy, and air force under a secretary of defense with limited powers.[1]

In the two years after it was established, SAC made little progress toward becoming an effective atomic strike force. Its first commander, General George C. Kenney, had aspired to be deputy chief of staff, but General Spaatz assigned him to SAC. As a consolation prize, Kenney was designated as the commander of the projected "International Air Force," to be developed by the United Nations, a project that fell victim to the emerging Cold War. Kenney's new command was the most prominent of the combat commands, with an authorized strength of 84,000 men and 1,300 aircraft, including 221 B-29s. But at the start of 1947, SAC was only at half strength in manpower and had 270 assigned aircraft, including 148 B-29s. As for its atomic strike mission, SAC possessed only 22 Silverplate (atomic capable) B-29s and lacked any access to the nuclear weapons or training in their assembly, both controlled by the new Atomic Energy Commission. The Soviet challenge posed by the Berlin Blockade underlined the need for SAC, but sufficient airplanes and experienced navigators and mechanics were not available. By the middle of 1948, with Cold War tensions increasing, SAC's readiness for combat was poor, a fact noted by a number of senior officers.[2]

SAC CHANGES COURSE

In April 1948, General Hoyt S. Vandenberg became air force chief of staff. From earlier service as the second director of the CIA, he had thought broadly about US strategy in dealing with a potential Soviet threat. After returning to the air force as deputy chief of staff, he had written the study proposing an "atomic strike force" to General Spaatz. Now as chief, with the Soviets placing restrictions on travel to West Berlin and aware of reports of poor readiness at SAC, Vandenberg sent special representatives to investigate his primary command. His personnel deputy examined staffing levels, training, and morale at numerous bases and reported in August that conditions were unsatisfactory—with high turnover, inadequate training for primary assignments, and emphasis on peacetime priorities rather than combat readiness. At a time of increased international tension, he concluded that the command was not adequately prepared. Asked to inspect SAC headquarters in Omaha, Colonel Paul W. Tibbets, who had been the pilot of the *Enola Gay* on its atomic bomb mission over Hiroshima and was a legendary figure in the air force, told the chief of staff that the headquarters was disorganized and the air crews were unprepared for their mission. Years later, he told interviewers that he had said: "There isn't anybody out there that knows what the hell they are doing. The crews don't know how to fly an airplane. The staff officers don't know what they are doing."[3]

To win credibility in the air force and beyond, Vandenberg asked his old friend Charles A. Lindberg, the famous aviator who flew the first nonstop transatlantic flight from New York to Paris, to thoroughly investigate SAC's operational readiness. A colonel in the air force reserve, Lindberg was widely respected for his aviation expertise and his commitment to public service. He had flown fifty combat missions with the AAF in the South Pacific in World War II and served as a consultant to the air force on aircraft and missile development after the war. He devoted ten weeks to his inspection tour and flew 100 hours with SAC crews. He reported his critical evaluation to Vandenberg on September 14. He began his findings with the general conclusion that the training and performance standards of World War II air forces were "inadequate for the specialized atomic forces we have today." On specific issues, he declared that "the personnel for atomic squadrons were not carefully enough selected, the average pilot's proficiency is unsatisfactory, teamwork is not properly developed, and maintenance of aircraft and equipment is inadequate. In general, personnel are not sufficiently experienced in their mission." He recommended that higher priority be devoted to making SAC a truly elite command, with the "highest-quality personnel," creation of integral crews with minimum turnover, and intensive training on realistic wartime missions emphasizing their primary mission as the nation's principal retaliatory force.[4]

The day after Lindbergh delivered his report to Vandenberg, General Kenney was scheduled to brief the joint chiefs on SAC and atomic preparedness. Kenney—who was known to have spent much of his time away from SAC headquarters making speeches about the importance of air power—gave a rambling presentation, appearing poorly prepared and uninformed. Immediately after the meeting, Lieutenant General Lauris Norstad, Vandenberg's trusted vice chief of staff, declared that it was critical to replace Kenney. Asked who he would suggest, Norstad posed a question of his own: Who would you want commanding SAC if we found ourselves at war tomorrow? Without hesitation, Vandenberg responded: LeMay! On September 21, Vandenberg called General Kenney to his office and relieved him of command. After official papers were prepared, Lieutenant General Curtis LeMay was appointed commander of SAC on October 19, 1948.[5]

When he was appointed, LeMay knew that SAC was unprepared for combat and had pursued the wrong priorities. His orders from General Vandenberg were simple and direct: Get your command ready to fight the day war breaks out. To achieve this level of readiness would demand complete change in training, equipment maintenance, discipline, and operational planning. To help manage the transformation of SAC, LeMay removed all the top staff in the command. Explaining his abrupt firing of so many senior officers, he brusquely declared: "We don't have time to distinguish between the unfortunate and the incompetent." He brought in trusted combat veterans who had worked closely with him in the South Pacific. In little time, he orchestrated the transfer to SAC of Brigadier General Thomas S. Power to be his vice commander, Brigadier General John B. Montgomery as operations chief, Brigadier General Walter Sweeney as director of plans, and Brigadier General August W. Kissner as chief of staff.[6]

Arriving at Offutt Air Force Base outside Omaha with his staff in November, LeMay found a poorly equipped airfield with a steeply sloping runway and an empty factory for his headquarters. But he was not very upset because he knew he would not be spending very much time at this base. SAC currently had 52,000 personnel, including 5,562 officers, and its men and aircraft were spread over twenty-one bases across the mainland United States. (See table 14.1 for a year-by-year overview of SAC's personnel and bases from 1946 to 1954.) Living conditions for the airmen and their families were often described as "genteel poverty." They lacked adequate housing, good schools for their children, and the

TABLE 14.1 Number of Personnel and Bases under the US
Strategic Air Command, 1946–54

Year	Officers	Enlisted	Civilians	Total	Active Bases
1946	4,319	27,871	4,903	37,093	18 CONUS
1947	5,175	39,307	5,107	49,589	16 CONUS
1948	5,562	40,038	6,365	51,965	21 CONUS
1949	10,050	53,460	7,980	71,490	17 CONUS
1950	10,600	66,000	8,273	85,473	19 CONUS /1 OS
1951	19,747	113,224	11,554	144,525	22 CONUS /11 OS
1952	20,282	134,072	11,667	166,021	26 CONUS /10 OS
1953	19,994	138,782	12,256	170,982	29 CONUS /10 OS
1954	23,447	151,466	14,193	189,106	30 CONUS /11 OS

Note: CONUS = continental United States; OS = overseas.

Source: Phillip S. Meilinger, *The Formation and Early Years of the Strategic Air Command, 1946–1957: Why the SAC Was Formed* (Lewiston, NY: Edwin Mellen Press, 2013), 339.

health and recreational benefits available to civilians in comparable jobs. Experienced pilots and mechanics, for example, could earn ten times the salary in commercial aviation as in the air force, and they worked fewer hours and were not away from home for months at a time. Training for pilots and aircrews was limited and unrealistic. Bombing tests were done at low altitude because pilots found their oxygen masks uncomfortable, and their radar frequently malfunctioned at combat altitudes of 30,000 feet. Tests were scheduled during daylight, using reflector targets for easy visual identification. Gunnery test scores were fudged upward to improve reports. Aircraft maintenance was poor, and many planes could not fly. When they did fly, the accident rate was unacceptably high. Discipline was lax, and pilots were urged to take an airplane on a long weekend jaunt to visit a girlfriend or a sick relative in order to use all the unit's fuel allotment.[7]

From earlier inspection reports and his own observations, LeMay knew that conditions at SAC were as bad as any he had seen in his military career. Yet the officers and men thought they were excellent at their jobs. The new commander devised a simple but devastating test to show them how broken the designated strike force was. It came to be known throughout the air force as the Dayton Exercise.

Without notice, LeMay walked into his office early one morning in January 1949 and directed his operations chief, John Montgomery, to organize a night attack by the entire command on Wright Field in Dayton. All 556 bombers in the command were to fly from around the country to "electronically" bomb military and industrial targets near Wright Field. Radar operators at Wright Field could track each simulated bomb and determine its accuracy. The planes were to fly at 30,000 feet, and crews were given photographs of their target area from 1938 to approximate the inadequate intelligence they would have vis-à-vis Soviet targets. They would not find any reflector targets on their mission. The results were predictably poor. Many bombers did not get off the ground; others had engine or radar malfunctions and turned back; some got lost and had to divert to other air bases. Of the aircraft that completed bombing runs, their accuracy was terrible, with their "bombs" missing their targets by 1 to 2 miles. In his memoirs, LeMay calls this exercise "just about the darkest night in American aviation history. Not one airplane finished the mission as briefed. *Not one.*"[8]

LeMay's statement to his command after this debacle was not to launch a tirade. He simply said: "I've been telling you you were in bad shape. We are in bad shape. Now let's get busy and get this fixed." Now that he had their full attention, the instruction could begin.[9]

What qualities persuaded US Air Force leaders that Curtis LeMay was the right man to transform SAC?

IRON ASS

On the basis of his background and education, no recruiter looking for a prospective talented military commander would have selected the twenty-two-year-old LeMay. He was stout and of average height. He looked forbidding, smiled infrequently, and often spoke with a snarl.

He possessed no social graces, came from a poor family, and had no political connections. He was not a West Point man, had poor grades as a civil engineer, and had lacked a few credits to graduate from Ohio State. Yet, as a recent biographer asserts, he became "the youngest and longest-serving general in modern American history." Another flatly declares "that in the minds of most military experts, General Curtis E. LeMay is the greatest air commander the United States has yet produced."[10]

Curtis was born in Columbus, Ohio, in 1906, the oldest of six children in a poverty-ridden family. His father was a steelworker and laborer who left school after the eighth grade and had trouble holding a job, which led the family to move to first Montana, then California, then Pennsylvania, and eventually back to Columbus. His mother was the resourceful anchor of the family; she managed what money they had, and created a supportive home life for her children. With his father often away from home looking for work, by the age of eight Curtis was "the responsible male" in the family. He worked hard at school, and to earn money he started a paper route and did odd jobs for neighbors. While in Montana, he learned to hunt with his father and made a nickel a bird killing sparrows for a neighbor's indolent cat with a borrowed BB gun. As a teenager, his interests were more in engines, electronics, and hunting than in what he called "the girl stuff." Most important, he continued to feed the ambition to become an army pilot, an interest initially sparked at age four when he chased the first airplane he saw across yards and fields in Columbus.[11]

In 1924, LeMay entered Ohio State to study civil engineering, and to pursue his dream of becoming a pilot, he joined the Army ROTC. He lived at home to save money, and also to supervise his younger brother and sisters when his parents were frequently away from home for work. To help pay expenses, he worked at a steel casting plant from 5 P.M. until 3 A.M. six days a week. The job paid well, but it proved costly to his studies because he slept through too many early classes to keep a good grade average. He did excel in his ROTC courses and was an honor graduate of the program. In his senior year, he focused on how to win an appointment in the Army Air Corps. As a result of the massive publicity surrounding Charles Lindbergh's solo flight to Paris the previous year, 3,000 young men were applying for only 100 positions in flight school. He learned that just 25 of those accepted were likely to complete the course and become pilots. Analyzing the selection process like an engineer, he found out that his commission as an ROTC honor graduate would give him extra points in the rating scheme. And being a member of the National Guard would add substantially more points. He immediately joined the National Guard and completed his application for the air corps. His strategy worked, and he was accepted as a flying cadet before the autumn college registration closed, so he decided to leave Ohio State a few credits short of his degree requirements. Four years later, when stationed in Ohio, he would complete his degree as a means of improving his qualifications for promotion. He was steadily improving the skills needed to operate successfully in a large bureaucracy.[12]

The US Army that Curtis LeMay entered in the autumn of 1928 was small and poorly funded. It was dominated by West Point graduates, most of whom served in the infantry or artillery branches. The primary mission of the air corps was support of the ground forces, not strategic bombing. Promotions came slowly, and the pay and benefits were modest. But after the economic crash of 1929, military officers appreciated having a steady job. LeMay showed an aptitude for flying and worked hard to master piloting skills and understand the rapidly evolving technology of aircraft design. After completing basic and advanced flight school courses, he was assigned to a pursuit squadron at Selfridge Field northeast of Detroit. He spent several years on routine assignments, and in 1933 he received an important opportunity to attend a new course on celestial navigation. Before this time, pilots had navigated by visual means—following highways, railroads, and rivers at low altitudes. LeMay understood at once the advantages of flying by instruments, which allowed operations at night and in bad weather, and he worked intensely to become one of the air corps' top navigators.[13]

Not long after completing his navigation course, LeMay took ten days leave in June 1934 to get married. His bride-to-be was Helen Maitland, the daughter of a successful Cleveland attorney and a direct descendant of Mary, Queen of Scots. They had met on a blind date three years earlier, when Helen was a student at the University of Michigan, and they had seen one another intermittently over the intervening period. They were married in a High Church Mass in an Episcopal Church, which made Curtis very uncomfortable, but which his bride wanted. They would make a strong, loving couple. "Helen was the perfect foil for Curtis's lack of social grace," argues his biographer, Warren Kozak. "She was extremely capable and loved to entertain. Her personality could fill a room just as his could darken it. . . . LeMay was devoted to her."[14]

During the next few years, LeMay used his assignments to master the skills that would put him at the cutting edge of an air corps destined to expand dramatically in wartime. A few weeks after his wedding, he received orders to go to Wheeler Field in Hawaii, where the new couple would spend two enjoyable years. While there, Curtis worked on his instrument navigation over water and ran a school on the subject for other pilots. Aware that the Army Air Corps had placed an order for a highly innovative long-range bomber, he calculated that in any future war, bombers would be the principal aviation weapon and would have the most resources. Wanting to work with the latest technology and advance his career, he requested to be transferred to a bomber squadron for his next post. His request was honored, and early in 1937 First Lieutenant LeMay arrived at Langley Field in Virginia to become the operations officer of a bomber squadron.[15]

This assignment proved doubly rewarding for LeMay's career. His new squadron was the only one in the air corps to be equipped with the new B-17 bomber. Quickly named the Flying Fortress for its five heavy machine guns and large bomb capacity, this new four-engine bomber reflected a huge advance in aircraft design. It flew higher and faster than any bomber in the world, carried a larger bomb load, and was sturdy while requiring less maintenance than any other plane at that time. But in its initial flight competition with two rival designs, the prototype B-17 crashed as a result of pilot error. Despite the air corps' pleas to continue a large order for B-17s, the ground soldiers who controlled the army budget selected a less-capable medium-range bomber that would be suitable for infantry support, not a strategic bomber. They placed a large order for a cheaper two-engine bomber and reluctantly approved a small order for thirteen B-17s to be used for further evaluation. LeMay would be in the vanguard of the group demonstrating how effective the B-17 could actually be.[16]

The second major benefit for LeMay from his Langley years was the opportunity to work closely with Lieutenant Colonel Robert Olds, a highly effective commander and a persuasive advocate of strategic bombing. From Olds, he learned how to be a strong leader who delegated responsibility, held his men accountable for good results, and rewarded those who performed well. Even more important were Olds's demand for a constant state of readiness for war and his insistence on personally leading his men on all important operations. These were policies that LeMay would adopt and refine as he advanced through his own commands. Bob Olds was the mentor LeMay needed at this stage of his career.[17]

With storm clouds rising in Europe and Asia in the late 1930s, air power advocates believed it was time to move beyond their role as a supporting arm for infantry forces. Olds had served on the staff of Brigadier General Billy Mitchell in the 1920s and had completely accepted his doctrine that air power would decide the outcome of the next major war. Now that he commanded a squadron of high performance B-17s, Olds wanted to demonstrate to the army and navy leadership as well as to the public the reach and power of strategic bombing. To achieve this, he organized a number of long flights and dramatic exercises for his unit, with himself as task force commander and LeMay as chief navigator.

The first exercise was a search-and-attack competition with the navy in August 1937. The challenge was structured for the navy to announce the position of the battleship USS *Utah* in the Pacific somewhere between Los Angeles and San Francisco and for the air corps, with a flight of eight B-17s, to locate the ship and attack it with water bombs within a 24-hour limit. On the initial attempt, Olds and LeMay could not find the battleship. LeMay calculated his navigation data again and was confident he had the right coordinates. When Olds pressed the navy for more details on the ship's location, he was told they had made a mistake of 1 degree in its announced position. This was a serious error, because 1 degree in celestial navigation equaled 60 miles of water. The air corps demanded a second test, and this time the B-17s found the *Utah* and hit it several times with their practice bombs. They also succeeded on a third attempt. Olds and his colleagues were elated by their demonstration that the air corps could defend the United States against attack from the sea. But this public relations victory was snatched away when the navy immediately classified all reports and photographs of the exercise. They were still classified when LeMay sought to use them for his memoirs twenty-seven years later. Ironically, the USS *Utah* was attacked from the air by the Japanese and sunk at Pearl Harbor on December 7, 1941, with the loss of fifty-eight lives.[18]

When the navy suppressed any publicity of the results of the USS *Utah* competition, air corps leaders decided to conduct their own public relations campaign. They approved a high-profile flight of six B-17s under Olds's command to Argentina to honor the inauguration of a new president in February 1938. The mission promised to generate significant publicity, but it also involved large risks. No crew had ever flown such long distances over water or operated for long periods at altitudes of 12,000 feet in aircraft that were not pressurized. The army had no maps of South America, and the Andes Mountains had not been fully charted, so LeMay had to rely on maps from the National Geographic Society and Pan-American Airways for his navigation. During the flight, LeMay and others realized that they were fatigued and inefficient due to oxygen deficiency, and they learned to use their oxygen tanks regularly to keep alert. The mission was a huge success. They flew nonstop without incident for 15 hours from Miami to Lima; and after their appearance in Buenos Aires, all the aircraft returned with no serious mechanical problems. During the next two years, Olds and LeMay made equally successful flights to Brazil and Colombia, perfecting their high-altitude performance and navigation skills each time. These trips won great public interest at each stop and created positive media coverage at home.

The most dramatic of the air corps' missions was an attempt in May 1938 to intercept the Italian luxury liner *Rex* over 600 miles at sea bound for New York. A team from NBC Radio was aboard Olds's plane broadcasting the search live. The widely read military correspondent of the *New York Times*, Hanson Baldwin, was also on the plane. Despite a huge storm on the scheduled day, air crews took off, knowing only the liner's course and approximate speed. LeMay predicted they would locate the

Rex at 12:25 P.M. if it was on course. Just before noon, they hit a large cold front and experienced heavy rain, very low visibility, and high turbulence. As the sighting time approached, they emerged from the clouds into a clear sky, and there was the *Rex*, exactly as predicted. The mission won extensive praise, and LeMay was proclaimed the top navigator in the air corps. In a broader context, columnists noted that at a time of Germany's annexation of Austria and Japan's full-scale war against China, the United States had shown it had an unmatched capability for long-range operations with its B-17 bombers. But Baldwin reported in a front-page article that, though the air corps had made "rapid strides in the last three years," it had too few airplanes to defend the country and no experience coordinating the flights of large numbers of aircraft.[19]

As Europe fell into total war in the months after the German invasion of Poland in September 1939, the United States slowly increased its military strength. This process involved major changes for LeMay. Production of B-17s rapidly expanded, and the number of bomber groups grew. The air corps received its first shipment of the secret Norden bombsight, which used an ingenious combination of gears, ball bearings, and gyroscopes to calculate the parabolic trajectory of bombs and made bombing much more accurate. As the operations officer for his squadron, LeMay spent hours mastering the new bombsight, which would become one of the key elements of American bombing success in the approaching conflict. Early in 1940, LeMay was promoted to captain and could now reach his cherished assignment as a B-17 pilot. There were family advances as well. The previous year, he and Helen had become the parents of a greatly desired baby girl, who was named Janie. Although his responsibilities were expanding, Curtis spent as much time with his family as possible. For much of 1941, he was involved in supporting Britain's desperate struggle against German air attacks. He spent several months ferrying new B-24 medium-range bombers from Canada to British bases. Later, he devoted several weeks to helping establish a new air route to Africa via Brazil to deliver supplies and weapons to British forces in Egypt. In May, he received another promotion, to major. After laboring as a lieutenant for eleven years, he vaulted from captain to major in fourteen months.[20]

After Pearl Harbor, the United States had to prepare for war on two fronts. Washington promptly declared war on Japan; and three days later, the Fascist leaders of Germany and Italy declared war on the United States. Germany and Italy were tied to Japan by the Tripartite Treaty, but this alliance required them to go to war only if any party was attacked by another state. For over a year, the United States and Germany had been engaged in an undeclared war over the American convoys of supplies going to Britain, and the Axis powers' decision clarified the legal situation and helped Franklin Roosevelt overcome his problem with isolationists in the United States. But in strategic terms, Hitler's impulsive decision for war with the United States is widely viewed as a major blunder—equal to his ill-fated invasion of the Soviet Union.[21]

The outbreak of war brought immense changes for the US Army Air Forces, as the service was now called. During the early months of 1942, the military recruited and drafted millions of young men and formed and started training new units, while factories worked overtime producing uniforms, trucks, packaged food, and weapons. There were big changes for LeMay as well. He was promoted to lieutenant colonel in January, and he took command of the 305th Bomb Group outside Salt Lake City in May. He had only three B-17s to train thirty-five air crews and only three pilots, including him, who knew how to fly these planes. His new pilots, navigators, and bombardiers had received only minimal training. Overall, he described his new group as "a raggle-taggle gypsy crowd." Using contacts in Washington, he brought into his unit several skilled specialists with whom he had previously worked to take charge of training pilots, managing supplies of ammunition and bombs, and ground support and maintenance. With this core of experienced staff officers, he instituted a 24-hour training schedule to prepare his men for early combat.[22]

For six months, LeMay's group trained as hard as their limited number of aircraft would allow in Utah and at an even more primitive base in the Mojave Desert in California. As new pilots and navigators joined the 305th Bomb Group, Major Joe Preston, the lead pilot instructor, advised them on how to deal with their gruff, taciturn commander: "When he gives you an assignment, get it right the first time. When he asks a question, get to the point. He doesn't want to hear any bullshit. . . . Performance is the beginning and the end for him. He's fair, but tough as nails." In this period, his men settled on a nickname for LeMay: "Iron Ass." It stuck, but was never uttered in his presence.

When the unit received orders in August to transfer to England, new pilots were still arriving from basic training, and the group had only four B-17s. They moved across the country to Syracuse to prepare for combat. Among the tasks occupying the staff was searching all over New England to find cold weather clothing to deal with temperatures that could reach 40 degrees below zero in the unheated B-17s at 20,000 feet. While in Syracuse, LeMay received a shock when he was diagnosed with Bell's Palsy, a partial paralysis of the right side of his face that made him look as if he were sneering. To disguise this appearance, he began to keep an unlighted cigar in the right corner of his mouth, a habit that enhanced his image as a tough character. By late October, the group had received and prepared its full complement of bombers and began to make the arduous trip across the North Atlantic.[23]

LeMay's unit flew its first combat mission just a month after leaving Syracuse. At their air base in England, they learned about the large losses suffered by British and American bombers as a result of deadly defenses put up by German fighters and antiaircraft artillery. Heavy casualties had convinced the British to restrict their air attacks to saturation bombing of cities at night. The commanders of the US Eighth Air Force wanted to concentrate on military targets with greater precision, and this approach required daytime bombing. When heavy antiaircraft fire, known as flak, caused a high level of lost aircraft, the Americans adopted zig-zag bombing runs to diminish damage. But this adjustment led to sharply reduced bombing accuracy.[24]

LeMay pondered these problems while talking to flight commanders and studying reconnaissance photos. Breaking down the issues into components, he concluded that fighter damage could be reduced by adopting a very tight bomber formation shaped in a wedge, with three squadrons of six or seven aircraft above or beside each other, to give clear lines of fire to each plane's set of nine powerful .50 caliber machine guns. Reports about the poor accuracy of zig-zag bombing runs disturbed

LeMay. He instinctively believed that it defeated the purpose of strategic bombing to place the safety of the crew and airplane above the mission of destroying the enemy's military capacity. One night, lying awake in his cot, an idea from his ROTC artillery class brought him upright. He found his old textbook in his footlocker and sat down to calculate how many rounds a German 88-millimeter battery would need to fire to hit a B-17-sized target at 25,000 feet. He found it would take 372 rounds and estimated that the guns could not fire that rapidly against an airplane flying 250 miles an hour. This led him to the conclusion that a tight wedge formation taking a straight and level bombing run could achieve much greater accuracy plus absorb less damage from flak. When he briefed his air crews on this new approach before their first combat mission, their reaction was stunned silence. Finally, a young pilot declared that he feared this tactic would be suicidal. LeMay response was a calm and supremely confident assertion that this *would* work, and that he was piloting the lead plane.[25]

On November 23, 1942, twenty bombers of the 305th Bomb Group launched their first combat mission against railroad yards and submarine pens in Saint Nazaire on the coast of Brittany. They achieved phenomenal success, greater than their commander had dared to hope. The B-17s spent a full 7 minutes on their straight and level bombing run and delivered twice as many bombs on target as any previous raid. Two aircraft were shot down by fighters on their route to Saint Nazaire, but none were lost to flak. Four other US bomb groups participated in this raid, and they had more planes shot down and much less bombing accuracy than LeMay with his innovative tactics. The air force was a young service, and strategic bombing was a completely new form of warfare. There was no rigid doctrine, and new approaches were welcomed. As a result, the senior commanders analyzed the results, and within two weeks the entire Eighth Air Force adopted LeMay's new tactics. This approach became known in the service as "the LeMay Doctrine."[26]

As he wrestled with the problem of how to attack German military targets effectively with as few casualties as possible, LeMay crystallized his ideas on the conduct of war. He believed that the top military leaders needed to analyze the situation carefully before recommending that the nation go to war. Political leaders held the ultimate responsibility to decide to declare war and should be very conscious of the costs involved and of their duty to provide the resources to fight it. Military commanders had the task of organizing and using the men and equipment they had as efficiently as possible to destroy the enemy's capacity and will to fight. Field commanders like him had to implement the plans and prepare the men for combat. They had to accept the fact that many lives would be lost and bodies would be damaged. Hard decisions would be necessary. But if the troops were rigorously trained and the mission were well designed and effectively executed, the conflict would be shorter, and many lives would be saved in the end. This tough, pragmatic approach to war would be refined through combat operations against Germany and Japan and would remain the core of LeMay's thinking on national security and the conduct of war.[27]

The way LeMay implemented his ideas is persuasively described by a close colleague in combat. Ralph Nutter was a student at Harvard Law School when he heard about the Japanese attack on Pearl Harbor. He left school and enlisted the next day, went to flight school, and became a navigator in the 305th Bomb Group. On the group's second mission over Germany, the navigator for the lead bomber got lost on the way back to base, and LeMay radioed all his aircraft, demanding, "Does anyone know where the hell we are?" Nutter knew, and he directed the group safely back to England. From then on, he became LeMay's lead navigator as a second lieutenant and remained by his side in Europe and later in the Pacific. Nutter explains how LeMay led his unit: "He analyzed every combat problem as an engineer. He considered every combat mission as if it were an engine with component parts, which had to mesh and interact perfectly. LeMay not only analyzed the performance of our crewmembers, the aircraft, and engines, but he studied the bombsights, armament, bomb trajectories, and bomb characteristics. He attempted to balance the cost and calculate the price of each mission. Those of us who flew with him knew that his rigid discipline and rigorous training program saved many lives." Nutter became a California Superior Court judge and was a lifelong liberal. He remained a great admirer and stout defender of his wartime boss.[28]

LeMay played an increasingly central role in the air war against Germany for almost two years before he was transferred to deal with another set of intractable problems in the Pacific theater. The Eighth Air Force faced difficult combat conditions. German fighter defenses and antiaircraft fire imposed severe losses as the American air arm grew from its start in February 1942 to a formidable force of 185,000 men and 4,000 aircraft by December 1943. At this point, more airplanes and new crews were arriving in England than the Nazis were destroying. By the time of the Normandy invasion in June 1944, German fighters had been swept from the skies, leaving Allied bombers greater freedom to operate. The leading British scholar of the air war, Richard Overy, concludes that Allied strategic bombing neutralized one-quarter of the German war economy and killed 350,000 civilians. Overall, the US combat losses in the air war against Germany were 18,400 aircraft, 30,000 dead, 13,000 wounded, and 51,000 missing or captured.[29]

During his remaining months as commander of the 305th Bomb Group, LeMay developed several new policies to improve the performance and morale of his men. After every mission, he had each crew sit for a debriefing with an intelligence officer. He moved from table to table, listening, asking questions, and seeking suggestions on how to achieve better results. He asked his officers and sergeants to identify men who were lazy, frozen with fear, or just stupid—a small group he called "no-goods"—and he had them transferred or removed from the air force. He had no tolerance for men who were ineffective or disruptive. "LeMay used to say," Ralph Nutter recalls, "whoever can't cut it or didn't like it here could always go to the infantry." Pleased with the performance of Nutter as his lead navigator, he made it a general policy to place his best navigator, bombardier, or gunner as the leader of their specialists on each mission to study the routes to and features of future targets. These policies—along with frequent training and his firm, hands-on leadership style—brought top results in bombing accuracy with minimal losses of aircraft and crews. With the air force expanding significantly, LeMay's success brought rapid promotions. In May 1943, he was promoted to colonel and became a wing commander in charge of four bomber groups. A month later, he moved up to division commander;

and with his promotion to brigadier general in September, he became the youngest general in the entire army at the age of thirty-six. To his dismay, his rise in command authority led his boss, the commanding general of the Eighth Air Force, to ground the new general as too valuable to be risked leading bombing raids.[30]

With the air war in Europe clearly on a path to victory, the air force needed LeMay for another big job. Recognized as his service's "most innovative problem solver," he was pulled out of Europe shortly after the successful Normandy invasion. Promoted to major general in March 1944, he returned to the United States at the end of June to prepare for the final push against Japan. The air force's chief of staff, General Henry H. "Hap" Arnold, personally chose the new two-star general to lead the Twentieth Air Force based in India. He gave LeMay a specific challenge: solve the growing list of problems with the new powerful weapon, the B-29 heavy bomber. Called the Superfortress, the B-29 was the most advanced airplane of its time, with great capabilities and many new technologies. It was the first pressurized, high-altitude bomber ever built, and it could operate at 30,000 feet for 3,700 miles without refueling. Its top speed was 350 miles per hour, and it could carry 20,000 pounds of bombs, three times the load of a B-17.

But this potential superweapon had two fundamental problems: It had been rushed into service before all its mechanical bugs were worked out, and its complex design was too difficult for the crews to operate without much more training than they were allowed. The harsh result was that the B-29 had a much higher accident rate during training than any other plane introduced during the war. Before going to India to lead a unit with many B-29s, LeMay insisted on going to the training facility to fly the new bomber and learn its problems from the test pilots and mechanics. He discovered enough to know that he had a challenging task ahead of him, and the B-29 would continue to present new issues as it flew in different environments.[31]

LeMay arrived at his new headquarters in Kharagpur, India, and took command of the Twentieth Air Force in August 1944. In addition to dealing with the mechanical problems of the B-29 and training crews, his operating area covered China, Burma, and India, known as the CBI theater. This immense area was a logistical black hole. Everything had to be flown in—bombs, spare parts, fuel, and food—over a great distance. The targets could only be reached by flying over the Himalayas to advance bases in China and then on to Manchuria and the Japanese home islands. The absurdity of the location was reflected in the cold fact that it required 7 gallons of fuel to deliver every gallon used in combat. Despite these obstacles, LeMay soon had his bombers flying missions, and they achieved a higher performance score than any other heavy bomber unit, except one in the Mediterranean that had much better weather and more efficient logistics.[32]

In Washington, the air force headquarters came under increasing pressure to use the B-29s for heavy attacks against the Japanese home islands. The Twenty-First Air Force in the newly liberated Mariana Islands was not achieving the desired results. In January 1945, General Arnold felt compelled to relieve his friend who commanded the underperforming unit and install the more aggressive and effective LeMay. Guam, the largest island in the Marianas Archipelago, had been recaptured from the Japanese after fierce fighting the previous August. The navy was in command of the island, and it brought in all the needed supplies, ammunition, and fuel. It also controlled the construction schedule, and the priorities of this schedule outraged LeMay.

The strategic value of the island was as a base for massive B-29 attacks on Japan. Runways for five large air bases were built, but little else for air force support. The Seabee construction corps had completed elegant houses for the theater commander and the island commander, as well as tennis courts for the officers. LeMay fumed when he found the air force's needs—barracks for the air crews, officers' quarters and briefing rooms, and facilities for ground support of the airplanes—listed on page 5 of the priority list he "acquired" from a construction supervisor. Adding to LeMay's anger was the indulgent military protocol of the senior navy commanders. Soon after LeMay's arrival, he received invitations for dinner at their homes from the theater commander and the island commander. Then he got an invitation from the submarine commander to dine on his yacht, a luxury vessel requisitioned from the Vanderbilt family for wartime use. LeMay hated formal social occasions and wanted to concentrate on his work for a maximum number of hours every day. But in this unwelcome situation, he saw an opportunity. He dressed in his wrinkled service uniform to attend each dinner and worked to remain on his best behavior. He then invited each of his hosts to dine with his staff in his tent, where they ate canned rations like all the air force officers and men. His message was received, and as he later wrote, "eventually they came up with the facilities we needed. And they built fine quarters for us."[33]

During his first seven weeks on Guam, LeMay's bombers achieved no better results against Japan than his predecessor. He struggled to understand why high-level precision bombing was so ineffective. The weather over Japan was a big part of the problem. There was constant heavy cloud cover, and the worst element was strong jet stream winds of 150 to 200 miles per hour at 30,000 feet, which blew bombs off their targets. LeMay studied reconnaissance photos of key target areas taken just before his arrival on what would be the "only crystal clear day for the next two years." These photos showed that Japanese war industries were widely dispersed in small shops and homes and most buildings were made of wood. From his days in India, he remembered the great destruction his bombers had created against a large supply base in China with new incendiary bombs. He learned from intelligence officers on Guam that the Japanese had no night fighter capability and that their antiaircraft guns were designed to hit targets at 20,000 feet and higher. Putting all these factors together, he saw the outlines of a new approach.[34]

With the help of a trusted wing commander, Colonel Thomas Power, LeMay worked out the details of dramatically new tactics against Japan. Instead of daytime precision bombing from high altitude, he would send a massive wave of B-29s against area targets in a night attack on Tokyo, flying at 5,000 to 7,000 feet with incendiary bombs. The bombers would no longer fly in tight formation but would attack in three staggered lines, producing a steady stream of air bursts of napalm and phosphorus incendiaries. On the afternoon of March 9, 1945, Power led a flight of 346 B-29s in three groups to Tokyo. The raid was a great success. Only twelve bombers were lost, with ninety-six men killed or missing. The damage was immense. The firestorm destroyed 16 square miles of central Tokyo with an estimated 100,000 dead. Two million people abandoned the city for the remainder of the war. The terse description of the raid's effect by the postwar US Strategic Bombing Survey states: "Probably more persons lost their lives by fire at in a 6-hour period than at any [equivalent period of] time in the history of man." Given the tenacity with which Japanese soldiers were fighting to the death on Iwo Jima and other islands close to their homeland, LeMay justified this mass attack to himself and his men as a way to shorten the war and save lives. He celebrated the raid's success with an expensive cigar and immediately began to push his crews to go back against other cities. They did so with equivalent results on four occasions, two to three days apart, until they ran out of incendiary bombs.[35]

In the last months of the war, LeMay worked long hours to support the air and ground assault on Japan. With new bombers and crews arriving from Europe and India each week, and aided by a new system of aircraft maintenance, he kept hundreds of B-29s attacking Japanese cities every two to three days, in addition to assisting the marines on Iwo Jima and Okinawa with air bombardment. At the navy's request, the Twentieth Air Force sowed the harbors and approaches of the home islands with 12,000 newly designed mines, cutting the delivery of critical raw materials by 90 percent.

LeMay personally supported the building of special facilities on Tinian for the units preparing the atomic bomb attacks and proposed the use of a single B-29 for delivery of the bombs against Hiroshima and Nagasaki on August 6 and 9. As Japanese leaders negotiated to limit the terms of surrender, LeMay was on the cover of *Time* on August 13. A stern, glaring photo of him, cigar in his mouth, with B-29 contrails in the sky behind him, appeared over the caption "LeMay of the B-29s: Can Japan stand twice the bombing that Germany got?" The Japanese emperor announced the surrender in a radio address to the nation on August 15, and preparations for the occupation began the next day. LeMay was on the first Allied plane to land in Japan, and at the formal surrender ceremony on September 2, he stood with other senior commanders on the deck of the battleship *Missouri*. Shortly after the Japanese representatives signed the surrender documents, a massive formation of 462 B-29s flew over Tokyo Bay in a thunderous statement of American air power.[36]

LeMay emerged from World War II as one of a handful of air force heroes, and his service bosses began to prepare him for a senior leadership position. His first postwar assignment was deputy chief of staff for research and development in the Pentagon. His principal objective was to put the United States at the forefront of aviation and space technology. He took several important steps in this direction by launching research on missiles and by creating the Research and Development Corporation (RAND) with a $10 million allocation from the air force budget. RAND would become a leading source of expertise on the strategy and technology of air power and would ultimately play a central role in developing the theoretical basis for nuclear deterrence, mutual assured destruction, and nuclear arms control. He helped shape nuclear weapons policies in a number of areas. He chaired a Joint Chiefs of Staff's subcommittee on nuclear testing, initiated a program of training air force officers to handle and arm nuclear bombs, and participated in adding nuclear weapons to an early war plan against the Soviet Union. As an important dimension of his Washington initiation, he learned about Congress and the budget process and testified many times before congressional committees justifying funding for research and weapons development. On July 26, 1947, along with his service colleagues, LeMay celebrated the president's signing of the National Security Act, which created the Department of Defense and the independent US Air Force. This was one of the rare occasions when the self-controlled general let loose and got roaring drunk.[37]

In October 1947, LeMay crossed the Atlantic again to take command of US Air Forces Europe. With this important post in Wiesbaden, Germany, he was promoted to lieutenant general, becoming the youngest three-star general in the air force. When he arrived in Germany, he immediately became involved in the local problems caused by the stagnant economy, high unemployment, and shortages of food and all basic necessities. In April 1948, he dealt with the start of the Marshall Plan for European economic recovery. One of the important preparatory steps was to unify the British, French, and American occupation zones in

Berlin in order to improve trade and industrial reconstruction. Soviet leaders prevented the governments of Central and Eastern Europe from participating in the Marshall Plan, and they strongly opposed having West Berlin used as a demonstration project for American capitalism. On June 24, the Soviet military blocked all the land and water routes into the city in an attempt to starve the residents and frustrate the Allied occupation government.

The military governor of the US zone, General Lucius Clay, proposed sending an armored convoy to break the blockade, while LeMay advocated an airlift to resupply the city. Finding Clay's suggestion too dangerous, President Truman endorsed the air force's recommendation. LeMay moved quickly to increase the number of transport planes available for the task and began a massive supply effort, which became known as the Berlin Airlift. When it was clear that the blockade would continue for a long period, he brought in more aircraft and the head of air force transportation to direct the airlift. Soon, the air force was operating 1,000 flights a day on a 24-hour schedule, bringing food, fuel, and equipment to West Berlin. With the airlift running smoothly, the new air force chief of staff, General Hoyt Vandenberg, recalled LeMay to the United States to take on another critical job: commander of the Strategic Air Command. To his new assignment, LeMay brought a strengthened concern about the challenge to US and European interests posed by aggressive Soviet actions. He also took to his new command a strong conviction that such behavior had to be resisted promptly and firmly.[38]

In addressing why Curtis LeMay was repeatedly chosen for the toughest jobs, including revitalizing SAC, the air force historian Herman S. Wolk explained: "LeMay came *naturally* to the bomber business. He was simply very good at it. He knew how to identify a problem, zero in on it, and solve it. [He had] an ability to convince the men he led that he knew his business—how to command and to protect his men when they were in the skies. Success leads to success. His men knew that he could accomplish the mission with the *lowest possible loss rate*. They liked to fly for him because they knew he was the best at what he did" (emphasis in the original).[39]

SAC TRANSFORMED

After the Dayton Exercise, LeMay and his trusted staff began the long process of motivating and reshaping an ineffective command. Although he had a mandate from the air force's chief of staff to revitalize the atomic strike force, he knew there would be few additional resources to use. Harry Truman had just been elected to a new term as president, and he was dedicated to holding down inflation and reducing the budget deficit. A key element in his agenda was to cap defense spending at $15 billion. LeMay had to work with the men and equipment he had. He instinctively turned to the leadership concepts he had developed with new commands in England, India, and Guam during the war. Each crew would work as a team, with every member having a specified role. Special courses were set up for pilots, navigators, bombardiers, radar operators, gunners, and mechanics. Lead teams were chosen to study selected targets in depth, so operations could be run without taking time for target analysis. Each crew member had a checklist to go through before takeoff as a means of reducing accidents. Every unit had constant drills to apply the lessons learned, with aircraft operating as close as possible to wartime conditions of altitude and limited intelligence.[40]

LeMay's leadership was based on teamwork and unit initiative. He gave wing commanders general instructions on what he wanted done and held them responsible for results. Successful innovations were praised and passed on for adoption by other wings. He seldom raised his voice. If an exercise was done poorly, he would direct the unit to do it again and get it right. After repeated poor performances, an individual would be transferred out of SAC. After successive unit failures, the commander would be replaced. Units were encouraged to compete in bombing accuracy, gunnery, and navigation at night and in bad weather. He persuaded the chief of air force personnel to transfer a large number of promotion vacancies to SAC, and he used them for instant promotions whenever an individual gave an outstanding performance in an exercise. If a crew remained in the top 15 percent of the rating system in competitions for several months, the entire crew won promotions.

The LeMay innovation that produced the greatest anxiety among commanders and airmen was the operational readiness inspection. A team from SAC headquarters, often with the boss in the lead, would fly without notice to a base and order the wing commander to implement the war plan. After observing how efficiently launch preparations advanced for several hours, the team leader would cancel the operation and either praise the unit or call for additional practice. If, as happened on at least one occasion, the wing commander appeared after some delay wearing golfing attire, he would soon find himself with a lot of time to practice his favorite sport.[41]

In order to limit rapid turnover of both officers and enlisted personnel, LeMay worked hard to improve living conditions on the often-remote SAC bases. When he arrived at Offutt Field, he found living arrangements to be primitive. The men were housed in tarpaper shacks with sparse furniture and ate mediocre cafeteria food. LeMay met with local Omaha business and civic groups to enlist their help in making the lives of his men more appealing. Developing adequate housing was his first priority. He found funds in his budget to design and build prefabricated houses for married men and their families. The airmen helped assemble them with assistance from local construction companies. For the single men, he designed barracks with two-person rooms and a bathroom between each pair of bedrooms. This allowed men on a night shift in SAC's 24-hour alert policy to obtain the sleep and rest that was impossible in traditional open barracks. On the initiative of the local brewery owner, a business group raised the money to furnish the housing for both families and single men. To improve the food, LeMay negotiated with top hotels to have air force cooks work with their chefs to learn how to prepare more appetizing meals. In part to satisfy his own love of repairing car engines, he set up a hobby shop for those who wanted to work on their cars or do woodworking. Over time, these improvements spread to all the SAC bases, and they proved their value in higher retention rates for experienced officers and airmen.[42]

In April 1949, a festering battle between the navy and the air force over the mission to deliver atomic weapons burst into public view when Secretary of Defense Louis Johnson canceled the navy's first supercarrier. This huge aircraft carrier was designed to launch planes capable of atomic bombing operations, and it was a direct challenge to the decision by the president, with the advice of the Joint Chiefs of Staff, to assign the atomic strike mission to the air force. The clash involved two congressional hearings focused on the navy's charges that the air force had fraudulently canceled four aircraft contracts so that it could buy more B-36 long-range bombers in an attempt to undercut the navy's need for a supercarrier. The admirals also charged that the B-36 had serious flaws, which had been covered up, and that it would not be capable of penetrating Soviet air defenses. Although the battle between the services generated a wave of press discussion and debate, it ultimately had little effect on the air force or SAC because it was disclosed that the navy's case rested on an anonymous document drafted by an aide to the assistant secretary of the navy. Testimony showed that this document was based completely on rumors and false accusations. This "revolt of the admirals" led to the firing of the chief of naval operations and the retirement of several other admirals. It was a clear victory for the air force and for SAC's atomic strike mission.[43]

During these hearings, LeMay testified once on the value of the B-36, but he did not have a major role in responding to the navy's charges. This failed power play did exacerbate his already well-established lack of respect for the US Navy. In a frequently quoted example of his attitude, he interrupted a captain's briefing when he referred to the Soviets as "enemies" to declare: "Young man, the Soviets are our adversaries; the Navy is our enemy."[44]

SAC'S CAPABILITIES AND WAR PLANS

Through 1954, the Strategic Air Command operated four types of bombers. When LeMay assumed command in the fall of 1948, SAC had 486 B-29s. We have seen how LeMay was assigned to the CBI theater in 1944 to resolve problems with the new bomber. Improvements continued to be made in the design of the airplane and in the power and stability of its engines. The fourth model, the B-29D, was introduced in May 1945, and it demonstrated significantly better capabilities. After the war ended, this model was redesignated the B-50, and when LeMay arrived, SAC possessed 35 B-50s in addition to many older models from the war years.[45]

Aviation technology advanced in many areas during the war, but the national priority was on maximizing production of proven aircraft such as the B-24 and B-29. The development and testing of the next long-range bomber, the B-36, was a clear case of delayed production. The contract for this airplane was issued in October 1941 and called for the production of a new class of heavy bomber that could carry a 10,000-pound bomb load for a 10,000-mile round trip. It should achieve a maximum altitude of 35,000 feet and an air speed of at least 240 miles an hour. The first flight test of the B-36, in August 1946, disclosed a wide range of problems. The airplane went through many changes before an acceptable version, the B-36D, had its initial flight test in March 1949. By adding four jet engines to the six propeller engines of earlier models this prototype showed marked improvement. It flew at 406 miles an hour up to a ceiling of 44,000 feet with a 10,000-pound bomb load, and could travel 5,000 miles and return to base. Despite its huge size and load capacity, the B-36D had major disadvantages. It required extensive maintenance to keep it operational; and more seriously, by the time it was introduced, the Soviet jet fighters then in service, such as the MiG-15, could match its speed and altitude, and the emerging next-generation MiG-17 would easily shoot it down. SAC's leaders realized that the B-36 was an interim bomber. But it served a purpose for several years, and the air force bought 385 of them, one-third of which were configured for reconnaissance missions. With the introduction of a more advanced all-jet bomber, these would all be retired by 1959. No B-36s ever participated in combat.[46]

The next major addition to SAC's inventory was an all-jet, medium-range bomber, the B-47 Stratojet. Boeing's initial proposal in 1943 did not promise major advances, but intelligence on innovations in jet engines and airframe design from German scientists and engineers after the war led to a completely new proposal. The new concept called for six jet engines to power a streamlined, swept-wing bomber. As with the B-29, the introduction of many new design elements in the B-47 required many modifications and changes. The new bomber did not become operational until October 1952. As the air power scholar Phillip Meilinger asserts,

"The Stratojet was worth the wait. One of the most beautiful bombers ever built, the B-47 was sleek, fast, and agile." It had a top speed of 600 miles an hour, a ceiling of 33,000 feet, a 25,000-pound bomb load, and a combat radius of 2,000 miles. It could deliver a new Mark 36 atomic bomb with a yield of 24 megatons, but not the early hydrogen bombs. LeMay called it his "workhorse bomber." By the end of 1953, SAC had 329 B-47s; and overall, 2,000 were built. The Stratojet operating from overseas bases was the designated nuclear delivery vehicle for the early 1950s, and equally important, many of its design features were used to build the highly successful next heavy bomber, the B-52.[47] (See figure 14.1.)

FIGURE 14.1 General Curtis LeMay describes the Strategic Air Command's latest heavy bomber, the B-52, to Field Marshal Viscount Montgomery, deputy supreme allied commander in Europe, at the Strategic Air Command headquarters in Omaha, Nebraska, on November 30, 1954.

Source: LeMay Papers, Library of Congress.

For its nuclear strike mission, SAC still needed a heavy bomber with greater range and bomb capacity to replace the B-36. In January 1946, the air force's leaders negotiated a contract with Boeing to develop a jet-powered heavy bomber. Boeing's top design team wanted to utilize some of the advanced elements of the B-47, but in order to obtain the speed and load capacity the air force required, they had to develop a more powerful engine. After finding that turboprop engines produced insufficient thrust for a heavy bomber, they pressed engine specialists to design a new, pure jet engine with greater power. The Boeing team then employed eight of the new engines in four pairs on a swept-wing airframe. After months of tests and modifications, the B-52 had its first flight test in April 1952, with promising results. Smaller than the B-36, it was still a large airplane: 152 feet long, with a 185-foot wing-span. The first operational model, the B-52B, entered service in March 1954. SAC received its first group of eighteen B-52s by the end of 1955. The new bomber quickly became SAC's new workhorse, starting in the mid-1950s, and it still is today; refitted and improved versions are still in use in conflicts in Iraq and Afghanistan. The most effective model was the B-52H, which was introduced in 1961. It had a maximum speed of 650 miles an hour, a bomb load of 70,000 pounds, a ceiling of 50,000 feet, and a range of 8,800 miles without refueling. The total of all models produced was 744, of which 76 are still in active service.[48] Tables 14.2 and 14.3 present year-after-year assessments of SAC's aircraft.

Until the B-52 became available in significant numbers, LeMay and his staff experimented with many options to design a strategy for a success-ful attack on the Soviet Union with minimum loss of aircraft and crews. These initiatives included using tankers for in-flight refueling, fighter escorts to combat enemy interceptors, and overseas bases for repair and refueling. Each of these efforts suffered from crippling problems. Tankers could not operate at the speed or altitude of the B-47; fighters had inad-equate altitude, range, and speed to accompany the bombers; and the overseas bases were vulnerable to enemy preemption. The United States built bases starting in Britain, Spain, Morocco, Turkey, and Guam, and expanded later to Canada, Newfoundland, and Greenland. SAC never resolved the fighter escort issues and eventually transferred its fighter

TABLE 14.2 Number of Aircraft under the US
Strategic Air Command, 1946–54

Year	Bombers	Tankers	Fighters	Reconnaissance
1946	148	—	85	31
1947	319	—	350	35
1948	556	—	212	58
1949	525	67	161	80
1950	520	126	167	112
1951	669	208	96	173
1952	857	318	230	193
1953	762	502	235	282
1954	1,082	683	411	410

Note: —= not available.

Source: Phillip S. Meilinger, *The Formation and Early Years of the Strategic Air Command, 1946–1957: Why the SAC Was Formed* (Lewiston, NY: Edwin Mellen Press, 2013), 339.

TABLE 14.3 The US Strategic Air Command's Bombers by Type, 1946–54

Year	B-29	B-50	B-36	B-47	Total
1946	148	—	—	—	148
1947	319	—	—	—	319
1948	486	35	35	—	556
1949	390	99	36	—	525
1950	286	196	38	—	520
1951	340	219	98	12	669
1952	417	224	154	62	857
1953	110	138	185	329	762
1954	—	78	209	795	1,082

Note: —= not available.

Source: Phillip S. Meilinger, *The Formation and Early Years of the Strategic Air Command, 1946–1957: Why the SAC Was Formed* (Lewiston, NY: Edwin Mellen Press, 2013), 340.

wings to other commands. Only with the B-52's intercontinental range combined with the introduction of the jet tanker, the KC-135, in 1957 was a solution feasible. The attack strategy developed with these new jets called for launching the mission from the United States, air refueling en route to the targets, and stopping at overseas bases for repairs and refueling on the return trip. SAC would be fully capable of implementing this strategy in 1958, when it had sufficient numbers of B-52s and KC-135s. Before then, any attempted large-scale nuclear attack on Soviet targets would have faced superior defenses in Moscow's more advanced jet fighters and surface-to-air missiles.[49] Tables 14.4, 14.5, and 14.6 show year-after-year assessments of SAC's tanker, fighter, and reconnaissance complements.

After the successful Soviet atomic test, the joint chiefs focused more attention on developing war plans. In October 1949, the Joint Outline Emergency War Plan OFFTACKLE received an updated target list that specified attacks on 104 Soviet urban targets using 220 atomic bombs with a reserve attack capability of 72 weapons. When the war in Korea intensified with the Chinese intervention, a new target annex of November 1950 concentrated attacks more heavily on the Soviet fuel, electric power, and atomic power industries. In the spring of 1951, Curtis LeMay successfully argued before the Joint Chiefs of Staff that the target list

TABLE 14.4 The US Strategic Air Command's Tankers by Type, 1949–54

Year	KB-29	KC-97	Total
1949	67	—	67
1950	126	—	126
1951	187	21	208
1952	179	139	318
1953	143	359	502
1954	91	592	683

Note: —= not available.

Source: Phillip S. Meilinger, *The Formation and Early Years of the Strategic Air Command, 1946–1957: Why the SAC Was Formed* (Lewiston, NY: Edwin Mellen Press, 2013), 340.

TABLE 14.5 The US Strategic Air Command's Fighters by Type, 1946–54

Year	P-51	P-80	F-82	F-84	F-86	Total
1946	85	—	—	—	—	85
1947	230	120	—	—	—	350
1948	131	—	81	—	—	212
1949	—	—	81	—	80	161
1950	—	—	—	167	—	167
1951	—	—	—	96	—	96
1952	—	—	—	230	—	230
1953	—	—	—	235	—	235
1954	—	—	—	411	—	411

Note: —= not available.

Source: Phillip S. Meilinger, *The Formation and Early Years of the Strategic Air Command, 1946–1957: Why the SAC Was Formed* (Lewiston, NY: Edwin Mellen Press, 2013), 341.

TABLE 14.6 The US Strategic Air Command's Reconnaissance Aircraft by Type, 1946–54

Year	F-2/9/13	RB-17	RB-29	RB-45	RB-50	RB-36	RB-47	Total
1946	31	—	—	—	—	—	—	31
1947	35	—	—	—	—	—	—	35
1948	—	24	30	4	—	—	—	58
1949	—	18	62	—	—	—	—	80
1950	—	—	46	27	19	20	—	112
1951	—	—	30	38	40	65	—	173
1952	—	—	18	22	39	114	—	193
1953	—	—	8	—	38	137	99	282
1954	—	—	—	—	12	133	265	410

Note: —= not available.

Source: Phillip S. Meilinger, *The Formation and Early Years of the Strategic Air Command, 1946–1957: Why the SAC Was Formed* (Lewiston, NY: Edwin Mellen Press, 2013), 341.

should be limited to designated industries in urban areas where greater damage could be assured. With this decision confirmed in mid-1951, SAC became, as the historian David Alan Rosenberg argues, "the dominant force in operational planning for nuclear war."[50]

Even with this refinement, the war plan was an inadequate program for crippling the war-making ability of the Soviet Union. In January 1950, the Weapons Systems Evaluation Group (WSEG), a technical advisory committee to the Joint Chiefs, briefed the president on their evaluation of the atomic war plan. The WSEG I Study discussed the lack of US intelligence about the location of targets, the strength of Soviet air defenses, and the damage that would be inflicted by the implementation of the war plan. The group concluded that the planned attack would be costly and would achieve limited results. Only 50 to 70 percent of the bombers would return, and about one-half to two-thirds of the targeted industrial plants would suffer major damage. The capabilities required to execute the war plan successfully—large numbers of B-52s and KC-135 tankers, improved aerial reconnaissance, electronic countermeasures, and improved bombing techniques—would not all be available until 1958.[51]

On the eve of the Korean War, leaders of the Truman administration saw the Soviet Union as the only potential adversary, but they believed that any conflict was unlikely in the next few years. Senior military officers and a few civilians, such as Paul Nitze, were concerned about the security implications of the new Soviet atomic capability. With some help from Republican congressional leaders and the press, these officials were able to win decisions for development of the H-bomb and a study of the changed security situation that would produce NSC Report 68. The air force pressed for additional funds for air defenses and more bombers than a force of forty-eight groups allowed. But the president was more concerned with inflation and domestic politics than defense spending, and he stuck firmly to his ceiling of $13 billion for defense in fiscal year 1951 and proposed cutting almost another billion for the following year. On April 24, 1950, Secretary of the Air Force Stuart Symington resigned over the stringent budget limits.[52]

At this point, SAC remained a work in progress: a military service designated as the nation's first line of deterrence and defense, but unable to fulfill this mission because of technology and budget constraints. LeMay's command possessed over 500 bombers, but more than half were obsolete B-29s of World War II vintage. Among operational aircraft were 196 B-50s (updated B-29s) and 38 B-36s. Of the total force, 224 were atomic-capable, with 263 combat-ready crews and 18 atomic bomb assembly teams. The US nuclear stockpile contained 450 weapons of all types, but these remained in the custody of the Atomic Energy Commission outside Roswell, New Mexico, and would take weeks to assemble for use by SAC.[53]

SAC AND THE KOREAN WAR

In the early days of the Korean War, when North Korean divisions were steadily driving South Korean and the small number of American troops down the peninsula, General MacArthur called urgently for support from SAC's bombers. The air force chief of staff ordered two SAC B-29 bomber groups to join the effort to stop the North Koreans. Two additional groups soon followed. These units, plus a reconnaissance squadron that joined later, would make up the Far East Air Force Bomber Command, under Major General Emmett "Rosie" O'Donnell, one of LeMay's most trusted senior officers. The command's initial missions focused on strategic targets such as communication hubs, transportation centers, and industrial plants. By the end of 1950, all but one of these strategic targets had been hit, most with multiple attacks. Despite sending his oldest aircraft to the Far East, LeMay objected to this assignment, viewing it as an unnecessary diversion of SAC resources from its primary mission of deterring war with the Soviet Union. He would later describe his attitude as "I don't want too many splinters to be whittled off the stick which we might have to wield."[54]

Starting July 11, with United Nations forces being pushed toward what would become the Pusan Perimeter, facing relentless North Korean attacks, the bomber command's priority shifted to "close air support and isolation of the battlefield." Steady pounding from the B-29s, combined with attacks by tactical aircraft, played a vital role in the successful defense at Pusan. On November 1, 1950, the dynamics of the air war changed with the appearance of new Soviet MiG-15 jet fighters, which had Chinese markings but were flown by Soviet pilots. These fast, maneuverable fighters proved deadly for the lumbering B-29s; and from this point on, bomber attacks had to be either accompanied by the limited number of American F-86 jet fighters or conducted at night with necessarily reduced visibility. For the remainder of the war, the main goals for SAC forces were close air support and maintaining air superiority, which in practice concentrated on preventing the operation of the thirty-four airfields constructed by the Chinese in North Korea.[55]

As the stalemate on the battlefield continued in 1952 and 1953, the Joint Chiefs of Staff asked the bomber command for additional target options that could apply pressure on the Soviets and Chinese to negotiate seriously on an armistice. The targeting unit quickly identified several high-value possibilities, and in June 1952 B-29s disabled eleven hydroelectric power plants along the Yalu River, blacking out all of North Korea for two weeks and reducing power in Manchuria by 23 percent. During August and September, bombers attacked oil refineries and storage depots across North Korea and again hit facilities in the capital, Pyongyang. When these attacks did not advance the stalled armistice talks, B-29s destroyed the North Korean dam and dike system in May 1953, flooding thousands of acres of rice fields and washing away rail lines and roads. After Stalin's death earlier in March, the new collective leadership in Moscow decided to end the war and had directed their Chinese allies to come to terms in Korea. An armistice agreement was signed on July 27, 1953, by the commanders of the UN forces, the North Korean Army, and the Chinese volunteers. There is no peace treaty ending the war, and today heavily armed units of the North Korean and South Korean armies taunt each other across a demilitarized zone at the 38th Parallel, where the war began in 1950.[56]

SAC's overall contribution to the Korean War effort was flying more than 21,000 missions and dropping nearly 160,000 tons of bombs. Interdiction attacks against railroads, bridges, and road junctions made up 80 percent of its targets, while 13 percent were support of ground operations. In three years of combat, the Bomber Command lost 24 aircraft to enemy fire, and 627 crew members were killed or missing. The Korean War was the final mission for the obsolete B-29s; all were retired from SAC by November 1954. In a conflict fought mainly by ground forces, LeMay's bombers provided important but limited support.[57]

THE WAR'S IMPACT ON SAC

The principal effect of the Korean conflict on SAC was to force its leadership to focus sharply on how to deal with a growing Soviet threat to the United States. Prototypes of new bombers regularly appeared at Soviet air shows, and intelligence estimates forecast a growing stockpile of nuclear weapons. Curtis LeMay and his commanders worked intensely to maintain an edge in aircraft design and technology, bombing accuracy, and crew training to deter and if necessary defeat a Soviet attack. Leaders of the air force and their proponents in Congress and the press persuaded the Truman administration to adopt an air-delivered nuclear strategy well before the war broke out. The war—with its widely accepted origin as a Soviet probe of the West's unity and will to resist aggression—provided the justification for the massive budgets that built SAC's capabilities. The wartime appropriations expanded SAC's bomber fleet from 520 (over half obsolete B-29s) in 1950 to 1,082 by 1954, with the basic design and technology established for the B-52s, which would form the core of the strike force for the next thirty years.[58]

As his bomber numbers grew and additional pilots and crews were trained to a high state of combat readiness, LeMay strengthened SAC's control of the nuclear mission in two critical areas. From its creation as an independent service in 1947, the US Air Force had argued that the Atomic Energy Commission's (AEC's) custody of all nuclear weapons made it impossible for SAC to conduct its atomic mission in an effective and timely manner. The fear at air force headquarters was that under the AEC's system, much of the bomber force and perhaps the weapons themselves could be destroyed by a Soviet attack before they could get off the ground. In November of that year, the Eighth Air Force conducted an exercise to implement its war plan, and the AEC's procedures for bomb assembly and transfer to bombers were so slow and cumbersome that the air force's point was proven. But the AEC, clinging to its legislative mandate to provide civilian control of nuclear weapons, refused to concede. After he assumed command of SAC, LeMay ordered a similar exercise in December 1948 to test the transfer procedures. The process went more smoothly, but it was still far too slow. Again, the AEC did not budge.[59]

It took the Korean War, with its heightened threat of war with the Soviet Union, to change minds in Washington. Early in 1951, with Chinese offensives pushing UN forces far below the 38th Parallel and reports of Soviet troops gathering in significant numbers near the North Korean border, LeMay urged the air force's chief of staff to plead the case for weapons custody again. In March, in a letter to the president, General Vandenberg made a strong argument for transferring most nuclear weapons to SAC so that a timely atomic response to an imminent attack would be possible. Under these more pressing circumstances, Truman accepted the air force's reasoning and justified his decision on the grounds that civilian control was maintained by the requirement that the president was the sole authority able to order the use of nuclear weapons. In coming weeks, nine nuclear bombs were transferred to SAC on Okinawa for use in Korea if needed. During the next two years, regional commands in Europe and the Middle East received their own supplies of nuclear weapons. By the end of the Korean conflict, these steps represented a significant advance in strategic readiness.[60]

LeMay's second major success in securing the atomic mission was to gain essential control of the targeting process for SAC. For several years after the 1948 nuclear tests, as the stockpile of weapons grew, the army and navy increased efforts to win some role in target selection. The army especially wanted some nuclear strikes assigned to slow or retard Soviet ground forces in Central and Eastern Europe, while the navy sought attacks against ports and shipyards along the Soviet coast. In August 1950, the Joint Chiefs of Staff sought to resolve this debate by assigning targets to three priorities: Soviet air units with an atomic mission; retardation of ground forces; and industrial centers for weapons, electricity, oil, and atomic production. LeMay contended that the lack of intelligence made it impossible to identify targets in the first two categories; and given the limited number of bombs available, he argued that the initial heavy strikes should focus on urban industrial centers, where most plants were located and whose coordinates were known. In July 1951, the Joint Chiefs agreed, and SAC for some years would dominate the process of target selection in the war plans.[61]

Curtis LeMay's greatest achievement in a long career was building SAC into the most powerful and best-prepared deterrent force in the world. He received his fourth star in October 1951, and he completed his highly successful command of SAC in 1957, when he returned to Washington as vice chief of staff of the air force. After four years, he would move up to become chief of staff from 1961 to 1965. By the mid-1950s, the air force received roughly half the overall defense budget, and SAC was its premier command, charged in the event of major war to "strike the initial, decisive blow."[62]

LeMay's success was not foreordained. He came from a poor family and worked his way through a large state university with a modest academic record. He did not move easily in the social company of the West Point graduates who dominated the army. Fascinated as a youth by airplanes, he was fortunate to select the air corps as his branch of the army. This new section of the service had no established doctrine on weapons or tactics and was open to young officers with energy and imagination who got results. LeMay advanced by hard work and a remarkable ability to solve problems of adapting new technologies to military needs as well as leading large numbers of men from widely different backgrounds. His experiences in World War II established his system of integrating new aircraft with untested tactics and organizing and training the crews to operate at a high level of effectiveness under harsh, dangerous conditions.

At SAC, LeMay applied the lessons and skills of wartime to transform an unfocused, dysfunctional unit into a world-class military organization. He took full advantage of the growth of the nuclear weapons stockpile and Truman's obsession with limiting defense spending to vault the

US Air Force, and especially SAC, over the US Army and US Navy as the nation's first line of defense. The Korean War provided the expanded budgets to fulfill his dreams and enable SAC to reach its full potential.

LeMay's strengths were not as well suited to the strategy of limited war that dominated much of the Cold War. He believed, once the nation was at war, that the military should use all its power to strike a decisive blow against the enemy. He was the warrior the country needed in the total war from 1941 to 1945. But in Korea, he chafed at the political constraints placed on the use of incendiary bombs, the prohibition of bombing Chinese and Soviet bases in Manchuria, and the refusal to use atomic weapons. His proposals for heavy bombing with atomic weapons would have split the Alliance fighting in Korea and seriously damaged the cohesion of NATO. He did not appreciate the complex political balance that was necessary to resist the North Koreans and Chinese while avoiding war with the Soviet Union. To his credit, he believed that political leaders should set policies, and that as a military commander, his job was to implement them. While at SAC, his more extreme views remained essentially within air force channels. But in later years, as chief of staff, his concepts of strategy and war led to numerous clashes with Secretary of Defense Robert McNamara and ultimately to his resignation at the demand of President Lyndon Johnson.

15

IGOR KURCHATOV DEVELOPS SOVIET NUCLEAR WEAPONS

At the end of World War II, Soviet nuclear science, when compared with the West, was in an underdeveloped state similar to the condition of its aeronautical science. In the 1930s, Soviet physics had been of high quality, rated by many as behind only Great Britain (the recognized world leader), France, and the United States. But Stalin's purges and wartime demands for improved weapons for combat had sharply reduced resources for basic research. Chemists had to develop better explosives, while physicists concentrated on radar and countermeasures against magnetic naval mines. The war also forced Soviet scientists to evacuate to the Urals and beyond to evade the advancing German armies.

Although not targeted as heavily as biologists, physicists were sent to the Gulag in significant numbers. Over a hundred physicists from Leningrad alone were sent to the camps. Even those who kept their jobs had to work under primitive conditions without much of their laboratory equipment and outside their field of specialization. They had two other inherent disadvantages. In order to test their theories about the structure of the atom and the properties of uranium, they had to construct large machines such as cyclotrons and atomic reactors, which cost billions of rubles. In addition, their research dealt with objects too minute to see and too dangerous to handle. One account, which is perhaps

apocryphal but is true to Stalin's suspicious nature and wartime priorities, describes the dictator completely rejecting Beria's November 1941
report that espionage from London stated that Britain was working an
on atomic bomb that could end the war in several years. Stalin declared:
"The Germans are already at Volokolamsk [about 60 miles northwest of
Moscow], and here you are launching into this fantasy! I do not believe
this. And I advise you not to believe that it is possible to win a war using
some kind of chemical element that no one has seen. Doesn't this seem
like pure propaganda to you? Done deliberately to distract our scientists
from work on new kinds of weapons for the army?"[1]

Working under such restrictive, intimidating conditions posed huge
challenges for Soviet scientists. But due to pragmatic leadership, creative
research skills, and great personal courage, a small group of physicists,
chemists, and engineers overcame a wide range of obstacles in their
drive to create a nuclear weapon.

EARLY STEPS

Before the Bolshevik Revolution, physics was one of the weaker disciplines within Russian science, while chemistry and mathematics had
long and solid reputations. The development of modern Russian physics
was largely the work of Abram F. Ioffe. Born in a small town in Ukraine
in 1880, Ioffe studied at the Saint Petersburg Technological Institute and
went on to receive a doctorate in Munich in 1905 for work on the electric conductivity of dielectric crystals under the supervision of Wilhelm
Röntgen, who had discovered X-rays. Ioffe returned to the institute in
Saint Petersburg, and after doing important research on semiconductors, he was appointed professor in 1913. During World War I, he continued his work on electricity and the magnetic field of cathode rays, and
in September 1918 he became one of the earliest scientists to endorse the
Bolshevik government. His research and teaching on the new physics
attracted a number of able students, and in 1921 he was named director
of the Leningrad Physicotechnical Institute, with many of his former

students becoming the research staff. Among his students were two future Nobel laureates, Peter Kapitsa and Nikolai Semenov, and others who would have distinguished careers in physics.[2]

Ioffe became the principal institution builder in Russian physics. Although he was recognized as a good scientist, his greatest strengths were as a teacher, a recruiter of talent, and a promoter of the rapidly expanding field of physics. Leningrad was the center of intellectual life in early-twentieth-century Russia, and the presence in the city of the Academy of Sciences made the area and its research institutes a magnet for the most talented students. The Academy of Sciences elected Ioffe as a corresponding member in 1918; and two years later, he became a full Academician. Ioffe excelled in recruiting the best students and faculty from the teaching institutions to work in his research laboratories. He maintained extensive contacts with leading research centers in Europe and sent his top students and staff members to do research in Cambridge, Paris, Strasbourg, and Munich. With operating funds scarce in the early Soviet years, he took advantage of the government's priority on rapid industrialization to propose in 1924 a new laboratory on applied research to benefit industry. He was successful, and his new research laboratory developed innovative methods and equipment for the electric power and metallurgical industries. By 1930, the institute and its affiliated applied physics laboratory employed over a hundred physicists, many of whom had studied in the West. Ioffe also sponsored physics and engineering institutes in four provincial cities with expanding industrial centers under the First Five-Year Plan. The most successful of these was in Kharkiv in northeastern Ukraine. The leading Western scholar of Soviet nuclear development, David Holloway, argues that by the early 1930s Ioffe's "institute had become a leading center of European physics at a time when quantum mechanics had revolutionized physics."[3]

A flurry of discoveries in nuclear physics during 1932 stimulated great interest and new departures in research among Soviet scientists. At the Cavendish Laboratory in Cambridge, James Chadwick discovered the neutron, while his colleagues, John Cockcroft and E. T. S. Wilson, split the lithium nucleus into alpha particles based on a theory advanced by the young Russian Georgii Gamov. Ernest O. Lawrence of the University of California at Berkeley built a cyclotron that could accelerate protons to an energy of 1.2 million electron volts. Carl Anderson of the California Institute of Technology discovered the positron, and Harold Urey of Columbia University identified deuterium. These breakthroughs in nuclear research led to new efforts in Kharkiv and at the Radium Institute in Leningrad. Ioffe created a nuclear department at his institute in December 1932 and named Igor Kurchatov, soon to be thirty years old, as head of the new department. Other physicists shifted their research to join the nuclear group, and by 1934 there were four laboratories with thirty researchers in the nuclear department. After reading Enrico Fermi's account of neutron bombardment of various elements in the spring of 1934, Kurchatov changed the focus of his research to examining the effects of irradiating a range of isotopes with neutrons. In the next two years, Kurchatov and his colleagues published seventeen papers on different aspects of artificial radioactivity.[4]

Unfortunately for the advancement of physics, the Soviet government began to make increasing demands on scientists at the very time when nuclear physics was expanding rapidly with a wave of new discoveries. Communist Party officials had always been suspicious of scientists because of their ties to the capitalist West and their questionable loyalty to the Soviet government. Scientists now faced restrictions on contacts with colleagues in the West and demands for loyalty to the regime. In 1933, Ioffe was banned from foreign travel, probably as a result of the defection of his young colleague, Georgii Gamov. The next year Peter Kapitsa, who had been in Cambridge for twelve years and was director of a laboratory at the Cavendish Laboratory, was ordered to remain in Russia when he came to visit colleagues in Moscow. In 1934, the government moved the Academy of Sciences from Leningrad to Moscow, taking with it a new physics institute, which tried unsuccessfully to recruit several top physicists from Ioffe's institute. The Academy of Sciences held a special conference in March 1936 to examine the relationship between physics and industry. Under detailed guidance from party leaders, senior physicists attacked Ioffe's institute for pursuing impractical theories, which did little to support the country's priority on industrialization. Under heavy pressure, Ioffe accepted some criticisms while trying to defend his institute's work. But of necessity, in the subsequent months he did shift some research to improve defense technology. As the purges accelerated in 1937–38, the Kharkiv Institute was basically destroyed when most of its top researchers were arrested. In Leningrad a hundred physicists were arrested, including several department heads from Ioffe's institute. The purges had a significant impact on the whole scientific community, including physics.[5]

Despite numerous obstacles, "Soviet nuclear physics reached a high standard in the 1930s," argues David Holloway. The progress can be measured by two conferences on the atomic nucleus held in 1933 and 1937. For the first conference, Ioffe wanted to expose his young colleagues to some of the prominent European physicists. Those presenting papers included Paul Dirac of Cambridge, who won the Nobel Prize in Physics in 1933; Frédéric Joliot-Curie of Paris, who with his wife would receive the Nobel Prize in Chemistry in 1935; Franco Rasetti of Rome; and Victor Weisskopf of Zurich. Among the rising stars of Soviet physics in attendance were Iulii Khariton, Igor Kurchatov, Lev Artsimovich, and Aleksandr Leipunskii. At the meeting four years later, Ioffe declared with pride that over one hundred Soviet scientists then specialized in nuclear physics, an increase of four times over the number involved in 1933. He also stated that many of their papers were of "fundamental importance." Reflecting the changed political atmosphere, no foreign physicists attended the 1937 conference.[6]

With the discovery of fission in December 1938, physicists in the Soviet Union, like their Western colleagues, immediately began a wide variety of experiments on fission in uranium and thorium. Successful research in Britain and Germany convinced scientists that making an atomic bomb was more possible than previously thought. Putting this information together with reports of advances in fission research in the United States, *New York Times* correspondent William Laurence wrote an important story about the possibility of building an atomic bomb and emphasized that teams of German scientists were already working on such a project. Laurence's story appeared on the front page of the Sunday *New York Times* on May 5, 1940; and in a rare coincidence, the Yale historian George Vernadsky saw the article and sent a copy to his father, the distinguished Soviet geochemist and Academician Vladimir Vernadskii. The senior Vernadskii passed this report to officials at the Academy of Sciences and to Nikolai Bulganin, deputy premier and chairman of the Council on the Chemical and Metallurgical Industries. The government did create a Uranium Commission to locate and mine uranium and to plan research on fission and isotope separation. In November 1940, some two hundred scientists gathered in Moscow for a week-long conference on nuclear physics. While presenting the major paper on fission, Igor Kurchatov discussed research findings of the last year and emphasized the point that in order to become competitive in the effort to achieve a chain reaction, the Soviet government would need to provide a massive allocation of national resources to the project. Although young physicists were eager to move ahead with fission research, senior Academicians and government officials remained reluctant to commit the necessary resources in light of the demands of military modernization and the uncertainty of timely results.[7]

With the fall of France in June 1940, Nazi Germany controlled most of continental Europe. Britain was under siege, and many in Moscow felt Russia might be the next victim. Even with resources being scarce, Soviet science made a few advances. A small cyclotron was built at the Radium Institute in Leningrad and began operation at the end of 1940. Two young physicists in Kurchatov's laboratory succeeded in creating spontaneous fission in U-238 without bombardment with neutrons, the first demonstration of a theory advanced earlier by leading physicists in Leningrad, Copenhagen, and Princeton. Khariton and a colleague used experimental data to develop a theory of chain reactions in uranium that would prove valuable in reactor design. Disappointed when the Academy of Sciences declined to fund his program of fission research, Kurchatov concentrated on building a large cyclotron at Ioffe's institute. The building was almost completed and the machine was under construction when a German attack stopped all basic research in nuclear physics. The cyclotron would not become operational until September 1944.[8]

THE DEMANDS OF WAR

Before dawn on June 22, 1941, a massive German attack on three fronts caught the Soviet Union completely by surprise. After the destruction of the Red Army's leadership in the purges of 1937–38 and the poor performance of Soviet forces in the winter war against Finland, Stalin had worked to rebuild the armed forces. He realized Hitler might attack the Soviet Union but convinced himself that this would come only after the defeat of Britain and not before 1942. In achieving strategic surprise, the German army of 3 million men, augmented by another half million troops from allies including Finland and Romania, made rapid advances. In the first week of the war, the German air force destroyed over 4,000 Soviet planes; and by mid-July, the armies had advanced far into Soviet territory and taken over 600,000 prisoners. When he realized the scope of the threat to the Soviet state and to his own continued rule, Stalin withdrew in a state of shock and depression.

Despite heavy initial Soviet losses, the outcome of the war was not yet sealed. Hitler's strategy was based on the premise of a massive initial attack destroying Soviet power within two months. The Germans had provided no reserves for the war in the East, and no additional troops or equipment. The Red Army gradually recovered and began to hold its ground. By December, with German forces preparing to attack Moscow, the Soviets launched their first counterattack. In the meantime, the Communist leadership in Moscow had regrouped around Stalin and formed a war cabinet, creating the State Defense Committee on June 30. With Stalin as chairman, the committee included Vyascheslav Molotov as deputy chairman, Marshall Klimenti Voroshilov as the token military representative, NKVD chief Lavrenti Beria, and secretary of the Central Committee Georgi Malenkov.[9]

Immediately after the German attack, Soviet scientists offered to devote their knowledge and energy to the war mobilization. The State Defense Committee created a Scientific-Technical Council to organize the work of research institutes and evaluate proposals for research to support national defense. The council included leading physicists and chemists such as Ioffe, Kapitsa, and Nikolai N. Semenov, who had worked in Ioffe's institute for over a decade before becoming director of the Leningrad Institute of Chemical Physics in 1931. The rapid advance of the German army forced drastic changes at all research institutes. Many junior scientists and technicians joined the military. Ioffe's institute lost 130 men to the Red Army in the first month of the conflict. All the research institutes evacuated their staffs and as much equipment as possible to safer areas in the East. Ioffe's institute moved, along with most of the physics institutes, to Kazan in Tartarstan during July and August. The physics institutes stopped almost all basic research and devoted roughly 90 percent of their work to the war effort. Kurchatov ended his fission research and closed his laboratory. For some months, he worked in Crimea with great success in demagnetizing ships to protect against German mines. At the beginning of 1942, he moved to Kazan but arrived with a severe case of pneumonia, which required two months of recuperation. When he returned to work, he had grown a long curly black beard, which became a permanent fixture. He pledged to his colleagues that he would not cut his beard until the Germans were defeated. From that point on, he was referred to as "the Beard." His new position at the Physicotechnical Institute was director of the armor laboratory assigned to improve the defenses of tanks and personnel carriers.[10]

While most physicists were heavily engaged in military support, a former member of Kurchatov's laboratory could not overcome his passion for fission research. Georgii Flerov, one of the physicists who discovered spontaneous fission early in 1940, had joined the military; but after six months studying aeronautical engineering, he decided he wanted to revive research on nuclear fission. He persuaded Ioffe to let him make a presentation to a seminar in Kazan, and his case for investigating fast-neutron chain reactions as a route to a bomb was well received by a group of physicists containing several prominent members of the Academy of Sciences. But ultimately, they were not convinced that the research could produce early results that would influence the outcome of the war. The twenty-eight-year-old Flerov was not deterred by this response. He wrote a long appeal to Kurchatov and later to Sergei Kaftanov, the chairman of the Scientific-Technical Committee, but neither replied to his letters. Then, in April 1942, he wrote directly to Stalin, urging a meeting of senior scientists who could decide on the validity of his proposal. The letter was passed on to Kaftanov and would later be used as a pretext for action.[11]

In contrast to Soviet scientists, top physicists in Britain and the United States concluded in 1941 that making a nuclear weapon was possible and could help decide the outcome of the war. The British government began a major bomb project in September 1941, and Washington initiated accelerated research the next month and expanded the Manhattan Project to a top priority in June 1942. The administration of Franklin Roosevelt built massive research and production facilities at Los Alamos, New Mexico; Oak Ridge, Tennessee; and Hanford, Washington. Only when American research moved ahead of British work was full cooperation established in August 1943. The leading British scientists moved to the Manhattan Project plants in the United States, soon to be joined by Canadian and French researchers. Once the basic facilities were completed, American scientists and their allies made rapid progress in their drive to win the race to develop a usable atomic bomb.[12]

Starting in September 1941, Stalin and his intelligence chief, Beria, learned quickly of each step taken in British and American research. Using effective propaganda and aggressive recruitment, the Soviet Union had created the world's best espionage service by exploiting the economic crisis of the Great Depression to attract many idealistic intellectuals in the West to serve as agents. Especially damaging were the Cambridge Five, who were recruited from Cambridge University in the 1930s and later worked as civil servants in the British Treasury, Secret Service, and Foreign Office, including in key positions in the Embassy in Washington. The initial information about the British decision to develop an atomic bomb came from John Cairncross, the "Fifth Man" of the Cambridge Five, who served as private secretary to Lord Hankey. As chairman of the Defence Services Panel of the Cabinet Scientific Advisory Committee, Hankey had supervised the panel review of the report of the Maud Committee, which had concluded that a uranium bomb could be made within two years and recommended steps to be taken in its development. On September 25, Anatolii Gorskii, the NKVD resident (chief of station) in London, sent a report to Moscow on the decision to launch a nuclear research program on an urgent basis, and a week later he forwarded a copy of the Maud Report itself. Soviet leaders had access to other sources of intelligence on the nuclear program. Klaus Fuchs, a naturalized British citizen of German birth, was a physicist working on British bomb development who volunteered to provide information on the project to the GRU, the military intelligence directorate of the Soviet General Staff. Fuchs would move to Los Alamos in December 1943 as a member of the British team on the Manhattan Project and would provide very helpful reports to Moscow. Other agents of Canadian and American nationality also provided information of varied value to Soviet intelligence. Espionage would prove important to the Soviet bomb program in showing the pace of the Anglo-American effort, along with which research methods were successful and which were not.[13]

Soviet leaders were slow to act on reports that nuclear weapons programs had begun in Britain, the United States, and Germany. The initial reports arrived in the fall of 1941, when Moscow was under siege and would soon see most of the government flee the city to Kuibyshev. There is evidence that both Stalin and Beria believed the intelligence from London was disinformation designed to persuade them to spend scarce resources on a program that would not help their war effort. As a result, only in March 1942—when he had more detailed reports from London and New York—did Beria send a memorandum to Stalin proposing how to respond to this intelligence. He recommended creating a high-level committee to direct all atomic research and having leading scientists evaluate the reports. The committee was not established, but consultations with prominent scientists went on through the remainder of 1942. Although most of the scientific advice opposed the creation of a uranium research program on the grounds that it would not produce results to decide the war, Sergei Kaftanov, chairman of the Scientific-Technical Committee, and his deputy recommended to Stalin that work on a bomb project should be started. With access only to GRU reports on German nuclear research, Kaftanov relied heavily on Flerov's letter when quizzed by Stalin on the basis for his recommendation. In early July, Stalin approved the start of a uranium research program;

and a few days later, Flerov was recalled from the southwestern front to advise on steps to be taken. In August, the physicist was reassigned to his old institute in Kazan to resume his research on fast-neutron chain reactions. After the German assault on Moscow was turned back, and he had time to consider the implications of the British and German bomb programs, Stalin made his decision to resume nuclear research but encouraged the bureaucracy to use Flerov's strong letter as the apparent reason for his decision. The intelligence reports from London and New York were shared with very few Soviet officials.[14]

On September 28, 1942, the State Defense Committee formally approved the resumption of nuclear research and allocated limited resources for the program. Kaftanov and a few colleagues devoted the next three months to deciding on the program's research agenda and who should direct it. They discussed these issues with as many as eight leading physicists. Kurchatov was summoned to Moscow twice to meet with this group, and at their request he drew up a program for research and a list of his preferred participants. A bit later, Mikhail Pervukhin—deputy premier and people's commissar for the chemical industry—joined the process. A longtime Bolshevik trained as an electrical engineer, Pervukhin was shown the intelligence on British nuclear research by Molotov and asked to meet with several potential project directors, including Kurchatov. In January 1943, after receiving Pervukhin's recommendations, Molotov asked Kurchatov to see him. Describing his decision on the project's new leader, Molotov said that the NKVD "gave me a list of reliable physicists who could be depended on." Kapitsa declared that the atomic bomb was a project for after the war, and Ioffe pleaded that he was too old for the job. "In short, I was left with the youngest, Kurchatov, who was not known to anyone," Molotov stated. "I summoned him, we had a talk, he made a good impression on me." In February, the State Defense Committee approved a plan submitted by Pervukhin and Kurchatov for the program on atomic energy. Pervukhin and Kaftanov were to supervise the project, which would establish a new laboratory in Moscow to conduct all nuclear research. On March 10, 1943, Kurchatov was formally named director of the nuclear program.[15]

THE GENERAL

Only days after turning forty, Igor Kurchatov found himself in charge of a program to create an atomic bomb. He was not sure that the task was possible under the current conditions in the Soviet Union, and he realized that he was not the obvious choice for the job. Physicists such as Kapitsa and Ioffe were more accomplished and better known. He was not even a member of the Academy of Sciences. When nominated to be a corresponding member in 1938, he was not elected, and some months later the academy declined to fund his research program on nuclear chain reactions. But there were solid reasons why the key authorities selected him. Among the physicists, he had valuable experience directing the department of nuclear research at Ioffe's institute; he had demonstrated strong leadership and management skills; he had never worked outside Russia; and though not a party member, he had never challenged the authority of the Communist Party.[16]

When Kurchatov returned to Kazan after his appointment, he had a candid discussion with his colleagues expressing his doubts about his qualifications to direct this important new program. As described by his friend and biographer, Igor Golovin, each of his concerns was answered. His colleagues concluded: "Then how come you've never failed to achieve success? Why is it you always keep things moving along and get results? You're the 'general,' and you've got to head these operations!"[17]

A telling example of Kurchatov's leadership and interpersonal skills had occurred in Leningrad between 1937 and 1940. When he was searching desperately for a way to measure the energy of neutrons, Kurchatov read that at Berkeley, Luis Alvarez had successfully performed this experiment with a cyclotron. The nearby Radium Institute was building a small cyclotron but having difficulty getting it to work. Despite the sharp rivalry with Ioffe's research groups, Kurchatov persuaded the Radium Institute staff to allow him to help resolve their problems. Soon, as a result of his energy and inventive approaches, the new colleague was in charge. He assigned tasks to researchers, brought in outside specialists to solve technical issues, and tried all options to get the cyclotron to work. The balky machine began to function for research in 1939; and by the end of 1940, it was in full operation. It was the first successful cyclotron in Europe.[18]

Kurchatov was a child of the Russian heartland and grew up without any advantages of family or wealth. Born in 1903 in the southern Urals, where his father was a surveyor and his mother was a teacher, Kurchatov at the age of nine moved with his family to Simferopol in the Crimea. He studied at the local gymnasium and then at Tauridian University, where his instruction in physics was uneven. Next, he moved to Petrograd to study shipbuilding; but after a year, he had to return home to help his family when his father was exiled for political activity. He soon moved to Baku to work as an assistant to a former physics professor. In 1925, he received a life-changing opportunity. His former classmate, Kirill Sinel'nikov, worked at Ioffe's institute and recommended Kurchatov as a researcher. Ioffe invited Kurchatov to join the institute and assigned him to work in his own laboratory on the physics of dielectrics. In his new work in Leningrad, Kurchatov made several discoveries that built his reputation as a physicist; but in 1932, he decided to move from the practical area of semiconductors to the rapidly expanding field of nuclear physics. In December of that year, Ioffe named Kurchatov head of a new nuclear department at the institute.[19]

By the time Kurchatov became a department head, he had a reputation as someone who took charge of projects, organized the tasks involved, and issued commands. His colleagues already called him "the general." They accepted directions willingly because he was fair, had an excellent sense of humor, and shared the work with them. Kurchatov's life revolved around physics. He married Marina, the sister of his friend and coworker Sinel'nikov, in 1927. Familiar with obsessed physicists when they met, she soon adjusted to her husband spending evenings in his laboratory. Most of the physicists who joined Kurchatov on the atomic bomb project had previously worked with him, including his younger brother, Boris. Kurchatov's friends remembered him as a highly focused, serious person behind his friendly, humorous manner. Later in life, his younger colleague, Igor Golovin, described Kurhatov to Holloway as "a man with many layers to his personality, and therefore ideally suited to secret work."[20]

In his work in Ioffe's nuclear department, Kurchatov studied a wide range of significant problems. His experiments included examining the effect of proton beams on boron and lithium, artificial radioactivity created by bombarding isotopes with neutrons, and the absorption of neutrons by the nuclei of different elements. Maurice Goldhaber, a physicist at the Cavendish Laboratory, said of Kurchatov's work in the 1930s that "I always guessed it was Kurchatov who was the most important man in atomic energy in Russia because I had read his papers. . . . There were always interesting papers coming out of Kurchatov's school." During the purges of 1937–38, Kurchatov continued his research and avoided foreign travel, which caused many of his fellow scientists to be exiled or executed. When Germany invaded the Soviet Union, he closed his laboratory and joined the war effort, first developing antimine technology for the navy and then as director of the armor laboratory. Through all these activities and during the search for a director of the atomic bomb project, Kurchatov always had the strong support of Abram Ioffe.[21]

One of the qualities that proved essential to his success was Kurchatov's understanding of the need to win and maintain the support of the key officials in the highly centralized Soviet system. When he was selected as the scientific director of the bomb project, Kurchatov was keenly aware that he had to have the backing of the two members of the State Defense Committee who would control his fate, Molotov and Beria. Before his appointment was formally approved, Kurchatov told Molotov that he was uncertain which path to follow in developing a bomb and whether he could succeed. The deputy premier decided to show him the intelligence from Britain, and later described how "Kurchatov sat in my office in the Kremlin for several days studying those materials."[22]

Realizing that neither Molotov nor Beria understood nuclear physics, Kurchatov worked to earn the trust and support of Mikhail Pervukhin, who was his immediate supervisor and who would report to Molotov as the top official responsible for the program and to Beria as the source of the intelligence from London. On March 7, 1943, Kurchatov wrote by hand a long memorandum for Pervukhin summarizing the state of nuclear research, explaining what the intelligence on British research added to knowledge on nuclear fission, and setting out research steps for the new program. He then searched through the published literature to analyze the meaning of a statement in the intelligence documents that pointed out that an isotope of element 94 (plutonium) might be an alternative to U-235 as a route to a bomb. Kurchatov then wrote a second memorandum to Pervukhin on March 22, contending that using a plutonium isotope would likely be a simpler and faster way to build a bomb because it would avoid the long, complex process of using isotope separation to obtain the fissionable U-235. He pointed out that his program would need to find a significant supply of uranium and build a large cyclotron before the plutonium route could be investigated, and he listed four questions he wanted intelligence agents to try to answer about the state of research in the United States. Kurchatov's campaign to win support soon showed results. Molotov relates in his memoirs that the physicist had declared that the secret papers were "wonderful materials; they fill in just what we were lacking." The old Bolshevik introduced Kurchatov to Stalin, who promised "every kind of support." Molotov concluded that "we began to be guided by him."[23]

Kurchatov also sought to win the confidence of Beria, a goal pursued by many but achieved by very few. When reading the intelligence on British research, he took notes by hand and later wrote his memoranda for Pervukhin by hand. He then gave his notes to Pervukhin's assistant to be destroyed. In organizing his research program, he needed to use the intelligence without indicating where the information originated. He accomplished this by dropping suggestions during brainstorming sessions and in conversation. After months of hard work, Kurchatov's team succeeded in starting their reactor and achieving their first self-sustaining nuclear chain reaction. A few days later, Beria wanted to see the reactor in operation but was disappointed only to see a few dials move and counters recording results as the reactor went critical. He asked to go see the reactor, and with trepidation Kurchatov replied that this would be impossible because it would be extremely dangerous. Kurchatov had prepared the way for handling this disappointment from the security chief. Realizing that Beria was accustomed to visiting the test flights of new fighters and the maneuvers of new tanks, he had carefully explained to Beria and his deputies that scientific research involved many failed experiments as a way of testing a range of theories and designs and that this was normal and not an effort to sabotage the equipment. He also emphasized that significant danger could accompany some experiment failures. Although these explanations bought the team some time, Beria remained a deeply suspicious boss.[24]

Though he would rely most heavily on young colleagues from Ioffe's institute, Kurchatov also needed to win the cooperation of several well-established physicists. This was a particularly delicate task for members of the Academy of Sciences who were jealous of Kurchatov's appointment and his broad authority. Especially challenging was the case of Vitali Khlopin, who was thirteen years older than Kurchatov, director of the Radium Institute in Leningrad, and a member of the Academy of Sciences. Angered that he had not been included in the discussions leading to the State Defense Committee's decision to resume work on nuclear fission, Khlopin wrote a letter on January 15, 1943, to Kaftanov insisting that he have a central role in the program. Any solution to the problem of nuclear energy, he asserted, required "the basic participation in this work of the Radium Institute of the USSR Academy of Sciences, which has been entrusted to me, and of myself personally." He identified isotope separation as the major issue and declared that the Radium Institute should be charged to perform this research. After Kurchatov and his trusted colleagues had developed the main lines of research and divided the key tasks among themselves, the scientific director moved to assuage Khlopin's feelings by urging the Radium Institute to assume responsibility for separating plutonium from irradiated uranium. Kurchatov accompanied this request with fulsome expressions of respect for Khlopin's role as "the creator of our radiochemistry." Khlopin accepted this assignment and cooperated with the program, eventually accomplishing the assigned mission. Ironically, Kurchatov also asked his brother Boris to work on the same problem, and in 1946 Boris was the first to separate plutonium from irradiated uranium using the newly completed cyclotron.[25]

Gaining the full cooperation of Abram Alikhanov involved a different set of issues. Alikhanov was a contemporary of Kurchatov at Ioffe's institute and had achieved more success as a physicist. Early in 1943, he was elected a corresponding member of the Academy of Sciences, and he had been interviewed for the position of scientific director of the bomb project. Kaftanov's deputy, S. A. Balezin, recorded that Alikhanov "was dying to take charge of this work" but had made a less favorable impression than Kurchatov, who was recommended for the job. Alikhanov wanted to be involved in the program, but made it clear that he would not work directly under Kurchatov. The solution devised by Kurchatov was to include Alikhanov in the early planning sessions, even in the first meeting with Pervukhin. Kurchatov then asked Alikhanov to build a heavy water reactor that was a significant part of the agenda but was not the plutonium path that Kurchatov had chosen as his top priority. The difficulty for Alikhanov was that the Soviet Union did not have a plant to produce heavy water and was not likely to get the resources for this construction until after the war. Alikhanov did get his own laboratory in 1945 and succeeded in building the first Soviet heavy water reactor.[26]

Kurchatov possessed another quality that would serve him well in a country likely to remain starved for resources long after the war. He had the audacity to challenge power at the highest level in order to advance his program. After his researchers had labored for over a year, Kurchatov was angry and depressed at their limited progress. He was especially disappointed that Molotov, Stalin's top deputy, had not provided the personal leadership the program needed. On May 19, 1944, he wrote a remarkable appeal to Stalin—declaring that for the nuclear project to succeed, the state had to make it a top priority for resources and personnel. In a cover letter, Pervukhin endorsed Kurchatov's plea and stated: "In order to catch up with the foreign [countries], we must make the development of the uranium problem into the task of first-rate State importance." To achieve this, he proposed transferring the supervision of the program to Beria. Believing that the bomb project was not an urgent issue, and knowing that Beria already had responsibility for the war industries, Molotov did not object. On Pervukhin's note, he wrote: "*Important.*—Report to Comrade Stalin." Apparently, the shift of authority was not urgent for Stalin either, because no action was taken.

Impatient for better support, Kurchatov wrote a more detailed request to Beria on September 29, 1944. Reporting that he had in the last month read 3,000 pages of new espionage materials on the Manhattan Project, Kurchatov emphasized that very important findings had come from the work of an unprecedented collection of scientific and technical talent. Compared with the US progress, Soviet developments were "completely unsatisfactory." He complained that the program lacked "unified leadership" and desperately needed essential raw materials, machinery, and scientists. He was sharply critical of the lack of cooperation from other institutions that did not appreciate the importance of his group's efforts. He concluded by asking Beria, despite his demanding responsibilities, to take charge of the project and "give instructions for the work to be organized in a way that corresponds to the possibilities and significance of our great state in world culture." This appeal was successful, and Beria began to campaign for the new authority. On December 3, 1944, the State Defense Committee ordered the entire nuclear project to be placed under NKVD supervision.[27]

LIMITED STEPS

Although he had gotten the administrative structure he wanted, Kurchatov's resource problems would not be solved for another year. The Soviet leadership had three basic reasons for ignoring Kurchatov's repeated pleas for more assistance. Most important was the need to devote all available funds and manpower to support the Red Army's drive across Central and Eastern Europe toward Berlin. Also working in the same direction was the distrust of Stalin and Beria, and other senior officials to a lesser degree, of the intelligence reports on US progress in developing nuclear weapons. A final contributing factor was the suspicion of all government leaders of the motives and loyalty of the scientists, most of whom were not party members and who were engaged in work the political elite did not understand or appreciate.[28]

Kurchatov's first task was to gather a core group of physicists in Moscow to work out the main elements of the project's research agenda. This group included Iulii B. Khariton, Isaak K. Kikoin, Abram Alikhanov,

Iakov Zel'dovich, Aleksandr I. Leipunskii, and Georgii N. Flerov. The group's members decided that their major initial goals would be to build a nuclear reactor and develop a method for separating large amounts of uranium isotopes. They were later joined by Leonid M. Nemenov, who would be responsible for building a large cyclotron, and Kurchatov's younger brother Boris. With an agenda settled, Kurchatov searched for an appropriate location for his growing staff and found a building that had been evacuated in the fall of 1941 by the staff of the Seismological Institute, located in the center of Moscow on Pyzhevski Lane. As the institute grew, it occupied another deserted building on Bolshaya Kaluzhskaya Street. Almost immediately, Kurchatov began looking for a new location to house a fully staffed and equipped Laboratory No. 2. He found a partially completed three-story building in the northwestern suburb of Silver Lake and began to organize the rapid construction of the new facility. By April 1944, when the institute started using its new building, the staff numbered seventy-four people, including twenty-five scientists, plus engineers, mechanics, and janitors. They conducted limited experiments and held stimulating seminars to discuss various theories of chain reactions, but their work was restricted by a lack of equipment, raw materials, and even furniture. The government had chosen Kurchatov as director of the atomic bomb project and directed that it be made an institute of the Academy of Sciences, and in September 1943 it took the next step and created a special position for the new director to become a full Academician, despite the opposition of some senior members.[29]

During the final two years of the war, the project's theoretical team, headed by Khariton, worked on ways to initiate and sustain a chain reaction and how to most efficiently separate uranium isotopes, while others concentrated on acquiring the needed equipment and raw materials. The three main problems, in order of increasing difficulty, were building a large cyclotron, purifying graphite, and mining and purifying uranium. Work on a cyclotron at Ioffe's institute had begun in early 1941, but the German invasion had brought this to a halt. The staff buried key parts on the institute property before evacuating to Kazan, and Leningrad had been under siege for 872 days before it was broken in late January 1943.

Soon afterward, Kurchatov sent Nemenov and an engineer back to the ravaged city to recover whatever they could find of the cyclotron's components. They were able to locate the generator, rectifier, and other parts; and most important, they found the 75-ton electromagnet at a plant 3 kilometers from the front lines. They packed these items on two freight cars and sent them to Moscow by the rail line recently opened through the German front. Nemenov's group devoted over a year to building the other key components and assembling the machine, which began operation in late September 1944. By the end of the next month, Boris Kurchatov succeeded in separating the first traces of plutonium from the uranyl nitrate irradiated in the cyclotron.[30]

Kurchatov knew from American physics journals that achieving a chain reaction with a uranium isotope would require some other element to act as a moderator to prevent premature and incomplete detonation. The intelligence reports told him that British and American scientists were using both heavy water and graphite as moderators. One of the early decisions of the core group was to build a reactor with a uranium-graphite core, largely because the Soviet Union lacked any supply of heavy water. With assistance from Pervukhin's staff, the project received several tons of graphite in the fall of 1943, but experiments showed that it contained far too many impurities to serve as a moderator. When the production plant declared that it could not remove the problematic amounts of ash and boron, the physicists at Laboratory No. 2 had to create a purification process. Even with this new technique, the plant produced uneven results, and each delivery of graphite had to be tested for purity. These delays meant that graphite of the necessary purity did not become available until the late summer of 1945.[31]

Locating an adequate supply of uranium ore was Kurchatov's most critical requirement, and the search was frustratingly slow. The quest for uranium had begun in July 1940, when the government, urged by Vladimir Vernadskii and Vitali Khlopin, had created a Commission on the Uranium Problem to find deposits of the valuable ore. The commission's work had been suspended without success because of the German attack, and only a small amount of uranium was available when Kurchatov wrote Pervukhin in April 1943 that he would need 50 to 100 metric tons of ore to advance fission research and build a reactor. Even with a government directive to produce the full amount of 100 tons, the Institute of Rare and Fine Metals completed its first ingot of pure uranium metal, weighing 1 kilogram, in November 1944. Only in September 1945 did a major exploration for uranium begin in Central Asia.[32]

The solution for the program's lack of uranium came, not from Central Asia, but from Central Europe. In March 1945, President Edward Beneš of Czechoslovakia signed a secret agreement in Moscow to deliver all his country's current and future uranium ore to the Soviet Union. Before the war, the Czech mines were one of the world's principal sources of uranium, yielding about 20 metric tons annually. Two months later, on May 2, the very day Berlin fell to the Red Army, a team of Soviet physicists led by an NKVD colonel-general and wearing the uniforms of NKVD lieutenant-colonels landed at the city's Templehof Airport to investigate the status of German nuclear research and seize any supply of uranium they could find. The team included Khariton, Kikoin, Nemenov, and Flerov, among others. They quickly learned from the few remaining German nuclear physicists (the most accomplished senior scientists had fled south to the American occupation zone) that their program had not gotten very far in building an atomic bomb. After days of painstaking detective work, they finally located a store of about 130 tons of uranium oxide stored in a tannery outside Berlin. This supply would provide fuel for the reactor, which would produce the initial plutonium for the Soviet bomb. Kurchatov later told Khariton that this discovery had saved their program "about a year." Ironically, the Soviet team had missed a much larger prize by two weeks. On April 17, a joint British-American unit quickly moved into what would become the Soviet occupation zone to capture 1,100 tons of uranium ore from a factory in Stassfurt. The Manhattan Project would use this seized ore to produce U-235 for the core of the bomb called Little Boy that was detonated over Hiroshima.[33]

At this point, Pervukhin and Kurchatov wrote directly to Stalin to urge that the nuclear program receive the government's top priority. Despite having Klaus Fuchs's report that the Americans were scheduled to test their plutonium bomb about July 10, the leaders who had ultimate authority over the project—Stalin, Molotov, and Beria—ignored this appeal. A puzzling question about the war in Europe is why Soviet leaders did not place a strong emphasis on building the bomb. Citing evidence from a senior KGB officer, David Holloway suggests that there are several likely reasons. Beria and Stalin did not trust the intelligence reports and were suspicious of the scientists working on the project. They also lacked any understanding of the science and technology involved in this complex undertaking. Holloway concludes: "Whatever the reasons, it is clear that . . . neither Stalin, Beria, nor Molotov understood the role that the atomic bomb would soon play in international relations." It would take a dramatic event to change this attitude.[34]

THE IMPACT OF HIROSHIMA

The effect of an atomic bomb destroying the city of Hiroshima provided this dramatic event. Within special government circles in the Soviet Union, Hiroshima caused a sharp acceleration of work on all phases of the bomb project, but Stalin and his top officials continued to present a public reaction of minimal concern over the new weapon's importance in both political and military arenas. Long before Hiroshima, Moscow's relations with Washington were already turning cool. In January 1945, Maksim Litvinov, former commissar for foreign affairs and ambassador in Washington, wrote Stalin that he believed the United States might "use Lend-Lease for obtaining economic and political compensation unacceptable to us." In fact, the Lend-Lease program was immediately terminated after victory in Europe in May, producing sharp complaints from Stalin to the visiting American emissary Harry Hopkins. Continuing difficulties ran through the spring, as Stalin repeatedly violated agreements made at Yalta on free elections in Romania and Poland. Documents released in the 1990s show that the Soviet dictator was suspicious of American motives in keeping the Manhattan Project a secret, even though he received regular espionage reports on its progress and knew about the scheduled test near Alamogordo. But he showed no reaction when Truman casually announced after a session at Potsdam in July that the United States had a powerful new weapon.[35]

In contrast to his public posture that the atomic bomb was just another weapon, Stalin's actions within his government showed deep concern and the need to build a Soviet bomb as soon as possible. His first initiative was to advance the date of the Soviet entry into the war against Japan. Having pledged to Truman that the Red Army would join the Pacific conflict in mid-August, Stalin now feared the bombing of Hiroshima on August 6 would lead to a Japanese surrender before the Soviet Union could enter the war and claim the territory and concessions he had been promised at Yalta. Stalin moved up the Soviet offensive to a few minutes after midnight, Manchurian time, on August 9. A few hours later, the United States dropped a plutonium bomb on Nagasaki. While the Red Army moved quickly south through Manchuria toward Korea, Japan began overtures for peace. On August 16, major combat operations ceased as the government in Tokyo accepted Allied terms for peace.[36]

Stalin's next significant reaction to Hiroshima was to call in Kurchatov and Boris Vannikov, the people's commissar of munitions, in mid-August to order a maximum effort to complete the atomic bomb. To emphasize the urgency, he declared: "Hiroshima has shaken the whole world. The balance has been destroyed." He announced that all the nation's resources would be available for the project, saying, "If a child doesn't cry, the mother doesn't know what he needs. Ask for whatever you like. You won't be refused." On August 20, the State Defense Committee created a new structure to manage the expanded program. A special committee chaired by Beria was to direct "all work" on atomic weapons. It would operate through a new First Chief Directorate of the Council of Ministers managed by Vannikov, with Kurchatov and Pervukhin among his deputies. With the exception of Kurchatov, the deputies were industrial managers who had extensive experience in organizing large projects of construction, mining, transportation, and production of all types of war matériel. Beria also had his own system of supervision based on NKVD generals placed near the director of each plant and research organization. Kurchatov relied on a Scientific-Technical Council within the First Directorate for advice on technical issues. Orders went out for new activity in many organizations. Intelligence agents in Canada, the United States, and Japan were directed to obtain specific details about the bombs used and the kind of damage they created. German scientists detained by the NKVD were assigned to work on isotope separation in two institutes on the Black Sea coast. Kurchatov and his colleagues developed plans for new research centers to be built in secret cities in the interior, new institutes for uranium and plutonium metallurgy, mining and refining facilities in Central Asia, and a test site in Kazakhstan—all to be special prison camps built and operated by Gulag labor. Reports and evidence from Hiroshima and Nagasaki—including pieces of melted rock and a severely burned human hand—were sent to Moscow and widely circulated at the top levels of government.[37]

An important task for Kurchatov was to explain in layperson's terms each step in the process to the industrial and security managers who would supervise the various aspects of the program. This involved describing why building isotope separation plants and plutonium production reactors was an essential element in making an atomic bomb to men who during the war had managed industries that made tanks and artillery shells as well as to those who had worked as senior internal security officers in the NKVD. Kurchatov and his top colleagues Khariton, Kikoin, Alikhanov, and Artsimovich were all involved as instructors, and when, on occasion, an explanation was too technical to be grasped by the managers, Kurchatov would intervene and rephrase the statement in more accessible terms. Kurchatov also served as a scientific counselor to Beria and Vannikov. "It is testimony to Kurchatov's extraordinary qualities as an organizer," Holloway asserts, "that he was able to work for Beria, collaborate with Vannikov and [his deputy] Zaveniagin, and retain the confidence and loyalty of his scientific colleagues."[38] (See figure 15.1.)

The order to agents in many countries to report on atomic research and deposits of critical metals produced so much material that Beria had to create a new system to manage the intake. He established Department S within the NKGB to translate, evaluate, and distribute the incoming intelligence. The new section was headed by Pavel Sudoplatov, a career NKGB officer noted for organizing the assassination of Leon Trotskii

FIGURE 15.1 Igor Kurchatov, director of the Soviet nuclear research program, was known by a wide circle as "the General" for his remarkable administrative skills. His closest colleagues referred to him as "the Beard," for obvious reasons. Here he is wearing three Hero of Socialist Labor medals and his Lenin Prize medal, circa 1954.

Source: Kurchatov House Museum, Moscow.

in Mexico in 1940. A young theoretical physicist from Moscow University, Iakov Terletskii, was recruited to evaluate and distribute appropriate material from the 10,000 pages of typewritten reports he was given when he arrived to begin work at Lubyanka. With his greatly expanded responsibilities, Kurchatov no longer received all the espionage material. Instead, Terletskii distributed the important documents to Kurchatov and his top associates. The intelligence reports strongly shaped decisions on the design and construction of the various parts of the project. They helped determine that isotope separation would proceed on a separate, slower track. Most crucially, Klaus Fuchs's two large reports in June and September 1945 dictated that effort would concentrate on the plutonium route to a bomb. In his reports, Fuchs described all the essential components of a plutonium bomb, including their materials and dimensions as well as a sketch of the design. Other useful material on the bomb's design came from David Greenglass, another spy who worked as a machinist at Los Alamos. When Beria reported the comprehensive nature of Fuchs's reports, Stalin ordered that Kurchatov copy the American plutonium bomb design in every detail.[39]

A final result of the Hiroshima bombing was the allocation of significantly increased resources for science and technology. Immediately after receiving the initial reports on Hiroshima, the Politburo ordered the preparation of a new five-year plan for 1946–50. The resources for science proposed in this plan were mainly to support the atomic bomb program, but other military projects were funded in radar, rocket, and jet engine development. Stalin organized a meeting with Kurchatov, Molotov, and Beria at the Kremlin late in the evening of January 25, 1946, to discuss the bomb project. He reaffirmed his decisions to copy the American design for the plutonium bomb and make available all the resources needed for the task. The dictator went on to emphasize the need for quick results and stated that he expected complete loyalty from the scientists during this intense period of work. He added that he planned to improve the lives of the scientists with increased salaries to allow them to have their own dachas and cars, and he proposed awarding prizes for major accomplishments. Stalin kept his promise, and in March the scientists received pay increases of two to three times their past salaries. The overall budget for science in 1946 was three times greater than that for the previous year. There was also an extravagant present for Kurchatov—a two-story, eight-room house to be built on the new grounds of Laboratory No. 2. Designed by a prominent architect in an Italianate style, the house had large windows, fine wood paneling, marble fireplaces, parquet floors, and a dramatic central staircase. Construction began early in 1946, and Kurchatov and his wife moved in the following November. Located in a forest of birch and pine trees, the elegant house was referred to by the general's colleagues as "the forester's cabin."[40]

Not long after Kurchatov's January meeting with Stalin, Beria became the object of the dictator's suspicion for his accumulation of near-total authority over the security services. After criticizing the security chief for having a senior staff composed entirely of loyal Georgians, Stalin essentially kicked him upstairs. In March 1946, he promoted Beria to be a full member of the Politburo and deputy chairman of the Council of Ministers. He increased the bureaucratic authority of the NKVD and the NKGB by making them ministries instead of commissariats. They were restyled as the Ministry of Internal Affairs (MVD) and the Ministry of State Security (MGB). Beria no longer had direct authority over the ministries, and his Georgian leaders were replaced by Russians. Stalin's paranoid logic was clear—Beria now had full responsibility for the government's top-priority project and would continue to receive nuclear intelligence from the MGB, but the project and Beria himself would be guarded by the MVD, whose leaders owed their promotions to the dictator.[41]

BUILDING A NUCLEAR INFRASTRUCTURE

Having finally received the government commitment as the top priority, the supervisors of the atomic bomb program now had to construct a complete nuclear industry in a country heavily destroyed and exhausted by four years of total war. A critical and time-consuming set of tasks confronted the organizers in locating, mining, and purifying a large supply of uranium. Begun in earnest only in September 1945, the uranium drive was also the most labor intensive. Stretching across the Soviet Union and into East Germany, Czechoslovakia, and Poland, the mining operation engaged up to 360,000 people (mostly prisoners), with the majority working in Eastern Europe, where the most productive deposits were found. Only in 1948 did the uranium supply begin to satisfy production demands, and extensive efforts to develop Soviet sources continued into the 1950s. More sustained labor was required to develop processes to purify the uranium ore of other metals and refine it into metal for use in the bomb core. Beria gave this difficult assignment to Nikolaus Riehl, who had been brought to Moscow in June 1945 along with several colleagues by the NKVD. Born in Saint Petersburg and fluent in Russian, Riehl had managed a program for uranium purification outside Berlin during the war. Using some of the machinery brought from Germany by Soviet forces, Riehl and his team encountered problems in two phases of his work: purification, and reducing uranium to powder for smelting into metal. With help from Soviet scientists and evidence from a recently published American report, he solved the issues that were slowing his progress, and by October 1946 his plant produced 3 metric tons of uranium metal a week for the program's effort to generate a chain reaction.[42]

The American report that provided some guidance to Kurchatov's extensive cadre of scientists is called the Smyth Report. Written by the Princeton physicist Henry D. Smyth, the report, titled *Atomic Energy for Military Purposes*, was a sanitized history of the Manhattan Project report issued by the US government on August 11, 1945, in an attempt at transparency just after the two atomic bombings in Japan. Six copies went to the Soviet press service Tass and were immediately forwarded to Moscow, where the text was translated into Russian and published in a print run of 30,000 copies on January 30, 1946. Although American scientists and policymakers who reviewed the manuscript before publication believed they had omitted all the highly sensitive information, helpful comments remained, and together with the intelligence provided by Klaus Fuchs and others, the Soviet program benefited from the combined information.[43]

Kurchatov personally assumed leadership in the important area of building an experimental reactor to test the purity and the most efficient combination of fuel elements to be used in a large plutonium production reactor. After having been delayed since 1943 by the lack of graphite and uranium, serious work on the reactor began only at the start of 1946. By the end of the year, the reactor group had expanded from eleven to seventy-six members. The reactor was called F–1 (Fizicheskii–1; Physical–1) by the staff and managers. In January, Kurchatov received the first group of cylindrical slugs of uranium metal. After experiments with small quantities of these slugs with a graphite moderator, the scientists concluded that the purity level of slugs was uneven. They had to devote several weeks to developing methods to obtain consistent purity levels in the vitally important uranium slugs and then instruct the manufacturing plant how to use the new technique. While these experiments were under way beneath two tents on the grounds of Laboratory No. 2, construction of a brick building to house the reactor began. In the center of the building, a large pit for the reactor was dug 23 feet deep to shield the operators from radiation. The building was 130 by 50 feet and two stories high, and it was connected by a tunnel to an underground control room, which was protected from radiation by walls of "lead blocks and hollow bricks filled with a mixture of boron and paraffin." The building was completed in June 1946, with its power supplied by two new electrical substations.[44]

The reactor core was built with a lattice of graphite blocks with uranium slugs inserted into holes. These blocks were surrounded on all sides by pure graphite blocks to give room for the fissioning neutrons to hit graphite and slow down until they contacted another U-235 nucleus in the next slug to sustain the chain reaction. Trial and error with precise measurement of the neutron absorption rate were used to determine the distance between the blocks and how many layers would be needed to achieve a self-sustaining chain reaction. The fission process was managed by three cadmium control rods, which would be gradually raised from their position in the center of the pile to start a chain reaction. They would be completely lowered to stop the process. By August, the necessary 400 metric tons of graphite were at the site, and the heavy labor of assembling the small first stage of the reactor began. This would not be sufficient to create a lasting chain reaction but would give measurements to determine how rapidly to add more layers. By November, the scientists were confident that their fourth assembly would work, and they began to add more layers of graphite and uranium-loaded graphite until they completed the sixty-first layer in the evening of December 24. Layer sixty-two was installed on Christmas Day. Kurchatov took over the reactor controls that afternoon and ordered everyone out of the control room except for four close associates. Gradually, he lifted the control rods, pausing after each step for the neutron intensity to be recorded before raising the rods another 4 inches. Finally, at 6 P.M., he raised the control rods 2 more inches, and the counters roared and the lights glowed steadily. Kurchatov calmly announced: "Well, we have reached it." The first nuclear reactor outside North America had gone critical on Christmas Day 1946.[45]

The achievement of building the first nuclear reactor in Europe created challenges in two forms. The first, discussed above, was when Beria asked to see the reactor in operation several days after Christmas, only to be disappointed and highly suspicious at seeing nothing more than noisy counters and flashing lights. As Golovin and Smirnov write: "Beria began suspecting that Kurchatov was swindling him." This suspicion was shared by the program's ever-present MVD officers. The bottom line, Golovin and Smirnov declare, was that "everyone understood that if the bomb didn't explode, the whole team would be in trouble."[46]

The other controversy revolved around whether Kurchatov's accomplishment is diminished because he simply copied what he learned from espionage about an experimental reactor designed at the University of Chicago for construction at the Hanford National Laboratory in Washington State. This debate is based on Arnold Kramish's 1959 volume *Atomic Energy in the Soviet Union*, which closely compares the specifications of the Hanford 305 reactor and the Soviet F–1, showing them to be remarkably similar. The one striking exception was in the F–1's use of 45 tons of uranium, compared with 27 tons for the Hanford 305, which Kramish correctly speculates was the result of impurities in the Soviet uranium slugs. In evaluating the fragmentary evidence available in

1958–59, Kramish strongly suggests that espionage provided the design specifications for Kurchatov's F–1.[47]

Subsequent research using declassified records has provided much additional information about espionage contributions to the Soviet atomic bomb program. The most direct evidence to support the Kramish theory was provided by Alexander Vassiliev, who took voluminous notes from MGB files in the early 1990s on atomic espionage in the United States. He reports that Engelbert Broda, an emigré Austrian physicist working at the Cavendish Laboratory in Cambridge, was a MGB agent who provided plans for a nuclear reactor designed at the University of Chicago's Metallurgical Laboratory to his handler in London. On March 29, 1944, the London KGB station chief sent these plans to Moscow, declaring that they contained "all the necessary information to build a plant, and [it] is exceptionally valuable." The design for the Hanford 305 reactor was started at the Chicago Metallurgical Laboratory in June 1943, and construction was completed at Hanford, Washington, in March 1944. Writing over a decade before Vassiliev's notes were published, Richard Rhodes accepted the Kramish argument that espionage probably provided the design for the F–1, but he goes on to contend that Kurchatov and his colleagues still had to test a series of neutron absorption rates, construct several lattice designs to identify the most efficient model, and develop critical improvements in the purification processes for both graphite and uranium in order to achieve their successful chain reaction. His persuasive conclusion is that, with a significant assist from American research, the Soviet program still made a substantial advance.[48]

Kurchatov had been planning a plutonium production complex as early as May 1945, and he realized that it would involve significant new issues in designing a large reactor to operate continuously at a high power level. In June 1946, he asked Nikolai Dollezhal', director of the Institute of Chemical Machine-Building and a specialist in heat and power stations, to help design the reactor. Many new problems had to be resolved, including how to structure a water cooling system, how to remove the irradiated uranium fuel slugs to separate the plutonium, how to seal the fuel slugs to prevent corrosion, how to set up remote controls to protect the operators, and how to arrange the lattices of graphite and the vertical holes for the fuel slugs. The biggest difficulties were with sealing (canning) the fuel slugs and constructing the aluminum cooling tubes.[49]

A new city, to be called Cheliabinsk–40, was constructed east of the Urals near a large power station, the Techa River, and four gulags. After trees were cleared and roads were built, construction began in the summer of 1946, with the labor of as many as 70,000 prisoners working under the supervision of an MVD major-general. A soldier working as a guard described the city as built in three concentric zones, each surrounded by barbed wire and guards. The outer zone was reserved for scientists, engineers, and technicians, some with families; the middle area was for soldiers and prisoners; and the center area was allocated to large buildings housing the reactor and the remote control rooms. The reactor itself was located underground in a pit 60 feet deep, which prisoners dug by hand. Water tanks lined the pit with 10-feet-thick walls inside surrounding the reactor.[50]

The building to house the reactor was completed by the end of 1947, and early the next year Kurchatov and Vannikov moved to Cheliabinsk–40 and lived in a railway car at the site. Materials for the reactor came from Moscow, and the large amount of graphite needed for the core was produced at a new plant in the complex. A shortage of trained personnel, especially chemists and engineers, delayed work at the new city by several months. Assembly of the reactor began in March. After three months of intense labor, the reactor was built, and testing of the instruments and controls began. The production reactor went critical on June 7 and advanced through several stages of increasing fuel and power output, until it reached its design level of 100,000 kilowatts on June 22, 1948. Serious problems developed with corrosion of the seals of the fuel slugs, and more critically, the slugs swelled and wrinkled so that they became lodged in the discharge pipes. The reactor had to be shut down, and the uranium removed. After considerable analysis of the problems, solutions were found and modifications were made in the reactor. The rebuilt reactor went into operation at the end of 1948.[51]

"In this most difficult period of his life," Golovin comments without further explanation, "in August 1948, Kurchatov became a member of the Communist Party of the Soviet Union." This may have resulted from Beria's sharp questioning of Kurchatov and his staff about the possibility of sabotage in the disaster with the reactor's swollen fuel slugs. But one can only speculate.[52]

Other phases of the production of usable plutonium proceeded at the same time in new facilities at Cheliabinsk–40. A second plant was responsible for separating plutonium from the irradiated uranium slugs. Following the precipitation method used successfully at the US Hanford Laboratory, the scientists dissolved the slugs in nitric acid, which produced large amounts of radioactive xenon and iodine gas, which in turn was released through a tall chimney to dissipate over a broad area. Resolving the technical and safety issues in this process proved complicated, and it took until early 1949 before the plant began producing plutonium. The plant designed to purify the plutonium and convert it into metal was still under construction, so the machinery for this process was set up in a temporary facility. The first nitrate solutions of plutonium were available at the end of February 1949. After purification, these solutions were sent to the metallurgical team in mid-April, and by June sufficient plutonium for a bomb was produced.[53]

Although Kurchatov personally directed the work on a plutonium implosion bomb, he organized teams of scientists to pursue alternative routes to nuclear weapons at different secret cities. One concentrated on isotope separation and uranium enrichment to build a uranium gun bomb, another focused on building a heavy water reactor for power generation, and a third began a program to develop a hydrogen bomb. The hydrogen, or thermonuclear fusion, bomb was the most significant course pursued. It began in January 1948 in Moscow at the Academy of Sciences' Institute of Physics, under the direction of the senior physicist and future Nobel laureate Igor Tamm. He recruited an outstanding team of young physicists, including Andrei Sakharov, Semyon Belensky, and Vitaly Ginzburg. By the end of 1948, Sakharov had already developed and refined a concept for a layer-cake design for a thermonuclear bomb, an idea that Edward Teller had independently conceived at Los Alamos. Early the next year, at Beria's insistence, Sakharov moved to Arzamas–16 at Sarov to work with Iulii Khariton.[54]

The main work at Arzamas–16 was to build and test the detonation mechanisms for the plutonium implosion bomb. Established in 1946 in a remote area 250 miles east of Moscow, the new research center was on the site of an old Orthodox monastery and near a labor camp, which would supply workers for construction and heavy tasks. Khariton selected a staff of specialists in the chemistry and physics of detonations and explosions. Their job was to build a high explosive case for a plutonium sphere that would when detonated compress the plutonium and create a chain reaction. The most complex aspect of this process was to design a system of lenses to convert the diffused shock waves into a focused spherical wave to compress the plutonium simultaneously and with equal force at each point. A related critical element was to build a neutron initiator at the center of the plutonium sphere to ensure that the chain reaction began at precisely the right microsecond. After multiple tests and revisions, these steps and the construction of an electrical system for detonation from a remote control center were completed by the spring of 1949.[55]

Constructing a completely new atomic industry within three years in a country devastated by war was an amazing accomplishment for the Soviet Union. It demonstrated that the nation had the scientific and engineering talent and a command economy able to concentrate resources for the leadership's top priority. But the crash program to build an atomic bomb came at tremendous costs. The most widespread damage was to the health of the prison labor working in mining and construction. There are no accurate statistics on deaths among the prisoners as a result of radiation exposure, accidents, malnutrition, or disease. But the clear result was that of the estimated 360,000 prisoners who worked in mining and construction on the project, very few ever returned to their homes. Another costly factor was the lack of adequate safety clothing and equipment for those who worked with radioactive materials. The scientists, engineers, and technicians who worked on reactors, the chemical separation and purification of uranium and plutonium, and bomb assembly reported frequent cases of radiation sickness and cancer starting in 1949. A final cost from creation of an atomic industry was severe damage to the environment. In only one example, the complex at Cheliabinsk–40 released 76 million cubic meters of high- and intermediate-level radioactive waste between 1948 and 1951. This discharge into the local river system required relocating 10,000 area residents and providing water from new sources for other towns and villages. There were at least six other atomic production facilities, plus many uranium mines in Central Asia and Central and Eastern Europe generating similar contamination.[56]

THE INITIAL TEST

Although Khariton had the design and specifications of the Fat Man plutonium bomb used at Nagasaki, he insisted that his team members perform all the calculations and experiments themselves to be as certain as possible that the bomb would work with the materials they had developed. As scientific director of Arzamas–16, he directed that each component of the ignition and explosive sequences be checked and rechecked.[57]

On top of the scientific demands and time pressure, Kurchatov's scientists and engineers had to work under the constant suspicion of security and party officials. One episode among many is illustrative. As Anatolii Aleksandrov was doing final work on the plutonium hemispheres at Cheliabinsk–40, Pervukhin arrived with a group of generals and the plant director. After explaining what he was doing, Aleksandrov writes,

They asked a strange question: "Why do you think it is plutonium?" I said that I knew the whole technical process for obtaining it and was therefore sure that it was plutonium and could not be anything else! "But why are you sure that some piece of iron hasn't been substituted for it?" I held up a piece to the alpha-counter, and it began to crackle at once. "Look," I said, "it's alpha-active." "But perhaps it has just been rubbed with plutonium on the outside and that is why it crackles," said someone. I grew angry, took that piece and held it out to them: "Feel it, it's hot!" One of them said that it did not take long to heat a piece of iron. Then I responded that he could sit and look till morning and check whether the plutonium remained hot. But I would go to bed. This apparently convinced them, and they went away.[58]

After the two plutonium hemispheres were finished at Cheliabinsk–40 in June 1949, they were transported to Arzamas–16, where Georgii Flerov carried out dangerous tests to ensure that the hemispheres would attain a critical mass when brought together under high explosive pressure. When Flerov's experiments were successfully concluded, Kurchatov reported to the Kremlin that the bomb was ready to be tested and asked for approval to move to the test site in Kazakhstan.[59]

Before the test was approved, Stalin directed the principal scientists and engineers to come to Moscow to report to him on the preparations. One by one they met with the premier and Beria. Kurchatov was first, followed by Khariton. In what would be his only meeting with Stalin, Khariton was asked if the available plutonium could be used for two less powerful bombs so that one could be on hand after the test. The nervous physicist replied that this would not be possible because all the plutonium used in the present core was necessary for the design of the bomb. Stalin accepted this answer without further discussion, and Kurchatov and Khariton noted his desire for a second bomb and made hasty preparations to produce more plutonium and fabricate another core before the test occurred. It is interesting to note that, in contrast to the many technical questions he asked when briefed on new tanks or aircraft, Stalin posed no technical questions for the nuclear scientists. Indeed, Kurchatov later stated that "when I was at meetings with Stalin, I had the impression that I bored him terribly. When I spoke to him, I did so briefly, finished quickly and fell silent as soon as possible. He never asked any questions about the technology. [I felt that he thought I] was droning on like an annoying fly and wanted me to finish quickly."[60]

As the time for the test of the bomb approached, security tightened at the main atomic cities. Although salaries and living conditions were very good for the scientists compared with the economic situation of most citizens, the climate of suspicion and fear made life uncomfortable. At Arzamas–16, the large complex was ringed by barbed wire and guards; no one could leave without special permission. Secrecy was tightly enforced, and research information was compartmentalized. When he first arrived at Arzamas–16, Andrei Sakharov was told "there are secrets everywhere, and the less you know that doesn't concern you, the better off you'll be." Top scientists such as Kurchatov, Khariton, and Zel'dovich had bodyguards who, in addition to providing security, also served as informants. As Khariton told an interviewer years later, "Beria's people were everywhere." Reminiscent of the purges of the 1930s, denunciation was encouraged. When Khariton attended a dinner to celebrate Kurchatov's birthday, Beria's senior agent remarked menacingly, "If you only knew how much they write against you!" After that thinly veiled threat had fully registered, he added, "But I don't believe them." The danger remained, as everyone present realized, because the accusations were on record and could be used at any time the security service chose.[61]

The scientists, including the physicists, were also threatened by a campaign against "cosmopolitans" launched in January 1949. This effort to enforce ideological purity focused on Jews and intellectuals with ties to the West. Kurchatov was regularly accused of surrounding himself with scientists who were Jewish or who were associated with Western scientists and their writings. Khariton was especially endangered; he was Jewish, he had received his PhD from Cambridge, and both his parents had fled Russia after the Bolsheviks seized power. In August 1948, Trofin Lysenko, with Stalin's active support, had led a purge of Mendelian genetics from biology and agriculture, with the argument that it was a bourgeois fabrication designed to invalidate Marxism-Leninism. There was already agitation among philosophers and physicists close to the government for a similar attack on foreign influences in physics. At this point, Kurchatov took precautionary action. In a section of his book on the final phase in making the bomb, his colleague, Igor Golovin, writes, "In this most difficult period of his life, in August 1948, Kurchatov became a member of the Communist Party of the Soviet Union."[62]

The desire to purify physics concentrated on preparations for a national conference of 600 specialists, who would debate the appropriate concepts for Soviet physics. This effort was a continuation of a 1930s battle between physicists at Moscow University and those at the Academy of Sciences. On the rhetorical level, the conflict was over the university scholars' charge that the theories of relativity and quantum mechanics were fallacious, Western inventions that were incompatible with dialectical materialism. But fundamentally, the university activists were outraged that the Academy had attracted the top physicists and garnered most of the government support for research as well as all the leading positions in the atomic project. Senior Academy physicists fought back, with little effect. Success came only when three prominent physicists, probably including Kurchatov, called on Beria to have the conference canceled on the grounds that it would damage Soviet physics and delay completion of the plutonium bomb. Beria took the issue to Stalin, who agreed to call off the conference only days before it was to convene on March 21. With regard to the physicists working on the bomb, Stalin told his security chief, "Leave them in peace. We can always shoot them later." Soviet physics survived as an independent intellectual discipline because it served the interests of the state. With classic Russian irony, Academy physicist Lev Landau declared that the vindication of Soviet physics was "the first example of successful nuclear deterrence."[63]

The test of the bomb was held on the steppes of Kazakhstan in late August 1949. A town to be called Semipalatinsk–21 was constructed about 85 miles northwest of a city of the same name. It would later be renamed Kurchatov. The test site was 43 miles south of the new town. Work on the test site had started two years earlier. The bomb would be detonated on top of a 100-foot steel tower built on a concrete foundation. Nearby was a reinforced concrete workshop, where the bomb would be assembled before being moved to the tower by a crane on rails. To examine the bomb's destructive power, workers had built small wooden buildings, four-story brick houses, bridges, tunnels, and water towers. Placed at various distances from the tower were railway engines and cars, tanks, and artillery pieces. Animals were left in outdoor pens and enclosed sheds close to the tower. Instruments were located widely to measure radiation levels and the pressure of the shock wave, and high-speed cameras were mounted to record the event.[64]

Kurchatov arrived at Semipalatinsk–21 in May. He was in charge of the test and of the thousands of scientists, engineers, and workers involved in preparations, including army units sent to provide maximum security. Kurchatov and Khariton supervised tests of all bomb components and organized two complete rehearsals to ensure that everyone involved in the detonation knew their roles and that the instruments and communications worked properly. A few days before the test, Beria arrived as chairman of a state commission composed of senior military and government officials that was assigned to monitor the event. The presence of the security chief with a contingent of MVD officers reminded anyone who might have momentarily forgotten that the forthcoming test of a bomb would also render a verdict on their personal safety and possibly their survival.[65]

The test, code-named First Lightning, was set for 6 A.M. on August 29, 1949. Engineers moved the bomb to the tower starting at 2 A.M., and physicists inserted sixty-four detonators into the outer high-explosive blocks and connected the cables that would fire them. When the bomb was moved from the workshop, Beria went to get a few hours' sleep, while Kurchatov returned to the command bunker to review once again the details of the test. Located 6 miles from ground zero, the command post was shielded behind a high earth berm. Other observation bunkers for scientists and senior military officers were several miles further away to the north and south of the test site. Light rain and poor visibility forced the test to be postponed until 7 A.M. Kurchatov and his senior colleagues and managers waited in the command bunker, along with Beria and his commission members, as the countdown began 30 minutes before the detonation. While Kurchatov paced back and forth, Beria, never the optimist, declared accusingly, "Nothing will come of it, Igor." The physicist replied, "I don't think so. We'll certainly get it."[66]

The detonation worked perfectly. Brilliant light suffused the whole area for a few seconds, a white fireball rose from the test site, and "the shock wave hit the bunker with a roar." With relief and rising pride, Kurchatov declared, "It worked. It worked!" Beria hugged Kurchatov and Khariton and kissed them on the forehead. Everyone shouted with joy and congratulated one another. Still, the security chief could not suppress his suspicions. He raced to a telephone to call one of his MVD scientists who had attended the US nuclear tests at Bikini in July 1946 and was now in the north observation post. "Did it look like the American one?" Beria asked. "Haven't we slipped up? Doesn't Kurchatov humbug us? Quite the same? Good! Good!" Beria immediately called the Kremlin to report the positive results to Stalin personally. When warned that the dictator was still asleep, he insisted that the boss be wakened, declaring, "It's urgent." An annoyed Stalin came on the line, saying, "What do you want? Why are you calling?" On hearing that the test was successful, he replied, "I know already," and hung up. Beria was furious and attacked the general on duty, charging, "Even here you spy on me! I'll grind you to dust!"[67]

While Beria fumed, scientists in two lead-lined tanks advanced to ground zero to record radiation levels and take soil samples. The deputy minister of health and chief of the Radiation Protection Service, A. I. Burnazian, was in charge of the tanks that entered the blast area. He writes: "The steel tower onto which the bomb had been hoisted had disappeared, together with the concrete foundation; the metal had vaporized. In place of the tower, there yawned a huge crater. The yellow, sandy soil around had coagulated, turned to glass, and crackled eerily beneath the tracks of the tank." On his way back to the command bunker, Burnazian met Kurchatov and his top scientists coming in light, unprotected trucks to inspect the test site. Later that day, Kurchatov wrote by hand a report on the test and sent it to Stalin by plane. Measurements showed that the yield of the explosion had been equivalent to about 20 kilotons of TNT, roughly the same as the Alamogordo test and the Nagasaki bomb yield.[68]

The leading scientists and managers soon received lavish awards and honors. Stalin signed a decree of the Council of Ministers on October 29 authorizing the rewards. Drafted by Beria, the decree was based on a logical but chilling principle, according to David Holloway: "Those who were to be shot in case of failure were now to become Heroes of Socialist Labor, those who would have received maximum prison terms were to be given the Order of Lenin, and so on down the list." Thirteen scientists received the highest honor, Hero of Socialist Labor—including Kurchatov, Khariton, Zel'dovich, Flerov, Khlopin, and the German Nikolaus Riehl, who had developed the processes for purifying uranium and fabricating it into metal. The top honorees won a large cash award, a luxury car (Kurchatov and Khariton got the executive model ZIS-110; the others received a Pobeda), the designation of Stalin Prize Laureate of the First Degree, free transportation within the Soviet Union for themselves and their families, free education for their children, and dachas outside Moscow. As the leader of the atomic project, Kurchatov received a dacha in the Crimea. Staff members with less responsibility were given other medals and awards.[69]

Building their first atomic bomb was a remarkable achievement for these Soviet scientists and managers. From the start of the top-priority program in August 1945, it took four years to achieve a successful test, only three months longer than the United States took after Roosevelt's decision in October 1941 to devote maximum effort to developing a bomb. The costs of the atomic project were high. Soviet estimates, for example, place the cost for the year 1950 at 8 billion rubles in a national gross domestic product of 600 billion rubles, or 1.3 percent of gross domestic product. Interestingly, a contemporary CIA estimate reached almost identical conclusions. The challenges for the Soviet economy were immense. The leaders had to develop an entire atomic industry in a country severely damaged by war. Given a political system based on coercion and fear, Stalin was shrewd to select Beria to drive the whole effort. Beria, in turn, was inspired to choose Kurchatov as scientific director over more accomplished and decorated physicists. Kurchatov had exceptional organizational skills and judgment of people to match his solid intellectual preparation in nuclear physics. He structured the steps to be taken and the scientists to lead each aspect of the program, and he proved able to work well with industrial managers, Beria's suspicious agents, and the scientists. Equally important was his ability to keep Stalin and Beria informed and supportive of his efforts.[70]

The largest obstacle for the program was the difficulty of locating an adequate supply of uranium. Soviet scientists showed that they were highly capable in their theoretical and experimental work and remarkably resourceful in designing and making, often by hand, the machinery needed for the separation and purification of graphite, uranium, and plutonium. Their progress at several points was delayed by the lack of uranium. Finally, there is the question of how much the Soviet program benefited from intelligence acquired from the United States and the United Kingdom. The best estimate by Soviet and American specialists is that information from Klaus Fuchs and others saved Kurchatov and his colleagues eighteen months in their race to make an atomic bomb. But even if the intelligence had not been available, the physicists without any outside help developed and tested in 1951 a gun-assembly U-235 bomb similar to the one used on Hiroshima.[71]

EXPANDING WEAPONS PRODUCTION

Before the first test, work had begun on an improved design for an implosion bomb. Tested in September 1951, this version produced twice the yield with only two-thirds the weight of the initial model. A further improvement of adding highly enriched U-235 to make a composite plutonium core for a bomb that was dropped from a Tu-4 bomber in October 1951 produced a slightly higher yield. In 1953, a significantly advanced implosion bomb with a levitation core design was tested in a drop from a medium-range IL-28 bomber. This miniaturized prototype produced a yield that was 70 percent of the composite core design but weighed only 38 percent of that bomb. The levitation design plutonium bomb was well suited for tactical use in the European theater. The final major advance in this period was the test of a boosted thermonuclear (hydrogen) bomb in August 1953. This model used a lithium deuteride core within a uranium shell boosted by tritium. It produced a yield ten times greater than any previous test. Although it was not a true thermonuclear weapon, it was an important step toward the ultimate goal, which Igor Tamm and Andrei Sakharov would achieve with a test of a two-stage thermonuclear bomb in November 1955, when their design produced a yield of 1,600 kilotons—roughly 100 times greater than the first test in 1949.[72]

While multiple weapons design teams were improving the weight-to-yield ratios, new facilities at Cheliabinsk–40 increased the production of fissile material dramatically. By June 1953, the complex operated four plutonium production reactors, one tritium production reactor, and one heavy water reactor for making uranium-233. These reactors produced 620 pounds per year of plutonium, 1,550 pounds per year of tritium, and

44 pounds per year of U-233. A comparable effort was made to produce enriched uranium with gas diffusion plants. Due to the high energy consumption and inefficient process of isotope separation, the production of enriched uranium only became significant in 1951. By 1954, production had increased by 350 percent, to 1,730 pounds a year.[73]

With this expanded production of fissile material, scientists and technicians created a growing stockpile of nuclear weapons. By the start of 1954, the Soviet Union possessed 154 nuclear weapons, a total that exceeded its planning objective by 55 (see table 15.1). A CIA estimate in February 16, 1954, calculated the number of weapons in the Soviet stockpile based on several yield combinations possible from an estimated amount of fissile material. The analysts acknowledged that they had inadequate evidence on the isotope separation capacity and therefore made an uncertain estimate of the U-235 available. Their best scenario argued that at the end of 1953, the Soviet stockpile contained 180 weapons of composite and plutonium design with a yield of 40 kilotons each. Their assumption was correct that the uranium enrichment program lagged behind the plutonium production level, but it overvalued the isotope separation capability, with the result that it forecast too many weapons in the stockpile.[74]

TABLE 15.1 Number of Soviet Nuclear Weapons Planned and Stockpiled, 1949–54

Date	Weapons Planned	Weapons Stockpiled
1949	2	1
1950	7	10
1951	18	35
1952	30	40
1953	42	68
Total (by 1954)	99	154

Source: Table compiled by Alexey Katukhov from data given by L. D. Riabeva, ed., *Atomnyi proekt SSSR: Dokumenty i materialy* [The atomic project of the Soviet Union: Documents and materials], 7 vols. (Moscow: Nauka, Fizmatlit, 1999), book 3, 342–44, and book 5, 342.

The steady expansion of fissile material production and the series of successful tests of fission and fusion weapons was a signal success for Soviet science and engineering. It also validated Stalin's decision to support multiple research programs simultaneously. The combination produced a range of deliverable bombs of both plutonium and enriched uranium design as well as rapid progress in developing usable thermonuclear weapons. Unlike their path on the atomic bomb, when they carefully followed an American design, Soviet physicists pursued their own distinctive route to thermonuclear weapons. The United States, after delays caused mainly by Edward Teller's insistence that Los Alamos concentrate on a maximum-yield fusion weapon, on November 1, 1952, tested a staged hydrogen device too massive to be delivered by air. The Soviets tested a more advanced hydrogen weapon capable of delivery by bomber nine months later, on August 12, 1953. An American test of a true two-stage thermonuclear bomb finally occurred on March 1, 1954, in the Castle Bravo test at Bikini Atoll. The Soviets closed the gap in thermonuclear weapons with the test of a comparable superbomb on November 22, 1955. From this point on, the nuclear arms race expanded in both numbers and types of weapons, going to unreasonable extremes in battlefield and tactical weapons and in the size of arsenals.[75]

An important question remains—what were Stalin's thoughts about the use of the nuclear weapons that his scientists and engineers had worked so intensely to develop?

STALIN ON STRATEGY AND THE ROLE OF NUCLEAR WEAPONS

In the years immediately after World War II, Stalin drew lessons from both Soviet and Anglo-American experiences during the conflict. He confirmed his commitment to the primacy of massive infantry and armor forces in defense of the homeland. He continued to improve the strength of tactical air power, including adopting jet-powered fighters and attack bombers to support ground operations. After studying the contributions of British and American strategic bombing to the defeat of Germany and Japan, he ordered significant resources devoted to a new air defense force supported by an extensive radar network. As discussed above, he also pressed his top airplane designers to develop long-range strategic bombers capable of delivering nuclear weapons against targets in Western Europe and the United States. This effort began with copying the B-29 to make the Tu-4 and moved on to the Tu-95. Starting in 1946, the Soviet leader urged the development of long-range missiles. Despite mounting pressure from the dictator, the leading missile designer, Sergei P. Korolev, faced difficulties similar to those confronted by Tupolev in creating missile engines with adequate thrust to obtain the desired transcontinental range. Shortly after Stalin's death in March 1953, Korolev's R-5 missile was successfully tested—but it only reached a range of 750 miles. Ironically, the Soviet military had a substantial stockpile of nuclear weapons before it had the strategic bombers or missiles to deliver them.[76]

Stalin never believed that nuclear weapons would be decisive in another world war. Following his principles, Soviet military analysts argued that nuclear bombs could destroy targets in the rear of land defenses but would have little effect on a dispersed, fortified ground force. The Soviets planned to use their shorter-range bombers to attack US air bases in Europe and the Middle East and to rely on their air defenses to limit damage to interior cities and industries. As tensions with the West grew over Berlin and the creation of NATO with the rearmament of Western European forces, Soviet policy shifted to increase its military strength in East Germany, build up the navy, and expand the military capabilities of its Central and Eastern European allies. Despite the huge growth of the US Strategic Air Command with the clear commitment to a nuclear strategy, Stalin clung to his belief that nuclear weapons would not be the determining factor in a major war. He told the Italian Socialist Party leader, Pietro Nenni, in July 1952 that the Americans lacked the massive army needed to win a war, declaring: "It is not enough for the Americans to destroy Moscow, just as it is not enough for us to destroy New York. We want armies to occupy Moscow and to occupy New York."[77]

The atomic bomb did not influence Stalin's foreign policy any more than it did his strategic calculations. From the time of the first American atomic test at Alamagordo in 1945, the Soviet leader was alert to the fact that the Truman administration would likely try to use its nuclear monopoly for diplomatic advantage. Stalin was determined to be tough and not be intimidated by atomic diplomacy. He would conduct what David Holloway calls a "war of nerves." This policy produced confrontations with the West over Germany, Poland, and Iran, and it had the undesired result of persuading Truman and most American leaders that the Soviet Union was an expansionist power that had to be resisted. Yet the dictator in the Kremlin tempered his aggressive policies with the realization that his nation was not prepared for war with the West. He was careful not to go too far and provoke a major war. The earliest evidence of his exercise of caution was in the Iran crisis of 1946, and it became clearer in the resolution of the Berlin Blockade two years later.[78]

The Korean War might seem to be an exception to this line of argument, but it is not. It is true that the successful Soviet atomic test in 1949 was a factor in Stalin's decision to support the North Korean invasion. But one must remember how this support was managed. From Truman's and Acheson's statements and policies for South Korea, Stalin had every reason to believe that the United States would not intervene in Korea. Even then he was careful to keep Soviet forces from direct engagement in combat. The North Koreans were expected to do all the fighting, and if they should get into trouble, the Chinese Communists were committed to bail them out. When the unexpected happened and the American-led United Nations forces were on the verge of victory over North Korea, the People's Republic of China honored Stalin's reinsurance policy and allowed the Soviet leader to maintain his limited role and avoid war with the United States.

16

WALTER BEDELL SMITH REFORMS
AND EXPANDS THE CIA

I n the closing months of World War II, officials in Washington prepared for the nation to play an expanded role in postwar international affairs. They drew up plans for the United Nations, the International Monetary Fund, and the World Bank. The increased international presence would be driven by diplomacy and economic engagement. Americans did not plan for significant overseas military involvement; and immediately after the end of the war, President Truman directed a mass demobilization of the armed services.[1]

One area where the president found it especially difficult to achieve agreement was policy for foreign intelligence. Only the pressures of the Korean War forced decisions on what type of intelligence agencies would be established and how they would be organized. There were several reasons for this policy deadlock. In general, Americans were uncomfortable with the concept that their government engaged in espionage. Policymakers also believed there was no pressing need to make a decision. Most important, numerous government departments and agencies had developed intelligence divisions during the war and did not want to relinquish this authority. Indeed, in the final months of the war, plans for continued and often expanded intelligence activity were drawn up in the State, Treasury, and War departments; the US Navy; the Federal Bureau of Investigation (FBI); the Office of Strategic Services (OSS); and the Bureau of the Budget.[2]

Confronted with a mass of competing interests and plans, Truman chose a proposal from the Joint Chiefs of Staff, which reflected an agreed-on solution among the military services. In doing so he rejected appeals from the State Department and Bureau of the Budget for a different plan. On January 22, 1946, he sent a letter to the secretaries of state, war, and the navy directing the creation of a National Intelligence Authority, which would in turn establish the Central Intelligence Group (CIG), to be formed by staff and facilities provided by their departments under the director of central intelligence (DCI), who was to be appointed by the president. The DCI was required to consult on all important initiatives and reports with the heads of the departmental intelligence agencies that would form the Intelligence Advisory Board (IAB). The loose structure outlined in Truman's letter left many basic questions unanswered. The mission of the CIG was to coordinate the activities of the departmental intelligence agencies and synthesize and present to the National Security Council (NSC) and the president the products of the departments that were related to strategic and national policy. But the DCI and the CIG's small staff could not collect intelligence themselves and had to work closely with the IAB, whose members' primary duties were collecting and analyzing intelligence for their departments. Furthermore, the CIG was prohibited from any domestic investigation or exercising any internal security function, a provision clearly designed to protect the counterintelligence power of the FBI and the military services.[3]

In January 1946, the president selected Rear Admiral Sidney W. Souers as the first DCI. Souers had drafted the joint chiefs' proposal on which Truman based his letter, and he agreed to serve for only a few months to get the CIG established while a permanent new DCI was chosen. His effort in the five months he was DCI concentrated on winning the support and cooperation of the members of the IAB. In June, Lieutenant General Hoyt S. Vandenberg replaced Souers as DCI. The decorated army air forces commander took the job in large part because he believed it would strengthen his chances of becoming chief of staff of the anticipated independent air force. While he held the position, Vandenberg wanted to impose his ideas on the CIG. His basic goal was to create a comprehensive central intelligence organization that would conduct covert operations, perform research and analysis, and prepare its own reports for the NSC and the president. Vandenberg sought to build a much more powerful CIG than Truman had authorized. It would sharply limit the power of the departmental intelligence divisions and was strongly resisted by all members of the IAB. As a result, most of Vandenberg's eleven months as DCI were consumed by disputes with the members of his advisory board.[4]

Meanwhile, legislation had been introduced in March 1947 to reorganize the military services and to authorize the NSC and CIA as federal agencies. The National Security Act of 1947 was passed and signed by the president in July. The act set the structure for the national security establishment for the remainder of the twentieth century. It created the position of secretary of defense, established an independent air force, and provided statutory authority for the NSC and CIA. The act was amended in 1949 to strengthen the power of the secretary of defense and to create the Department of Defense. Hoyt Vandenberg left his post as DCI in May and became vice chief of staff of the air force in October with the rank of general. He would move up to become chief of staff in April 1948.[5]

Rear Admiral Roscoe H. Hillenkoetter, an experienced intelligence officer, became the third DCI in May 1947. In taking up his duties, the new director faced two significant obstacles: The IAB remained aggressive in resisting any increase of the DCI's authority, and Hillenkoetter was junior in personal rank to all the military members of the board. Although the language of the National Security Act supported a more powerful CIA and made no mention of an IAB, Hillenkoetter sought to win the support of the members by continuing their service as an Intelligence Advisory Committee (IAC) and accepting a number of limitations on his authority. The DCI's effort to accommodate the IAC failed to achieve the cooperation he needed; and after weeks of conflict, he appealed to the secretary of defense for a decision. Forrestal and other members of the NSC recommended that the president appoint an outside committee to review the structure and effectiveness of the CIA along with its relations with other departments and agencies and the quality of its personnel and products. In January 1948, Truman approved Forrestal's recommendation to appoint three New York lawyers with different experiences in government as a review committee. The group would be chaired by Allen W. Dulles, a former senior official in the OSS; William H. Jackson, a former intelligence aide to General Omar Bradley; and Matthias Correa, a former military aide to Forrestal who had worked extensively on criminal investigations and security issues.[6]

THE DULLES REPORT

The three committee members and a small staff devoted a year to research, interviews, and preparation of their report, which was presented to the NSC on January 1, 1949. The report started from the premise that the current international situation was dramatically more dangerous than any time before World War II. It cited increasing Soviet aggressive tactics including espionage and subversion, closed societies in the Soviet Bloc, and the prospect of an early Soviet atomic weapons capability. Intelligence was now a full-time necessity, the committee asserted, going beyond traditional military assessments to cover political, economic, and scientific developments. The CIA had failed in its mission to coordinate the intelligence activities of the other agencies and produce top-quality national estimates. The CIA should not compete or duplicate the work of the military intelligence sections but should coordinate their work and cooperate on final products relevant to national policy. The committee's criticism was sharp and direct: "The principal defect of the Central Intelligence Agency is that its direction, administrative organization and performance do not show sufficient appreciation of the Agency's assigned functions, particularly in the fields of intelligence coordination and the production of intelligence estimates. The result has been that the Central Intelligence Agency has tended to become just one more intelligence agency producing intelligence in competition with older established agencies of the Government departments."[7]

The committee acknowledged that difficulties had been created for the CIA by the lack of clear guidance from policymakers about their needs and by obstruction from the established intelligence agencies. But the authors asserted that the obligation rested with the CIA to resolve these problems and perform its assigned missions. They placed specific responsibility for the failure on "inadequacies of direction" from DCI Hillenkoetter. The committee devoted substantial attention to the preparation of national intelligence estimates. It called for the creation of an Estimates Division, and it strongly recommended that all the main intelligence agencies participate in preparing these estimates and approve them. The report urged improved coordination of counterintelligence activities, especially between the CIA and the FBI. In their conclusion, the authors stated firmly that the next DCI should be a civilian. The report had a significant impact. Two prominent intelligence historians contend that "the Dulles Report was one of the most influential outside evaluations in the history of the Intelligence Community. It owed its success in no small portion to its authors' understanding that Congress and the White House had intended the Central Intelligence Agency to coordinate both operations and analysis—that the definition of 'intelligence' in its title had to include both activities."[8]

The NSC asked the secretaries of state and defense to review the extensive reactions of the DCI and the members of the IAC to the Dulles Report and recommend actions to be taken. The new secretary of state, Dean Acheson, and James Forrestal both favored a strong, centralized CIA, and their report reflected this conviction. They recommended adopting almost all the Dulles Report's proposals for reorganization and reform—with one significant exception. They strongly opposed the view that national intelligence estimates should be approved both by members of the advisory committee and also the DCI, arguing that such a process would produce diluted, compromise judgments. Instead, they insisted that the DCI have the final decision after consulting with the IAC. On July 7, 1949, the NSC accepted the report of the two secretaries as NSC Report 50, including the provision for the DCI's final authority on National Intelligence Estimates.[9]

Although the NSC had found the criticism of Admiral Hillenkoetter in the Dulles Report "too sweeping" and had endorsed the DCI's power to coordinate the other intelligence agencies and have the final word on national estimates, the conclusions of NSC 50 "crushed" his spirit. This observation comes from Ludwell Lee Montague, who at the time was serving as the CIA's representative on the NSC staff. Montague goes on to contend in his official history that "instead of being stimulated to exert the 'forthright leadership' called for by the Dulles Report and NSC 50, he became psychologically withdrawn—still amiably approachable, but more than ever unwilling to exercise initiative and leadership." Further complicating any reform in the intelligence community, senior officials were immersed in debates over how to respond to the first Soviet atomic test and whether to accelerate research on a hydrogen bomb. As a result, no action was taken on replacing the ineffectual Hillenkoetter until the totally unexpected North Korean attack forced a change.[10]

THE CHALLENGE

Whoever Harry Truman chose to take over the CIA would face an agency without a clear mission or a tradition of firm leadership. It had many bureaucratic competitors with larger budgets and strong leaders. Among the rivals were the established military intelligence agencies; the State Department, which had the former OSS section for research and analysis; and the FBI, which sought an international mandate. Within the administration, there were several different concepts of foreign intelligence. The president himself wanted nothing more than "a global news service, delivering daily bulletins," according to Tim Weiner in his critical history of the CIA. Some civilian and military officials—many with wartime experience in the OSS—wanted active covert operations, both political disruption and sabotage, to match the tactics of the Soviet Union. Conversely, DCI Hillenkoetter, who had a covert action division in his agency, opposed the policy of conducting destabilizing secret operations inside other nations in peacetime.[11]

The largest practical problem for a new director was that as the Cold War heated up after 1946 the pressure for active measures had produced a CIA covert action program that lacked supervision, legal authorization, and an approved budget. How this unprecedented peacetime program began is a tortured tale. On May 4, 1948, George F. Kennan, the top adviser on Soviet affairs to Secretary of State George C. Marshall, proposed a new program of covert operations to complete the strategy against Stalin begun with the Truman Doctrine and the Marshall Plan. This secret initiative came at a time when a communist coup had recently occurred in Czechoslovakia and the Soviets were restricting land access to the Western occupation zones of Berlin. Kennan's recommendation was well received in high policy circles, and the program was created with a broad mandate in NSC Report 10/2, which was approved on June 18, 1948. The covert action group was housed in the CIA and ultimately given the intentionally misleading name of the Office of Policy Coordination (OPC). In part because Admiral Hillenkoetter opposed the program, the director of OPC was to report to the secretaries of state and defense, who were enthusiastic sponsors.[12]

Faced with increasing Soviet obstruction in Germany, the United States, Britain, and France agreed in early June 1948 to unify their occupation zones to create a West German state with full participation in the Marshall Plan. Moscow protested these steps strongly, and when the Western powers introduced a new currency in their merging zones, the Soviets imposed a total land blockade of Berlin. One of the most enthusiastic advocates for the new German currency was Frank Wisner, deputy assistant secretary of state for the occupied areas. A New York corporate lawyer from Mississippi who had led covert operations in Romania and in occupied Germany for the OSS, Wisner was the obvious choice of Kennan, Marshall, and Forrestal to head OPC. He took over on September 1, 1948, and immediately began to develop an ambitious strategy for his program and a rapid expansion of his initial staff of ten.[13]

Unlike other national security officials, Wisner did not have to worry about funding in his first years at OPC. The architects of the Marshall Plan had designed an ideal solution for espionage expenses. The legislation authorizing and appropriating $13 billion over five years called for the creation of counterpart funds to be supplied by the countries receiving aid in matching amounts of local currency. Terms of the individual national plans specified that 5 percent of the counterpart funds be set aside for administrative costs. Frank Wisner negotiated for these administrative funds to be provided to OPC as an untraceable supply of local currency for operations in each country hosting a Marshall Plan office. This made available a pool of roughly $685 million for OPC activities in the period 1948–53.[14]

Just forty years old, Frank Wisner was intense, impatient, and highly competitive. Working very long hours, he developed his grand plan for the coming five years during his first month at OPC. He began hiring old hands from the OSS, and also lawyers, bankers, and fresh graduates from top colleges—anyone with ideas, patriotism, and a desire for action. Within a year, his small group had grown to 450, and it soon outnumbered the rest of CIA. In his first three years, he opened forty-seven overseas stations. In most of these locations, there were two CIA station chiefs, one for managing agents who collected information for the Office of Special Operations and another for OPC's covert activities. Rivalry often became heated between the two branches over the value of their respective missions and over the competition for talented agents.[15]

Among the operations launched in his first year, Wisner had agents in Western Europe provide cash for support to center-right politicians, publishers, journalists, generals, spy chiefs, and union leaders. He won cooperation from Christian Democrats and Catholic leaders to break the influence of communists in important unions, such as those for railroad and shipping workers in France and Italy. When communist longshoremen refused to unload Marshall Plan aid and military equipment in Marseilles, OPC agents hired the Corsican mafia to break up their strike and unload the ships. Wisner took a special interest in trying to penetrate Central and Eastern Europe and to stimulate resistance to communist rule. His men recruited Central and Eastern European and Soviet exiles to conduct espionage and sabotage in their home countries. On the political side, OPC set up and funded the Congress for Cultural Freedom to support intellectuals advocating democracy and free enterprise in conferences, newspapers, and magazines like the monthly

Encounter. With the advice of Kennan and his old OSS boss Allen Dulles, Wisner laid plans for the start of Radio Free Europe, to be run by Central and Eastern European exiles broadcasting news and cultural programs into their homelands.[16]

In February 1949, concerned that these operations had no legal authority and no directly appropriated funds, DCI Hillenkoetter urged key leaders of Congress to provide the legislation to support these activities. A handful of senior members of the House and Senate armed services committees agreed that covert operations were a valuable means of combating communist aggression and deserved legal cover from Congress. Representative Dewey Short (R-MO), the ranking Republican on the House Armed Services Committee, expressed the opinion of the bipartisan leadership when he said: "The less we say about this bill, the better off all of us will be." Congress quietly passed Hillenkoetter's draft of the Central Intelligence Agency Act of 1949 with only minor changes on May 27. Reflecting the strong anticommunist attitudes of the day, the act provided the CIA with remarkably broad powers. The agency could do anything it deemed necessary except operate a secret police force within the United States, as long as Congress provided the funds that would be approved by a small subcommittee and buried in the Department of Defense budget.[17]

The new act included a provision authorizing the CIA to bring up to 100 foreigners into the United States as permanent residents regardless of any past deeds if they were valuable to national security activities. On the very day the president signed the act, the head of the Office of Special Operations took steps to bring into the country a Ukrainian warlord named Mikola Lebed, who had fought with the Nazis in World War II and was classified as a war criminal by the Justice Department. In July, the agency assumed responsibility from the army for an intelligence group run by General Reinhard Gehlen, who had been chief of military intelligence on the eastern front for Hitler. Both Lebed and Gehlen commanded groups of Fascist exiles, but their anticommunist beliefs and their experience fighting the Soviets made them desirable partners. The Gehlen group would go on to become the core of the West German Federal Intelligence Service, the Bundesnachrichtendienst. Unfortunately, the organization had been penetrated earlier by East German and Soviet intelligence, and it was discovered much later that Gehlen's counter-intelligence chief had worked for the KGB for years.[18]

The legislative endorsement and appropriated funds encouraged a significant expansion of covert operations by both the Office of Special Operations and OPC after June 1949. There were attempts to parachute Ukrainian exiles into their homeland to establish coordination with an underground resistance group. Wisner also sent teams of Albanian émi-grés into their country to conduct sabotage. Working from Munich, OPC dispatched Russian, Polish, and Baltic exiles to their countries. Most of these agents were killed shortly after they landed. Some were kept as prisoners and used to send false reports back to their station chiefs creating a stream of disinformation. The causes of such widespread failures were twofold. The émigré groups were infiltrated by Soviet agents in their displaced persons camps, and the CIA official responsible for the security of covert operations, James J. Angleton, shared information on these missions with a senior member of the British Embassy in Washington, Kim Philby. It turned out that Philby, who was British liaison with the CIA and with the Atomic Energy Commission, was Moscow's top spy in the United States. Every mission was compromised from the start. Overall, hundreds of CIA's exile agents were killed in these years. No careful evaluations were made at the time, and no publicity was allowed. A declassified CIA history acknowledges dryly that after five years of "abortive missions, CIA discontinued this approach."[19]

Compounding its failure to penetrate the Soviet Union or its satellites with exiles was the CIA's lack of reliable agents inside any communist government, with the exception of East Germany, where a few sources provided valuable information. The United States had very little intelligence about activities within the Soviet Union, North Korea, or the People's Republic of China. The closest American Allies in East Asia were Jiang Jieshi in Taiwan and Syngman Rhee in Seoul, both highly manipulative and heading deeply corrupt regimes. Their agents did supply reams of reports on activities in mainland China and North Korea, but almost all were self-serving and inaccurate, if not totally fabricated. Interviewed some years later, James Lilley, a CIA officer in Taiwan, declared: "We thought it was going to be like World War II. Instead we got led into lies, deceit, deception, and traps. We were children in a big boy's game." The ultimate blow came with the loss of signals intelligence, the only source of useful intelligence in East Asia. In the spring of 1950, just as Kim Il-sung was negotiating with Stalin and Mao for support of his invasion of South Korea, a Soviet spy working for the code-breaking center outside Washington informed Moscow that the United States had broken the code used in encrypted telegrams to Soviet representatives in China and North Korea. The codes were quickly changed, and American intelligence went completely dark.[20]

In the three years after its creation in the 1947 National Security Act, the CIA had been by any measure a nearly total failure. It had not anticipated and informed the president about the Czech coup, the Berlin Blockade, the Soviet atomic test, the North Korean invasion, or the Chinese intervention in the war. The first three DCIs had failed to develop productive working relationships with the existing intelligence agencies or mechanisms for producing coordinated intelligence estimates for the NSC and the president. By 1950, the rapidly expanding program of covert operations was spending millions of dollars a year and sacrificing the lives of hundreds of foreign agents without any substantial results. President Truman was desperate to obtain valuable intelligence, and it is surprising to see whom he chose to put the CIA in working order.

IKE'S HATCHET MAN

Beetle Smith was born in 1895 into "a family of moderate means" in Indianapolis. He lived a comfortable life with the normal pleasures of childhood and performed well in school. But in 1909, his father's business career suffered a sharp downturn, and the family found itself under serious economic pressures. "Beetle spent his first thirteen years in a warm, secure home," argues his biographer, D. K. R. Crosswell: "His family's suddenly reduced circumstances came as a rude shock. He now shouldered adult responsibilities while still just a boy. This boyhood trauma shattered Beetle's dependence on others but instilled in him the lessons of loyalty and self-reliance." To help with family expenses, he had to take a part-time job as a worker in an automobile factory. He won admission to the top public high school with strong programs in English and mathematics as well as advanced technical vocational subjects. But after the first year, his interest in academic work declined, along with his grades. Under the pressures of school and work as he entered adolescence, his personality changed sharply. The once lively boy with a sardonic sense of humor became a withdrawn, moody, even surly young man.[21]

Smith's final two years in high school saw his opportunities narrow further. In 1911, he took a second part-time job at a soda fountain near his home. Upon turning sixteen that year, he joined the Indiana National Guard on the first day he was eligible, fulfilling a boyhood dream to become a soldier but creating another diversion from his studies. A serious blow came in 1913, when his father became incapacitated and had to stop work. After barely completing enough credits to graduate from high school, Beetle had to take a full-time job as a die maker for a heavy equipment manufacturer. His responsibility as the primary earner for his family required him to withdraw his application to Butler University. Not only was he unable to compete for a cherished appointment to West Point, but his family's financial needs also prevented him from attending the local university. His formal education ended at the age of eighteen.[22]

At this point, Beetle had two positive aspects to his life when other possibilities were closed. He had met a girl and fallen in love with her. She was Mary Eleanor (Nory) Cline, who lived three blocks away but inhabited a different, more prosperous world. She and Beetle shared the Catholic faith and continued to see each other despite her parents feeling that he did not have suitable career prospects. The other bright spot in his life was his rapid advance in the Indianapolis National Guard company. His military deportment and performance earned an early promotion to sergeant, and after very effective leadership during the city's flood emergency of March 1913, he was promoted at the age of eighteen to first sergeant of his unit. He wanted his company to be the best in Indiana, and he pressed his men hard in drill and training exercises, perhaps too hard. The troops cursed him and resisted his strict discipline, but this only made him push them harder. When the company was activated to join the punitive expedition against Pancho Villa along the southwest border, Beetle, as the primary support for his family, had to remain at home as part of the headquarters staff. His troops no doubt celebrated his absence with a few rounds of drinks.[23]

Beetle Smith's personality was formed in the years 1913–16, driven by his difficult family situation. "He was," writes Crosswell, "combative, inarticulate when expressing personal feelings, covetous and resentful of those better off, a secretive loner bordering on antisocial." His good qualities also took shape in this period. He had an excellent mind, which was "analytical and retentive." He was deeply committed to his family and his church. He respected authority and was clear and direct in his speech. His most distinctive strengths were his "unquestioned loyalty and his remarkable capacity for work." Those who worked with him later in his life did not see the positive qualities right away because Beetle always preferred to appear as the tough drill sergeant. He had a substantial chip on his shoulder.[24]

America's entry into World War I opened a career in the army for Beetle Smith. As part of the mobilization after the declaration of war in April 1917, he was nominated for officer candidate school. Just before leaving for training, he married Nory Cline in July. After a brief training program, Second Lieutenant Smith embarked for Europe, where he joined a French division fighting to stem the German attack at the Marne. Wounded after only 36 hours of combat, Beetle returned to Washington to join the army General Staff in the preparation of new regiments going to France. With the armistice in November 1918, he spent several months at Camp Dodge in Iowa managing the demobilization of a division. Unlike most young officers, he wanted to remain in the army, which required taking an examination. To his surprise, he was one of 5,200 out of 14,000 who passed the exam and received a regular commission. He was also fortunate to retain his newly acquired rank of first lieutenant.[25]

In the small interwar army dominated by West Point graduates, Smith had limited prospects for advancement. Being socially awkward and lacking a college degree, he resolved to learn important skills at each post and to outwork his colleagues in order to prove his value to his superior officers. In his spare time, he read widely in history, philosophy, literature, and military affairs to make up for his limited formal education. His next assignments taught Smith important lessons at each post: how to train National Guard civilians for military service, how the War Department budget was shaped, and how to resolve problems of US forces in a restive Asian dependency like the Philippines. Now a captain, Beetle's organizational and administrative talents won him high ratings in his performance evaluations and helped him receive a valuable assignment to attend the Army Infantry School in Fort Benning, Georgia.[26]

Smith's two years at the Infantry School "proved to be the most valuable in his career," argues his biographer Crosswell, because it provided brief but important contact with Colonel George C. Marshall, who would be "the most influential figure in his life." One day, Marshall—who was assistant commandant and head of the academic department—dropped in on a course when Beetle was making a presentation on the Battle of the Marne. The colonel found him to be cogent and concise in his analysis, and suggested to his deputy that Smith would make a fine instructor. For the next year, Smith worked as an assistant in the weapons course with Major Omar Bradley, who was highly impressed, later saying that Beetle "had an absolutely brilliant and analytical mind." After his time as an instructor, Smith sought and won assignment to the Command and Staff School in Fort Leavenworth, Kansas. This two-year course was an essential step toward being eligible for senior command appointments. He worked intensely and showed he could keep pace with the West Point graduates, but it came at the cost of leaving with an ulcer. Finishing in the top third of the class, he "punched his ticket for admission to the War College," the last critical course toward a top position. His assignments in the late 1930s were devoted to teaching tactics and weapons and attending the War College. Finally, on New Year's Day 1939, after over twenty-one years in the army, he was promoted to major.[27]

Smith's career soon began to advance as Hitler's aggressive policies threatened to engulf Europe in war. The element propelling Beetle to the center of war preparations was the reputation he had established in the army schools. General George C. Marshall became army chief of staff on September 1, 1939, the day that World War II began with the German invasion of Poland. He brought Lieutenant Colonel Omar Bradley, one of his protégés from the Infantry School, to be an assistant secretary on his personal staff. With Marshall heavily involved in preparing for mass mobilization if the United States were to enter the war, his three-man secretariat sorted and referred the mail and messages to appropriate responders and themselves drafted over two-thirds of the replies. Marshall became irritated when he had to correct and revise almost all the drafts submitted by his two assistant secretaries, and he asked them to find someone with a good command of the English language who could write clear, concise responses. Bradley strongly recommended Beetle for the job, reminding the chief that he had been impressed with Smith at Fort Benning. Marshall accepted Bradley's proposal and directed that Major Smith be assigned as an assistant secretary to the Office of the Chief of Staff. The Smiths arrived in Washington in October 1939 to face a rapidly expanding set of challenges.[28]

Marshall was a very demanding boss, but Beetle Smith had the talent and experience to succeed as a member of his small personal staff. The general wanted his staff to take the initiative to solve problems themselves and bring only the major issues to him. When a staff member made a decision on a problem, he would briefly tell the chief what had been done, and he would back them fully. If they did present an issue to Marshall, they had to think through all the pros and cons and be thoroughly prepared to present the problem with a recommended action in no more than a single page. Officers who came to Marshall poorly prepared or indecisive were soon replaced. Beetle thrived in this environment. He worked extra hours to master the details of all issues likely to come before his boss; he had a near-photographic memory; and he wrote succinct prose with clear recommendations. His memory and analytical skills enabled him to listen to a 2-hour presentation and with no notes write a one-page summary and evaluation. This ability soon led Marshall to take Beetle with him when he had appointments with the president, because Franklin Roosevelt did not allow notes to be taken during private meetings. The chief of staff also used Smith as his liaison with the White House, especially with Roosevelt's most trusted assistant, Harry Hopkins.[29]

Beetle Smith was more than a scribe with an excellent memory. He had the initiative and self-confidence to analyze situations and make bold proposals. A favorite example of Marshall's was Beetle's handling of an automobile salesman who had been referred to the chief of staff by the secretary of war. The salesman was promoting a new model of "a small, low silhouette truck." Smith studied the truck's specifications, checked with several colleagues commanding infantry and cavalry units, and on the basis of his experience with heavy weapons decided to recommend the purchase of forty vehicles for field testing. He interrupted the chief in a meeting with several generals, briefly explained the truck's capabilities, and said it would be a valuable addition for carrying machine guns and mortars in combat. Marshall approved his proposal on the spot, and the "jeep" became one of the essential means of transportation for the army in the war years and afterward.[30]

Although he was the junior man in the secretariat, Smith quickly caught Marshall's eye as the most organized and effective member of his staff. This was largely due to his ability to understand what the chief wanted done on most issues and to his willingness to tackle problems he thought he could resolve in order to free his boss to deal with larger questions. As a result of his efficient and discreet style, Beetle soon became Marshall's liaison with Harry Hopkins and with Roosevelt's influential personal adviser, Bernard Baruch. In April 1940, Smith was promoted to lieutenant colonel, and by the summer he had become, according to Crosswell, Marshall's "top troubleshooter." He helped gain authorization and funds from Congress for the Lend-Lease Act to aid Britain after the fall of France, and in August 1941 he was named to the important post of secretary of the General Staff and promoted to colonel. As preparations for war accelerated, Smith expanded the role of the secretary of the General Staff to become "gatekeeper" for information and for people wanting to see the overburdened chief of staff. In the process, he became an expert on all aspects of the army's preparations for war. When the Japanese attacked Pearl Harbor in December 1941, Beetle had established himself as "Marshall's de facto chief of staff." His role would soon expand even more.[31]

When Germany and Italy went beyond their alliance commitment to Japan under the Tripartite Pact and declared war on the United States on December 11, they solved a huge political problem for Franklin Roosevelt. Overnight, the country was unified behind a major two-front war, and most isolationist voices fell silent. Yet the government and the population were not in any way prepared for war. Field Marshal Sir John Dill, the head of the British military mission in Washington for much of the war, declared that the United States had "not the slightest conception of what the war means," and that the American military was "more unready than it is possible to imagine." The US lacked an integrated military force. The War Department and Navy Department had no coordination—and, indeed, viewed each other as bitter rivals. There was no cooperation across the services on intelligence, logistics, or supply. British prime minister Winston Churchill led a military delegation to Washington to negotiate aid for a desperate United Kingdom and to develop a grand strategy for the war. The delegation arrived on December 22, and the key leaders held twelve meetings over the next three weeks. The British, who had been at war for over two years and had a fully integrated military with a combined staff, found it difficult to do business with the disorganized and understaffed American officials.[32]

The Washington meetings, code-named Arcadia, proved stressful for both sides; but by their end, the two governments had hammered out important agreements on strategy and organization. In broad context, the British had to obtain full US support in order to defeat the Axis and survive as a world power, so they urgently needed men and supplies while recognizing the need to be patient in bringing the Americans up to speed. For their part, the Americans did not appreciate how totally unprepared for modern war they were. On strategic priorities, the parties agreed to make Europe the first theater of offensive action and to consider mounting an initial attack against German forces in North Africa. With regard to organizing for war, the British gave up their preferred principle of command by committee to accept the American insistence on unity of command in each theater. Overall military policy would be shaped by the Combined Chiefs of Staff (CCS), who would be based in Washington. Most important for the long range, Arcadia generated a close, trusting relationship between Roosevelt and Churchill which would help in resolving future problems between the two Allies.[33]

Beyond the two national leaders, the conference produced several significant insights. Churchill realized that, after Roosevelt, Marshall was the most critical American in building close cooperation. The American chief and Sir John Dill formed a close friendship that boded well for Anglo-American coordination in the CCS. Marshall now understood the immediate need for a stronger staff organization, and the president created the Joint Chiefs of Staff by executive order in February 1942, with Beetle Smith as secretary. He also realized the necessity of having an able, trusted manager of the US relationship with the British military mission in Washington. This led him to choose Smith as the head of the joint secretariat of the CCS. Beetle now had to coordinate two very active groups, and everyone involved understood he was Marshall's man. This dual responsibility brought him another promotion, to brigadier general, early in February.

Smith took seriously his instructions from Marshall to facilitate understanding and cooperation with the British. This became easy due to the instant liking that Smith took to the secretary of the British mission, Brigadier Vivian Dykes. Beetle arranged for Dykes to occupy quarters next door to him at Fort Myer, and Nory looked after Dykes, often including him for dinner and holiday excursions. As a result of this close relationship, Beetle developed contrasting reputations with the Americans and British who regularly dealt with him. His own military colleagues viewed him as hard, often even harsh, in communicating assignments and instructions, whereas the British saw him as a genial, informal, decisive, and "willing collaborator" with an excellent sense of humor. Four men played the key roles in shaping Allied military cooperation. The "genuine partnership" between Marshall and Dill led the way in the CCS. Smith and Dykes put the detailed pieces together and made the group operate smoothly. "No one could have predicted," asserts Crosswell, "that the charismatic Dykes and the enigmatic Smith would hit it off, but they did."[34]

After the Arcadia conference, Smith spent most of the next five months working to devise an American strategy that would win British approval. The president insisted that US ground troops had to engage the Germans sometime in the autumn of 1942. Marshall pressed for a cross-channel invasion, even on a limited scale, in 1942 or early the next year. The British faced an increasingly deteriorating situation. They experienced defeats by the Germans and Italians at Tobruk in Libya and by the Japanese in the Indian Ocean. Their leaders feared that the Soviet Union might collapse and thus free German units to shift to strengthen their hold on Western Europe. Further complicating London's planning was the perception that American troops were unprepared for battle with inadequate training, few landing craft, and no commanders with combat experience.

In a final showdown in London in July, the British vetoed any cross-channel operation in 1942 and argued for an offensive in North Africa to satisfy Roosevelt's desire to engage the Germans in the autumn. With Smith and Dykes helping their colleagues appreciate the realities felt by their opposite numbers, the two sides reached a grudging agreement on July 24 for an offensive in North Africa in the autumn, code-named Torch, to be commanded by an American. The next day, Marshall informed Lieutenant General Dwight Eisenhower that he would most likely be the commander for Torch. Already in London as the commander of American forces in Europe, Eisenhower repeated his request for Beetle Smith as his chief of staff. For another six weeks, Marshall kept Smith in Washington to broker decisions on how large an operation Torch should be and when it could be launched. Smith finally arrived in the United Kingdom on September 7, to Eisenhower's immense relief.[35]

Second only to his time on Marshall's personal staff, Beetle's three years with Eisenhower constituted one of the most formative periods of his adult life. Ike, as he was known to everyone, had a very complex personality. Outwardly, he was warm, optimistic, charming, and highly sociable. Inwardly, he had a compulsive need to be liked, was masterful at relating to all types of people, and was very adept at manipulating them to get his way. Ike avoided conflict with superiors or peers, invariably delegating difficult, thankless tasks to others. He was often indecisive when the outcome of a major decision was unclear, and he had a terrible temper—which he kept under control, most of the time. An accomplished poker player, Ike's constant smile gave no hint of his intentions.

Beetle had similar values and intellect to Ike but possessed a dramatically different personality. He was cautious in his personal relationships and did not need to be liked. He was intense, often blunt in giving directions or reprimands. He was an excellent judge of character and quickly discerned someone's strengths and vulnerabilities. Capable of charm and warmth, he reserved these qualities for a few kindred souls, like Vivian Dykes. Those who were close to Smith called him "Beetle," a play on his middle name that emphasized his "hyperactivity." He welcomed the nickname, and "had a small black beetle embossed on his personal stationery." But he was harsh with colleagues who did not match his demanding standards. A bold administrator who organized complex tasks quickly, he readily took on difficult assignments. "Smith frequently made key policy decisions in areas Eisenhower would not deign to touch, mostly related to military government and civil affairs programs. In effect," Crosswell contends, "Smith acted as the headquarters 'general manager' and as Eisenhower's foreign minister," especially in managing Churchill and the French. "In many ways, Beetle was born to play his assigned role of 'bad cop' to Ike's 'good cop.'"[36]

In London, Smith immediately plunged into organizing a headquarters staff for US forces and then building a joint Allied staff with the British. Eisenhower served as both commander of US forces in Europe and as supreme commander of Allied forces in the Mediterranean. At Ike's request, Beetle served as chief of staff of both headquarters and spoke for him on almost all issues. He found that developing an effective staff was more difficult with the Americans than with the British, who had a pool of very competent staff officers seasoned by three years of war. American officers had two inherent problems: very few had training and experience as staff officers; and the US Army was organized by functional bureaus, so supply and intelligence specialists worked through their chief in the War Department and did not integrate at each command level. Beetle would have continuing difficulties getting these two specialties in particular to cooperate in an integrated command staff. At the same time, new American troops were pouring into the British bases, and planning for the invasion of North Africa was speeding ahead under pressure from Roosevelt and Marshall for early action against the Germans.[37]

Despite the abbreviated training given the American troops and a shortage of equipment and shipping, the invasion went ahead on November 8, 1942, with US and British landings at three points in Vichy-occupied Morocco and Algeria. The landings went smoothly; and after token resistance, the French units surrendered. But soon the deficiencies of American forces took their toll, as inadequate transportation and supplies along with poor leadership produced a series of defeats by the German and Italian armies. Smith worked intensely to resolve the supply problems, and by March he found success as a huge convoy arrived with masses of trucks, weapons, ammunition, and railroad equipment. Superior Allied numbers ground down the Axis forces, and in mid-May they were cornered and surrendered. Operation Torch can be compared with preseason games in a major sport—the troops made many mistakes; but by the end, a more effective military force came together, and greatly improved logistics proved to be a large part of Allied success. Beetle Smith had been at the center in meeting these challenges of organization and leadership.[38]

To keep pressure on the Axis in the West and provide some relief to the Soviet Union, the Allies worked quickly to prepare the invasion of Sicily. A large British and American force landed at multiple points on July 10, and from the start confused lines of command hampered the operation. Eisenhower did not impose an overall strategic plan on the unit commanders, and as the supreme commander he allowed multiple command centers on the ground to compete for advantage. Despite an eight-to-one ratio in manpower over the Axis, the Anglo-American force took thirty-eight days to capture the island and failed to cut off the enemy's successful withdrawal to the Italian mainland. Beetle tried to establish order in a chaotic situation punctuated by frequent intrusions from an impatient Churchill. Much of his time was taken up drafting multiple plans for the next attack in Southern Italy as instructions from Washington and London changed almost daily.[39]

Smith visited Sicily in late July to assess the situation and meet with the commanders, but he was urgently called back to Algiers by

Eisenhower to undertake an important diplomatic mission. In Rome, King Victor Emmanuel III had removed Prime Minister Benito Mussolini from office and had arrested him, replacing him with Marshall Pietro Badoglio. This opened the possibility of Italy withdrawing from the war. Members of the new Italian government wanted peace but had a greatly exaggerated view of their negotiating strength. The government was split into several factions, and Smith soon found himself in Lisbon in an opera buffa of negotiations with military representatives of two different groups. Beetle had authority to discuss only a military armistice, not broader terms of a settlement. He told the Italian general representing the prime minister that any discussion of Italy's status or participation in the war against the Germans would be decided later by political leaders, carefully avoiding any mention of the actual policy of unconditional surrender. Hearing how afraid the Italians were of German retaliation, Smith knew that announcement of an armistice had to be carefully coordinated with an Allied invasion in order to prevent a Nazi takeover of the entire country. He sent the general back to Rome with instructions to get the prime minister's approval to return to Sicily and sign an armistice.[40]

After Smith returned to Algiers and briefed Ike on his negotiations, the situation took a dangerous turn. Another Italian general representing the army chief of staff appeared in Lisbon and sought to negotiate with the British ambassador. Obeying misguided instructions from London, the ambassador gave the general the full terms of unconditional surrender recently agreed on by Roosevelt and Churchill. This news struck Ike and Beetle like a thunderbolt. They feared that if news of these terms reached Rome, their attempt to get a military armistice would be immediately rejected. Smith persuaded the British diplomat to get the copy of the terms back from the Italian and, under the pretense of touring an Allied military base, send him via Gibraltar to Algiers, where he was detained and questioned intensively. Smith pressured the Italian general to write a letter to his superior urging acceptance of the armistice terms. Beetle, accompanied by British and American diplomats, went to Sicily to meet the general representing the prime minister, taking the general sent by the chief of staff with them. Smith quickly learned that the representative from Rome had no authority to sign an armistice, and instead, as a condition of signing, he wanted significant Allied commitments to protect the security of the king, the government, and the capital city.[41]

Beetle flatly rejected these commitments and stated that the Allied invasion would occur with or without an armistice. If there was not a prior armistice, Anglo-American diplomats would surely demand harsher terms of surrender. Understanding that the Germans now had nineteen divisions in Italy, Smith was confident that he held all the cards. With Ike's authorization, Beetle proposed providing security to the government in Rome, and the Italian representatives seemed relieved. He told them that the Badoglio government had until midnight September 2 to accept the armistice with these terms. The generals flew back to Rome; and, after considerable debate, they responded that the prime minister accepted the terms and would send a representative to sign the armistice in Sicily on September 2.[42]

Smith soon discovered that he had to overcome more Italian ruses. Badoglio's representative, General Giuseppi Castellano, arrived in Sicily at the last moment, and, when asked to sign the armistice, admitted that he had no written authority to do so and had come "to work out the details of military cooperation." Beetle was furious, and let Castellano know it. He detained the general and his aides in a guarded tent while deciding how to respond. After consulting his top commanders, he orchestrated his own "amateur theatricals" to pressure the Italians. Following some delay, the tall, imposing figure of General Sir Harold Alexander arrived in dress uniform with an escort of similarly attired Irish Guards. When he learned that Castellano had no authority to sign the armistice, the British general exploded, calling the Italian a spy and ordering his arrest. For this perfidy, Alexander threatened that Allied bombers would destroy Rome the next day.

Sometime after Alexander stormed out, the Foreign Office representative, Harold Macmillan, told Castellano that the only way to escape this debacle was to cable the prime minister for immediate authority to sign. This was done, but failed to produce a prompt response because Badoglio was afraid to take responsibility for authorizing the armistice.

Early in the morning of September 3, Smith pressured Castellano to cable the prime minister again, and more waiting followed. When another ambiguous reply came from Rome, Smith himself cabled Badoglio, insisting on an unqualified authorization to sign. The desired authority finally arrived about 5 P.M. on September 3, and within 15 minutes the armistice was signed. After a congratulatory dinner hosted by General Alexander, Smith gave Castellano the full terms of settlement, which, to the Italian's surprise and dismay, called for unconditional surrender.[43]

The entire episode of the Italian surrender reveals a great deal about Beetle Smith's skills as a bold and adroit negotiator as well as his unusual relationship with his boss Dwight Eisenhower. In the early days of Operation Torch, Ike had initiated a deal with Admiral François Darlan, the senior Vichy representative in North Africa, to make him senior commander of French forces in the region in exchange for cooperation with the Allied forces in their control of French colonial territory. When the bargain became publicly known, a huge outcry arose from British and American politicians and media about collaborating with the brutal Vichy fascists. "Badly burned in the Darlan affair," Crosswell argues, "Eisenhower avoided political entanglements like the plague." For future efforts, to protect his own reputation, Ike assigned Beetle Smith to conduct political and diplomatic missions that might result in failure, embarrassment, and possibly removal from command.

As a result of Ike's decision, Beetle handled the tortured series of negotiations with Italian representatives. He undertook the secret mission to Lisbon to meet Castellano, arranged to divert the chief of staff's representative to Algiers and keep him quiet about the actual surrender terms, pressured Castellano through multiple sessions in Sicily, and ultimately forced Badoglio to authorize signing the armistice that took Italy out of the war. Remarkably, Smith accomplished all this as the junior officer orchestrating several senior generals with immense egos. Smith was a recently promoted, two-star general, whereas Alexander and Montgomery had four stars and Patton had three. For his efforts, Smith received high praise from British and American officials. But given the continued fragile relationship with the Italian government, the details of his role remained secret for many years.[44]

Unfortunately for the Allied invasion forces, the Italian problem was far from solved. The amphibious landings proceeded as scheduled, but the Badoglio government took no action on any of its promises to assist the Allies. Faced with an Italian double-cross, Eisenhower canceled the promised security for Rome and announced the signature of the armistice, which the Italians had hoped to keep secret longer. After a period of confusion, the Germans responded firmly by releasing Mussolini from prison and naming him head of a puppet government while preparing for a stout defense of Southern Italy. Anglo-American strategy was already shifting to prepare for an invasion of France. Troops and naval units began to withdraw to Britain for a major cross-channel attack in the late spring of 1944. Eisenhower was designated supreme commander for the invasion, code-named Overlord, with Smith as his chief of staff.[45]

Moving to London in December, Smith spent the first three months of 1944 organizing and filling a large staff with the right combination of British and American officers. He received recognition for his hard work on Italy when he was promoted to lieutenant general in January. Building an efficient headquarters staff required Beetle to utilize a great deal of personal diplomacy because the British felt they had more experience in war and had a superior staff system, while the Americans who were steadily becoming the largest military force and the greatest source of weapons and supplies believed they had the right to lead the war effort. British officers, with the exception of Air Chief Marshal Sir Arthur Tedder, all praised Smith for his organization, consultation, and efficiency, whereas the Americans felt that Beetle gave priority to British views and was harsher with his own colleagues. In mid-March, Smith moved his headquarters, known as SHAEF, to Bushy Park outside London to have more room and separation from the heavy hand of the British ministries in Whitehall. When American officers who enjoyed London's nightclubs complained that they had no evening activities in their new location, Beetle replied bluntly: "Why not work? That's what I [do]." Throughout his invasion planning, Smith concentrated on implementing Eisenhower's priorities and protecting against any challenges to his full authority as supreme commander.[46]

As the chief planner for Overlord, Smith had to deal with many complex issues. Foremost was determining how large an invasion force could be transported to the Normandy beaches and sustained through the initial month of hard fighting needed to establish a defensible beachhead. This analysis included estimating how many landing craft would be available by late May and how many tons of supplies would need to be delivered each day. There were also disputes with the British over centralized control over the two nations' air forces and continuing conflicts with the leader of the French forces, General Charles de Gaulle, about the role of French troops and the administration of French territory under Allied control. On top of these and many lesser issues, Ike insisted also that Beetle handle the frequent demands of Churchill, Montgomery, and Patton. Dealing with all these problems required intense, 16-hour days and left Smith exhausted. By early May, he was suffering greatly from his inflamed stomach ulcer.[47]

Aided by a successful deception of the German defenders and a break in a period of stormy weather, the invasion of Normandy began on June 6, 1944. During the rest of the year, as Allied forces slowly fought their way out of Normandy, Smith concentrated on logistical problems and left the direction of combat to Eisenhower and his operations staff. During the entire fall of 1944, supply and transportation problems became so severe that the Allied advance stalled. By late January, most of the issues had been patched over, and supplies and new divisions flowed to Allied units at the front.

With increasing amounts of French territory liberated, Smith had to deal with the repeated appeals of General de Gaulle to establish a provisional government under his leadership. Such a decision was delayed for several months because Roosevelt and Churchill had decided that the Allies should not choose the new leader for France; instead, this should be done by national elections after the country was fully liberated. But this delay became untenable because the French people enthusiastically welcomed de Gaulle and the general cooperated on military affairs with the Allied commanders. On his own initiative, Smith developed a plan to persuade American diplomats and ultimately the president to recognize de Gaulle as head of a provisional government for France. This was implemented by the Big Three and five other governments on October 23.[48]

Smith soon found himself in the middle of a bitter struggle between British and American leaders over strategy for the final drive against Germany. Ever since the Allied invasion of North Africa, British officials had focused on the political dimensions of the war and sought to preserve their position as a global power. Churchill and his generals wanted to play a leading role in the fight against Germany while conserving their military strength to protect their empire in the Middle East and South Asia. In contrast, the Americans believed the goal of the war was to destroy the enemy's fighting power and insisted that political issues be addressed only after the Axis powers were all defeated. By 1944, British military and economic power was severely depleted, and leaders in London wanted to end the war as quickly and with as few casualties as possible. This led them to push repeatedly for forces, including several American armies, to be concentrated under Field Marshal Montgomery for a drive on Berlin and an early German surrender.

American leaders preferred a classic offensive strategy of pressure against Germany all across the western front with attacks launched at several points to tie down as many German troops as possible while the Soviets mounted a massive offensive from the east. Because the United States was now providing by far the most troops, supplies, and weapons for the war, leaders in Washington insisted on setting the strategy and commanding the forces. The strategy developed by Eisenhower and Smith had been approved months before by the CCS as well as the Big Three Allied leaders.[49]

Nevertheless, British leaders forced a confrontation on strategy at a hastily organized conference on Malta in January and February 1945, as Churchill and Roosevelt were on their way to meet Stalin at Yalta. Field Marshal Sir Alan Brooke, chief of the Imperial General Staff and chairman of the Chiefs of Staff Committee, led the fight to change Eisenhower's strategy and endorse a conclusive push to Berlin under Montgomery. In addition, he insisted that Field Marshal Sir Harold Alexander, Churchill's favorite general, be made commander of all ground forces in France. Brooke's remarks were sharp and personal, and part of his animus stemmed from his deep disappointment at having learned from Churchill over a year earlier that the assignment to lead the invasion of France had been given to the Americans after the prime minister had promised the prized position to him on three separate occasions.

George Marshall was initially slated to become the supreme commander for Overlord. But Roosevelt required him to stay in Washington to manage the overall war effort, and Eisenhower became the supreme commander for the invasion and campaign in France. On behalf of an offended and united Joint Chiefs of Staff, Marshall and the chief of naval operations, Admiral Ernest J. King, returned fire, vigorously attacking Brooke for his unwarranted criticism of Eisenhower and going on to berate Montgomery as overly cautious, arrogant, and insubordinate. To clinch his case, Marshall emphasized that Eisenhower was an Allied, not just an American, commander and pointed out that he had persuaded Roosevelt to have no direct contact with him for this reason. In contrast, Churchill constantly violated agreed-on procedures and argued points both large and small with Eisenhower. The meeting wound down without a decision beyond a plan to meet again in the morning.[50]

Seething in his room after a long dinner, Smith, who was representing Eisenhower at the conference, decided to break the deadlock. Just after midnight, when Brooke returned to his room, Beetle came to see him to set him straight. Smith defended Eisenhower's strategy and pointed out that his plan included a major thrust by Montgomery using an American army with his own Anglo-Canadian army group and added a secondary attack toward Frankfurt. He challenged Brooke's criticism of Ike's performance as supreme commander and concluded by threatening that if the British insisted on showing no confidence in Eisenhower by making Alexander commander of all ground forces, he was certain that Ike would resign. Brooke retreated, saying that there was no idea of replacing Eisenhower. Major General Ian Jacob, who was present, stated in a subsequent interview: "It wasn't everybody who dared stand up like that to Sir Alan Brooke—who was a very formidable character. But that's what Beetle Smith said—and he obviously meant it! Brooke was stunned." At the final Malta session, the CCS approved the strategy, and Churchill and Roosevelt then endorsed the decision. In a later addition to his diary, Brooke stated: "My talk with Bedell Smith on the previous evening had at any rate shown to me that Bedell was quite able to appreciate the dangers of Ike's strategy and I felt satisfied that he would use his influence to guide him."[51]

Starting in February, the final Allied offensive steadily accelerated to a German collapse in early May. In this last stage of the war in Europe, Beetle Smith was very busy dealing with plans for the occupation and civil government of Germany, the danger of mass starvation among 3.6 million civilians in the German occupied portion of the Netherlands, and the surrender of all German forces. Negotiating the terms of surrender among the Allies and with the Germans proved to be highly demanding and stressful. Smith later recorded that the first week of May was the most frenetic period of the war, when he and his staff worked around the clock dealing with the details of surrender along with other crises.

Following Hitler's suicide on April 30, the new head of Germany's government began searching for the best way to end the war. On May 4, German forces in the northwest surrendered to Montgomery; and, after signing the appropriate documents, the senior officer indicated privately to the British that all German forces were ready to surrender unconditionally but wanted to do so to the Western forces to avoid the retribution they feared from the Soviets. The German delegation was flown to Eisenhower's headquarters in Reims to negotiate the surrender of the remaining majority of German units with Smith. Because Allied political leaders had not resolved the political issues of a settlement with Germany, Beetle—with Ike's approval—used the same approach he had with the Italians: specifying only the narrow terms of military surrender and leaving open the possibility of imposing "unconditional" terms and "dismemberment," as some in Washington advocated. The delegation sought to delay agreeing to terms to allow more units to surrender to the Western Allies, but Eisenhower instructed Smith to insist on the simultaneous surrender of all German forces on every front.[52]

When the Germans sought further delay, Smith resorted to psychological pressure, as he had with the Italians. In the War Room, he had his staff prepare current situation maps showing the location of Allied and

German units and a chart in the shape of a thermometer marking the current number of German prisoners (over 4 million). In his office, they placed a new map on his desk displaying current troop dispositions plus two large red arrows representing offensives from east and west cutting through German formations and foretelling complete disaster. Upon arrival at Allied headquarters, the German delegation was kept waiting for some time in the War Room, where they could ponder their difficult military situation and the large number of their colleagues who were already prisoners. Then the Germans were brought into Smith's office to present their appeals while standing above the new map on his desk. Beetle insisted that all German units on every front had to surrender at the same time, and he assured the dispirited Germans that their troops in all locations would be treated according to the Geneva Conventions. The Germans had to refer these conditions to their head of government, while Smith had to wait for Soviet approval of the terms. After a tense day on May 6, affirmative replies came from both sides.[53]

At this point, the Germans returned, led by Colonel General Alfred Jodl, who had been commander of the Operations Staff for the armed forces throughout the war. Jodl firmly restated the old demands to surrender only on the western front, and he asked for a 24-hour cease-fire to implement the surrender. Smith flatly rejected these requests and said the Germans had to surrender on all fronts simultaneously and had to accept these terms by midnight or the Allies would seal the front and resume offensive operations. Ike authorized Beetle to add that the Germans could have a 48-hour delay for implementation. Shortly after midnight, the authorization to sign came from the head of the German government. The two delegations assembled 2 hours later, and after a 10-minute exchange, officers from each nation signed the surrender documents at 2:41 A.M. on May 7. Beetle Smith signed for the United States. The next day, Secretary of War Henry L. Stimson cabled him: "It is fitting you should have been the one to sign [the] historic documents."[54]

Like Curtis LeMay, Beetle Smith shaped his methods of leadership and administration in the crucible of World War II. He was intense, highly efficient, and demanding of himself and those who worked with him. He could be charming and considerate with foreigners, visitors, and his junior and enlisted staff. But his default style was the stern task-master. When colleagues did not meet his high standards, he was often sharp and brutal in his criticism. With the end of the war in Europe in the late spring of 1945, Beetle was a few months shy of turning fifty. He was exhausted and had lost a great deal of weight due to his multiple stomach problems. After some rest and improvement in his health, he faced disappointment in the autumn as several posts he wanted badly were awarded to others. Included were European theater commander and military governor of Germany. At the end of the year, Ike—having replaced Marshall as army chief of staff—brought Smith to Washington to be his assistant chief of staff for operations and planning. Before he was fully settled in his new job, the president chose him for a very different and challenging position.[55]

Truman appointed Smith as his ambassador to the Soviet Union. Wanting to continue a cooperative relationship with Moscow, the president believed this could best be achieved by a forceful military man as ambassador who would not be pushed around by Stalin and his top diplomats Vyacheslav Molotov and Andrei Vishinsky. Marshall and Eisenhower both praised this choice. Referring to the Soviet leaders more frankly, Ike declared that it "serves those bastards right." Beetle arrived in Moscow at the end of March 1946, a month after George F. Kennan sent his famous "long telegram" to the State Department. In this seminal analysis, and in his "X" article in Foreign Affairs the next year, the chargé d'affaires argued that the repressive Soviet regime was inherently expansionist and that the United States should counter this tendency with a policy of containment in areas of its vital national interests. Kennan remained in Moscow for another month after Smith's arrival, and the new ambassador quickly came to appreciate Kennan's assessment of Soviet policy. On his initial visit to the Kremlin, on April 5, Beetle found Stalin and Molotov to be cold and unyielding in their suspicion of American policies. When he said the United States wanted to cooperate with the Soviet Union on important international questions but would respond appropriately to any aggressive behavior, the Soviet ruler accused Washington of obstructing his government's attempts to win oil concessions in Iran and of forming "a definite alignment" with

Britain "against the USSR," as demonstrated by allowing Churchill's "unfriendly" and "unwarranted attack on himself and the USSR" in his speech in Fulton, Missouri. It was not an auspicious beginning.[56]

Smith served as ambassador for three years, until March 1949. During this period, the administration adopted Kennan's recommendations and implemented a containment policy through such milestones as the Truman Doctrine and the Marshall Plan. Less than three months after the economic recovery plan for Europe went into effect, in June 1948 the Soviet Union imposed a blockade on land access to the Western zones of Berlin. Behind the effort to starve the occupying powers out of Berlin was the main Soviet objective of disrupting the plan of Western governments to create a West German government from their three zones. Instead, the Western powers collaborated on a massive airlift of food and fuel to supply the city for ten months. From the early days of the blockade, Beetle worked closely with the British and French ambassadors in Moscow to negotiate an end to the crisis and agree with the Soviets on assured Western access to Berlin. The ambassadors met separately with Stalin, and then five times with Molotov, in an effort to find agreement; but the Soviets would not accept the Western governments' insistence on full access to Berlin and the right to create a West German state. By the end of 1948, Smith wanted to leave Moscow, which had become a hostile and unproductive situation. He returned to Washington in December and submitted his resignation to the president after the election, following tradition. He spent several months in and out of Walter Reed General Hospital for treatment of his stomach ailments. Truman finally accepted Beetle's resignation in March and offered him a senior post in the State Department. Smith declined this proposal and asked to return to active duty.[57]

The president approved Smith's request, and he was named commander of the First Army, with headquarters on Governor's Island in Upper New York Bay. In practice, this post served as a preretirement assignment for richly deserving senior officers, and Beetle devoted much of his time to writing about his experiences as ambassador in Moscow. Starting in November, portions of his work were serialized in the *New York Times* and the *Saturday Evening Post*, and the entire account was published early in 1950 as *My Three Years in Moscow*. Compared with all the documents available after the breakup of the Soviet Union Smith's portrait of the country and its leaders between 1946 and 1949 is remarkably accurate. He paints the country as drab and recovering slowly from a terribly destructive war, with the government imposing rationing on food, fuel, and many of the essentials of life. The Communist Party dominated all aspects of society and ruled by severe repression of intellectual dissidents and political opponents. The party's Politburo ruled the country and controlled the bureaucracy. Its twelve to fourteen members were capable, hard-working, and loyal to Stalin, who had provided the opportunities for their careers. There were differences of opinion on policy and process within the group, and Stalin, though not "an absolute dictator," was like a "chairman of the board with the decisive vote." In 1946, when Smith held his first of four long meetings with the leader, Stalin was sixty-seven years old and had been in power for over fifteen years. His rivals, real and imagined, had all been eliminated. Based on discussions with experts such as George Kennan, Charles Bohlen, and Foy Kohler and his own observations, Smith described Stalin as "courageous but cautious; suspicious, revengeful and quick to anger, but coldly ruthless and pitilessly realistic; decisive and swift in the execution of his plans when the objective is clear, but patient, deceptive and Fabian in his tactics when the situation is obscure." Because the leader did not meet with his own citizens or travel outside Soviet territory, all his information came through trusted aides such as Politburo members or his personal staff. Beetle sought to learn as much as possible about this small group that controlled the reports going to Stalin.[58]

With regard to Soviet policies, Smith declared that his experience over three years in Moscow led him to conclude that the leaders' "ultimate goal . . . [was] world revolution and Communist world domination." He predicted that the "Soviet Union is not likely to resort to deliberate military aggression in the immediate future if the Atlantic Pact nations do not waver in the positive application of their program. The USSR leadership is not likely to gamble without favorable odds." Emphasizing the importance of NATO and the new program of military assistance, he stated: "The greatest single achievement toward the creation of conditions that would assure lasting peace in the world would be the re-establishment in Europe of a group of strong, free, virile and progressive states, living together in harmony and cooperating politically, economically and militarily." In conclusion, he urged his readers to be prepared to sustain these policies over the long term: "The fundamental fact [is] that we are forced to a continuing struggle for a free way of life that may extend over a period of many years. We dare not allow ourselves any false sense of security. We must anticipate that the Soviet tactic will be to attempt to wear us down, to exasperate us, to keep probing for weak spots, and we must cultivate firmness and patience to a degree we have never before required."[59]

Shortly after this volume was published, Smith faced a serious health crisis. He was in constant pain, and his weight had fallen from a normal 174 to 135 pounds. His doctors insisted on a major operation to remove half of his stomach. He was in Walter Reed for three and a half months; and after his release, he required a long recovery period, physical therapy, and special diets. While Smith was still in the hospital, President Truman visited him and urged him to become director of the CIA. Smith declined this offer, as he had once done previously. After the Korean War broke out, and the nation was in a national emergency, the president urgently restated his request. The still-frail soldier knew that under these circumstances he could not refuse the commander in chief a third time, and he agreed to take up the unwelcome assignment. He wrote a friend: "I expect the worst, and I am sure I won't be disappointed."[60]

DEVELOPING A PLAN

When Smith reluctantly agreed in July 1950 to become head of the CIA, he turned to Rear Admiral Sidney W. Souers for advice on who best knew the problems at the agency and could serve as a strong deputy. As the executive secretary of the NSC who had been involved in establishing the Dulles Committee to review the agency, Souers immediately recommended William H. Jackson. A member of the three-man review group, Jackson was considered the most balanced of the team. He had studied the structure and operation of British intelligence, and during the war he had served as deputy chief of intelligence for General Omar Bradley. In that post, he had absorbed his boss's dislike of Beetle Smith as "the ogre of SHAEF." When, over lunch at the 21 Club in New York, Smith had urged Jackson to become his deputy, with a mandate to reorganize the CIA, Jackson's reaction was negative. Beetle employed his charm in arguing that he needed Jackson's experience to perform a critical job at a time when the nation could be facing the beginning of World War III. Jackson eventually agreed to leave his remunerative position as head of a major investment bank to assume the difficult task of creating a functioning intelligence agency—on the conditions that he have full control of the reorganization, that he would stay for only six months, and that Smith would not subject him to any of his infamous caustic attacks. Beetle readily accepted these terms, and when his appointment as DCI was announced on August 18, he issued a statement the same day saying that Jackson would be his deputy.[61]

In light of the ongoing war in Korea and the obvious disarray in the US intelligence agencies, the Senate treated Smith's nomination as an urgent matter. He testified before the Senate Armed Services Committee on August 24, and the Senate confirmed his appointment by unanimous vote on the 28th. Due to his continuing recovery from surgery, Beetle did not take up his duties as DCI until October 7. He would remain on active duty as a lieutenant general in the US Army.[62]

While still regaining his strength before formally beginning as director, Smith sought information on the current state of the CIA and its relations with the departmental intelligence agencies. He first consulted Lawrence Houston, the CIA's general counsel, about the organization and performance of the top agency officials and asked him for a memorandum on the problems he would face as DCI. Houston's August 29 memorandum described in detail a series of problems that stemmed from a lack of specific authority for the DCI to act as the coordinator and final judge of the contents of National Intelligence Estimates and the refusal of the departmental agencies to provide information requested, make substantive comments on drafts, and accept the authority of the

DCI as set forth in NSC Report 50. The DCI, Houston argued, could not rely on goodwill and cooperation to improve the agency's performance but needed clear authority from the NSC to direct the process of creating useful national estimates. To his memorandum, the general counsel attached seven documents, which provided examples of the problems he identified and suggested remedies for them. In addition, Beetle had discussions with the former head of the wartime OSS, William Donovan; with Allen Dulles; and with several senior CIA officials. After assuming his new position, he met with the secretaries of state and defense and then with the NSC on October 12. He told the council members he would carry out the requirements of NSC 50—with the single exception that he did not want to merge the two branches that dealt with covert affairs, the Office of Special Operations (OSO), which collected information secretly and analyzed it; and the Office of Policy Coordination (OPC), which ran active disruption operations. The NSC approved this change in its directive and did not explore what Smith planned to do any further.[63]

COORDINATING THE INTELLIGENCE COMMUNITY

From his preparatory reading and discussions, Smith understood that developing a satisfactory working relationship with the Intelligence Advisory Committee was his first challenge. The Dulles Report and NSC 50 clearly established that the conflict between the advisory committee members and the DCI had proven to be a major obstacle in producing timely, solid estimates for the president. In approving NSC 50, the secretaries of state and defense had expressed strong support for the view that the DCI should be the final arbiter of the contents of National Intelligence Estimates, as his title implied. Reflecting on his experiences with Eisenhower's artful handling of relations with Allied political and military leaders and on Brigadier Kenneth Strong's methods of cooperative leadership of an intelligence staff composed of representatives from different services and nationalities in North Africa and later in

Europe, Beetle chose not to follow Lawrence Houston's advice to get specific authority from the NSC and if necessary from Congress to buttress his role as the senior figure in the intelligence community. Instead, he decided to rely on his reputation as a forceful leader and on the positive endorsements he had from the president and from Congress to develop a relationship of mutual respect and cooperation with the IAC. His first opportunity to employ this approach came sooner than expected.[64]

At the end of the working day on October 10, Smith's second day on the job, he received an urgent request from the president for six estimates on issues that he would discuss with General MacArthur on Wake Island. The White House needed these estimates within 20 hours, when Truman would be leaving for the Pacific island base. These reports were to analyze the threats of major Chinese or Soviet intervention in Korea; Chinese aggression against Formosa, Indochina, or the Philippines; and general Soviet and Chinese capabilities and intentions in the Far East. Smith personally called each member of the IAC to attend a meeting at his office at 7 P.M. When one member objected to interrupting his dinner, Beetle "straightened him out in the language of a drill sergeant addressing a lackadaisical recruit," reports Montague. Briefed on the president's needs and instilled with a sense of urgency, the seven intelligence leaders returned to the Pentagon to gather six joint working groups to produce the desired estimates. Smith directed Ludwell Montague of the CIA's Office of Research and Evaluation to join the groups to supervise the assembly of the combined estimate. The conclusions reached in this overnight blitz were negative in all estimates. On the most pressing issue, the analysts stated: "While full-scale Chinese Communist intervention in Korea must be regarded as a continuing possibility, a consideration of all known factors leads to the conclusion that barring a Soviet decision for global war, such action is not probable in 1950. During this period, intervention will probably be confined to continued covert assistance to the North Koreans." The collection of estimates was delivered to the White House in time for the president's trip. This inadvertent initial engagement of the IAC with the new DCI was a rushed version of the type of collective effort that Beetle wanted to establish as routine procedure.[65]

General Smith held his first formal meeting with the members of the IAC on October 20. In explaining several of his early decisions as DCI he stated that he had won the agreement of the secretaries of state and defense that no further discussion of ways to implement NSC 50 was necessary and that he would proceed "promptly" to implement the recommendations of that directive with the exception of not merging the OSO and the Office of Policy Coordination, a decision the NSC had endorsed. He then reported that he had the approval of the secretaries of state and defense for the Office of Policy Coordination to continue receiving guidance from their departments but that OPC "would act under the authority and subject to the control" of the DCI. Having confirmed his authority in two important areas, the new director turned to relations with the advisory committee. He stated that in future the committee would meet more frequently and "for longer periods" and declared that the members "must be geared for rapid cooperative work." Next Beetle addressed the sensitive issue of compiling National Intelligence Estimates (NIEs) by reading a passage from a memorandum by his deputy, William H. Jackson, which was taken verbatim from the Dulles Committee report. This section established that the CIA had "the clear duty and responsibility" to obtain the best available information from all intelligence agencies to coordinate and produce NIEs.

To organize and direct this "collective effort," Smith announced he was establishing an Office of National Estimates (ONE) within the CIA. A separate Office of Research and Reports (ORR) would conduct research on issues "of common concern in fields assigned specifically by directives of the National Security Council." In future, the committee agreed that NIEs would be produced under a priority list of subjects adopted by the IAC. The ONE would draft an outline and request submissions from the appropriate agencies within a fixed schedule. The ONE would complete a first draft, obtain comments and changes from the agencies, do a second draft, and submit it to the IAC for discussion and approval. In the case of crisis estimates, such as those recently requested by the president, the procedure used on that occasion would be repeated. In this opening session, Smith had established his authority in several important areas and won the approval of the IAC for a new cooperative effort for producing NIEs. As Montague concludes: "His performance that afternoon was masterful."[66]

Cooperation between the CIA and the IAC worked smoothly and efficiently after Smith's firm invitation to collaborate. By the end of 1950, ten new estimates had been completed, half dealing with potential threats around the periphery of the Soviet Union and China and half related to Chinese intervention in Korea and the security capabilities of Western Europe. Beetle could now devote his attention to restructuring the CIA itself and to meeting the needs of the president and key members of the NSC.[67]

TIGHTENING THE CHAIN OF COMMAND

When Smith arrived at the CIA, he knew the agency was a poorly managed series of feudal baronies. In order to create an organization that would be the vital center of the intelligence community with the capability to provide the information needed by the decisionmakers of a global power, he had three overriding objectives. He wanted to centralize the management so that the DCI could be in full control of the agency. He worked steadily to improve the quality and commitment of the division heads and the officials under them with the goal of building intelligence into an attractive career service. And he sought to develop a culture that called for cooperation among division chiefs, who would resolve differences between them in a spirit of collaboration in a common mission. With the country in a crisis, as masses of Chinese "volunteers" drove US and Allied forces back below the 38th Parallel, Beetle realized he could not make his changes too rapidly.

To signal that a very different leader was now in charge at the agency, Smith won everyone's attention at his first staff meeting in October by calmly stating: "It's interesting to see all you fellows here. It'll be even more interesting to see how many of you are here a few months from now."[68]

One problem that complicated Beetle's ability to reshape the CIA was its dysfunctional office arrangement. In October 1950, the CIA was scattered among ten buildings, centered in the former OSS headquarters at 2430 E Street, NW. This group included four old brick buildings on the hill west of 23rd Street and four wartime temporary structures at the foot of the hill on the Mall. The offices for OSO and OPC were in temporary buildings further away on the opposite side of the Mall, beyond the Reflecting Pool. The following April, the burst of growth in OPC required two additional temporaries and a recreation center nearby. This dispersion of his staff would limit Smith's efforts to supervise the divisions of the agency closely. This would pose particular difficulties in gaining control over covert operations. But the pressing demands of the war meant that the DCI's plans would need to adapt to the dismal housing arrangement for the foreseeable future.[69]

His initial steps were to bring in excellent key people who would work directly with him. His basic plan was to organize the CIA along the lines that had worked well for him at SHAEF. His deputy, Bill Jackson, would function as chief operating officer, as Beetle did for Ike. He would be involved in all decisions and available for special projects. The director's small personal staff would be run by an executive assistant who knew the agency and had worked with Jackson on Bradley's intelligence staff during the war. He was in charge of scheduling all appointments; keeping a daily log of all important communications, meetings, and conversations; relaying the director's decisions to those responsible for carrying them out; and checking on implementation. Smith knew he needed expert assistance in trying to gain control over the rapidly expanding covert operations run by Frank Wisner of OPC. Despite differences on policy and organization, he persuaded Allen W. Dulles to join the top staff, first as a consultant, then as deputy director for plans, with responsibility for both OPC and OSO. For the first three months, Beetle met daily with the assistant directors of all offices and his deputies to set out his priorities and assert his leadership as the director. Later, Jackson began to chair these meetings; and after March 1951, the executive assistant ran them as preparation for the three specialized deputies to meet with Jackson and Smith. Beetle's position was strengthened in making these changes when he was promoted, at Truman's insistence, to four-star general on July 1, 1951.[70]

Several other administrative arrangements depended on Beetle's evaluation of inside candidates for senior positions and resolving questions of jurisdiction. During his first year, Smith created two additional groups of offices headed by deputy directors. First was the deputy director for administration, who covered a wide range of administrative duties. When Jackson left the agency, to be replaced in August 1951 by Allen Dulles, Beetle put together six offices—some of which Jackson had supervised—headed by the deputy director for intelligence (DDI). The intelligence directorate included groups that collected intelligence from all sources, prepared the daily briefing for the president, coordinated relations with other intelligence agencies, performed basic intelligence and scientific research, and prepared NIEs. Smith and Jackson placed great importance on producing high-quality NIEs and recruited prominent academics, including William Langer of Harvard, Sherman Kent of Yale, and Raymond Sontag of the University of California at Berkeley. When problems developed between the academics and the DDI, Smith ordered the members to report directly to him on the substance of the estimates while remaining under the management of the DDI for scheduling and producing the finished NIEs. To ensure that his policies of coordination and cooperation were carried out as part of the effort to create a new agency culture, Beetle had three other offices—personnel, training, and communications—report directly to him for an initial period.[71]

Starting in March 1951, Smith relied for administrative control on a daily meeting with Jackson, his three specialized deputies, his executive assistant, and one or two office heads as appropriate. In practice, the great majority of their time in these meetings was devoted to the management of the clandestine services. These services had expanded rapidly and haphazardly in the early months of the Korean conflict. Recruitment standards were lax, training was very brief, and administration was loose. All three of these functions were controlled by OPC and were not integrated with the rest of the CIA. Smith worked to change this in all three areas; and after a series of battles with Dulles and Wisner, he succeeded. Even then, the leadership of the plans directorate stretched the limit of their orders as much as possible without crossing into outright violation.[72]

The case of cable traffic presented an extreme example. During the rapid growth of the clandestine services and overseas posts after the Chinese intervention, cable traffic from overseas increased sharply. Smith was intensely irritated when he discovered in early 1952 that all cables from overseas agents went directly to the Directorate of Plans, which distributed them to action officers and decided which cables should go to the DCI, often several days after their initial distribution. He ordered the process changed as part of the reorganization of the clandestine services in August 1952. All cables would now be sent to a small staff in his office, whose members would decide how to distribute the cables, including which ones should be brought to the attention of the DCI. For the contents of the cables to be intelligible, this change required revealing the names of the agents mentioned in the messages, a disclosure that caused furious arguments and was resolved only after what were described as "some explosive remarks" from Beetle Smith.[73]

In the spring of 1952, Smith submitted a report to the NSC on the reorganization of the CIA in response to the changes directed by NSC 50. He began by stating that the elements of the directive "have been carried out in all substantial respects." To illustrate "the general scope of the reorganization," he attached tables of organization as of October 1950, when he became DCI, and as of December 31, 1951. Beetle noted that several new units were established during his first fifteen months, and leading his list was the creation of the Office of National Estimates and refinement of the production of NIEs. Also mentioned were the Office of Current Intelligence and the Office of Research and Reports, which, with the Interdepartmental Economic Intelligence Committee, focused on coordinating economic intelligence on the Soviet Bloc, a task previously spread over twenty-four government agencies. He concluded by describing the Interdepartmental Watch Committee within the Department of Defense, which provided a "constant and periodic review of indications of possible enemy action," and the establishment of a career training program to build a service of "high-caliber personnel."[74]

The DCI summarized four special studies of new areas done at the request of the NSC. He devoted by far the greatest detail to a paper that "redefines the Central Intelligence Agency's responsibilities" for covert activities. He pointed out that over the previous three years, requirements have "produced a threefold increase in the clandestine operations of the Agency and will require next year a budget three times larger than that required for our intelligence activities." These operations were spread around the world and ranged from psychological warfare to paramilitary operations to stockpiling strategic materials and organizing "escape and evasion networks and stay-behind movements for use in the event of war." Stating that the agency could meet these new obligations if it were provided with the additional funds and personnel, he bluntly asked the council members to understand three things: These new duties were not "essential" to performing the agency's "intelligence responsibilities"; the CIA was assigned these tasks because no other agency "could undertake them"; and the covert activities "will inevitably militate against the performance by Central Intelligence Agency of its primary intelligence functions and are a continuing and increasing risk to its security. Regrettably, (from my personal viewpoint) it seems impracticable, for reasons of coordination and security, to divorce these from other covert operations."[75]

In conclusion, Smith emphasized two factors limiting the "accuracy and timeliness" of the CIA's intelligence. First was the depth and strength of the Soviet security system, which, despite every effort of the United States in cooperation with its Allies, prevented certainty in providing advance warning of a surprise attack. Second was the agency's dependence on a diverse group of partners. The CIA "is basically an assembly plant for information produced by collaborating organizations of the Government, and its final product is necessarily dependent upon the quality of the contributions of these collaborating organizations."[76]

In this candid report to the NSC, the director made four basic points beyond describing his restructuring of the CIA. He highlighted his view that collecting and analyzing intelligence was the CIA's primary mission; he pointed out that clandestine operations were not "essential" to this mission; he expressed concern that the rapid expansion of covert operations was threatening the agency's ability to achieve its basic mandate; and he insisted that these operations should be paid for in full by the government agencies that needed them—that is, the Defense and State departments. (See figure 16.1.)

FIGURE 16.1 Lieutenant General Walter Bedell Smith (*right*), director of the US Central Intelligence Agency, arrives in Taegu, Korea, and confers on the current military situation with Major General Charles A. Willoughby, MacArthur's intelligence chief (*left*), and Lieutenant General Matthew B. Ridgway, commander of the US Eighth Army (*center*), January 17, 1951.

Source: US Army photo, National Archives.

DEALING WITH COVERT OPERATIONS

From his time as Eisenhower's chief of staff in Europe, when one of his duties was coordinating the activities of Allied intelligence agents with resistance groups in Axis-occupied areas, Smith developed a critical view of covert operations. He believed these missions were inefficient and diverted resources from combat units. This judgment carried over to his years as DCI. He felt strongly that the principal task of the CIA was to generate intelligence to inform the decisions of top policymakers. As DCI, he "was dismayed by the variety and magnitude of the covert action operations that he was called upon to conduct," asserts Montague.

The conflict in Korea produced a great clamor in government circles for a massive effort to destabilize the Soviet Bloc through clandestine activities. This pressure made it difficult for Smith to curtail the level of covert operations. For most of his final two and a half years as director, he fought a sustained battle on two fronts to reduce the number of these activities and strengthen quality control for them. The first front was a fundamental heated battle with the Joint Chiefs of Staff (JCS) about their attempt to gain control over guerrilla warfare in combat zones and at a later stage to control all covert operations, including the clandestine collection of information. The second front was mainly inside the CIA, as he worked to restrain and reduce the covert operations aggressively sponsored by Allen Dulles and Frank Wisner. In the end, he was successful against the JCS, but he could do little more than improve the quality of the covert operations run by the Directorate of Plans.[77]

After the Chinese intervention showed that the war in Korea would not end quickly, the NSC staff debated which department or agency should have control of what NSC 68 had designated "psychological warfare." This term covered propaganda, secret espionage, and covert actions. In December 1950, the NSC staff proposed the creation of a Psychological Strategy Board (PSB) to evaluate and approve proposals for clandestine operations of all types. This proposal was studied and revised by an interdepartmental committee and was approved by the NSC and the president on April 4, 1951. The PSB was made up of three senior officials: Undersecretary of State James Webb, Deputy Secretary of Defense Robert Lovett, and the DCI. The board would have a staff and a director appointed by the president. The members of the board chose Beetle Smith as chairman.[78]

In a memorandum on the "Scope and Pace of Covert Operations" on May 8, Smith attempted to persuade the NSC to clarify the division of responsibilities among the sponsors of clandestine operations. His more specific objective was to have all paramilitary and guerrilla activities in war zones assigned to the Department of Defense, not to the CIA. He was only partially successful. In extensive interagency debate, an attempt by the JCS to win control of all covert operations in war zones was defeated. In a decision made on October 23, 1951, the NSC directed that the DCI had the authority to conduct all covert operations, subject to the approval of the PSB; that OPC should significantly increase its covert activities; and that the PSB should determine "the desirability and feasibility" of major covert operations as well as their scope and pace and should ensure that the State and Defense departments provide sufficient support to conduct these operations. This drawn-out bureaucratic struggle was a victory for Allen Dulles and Frank Wisner, who had consistently argued that the clandestine collection of intelligence and active covert operations were closely connected parts of the same form of secret warfare. The JCS lost in its attempt to take over large parts of wartime covert operations, although the State and Defense departments had to provide the funds, equipment, and personnel under CIA direction.[79]

The decisions in the "Scope and Pace of Covert Operations" directive in October 1951 marked a defeat for Smith's effort to significantly reduce the covert activities of the Office of Policy Coordination. Indeed, this short document, known in the bureaucracy as NSC 10/5, signaled the dominance of a wide range of covert activities within the CIA. This shift was also reflected in changes in agency leadership and structure. In August 1951, William Jackson resigned as deputy director for central intelligence to return to business, and he was replaced by Allen Dulles. Frank Wisner moved up to become deputy director for plans. Through the first half of the year, Dulles and Wisner had moved steadily to integrate the operations of OSO and OPC, against the stated policy of Smith. This process did not go smoothly, because the staff members of OSO worked to remain independent. They viewed themselves as the experienced intelligence professionals and resented the higher salaries, rapid promotions, and freewheeling methods of the operators of OPC, whom they saw as overly enthusiastic amateurs. Competition developed in overseas stations as OPC officials recruited agents away from OSO with higher pay and more exciting, if more dangerous, work.

In January 1952, Beetle finally accepted the merger of the two offices in principle; and after more fights at headquarters over missions and command authority, a final merger was announced by Smith in a directive of July 15, 1952, on the "Organization of the Clandestine Services."

The new organization created leadership positions to protect "the long-term espionage mission of CIA from becoming lost in multifarious opportunistic and urgent covert operations." A chief of operations, Richard Helms, came from OSO, and a separate office was set up to manage foreign intelligence. Other divisions within the Directorate of Plans were for political and psychological warfare (basically OPC), paramilitary operations, technical support, and administration.[80]

THE EXPANSION OF COVERT OPERATIONS

The rapid growth of CIA covert operations began after the adoption of NSC 10/2 in June 1948. This built upon the successful clandestine intervention in the Italian election the previous April, when, with widespread propaganda and political support of center-right candidates, the agency had prevented a threatened Communist Party victory. President Truman was a strong advocate of psychological warfare, which was understood to include clandestine propaganda and political action. Many in the State Department, including Secretary Marshall and George F. Kennan, shared this view. A large number of senior officials in the Pentagon wanted more disruptive operations—including sabotage; forming underground resistance groups within the Soviet Bloc; and, if needed, paramilitary warfare. These missions would be the mandate of the OPC, which began active recruitment with the appointment of Wisner as its head in September 1948. Within Congress, the handful of members who reviewed the CIA's budget also supported active OPC measures. After the first Soviet atomic test and the outbreak of the Korean War, demand for OPC operations grew dramatically.[81]

When Beetle Smith took over as director, OPC's projects were expanding without effective control. By early 1951, "Wisner's operations had multiplied fivefold since the start of the war," asserts Tim Weiner. He "was hiring hundreds of college kids every month, running them through a few weeks of commando school, sending them overseas for half a year, rotating them out, and sending more raw recruits to replace them. He was trying to build a worldwide military machine without a semblance of professional training, logistics, or communications." After William Jackson resigned and Allen Dulles became deputy director for central intelligence, Smith saw no other choice but to promote Wisner to be deputy director for plans, in charge of all clandestine operations. "When he saw the first CIA budget the two men proposed, he exploded," says Weiner. "It was $587 million, an elevenfold increase from 1948. More than $400 million was for Wisner's covert operations—three times the cost of espionage and analysis combined."[82]

Most of the covert operations Smith found were in Europe and were focused on the Soviet Union and its satellites. The prime recruiting grounds for agents were in the camps for displaced persons and the exile communities scattered across Western Europe. Wisner's young operators searched these groups for agents to be trained quickly and sent back to their countries to report on any mobilization of Soviet forces and to organize resistance and sabotage cells. One of the largest operations recruited Ukrainians to return to their country to work with a guerrilla brigade based in the Carpathian Mountains. Almost all these contract agents were captured, and some were turned to feed disinformation back to their handlers. Eventually, all were killed after a Soviet assault in 1954.

This series of failed missions had multiple causes. One problem was that Soviet intelligence had infiltrated the exile groups and could identify many who became American agents. Some of these were captured and forced to send false reports back to their station in Munich. These reports were later described as coming from "paper mills." Other Soviet agents were recruited by the CIA and became double agents reporting on forthcoming missions. A more serious issue was that James J. Angleton, the CIA's head of foreign intelligence and liaison with friendly services such as Britain's MI6, met frequently with Kim Philby, the senior MI6 officer in Washington, and shared the details of all operations in the Soviet Bloc. The tragic fact was that Philby was the top Soviet spy in the United States. If Soviet agents in Europe did not identify CIA recruits returning to the communist bloc, Philby's reports to Moscow would make certain that their missions and probably their lives ended abruptly.[83]

Other major paramilitary operations in Poland and Albania also failed dramatically. A Polish resistance group, the Freedom and Independence movement (WIN was its Polish acronym), claimed to have 500 active members and as many as 100,000 ready to support a retardation effort to slow any Soviet advance against the West. Starting in the summer of 1950, OPC agents dropped military equipment, radios, and money from chartered aircraft for WIN leaders to use in their planned action against the Red Army. In December 1952, Polish government radio announced that the security forces had broken up an attempt by Britain and the United States to sponsor a revolt against the communist regime. In fact, WIN had begun as a legitimate resistance group, but it had been taken over by Polish internal security in 1947 and run as a false front since then. The repressive Polish government was the beneficiary of the equipment and funds dropped by the CIA.

The Albanian fiasco had different origins but ended the same. British and American intelligence planners decided to use the sizable community of royalist Albanian exiles in Italy, Greece, and Egypt to send teams of paramilitary agents to organize local opposition groups to create a civil war and overthrow the communist government. Beginning in the spring of 1950, a series of teams were sent into Albania by air, land, and sea. Virtually every one was captured on arrival. Despite repeated failures, the missions continued until 1954, when the Albanian government staged a show trial to demonstrate how it had foiled the Anglo-American attempt at regime change. Again the reason for the total failure was Kim Philby, who was one of the operation's sponsors in Washington until 1951 and became its supervisor when he returned to headquarters in London. "All told, hundreds of the CIA's foreign agents were sent to their deaths in Russia, Poland, Romania, Ukraine, [Albania], and the Baltic states during the 1950s," charges Tim Weiner. "Their fates were unrecorded; no accounts were kept and no penalty assessed for failure. Their missions were seen as a matter of national survival for the United States."[84]

Given Smith's doubts about the efficacy of covert operations, one might reasonably ask why he did not stop the poorly proposed and obviously failing missions that he found when he became DCI. There are several reasons why he moved slowly. Despite his repeated tough interrogation of Dulles and Wisner about the results of their dozens of operations, he did not receive details of the scope of their activities or reports of their frequent failures. In a very hectic wartime environment, he simply could not get an adequate picture of what was going on in Europe. After the massive Chinese intervention, Washington had to confront the prospect of being driven off the Korean Peninsula in defeat. Any effort to dissuade Soviet leaders from aggression in Europe, the most valuable prize, quickly won support from the US president and his advisers. Smith understood that his most important task was to build a professional intelligence service from a dysfunctional group of fiefdoms. He had to work steadily toward this objective and accept failures along the way.

An accurate reflection of this attitude was his handling in May and June 1951 of the British MI6 report asserting strong suspicion that Kim Philby was a Soviet spy who had facilitated the escape of fellow KGB agents Guy Burgess and Donald Maclean. Smith gathered evaluations of Philby's activities while serving as British liaison to the CIA from senior colleagues who had worked closely with him and concluded that Philby was almost certainly a Soviet agent who had done serious damage to agency operations and US interests. Beetle then wrote a very strong personal letter to the head of MI6 (known as "C"), demanding that Philby be fired or the United States would terminate its special intelligence relationship with the United Kingdom. The British complied with the CIA director's demand and fired Philby. As the news spread within the CIA, the impact was severe; many officials criticized colleagues who were thought to have cooperated too freely with the treasonous British agent. Not wanting the internal turmoil to become public and further fuel McCarthyism, Beetle Smith put a lid of secrecy on the whole affair to protect the reputation of the fledgling agency.[85]

Smith's concern about the CIA's professional repute continued into late 1952 when he buried a report about massive intelligence failures in Korea. The new station chief in Seoul, John Limond Hart, had conducted a three-month investigation of the poor performance of the agents managed from Seoul. He removed all the double agents and fabricators from the payroll and recommended that his station cease operations. One of Beetle's deputies on an inspection tour delivered a firm negative reply from the director, saying: "The CIA, being a new organization whose reputation had not yet been established, simply could not admit to other branches of Government—least of all to the highly competitive US military intelligence services—its inability to collect intelligence on North Korea."[86]

When, in the summer of 1952, Smith learned of the excesses in OPC operations and some of the paramilitary failures became public, he had to act. He devised a process to send trusted representatives—mostly senior military officers—to each of the five overseas regions to review ongoing operations and proposals for new projects. One of the most active of these senior representatives was Lieutenant General Lucian K. Truscott, a tough, highly decorated commander in World War II, who went to Berlin to oversee all OSO and OPC operations. Truscott discovered a number of questionable projects. Potentially the most explosive was a program of secret prisons where harsh interrogation techniques and mind control drugs were used to extract confessions from suspected double agents. Forerunners of the secret prisons after 9/11 were operated in Germany, in Japan, and in the Panama Canal Zone (which was the largest one). Most of the records of these operations were destroyed, but the fragments that survived show that Russians were taken to Panama and North Koreans to Japan for brutal questioning and experiments with heroin, amphetamines, and the recently discovered LSD. The prison program began in 1948 and sharply expanded with the outbreak of war in Korea. It operated until the late 1950s. Dulles, Wisner, and Helms supervised the program of secret prisons, and it is hard to believe that Smith and some more senior officials did not know about it and approve it.[87]

Among the large number of projects Truscott canceled was support for a resistance group called the Young Germans. This organization of 20,000 in West Germany was led by former Hitler Youth members. They buried weapons and radios across West Germany for use against a Soviet invasion. But they had a dangerous private agenda. The leaders had developed a list of centrist democratic West German politicians to be assassinated if war broke out. This group and its hit list became public, creating a major scandal and leading to the cancellation of the CIA's support and the dissolution of the organization.

Another project within Truscott's purview was hijacked and taken to its demise by Frank Wisner. This involved the Free Jurists' Committee in East Germany. The group of young lawyers and paralegals compiled a record of state crimes they planned to unveil at an International Congress of Jurists in West Berlin in July 1952. Over the objections of the project's OSO handler, Wisner approved a plan by an OPC officer to transform the group into an armed underground. The project came to a sad conclusion when Soviet soldiers kidnapped a group leader and tortured him into identifying the other members, all of whom were arrested just before the conference opened. This competition between two CIA offices was recorded as the sacrifice of a useful propaganda and disruption mission for a poorly planned and ultimately fatal resistance operation. Although the record of Beetle's senior representatives was far from perfect, overall, across the five regions they terminated about one-third of the proposals and projects they reviewed. Smith himself took decisive action in the fall of 1952 to cancel a proposed attempt to assassinate Stalin on a trip to Paris. Dulles and Wisner had approved the project, but Smith saw the immense political problems if it were attempted and ended the discussion. As it turned out, the Soviet dictator did not make the trip.[88]

COVERT OPERATIONS IN ASIA

Operating in Asia posed even greater problems for the CIA than those found in Europe. The agency had very few officers in the entire region because General MacArthur, as Far East commander, had banned CIA operations from his domain—just as he had kept the OSS out during World War II. Even worse, a Soviet spy in Washington had cut off signals intelligence of Moscow's communications with China and North Korea when he discovered that the US Army had broken their encryption codes. After the Chinese intervened massively without being detected, Smith made an urgent trip to Tokyo in January 1951 and persuaded the general to cooperate with CIA officers in the region. A major station and training center was set up in Japan a few weeks later.

Meanwhile, Frank Wisner had been recruiting and training hundreds of new agents. By early 1951, he had dispatched 1,000 officers to Korea and 300 to Taiwan. One of the young agents training the recruits was Donald Gregg, a recent graduate of Williams College who himself had been hastily trained in paramilitary operations. Sent to a new $28 million training base on the mid-Pacific island of Saipan, Gregg said in a later interview that he "took tough Korean farm boys plucked from refugee camps, brave but undisciplined men who spoke no English, and tried to turn them into instant American intelligence agents. The CIA sent them on crudely conceived missions that produced little save a lengthening roster of lost lives." He summed up his experience: "We didn't know what we were doing. . . . It was swashbuckling of the worst kind. We were training Koreans and Chinese and a lot of other strange people, dropping Koreans into North Korea, dropping Chinese into China just north of the Korean border, and we'd drop these people in and we'd never hear from them again."[89]

In Korea, many CIA missions failed due to poor training and fabricated reports by senior station officials. From February through April 1951, Hans Tofte, an OSS veteran who was chief of operations in Korea, trained over 1,200 North Korean exiles to return to their country as guerrilla fighters who would gather intelligence, conduct sabotage, and rescue downed American air crews. Organized into forty-four teams, they were sent into North Korea by boat and parachute between April and November. Tofte regularly cabled expansive reports of their successful activities to headquarters. But in fact, almost all these paramilitary agents were killed or captured and were forced to send false reports back to the agency station. None came out alive.[90]

In the spring and summer of 1952, the station chief in Seoul, army colonel Albert Haney, sent positive reports of the great accomplishments in intelligence collection and guerrilla attacks by the over 1,500 Korean agents parachuted into the north. When John Limond Hart replaced Haney as station chief in September 1952, he was alert to the problems of fabrication and disinformation from his earlier experience managing untrustworthy Albanian agents out of the Rome station. He found that Haney had directed 200 agency officers at the station, but none spoke Korean. To manage the hundreds of agents operating in North Korea, these American officers had hired South Korean contract agents to supervise intelligence collection and guerrilla operations. Suspicious of his predecessor's reports of "miraculous achievements," Hart spent three months investigating the basis of Haney's claims and "determined that nearly every Korean agent he had inherited had either invented his reports or worked in secret for the communists. Every dispatch the station had sent to CIA headquarters from the front for the past eighteen months was a calculated deception." Hart even learned that all the Koreans supervising agents in the field were "con men who had for some time been living happily on generous CIA payments supposedly being sent to 'assets' in North Korea. Almost every report we had received from their notional agents came from our enemies."[91]

We have seen earlier in the chapter how Beetle Smith overruled Hart's request to close down the Seoul station while he cleaned house on the grounds that the CIA, as a new intelligence organization, had to protect its reputation. After the war ended, a brave air force colonel, James G. L. Kellis, wrote a personal letter to President Dwight Eisenhower disclosing how this fiasco in Seoul had been covered up by the CIA and misrepresented by Allen Dulles, then CIA director, in testimony before Congress. Kellis, who had been Wisner's director of paramilitary operations, wrote that before his testimony Dulles, had been alerted that the "'CIA's guerrillas' in North Korea were under the control of the enemy" and that the "CIA was being duped." "The inability to penetrate North Korea," Weiner concludes, "remains the longest-running intelligence failure in the CIA's history."[92]

Operations in China were no more successful than in Korea. The Chinese intervention in the war caused panic in the CIA and also in the rest of the US government. Despite having very few assets in China, OPC planners wanted to apply pressure to destabilize Mao's new regime. Jiang Jieshi's intelligence officers in Taiwan and various freelance operators in Hong Kong and on the mainland quickly responded, with reports of as many as 1 million Nationalist supporters ready to join resistance activities against the Communists. Despite the fact that these reports were unconfirmed and were mostly self-interested pleas, the agency dropped hundreds of Chinese agents into the mainland along with tons of weapons and supplies to Muslim clans in far northwestern China. Michael Coe, a Harvard graduate student recruited in the fall of 1950, spent months assigned to a CIA front group on Taiwan called Western Enterprises. After eight months as part of a Nationalist intelligence team on a small offshore island, he worked over a year in Taipei sending agents into China with very vague instructions. He lived with some six hundred colleagues in a "gated community with its own PX and officers club," as he described his experience in a later interview. He stated that the entire effort "was a waste of money. [The CIA] had been sold a bill of goods by the Nationalists." There was no large guerrilla force waiting to be activated.[93]

Burned numerous times by the corruption and deception of the Nationalists, CIA officials nevertheless pursued claims by Chinese exiles that a "Third Force" opposed to both the Nationalists and the Communists existed on the mainland. From April 1951 until late 1952, OPC invested $100 million in arms and support for groups declaring that they represented a force of 200,000 guerrillas. One well-documented attempt to contact these resistance fighters in July 1952 came to a disastrous end. A four-man team of Chinese agents was parachuted into Manchuria. Four months later, they radioed that they had information about the guerrillas and asked for a rescue team to extract them. This was an ambush. The team had been captured and turned into double agents by Chinese troops. The agency station in Taipei sent a C-47 transport and two young officers, Dick Fecteau and Jack Downey, on their first operational mission to bring the team back for debriefing. As the plane swooped low to catch the team members in a special sling, it was hit by a barrage of Chinese machine gun fire. The pilots were killed in the crash. Fecteau and Downey were captured, tried, and imprisoned in harsh conditions for nineteen and twenty years, respectively. They were finally released after special appeals by President Richard Nixon at the time of the US recognition of the People's Republic of China. Further deepening this tragic tale was the disclosure years later that an operations officer in the same unit in Taipei had been suspicious of the language in two messages from the team requesting rescue and was "90 percent" sure that the team had been doubled. When he raised his concern with the mission chief, he was rebuffed and the rescue went ahead. After the plane failed to return, the chief instructed him never to mention his suspicion again.[94]

Early in 1951, Wisner's Far East division launched an operation to put pressure on the Chinese military by exploiting an opportunity in northern Burma. Li Mi, a Nationalist general, was stranded with some 1,500 men in Burma near the Chinese border. He requested arms and money to launch attacks against the Communists, and the NSC and the president approved his request over Beetle Smith's objections. The CIA trained Nationalist troops from Taiwan and dropped them into Burma with weapons and supplies to reinforce Li Mi's brigade. When Li Mi led his forces into China, they were quickly routed by the People's Liberation Army and retreated back to Burma. Even with the CIA urging and more weapons and supplies, they refused to fight. When Wisner's deputy for the Far East, Colonel Richard G. Stilwell, reported to Smith that Li Mi was about to enter China, he had to correct himself several days later, saying that he had not yet advanced. Smith's caustic reaction, according to Stilwell, was: "All that guy does is skate up and down the wrong side of the border." As it turned out, Li Mi's troops gave up fighting, settled in the mountainous Golden Triangle, married local women, and cultivated opium poppies, eventually creating a drug empire that provided roughly one-third of the global opium supply. Li Mi's group later clashed with the Burmese government—which, suspecting CIA involvement, broke diplomatic relations with the United States, beginning fifty years of isolation from the West, and developed a highly repressive military regime. In April 1952, Smith wrote General Matthew Ridgway, the Far East commander, apologizing for a series of failed operations. "There is no point," he said, "in bemoaning opportunities lost . . . nor attempting to alibi past failures. I have found, through painful experience, that secret operations are a job for the professional and not for the amateur."[95]

The CIA achieved very little success running agents in Korea and China. In intelligence terms, human intelligence (HUMINT) was a "debacle" in the Far East, due to a combination of poor training, inexperienced management, and fluid loyalties among impoverished soldiers and greedy information peddlers. The prominent intelligence historian Christopher Andrew contends that signals intelligence (SIGINT) was by far the best source of information on enemy strength and movements for United Nations forces. He quotes John Hart as saying: "SIGINT was almost the only intelligence worth having in Korea." It proved valuable in disclosing the course of Chinese and North Korean advance in late 1950, and it discovered the buildup of Chinese forces before the major offensives in 1951. SIGINT also confirmed that Soviet pilots were flying MiG-15s in late 1950, and in March 1951 revealed the basing of a large number of Soviet bombers in Manchuria. In the United States, SIGINT provided critical evidence in identifying Soviet espionage activities, including the work of the atomic spies Julius and Ethel Rosenberg and the British spies Donald Maclean and Guy Burgess.[96]

As the fighting in Korea settled into a stalemate in the summer of 1951, Beetle Smith became increasingly frustrated by his inability as head of the intelligence community to win the cooperation of the military intelligence services on SIGINT. He gradually won Truman's support for a thorough review of the management of all communications intelligence. This led to the creation of a committee headed by George A. Brownell and including senior officials of the State and Defense departments and the CIA. The committee reported in June 1952 and strongly recommended the strengthening of the Armed Forces Security Agency and giving the DCI a leading role in coordinating SIGINT with other intelligence activities. In November, in a top secret directive, Truman ordered the implementation of these proposals and designated the strengthened Armed Forces Security Agency as the National Security Agency (NSA). DCI Smith had been the driving force behind this important step in coordinating and strengthening US communications intelligence.[97]

SMITH'S LEGACY

Beetle Smith confronted huge problems when he became DCI. He inherited an agency that was dysfunctional with a rapidly growing program of covert operations that lacked adequate supervision. He entered the job when US intelligence had suffered several major failures; and within his first six weeks, he would fail again when it missed the buildup for a massive Chinese intervention. Despite having the position as head of the intelligence community, he received very little cooperation from the military intelligence services and the FBI, which refused to share much critical information with the CIA. And he had just undergone major surgery to remove half his stomach and still suffered from painful ulcers.

However, Smith had several advantages—if he could manage to utilize them. He had the full support of the president and his key national security advisers, Dean Acheson and George Marshall, who had been Smith's main career mentor and had just returned to government as secretary of defense. In a crisis situation, he had a mandate for change and an approved blueprint in the Dulles Report for what the administration wanted to be done. And he had broad experience in restructuring and motivating large organizations from his service as Eisenhower's wartime chief of staff.

Among his most important accomplishments, Smith shaped the CIA into a modern intelligence service. Its structure and procedures remained largely intact until the reforms of the mid-1970s following the Church Committee reports. He took the leading role in producing strategic intelligence for the president and national security leaders. Foremost within this area were the National Intelligence Estimates and the president's daily briefing. He achieved considerable success in winning cooperation from the military intelligence services and the FBI, and in the process creating a functioning intelligence community. And he took substantial steps toward making the CIA a professional career service.

Despite great sustained effort, Beetle made only limited progress in reviewing the feasibility and restraining covert operations. His outbursts over failed missions and biting personal criticism had only a marginal effect on controlling the operations enthusiastically sponsored by Allen Dulles and Frank Wisner. His ineffectiveness was largely due to widespread attitudes about the limited strategic value of Korea and the lack of concern for the lives of Korean and Chinese agents. Tim Weiner describes this mind-set in discussing Allen Dulles's opening remarks to a secret conference of his trusted friends at a May 1952 meeting of the National Committee for a Free Europe at the Princeton Inn: "For Dulles, Asia was always a sideshow. He believed that the real war for Western civilization was in Europe." Dulles contended: "After all, we have had a hundred thousand casualties in Korea. . . . If we have been willing to accept these casualties, I wouldn't worry if there were a few casualties or a few martyrs behind the iron curtain. . . . You have got to have a few martyrs. Some people have to get killed."[98]

Smith's accomplishments owed a great deal to his close personal relationship with Harry Truman. From his time as an artillery captain in World War I, the president suspected most generals, especially those from West Point, of being cautious career builders. But he idolized George Marshall and knew Smith was his protégé. He also respected the fact that Smith was a self-made man, just as he was. As a result of their mutual respect, Smith had a regular private meeting with the president every Friday morning. During the most difficult period of the war, he would bring a detailed order-of-battle map to provide a more candid picture of the conflict than that presented by General Omar Bradley, chairman of the JCS, at the Thursday meetings of the NSC. On one occasion, when Smith was concerned about the legality of a covert operation he had been asked to approve, Truman reached into his desk for a piece of stationery, wrote a brief note giving the DCI a full pardon for any decision he made, signed it, and left it undated. This was his strongest possible demonstration of support. This level of endorsement helped Smith win his final battle to get a strengthened organization for communications intelligence established as the NSA, one of his most significant achievements.[99]

17

KOREA TRANSFORMS
THE COLD WAR

The principal argument of this study is that a series of decisions made by the Truman administration during the first six months of the Korean War transformed the Cold War into a militarized competition between the two superpowers. Leaders in Washington did not expect or want this result, but they responded to events in Korea. The critical turning point was China's intervention in the conflict in October 1950. The flawed assumption driving the US response was the belief that the People's Republic of China was totally under the control of Soviet leaders in Moscow. Further complicating the situation was the USSR'S decision to accelerate its own strategic weapons programs while providing all the necessary assistance to the Chinese "volunteer" forces in Korea.

But in June 1950, when North Korea attacked the South, the United States found itself completely unprepared for a war in Asia. Leaders of both political parties viewed the country's primary interests as residing in the security of a stable and prosperous Western Europe. The Truman administration had thwarted the Soviet blockade of Berlin, created a West German state, and negotiated a defensive alliance in NATO. Europe appeared secure and politically stable, with improving national economies. However, members of the administration and Congress believed that the nation's security was protected by two elements that proved to be inadequate. They were convinced that America's sizable stockpile of nuclear weapons would deter any military aggression by an adversary. And they thought the destruction and exhaustion from six years of war would prevent any major confrontation with the Soviet Union for at least five years and probably for as long as ten or fifteen years. As a result, the president and a strong majority of Congress were not prepared to endorse the major buildup of conventional and nuclear strength called for by Paul Nitze in National Security Council (NSC) Report 68.

After the Japanese surrender, the US military rapidly demobilized, with millions of servicemen returning to their civilian lives. Large amounts of military equipment were abandoned, sold as surplus, or sent as military assistance to the European Allies. Only the air force was moderately prepared for combat, and this evaluation applied mainly to Curtis LeMay's Strategic Air Command. The United States had a significant advantage over the Soviet Union in long-range bombers, with the B-29 deployed in an advanced model. The air force also had the B-52 under development. This innovative airplane, which would have its initial flight tests in April 1952, would change the parameters for strategic bomber capabilities. However, as dogfights with the new MiG-15 over Korea would demonstrate, the United States was behind the Soviet Union in jet fighter technology. The B-29s paid a high price, because they were forced to fly only at night, when their American escort fighters proved no match for the new MiGs. The army and navy were on a purely peacetime status, with very limited funds for operational training or new equipment. The wartime industries that had produced millions of weapons, supply items, and uniforms for American and Allied forces had all converted to the production of consumer goods. It would take months for them to refit to manufacture tanks, trucks, howitzers, and aircraft for use in Korea.

American intelligence was even less effective in fulfilling its mission than the military services. The top policymakers received very little useful information from the intelligence services about the Soviet Union, China, and North Korea. The numerous agents sent into these countries were quickly rolled up and eliminated or turned to send back fabricated reports. There was almost no cooperation between the CIA and the military intelligence services and the FBI. Signals intelligence, which had been the best source for information on Soviet communications with China and North Korea, was abruptly cut off in the spring of 1950, when a Soviet spy reported that the army 's decoders had broken the encryption codes and Moscow quickly changed them.

Politically, the Truman administration was under sustained challenges from a desperate Republican Party, which had lost five presidential elections in a row. Even though the Democrats had a majority in both houses of the Eighty-First Congress, Republicans and some Democrats were strong supporters of Senator Joseph McCarthy's attacks on the administration for protecting communists in important government positions, especially in the State Department. Concerned with budget deficits and inflation, Truman wanted to cut defense spending, which he saw as a drag on economic growth, to $13 billion in the fiscal year (FY) 1951 request. To underline his conviction, he had refused to spend the $800 million for long-range bombers that Congress had added to his FY 1950 appropriation proposal.

The Soviet Union also found itself unprepared for major war. Much of the western part of the country had been devastated by war. The population was exhausted after six years of brutal combat and suffered continued shortages of fuel, food, and consumer goods. Yet Stalin and the Politburo had significant advantages to exploit. During the previous twenty years, Stalin had established full control over the Soviet Union's government and political institutions. His designers, scientists, and engineers were making remarkable progress on highly enriched uranium and plutonium weapons; and, despite severe limitations in electronics and metallurgy, they were also advancing in the development of long-range bombers that could deliver nuclear weapons against the United States. The government had at its disposal the world's largest and most professional intelligence and disinformation services, including spies in key positions in all the major Western governments. The Soviet Union had contiguous borders with the People's Republic of China and North Korea. And more important, these client states were willing to take geopolitical risks in exchange for the military and economic assistance Moscow could provide.

The new government of the People's Republic of China was not fully in control of its territory and was not ready for war with a Western military power. The People's Liberation Army (PLA) was still working to suppress armed opponents and win the support of the population in the cities and western provinces. The economy had been disrupted by fourteen years of war against Japan followed by a four-year civil war. Mao Zedong had a massive army trained in the tactics of revolutionary people's war, but this army was poorly armed and equipped. The decisive factor in Chinese policy was Mao's strong desire to become the leader of a communist revolution in Asia fueled by his enormous confidence in his ability to impose his will on difficult situations.

The Soviet-supported regime in North Korea had only recently consolidated its control over both state and political institutions, and Kim Il-sung was untested as a national leader, with several rival factions eager for power. Despite having spent most of his life outside Korea and speaking only rudimentary Korean, Kim had the driving ambition to be the leader who would unify Korea under communism. His obsession with conquering South Korea blinded the thirty-eight-year-old ruler to problems that his invasion could face. Although his army was stronger and better prepared than that of South Korea, it still had limitations. More than 72,000 of his troops had fought with Mao in the Chinese Civil War, but they had not been integrated with the poorly trained units formed in North Korea. The Korean People's Army (KPA) used many different types of weapons acquired from Japan, China, and the Soviet Union. This wide range of weapons created serious problems of ammunition supply. The army lacked adequate logistics and ground transportation for operations deep into South Korea. Kim's strategy relied on an insurrection of 200,000 communist guerrillas to join the invading army, but the Rhee government in Seoul had succeeded in suppressing these groups in the spring of 1950. Ignoring these factors, Kim was able to persuade Stalin that he could capture Seoul and, with the help of a communist revolt, defeat South Korea within a week. He received supplies, heavy weapons, and advisers from Moscow, but Stalin made it clear that Soviet forces would not join the war. If problems arose, Mao was to provide the reserve forces needed.

After war broke out with the North Korean invasion, hopes and expectations collapsed for all sides when confronted with the realities of combat. The United States quickly determined that it would come to the assistance of South Korea. Within three months, the American-led international force, operating under a United Nations mandate, was approaching the North Korean border with China and Russia. Within another month, the Chinese had entered the war as the result of a double gamble by Mao. The chairman had wagered that he could drive a hard bargain with Stalin, only to discover that the Soviet leader had boxed him into a corner and forced him to backstop the North Korean attack. Mao's second bet was that he could accept this obligation with, at most, limited responsibility for suppressing final resistance and occupation duties. After the United States entered the war, Mao decided to intervene to honor his commitment and to use the war emergency to escalate his revolutionary purges at home while emphasizing nationalism to build support for his government. When the Americans were on the verge of destroying the KPA, Mao concluded that in order to achieve his ambitious goals for China, he needed to act immediately, reasoning that it was better to conduct this battle on Korean rather than Chinese territory. A closer examination of the context of these decisions will show how the transformation of the Cold War evolved.

WASHINGTON'S GAME CHANGER

Harry Truman's immediate decision to intervene in Korea was the principal factor in forcing the two sponsors of the North Korean attack to revise their plans. The United States had to make even greater changes in policy. The president and his top advisers believed the Soviet Union orchestrated the attack to test American will to support a friendly government. They thought that if they did not respond with force in Korea, there would be more aggressive communist actions in Western Europe or Iran. Almost all American political leaders supported the president's decision to assist South Korea, as did the public. Within the government, intelligence officials were concerned and embarrassed that they had missed the North Korean buildup of troops and weapons and had misread the regime's intentions. Military and diplomatic leaders regretted withholding tanks, artillery, and combat aircraft from South Korea in the belief that Syngman Rhee was the more likely aggressor.

The US military response in Korea evolved gradually. Initially, the administration ordered bombers to attack advancing columns of North Korean forces and their supply lines. When the South Korean army collapsed within days before the power of the KPA's tanks and artillery, General MacArthur gathered whatever units he had in Japan, and the president ordered them to help stem the North Korean drive. As the Americans and the remnants of the South Korean forces were pushed back to a pocket around Pusan, Washington endorsed MacArthur's daring plan to prepare an amphibious envelopment at Inchon. At the same time, the Pentagon assembled all the troops available in the United States, except the strategic reserve, for rapid transfer to Korea. When the Inchon landing achieved great success, MacArthur moved swiftly to cut the North Korean supply lines to the south and capture a large proportion of the KPA.

In Washington, the administration prepared to complete the destruction of the North Korean armed forces and expand overall US military capabilities. Truman approved the NSC 68 proposals for a significant buildup, and Congress passed the FY 1951 defense appropriation of $13.3 billion and the first supplemental appropriation of $11.7 billion, providing a total of $25 billion for the armed services.

At this point in late September, national security leaders began to make a series of mistakes based on overconfidence in MacArthur's strategic judgment and another disastrous intelligence failure. The Far East commander insisted on pursuing the KPA across the 38th Parallel and driving to the Yalu River border before the enemy could escape into Manchuria to reorganize and rearm. The Joint Chiefs of Staff placed minor limits on his freedom to operate, but MacArthur ignored them. Making his forces even more vulnerable, the imperious general divided his armies, sending the X Corps and the First Marine Division along with several ROK units up the east side of the peninsula, while the

Eighth Army moved up the west side, leaving a large mountainous gap between them. When military intelligence reported that Chinese units were massing in Manchuria, MacArthur's headquarters staff and analysts in Washington concluded that they would not intervene, but were deployed to protect Chinese territory. Days later, intelligence officers with advance units reported that they had questioned captured soldiers and confirmed they were members of Chinese divisions, but MacArthur's staff rejected this interpretation and claimed they must be ethnic Koreans who lived in Manchuria or a small group of Chinese volunteers.

Meanwhile, Peng Dehuai laid a trap for the advancing American and Allied armies. Beginning on October 19, large numbers of PLA soldiers moved at night across bridges into Korea. They launched a surprise attack against elements of the Eighth Army and several South Korean units on October 25, inflicting heavy casualties and leaving the right flank of US forces vulnerable. Other limited attacks occurred until November 6, when the Chinese withdrew and set up defensive positions in the mountains on both flanks of the divided Allied forces. Still convinced that the Chinese had committed only small volunteer units, MacArthur's intelligence staff insisted that there were no more than 35,000 PLA troops in Korea. From detailed Chinese histories, we now know that as of mid-November, there were 388,000 Chinese soldiers facing the UN divisions. Eager to finish off the North Korean army and whatever Chinese allies it had, MacArthur began what he hoped would be his victorious drive to the Yalu on November 15. In what would become a classic expression of hubris, the commander exclaimed that the troops would be "home by Christmas." Peng Dehuai sprang his trap with a massive offensive nine days later. The Allied forces were driven back south of Pyongyang in disarray. In their retreat, they suffered 50,000 casualties, many from frostbite due to a sustained early cold wave that caught the American and Allied forces without winter clothing and equipment.

After the debacle created by the Chinese intervention, the Truman administration conducted a thorough strategic review. Led by Acheson, Marshall, and Lovett and prodded by the president, the National Security Council (NSC) concluded that there was a real possibility that the crisis in Korea could be the start of World War III. In order to win

the funding to defend South Korea and protect Europe against anticipated Soviet aggression, they determined to argue to Congress and the
American people that the country faced a "worst case" emergency that
required a major defense buildup. Their strategic review asserted that
the Soviet Union was the principal threat; that Europe was the first priority for defense, after the homeland; and that after regaining strategic
initiative in Korea, the United States would seek negotiations for an end
to the conflict with a divided Korea. These decisions meant that Korea
would be a limited war, that MacArthur would need to recover with the
forces he had, and that the buildup of military strength would continue.
The leaders also approved an expansion of all forms of covert operations
to increase the costs of aggressive policies for the Soviet Union and its
satellites. Though it was seldom mentioned, the continuing challenge of
McCarthyism remained a tacit encouragement throughout the strategic
review to stand firmly against communist advances around the world.

The visit of a British delegation led by Prime Minister Clement Attlee
in early December solidified the administration in its recent decisions.
Serious British concern over Truman's unconsidered statement that the
government would keep open the option to use atomic weapons if necessary forced the president to pledge that before any decision to use the
powerful weapons, he would consult with America's closest ally. This
commitment and the agreement to abandon any further effort to unify
Korea were the only concessions made to British demands. The president rejected proposals to extend diplomatic recognition to the People's
Republic of China and to replace General MacArthur as UN commander, and he lectured the visiting delegation to focus on the Soviet
Union as the source of problems facing the Allies in Asia and in Europe.

Before the administration could regain the initiative in Korea, two
additional blows deepened the crisis atmosphere in Washington. As he
was managing a strategic withdrawal, Lieutenant General Walton H.
Walker, the commander of the Eighth Army, was killed on December 23
in a jeep accident on a chaotic Korean road packed with retreating soldiers and refugees. His designated replacement, Lieutenant General
Matthew B. Ridgway, rushed to Tokyo to prepare for the huge challenges
awaiting him in Korea. Soon after Ridgway was briefed by General

MacArthur and assumed command in Korea, Peng Dehuai launched the second major Chinese offensive, on December 31. This bold effort to drive UN forces off the peninsula increased the pressure on Washington to hold as much territory as possible. Ridgway did his part in reorganizing and motivating the Eighth Army, and the administration pushed a large second supplemental appropriation of $16.8 billion through Congress on January 6, 1951. These funds provided the resources for the significant increase of strength called for in NSC 68.

For General Ridgway, the next phase of the war was taking the offensive to advance beyond the 38th Parallel to a natural defensive line. In the course of these carefully planned initiatives, he used aggressive tactics—combined with closely coordinated armor, artillery, and air operations—to raise the cost of continuing the war and persuade the three communist governments to begin armistice negotiations. During this series of offensives, there were heated debates between General MacArthur and Washington officials over expanding bombing to China and using atomic weapons. MacArthur's appeal for Republican support in Congress was the final straw for President Truman, who fired the UN commander on April 11, 1951, and promoted Ridgway to his multiple commands in Tokyo. In the process, American officials confirmed their earlier decisions on no first use of nuclear weapons and keeping Korea a limited war. United Nations forces reached a suitable defensive line by the end of June 1951, and negotiations for an armistice began early in July. The talks dragged on for over two years, becoming deadlocked over a cease-fire line and the return of prisoners. Only after Dwight Eisenhower's election as president in November 1952 and Stalin's death in March 1953 were Soviet and Chinese leaders ready for an armistice, which was signed on July 27, 1953.

THE STRATEGIC BUILDUP

During the war in Korea, Dean Acheson kept the government focused on the priority of rebuilding the defenses and increasing the security of

Western Europe. In earlier years, he had been a strong supporter of the Truman Doctrine and the Marshall Plan, and he was a leading advocate for the integration of the economies of the European Allies. Emphasizing the significance of the Soviet threat to Europe, Acheson led the effort to include the Federal Republic of Germany (West Germany) in Western institutions and worked intensively with the leaders of Britain and France to rearm West Germany as a member of NATO. He orchestrated the transformation of the Alliance from a loose organization for political reassurance into a functioning defensive Alliance with an international staff led by an American as supreme commander and dedicated forces, including six divisions of US troops stationed in Europe. Acheson worked closely with George Marshall and Robert Lovett in winning congressional support for the funding of the strategic buildup, and he was an early proponent of the reform and expansion of the CIA and its burgeoning program of covert operations against the Soviet Bloc. In expanding the protection of US interests in the Mediterranean and the Middle East, he brought about the admission of Greece and Turkey to NATO and the acquisition of basing rights for Strategic Air Command bombers in Europe, Turkey, and North Africa.

As the war ground to a stalemate in Korea, military leaders in Washington and Moscow concentrated on building up their strategic forces. Both sides pursued multiple avenues of development for long-range bombers and varied types of nuclear weapons, and both devoted more resources to these programs than they planned or preferred. The United States had a clear lead in both bombers and nuclear weapons. By 1954, American forces had an operational B-52 bomber and miniaturized nuclear weapons that included tactical bombs and atomic artillery deployed in Europe. Curtis LeMay used the increased budgets of the Korean War to prepare the Strategic Air Command to play the leading offensive role in a strategy of nuclear deterrence against Moscow. He pressed the air force leadership to obtain the funds to expand the command from 48 to 83 groups between 1950 and 1953, with a pledge to increase to 126 groups in the next two years. He also trained and exercised his air crews to use in-air refueling and overseas bases for potential attacks on Soviet cities and military facilities.

The United States also made significant progress in developing an effective intelligence service. Walter Bedell Smith created a substantial analytic staff in the Office of National Estimates, which provided greatly improved assessments to the political leadership. He continued the expansion of covert activities and canceled some of the more extravagant and dangerous missions. Still, the intelligence collection efforts of the CIA were not as successful as the administration desired, due to poor tradecraft and the Soviet Bloc's vastly superior counterintelligence services. Covert operations proved even less effective, and most agents were captured and killed or turned against the United States before they could provide any useful information or disruptive activity. The Soviet Union and its allies had a clear advantage in all aspects of intelligence.

THE SOVIET RESPONSE

An important product of Stalin's intelligence services was the prompt receipt of reports about the United States' development of both an intercontinental bomber, the B-29, and an atomic bomb. Early in 1943, he directed his scientists and engineers to begin work on similar weapons. But because the Soviet Union was in the midst of an existential struggle for survival against the Nazi invasion, these projects received only limited resources until Germany was defeated. The initial Soviet strategic bomber program had modest goals. In September 1943, the Aviation Ministry ordered Andrei Tupelov to design and build a bomber with a range of 3,700 miles and a bomb capacity of 10 tons. The American B-29, which took its first test flight in September 1942, had a range of 5,600 miles with a bomb capacity of 10 tons. But the requirements set for Tupelov were beyond the capacity of Soviet technology at the time. His design team had great difficulty developing automated controls, pressurized cabins, and engines powerful enough to reach the range and load specifications.

Within a month after the German surrender, Stalin and Beria decided to abandon the indigenous strategic bomber project and ordered

Tupelov to copy the B-29 in every detail. The Soviet Union possessed three of these American bombers, which had made emergency landings in Siberia, and the Kremlin had rejected Washington's requests to return them. The urgency for progress on this assignment and on an atomic bomb increased sharply when Stalin and his colleagues understood the military and political significance of the atomic bomb attacks on Hiroshima and Nagasaki. Adding further pressure was the celebration of US air power represented in the flyover of 462 B-29s at Tokyo Bay immediately after the formal Japanese surrender on September 2, 1945.

However, reverse-engineering and copying the B-29 proved to be much more difficult than Soviet leaders assumed. At the most basic level, all Soviet machine tools and instruments used metric measurements, not the imperial system of inches and pounds used in the United States. Tupelov's engineers had to learn how to make or substitute for the American electronics, metal alloys, plastics, and mazes of wiring. The project took four years of hard work before the new Tu-4 entered air force service in May 1949. It would soon be outdated and vulnerable to new models of jet fighters, as the Korean War demonstrated. The process of reproducing the B-29 forced the modernization of the Soviet aviation industry; but at the same time, it stimulated the United States to establish an air defense network of radar installations and fighter bases that could defeat any air offensive that Moscow could launch.

Using multiple design and engineering teams, Tupelov pursued several projects simultaneously. The most successful offensive product was a medium-range bomber designated the Tu-16. Combining technologies from the Tu-4 with new design concepts, this compact airplane had swept wings, turbojet engines, and a range of 4,000 miles with a load of 3 tons. Initially tested in 1952, the Tu-16 was the first Soviet bomber to drop a hydrogen bomb. It threatened US bases in Europe and Asia and was used extensively in Afghanistan. A less successful airplane was the long-range bomber, the Tu-85. It was powered by piston engines and had a range of 7,500 miles. But it was too slow to survive attacks by jet interceptors and was canceled in November 1951.

Tupelov continued working to build an effective long-range bomber, and inadequate engine thrust remained his biggest obstacle. He began a new design in February 1951. His careful calculations showed that he could not satisfy the range, speed, and load requirements with jet engines, as Stalin had demanded. When he reported this to the disgruntled dictator, Stalin replied that another designer had proposed a turbojet-powered bomber with a range of 7,500 miles and he had awarded him a full design bureau to build it. This decision led to the ill-fated M-4 bomber designed by Vladimir Miasishchev which began development in March 1951. An early model flew in the May Day parade of 1954 but had major engine problems that caused crashes. An improved model was produced by 1957, yet the engine issues remained, and it was canceled the next year, with only thirty-five manufactured.

Eventually, Tupelov completed his bomber, the Tu-95, which reached the desired range of 8,200 miles using an unusual design of eight turboprop engines mounted in pairs with counterrotating propellers. It was capable of delivering an atomic bomb against targets in much of the continental United States. But by the time it entered service in 1957, it was also vulnerable to jet fighters and would be used mainly for reconnaissance, antisubmarine warfare, and later bombing in the Afghan war. Overall, 175 aircraft of various models were built until its cancellation in 1959. In the United States, inflated intelligence estimates of Soviet bomber capabilities, called the "Bomber Gap," led to further strengthening of air defenses.

The Soviet nuclear weapons program faced all the difficulties of the strategic bomber effort, including a weak economy, the primitive state of technology, and the constant suspicion and interference of the security services. And it had two further challenges: its huge expense, and the lack of observable progress as it developed. The fact that none of the top officials who knew about the secret program understood elementary physics was an immense problem for Igor Kurchatov and his colleagues. Although the bomb project started in late 1942, at roughly the same time as the American effort, it became a high priority only after Hiroshima and Nagasaki, when Stalin and his most trusted lieutenants saw the political and military utility of nuclear weapons. Only when Stalin met Molotov, Beria, and Kurchatov on January 25, 1946, did the nuclear program become the regime's top priority. At this time, the premier directed

Kurchatov to ask for whatever he needed and authorized salary increases of two to three times for the top scientists working on the program.

In structuring his research agenda, Kurchatov identified four major issues. His teams had to build a cyclotron, build several types of reactors, purify graphite, and locate large uranium deposits while learning how to separate high-quality ore from other materials. Researchers encountered unexpected problems in each of these areas. Building a reactor required innovative work by a team recruited from Germany to create a process for purifying graphite that would be inserted as a moderator in the initial machine. The first significant achievement came on Christmas Day 1946, when the first reactor went critical. Based on valuable intelligence from Klaus Fuchs at Los Alamos, Kurchatov knew that the construction of a plutonium implosion bomb would be much faster than using isotope separation to build a uranium weapon. Most of the work on the plutonium bomb was conducted at a hastily built secret city called Cheliabinsk-40. Kurchatov personally directed work on the plutonium bomb, while other teams pursued different approaches at other secret cities. These projects included uranium enrichment to build a U-235 gun assembly bomb, a heavy water reactor for power generation, and a hydrogen bomb. Major problems developed, however, in separating the plutonium from the irradiated uranium processed in a production reactor. Resolving these issues took until early 1949.

The first test of a plutonium bomb came on August 29, 1949. It was a great success. The Soviet Union created an entire nuclear industry in three years, using a command economy to mobilize hundreds of thousands of workers to build a group of secret cities for research and production facilities. The physicists led the effort and resolved the problems they encountered. Espionage reports from the US Manhattan Project probably saved eighteen months in building the plutonium bomb; yet it needs to be noted that Soviet scientists had no similar intelligence to assist then in designing and building the uranium gun assembly bomb and the hydrogen bomb. By 1953, the Soviet Union possessed a powerful and diverse stockpile of slightly over 150 nuclear weapons, but it lacked the bombers and missiles it was developing to deliver them.

Though Stalin considered it very important to have this nuclear capability, he did not think it would be crucial in a general war. He and his military chiefs continued to rely on massive ground and armor forces backed by artillery and tactical air support for their defense. More important, the premier knew that the Soviet Union was not ready for a major war, and he took precautions to avoid stumbling into such a conflict.

THE TRANSFORMATION

Now, seventy years since the conflict began, we have the sources to understand the choices made on all sides in the Korean War. Recent official histories and new documents have enriched the familiar narrative of decisions made by the Truman administration. A trove of newly released documents on Soviet and Chinese policies shows that Kim Il-sung initiated the war with repeated requests for support to Stalin. The Soviet dictator was prepared to take a limited risk in supporting a North Korean invasion of the South. He was determined to avoid a general war with the United States. Moreover—given his knowledge of low American combat readiness, and his excellent espionage sources on Washington policy decisions—he thought it very unlikely that the United States would intervene in Korea. To cover the small risk, he told Kim that no Russian forces would be engaged in the war, and he maneuvered Mao Zedong into providing a reinsurance policy by agreeing to serve as the backup if North Korean armies got into difficulty. Given Stalin's actions, from today's perspective Truman was correct in his instinctive decision to enter the Korean War. Yet, in entering the war without the approval of Congress, he made a costly mistake that would pose later problems for him and set a dangerous precedent for future administrations.

For the United States, Mao was the wild card about whom Washington officials knew very little. They assumed that Mao and the People's Republic of China were willing instruments of the Kremlin. They knew nothing of Mao's harsh negotiations to secure the treaty of alliance and assistance with Moscow or of the Chinese leader's commitment to support Kim. Washington policymakers and MacArthur's staff in Tokyo had no hint of Mao's personal decision in July 1950 to intervene in Korea, regardless of how the United States conducted its military campaign. Nor could they imagine that the Chinese leader would accept hundreds of thousands of casualties to achieve his ambitious goals. Based on what was known in Washington, the Truman administration was justified in directing MacArthur to cross the 38th Parallel and try to crush the disorganized North Korean Army.

However, the Far East commander and Washington leaders had solid intelligence that several hundred thousand PLA troops were massed in northeastern China just beyond the Yalu River border with North Korea. Even later, when confronted with evidence of PLA soldiers fighting in North Korea, MacArthur did not seriously consider that China would intervene. He should at the least have been more cautious in his strategy and not have divided his main forces while stretching his supply lines to the limit. American political and military leaders violated a basic principle of strategy in allowing the regional commander to launch a vulnerable offensive surge when intelligence on Chinese and Soviet capabilities and intentions was very poor. The Joint Chiefs of Staff, the NSC, and the president should have taken firm steps to restrain MacArthur's high-risk race to the Chinese border.

With the exception of these costly mistakes, the overall strategy of the Truman administration for the Korean War was sound. Europe was the top priority, and European nations received the largest proportion of assets from the broad military buildup. Deciding on a limited war in Korea was a wise choice after the Chinese intervened. Although it left an unresolved conflict on the Korean Peninsula, this decision avoided the real possibility of a larger war with China and possibly the Soviet Union. Limited war also dictated rejecting MacArthur's pleas to use nuclear weapons against China. This established an important precedent in the expanding Soviet-American strategic competition in creating the policy of "no first use" of nuclear weapons.

One large question remains: Was the full US strategic buildup necessary? This is an issue on which diplomats and scholars still disagree. As the epigraph of this book, I quote with approval the statement by one of the nation's leading experts on the Soviet Union, Ambassador Charles E. Bohlen, who wrote in 1973: "It was the Korean War and not World War II that made us a world military-political power." This experienced diplomat placed this judgment within a section of his memoirs where he argued that the significant US military buildup was a mistake based on an exaggerated estimate of Soviet intentions. He goes on to contend that "the militarization of NATO was not a wise policy. A slight increase in the American military budget would have been sufficient to reassure our friends in Europe."[1]

My reading of the evidence leads to a different judgment about the US strategic buildup. After analyzing the immense resources Stalin invested in his programs for nuclear weapons and long-range bombers and the difficulties the Truman administration had in winning congressional support for the necessary funding, I have concluded that it was necessary for the administration to argue that the Korean conflict could develop into a global war if the United States did not make a strong stand for strategic superiority. The administration could have positioned the country in an even stronger position if it had not invested so heavily in strategic air power but had structured a more balanced force of ground and naval forces to accompany the Strategic Air Command's armada. General George Marshall had urged this balanced approach in his final months as secretary of defense. American leaders were justified in making a worst case argument for the funding to fully implement the programs approved under NSC 68.

After the massive Chinese intervention, when the Truman administration made its initial worst case arguments for the second supplemental appropriation in December 1950, officials actually believed they faced World War III. This belief was justified in part by the CIA report that Zhou Enlai had declared on December 5 that "a third world war is inevitable as long as neither UN nor Chinese forces are willing to leave Korea." Soon after reading this report, Truman entered in his diary: "It looks like World War III is here." Later, in the last half of 1951, when congressional resistance to continued high defense appropriations strengthened, Acheson, Marshall, and Lovett were convinced that only continued invocation of worst case justification would win passage of the 1952 defense funding bill. They were proved correct. Now, years later—when the documentation is available about Soviet strategic ambitions, about the high level of expenditures, and about Chinese willingness to take risks and absorb huge numbers of casualties—it is obvious that in the medium term, the prospect of a broader war with China was indeed a worst case.[2]

We now know that the ambitions and defense programs advanced by Soviet leaders can easily justify the worst case presented by the president and his colleagues to win the additional appropriations needed to maintain strategic superiority. Decisions made by the Truman administration after the Chinese intervention in Korea fundamentally transformed the Cold War. Moscow's aggressive designs would continue after Stalin's death and come to a dangerous peak with the Cuban missile crisis in 1962. At that time, the United States' air and naval strength created by the Korean buildup provided the instruments to allow President John F. Kennedy to employ coercive diplomacy to force the Soviets to back down and remove their nuclear weapons and missiles from Cuba. That major crisis is worthy of another book focused on the strategic issues within a broad international context.

·

CHRONOLOGY

1941

September: The British government begins research on nuclear weapons.

October: The US government begins research on nuclear weapons.

1942

June: President Roosevelt accelerates nuclear research with start of the Manhattan Project. In the fall of 1943, British, French, and Canadian scientists and engineers move to the United States and join the project.

September 28: The Soviet State Defense Committee, stimulated by espionage reports on British and US programs, approves resumption of a small nuclear research program.

1943

March 10: Igor Kurchatov is appointed director of the Soviet nuclear program.

September: Andrei Tupelov is ordered to design a strategic bomber with a range of 6,000 kilometers and a bomb capacity of 10 tons. Unknown to him, this airplane was to be the delivery vehicle for an atomic bomb.

1944

April: Kurchatov and the nuclear program occupy a new building in Moscow with a staff of seventy-four, including twenty-five scientists.

December 3: Lavrenti Beria, head of the NKVD, is appointed supervisor of the nuclear program at Kurchatov's urging.

1945

June 5: Stalin orders Tupelov to stop work on the strategic bomber begun in 1943 and instead copy a captured American B-29. He is given two years to complete the project.

August 20: Stalin approves sharp acceleration of the nuclear program after seeing the great political and military effects of the American atomic bombs dropped on Hiroshima and Nagasaki.

September: Klaus Fuchs's reports from Los Alamos in June and September provide a detailed description of the American plutonium bomb's design and specifications. He strongly urges Soviet leaders to develop a plutonium bomb as a faster process than pursuing a uranium weapon. Stalin orders Kurchatov to copy the American bomb in every detail.

1946

January 25: Stalin meets with Molotov, Beria, and Kurchatov to finalize plans for an accelerated nuclear program and to announce his intention to increase the salaries of the scientists by two to three times.

December 25: Kurchatov's nuclear reactor achieves criticality—the first outside North America. He had personally directed the reactor construction and was at the controls when it went critical.

1947

March 12: President Harry S. Truman announces the Truman Doctrine expressing America's intent to contain the spread of communism.

June 5: The Marshall Plan is announced, and the Central and Eastern European countries—including the Soviet Union—are invited to join; all Eastern Bloc countries reject the offer under Soviet pressure.

July 26: Truman signs the National Security Act of 1947, creating the position of secretary of defense and an independent department of the air force and providing statutory authority for the National Security Council and the CIA.

1948

January: The Soviet nuclear program begins research on a thermonuclear (hydrogen) bomb in Moscow, led by physicist Igor Tamm.

March 17: The Brussels Pact is signed by Britain, France, Belgium, the Netherlands, and Luxembourg, forming a defensive alliance, which the Truman administration will support.

June: The split between the Soviet Union and Yugoslavia occurs.

June 18: The National Security Council approves a program of covert operations in NSC 10/2. A group, which was soon named the Office of Policy Coordination, was based in the CIA.

June 22: The first Soviet plutonium production reactor achieves the design level for sustained operation at the new secret city Cheliabinsk–40. Problems with the corrosion of fuel slugs caused a redesign of the reactor, and production resumed at the end of 1948.

June 24: The Berlin Blockade begins.

September 9: The Democratic People's Republic of Korea (North Korea) is established.

October 19: Lieutenant General Curtis E. LeMay is appointed commander of the Strategic Air Command.

1949

January 1: The Dulles Report on reform of the CIA and the intelligence community is submitted to the National Security Council.

Early March: Kim Il-sung meets with Joseph Stalin in Moscow to request material military aid and economic assistance.

March: Louis Johnson is appointed secretary of defense.

May: The Tu-4, a copy of the B-29, goes into service with the Soviet Air Force. With a range of 1,700 miles, it could only attack targets in the western United States on a one-way mission. Given US fighter capabilities, it posed no threat to American targets.

May 27: Congress passes the CIA Act of 1949, providing statutory authority and a dedicated budget for covert operations.

April 4: The North Atlantic Treaty is signed by Belgium, Canada, Denmark, France, Iceland, Italy, Luxembourg, the Netherlands, Norway, Portugal, the United Kingdom, and the United States—thus forming NATO.

May 12: The Berlin Blockade ends.

June: The Soviet nuclear program has produced sufficient plutonium to build a bomb.

June 4: The Soviet Union agrees to send North Korea military aid.

June 29: The US occupation of South Korea ends, and all remaining combat forces are withdrawn.

July: The B-36D starts production. A strategic bomber with six piston and four jet engines, it has a top speed of 406 miles per hour, a range of 5,000 miles with a bomb load of 10,000 pounds, and a ceiling of 44,000 feet.

August 29: The Soviet Union successfully tests its first atomic bomb.

September 2: John J. McCloy is appointed the first US high commissioner for Germany.

September 21: The Federal Republic of Germany (West Germany) is founded.

September 23: President Truman announces publicly that the Soviet Union has successfully tested an atomic bomb.

September–June 1950: More than 47,000 soldiers of the Korean People's Army return from helping the Communists during the Chinese Civil War, bringing their combat experience back to North Korea, where they would form the core of Kim Il-sung's invasion force.

October 1: The People's Republic of China is proclaimed by Mao Zedong.

October 6: President Truman signs the bill approving the Mutual Defense Assistance Program, which authorizes $1.3 billion in military aid to Allied and friendly nations with European members of NATO receiving over 75 percent of the funds.

October 7: The German Democratic Republic (East Germany) is founded.

December 16: Mao Zedong arrives in Moscow for his first official foreign visit as head of the People's Republic of China. He remains until February 14 to negotiate a treaty of alliance and assistance with the Soviet Union.

1950

January 1: Paul Nitze assumes the duties of director of the US State Department's Policy Planning Staff.

January 5: President Truman announces that the United States will no longer provide military aid to Chinese forces resisting the Communists from Formosa (Taiwan).

January 12: US secretary of state Dean Acheson and the Truman administration declare a consolidated security perimeter for Asia, which technically excludes South Korea and Taiwan from areas designated as vital to US interests.

January 25: Former State Department employee Alger Hiss, alleged to have been a member of a secret Communist Party organization and a Soviet spy, is convicted of perjury.

January 27: The agreement to implement the Mutual Defense Assistance Program in France is signed. A US military assistance team begins operating in Paris the following May.

January 30: Joseph Stalin informs Kim Il-sung that he is willing to discuss Kim's plans to invade South Korea.

January 31: A special committee of the National Security Council recommends to President Truman that the United States should develop the hydrogen bomb and that US strategic programs be reviewed. This review would result in the drafting of NSC 68.

February 14: A new Sino-Soviet treaty of alliance is signed.

February 20: Senator Joseph McCarthy delivers a speech before the Senate asserting that the State Department had been infiltrated by Communists. The Second Red Scare begins.

March 8: The Tydings Committee hearings investigating the loyalty of State Department employees begins.

March 30: Kim Il-sung arrives in Moscow for three weeks of discussions with Soviet leaders and meets with Stalin three times. Stalin tacitly approves Kim's invasion plans, provided that Kim also receives Mao's consent.

April: The amount of Soviet military aid being sent to North Korea increases dramatically.

April 9: French foreign minister Robert Schuman announces the Schuman Plan to create the European Coal and Steel Community, a six-nation consortium to manage the coal and steel industries of the member states.

May 13–16: Kim Il-sung goes to Beijing to meet with Mao and get confirmation of China's support for North Korea's plans to invade South Korea. On May 15, Mao agrees to support North Korea in the event of an American intervention in the conflict.

June 1: President Truman requests that only $1.2 billion be appropriated for military aid for fiscal year 1951.

June 25: North Korea invades South Korea.

June 27: President Truman informs Congress and the public of his decision to send US air and naval forces to support South Korea.

June 27: South Korean president Syngman Rhee and his cabinet evacuate the capital, Seoul. The US Air Force begins sorties against the North Korean advance. The United Nations Security Council calls on its members to help the South Koreans.

June 29: Seoul is captured by the North Koreans.

June 29: On his own initiative, General MacArthur orders strikes on airbases north of the 38th Parallel, a day before the Joint Chiefs of Staff authorize such actions.

June 30: President Truman authorizes the deployment of US ground troops to Korea from their bases in Japan.

July 19: Total authorized military manpower is increased from the 1.5 million outlined in the fiscal year 1951 defense budget to 2.1 million, a 41 percent increase. President Truman addresses Congress about the Korean crisis for the first time and asks not for approval of his decisions but for legislation to prosecute the conflict and for supplemental appropriations.

July 24: Congress begins reviewing the first supplemental defense appropriation request for fiscal year 1951, increasing the budget from $13 billion to $25 billion.

End of July: A force of 260,000 Chinese troops had amassed on their border with North Korea.

July 31: President Truman approved studying the idea of including German forces under NATO command amid pressures to strengthen European defenses.

Mid-August: The State Department proposes to the Pentagon that the continuation of Marshall Plan aid to Europe be linked to the assignment of four to six additional divisions to Europe to be under NATO, with a US supreme commander.

August 18: Truman announces the appointment of Lieutenant General Walter Bedell Smith as the new director of central intelligence. He will take up his duties October 7.

August 25: General MacArthur releases a statement stressing the strategic importance of Formosa and a desire for US military bases on the island. The statement contradicts official US policy, and the next day President Truman demands that MacArthur withdraw it.

September 3: In what would evolve into the Pleven Plan, Jean Monnet writes to his friend, French prime minister René Pleven, urging him to add a defense component to the Schuman Plan for the creation of the European Coal and Steel Community.

September 9: President Truman announces his intention to send additional US ground troops to Europe to join NATO forces.

September 11: President Truman approves NSC 81/1, which would allow troops to cross the 38th Parallel with prior presidential approval.

September 12: President Truman demands the resignation of Secretary of Defense Louis Johnson and announces that George C. Marshall will replace him.

September 12–14: Secretary of State Dean Acheson, at a meeting in New York with British foreign secretary Ernest Bevin and French foreign minister Robert Schuman (known as the "Big Three"), proposes that the commitment of more US troops and financial aid to Europe be linked with an American commander for NATO and German rearmament in a single package.

September 15: American forces land at Inchon.

September 21: General George C. Marshall is sworn in as secretary of defense.

September 27: Congress passes the fiscal year 1951 defense appropriation of $13.3 billion, plus the first supplemental request of $11.7 billion, for a total of $25 billion.

September 27: George Marshall and the Joint Chiefs of Staff authorize General MacArthur to cross the 38th Parallel.

September 29: US and South Korean troops retake Seoul.

September 30: Kim Il-sung requests direct military assistance from the Soviet Union.

September 30: President Truman approves the conclusions made in NSC 68—for increased military spending, development of the hydrogen bomb, and a tougher stance against the Soviet Union—and directs that they be implemented as policy.

October 1: South Korean troops unilaterally push north of the 38th Parallel. Stalin asks Mao to deploy Chinese troops into North Korea. Kim Il-sung requests direct Chinese military intervention in Korea.

October 7: UN forces cross the 38th Parallel.

October 14: The Soviet Union pledges to provide Chinese troops with arms and equipment on credit and send sixteen regiments of fighter jets to defend Chinese cities and reserve forces.

October 19: A total of 260,000 Chinese volunteers begin to enter North Korea. Another 120,000 troops will enter in November.

October 24: The Pleven Plan to create an integrated European defense force of about 100,000 troops is introduced and is approved by the French National Assembly. This force would be independent of NATO, and it would be commanded by a European general reporting to a European defense minister, who would be responsible to a European political assembly. Although German troops would be included in the defense force, there would be no division-sized German units and no German military staff.

October 25: The first Chinese offensive begins.

November 1: The five-year budget for NSC 68 programs is calculated to be $191 billion.

November 1: MiG-15 fighter jets with Soviet pilots appear over the Yalu River and began attacking US bombers and their fighter escorts.

November 21: A lead patrol of Americans reaches the Yalu River near the Chinese–North Korean border.

November 24: MacArthur begins what he calls his "final" offensive, and on the same day the Chinese launch a massive counterattack, forcing Allied units to retreat.

November 28: Allied defeats force Washington officials to launch an urgent strategic evaluation of the war.

December 4–8: A British delegation led by Prime Minister Clement Attlee visits Washington to try to persuade the Truman administration to end the war quickly. Almost all their proposals are rejected.

December 5: Zhou Enlai declares to the East German ambassador in Beijing that "a third world war is inevitable as long as neither UN nor Chinese forces are willing to leave Korea," according to a December 7 CIA report.

December 8: After sustained negotiations, the French government accepts the Spofford Plan, a compromise proposal that offers new US commitments to NATO and US support for the Pleven Plan's efforts to create the European Defense Community. In exchange, the French are to accept the principle of German rearmament and the inclusion of German regimental combat teams in NATO.

December 18–19: At a meeting in Brussels, the North Atlantic Council approves the Defense Committee's recommendations on German participation in a European force within NATO and requests that President Truman name General Dwight Eisenhower as supreme Allied commander for Europe, which he promptly did, on December 18.

December 19: President Truman announces to the public that more US divisions will be sent to augment NATO forces in Europe.

December 20: Truman's announcement provokes strong opposition, which sparks the "Great Debate," opening with a national radio broadcast of a speech by former president Herbert Hoover, in which he opposes sending more US troops to Europe, instead calling for building up the air force and navy, concentrating on the defense of the Western Hemisphere and relying on atomic weapons to defend American interests.

December 23: Lieutenant General Walton H. Walker is killed in a jeep accident in Korea; he is replaced by Lieutenant General Matthew B. Ridgway as commander of the US Eighth Army.

December 25: Most of the territory north of the 38th Parallel is retaken by the North Korean and Chinese armies.

December 31: Peng Dehuai launches his third offensive and pushes UN forces below the Han River.

1951

January 4: Seoul is retaken by Communist troops.

January 5: Prominent Republican senator Robert A. Taft of Ohio delivers a speech to the Senate supporting Hoover's arguments and charging that Truman's plan to send troops to Europe is provocative and unconstitutional because the president needs congressional authorization to send troops overseas in peacetime.

January 6: Congress passes a second supplemental appropriation bill for fiscal year 1951 of $16.8 billion for the Defense Department, and President Truman signs it into law.

January 8: Senator Kenneth Wherry (R-NE) introduces a resolution stating that it is the sense of the Senate that no ground troops should be deployed in Europe until Congress has given its approval. This sparks a prominent public debate on the limits of presidential authority.

January 15: American troops begin a counteroffensive.

January 29: The Joint Chiefs of Staff recommend that four divisions be sent to Europe. President Truman approves this number but directs that it not be made public immediately.

February 11: China begins its fourth offensive, but revitalized UN forces counterattack, with considerable success.

February 15: Joint formal hearings are held before the Senate Foreign Relations and Armed Services committees on the decision to send US troops to Europe.

Mid-February: The Truman administration reaches a consensus on conduct of the war; the United States will continue to fight to improve its military situation, and then will seek a cease-fire. Also, it will avoid any wider war with China or the Soviet Union. Korea will be a limited war, and Europe will remain the first priority.

March: The Air Force chief of staff, General Hoyt Vandenberg, urges Truman to approve the transfer of the custody of nuclear weapons from the Atomic Energy Commission to the Strategic Air Command, as a matter of preparedness. The president authorizes the transfer.

March 15: UN troops recapture Seoul.

March 24: General MacArthur issues a press release declaring that China should either negotiate a peace settlement or face an expanded war. The incident greatly angers Truman and causes concern among Allied diplomats.

April 2: An amendment to the Wherry Resolution, proposed by Senator John L. McClellan (D-AR), stating that no more than four divisions should be sent to Europe "without further congressional approval," passes 49–43.

April 4: The Senate passes the Wherry Resolution as amended 69–21, with over half the Senate Republicans, including Senator Taft, voting in favor of the measure. This approves, in principle, the deployment of four divisions to Europe as well as the appointment of General Eisenhower as supreme Allied commander for Europe.

April 11: President Truman relieves MacArthur of his commands, replacing him with General Matthew Ridgway.

April 22: Peng Dehuai launches his fifth offensive. UN forces give some ground but hold Seoul and exact heavy casualties on the Communist units.

April 30: President Truman submits a proposed $56.2 billion defense budget to Congress for fiscal year 1952.

May 3: The Soviet Union begins hinting to the United States that it would be open to discussing a cease-fire in Korea.

May 16: The Chinese begin their sixth offensive but are stopped by UN forces and driven back north of the 39th Parallel by mid-June.

May 31: President Truman signs into law a fourth supplemental appropriations bill of $6.4 billion for fiscal year 1951. Thus total defense appropriation for fiscal year 1951 reached $48.2 billion, and the size of the armed forces grew from 1.5 million to 3.3 million men.

June: The United States–led talks on German participation in a European defense force are held at the Petersberg Hotel outside Bonn, among representatives of the high commissioners and West Germany. These talks conclude with a plan for twelve German divisions—with tanks, artillery, and tactical air units—to be part of NATO. The French reject the Petersberg Plan, leaving the European Defense Community negotiations, in which the United States was not a direct participant, as the only option for creating an integrated European defense force.

End of June: The fighting in Korea reaches a stalemate.

June–July: The national security programs established under NSC 68 are reviewed; this review leads to the adoption on August 8 of NSC 114, which estimates that the Soviet threat was more imminent than was thought when NSC 68 was drafted before the Korean War.

July: The Strategic Air Command wins control of the nuclear target list and concentrates on urban industrial targets whose coordinates are known.

July 10: The first cease-fire negotiation meeting is held in Kaesong. The truce talks will carry on intermittently for two years.

July 30: President Truman approves a State Department proposal to implement a program formulated by John McCloy and David Bruce, the US ambassador to France, to strengthen European defenses that satisfies both German desires for equal rights and French security needs. This program, later designated NSC 115, will be achieved by giving full US support to the European Defense Community, using General Eisenhower to help make a European force militarily effective while including German units, and negotiating contractual agreements to restore most elements of German sovereignty.

September 17: Robert Lovett replaces George Marshall as secretary of defense.

October 18: A revised defense budget for fiscal year 1952 is passed; at $60.4 billion, it is the largest defense budget to be approved since 1945.

October 23: The National Security Council approves NSC 10/5, "The Scope and Pace of Covert Operations." This represents a compromise— in which the director of central intelligence retains control over all covert operations, defeating an attempt by the Joint Chiefs of Staff to control operations in war zones, but loses his fight to restrict the number and types of covert operations to be carried out.

1952

January 21: President Truman asks Congress for $48.6 billion in defense spending for fiscal year 1953.

February: At the North Atlantic Council meeting in Lisbon, Dean Acheson succeeds in winning commitments for higher force levels from the Allies; but as domestic demands increase, the governments soon ignore these pledges.

February 18: Greece and Turkey join NATO.

April: The Tu-16 has its first flight test. This medium-range bomber has twin turbojet engines, swept wings, a top speed of 590 miles per hour, and a range of 4,000 miles, with a bomb load of 3 tons. It becomes the first Soviet airplane to drop a hydrogen bomb.

May 26: After ten months of negotiations, the United States, Great Britain, and France sign the contractual agreements with West

Germany. The US Senate approves the contractual agreements on July 1 of this year.

May 27: Germany, France, Italy, and the Benelux governments sign the European Defense Community Treaty.

July 10: A defense budget for fiscal year 1953 of $44.3 billion in new obligations is signed into law, for a total defense budget of $47 billion.

October: The B-47E becomes operational. This strategic bomber has six turbojet engines, swept wings, a top speed of 600 miles per hour, a ceiling of 33,000 feet, a combat radius of 2,000 miles, and a bomb load of 25,000 pounds. It becomes the designated nuclear delivery vehicle for the early 1950s, operating from overseas bases with midair refueling.

1953

March 5: Joseph Stalin dies.

July 27: The Korean Armistice Agreement is signed, formally ending hostilities.

1954

March: The B-52B enters service with the US Air Force. The Strategic Air Command receives its first group of B-52Bs at the end of 1955.

March 1: The United States tests a two-stage thermonuclear bomb.

July: A squadron of ten M-4 strategic bombers flies in the Moscow Air Show. This four-engine turbojet bomber has a range of 6,000 miles and causes great concern among Western military attachés. But it has serious engine and electrical problems and will never pose a threat to the United States.

August 30: After months of debate, the French National Assembly defeats both the European Defense Community Treaty and the contractual agreements with Germany by a vote of 319–264.

1955

November 22: The Soviet Union tests a two-stage thermonuclear bomb.

1957

September: The Tu-95 strategic bomber enters service in the Soviet Air Force. This turboprop, swept-wing bomber has eight engines mounted in pairs, a maximum speed of 562 miles per hour, and a range of 8,200 miles flying at a slower speed. Given US air defenses, it is too slow to be used as a bomber, but it will serve for decades as a reconnaissance aircraft.

NOTES

1. STALIN ENDORSES WAR IN ASIA

1. John Barber and Mark Harrison, "Patriotic War, 1941–45," in *The Cambridge History of Russia*, vol. III, ed. Ronald Grigor Suny (Cambridge: Cambridge University Press, 2006), 225–42; Abbott Gleason, ed., *A Companion to Russian History* (New York: Wiley-Blackwell, 2009), 409.

2. Barber and Harrison, "Patriotic War," 233–42; Naum Jasny, "A Close-Up of the Soviet Fourth Five-Year Plan," *Quarterly Journal of Economics* 66 (May 1952): 139–71.

3. Adam B. Ulam, *Stalin: The Man and His Era* (New York: Viking Press, 1974), 369–462; David E. Murphy, *What Stalin Knew: The Enigma of Barbarossa* (New Haven, CT: Yale University Press, 2005), xviii–xx.

4. Svetlana Alliluyeva, *Only One Year* (New York: Harper & Row, 1969), 141–47, 387.

5. Roy A. Medvedev, "New Pages from the Political Biography of Stalin," in *Stalinism: Essays in Historical Interpretation*, ed. Robert C. Tucker (New York: W. W. Norton, 1977), 226.

6. Anastas Ivanovich Mikoian, *Tak Bylo: Razmyshleniia o minuvshem* (Moscow: Vagrius, 1999), 530–33; Milovan Djilas, *Conversations with Stalin* (New York: Harcourt, Brace & World, 1962), 152; Oleg Troianovskii, *Cherez gody i rasstoianiia: Istoriia odnoi sem'i* (Moscow: Vagrius, 1997), 148.

7. Nikita S. Khrushchev, *Khrushchev Remembers* (Boston: Little, Brown, 1970), 297–99; Mikoian, *Tak Bylo*, 534–37.

8. S. M. Shtemenko, in *Vstrechi so Stalinym*, ed. Pavel Aleksandrovich Zhuravlev (Moscow: Al'ternativa, 2004), 358; Troianovskii, *Cherez gody*, 159; Felix Chuev, *Molotov Remembers: Inside Kremlin Politics—Conversations with Felix Chuev* (Chicago: Ivan R. Dee, 1993), 211.

9. Mikoian, *Tak Bylo*, 527, 530–33.

10. Khrushchev, *Khrushchev Remembers*, 299–305; Djilas, *Conversations with Stalin*, 76, 92, 153.

11. Both quotations are in *Cold Peace: Stalin and the Soviet Ruling Circle, 1945–1953*, by Yoram Gorlizki and Oleg Khlevniuk (New York: Oxford University Press, 2004), 54.

12. Gorlizki and Khlevniuk, *Cold Peace*, 45, 52–59.

13. Gorlizki and Khlevniuk, *Cold Peace*, 46–50, 58–65; Djilas, *Conversations with Stalin*, 73–74.

14. Gorlizki and Khlevniuk, *Cold Peace*, 74–78. The resolutions to replace Molotov and Mikoyan were voted on at a Politburo meeting at Stalin's dacha attended by Georgi Malenkov, Lavrenti Beria, and Nikolai Bulganin. When canvassed by telephone, all the other members voted in favor of the resolutions, including the two ministers being fired.

15. Gorlizki and Khlevniuk, *Cold Peace*, 78–79.

16. Ulam, *Stalin*, 706 14; Gorlizki and Khlevniuk, *Cold Peace*, 79–87.

17. Gorlizki and Khlevniuk, *Cold Peace*, 88–89.

18. Gorlizki and Khlevniuk, *Cold Peace*, 113.

19. Gorlizki and Khlevniuk, *Cold Peace*, 113–19. In December 1954, a special open tribunal was held in Leningrad for Abakumov and his colleagues. They were found guilty of falsifying evidence in the Leningrad Affair and were condemned to death. See Ulam, *Stalin*, 711.

20. Gorlizki and Khlevniuk, *Cold Peace*, 89–94, quotation at 94; Chuev, *Molotov Remembers*, 232–33.

21. Gorlizki and Khlevniuk, *Cold Peace*, 101–08, 119–20, quotation at 107.

22. Mikoian, *Tak Bylo*, 517, 530–33; Khrushchev, *Khrushchev Remembers*, 307–15; William Taubman, *Khrushchev: The Man and His Era* (New York: W. W. Norton, 2003), 216–22; Alliluyeva, *Only One Year*, 379.

23. William Taubman, *Stalin's American Policy: From Entente to Détente to Cold War* (New York: W. W. Norton, 1982), 172–75, quotation at 175; Vladislav Zubok and Constantine Pleshakov, *Inside the Kremlin's Cold War: From Stalin to Khrushchev* (Cambridge, MA: Harvard University Press, 1996), 50–51, 103–08.

24. Taubman, *Stalin's American Policy*, 175–77; Gorlizki and Khlevniuk, *Cold Peace*, 31–38; Zubok and Pleshakov, *Kremlin's Cold War*, 125–33; Robert Dallek, *The Lost Peace: Leadership in a Time of Horror and Hope, 1945–1953* (New York: HarperCollins, 2010), 251–52.

25. Jeronim Perović, "The Tito-Stalin Split: A Reassessment in Light of New Evidence," *Journal of Cold War Studies* 9 (Spring 2007): 32–63; Zubok and Pleshakov, *Kremlin's Cold War*, 134–36; Taubman, *Stalin's American Policy*, 181–82, quotation at 182.

26. Marshall D. Shulman, *Stalin's Foreign Policy Reappraised* (New York: Atheneum, 1965), 36–38; Zbigniew Brzezinski, "The Pattern of Political Purges," *Annals of the American Academy of Political and Social Science* 317 (May 1959): 79–87.

27. Taubman, *Stalin's American Policy*, 182–87; Zubok and Pleshakov, *Kremlin's Cold War*, 50–52; Dallek, *Lost Peace*, 256–60; Melvyn P. Leffler, *A Preponderance of Power: National Security, the Truman Administration, and the Cold War* (Stanford, CA: Stanford University Press, 1992), 214–17.

28. Taubman, *Stalin's American Policy*, 187–92; Zubok and Pleshakov, *Kremlin's Cold War*, 51–53; Dallek, *Lost Peace*, 259–63; Leffler, *Preponderance of Power*, 318.

29. David Holloway, *Stalin and the Bomb: The Soviet Union and Atomic Energy, 1939–1956* (New Haven, CT: Yale University Press, 1994), 265; Leffler, *Preponderance of Power*, 333–38.

30. Ulam, *Stalin*, 688–94; Henry Kissinger, *On China* (New York: Penguin Press, 2011), 113–15. Jiang Jieshi is the current transliteration for the older Chiang Kai-shek.

31. Ulam, *Stalin*, 695.

32. Zhihua Shen and Danhui Li, *After Leaning to One Side: China and Its Allies in the Cold War* (Washington, DC, and Stanford, CA: Woodrow Wilson Center Press and Stanford University Press, 2011), 5–10.

33. Shen and Li, *After Leaning to One Side*, 10–13, quotation at 11. For the latest details from Moscow archives on the Sino-Soviet treaty negotiations, see Zhihua Shen and Yafeng Xia, *Mao and the Sino-Soviet Partnership, 1945–1959: A New History* (Lanham, MD: Lexington Books, 2015), 52–56. Henry Kissinger begins his profile of Zhou Enlai by saying: "In some sixty years of public life, I have encountered no more compelling figure than Zhou Enlai." Kissinger, *On China*, 241–55.

34. Shen and Li, *After Leaning to One Side*, 12–15; for a different assessment of the Sino-Soviet negotiations, see Kissinger, *On China*, 117.

35. Dae-Sook Suh, *Kim Il Sung: The North Korean Leader* (New York: Columbia University Press, 1988), 30–105; Yeongtae Im, *Fifty-Year History of North Korea*, vol. 1, *Liberation to Chollima Movement* (Seoul: Deulnyeok Publications, 1999), 27 (in Korean).

36. Conversation between Stalin and a delegation from North Korea led by Kim Il-sung, March 7, 1949, Archives of the President of Russia, in "The Korean Conflict, 1950–1953: The Most Mysterious War of the 20th Century—Based on Secret Soviet Archives," by Evgeniy P. Bajanov and Natalia Bajanova, unpublished typescript, n.d., copy in archives of North Korea International Documentation Project, Woodrow Wilson Center, 17–18; T. Shtykov to A. Vyshinsky (telegram), January 19, 1950, Stalin to Shtykov (telegram), January 30, 1950, in "To Attack, or Not to Attack? Stalin, Kim Il Sung, and the Prelude to War," by Kathryn Weathersby, Cold War International History Project *Bulletin*, No. 5, Woodrow Wilson Center, Spring 1995, 1–9, quotation at 9.

2. KIM IL-SUNG PLANS AN ATTACK

1. Bruce Cumings, *The Origins of the Korean War*, vol. I, *Liberation and the Emergence of Separate Regimes, 1945–1947* (Princeton: Princeton University Press, 1981), 120–121.

2. Bruce Cumings, *The Korean War: A History* (New York: Modern Library, 2010), 3–4, 41–42, 103–5; Allan R. Millett, *The War for Korea, 1945–1950* (Lawrence: University Press of Kansas, 2005), 44–45.

3. Cumings, *Korean War*, 104–17; Millett, *War for Korea*, 44–46.

4. Millett, *War for Korea, 1945–1950*, 47–48; Cumings, *Origins of the Korean War*, I, 190–91.

5. Cumings, *Korean War*, 108–112, at 109; Millett, *War for Korea, 1945–1950*, 52–71.
6. Robert J. Donovan, *Conflict and Crisis: The Presidency of Harry S Truman, 1946–1948* (New York: W. W. Norton, 1977), 284, 288–91; Cumings, *Korean War*, 109–12.
7. Cumings, *Origins of the Korean War*, I, 351–81.
8. Cumings, *Korean War*, 112–13; Millett, *War for Korea, 1945–1950*, 148–55.
9. Millett, *War for Korea, 1945–1950*, 142–48; Cumings, *Korean War*, 121–31. Based on extensive research in US military records containing interviews with US and Korean officials, prisoners, and survivors, Millett places significantly greater emphasis on communist leadership of the revolt than Cumings, who relies more heavily on Korean sources.
10. Cumings, *Korean War*, 138–42; Millett, *War for Korea, 1945–1950*, 166–75, 198–212.
11. Cumings, *Korean War*, 139–45; NSC 48/2, "The Position of the United States With Respect to Asia," December 30, 1949, in *Foreign Relations of the United States, 1949*, vol. VII, part 2 (Washington, DC: US Government Printing Office, 1976), 1215–20. Hereafter, throughout the book, these *Foreign Relations* volumes are simply referred to as *Foreign Relations* with the year.
12. Andrei Lankov, *From Stalin to Kim Il-sung: The Formation of North Korea, 1945–1960* (New Brunswick, NJ: Rutgers University Press, 2002), 17, 58–59.
13. Lankov, *From Stalin to Kim Il-sung*, 50–53; Haruki Wada, *North Joseon* (Paju, South Korea: Dolbaegae, 2002), 38–41; Charles K. Armstrong, *The North Korean Revolution, 1945–1950* (Ithaca, NY: Cornell University Press, 2003), 27–28. The nom de guerre Kim Il-sung was adopted about 1935. The historical background of the founding leader of North Korea is difficult to establish because official historians of the regime rewrote his biography frequently to obscure or eliminate influences from Christian, Chinese, and Soviet sources in order to present Kim Il-sung as the heroic military genius who singlehandedly created North Korea.
14. Suh, *Kim Il Sung*, 17–38; Wada, *Joseon*, 53–60; Lankov, *From Stalin to Kim Il-sung*, 54–57.
15. Armstrong, *North Korean Revolution*, 26, 38–41; Suh, *Kim Il Sung*, 60–61; Lankov, *From Stalin to Kim Il-sung*, 12–22.
16. Cumings, *Origins of the Korean War*, I, 401–7; Suh, *Kim Il Sung*, 61–68; Armstrong, *North Korean Revolution*, 66–70; Lankov, *From Stalin to Kim Il-sung*, 19–27.
17. Lankov, *From Stalin to Kim Il-sung*, 2–3; Suh, *Kim Il Sung*, 62–63.
18. Wada, *Joseon*, 83; Suh, *Kim Il Sung*, 68–69, 72, 95–102; Cumings, *Origins of the Korean War*, I, 409–13; Lankov, *From Stalin to Kim Il-sung*, 29–47; for a detailed analysis of Kim Il-sung's "democratic reforms," see Armstrong, *North Korean Revolution*, 71–106, 136–65.
19. Suh, *Kim Il Sung*, 70–71, 74–94; Wada, *Joseon*, 83–84.
20. Shtykov to Foreign Minister Molotov, February 3 and 4, 1949, Stalin's conversation with Kim and North Korean delegation, March 5, 1949, Archives of the President of Russia; Evgeniy Bajanov and Natalia Bajanova, "The Korean Conflict, 1950–1953: The Most Mysterious War of the 20th Century—Based on Secret Soviet Archives," unpublished typescript, n.d., copy in archives of North Korea International Documentation Project, Woodrow Wilson International Center for Scholars, 3–6, at 6; Millett, *War for Korea,*

1945–1950, 204–12; Bruce Cumings, *The Origins of the Korean War*, vol. II, *The Roaring of the Cataract, 1947–1950* (Princeton, NJ: Princeton University Press, 1990), 388–406.

21. Cumings, *Origins of the Korean War*, II, 358–374; Kim Il-Sung to Stalin, April 28, 1949, Shtykov to Stalin, May 1, 1949, Soviet Ministry of Armed Forces to Shtykov, June 4, 1949, Archives of the President of Russia, Bajanov and Bajanova, "Korean Conflict," 54–56; Chen Jian, *China's Road to the Korean War: The Making of a Sino-American Confrontation* (New York: Columbia University Press, 1994), 110–11; Millett, *War for Korea, 1945–1950*, 243–44.

22. Stalin to Shtykov, January 30, 1950, Report on Kim Il-sung's visit to the USSR, March 30–April 25, 1950, International Department of the Central Committee of the Communist Party, Archives of the President of Russia, in Bajanov and Bajanova, "The Korean Conflict," 36, 40–42; Kapitsa, quoted in Shen and Li, *After Leaning to One Side*, 29.

23. Roshchin (Soviet ambassador in Beijing) to Stalin, May 13, 1950, Archives of the President of Russia, Stalin to Mao, May 14, 1950, Archives of the Soviet Foreign Ministry, Bajanov and Bajanova, "Korean Conflict," 48–51.

24. Roshchin to Stalin, May 15 & 16, 1950, Archives of the President of Russia, Bajanov and Bajanova, "Korean Conflict," 51–53; Shen and Li, *After Leaning to One Side*, 30–32.

25. Millett, *War for Korea, 1945–1950*, 193–96, 241–44, 249.

3. TRUMAN CONSOLIDATES US COMMITMENTS

1. Robert J. Donovan, *Tumultuous Years: The Presidency of Harry S Truman, 1949–1953* (New York: W. W. Norton, 1982), 98–99; Richard G. Hewlett and Francis Duncan, *Atomic Shield, 1947–1952* (Washington, DC: US Atomic Energy Commission, 1972), 362–69; Dean Acheson, *Present at the Creation: My Years in the State Department* (New York: W. W. Norton, 1969), 321, 355, 362; Paul H. Nitze, "Recent Soviet Moves," February 8, 1950, in *Foreign Relations of the United States, 1950*, vol. I (Washington, DC: US Government Printing Office, 1977), 145; Melvyn P. Leffler, *A Preponderance of Power: National Security, the Truman Administration, and the Cold War* (Stanford, CA: Stanford University Press, 1992), 312–13.

2. Leffler, *Preponderance of Power*, 304–17; Donovan, *Tumultuous Years*, 123, 131–32.

3. Donovan, *Tumultuous Years*, 114–127.

4. Alonzo L. Hamby, *Man of the People: A Life of Harry S. Truman* (New York: Oxford University Press, 1995), 278–84.

5. Donovan, *Tumultuous Years*, 14; Hamby, *Man of the People*, 467–78.

6. Hamby, *Man of the People*, 7–199 passim.

7. Hamby, *Man of the People*, 200–273 passim; *Time*, March 8, 1943, 13–15; *Look*, May 16, 1944, 26–27.

8. Donovan, *Conflict and Crisis*, 72–93. We now know that Stalin was well aware of the US progress in developing an atomic bomb from his spies in the Manhattan Project. See Christopher Andrew and Oleg Gordievsky, *KGB: The Inside Story of Its Foreign Operations from Lenin to Gorbachev* (New York: HarperCollins, 1990), 311–17.

9. Leffler, *Preponderance of Power*, 100–140, at 109; Donovan, *Conflict and Crisis*, 187–97, 219–28.

10. Donovan, *Conflict and Crisis*, 275–91, 357–68, at 284.

11. Donovan, *Conflict and Crisis*, 395–418, at 416 and 418; Hamby, *Man of the People*, 445–51.

12. Donovan, *Conflict and Crisis*, 415–31, at 430; Hamby, *Man of the People*, 452–63, at 459.

13. To win the farm vote, Truman exploited a provision in a Republican-passed farm bill that prohibited the government from adding storage facilities for grain if the harvest exceeded current commercial capacity. A bumper harvest developed over the summer, and farmers lost money by having to sell their expanded yields of corn and wheat at low prices due to the lack of storage facilities. Truman attacked the grain elevator operators and large grain traders who profited from the farmers' distress. Donovan, *Conflict and Crisis*, 420–23, 432–39; Hamby, *Man of the People*, 463–66.

14. Leffler, *Preponderance of Power*, 260–65, at 264 and 265; Samuel R. Williamson Jr. and Steven L. Rearden, *The Origins of US Nuclear Strategy, 1945–1953* (New York: St. Martin's Press, 1993), 93–95.

15. Dean Acheson had served as undersecretary of state from 1945 to 1947 and played a central role in the formulation of the Truman Doctrine and the Marshall Plan. Acheson, *Present at the Creation*, 257–63, 277293; Robert L. Beisner, *Dean Acheson: A Life in the Cold War* (New York: Oxford University Press, 2006), 130–34, 143–45; Leffler, *Preponderance of Power*, 277–86, at 277 and 285.

16. The Allied airlift to West Berlin continued until September 30 to build up adequate supplies in case of a new blockade. The total cost of the US portion of the airlift was $224 million in 1949 dollars. Leffler, *Preponderance of Power*, 280–86; Steven L. Rearden, *The Formative Years, 1947–1950: History of the Office of the Secretary of Defense*, vol. I (Washington, DC: Historical Office, Office of the Secretary of Defense, 1984), 285–308, 472–79; Acheson, *Present at the Creation*, 267–293; W. R. Smyser, *From Yalta to Berlin: The Cold War Struggle Over Germany* (New York: St. Martin's Press, 1999), 73–96.

17. Gordon H. Chang, *Friends and Enemies: The United States, China, and the Soviet Union, 1948–1972* (Stanford, CA: Stanford University Press, 1990), 11–21; Leffler, *Preponderance of Power*, 85–88, 127–30, 169–70, 246–51, 291–95.

18. US Department of State, *The China White Paper, August 1949*, reissued (Stanford, CA: Stanford University Press, 1967), xvi; for a detailed study of the China lobby, see Ross Y. Koen, *The China Lobby in American Politics* (New York: Harper & Row, 1974); Chang, *Friends and Enemies*, 35–41; Leffler, *Preponderance of Power*, 295–98.

19. Leffler, *Preponderance of Power*, 298–99; for an excellent, detailed account of the Allied occupation of Japan, 1945–1952, see John W. Dower, *Embracing Defeat: Japan in the Wake of World War II* (New York: W. W. Norton, 1999).

20. Leffler, *Preponderance of Power*, 300–303.

21. Millett, *War for Korea, 1945–1950*, 186–93, at 187; Leffler, *Preponderance of Power*, 251–53, 300; Donovan, *Tumultuous Years*, 179–81.

22. Rearden, *Formative Years*, 361–72; Leffler, *Preponderance of Power*, 304–8.

23. Leffler, *Preponderance of Power*, 305–8.

24. Robert M. Blum, *Drawing The Line: The Origin of the American Containment Policy in East Asia* (New York: W. W. Norton, 1982), 135–77; Rearden, *Formative Years*, 230–38; NSC Report 48/2, "The Position of the United States With Respect to Asia," December 30, 1949, US Department of State, *Foreign Relations of the United States, 1949*, vol. VII, part 2 (Washington, DC: US Government Printing Office, 1976), 1215–20.

25. David S. McLellan, *Dean Acheson: The State Department Years* (New York: Dodd, Mead, 1976), 204–6, at 206.

26. Acheson's main point with regard to South Korea was to urge Congress to pass an aid bill to assist the Rhee government in establishing a sound economy. Dean G. Acheson, "Crisis in Asia: An Examination of US Policy," US Department of State, *Bulletin*, XXII (January 23, 1950), 111–18, at 115; McLellan, *Acheson*, 206–15; Donovan, *Tumultuous Years*, 136–38.

27. Shen and Li, *After Leaning to One Side*, 13–14; Chen Jian, *China's Road to the Korean War: The Making of the Sino-American Confrontation* (New York: Columbia University Press, 1994), 101–2; Andrew and Gordievsky, *KGB*, 393–95.

4. JOSEPH McCARTHY SELLS THE POLITICS OF FEAR

1. Richard M. Fried, *Men Against McCarthy* (New York: Columbia University Press, 1976), 43–44, at 44; Richard M. Fried, *Nightmare in Red: The McCarthy Era* (New York: Oxford University Press, 1990), 121–23. This version of the Wheeling speech is reprinted in US Senate, Subcommittee of the Committee on Foreign Relations, *A Resolution to Investigate Whether There Are Employees in the State Department Disloyal to the United States. Hearings Pursuant to S.Res. 231, 81st Cong., 2d Sess., 1950*, 1759–67 (referred to hereafter as *The Tydings Committee Hearings/Report*).

2. Alonzo L. Hamby, *Man of the People: A Life of Harry S. Truman* (New York: Oxford University Press, 1995), 530.

3. Fried, *Men Against McCarthy*, 45–51; Robert J. Donovan, *Tumultuous Years: The Presidency of Harry S Truman, 1949–1953* (New York: W. W. Norton, 1982), 164.

4. Fried, *Men Against McCarthy*, 33–35.

5. Arthur Herman, *Joseph McCarthy: Reexamining the Life and Legacy of America's Most Hated Senator* (New York: Free Press, 1999), 30; David M. Oshinsky, *A Conspiracy So Immense: The World of Joe McCarthy* (New York: Oxford University Press, 2005), 32; Fried, *Men Against McCarthy*, 35.

6. Richard H. Rovere, *Senator Joe McCarthy* (Berkeley: University of California Press, 1959), 97, 102; Arnold Beichman, "The Politics of Self-Destruction," *Policy Review* 135 (February–March 2006): 70–72.

7. Robert Griffith, *The Politics of Fear: Joseph R. McCarthy and the Senate* (Amherst: University of Massachusetts Press, 1987), 26–28; Fried, *Men Against McCarthy*, 37–43; Fried, *Nightmare in Red*, 122–123; Herman, Joseph *McCarthy*, 51.

8. Ross Y. Koen, *The China Lobby in American Politics* (New York: Harper & Row, 1974), 29–55; Donovan, *Tumultuous Years*, 29–31.

9.   Koen, *China Lobby*, 33–35; Donovan, *Tumultuous Years*, 29–31.

10. Allen Weinstein, *Perjury: The Hiss-Chambers Case* (New York: Random House, 1997), 3–8, 62–72, 116–38; Donovan, *Tumultuous Years*, 31–32.

11. Weinstein, *Perjury*, 141–513 passim; Donovan, *Tumultuous Years*, 133–35.

12. Weinstein, *Perjury*, 337–513 passim, at 512 and 513; Hamby, *Man of the People*, 521–23; Alger Hiss, *In the Court of Public Opinion* (New York: Alfred A. Knopf, 1957); Alger Hiss, *Recollections of a Life* (New York: Henry Holt, 1988); Allen Weinstein and Alexander Vassiliev, *The Haunted Wood: Soviet Espionage in America—The Stalin Era* (New York: Random House, 1999); John Earl Haynes and Harvey Klehr, *Venona: Decoding Soviet Espionage in America* (New Haven, CT: Yale University Press, 2000). The most recent volume on the case is from a retired Defense Intelligence Agency analyst, Christina Shelton, *Alger Hiss: Why He Chose Treason* (New York: Threshold Editions, 2012). Emblematic of the secrecy culture permeating postwar Washington is the fact that the head of the Armed Forces Security Agency (predecessor of the National Security Agency), the FBI director, and the chairman of the Joint Chiefs of Staff knew the contents of the Venona telegrams but refused to tell President Truman. See Daniel Patrick Moynihan, *Secrecy: The American Experience* (New Haven, CT: Yale University Press, 1998), 62–73.

13. Koen, *China Lobby*, 171.

14. Hamby, *Man of the People*, 453.

15. Fried, *Men Against McCarthy*, 48–49, at 49.

16. Fried, *Men Against McCarthy*, 49–53; Donovan, *Tumultuous Years*, 164–65.

17. Donovan, *Tumultuous Years*, 162–65; Fried, *Men Against McCarthy*, 59–63.

18. Fried, *Men Against McCarthy*, 53–58, 68, 93, at 57.

19. Fried, *Men Against McCarthy*, 61–63.

20. Fried, *Men Against McCarthy*, 64–67, at 67 and 68; Robert L. Beisner, *Dean Acheson: A Life in the Cold War* (New York: Oxford University Press, 2006), 305–7; David S. McLellan, *Dean Acheson: The State Department Years* (New York: Dodd, Mead, 1976), 225–27; Letters to the Times, *New York Times*, March 27, 1950.

21. Fried, *Men Against McCarthy*, 67–70, at 69 and 70; Donovan, *Tumultuous Years*, 170.

22. Robert P. Newman, *Owen Lattimore and the "Loss" of China* (Berkeley: University of California Press, 1992), 22–204 passim; Eric Pace, "Owen Lattimore, Far East Scholar Accused by McCarthy, Dies at 88," *New York Times*, June 1, 1989; Griffith, *Politics of Fear*, 76.

23. Fried, *Men Against McCarthy*, 71–74; Griffith, *Politics of Fear*, 77–84.

24. Beisner, *Dean Acheson*, 307–8; McLellan, *Dean Acheson*, 232; Fried, *Men Against McCarthy*, 74–85.

25. *The Tydings Committee Report*, 151–54, 159–63, 167; Fried, *Men Against McCarthy*, 85–89, at 86 and 88–89.

26. Donovan, *Tumultuous Years*, 165; Fried, *Men Against McCarthy*, 60–63, 89–94, at 89; Newman, *Owen Lattimore*, 300.

27. Ellen Schrecker, *Many Are the Crimes: McCarthyism in America* (Boston: Little, Brown, 1998), 158–59; Newman, *Owen Lattimore*, 318–81 passim; Beisner, *Dean Acheson*, 308–13; Fried, *Men Against McCarthy*, 93–94, 129–40, 156–69.

28. Griffith, *Politics of Fear*, 216–35, 254–69 ; Fried, *Men Against McCarthy*, 169–81, 188–92, 247–53, 279–88, 297–300, 310–15; Oshinsky, *Conspiracy So Immense*, 457–71.

29. Fried, *Nightmare in Red*, 119.

30. Rovere, *Senator Joe McCarthy*, 148–49. Rovere wrote widely read articles on McCarthy's activities as they occurred for *The New Yorker* and published a revised version as a book in 1959. In a second edition, in 1996, this volume remains one of the most pungent and readable accounts of a tragic era.

5. PAUL NITZE SOUNDS THE TOCSIN

1. Samuel R. Williamson Jr. and Steven L. Rearden, *The Origins of US Nuclear Strategy, 1945–1953* (New York: St. Martin's Press, 1993), 101–111; Richard G. Hewlett and Francis Duncan, *Atomic Shield, 1947–1952: A History of the US Atomic Energy Commission*, vol. II (Washington, DC: Atomic Energy Commission, 1972), 161–65; Melvyn P. Leffler, *A Preponderance of Power: National Security, the Truman Administration, and the Cold War* (Stanford, CA: Stanford University Press, 1992), 271.

2. Hewlett and Duncan, *Atomic Shield*, 373–394, at 394; Williamson and Rearden, *Origins*, 111–16; David Alan Rosenberg, "American Atomic Strategy and the Hydrogen Bomb Decision," *Journal of American History* 66 (June 1979): 62–87.

3. Hewlett and Duncan, *Atomic Shield*, 394–405; Paul Nitze, memorandum of December 19, 1949, Records of the Policy Planning Staff, RG 59, National Archives, Washington, DC; Williamson and Rearden, *Origins*, 117–25.

4. Report by the Special Committee of the NSC to the President, January 31, 1`950, President to the Secretary of State, January 31, 1950, *Foreign Relations, 1950*, I, 513–17, 141–42.

5. Hewlett and Duncan, *Atomic Shield*, 371–80; General Omar Bradley, "This Way Lies Peace," *Saturday Evening Post*, 222 (October 15, 1949), 168–96.

6. Hewlett and Duncan, *Atomic Shield*, 378–86, at 379. For detailed evidence on the US Navy's opposition to an atomic strategy and the activity of the Joint Chiefs of Staff in urging rapid development of the H-bomb, see Rosenberg, "American Atomic Strategy."

7. Kennan served as both counselor and director of the Policy Planning Staff from October 1 until December 31, 1949. Paul Nitze assumed the latter post on January 1, 1950. Discouraged over recent trends in department policy, Kennan had asked on September 29, 1949, to give up his duties on the Planning Staff as soon as possible and to retire the following June. Two months later, he stated in his diary that his decision to retire rested on the fact that his view of diplomatic priorities was not shared by the secretary of state or by the senior officials who would advise him, so he felt it best for him to leave government service. See George F. Kennan, *Memoirs, 1925–1950* (Boston: Little, Brown, 1967), 468.

8. Kennan, "International Control of Atomic Energy," January 20, 1950, *Foreign Relations, 1950*, I, 22–29. For the evolution of Kennan's views on nuclear weapons up to this point, see John Lewis Gaddis, *George F. Kennan: An American Life* (New York: Penguin Press, 2011), 374–81.

9. Kennan, "International Control," 35–36.

10. Kennan, "International Control," 37–40.

11. Kennan, "International Control," 40–44. In his *Memoirs*, Kennan says that this personal memorandum was "in its implications one of the most important, if not the most important, of all the documents I ever wrote in government." In recounting his arguments from memory, Kennan contends mistakenly that he made a plea against development of a thermonuclear bomb. He argued against first use of atomic weapons, but made no mention of thermonuclear development. See Kennan, *Memoirs*, 471–76.

12. Gaddis, *Kennan*, 381. In his *Memoirs*, Kennan says he "did not believe in the reality of a Soviet military threat to Western Europe." Kennan, *Memoirs*, 464; see comments on Kennan's draft paper by Arneson, Rusk, Hickerson, and Nitze, *Foreign Relations, 1950*, I, 1–17.

13. Robert A. Pollard, *Economic Security and the Origins of the Cold War, 1945–1950* (New York: Columbia University Press, 1985), 153–56, 224, 228–32; Louis Fisher, *Presidential Spending Power* (Princeton, NJ: Princeton University Press, 1975), 162–63; Alonzo L. Hamby, *Man of the People: A Life of Harry S. Truman* (New York: Oxford University Press, 1995), 398–400, 514; Congressional Quarterly, *Congress and the Nation, 1945–1964* (Washington, DC: Congressional Quarterly, 1965), 253–54.

14. Congressional Quarterly, *Congress and the Nation*, 253–54.

15. Paul H. Nitze, *From Hiroshima to Glasnost: At the Center of Decision—A Memoir* (New York: Grove Weidenfeld, 1989), x–xv, at xii.

16. Nitze, *From Hiroshima to Glasnost*, xv–xxii; Steven L. Rearden, *The Evolution of American Strategic Doctrine: Paul H. Nitze and the Soviet Challenge* (Boulder, CO: Westview Press, 1984), 2.

17. Nitze, *From Hiroshima to Glasnost*, 6–37; Rearden, *Evolution*, 2–3.

18. Nitze, *Hiroshima to Glasnost*, 37–43; Nicholas Thompson, *The Hawk and the Dove: Paul Nitze, George Kennan, and the History of the Cold War* (New York: Henry Holt, 2009), 64–66, at 66. Thompson points out that in this instance, Nitze "let his conclusions outrun his facts" and confirm a preconceived view that atomic bombs were "just another weapon."

19. Rearden, *Evolution*, 3; Nitze, *Hiroshima to Glasnost*, 43–45; United States Strategic Bombing Survey, *Summary Report (Pacific War)* (Washington, DC: US Government Printing Office, 1946), 30–32.

20. Nitze, *Hiroshima to Glasnost*, 46–77; Thompson, *Hawk and the Dove*, 80–82.

21. Thompson, *Hawk and the Dove*, 94–97, 101–9; Nitze, *Hiroshima to Glasnost*, 82–92.

22. President to the Secretary of State, January 31, 1950, *Foreign Relations, 1950*, I, 141–42. Chaired by Paul H. Nitze, the State-Defense Policy Review Group consisted of ten other regular members and four occasional participants. Representing the Department of State were Nitze, George H. Butler, Carlton Savage, Harry H. Schwartz, and Robert Tufts of the Policy Planning Staff; and R. Gordon Arneson, special assistant to the undersecretary for atomic energy policy. The Defense representatives included Major General James H. Burns (ret.), assistant to the secretary of defense for foreign military affairs; Major General Truman H. Landon, the US Air Force member of the

Joint Strategic Survey Committee of the Joint Chiefs of Staff; Najeeb E. Halaby, director of the Office of Foreign Military Affairs; and Robert LeBaron, chairman of the
Military Liaison Committee to the Atomic Energy Commission and adviser to the
secretary of defense on atomic energy affairs. The National Security Council was represented by its executive secretary, James S. Lay Jr. Among those attending at least one
meeting were Joseph Chase and Adrian S. Fisher of the State Department, Lt. Col.
William Burke of Defense, and S. Everett Gleason of the NSC. From its first meeting on February 8, this group labored steadily until it had a working draft to present
to selected outside experts by February 27. Evidence suggests that this draft closely
resembled the final report, except that it lacked the section on atomic armaments and
the conclusion.

23. Policy Planning Staff, Record of Meeting on February 2, 1950, Nitze, "Recent Soviet
     Moves," February 8, 1950, *Foreign Relations, 1950*, I, 142–43, 145–47.

24. US Department of State, *Bulletin*, January 23, 1950, 114–15; February 20, 1950, 274;
     March 20, 1950, 427; and March 27, 1950, 473–78.

25. Lt. Gen. Alfred M. Gruenther to Deputy Secretary of Defense, January 31, 1950, Records
     of the Office of the Secretary of Defense, RG 330, Department of Defense; CIA Report
     (ORE 91–94), "Estimate of the Effects of the Soviet Possession of Atomic Bomb upon
     the Security of the United States and Upon the Probabilities of Direct Soviet Military
     Action," February 10, 1950, RG 330.

26. LeBaron, memorandum for secretary of defense, February 20, 1950 (based on a report
     by Maj. Gen. Kenneth D. Nichols and Brig. Gen. Herbert B. Loper), Halaby, memoran-
     dum for secretary of defense, February 24, 1950, RG 330; Hewlett and Duncan, *Atomic
     Shield*, 415–16.

27. Kennan, draft memorandum to secretary of state, February 17, 1950, *Foreign Relations*,
     I, 1950, pp. 160–67. The counselor communicated these views orally to the secretary,
     and left the draft memorandum for the information of the Policy Planning Staff. Ken-
     nan also took to the public his argument for a multifaceted program of containment
     against a Soviet threat that was essentially political in nature. See George F. Kennan, "Is
     War with Russia Inevitable? Five Solid Arguments for Peace," Department of State, *Bul-
     letin*, February 20, 1950, 267–71, 303. This article was reprinted in *The Reader's Digest*
     for March 1950.

28. Francis H. Russell, memorandum for assistant secretary of state for public affairs,
     March 6, 1950, Barrett, memorandum for undersecretary of state (James E. Webb),
     March 6, 1950, *Foreign Relations, 1950*, I, 185–87.

29. State-Defense Policy Review Group, Record of Meetings with Oppenheimer and
     Conant, *Foreign Relations, 1950*, I, 168–82.

30. State-Defense Policy Review Group, Record of Meeting with Lovett, *Foreign Relations,
     1950*, I, 196–200. The other three consultants were Chester I. Barnard, Henry R. Smyth,
     and Ernest O. Lawrence; for their positive reactions, see *Foreign Relations, 1950*, I,
     190–95, 200–201. Of all the suggestions made by these six consultants, the only change
     that can be identified is the removal from the final version of the objective "restoring
     freedom to the victims of the Kremlin," which had so disturbed Conant.

31. Nitze, memorandum for secretary of state, March 22, 1950, memorandum of conversation at the Department of State, March 22, 1950, *Foreign Relations*, I, 202–6; Nitze, *Hiroshima to Glasnost*, 94–95; Halaby, memorandum for secretary of defense, February 24, 1950, RG 330; Burns, memorandum for secretary of defense, March 13, 1950, RG 330; Rearden, *Evolution*, 24–25.

32. Johnson to senior officials of Defense Department, March 31, 1950, Johnson to President, April 11, 1950, RG 330; Robert L. Beisner, *Dean Acheson: A Life in the Cold War* (New York: Oxford University Press, 2006), 238–41; Acheson, *Present at the Creation*, 373–74. Acheson's account of these events contains several errors; for details, see Samuel. F. Wells Jr., "Sounding the Tocsin: NSC 68 and the Soviet Threat," *International Security* 4 (Autumn 1979): 131n26.

33. "NSC 68," April 7, 1950, *Foreign Relations, 1950*, I, 237–38; the full report can be found at 235–92.

34. NSC 68, *Foreign Relations*, 1950, I, 239–40.

35. NSC 68, *Foreign Relations*, 1950, I, 242. For the text of NSC 20/4, see *Foreign Relations*, 1948, I, part 2, 662–69.

36. NSC 68, *Foreign Relations*, 1950, I, 244.

37. NSC 68, *Foreign Relations*, 1950, I, 245–46, 249–52.

38. NSC 68, *Foreign Relations*, 1950, I, 263–64.

39. NSC 68, *Foreign Relations*, 1950, I, 265–66.

40. NSC 68, *Foreign Relations*, 1950, I, 267–71.

41. NSC 68, *Foreign Relations*, 1950, I, 276–81.

42. NSC 68, *Foreign Relations*, 1950, I, 282–85.

43. NSC 68, *Foreign Relations*, 1950, I, 285–92.

44. For the reactions of these and other State Department policymakers, see NSC 68, *Foreign Relations*, 1950, I, 213–21, 225–26.

45. Despite the claim in his memoirs of no involvement with NSC Report 68, Bohlen returned from his new post as minister in Paris to evaluate the study. See Charles E. Bohlen, *Witness to History* (New York: W.W. Norton, 1973), 290, and Bohlen, memorandum for Nitze, April 5, 1950, *Foreign Relations, 1950*, I, 221–25.

46. *Foreign Relations, 1950*, I, 213–26 passim; the Thompson and Bohlen statements are at 214 and 225, respectively.

47. Truman to James S. Lay Jr. (executive secretary of the NSC), April 12, 1950, Lay to Ad Hoc Committee on NSC 68, April 28, 1950, *Foreign Relations, 1950*, I, 234–35, 293–96.

48. James S. Lay, Jr., memorandum of discussion at 1st meeting of Ad Hoc Committee on May 2, 1950 and 4th meeting on May 12, 1950, *Foreign Relations, 1950*, I, 297–98, 312–13.

49. Frank Whitehouse, memorandum for Gen. James H. Burns, May 22, 1950, Louis Johnson, memorandum for service secretaries and senior defense officials, May 25, 1950. RG 330; Steven L. Rearden, *The Formative Years, 1947–1950: History of the Office of the Secretary of Defense*, vol. I (Washington, DC: Historical Office, Office of the Secretary of Defense, 1984, 534–35; unsigned memorandum from National Security Resources Board, May 29, 1950, W. J. McWilliams, memorandum of discussion at meeting of under secretary of state's advisory committee, June 6, 1950, *Foreign Relations, 1950*, I, 316–24.

50.   James S. Lay Jr., report to the NSC, September 30, 1950, *Foreign Relations, 1950*, I, 400.

51.   John Paton Davies, quoted by Gaddis, *Kennan*, 392.

52.   Acheson, *Present at the Creation*, 374; Beisner, *Dean Acheson*, 243–46.

6. NORTH KOREA DRIVES SOUTH

1.   Charles K. Armstrong, *The North Korean Revolution, 1945–1950* (Ithaca, NY: Cornell University Press, 2003), 237–39.

2.   Armstrong, *North Korean Revolution*, 231–35; Wada Haruki, *Kin Nichisei to Manshu konichi senso* [Kim Il Sung and the Anti-Japanese War in Manchuria] (Tokyo: Heibon-sha, 1992), 377.

3.   Armstrong, *North Korean Revolution*, 233; Bruce Cumings, *The Origins of the Korean War*, vol. II, *The Roaring of the Cataract, 1947–1950* (Princeton, NJ: Princeton University Press, 1990), 443–55.

4.   Chen Jian, *China's Road to the Korean War: The Making of the Sino-American Confrontation* (New York: Columbia University Press, 1994), 106–10, at 108 and 109; Cumings, *Origins of the Korean War*, II, 358–64.

5.   Chen, *China's Road to the Korean War*, 110–11; Armstrong, *North Korean Revolution*, 234; Cumings, *Origins of the Korean War*, II, 363–64.

6.   Chen, *China's Road to the Korean War*, 111.

7.   Armstrong, *North Korean Revolution*, 233; Cumings, *Origins of the Korean War*, II, 446–47; Kim Il-sung to Stalin, April 28, 1949, Shtykov to Stalin, May 1, 1949, USSR Ministry of Armed Forces to Shtykov, June 4, 1949, Archives of the President of Russia, in the "The Korean Conflict, 1950–1953: The Most Mysterious War of the 20th Century—Based on Secret Soviet Archives," by Evgeniy Bajanov and Natalia Bajanova, unpublished typescript, n.d., copy in archives of North Korea International Documentation Project, Woodrow Wilson International Center for Scholars, 54–56.

8.   Shtykov to Stalin, June 22, 1949, Stalin to Shtykov, October 30, 1949, Shtykov to Stalin, October 31, 1949, Stalin to Shtykov, November 20, 1949, Archives of the President of Russia, in "Korean Conflict," by Bajanov and Bajanova, 10–12; Allan R. Millett, *The War for Korea, 1950–1951: They Came from the North* (Lawrence: University Press of Kansas, 2010), 46–47.

9.   Shtykov to Stalin, January 1, 1950, Archives of the President of Russia, in "Korean Conflict," by Bajanov and Bajanova, 56; Millett, *War for Korea, 1950–1951*, 47; Sergei N. Goncharov, John W. Lewis, and Xue Litai, *Uncertain Partners: Stalin, Mao, and the Korean War* (Stanford, CA: Stanford University Press, 1993), 147.

10.   Millett, *War for Korea, 1950–1951*, 48–50; Wada Haruki, *Hanguk Chonjaeng* [The Korean War] (Korean translation of Japanese edition) (Seoul: Changbi, 1999), 67–69.

11.   Millett, *War for Korea, 1950–1951*, 48–50; Shtykov to Stalin, May 29, 1950, Archives of the President of Russia, in "Korean Conflict," by Bajanov and Bajanova, 57.

12.   Wada, *Hanguk Chonjaeng*, 100, 337; Robert A. Scalapino and Chong-sik Lee, *Communism in Korea: Part I* (Berkeley: University of California Press, 1972), 394; Millett,

War for Korea, 1950–1951, 49–50; Shtykov to Stalin six cables, June 12–21, 1950, Stalin to Shtykov, June 21, 1950, Archives of the President of Russia, in "Korean Conflict," by Bajanov and Bajanova, 58–60.

13.   The detailed reports of North and South Korean military capabilities come from the semiannual report by the US Army KMAG of June 15, 1950, various US and South Korean intelligence estimates of KPA strength, and North Korean documents captured by US forces when they advanced to Pyongyang and beyond in the fall of 1950. Millett, *War for Korea, 1950–1951*, 29–31, 51; James F. Schnabel, *Policy and Direction: The First Year—The United States Army in the Korean War* (Washington, DC: Office of the Chief of Military History, US Army, 1972), 36–40; Armstrong, *North Korean Revolution*, 235.

14.   Millett, *War for Korea, 1950–1951*, 30–37, 51, at 37; Chen, *China's Road to the Korean War*, 110–11; Zhihua Shen and Yafeng Xia, *A Misunderstood Friendship: Mao Zedong, Kim Il-sung, and Sino-North Korean Relations, 1949–1956* (New York: Columbia University Press, 2018), 30.

15.   Zhihua Shen and Danhui Li, *After Leaning to One Side: China and Its Allies in the Cold War* (Washington, DC, and Stanford, CA: Woodrow Wilson Center Press and Stanford University Press, 2011), 32–35, at 32; Goncharov, Lewis, and Xue, *Uncertain Partners*, 152–53.

16.   Millett, *War for Korea, 1950–1951*, 85–89.

17.   Schnabel, *Policy and Direction*, 70; Millett, *War for Korea, 1950–1951*, 27–28, 89–96.

18.   Millett, *War for Korea, 1950–1951*, 96–100, at 97 and 99.

19.   Millett, *War for Korea, 1950–1951*, 100–106.

20.   Doris M. Condit, *The Test of War, 1950–1953: History of the Office of the Secretary of Defense*, vol. II (Washington, DC: Historical Office, Office of the Secretary of Defense, 1988), 47–51; Millett, *War for Korea, 1950–1951*, 85–86, 110–21.

7. TRUMAN REVERSES POLICY

1.   Allan R. Millett, *The War for Korea, 1950–1951: They Came From the North* (Lawrence: University Press of Kansas, 2010), 37–45. Millett gives a detailed analysis of intelligence activities leading up to the outbreak of hostilities and why they failed to forecast the conflict.

2.   Millett, *War for Korea, 1950–1951*, 38–43, at 43.

3.   Associated Press, "Bradley, Johnson in Tokyo For Talks," *New York Times*, June 18, 1950; Associated Press, "Bradley and Johnson Hear MacArthur on Asian Security," *New York Times*, June 19, 1950; Lindesay Parrott, "Tokyo Conference Is Held In Secrecy," *New York Times*, June 20, 1950; Bruce Cumings, *The Origins of the Korean War*, vol. II, *The Roaring of the Cataract, 1947–1950* (Princeton, NJ: Princeton University Press, 1990), 500–507; Millett, *War for Korea, 1950–1951*, 21–22. A survey of the *New York Times*, *Washington Post*, and *Los Angeles Times* for June 18–24 shows no mention of heightened tension in Korea.

4.   Associated Press, "McCarthy Charges Peurifoy 'Pay-Off,'" *New York Times*, June 16, 1950; William S. White, "81 Files On Loyalty Held Inconclusive," *New York Times*, June 24, 1950; Rusk, quoted by Donovan, *Tumultuous Years*, 182.

5. Donovan, *Tumultuous Years*, 187–89; Hamby, *Man of the People*, 533.

6. Hamby, *Man of the People*, 533–35; Donovan, *Tumultuous Years*, 191–92.

7. Muccio to secretary of state, June 25, 1950 (2 cables), *Foreign Relations, 1950*, VII, 129, 132–33, at 133; Donovan, *Tumultuous Years*, 192–93; Hamby, *Man of the People*, 534–35.

8. Barbour to secretary of state, June 25, 1950, Dulles and Allison to secretary of state, June 25, 1950, Muccio to secretary of state, June 26,1950, *Foreign Relations, 1950*, VII, 139–43, at 139, 140, 142; Donovan, *Tumultuous Years*, 194.

9. Dean Acheson, *Present at the Creation: My Years in the State Department* (New York: W. W. Norton, 1969), 404; Donovan, *Tumultuous Years*, 194–96; ; Robert L. Beisner, *Dean Acheson: A Life in the Cold War* (New York: Oxford University Press, 2006), 338–40; James F. Schnabel and Robert J. Watson, *The Korean War, History of the Joint Chiefs of Staff—The Joint Chiefs of Staff and National Policy*, vol. III (2 parts) (Washington, DC: Office of Joint History, Office of the Chairman of the Joint Chiefs of Staff, 1998), part one, 31–32.

10. Resolution adopted by UN Security Council, June 25, 1950, Office of Intelligence Research, Intelligence Estimate on Korea, June 25, 1950, *Foreign Relations, 1950*, VII, 155–56, 148–54, at 155–56, 149, 154; Donovan, *Tumultuous Years*, 196–97.

11. Hamby, *Man of the People*, 535–36; Donovan, *Tumultuous Years*, 197–98, at 197; memorandum of General MacArthur on Formosa, June 14, 1950, *Foreign Relations, 1950*, VII, 161–65; Acheson, *Present at the Creation*, 405–6.

12. Schnabel and Watson, *Korean War*, 34–35; memorandum of Blair House conversation by Ambassador at Large Philip Jessup, June 25, 1950, *Foreign Relations, 1950*, VII, 157–61, at 158 and 160; Acheson, *Present at the Creation*, 406–7; Donovan, *Tumultuous Years*, 198–99, at 199.

13. Muccio to secretary of state, June 26, 1950, *Foreign Relations, 1950*, VII, 170; statement by the president on the violation of the 38th Parallel in Korea, June 26, 1950, *Public Papers of the President*, 1950 (Washington, DC: US Government Printing Office, 1965), 491–92.

14. Donovan, *Tumultuous Years*, 204–5.

15. Bohlen to Kennan, June 26, 1950, *Foreign Relations, 1950*, VII, 174–75; George F. Kennan, *Memoirs, 1950–1963*, vol. II (Boston: Little, Brown, 1972), 3–4.

16. Schnabel and Watson, *Korean War*, 36–38, at 37; Beisner, *Dean Acheson*, 342–43; Muccio to secretary of state, June 27, 1950 (received June 26), memorandum of Blair House conversation by Ambassador Jessup, June 26, 1950, *Foreign Relations, 1950*, VII, 173, 178–83.

17. Memorandum of Blair House conversation, June 26, 1950, *Foreign Relations, 1950*, VII, 180–83, at 183.

18. Memorandum of conversation by Ambassador Jessup, June 27, 1950, statement issued by the president, June 27, 1950, resolution adopted by UN Security Council, June 27, 1950, *Foreign Relations, 1950*, VII, 200–203, 211, at 202; Donovan, *Tumultuous Years*, 208–9, at 209.

19. Schnabel and Watson, *Korean War*, 42–44, at 43 and 44; Donovan, *Tumultuous Years*, 210–11.

20. Millett, *War for Korea, 1950–1951*, 122.

21. Schnabel and Watson, *Korean War*, 44–45, 47.

22. Millett, *War for Korea, 1950–1951*, 124.

23. Schnabel and Watson, *Korean War*, 45–47; minutes of NSC meeting, June 29, 1950, NSC meetings, President's Secretary's Files, Harry S Truman Library, Independence, Missouri; Donovan, *Tumultuous Years*, 211–12, at 212.

24. MacArthur to JCS and secretary of state, June 30, 1950, *Foreign Relations, 1950*, VII, 248–49, at 249.

25. Memorandum of teletype conference, June 30, 1950, *Foreign Relations, 1950*, VII, 250–53, at 251; Donovan, *Tumultuous Years*, 214–15.

26. Glenn D. Paige, *The Korean Decision: June 24–30, 1950* (New York: Free Press, 1968), 257–21; Donovan, *Tumultuous Years*, 216–18; Beisner, *Dean Acheson*, 345–47; Schnabel and Watson, *Korean War*, 49–52.

27. Millett, *War for Korea, 1950–1951*, 132–55, at 154.

28. Millett, *War for Korea, 1950–1951*, 135–38.

29. Donovan, *Tumultuous Years*, 249–53; Millett, *War for Korea*, 138–40, 151–67, 186–201. Despite the need for more troops, the president and his secretary of defense remained reluctant to order a broad mobilization. Congress extended authority for the draft by a year in June, and reservists were called up in late July and August. But no longer-term solution to the manpower shortage was developed until later in the fall. See Schnabel and Watson, *Korean War*, 77–79.

30. Millett, *War for Korea*, 215–31; Schnabel, *Policy and Direction*, 125–38.

31. Robert Dallek, *The Lost Peace: Leadership in a Time of Horror and Hope, 1945–1953* (New York: HarperCollins, 2010), 313.

32. Donovan, *Tumultuous Years*, 219–24, at 219.

8. DOUGLAS MacARTHUR GAMBLES AND WINS

1. Glenn D. Paige, *The Korean Decision (June 24–30, 1950)* (New York: Free Press, 1968), 221–26; Allan R. Millett, *The War for Korea, 1950–1951: They Came From the North* (Lawrence: University Press of Kansas, 2010), 123; Melvyn P. Leffler, *A Preponderance of Power: National Security, the Truman Administration, and the Cold War* (Stanford, CA: Stanford University Press, 1992), 363–64.

2. Leffler, *Preponderance of Power*, 363–64; Forrest C. Pogue, *George C. Marshall: Statesman, 1945–1959* (New York: Viking Press, 1987), 420–23, 436–39.

3. Quoted by Robert J. Donovan, *Tumultuous Years: The Presidency of Harry S Truman, 1949–1953* (New York: W. W. Norton, 1982), 219–21, at 220 and 221; Robert L. Beisner, *Dean Acheson: A Life in the Cold War* (New York: Oxford University Press, 2006), 347–49.

4. Dean Acheson, *Present at the Creation: My Years in the State Department* (New York: W. W. Norton, 1969), 414–15; Donovan, *Tumultuous Years*, 220–24; Alonzo L. Hamby, *Man of the People: A Life of Harry S. Truman* (New York: Oxford University Press, 1995), 539.

For a persuasive argument by a top constitutional specialist that Truman had no legal basis to act in this "police action," but that Congress accepted with minor complaint his fait accompli, see Louis Fisher, "The Korean War: On What Legal Basis Did Truman Act?" *American Journal of International Law* 89 (January 1995): 21–39.

5. Hamby, *Man of the People*, 248–60; Donovan, *Tumultuous Years*, 257–59, at 258 and 259.

6. D. Clayton James, *The Years of MacArthur*, vol. III, *Triumph and Disaster, 1945–1964* (Boston: Houghton Mifflin, 1985), 452–54, at 454; Donovan, *Tumultuous Years*, 259–60, at 260.

7. James, *Years of MacArthur*, III, 454–57, at 454 and 457; Donovan, *Tumultuous Years*, 260–62; Beisner, *Dean Acheson*, 350–51.

8. Memorandum of conversation by Troy L. Perkins, deputy director of the office of Chinese affairs, August 25, 1950, with note about Zhou Enlai letter of August 24, secretary of state to certain diplomatic offices including sections of MacArthur message to VFW, August 26, 1950, memorandum by Lucius D. Battle, special assistant to secretary of state, record of events of August 26, 1950, *Foreign Relations, 1950*, VI, 450–54; Donovan, *Tumultuous Years*, 259–63.

9. Battle memorandum on events of August 26, 1950, *Foreign Relations, 1950*, VI, 454–60; Millett, *War for Korea, 1950–1951*, 213–14; Donovan, *Tumultuous Years*, 263–65, at 264.

10. Donovan, *Tumultuous Years*, 265–67.

11. James F. Schnabel and Robert J. Watson, *The Korean War, History of the Joint Chiefs of Staff: The Joint Chiefs of Staff and National Policy*, vol. III (2 parts) (Washington, DC: Office of Joint History, Office of the Chairman of the Joint Chiefs of Staff, 1998), 73–74, at 73.

12. Schnabel and Watson, *Korean War*, 74–79; Condit, *Test of War*, 223–225.

13. Doris M. Condit, *The Test of War, 1950–1953—History of the Office of the Secretary of Defense*, vol. II (Washington, DC: Historical Office, Office of the Secretary of Defense, 1988), 225–27, at 227.

14. Condit, *The Test of War*, 227–30, at 228.

15. Condit, *The Test of War*, 230–33; NSC 68/2, September 30, 1950, *Foreign Relations, 1950*, I, 400.

16. Millett, *War for Korea, 1950–1951*, 207–10.

17. Robert Debs Heinl Jr., *Victory at High Tide: The Inchon-Seoul Campaign* (Washington, DC: Naval & Aviation Publishing Co. of America, 1979), 38–40; Millett, *War for Korea, 1950–1951*, 208–10.

18. Heinl, *Victory at High Tide*, 40; Millett, *War for Korea*, 208–12.

19. Heinl, *Victory at High Tide*, 40–42, at 41 and 42; Millett, *War for Korea, 1950–1951*, 210–12, at 210. For those not familiar with the history of the French and Indian War, British General James Wolfe defeated his French counterpart, the Marquis de Montcalm, in this critical battle of 1759, which determined the outcome of the war and ultimately ended French rule in what became British Canada.

20. Heinl, *Victory at High Tide*, 41.

21. Heinl, *Victory at High Tide*, 10–11, at 11.

22. James, *Years of MacArthur*, III, 355–65, 371–74.

23. James, *Years of MacArthur*, III, 366–67.

24. Millett, *War for Korea, 1950–1951*, 68–70, at 69; James, *Years of MacArthur*, III, 61–62.

25. Millett, *War for Korea, 1950–1951*, 38–44.

26. James, *Years of MacArthur*, III, 355–56, 378–79; Millett, *War for Korea, 1950–1951*, 68.

27. James, *Years of MacArthur*, III, 359–60, 458–60, at 460; Millett, *War for Korea, 1950–1951*, 67–68, 167–68.

28. James, *Years of MacArthur*, III, 370.

29. James, *Years of MacArthur*, III, 370–71, at 371.

30. Heinl, *Victory at High Tide*, 17–24, 35–38, 55–56; Millett, *War for Korea, 1950–1951*, 244–46. Most of the South Korean conscripts were refugees who were rounded up by the US military police and sent to Japan to join the Seventh Division wearing the shirts, shorts, and sandals they had on when pressed into military service.

31. Heinl, *Victory at High Tide*, 52, 69; Millett, *War for Korea, 1950–1951*, 242, 248–49; James, *Years of MacArthur*, III, 471–79; Chen Jian, *China's Road to the Korean War: The Making of the Sino-American Confrontation* (New York: Columbia University Press, 1994), 147–49.

32. James, *Years of MacArthur*, III, 473–75.

33. Heinl, *Victory at High Tide*, 73–77, 87–89; Millett, *War for Korea, 1950–1951*, 248–49; James, *Years of MacArthur*, III, 474–75.

34. Heinl, *Victory at High Tide*, 80–82, 87–120; Millett, *War for Korea, 1950–1951*, 249–51.

35. Heinl, *Victory at High Tide*, 70–76, 102.

36. Heinl, *Victory at High Tide*, 132–41, 149–50, 225–58; James, *Years of MacArthur*, III, 481–85; Millett, *War for Korea, 1950–1951*, 250–56; J. Lawton Collins, *War in Peacetime: The History and Lessons of Korea* (Boston: Houghton Mifflin, 1969), 135–42, at 141–42.

37. Allison to Rusk, July 1, 1950, *Foreign Relations, 1950*, VII, 272.

38. Policy Planning Staff draft memorandum, July 22, 1950, *Foreign Relations, 1950*, VII, 449–54; Acheson to Embassy of Korea, July 14, 1950, *Foreign Relations, VII*, 387; Truman news conference, July 13, 1950, *Public Papers of the President, 1950*, 523.

39. Chen, *China's Road to the Korean War*, 125–37; Shen Zhihua, *Mao, Stalin and the Korean War: Trilateral Communist Relations in the 1950s* (London: Routledge, 2012), 138–42; Bohlen remarks in Minutes of Meeting of Representatives of France, the United Kingdom and the United States, August 4, 1950, *Foreign Relations, 1950*, VI, 420; Rusk to Douglas, August 13, 1950, *Foreign Relations, 1950*, VI, 432–33; Michael H. Hunt, "Beijing and the Korean Crisis, June 1950–June 1951," *Political Science Quarterly* 107 (Fall 1992): 458–59; Hao Yufan and Zhai Zhihai, "China's Decision to Enter the Korean War," *China Quarterly* 121 (March 1990): 100–102; Beisner, *Dean Acheson*, 395–98.

40. James S. Lay Jr. to NSC, July 17, 1950, draft memorandum from Defense Department, July 31, 1950, draft memorandum by John M. Allison and John K. Emmerson, Office of Northeast Asian Affairs, State Department, *Foreign Relations, 1950*, VII, 410, 506–7, 620–23, at 506 and 622.

41. Schnabel and Watson, *Korean War*, 95–98, 102; Leffler, *Preponderance of Power*, 376–77; NSC 81/1, September 9, 1950, approved by the president on September 11, *Foreign Relations, 1950*, VII, 712–21, at 716; Beisner, *Dean Acheson*, 398–99.

42. Donovan, *Tumultuous Years*, 269–77, at 271; James, *Years of MacArthur*, III, 484–87; Millett, *War for Korea, 1950–1951*, 274–75.

43. Schnabel and Watson, *Korean War*, 99–100; Marshall to Truman, September 27, 1950, *Foreign Relations, 1950*, VII, 792–93.

44. Marshall to MacArthur, September 29, 1950, *Foreign Relations, 1950*, VII, 826; Forrest C. Pogue, *George C. Marshall: Statesman 1945–1959* (New York: Viking Press, 1987), 457; Donovan, *Tumultuous Years*, 276; Millett, *War for Korea, 1950–1951*, 276–77; Beisner, *Dean Acheson*, 399–401.

9. MAO ZEDONG INTERVENES MASSIVELY

1. John K. Fairbank, "The Reunification of China," 14–23 (at 14), and Frederick C. Teiwes, "Establishment and Consolidation of the New Regime," 67–69, both in *The People's Republic, Part I: The Emergence of Revolutionary China, 1949–1965—Volume 14, The Cambridge History of China*, ed. Roderick MacFarquhar and John K. Fairbank (Cambridge: Cambridge University Press, 1987).

2. Teiwes, "Establishment and Consolidation," 76–78; Mao Zedong, "Don't Hit Out in All Directions," June 6, 1950, in *Selected Works of Mao Tse-Tung* (Beijing: Foreign Languages Press, 1977), V, 35.

3. Fairbank, "Reunification of China," 22, 78–85; Mao, *Selected Works*, V, 29.

4. Teiwes, "Establishment and Consolidation," 73–76.

5. Chen Jian, *China's Road to the Korean War: The Making of a Sino-American Confrontation* (New York: Columbia University Press, 1994), 92–94.

6. Ibid., 94–96, at 96.

7. Teiwes, "Establishment and Consolidation," 83–92; Chen, *China's Road to the Korean War*, 137–41.

8. Chen Jian, "Reorienting the Cold War: The Implications of China's Early Cold War Experience, Taking Korea as a Central Test Case," in *The Cold War in East Asia, 1945–1991*, ed. Tsuyoshi Hasegawa (Washington, DC, and Stanford, CA: Woodrow Wilson Center Press and Stanford University Press, 2011), 83–84, 89–90; Zhihua Shen and Yafeng Xia, "Leadership Transfer in the Asian Revolution: Mao Zedong and the Asian Cominform," *Cold War History* 14 (May 2014): 195–213.

9. Mao, "Carry the Revolution Through to the End," December 30, 1948, in *Selected Works*, IV, 306; Chen, *China's Road to the Korean War*, 93–102, at 101.

10. Chen, *China's Road to the Korean War*, 100–102.

11. Ibid., 102–6; Doris M. Condit, *The Test of War, 1950–1953—History of the Office of the Secretary of Defense*, vol. II (Washington, DC: Historical Office, Office of the Secretary of Defense, 1988), 205–7; Melvyn P. Leffler, *A Preponderance of Power: National Security, the Truman Administration, and the Cold War* (Stanford, CA: Stanford University Press, 1992), 338–41, 346, 353–55.

12. Chen, *China's Road to the Korean War*, 106–11; Bruce Cumings, *The Origins of the Korean War*, vol. II, *The Roaring of the Cataract, 1947–1950* (Princeton, NJ: Princeton

University Press, 1990), 358–64; Charles K. Armstrong, *The North Korean Revolution, 1945–1950* (Ithaca, NY: Cornell University Press, 2003), 234; Chen, "Reorienting the Cold War," 82.

13. Chen, *China's Road to the Korean War*, 106, 111–12; Chen, "Reorienting the Cold War," 86–87; Shen Zhuhua and Danhui Li, *After Leaning to One Side: China and Its Allies in the Cold War* (Washington, DC, and Stanford, CA: Woodrow Wilson Center Press and Stanford University Press, 2011), 29–33.

14. Chen, *China's Road to the Korean War*, 94.

15. Ibid., 131.

16. Shu Guang Zhang, *Mao's Military Romanticism: China and the Korean War, 1950–1953* (Lawrence: University Press of Kansas, 1995), 58–59; Shen and Li, *After Leaning to One Side*, 34–35; Chen, *China's Road to the Korean War*, 135–37.

17. Zhihua Shen and Yafeng Xia, *Mao and the Sino-Soviet Partnership, 1945–1959: A New History* (Lanham, MD: Lexington Books, 2015), 69–73; Hasegawa, *Cold War in East Asia*, 82–84; Chen, *China's Road to the Korean War*, 128–41.

18. Shen and Li, *After Leaning to One Side*, 35; Chen, *China's Road to the Korean War*, 142–43.

19. Chen, *China's Road to the Korean War*, 143–45, at 143; Alan R. Millett, *The War for Korea, 1950–1951: They Came from the North* (Lawrence: University Press of Kansas, 2010), 234–35; Zhang, *Mao's Military Romanticism*, 62–63.

20. Chen, *China's Road to the Korean War*, 147–48, at 148; Zhang, *Mao's Military Romanticism*, 72–73.

21. Shen and Xia, *Mao and the Sino-Soviet Partnership*, 73–76; Chen, *China's Road to the Korean War*, 148–151, quotations at 150; Zhang, *Mao's Military Romanticism*, 64–67, 73; Zhou Enlai, *Zhou Enlai Jun Shi Wen Xuan* [Selected Military Works of Zhou Enlai] (Beijing: People's Press, 1997), vol. 4, 44–45.

22. Chen, *China's Road to the Korean War*, 152–54.

23. Shen and Xia, *Mao and the Sino-Soviet Partnership*, 75–76; Shen and Li, *After Leaning to One Side*, 37–38; Chen, *China's Road to the Korean War*, 155–57.

24. Alexander V. Pantsov with Steven I. Levine, *Mao: The Real Story* (New York: Simon & Schuster, 2012), 12–17.

25. Ibid., 17–20, at 20.

26. Ibid., *Mao*, 28–40, at 38; Jung Chang and Jon Halliday, *Mao: The Unknown Story* (New York: Alfred A. Knopf, 2005), 10–14.

27. Pantsov and Levine, *Mao*, 31–52; Edgar Snow, *Red Star over China* (London: Victor Gollancz, 1937), 145–46, at 146.

28. Pantsov and Levine, *Mao*, 56–80; Snow, *Red Star*, 148–52.

29. Pantsov and Levine, *Mao*, 90–102, at 94; Snow, *Red Star*, 154–55; Chang and Halliday, *Mao*, 18–27.

30. Pantsov and Levine, *Mao*, 119–85; Chang and Halliday, *Mao*, 27–46.

31. Pantsov and Levine, *Mao*, 186–288; Gao Wenqian, *Zhou Enlai: The Last Perfect Revolutionary* (New York: PublicAffairs, 2007), 69–83; Chang and Halliday, *Mao*, 49–167.

32. Pantsov and Levine, *Mao*, 283–342; MacFarquhar and Fairbank, *People's Republic*, 59–60; Chang and Halliday, *Mao*, 184–269.

33. Pantsov and Levine, *Mao*, 345–48; Odd Arne Westad, *Decisive Encounters: The Chinese Civil War, 1946–1950* (Stanford, CA: Stanford University Press, 2003), 28–66, at 60; Chang and Halliday, *Mao*, 281–92.

34. Westad, *Decisive Encounters*, 69–199, at 198–99.

35. Mao to Stalin, January 13, 1949 in Decisive *Encounters*, by Westad, 215–18, at 218.

36. Westad, *Decisive Encounters*, 236–55; Chang and Halliday, *Mao*, 317322; Pantsov and Levine, *Mao*, 351–59.

37. Pantsov and Levine, *Mao*, 4, 326–30, 364–65, at 364; Chang and Halliday, *Mao*, 6–7, 13–14, 23–25, 148–50, 194–97, 332–33, at 333.

38. Chang and Halliday, *Mao*, 329–33, at 329, 331, 333.

39. Pantsov and Levine, *Mao*, 363–70.

40. Ibid., 367.

41. MacFarquhar and Fairbank, *People's Republic*, 59–63, at 61.

42. Shen and Li, *After Leaning to One Side*, 38; Chen, *China's Road to the Korean War*, 158–63.

43. Stalin's instructions to Kim Il-sung are summarized in his cable to Mao and Zhou Enlai, October 1, 1950, A. I. Matveev (a pseudonym for Zakharov) to Stalin, September 27, 1950, in "The Korean Conflict, 1950–1953: The Most Mysterious War of the 20th Century—Based on Secret Soviet Archives," by Evgeniy Bajanov and Natalia Bajanova, unpublished typescript, n.d., copy in archives of North Korea International Documentation Project, Woodrow Wilson International Center for Scholars, 72–74, 97–98; Chen, *China's Road to the Korean War*, 160–61; Shen and Li, *After Leaning to One Side*, 38; Zhihua Shen and Yafeng Xia, *A Misunderstood Friendship: Mao Zedong, Kim Il-sung, and Sino-North Korean Relations, 1949–1956* (New York: Columbia University Press, 2018), 35–42.

44. Chen, *China's Road to the* Korean *War*, 161–62; Shen and Li, *After Leaning to One Side*, 38–39, at 38.

45. Kathryn Weathersby, "The Soviet Role in the Early Phase of the Korean War: New Documentary Evidence," *Journal of American–East Asian Relations* 2 (Winter 1993): 455–56, at 456; Shen and Li, *After Leaning to One Side*, 39; Shen and Xia, *Mao and the Sino-Soviet* Partnership, 77–78; Stalin to Mao, October 1, 1950, in "Korean Conflict," by Bajanov and Bajanova, 97–98.

46. Shen Zhihua, "The Discrepancy Between the Russian and Chinese Versions of Mao's 2 October 1950 Message to Stalin on Chinese Entry into the Korean War: A Chinese Scholar's Reply," *CWIHP Bulletin*, nos. 8–9 (Winter 1996–97): 237–40; Shen and Li, *After Leaning to One Side*, 39.

47. Ibid., 238–39, at 239; Roshchin to Stalin, October 3, 1950, in "Korean Conflict," by Bajanov and Bajanova, 98–100.

48. Lin Biao, citing his illness, refused Mao's proposal that he serve as the commander of the Chinese volunteers in Korea. Zhang, *Mao's Military Romanticism*, 80–81; Shen and Li, *After Leaning to One Side*, 40.

49. Zhang, *Mao's Military Romanticism*, 81; Sulmaan Wasif Khan, *Haunted by Chaos: China's Grand Strategy from Mao Zedong to Xi Jinping* (Cambridge, MA: Harvard University Press, 2018), 57–59.

50. Zhang, *Mao's Military Romanticism*, 82; Shen and Li, *After Leaning to One Side*, 40–42.

51. Shen and Li, *After Leaning to One Side*, 41–42; Shen and Xia, *Mao and the Sino-Soviet Partnership*, 78; Stalin summarized this telegram to Mao and the reply in Stalin to Kim Il-sung, October 8, 1950, in "Korean Conflict," by Bajanov and Bajanova, 100–102.

52. Shen and Li, *After Leaning to One Side*, 42–43; Zhang, *Mao's Military Romanticism*, 83; Chen, *China's Road to the Korean War*, 196–200.

53. Shen and Li, *After Leaning to One Side*, 43; Chen, *China's Road to the Korean War*, 200–202, at 202; Zhang, *Mao's Military Romanticism*, 83–84; Khan, *Haunted by Chaos*, 59–61.

54. Shen and Li, *After Leaning to One Side*, 44; Zhang, *Mao's Military Romanticism*, 94; Mao Zedong, *Mao Zedong Jun Shi Wen Ji* [*Military Works of Mao Zedong*] (Beijing: Military Science Press and Zhong Yang Wen Xian Press, 1993), vol. 6, 108.

55. Stalin to Kim Il-sung, October 12 & 13, 1950, Bajanov and Bajanova, "The Korean Conflict," 102–103 with quotations; Shen and Li, *After Leaning to One Side*, 45.

56. Shen and Li, *After Leaning to One Side*, 45–46, quotation at 46; Shen and Xia, *Mao and the Sino-Soviet* Partnership, 78–81; Chen, *China's Road to the Korean War*, 207–209.

57. Yeh Wen-hain used the term "perpetually enigmatic" to describe Mao's behavior in the Korean War and later in comments at the conference "New Sources and New Perspectives on China's Frontiers during the Cold War," August 4, 2014, Woodrow Wilson International Center for Scholars.

10. PENG DEHUAI AND MATTHEW RIDGWAY FIGHT TO A STALEMATE

1. Allan R. Millett, *The War for Korea, 1950–1951: They Came From the North* (Lawrence: University Press of Kansas, 2010), 300–302, 317–19, 334; Shu Guang Zhang, *Mao's Military Romanticism: China and the Korean War, 1950–1953* (Lawrence: University Press of Kansas, 1995), 86–94.

2. Millett, *War for Korea, 1950–1951*, 300–302, 312–13; Zhang, *Mao's Military Romanticism*, 89–92.

3. Zhang, *Mao's Military Romanticism*, 95–107; Millett, *War for Korea, 1950–1951*, 300–305, at 301; Clay Blair, *The Forgotten War: America in Korea 1950–1953* (Annapolis, MD: Naval Institute Press, 2003), 375–402; Zhihua Shen and Yafeng Xia, *A Misunderstood Friendship: Mao Zedong, Kim Il-sung, and Sino-North Korean Relations, 1949–1956* (New York: Columbia University Press, 2018), 45–67.

4. Millett, *War for Korea, 1950–1951*, 306–10.

5. James F. Schnabel, *Policy and Direction: The First Year—The United States Army in the Korean War* (Washington, DC: Office of the Chief of Military History, US Army, 1972), 266, 272; Millett, *War for Korea, 1950–1951*, 306.

6. NIE-2, "Chinese Communist Intervention in Korea," November 8, 1950, *Foreign Relations, 1950*, VII, 1101–1106; Millett, *War for Korea, 1950–1951*, 312–13.

7. Millett, *War for Korea, 1950–1951*, 313–15, at 314; Robert L. Beisner, *Dean Acheson: A Life in the Cold War* (New York: Oxford University Press, 2006), 406–7.

8. Schnabel, *Policy and Direction*, 257–82, 300–304; Zhang, *Mao's Military Romanticism*, 107–19; Millet, *War for Korea, 1950–1951*, 334–57, 373; Joseph C. Goulden, *Korea: The Untold Story of the War* (New York: Times Books, 1982), 311–81, at 317. For a dramatic account of the risky strategy developed by General Douglas MacArthur and his protégé, Major General Edward Almond, that led to the First Marine Division being trapped by a large Chinese force at Chosin Reservoir and how the marines under the inspired leadership of Major General Oliver Prince Smith fought their way out, see Hampton Sides, *On Desperate Ground: The Marines at the Reservoir—The Korean War's Greatest Battle* (New York: Doubleday, 2018).

9. Schnabel, *Policy and Direction*, 305–10; Millett, *War for Korea, 1950–1951*, 356–57, 372–73; Blair, *Forgotten War*, 436–556.

10. Memorandum of National Security Council meeting, November 28, 1950, *Foreign Relations, 1950*, VII, 1242–249; memorandum of meeting of Defense and State Department officials, December 1, 1950, *Foreign Relations, 1950*, VII, 1276–81; CIA memorandum, "Soviet Intentions in the Current Situation," December 2, 1950, *Foreign Relations, 1950*, VII, 1308–10, at 1310 (this memorandum was issued as NIE-11 on December 5, 1950); memorandum of Acheson-Franks conversation, December 4, 1950, *Foreign Relations, 1950*, VII, 1374–77; memorandum of Acheson meeting with senior staff, December 5, 1950, *Foreign Relations, 1950*, VII, 1382–86; Millett, *War for Korea, 1950–1951*, 357–61; Beisner, *Dean Acheson*, 410–16.

11. Beisner, *Dean Acheson*, 417–419; minutes of meeting of Truman and Attlee, December 4, 1950, *Foreign Relations, 1950*, VII, 1361–74, at 1366, 1367, and 1395.

12. Lucius D. Battle, memorandum of discussion at British Embassy dinner on December 6, 1950, December 7, 1950, *Foreign Relations, 1950*, VII, 1430–32, at 1431; Beisner, *Dean Acheson*, 420–21; Robert J. Donovan, *Tumultuous Years: The Presidency of Harry S Truman, 1949–1953* (New York: W. W. Norton, 1982), 316–18; Millett, *War for Korea, 1950–1951*, 361–364.

13. See US Central Intelligence Agency, "President's Daily Report, December 7, 1950: 'Chou-En-lai's Views on World War,'" https://www.cia.gov/centerforthestudyof intelligence/foiaelectronicreadingroom/historicalcollections/, at koreanwarcollection /daily reports/1950/1950-12-7.pdf; Truman diary entry, December 9, 1950, PSF, Truman Library.

14. Statement of Zhou Enlai, December 22, 1950, in Austen to Acheson, December 24, 1950, *Foreign Relations, 1950*, VII, 1594–98, at 1597; Millett, *War for Korea, 1950–1951*, 364–65.

15. Millett, *War for Korea, 1950–1951*, 365; Doris M. Condit, *The Test of War, 1950–1953—History of the Office of the Secretary of Defense*, vol. II (Washington, DC: Historical Office, Office of the Secretary of Defense, 1988), 90–93; JCS to CICFE, December 29, 1950, *Foreign Relations, 1950*, VII, 1625–26.

16. Schnabel, *Policy and Direction*, 316–26; D. Clayton James, *The Years of MacArthur: Triumph and Disaster, 1945–1964*, vol. III (Boston: Houghton Mifflin, 1985), 550–56; Beisner, *Dean Acheson*, 421–22.

17. Peng Dehuai, *Memoirs of a Chinese Marshal: The Autobiograhical Notes of Peng Dehuai (1898–1974)*, trans. Zheng Longpu (Beijing: Foreign Languages Press, 1984), 1–5, 13–82; Jurgen Domes, *Peng Te-huai: The Man and the Image* (Stanford, CA: Stanford University Press, 1985), 9–17. Peng's *Memoirs* are based on notes written when he was under detention and in response to interrogations during the Cultural Revolution, 1966–74.

18. Peng, *Memoirs*, 5–6, 95–406 passim; Domes, *Peng Te-huai*, 18–37.

19. Domes, *Peng Te-huai*, 37–42; Barbara Barnouin and Yu Changgen, *Zhou Enlai: A Political Life* (Hong Kong: Chinese University of Hong Kong, 2006), 91–96; Frederick C. Teiwes, "Peng Dehuai and Mao Zedong," *Australian Journal of Chinese Affairs*, no. 16 (July 1986): 85–86; Peng, *Memoirs*, 407–47.

20. Domes, *Peng Te-huai*, 42–46; Barnouin and Yu, *Zhou Enlai*, 109–12; Peng, *Memoirs*, 448–71.

21. Domes, *Peng Te-huaii*, 46–47.

22. Teiwes, "Peng and Mao," 81–84; Peng, *Memoirs*, 7–8, 48–49, 226–31; Domes, *Peng Te-huai*, 47–48.

23. Peng, *Memoirs*, 286–302, 415–25; Domes, *Peng Te-huai*, 31–35, 73; Teiwes, "Peng and Mao," 84.

24. Teiwes, "Peng and Mao," 81, 84.

25. Peng, *Memoirs*, 479–84; Teiwes, "Peng and Mao," 84, 86; Barnouin and Yu, *Zhou Enlai*, 147–48; Domes, *Peng Te-huai*, 54–64.

26. Teiwes, "Peng and Mao," 89–92; Peng, *Memoirs*, 9–10, 485–520; Domes, *Peng Te-huai*, 77–124 passim.

27. Matthew B. Ridgway, *Soldier: The Memoirs of Matthew B. Ridgway* (Westport, CT: Greenwood Press, 1974), 19–28; George C. Mitchell, *Matthew B. Ridgway: Soldier, Statesman, Scholar, Citizen* (Mechanicsburg, PA: Stackpole, 2002), 1–10.

28. Mitchell, *Ridgway*, 11–36; Ridgway, *Soldier*, 45–46; Clay Blair, *Ridgway's Paratroopers: The American Airborne in World War II* (New York: Dial Press, 1985), 4–10, at 10.

29. Blair, *Ridgway's Paratroopers*, 5, 21, 80, at 5; Ridgway, *Soldier*, 53.

30. Blair, *Ridgway's Paratroopers*, 32–50, 70, at 32; Ridgway, *Soldier*, 53–54.

31. Blair, *Ridgway's Paratroopers*, 57–102; Ridgway, *Soldier*, 68–73.

32. Blair, *Ridgway's Paratroopers*, 102–11, at 110 and 111; Ridgway, *Soldier*, 73–80, at 74.

33. Blair, *Ridgway's Paratroopers*, 111–15.

34. Ibid., 115–43.

35. Ibid., 143–60, at 143; Ridgway, *Soldier*, 80–86, 93–98.

36. Blair, *Ridgway's Paratroopers*, 160–68, at 162; Ridgway, *Soldier*, 87–92.

37. Blair, *Ridgway's Paratroopers*, 177–209; Ridgway, *Soldier*, 100–101.

38. Kroos served with Ridgway throughout the Normandy operation, and after that the general encouraged him to leave for a combat unit so he could be promoted and join the fighting. In September 1944, his glider was shot down in the attack on Arnhem,

and Kroos spent the rest of the war in a German prisoner of war camp. Blair, *Ridgway's Paratroopers*, 196, 331, at 196.

39. Ibid., 213–97, at 294 and 295; Ridgway, *Soldier*, 102–4.

40. The Distinguished Service Cross is the second-highest award that can be given to a member of the US Army for bravery in combat. Blair, *Ridgway's Paratroopers*, 296–97.

41. Ibid., 298–301, 317–45.

42. Ibid., 345; Max Hastings, *Armageddon: The Battle for Germany, 1944–1945* (New York: Alfred A. Knopf, 2004), 36.

43. Blair, *Ridgway's Paratroopers*, 353–68, at 366; Ridgway, *Soldier*, 111–16; Hastings, *Armageddon*, 197–220.

44. Blair, *Ridgway's Paratroopers*, 368–406; Ridgway, *Soldier*, 116–22; Hastings, *Armageddon*, 220–29, at 225.

45. Blair, *Ridgway's Paratroopers*, 400–404, at 404; Ridgway, *Soldier*, 117–22, at 121.

46. Blair, *Ridgway's Paratroopers*, 409–25, at 416; Hastings, *Armageddon*, 228–37.

47. Blair, *Ridgway's Paratroopers*, 443–87, at 485 and 486; Hastings, *Armageddon*, 344–80, 418–19.

48. Blair, *Ridgway's Paratroopers*, 488–95, at 495; Hastings, *Armageddon*, 420–37.

49. Schnabel, *Policy and Direction*, 308–10, 315–25; Zhang, *Mao's Military Romanticism*, 120–32; Millett, *War for Korea, 1950–1951*, 380–89.

50. Schnabel, *Policy and Direction*, 306–8, 326–29; Millett, *War for Korea, 1950–1951*, 389–92; Zhang, *Mao's Military Romanticism*, 136–40; Max Hastings, *The Korean War* (New York: Simon & Schuster, 1987), 189–90; Blair, *Forgotten War*, 570–668.

51. Schnabel, *Policy and Direction*, 329–30, Marshall quotation at 330; James F. Schnabel and Robert J. Watson, *The Korean War, History of the Joint Chiefs of Staff: The Joint Chiefs of Staff and National Policy*, vol. III (2 parts) (Washington, DC: Office of Joint History, Office of the Chairman of the Joint Chiefs of Staff, 1998), 439–40; Beisner, *Dean Acheson*, 422–23; James, *Years of MacArthur*, III, 559.

52. Millett, *War for Korea, 1950–1951*, 399–416; Schnabel, *Policy and Direction*, 336–40; Zhang, *Mao's Military Romanticism*, 140–44.

53. James, *Years of MacArthur*, III, 582–85; Millett, *War for Korea, 1950–1951*, 414–15.

54. James, *Years of MacArthur*, III, 585–604; Millett, *War for Korea, 1950–1951*, 420–26; Beisner, *Dean Acheson*, 426–30; for a vivid description of the storm of criticism that met Truman's decision and the triumphal return of MacArthur to the United States and his speech before a joint session of Congress on April 19, see Donovan, *Tumultuous Years*, 355–62, at 361.

55. Millett, *War for Korea, 1950–1951*, 426–48; Zhang, *Mao's Military Romanticism*, 146–52.

56. Quoted by Scott S. Smith, "Gen. Matthew Ridgway Stopped the Communists Cold in Korea," *Investor's Business Daily*, April 23, 2016.

57. Sheila Miyoshi Jager, *Brothers at War: The Unending Conflict in Korea* (New York: W. W. Norton, 2013), 190–92; Millett, *War for Korea, 1950–1951*, 448–55; Hastings, *Korean War*, 228–31.

58. Dean Acheson, *Present at the Creation: My Years in the State Department* (New York: W. W. Norton, 1969), 529–33; George F. Kennan, *Memoirs, 1950–1963*, vol. II, (Boston:

Little, Brown, 1972), 35–37; Beisner, *Dean Acheson*, 436–437; Millett, *War for Korea, 1950–1951*, 454–455.

59. For exchanges among the communist leaders, see Evgeniy Bajanov and Natalia Bajanova, "The Korean Conflict, 1950–1953: The Most Mysterious War of the 20th Century—Based on Secret Soviet Archives," unpublished typescript, n.d., copy in archives of North Korea International Documentation Project, Woodrow Wilson International Center for Scholars, 132–140; Acheson, *Present at the Creation*, 533–34; Millett, *War for Korea, 1950–1951*, 455–57; Jager, *Brothers at War*, 192–95.

60. Jager, *Brothers at War*, 195–200; Schnabel and Watson, *Korean War*, III, part two, 251–53.

61. The US charges were basically proven to be true, while those of the communists were found to be totally falsified. Jager, *Brothers at War*, 200–257; Schnabel and Watson, *Korean War*, III, part two, 16–180 passim; Beisner, *Dean Acheson*, 437–41; Shen and Xia, *Misunderstood Friendship*, 67–4.

62. Robert Dallek, *The Lost Peace: Leadership in a Time of Horror and Hope, 1945–1953* (New York: HarperCollins, 2010), 346–55; Jager, *Brothers at War*, 268–76; Kathryn Weathersby, "Stalin, Mao, and the End of the Korean War," in *Brothers in Arms: The Rise and Fall of the Sino-Soviet Alliance, 1945–1963*, ed. Odd Arne Westad (Washington, DC, and Stanford, CA: Woodrow Wilson Center Press and Stanford University Press, 1998), 107–10; USSR Council of Ministers, Resolution with draft letters to Mao Zedong, Kim Il-sung, and the Soviet delegation to the UN, March 19, 1953, *CWIHP Bulletin*, nos. 6–7 (Winter 1995): 80.

63. Schnabel and Watson, *Korean War*, III, part two, 225–60; Jager, *Brothers at War*, 278–286; Dallek, *Lost Peace*, 350–53.

64. On Kim's purges, see Dae-Sook Suh, *Kim Il Sung: The North Korean Leader* (New York: Columbia University Press, 1988), 126–36; the most thorough compilation of casualties is in Wikipedia, which uses US, South Korean, Chinese, and Soviet sources. The figures for civilian casualties are estimates. See en.wikipedia.org/wiki/Korean_War.

65. Jager, *Brothers at War*, 311–12: Sulmaan Wasif Khan, *Haunted by Chaos: China's Grand Strategy from Mao Zedong to Xi Jinping* (Cambridge, MA: Harvard University Press, 2018), 60–62; Shen and Xia, *Misunderstood Friendship*, 75–76.

66. Henry Kissinger, *On China* (New York: Penguin Press, 2011), 147.

67. Craig Whitlock, "Hagel Visit to South Korea," *Washington Post*, October 2, 2013.

68. The literature on the Korean War is huge and diverse. For a well-written account of the war between the two Koreas up to the present, see Jager, *Brothers at War*; for the best coverage of all sides of military activity, see Millett, *War for Korea, 1950–1951*, with a final volume covering 1952–53; for an overall history of the war from a US perspective, see Goulden, *Korea*; for Mao's strategy, see Zhang, *Mao's Military Romanticism*. And for the interactions between Stalin, Mao, and Kim Il-sung, see Shen Zhihua, *Mao, Stalin and the Korean War: Trilateral Communist Relations in the 1950* (New York: Routledge, 2012); Zhihua Shen and Danhui Li, *After Leaning to One Side: China and Its Allies in the Cold War* (Washington, DC, and Stanford, CA: Woodrow Wilson Center Press and Stanford University Press, 2011); Zhihua Shen and Yafeng Xia, *Mao and the Sino-Soviet Partnership, 1945–1959: A New History* (Lanham, MD: Lexington Books, 2015); and Shen and Xia, *Misunderstood Friendship*.

11. GEORGE C. MARSHALL AND ROBERT LOVETT
GUIDE A US BUILDUP

1. Gen. Walter Bedell Smith, director of the CIA, to the president, November 1, 1950, John P. Davies, memorandum on courses of action in Korea, November 17, 1950, Philip Jessup, memorandum on meeting at Pentagon, November 21, 1950, *Foreign Relations, 1950*, VII, 1025–26, 1178–83, 1204–8; Alan R. Millett, *The War for Korea, 1950–1951: They Came from the North* (Lawrence: University Press of Kansas, 2010), 313–15; Robert L. Beisner, *Dean Acheson: A Life in the Cold War* (New York: Oxford University Press, 2006), 409–10.

2. Millett, *War for Korea, 1950–1951*, 334–55.

3. Forrest C. Pogue, *George C. Marshall: Education of a General, 1880–1939* (New York: Viking Press, 1963), 19–69.

4. Pogue, *Marshall: Education*, 70–269 passim, at 268.

5. Pogue, *Marshall: Education*, 270–307.

6. Pogue, *Marshall: Education*, 307–33.

7. Frank A. Settle, *General George C. Marshall and the Atomic Bomb* (Santa Barbara, CA: Praeger, 2016), 4–5, at 4, 5; Forrest C. Pogue, *George C. Marshall: Ordeal and Hope, 1939–1942* (New York: Viking Press, 1966), 13–26.

8. Pogue, *Marshall: Ordeal*, 9–150 passim, at 11.

9. Pogue, *Marshall: Ordeal*, 261–24, at 408; D. K. R. Crosswell, *Beetle: The Life of General Walter Bedell Smith* (Lexington: University Press of Kentucky, 2012), 223–41.

10. Pogue, *Marshall: Ordeal*, 290–98; Walter Isaacson and Evan Thomas, *The Wise Men: Six Friends and the World They Made* (New York: Simon & Schuster, 2013), 194–207.

11. Pogue, *George C. Marshall: Statesman, 1945–1959* (New York: Viking Press, 1987), 149–50, at 150; Isaacson and Thomas, *Wise Men*, 60–64, 90–93, quotation at 64.

12. Isaacson and Thomas, *Wise Men*, 109–17, at 112.

13. Isaacson and Thomas, *Wise Men*, 183–207, at 194 and 195; Herman S. Wolk, "Lovett," *Air Force Magazine*, September 2006, 91–94; Pogue, *Marshall: Statesman*, 149–50.

14. Isaacson and Thomas, *Wise Men*, 337–38.

15. Pogue, *Marshall: Statesman*, 149–415 passim, quotations at 150; Isaacson and Thomas, *Wise Men*, 414–68 passim, at 418.

16. Philip Jessup, memorandum of conversation, December 1, 1950, *Foreign Relations, 1950*, VII, 1276–81, at 1276, 1277, 1279, 1281; Beisner, *Dean Acheson*, 410–12. The CIA estimate mentioned by General Smith was submitted on December 5, 1950, as NIE 11, "Soviet Intentions in the Current Situation," *Foreign Relations, 1950*, VII, 1308–10.

17. MacArthur to Joint Chiefs of Staff, December 3, 1950, Philip Jessup, memorandum of conversation, December 3, 1950, Lucius Battle, memorandum of secretary's staff meeting, December 4, 1950, *Foreign Relations, 1950*, VII, 1320–22, 1323–34, 1345–47, at 1321, 1326, 1346–47; Beisner, *Dean Acheson*, 412–16. George Kennan had been called back from his leave at the Institute for Advanced Study to advise Acheson on likely Soviet actions. For a discussion of the drafting and contents of his memorandum, see Kennan. *Memoirs*, II, 26–33.

18.   In order to protect its rule of Hong Kong and its property and trading rights in China, the United Kingdom extended diplomatic recognition to the PRC on January 6, 1950. Philip Jessup, memorandum of conversation with British ambassador, December 4, 1950, William McWilliams, memorandum of conversation with senior staff, December 5, 1950, *Foreign Relations, 1950*, VII, 1374–77, 1382–86; Millett, *War for Korea, 1950–1951*, 361.

19.   Memoranda on the Anglo-American discussions on policies for Korea and Asia, *Foreign Relations, 1950*, VII, 1361–74, 1392–1408, 1430–32, 1435–42, 1449–61, 1468–79, at 1395; Beisner, *Dean Acheson*, 417–21; Millett, *War for Korea, 1950–1951*, 361–64.

20.   Truman diary entry for December 9, 1950, PSF, Truman Library; Joint Chiefs of Staff memorandum for secretary of defense, January 12, 1951, *Foreign Relations, 1951*, VII, 71–72, at 71; Millett, *War for Korea, 1950–1951*, 395–96.

21.   Truman to MacArthur included in Joint Chiefs of Staff to MacArthur, January 13, 1951, *Foreign Relations, 1951*, VII, 77–78, at 77, 78; Millett, *War for Korea, 1950–1951*, 396–97.

22.   Millett, *War for Korea, 1950–1951*, 388–92, 397–98, at 398; Beisner, *Dean Acheson*, 422–23.

23.   Doris M. Condit, *The Test of War, 1950–1953—History of the Office of the Secretary of Defense*, vol. II (Washington, DC: Historical Office, Office of the Secretary of Defense, 1988), 223–27, 230–36, at 232.

24.   Nitze to Acheson, November 22, 1950, *Foreign Relations, 1950*, I, 418–420; Condit, *Test of War*, 235–37, at 237.

25.   Condit, *Test of War*, 237–39; Truman, message to Congress requesting additional appropriations for defense, December 1, 1950, *Public Papers of the Presidents, 1950*, 728–31, at 730.

26.   "Mr. Truman to the Country," *New York Times*, December 16, 1950; The 'Sense of Urgency,'" *New York Times*, October 29, 1950; George H. Gallup, *The Gallup Poll: Public Opinion, 1935–1971*, 3 vols. (New York: Random House, 1972), II, 949–55, at 949, 955.

27.   "Taft's Speech Challenging Truman's Sending Troops Abroad," *New York Times*, January 6, 1951; "Hoover's Speech Presenting Defense Program for Peace," *New York Times*, February 10, 1951; "Here's the Bill: Is It Worth It?" *Chicago Tribune*, January 17, 1951; Walter Lippmann, "The Isolationist Tide," *Washington Post*, December 19, 1950.

28.   Condit, *Test of War*, 243–49.

29.   Condit, *Test of War*, 239; Congressional Quarterly, *Congress and the Nation, 1945–1964* (Washington, DC: Congressional Quarterly, 1965), 260.

30.   A third supplemental appropriation was passed for the FY 1951 budget, but it contained no funds for the Department of Defense. Condit, *Test of War*, 239–42; Congressional Quarterly, *Congress and the Nation*, 260, 265; Edward A. Kolodziej, *The Uncommon Defense and Congress, 1945–1963* (Columbus: Ohio State University Press, 1966), 129–39.

31.   Condit, *Test of War*, 259–54; Congressional Quarterly, *Congress and the Nation*, 266.

32.   Condit, *Test of War*, 256; Kolodziej, *Uncommon Defense*, 140–50, at 146, 147.

33.   Condit, *Test of War*, 257–60, at 257; Kolodziej, *Uncommon Defense*, 148–52. The term "Organizer of Victory" is the subtitle of Forrest C. Pogue's third volume in his

masterful biography of George C. Marshall covering his role as army chief of staff in World War II.

34. Condit, *Test of War*, 261–64, at 261; Kolodziej, *Uncommon Defense*, 150–52.

35. NIE 25, "Probable Soviet Courses of Action to Mid-1952," August 2, 1951, W. Park Armstrong Jr. to Acheson, August 6, 1951, *Foreign Relations, 1951*, I, 119–27, at 119, 120, 121, 127.

36. Bohlen to Nitze, July 28, 1951, *Foreign Relations, 1951*, I, 106–9, at 107, 108. 109.

37. NSC 114/1, "Preliminary Report by the NSC on Status and Timing of Current US Programs for National Security," August 8, 1951, James S. Lay Jr. to NSC, August 9, 1951, *Foreign Relations, 1951*, I, 127–59, at 132, 147; Condit, *Test of War*, 262–65.

38. NSC 114/1, August 8, 1951, *Foreign Relations, 1951*, I, 127–57, at 130, 150, 152.

39. Condit, *Test of War*, 261–62, 265–69; Congressional Quarterly, *Congress and the Nation*, 270.

40. Condit, *Test of War*, 269–79; Kolodziej, *Uncommon Defense*, 152–56; Congressional Quarterly, *Congress and the Nation*, 270.

41. Condit, *Test of War*, 279–84, at 282; Kolodziej, *Uncommon Defense*, 156–66; Congressional Quarterly, *Congress and the Nation*, 270–71.

12. DEAN ACHESON LEADS THE DEFENSE OF EUROPE

1. Melvyn P. Leffler, *A Preponderance of Power: National Security, the Truman Administration, and the Cold War* (Stanford, CA: Stanford University Press, 1992), 277.

2. Doris M. Condit, *The Test of War, 1950–1953—History of the Office of the Secretary of Defense*, vol. II (Washington, DC: Historical Office, Office of the Secretary of Defense, 1988), 395–400, 413; Irwin M. Wall, *The United States and the Making of Postwar France, 1945–1954* (Cambridge: Cambridge University Press, 1991), 190.

3. Thomas Alan Schwartz, *America's Germany: John J. McCloy and the Federal Republic of Germany* (Cambridge, MA: Harvard University Press, 1991), 38–58.

4. Schwartz, *America's Germany*, 1–57 passim.

5. Record of meeting of US ambassadors at Paris, October 21–22, 1949, *Foreign Relations, 1949*, IV, 485–88; Beisner, *Dean Acheson*, 253–54; Schwartz, *America's Germany*, 89–91, at 90.

6. Schwartz, *America's Germany*, 61–65; Wall, *United States and the Making of Postwar France*, 155–57; US negotiations over devaluation of the German mark, September 20–October 1, 1949, *Foreign Relations, 1949*, III, 448–77.

7. Schwartz, *America's Germany*, 33–39; Acheson to Truman, memorandum on German policy, March 31, 1949, *Foreign Relations, 1949*, III, 142–55; Dean Acheson, *Present at the Creation: My Years in the State Department* (New York: W. W. Norton, 1969), 291–301.

8. Sherrill Brown Wells, "Robert Schuman," in *Encyclopedia of the European Union*, ed. Desmond Dinan (Boulder, CO: Lynne Rienner, 1998), 414–17; Jean-Pierre Rioux, *The Fourth Republic, 1944–1958* (Cambridge: Cambridge University Press, 1987), 142–44; Robert L. Beisner, *Dean Acheson: A Life in the Cold War* (New York: Oxford University

Press, 2006), 162–63; Acheson, *Present at the Creation*, 271–73; Acheson to Webb, September 26, 1949, *Foreign Relations, 1949*, III, 460–62, at 461 and 462.

9.   Acheson to George Perkins, October 19, 1949, *Foreign Relations, 1949*, IV, 469–72, at 469 and 470.

10.   Record of a meeting of US ambassadors at Paris, October 21–22, 1949, *Foreign Relations, 1949*, IV, 489–94, at 490 and 492.

11.   Schwartz, *America's Germany*, 84–95; Leffler, *Preponderance of Power*, 313–47.

12.   Beisner, *Dean Acheson*, 7–11; Robert J. Donovan, *Tumultuous Years: The Presidency of Harry S Truman, 1949–1953* (New York: W. W. Norton, 1982), 34–36; David S. McLellan, *Dean Acheson: The State Department Years* (New York: Dodd, Mead, 1976), 4–35.

13.   McLellan, *Dean Acheson*, 1–13.

14.   McLellan, *Dean Acheson*, 13–21.

15.   Gaddis Smith, *Dean Acheson* (New York: Cooper Square, 1972), 10–24; Beisner, *Dean Acheson*, 11–23; McLellan, *Dean Acheson*, 44–56.

16.   Smith, *Acheson*, 25–53; McLellan, *Dean Acheson*, 57–135 passim; Beisner, *Dean Acheson*, 24–79 passim.

17.   McLellan, *Dean Acheson*, 142–49, 211–14; Donovan, *Tumultuous Years*, 34–36; Beisner, *Dean Acheson*, 88–90, at 89.

18.   McLellan, *Dean Acheson*, 5; Beisner, *Dean Acheson*, 104–9; Donovan, *Tumultuous Years*, 34–36, at 36.

19.   Beisner, *Dean Acheson*, 259–61; McLellan, *Dean Acheson*, 246–53.

20.   Sherrill Brown Wells, *Jean Monnet: Unconventional Statesman* (Boulder, CO: Lynne Rienner, 2011), 128–62 passim, at 130; Douglas Brinkley, "Dean Acheson and Jean Monnet: On the Path to Atlantic Partnership," in *Monnet and the Americans: The Father of a United Europe and His US Supporters*, ed. Clifford P. Hackett (Washington, DC: Jean Monnet Council, 1995), 82–84; Beisner, *Dean Acheson*, 262–63; McLellan, *Dean Acheson*, 152–53; Acheson to Webb, May 9, 1950, chargé in Paris to Webb (transmitting the Schuman proposal), May 9, 1950, Acheson to Webb, May 10, 1950, *Foreign Relations, 1950*, III, 691–95.

21.   Leffler, *Preponderance of Power*, 349–51; Steven T. Ross, *American War Plans, 1945–1950* (New York: Garland, 1988), 115–19; Beisner, *Dean Acheson*, 260–61, 263–65; Johnson to NSC with views of JCS, June 8, 1950, Truman to Acheson, June 16, 1950 (two memos), Acheson to NSC, July 3, 1950, *Foreign Relations, 1950*, IV, 686–95, at 688. Ross shows that, despite the lack of critical resources to implement it, the war plan OFFTACKLE of November 8, 1949, was approved by the Joint Chiefs of Staff in December 1949 and remained the basic US war plan against the Soviet Union until mid-1951.

22.   Schwartz, *America's Germany*, 124–28, at 127; Beisner, *Dean Acheson*, 333–52; McLellan, *Dean Acheson*, 273–81, 327–28; Acheson, memorandum on cabinet discussion, July 14, 1950, *Foreign Relations, 1950*, I, 344–46, at 345.

23.   Schwartz, *America's Germany*, 129–34; McLellan, *Dean Acheson*, 327–29; Beisner, *Dean Acheson*, 356–60; Gallup, *Gallup Poll*, II, 914, 932.

24.   Acheson's suite at the Waldorf-Astoria Hotel was the site of many private meetings of the Big Three. Beisner, *Dean Acheson*, 362–67; Schwartz, *America's Germany*, 135;

Acheson to Webb (for the president), September 15, 1950, *Foreign Relations, 1950*, III, 1229–31, at 1230; *Washington Post*, September 9, 1950; *New York Times*, September 10, 1950.

25. Beisner, *Dean Acheson*, 368–69; Schwartz, *America's Germany*, 135–40; McLellan, *Dean Acheson*, 329–32; Acheson to Webb, including North Atlantic Council, "Resolution on the Defense of Western Europe," September 26, 1950, *Foreign Relations, 1950*, III, 350–52.

26. Wells, *Jean Monnet*, 140–42; Schwartz, *America's Germany*, 128–33, 140–42; Beisner, *Dean Acheson*, 369–70; Condit, *Test of War*, 323–26.

27. Beisner, *Dean Acheson*, 370–72, at 370; Schwartz, *America's Germany*, 142–45, 150–52; Condit, *Test of War*, 325–32; Acheson to Bruce (for Schuman), November 29, 1950, Spofford to Acheson, December 8, 1950, *Foreign Relations, 1950*, III, 496–98, 528–30, at 497 and 498.

28. Schwartz, *America's Germany*, 145–46, 152, at 152. For Adenauer's views, see McCloy to Acheson, December 1, 1950, *Foreign Relations, 1950*, IV, 789–92.

29. Schwartz, *America's Germany*, 154–55.

30. US delegation, minutes of North Atlantic Council, December 19, 1950, Truman to Eisenhower, December 19, 1950, *Foreign Relations, 1950*, III, 595–605; Condit, *Test of War*, 332–35; Beisner, *Dean Acheson*, 373–74, at 373.

31. Leffler, *Preponderance of Power*, 390; Beisner, *Dean Acheson*, 452–53.

32. Condit, *Test of War*, 329–35; Beisner, *Dean Acheson*, 453.

33. McLellan, *Dean Acheson*, 337–40; Beisner, *Dean Acheson*, 449; Ronald J. Caridi, *The Korean War and American Politics: The Republican Party as a Case Study* (Philadelphia: University of Pennsylvania Press, 1968), 126.

34. Herbert Hoover, "Our National Policies in This Crisis," December 20, 1950, *Vital Speeches of the Day* (January 1, 1951), 165–67, at 166; Donald J. Mrozek, "Progressive Dissenter: Herbert Hoover's Opposition to Truman's Overseas Military Policy," *Annals of Iowa* 43 (1976): 275–91; McLellan, *Dean Acheson*, 340–41.

35. McLellan, *Dean Acheson*, 341; Acheson, *Present at the Creation*, 488–90, at 490.

36. Sen. Robert A. Taft, "Constructive Criticism of American Foreign Policy Is Essential to the Safety of the Nation," January 5, 1951, *Congressional Record*, US Senate (82nd Cong., 1st Sess.), 54–69, at 61; McLellan, *Dean Acheson*, 341–42; James T. Patterson, *Mr. Republican: A Biography of Robert A. Taft* (Boston: Houghton Mifflin, 1972), 470–78.

37. McLellan, *Dean Acheson*, 343; Beisner, *Dean Acheson*, 449.

38. Eisenhower testimony, February 1, 1951, Committees on Foreign Relations and Armed Services, US Senate, "Assignment of Ground Forces of the United States to Duty in the European Area," *Hearings* (82nd Cong., 1st Sess.), 1–35; Condit, *Test of War*, 339–40.

39. Marshall testimony, February 15, 1951, Senate Committee on Foreign Relations, "Assignment of Ground Forces," *Hearings*, 38–42, 46–47, 67–69, at 40 and 41; Condit, *Test of War*, 340.

40. Acheson testimony, February 16, 1951, Senate Committee on Foreign Relations, "Assignment of Ground Forces," *Hearings*, 77–94, at 78, 79, and 85; Beisner, *Dean Acheson*, 451–52; McLellan, *Dean Acheson*, 344–46.

41. Beisner, *Dean Acheson*, 451.

42. Condit, *Test of War*, 340–41, at 341; McLellan, *Dean Acheson*, 346; Beisner, *Dean Acheson*, 452.

43. Schwartz, *America's Germany*, 210–26; Beisner, *Dean Acheson*, 452–54; Wall, *United States and the Making of Postwar France*, 204–212.

44. Schwartz, *America's Germany*, 226–78 passim; Wells, *Jean Monnet*, 151–54; Beisner, *Dean Acheson*, 589–99; Eisenhower to Marshall, July 18, 1951, Bruce to Acheson, July 19, 1951, NSC 115, "US Policy on Problems of the Defense of Europe and the German Contribution," July 30, 1951, *Foreign Relations, 1951*, III, 838–42, 849–52; Edward Fursdon, *The European Defence Community: A History* (New York: St. Martin's Press, 1980), 147, 186. The United States and the United Kingdom did not sign the EDC Treaty, but with France they attached a Tripartite Declaration extending NATO security guarantees to the EDC nations if any member faced a threat to its security.

45. Schwartz, *America's Germany*, 279–94; Wells, *Jean Monnet*, 176–79; Condit, *Test of War*, 377–84, 392–93; Beisner, *Dean Acheson*, 589–603.

46. Beisner, *Dean Acheson*, 602–5; Wall, *United States and the Making of Postwar France*, 265–96; Wells, *Jean Monnet*, 176–79; Simon W. Duke and Wolfgang Krieger, eds., *US Military Forces in Europe: The Early Years, 1945–1970* (Boulder, CO: Westview Press, 1993), 177–79.

47. Condit, *Test of War*, 347–67; Duke and Krieger, *US Military Forces in Europe*, 55–58, 173–79.

13. ANDREI TUPOLEV CREATES A STRATEGIC BOMBER FORCE

1. Yu. A. Ostapenko, *Tovarishch ministr: Povest' o rukovoditele aviatsionnoi promyshlennosti SSSR P. V. Dement'eve* [Comrade Minister: A narrative about P. V. Dement'ev, the head of the aviation industry in the USSR] (Moscow: Aerosphere, 2006), 60–68, at 60 and 67; A. Sul'anov, "Foreword" in *Reaktivnye samolety Vooruzhennyh Sil SSSR i Rossii* [Soviet and Russian Turbojet Aircraft], by M. Arkhipova (Moscow: AST, 2002), 5.

2. Steven J. Zaloga, *The Kremlin's Nuclear Sword: The Rise and Fall of Russia's Strategic Nuclear Forces, 1945–2000* (Washington, DC: Smithsonian Institution Press, 2002), 4; quoted in *Dal'niaia Aviatsiia, pervye 90 let* [Long-range aviation, the first 90 years], ed. V. Zotov (Moscow: Polygon Press, 2004), 181.

3. V. Rigmant, *Samolety OKB A. N. Tupoleva* [The aircraft of A. N. Tupolev's design bureau] (Moscow: Rusavia, 2001), 111; Steven J. Zaloga, *Target America: The Soviet Union and the Strategic Arms Race, 1945–1964* (Novato, CA: Presidio Press, 1993), 34–35, 68; Christopher Andrew and Oleg Gordievsky, *KGB: The Inside Story of Its Foreign Operations from Lenin to Gorbachev* (New York: HarperCollins, 1990), 311–20.

4. L. L. Kerber and Von Hardesty, *Stalin's Aviation Gulag: A Memoir of Andrei Tupolev and the Purge Era* (Washington, DC: Smithsonian Institution Press, 1996), 20–27; Yefim Gordon and Vladimir Rigmant, *OKB Tupolev: A History of the Design Bureau and Its Aircraft* (Hinckley, UK: Midland, 2005), 13.

5. Kerber and Hardesty, *Stalin's Aviation Gulag*, 28–35; Zaloga, *Target America*, 63–64.

6. Kerber and Hardesty, *Stalin's Aviation Gulag*, 32; Zaloga, *Target America*, 63.

7. Kerber and Hardesty, *Stalin's Aviation Gulag*, 47–50, 64–73, at 72.

8. Kerber and Hardesty, *Stalin's Aviation Gulag*, 76–106; Rigmant, *Samolety OKB A. N. Tupoleva*, 31; Zaloga, *Target America*, 64.

9. Kerber and Hardesty, *Stalin's Aviation Gulag*, 107–25.

10. Kerber and Hardesty, *Stalin's Aviation Gulag*, 35, 40–46, 61–63, 100–104, 128–33, 135–39.

11. Kerber and Hardesty, *Stalin's Aviation Gulag*, 12, 220–21, 157–58, at 158.

12. Kerber and Hardesty, *Stalin's Aviation Gulag*, 157–59, 221–24; Chuev, *Molotov Remembers*, 141.

13. Kerber and Hardesty, *Stalin's Aviation Gulag*, 154–67, 175–78, 191–92.

14. Kerber and Hardesty, *Stalin's Aviation Gulag*, 188–90, at 189.

15. Kerber and Hardesty, *Stalin's Aviation Gulag*, 190–91. Despite Lavrenti Beria's well-earned reputation for brutality, he was widely respected for his hard work, intelligence, and effective administrative ability—as demonstrated during World War II, when he supervised the relocation of defense industries beyond the Urals and managed wartime production across many industries. See Amy Knight, *Beria: Stalin's First Lieutenant* (Princeton, NJ: Princeton University Press, 1993), 112–13, 137–38.

16. Kerber and Hardesty, *Stalin's Aviation Gulag*, 210–11, at 211.

17. Kerber and Hardesty, *Stalin's Aviation Gulag*, 200–206, 213–19, 224–28; Zaloga, *Target America*, 66–67; Paul Duffy and Andrei Kandalov, *Tupolev: The Man And His Aircraft* (Warrendale, PA: SAE, 1996), 14.

18. Kerber and Hardesty, *Stalin's Aviation Gulag*, 238–46; Gordon and Rigmant, *OKB Tupolev*, 13; Robert Jackson, *Aircraft of World War II: Development, Weapons, Specifications* (Leicester, UK: Amber Books, 2003), 154; Zaloga, *Target America*, 67.

19. V. Rigmant, "Neizvestnaia 'Shest' desyatchetverka" [The Unknown "64"], *Aviatsiia i Kosmonavtika* 1(1996): 21–26; Zaloga, *Kremlin's Nuclear Sword*, 13; Christopher Andrew and Vasili Mitrokhin, *The Sword and the Shield: The Mitrokhin Archive and the Secret History of the KGB* (New York: Basic Books, 1999), 114; Gordon and Rigmant, *OKB Tupolev*, 13; Kerber and Hardesty, *Stalin's Aviation Gulag*, 247–55, at 248.

20. Rigmant, "Neizvestnaia," 27–28; Kerber and Hardesty, *Stalin's Aviation Gulag*, 255.

21. Rigmant, "Neizvestnaia," 27; Rigmant, "Samolety," 113; E. Podol'nyi, "V labirinte modernizatsii" [In the labyrinth of modernizations], *Kryl'ia Rodiny* 10 (2004): 4; Zaloga, *Target America*, 71.

22. N. Iakubovich, "Nash otvet SShA" [Our answer to the USA], *Kryl'ia Rodiny* 1(2002);3; Rigmant, "Samolety," 112–14; Kerber and Hardesty, *Stalin's Aviation Gulag*, 255–56; L. Kerber and M. Saukke, "Ne kopiia, a analog" [Not a copy, but an analog], *Kryl'ia Rodiny* 1 (1989): 25.

23. Kerber and Hardesty, *Stalin's Aviation Gulag*, 257–63, at 257; Zaloga, *Target America*, 71–72.

24. Kerber and Hardesty, *Stalin's Aviation Gulag*, 263–67; Kerber and Saukke, "Ne kopiia," 25; Rigmant, "Samolety," 117; Zaloga, *Target America*, 71–72.

25. Duffy and Kandalov, *Tupolev*, 15, 96–101; Kerber and Hardesty, *Stalin's Aviation Gulag*, 258–69, at 259; Zaloga, *Target America*, 71–74.

26. Podol' nyi, "V labirinte," 3; Kerber and Saukke, "Ne kopiia," 34; Rigmant, "Samolety," 117; Iakubovich, "Nash otvet," 4–5; Kerber and Hardesty, *Stalin's Aviation Gulag*, 269–70.

27. Rigmant, "Samolety," 118–20; Duffy and Kandalov, *Tupolev*, 108–10; Zaloga, *Target America*, 74–79.

28. Duffy and Kandalov, *Tupolev*, 14–17, 108–10.

29. Rigmant, "Samolety," 126–28; N. Iakubovich, "Mertvorozhdennyi monstr" [The stillborn monster], *Kryl'ia Rodiny* 2 (1997): 4; Kerber and Hardesty, *Stalin's Aviation Gulag*, 279–83; V. Rigmant, "Tu-85: Konets evolyutsionnogo puti" [Tu-85: The end of evolution], *Aviatsiia i Kosmonavtika* 7 (1997): 29.

30. Rigmant, "Tu-85," 30–31; N. V. Iakubovich and V. N. Lavrov, *Samolety V. M. Miasishcheva* [The airplanes of V. M. Miasishchev] (Moscow: Rusavia, 1999), 45–46, at 46; Zaloga, *Target America*, 79–80.

31. Iakubovich and Lavrov, *Miasishcheva*, 47; Kerber and Hardesty, *Stalin's Aviation Gulag*, 286; Rigmant, "Neizvestnaia," 30; Zaloga, *Target America*, 81.

32. Kerber and Hardesty, *Stalin's Aviation Gulag*, 286.

33. Iakubovich and Lavrov, *Miasishcheva*, 34–35, 43, 46–48; L. Seliakov, *Maloizvestnye stranitsy tvorcheskoj deiatel'nosti aviatsionnogo konstruktora Vladimira Mikhailovicha Miasishcheva* [Little-known pages from the creative work of aviation designer Vladimir Mikhailovich Miasishchev] (Moscow: AO ANTK im. A. N. Tupoleva, 1997), 13; Zaloga, *Target America*, 81–82, at 82.

34. Iakubovich and Lavrov, *Miasishcheva*, 49–66; Ostapenko, *Dement'eve*, 144, 155; S. Moroz, *Dal'nie bombardirovschiki M-4 i 3M* [Long-range bombers M-4 and 3M] (Moscow: Exprint, 2005), 5–6, 10–15; Zaloga, *Target America*, 82–85; CIA, "Main Trends in Soviet Capabilities and Policies, 1957–1962," NIE 11-4-57, November 12, 1957, 33.

35. Rigmont, "Samolety," 130–32; Iakubovich and Lavrov, *Miasishcheva*, 47; Kerber and Hardesty, *Stalin's Aviation Gulag*, 297–98; Piotr Butowski, "Tu-95/Tu-142 'Bear,'" in *Tupolev Bombers*, ed. David Donald and Rob Hewson (Norwalk, CT: AIRtime, 2002), 8; N. Kuznetsov, "Uchilsya u nego vsemu" [He taught me everything], in *Andrei Nikolaevich Tupolev: Grani derznovennogo tvorchestva* [Andrei N. Tupolev: The limits of daring creation] (Moscow: Nauka, 1988, 171–72.

36. Kerber and Hardesty, *Stalin's Aviation Gulag*, 299–303, at 302; Rigmant, "Samolety," 131–32.

37. Gordon and Rigmant, *OKB Tupolev*, 150–54; Yefim Gordon and Peter Davison, *Tupolev: Tu-95 Bear* (North Branch, MN: Specialty Press, 2006), 14–21, 96–97; Duffy and Kandalov, *Tupolev*, 113–15.

38. Gordon and Rigmant, *OKB Tupolev*, 151.

39. Zaloga, *Target America*, 87–88; Allen W. Dulles, "Present and Planned Strengths of the US Air Force: Briefing on Air Intelligence," Subcommittee on the Air Force, US Senate Armed Services Committee, 12–13. CIA–RDP 80M01389R000400110009-4, CIA Records Search Tool (CREST), National Archives, College Park, MD; Dulles, Draft for Symington Committee, April 13, 1956, 7. CIA-RDP80M01389R000400110002-1, CREST.

40. Zaloga, *Target America*, 87–88.

14. CURTIS LᴇMAY BUILDS THE STRATEGIC AIR COMMAND

1. Phillip S. Meilinger, *The Formation and Early Years of the Strategic Air Command, 1946–1957: Why the SAC Was Formed* (Lewiston, NY: Edwin Mellen Press, 2013) (hereafter, *Early Years of SAC*), 70–78, 83–84, 100–101; Robert Frank Futrell, *Ideas, Concepts, Doctrine: A History of Basic Thinking in the United States Air Force, 1907–1964* (Maxwell Air Force Base, Ala.: Air University Press, 1974), 95–104.

2. Meilinger, *Early Years of SAC*, 76–88; Warren Kozak, *Curtis LeMay: Strategist and Tactician* (Washington, DC: Regnery History, 2014), 279–85; Harry R. Borowski, *A Hollow Threat: Strategic Air Power and Containment Before Korea* (Westport, CT: Greenwood Press, 1982), 39–71, 87–88, 91–107, 137–49.

3. Meilinger, *Early Years of SAC*, 94–95, 118–20, at 120; Borowski, *Hollow Threat*, 145–47.

4. Borowski, *Hollow Threat*, 145–46, at 146; Meilinger, *Early Years of SAC*, 119–20; Charles A. Lindberg, *Autobiography of Values* (New York: Harcourt Brace Jovanovich, 1978), 220–23.

5. Borowski, *Hollow Threat*, 148–49; Meilinger, *Early Years of SAC*, 120.

6. Borowski, *Hollow Threat*, 163–65; Kozak, *Curtis LeMay*, 286–87, at 286; Meilinger, *Early Years of SAC*, 127–28.

7. Kozak, *Curtis LeMay*, 282–94, at 284; Borowski, *Hollow Threat*, 165–66.

8. Kozak, *Curtis LeMay*, 285–86; Borowski, *Hollow Threat*, 166–67; Meilinger, *Early Years of SAC*, 132; General Curtis E. LeMay with MacKinlay Kantor, *Mission with LeMay: My Story* (Garden City, NY: Doubleday, 1965), 432–33, at 433.

9. Kozak, *Curtis LeMay*, 286.

10. Kozak, *Curtis LeMay*, ix–xi, at ix; Thomas M. Coffey, *Iron Eagle: The Turbulent Life of General Curtis LeMay* (New York: Crown. 1986), 3–5, at 3.

11. Kozak, *Curtis LeMay*, 1–11, at 8 and 10; Barrett Tillman, *LeMay* (New York: Palgrave Macmillan, 2009), 4–5; Coffey, *Iron Eagle*, 185–94.

12. Kozak, *Curtis LeMay*, 11–17, 31–32; Coffey, *Iron Eagle*, 195–202; Tillman, *LeMay*, 5–6.

13. Kozak, *Curtis LeMay*, 19–41; Coffey, *Iron Eagle*, 206–23; Tillman, *LeMay*, 6–8.

14. Kozak, *Curtis LeMay*, 28–31, 41–43, at 42; Coffey, *Iron Eagle*, 216–17, 223–29; Tillman, *LeMay*, 9.

15. Kozak, *Curtis LeMay*, 43–53; Meilinger, *Early Years of SAC*, 15–34; Tillman, *LeMay*, 9–11.

16. Kozak, *Curtis LeMay*, 48–52; Meilinger, *Early Years of SAC*, 34–35, 58–59; Tillman, *LeMay*, 13–14.

17. Kozak, *Curtis LeMay*, 52–53; Coffey, *Iron Eagle*, 17, 41–43, 231–33; Tillman, *LeMay*, 14–15.

18. Kozak, *Curtis LeMay*, 52–58; Coffey, *Iron Eagle*, 231–40; Tillman, *LeMay*, 14–15; for an account of the earlier battle between Billy Mitchell and the navy, see Samuel F. Wells Jr., "William Mitchell and the *Ostfriesland*: A Study in Military Reform," *The Historian* 26 (August 1964): 538–62.

19. LeMay, *Mission with LeMay*, 152–93; Kozak, *Curtis LeMay*, 58–64; Coffey, *Iron Eagle*, 240–43; Tillman, *LeMay*, 15–18; Hanson Baldwin, "War Games Show Air Force Is Weak: But Rapid Strides in 3 Years Are Evident," *New York Times*, May 15, 1938.

20. Kozak, *Curtis LeMay*, 53, 62–68; Coffey, *Iron Eagle*, 242–44; Tillman, *LeMay*, 18–20.

21. Gerhard L. Weinberg, *A World At Arms: A Global History of World War II* (New York: Cambridge University Press, 1994), 238–64; Robert Dallek, *Franklin D. Roosevelt and American Foreign Policy, 1932–1945* (New York: Oxford University Press, 1979), 269–313; Andrew Gilmour, "Escape from Dunkirk: Hitler's Four Strategic Mistakes," *Newsweek*, June 5, 2015, www.europe.newsweek.com/escape-dunkirk-hitlers-four-strategic-mistakes-328274.

22. Kozak, *Curtis LeMay*, 72–80, at 78; Coffey, *Iron Eagle*, 16–18; Tillman, *LeMay*, 21–25.

23. The flight surgeon told LeMay that Bell's palsy was due to sustained cold temperatures at high altitudes, but today we know that it is caused by a virus. In any event, the paralysis did diminish significantly over the next decade. Kozak, *Curtis LeMay*, 80–89, at 83; Coffey, *Iron Eagle*, 18–27, at 21; Tillman, *LeMay*, 24–26.

24. Kozak, *Curtis LeMay*, 94–96; Coffey, *Iron Eagle*, 29–30; Tillman, *LeMay*, 26–27.

25. Kozak, *Curtis LeMay*, 95–107, 114; Coffey, *Iron Eagle*, 28–36; Tillman, *LeMay*, 26–29.

26. Kozak, *Curtis LeMay*, 96, 109–12; Coffey, *Iron Eagle*, 36–38; Tillman, *LeMay*, 29.

27. Kozak, *Curtis LeMay*, 96–97; Coffey, *Iron Eagle*, 39–50.

28. Kozak, *Curtis LeMay*, 73, 121–22, 201, 390, at 121 and 201.

29. Kozak, *Curtis LeMay*, 112–63; Richard J. Overy, *The Air War, 1939–1945* (New York: Stein & Day, 1980), 122–26; Richard Overy, *The Bombers and the Bombed: Allied Air War Over Europe, 1940–1945* (New York: Penguin Press, 2015), 306–7; Office of Statistical Control, Headquarters, Army Air Force, *Army Air Force Statistical Digest: World War II* (1945), tables 35 and 100, www.ibiblio.org/hyperwar/AAF/StatDigest/index.html.

30. Kozak, *Curtis LeMay*, 116–65, at 118; Coffey, *Iron Eagle*, 47–102; Tillman, *LeMay*, 30–37.

31. The most serious problem with the B-29 appeared in early test flights, when engines caught on fire and dropped off the wing or caught the wing on fire, causing a crash. The latter occurred with the top test pilot and nine senior Boeing engineers aboard when the burning airplane crashed into a meat packing plant in downtown Seattle with a large number of casualties, including everyone on the plane. Kozak, *Curtis LeMay*, 165–79, at 165; Coffey, *Iron Eagle*, 103–11; Tillman, *LeMay*, 38–43.

32. Kozak, *Curtis LeMay*, 180–98; Coffey, *Iron Eagle*, 111–28; Tillman, *LeMay*, 43–52.

33. Kozak, *Curtis LeMay*, 198–210; LeMay, *Mission with LeMay*, 341–42, at 342; Coffey, *Iron Eagle*, 129–37.

34. Kozak, *Curtis LeMay*, 196–97, 210–14, at 196; Coffey, *Iron Eagle*, 137–56; Tillman, *LeMay*, 55–60.

35. Kozak, *Curtis LeMay*, 215–27, at 224; Coffey, *Iron Eagle*, 155–68; Tillman, *LeMay*, 60–63.

36. Kozak, *Curtis LeMay*, 238–59, at 255; Coffey, *Iron Eagle*, 168–82; Tillman, *LeMay*, 64–77.

37. Kozak, *Curtis LeMay*, 261–71; Lawrence Freedman, *The Evolution of Nuclear Strategy* (New York: St. Martin's Press, 1981), 178–207, 247–49, 258–61; Fred Kaplan, *The Wizards of Armageddon* (New York: Simon & Schuster, 1983), 55–124; Coffey, *Iron Eagle*, 252–57; Tillman, *LeMay*, 79–85.

38. The Berlin airlift continued until the Soviets lifted the blockade on May 12, 1949. Kozak, *Curtis LeMay*, 272–78; Coffey, *Iron Eagle*, 258–69; Tillman, *LeMay*, 85–91.

39. Quoted in a 2008 letter to the author, Kozak, *Curtis LeMay*, 166.

40. Kozak, *Curtis LeMay*, 290–93; Meilinger, *Early Years of SAC*, 133–39; Coffey, *Iron Eagle*, 280–84; Tillman, *LeMay*, 101–2.

41. Kozak, *Curtis LeMay*, 292–93, 300; Meilinger, *Early Years of SAC*, 139–40; Coffey, *Iron Eagle*, 293–94; Tillman, *LeMay*, 102–3.

42. Kozak, *Curtis LeMay*, 294–97; Meilinger, *Early Years of SAC*, 130–31; Coffey, *Iron Eagle*, 294–98.

43. Meilinger, *Early Years of SAC*, 140–50; Coffey, *Iron Eagle*, 284–90; Tillman, *LeMay*, 104–5; for the navy's side of this episode, see Jeffrey G. Barlow, *Revolt of the Admirals: The Fight for Naval Aviation, 1945–1950* (Washington, DC: Naval Historical Center, 1994).

44. Meilinger, *Early Years of SAC*, 140.

45. Meilinger, *Early Years of SAC*, 255–56, 340.

46. Effective in 1950, the air force established a new class of heavy bomber with the B-36D; the B-29 and B-50 were redesignated medium-range bombers at this time. Meilinger, *Early Years of SAC*, 252–56; Meyers K. Jacobsen and Scott Deaver, *Convair B-36: A Comprehensive History of America's "Big Stick"* (Atglen, PA: Schiffer, 1997), 254–56.

47. Meilinger, *Early Years of SAC*, 257–59, at 257 and 258; Alwyn T. Lloyd, *Boeing's B-47 Stratojet* (North Branch, MN: Specialty Press, 2005), 62–72.

48. Meilinger, *Early Years of SAC*, 255–56; Kozak, *Curtis LeMay*, 303–4; Eric Adams, "How on God's Green Earth Is the B-52 Still in Service?" *Wired*, April 19, 2016, https://wired .com/2016/04/gods-green-earth-b-52-still-service/.

49. Ibid., 259–70, 340; Tillman, *LeMay*, 106–10.

50. David Alan Rosenberg, "The Origins of Overkill: Nuclear Weapons and American Strategy, 1945–1960," *International Security* 7 (Spring 1983): 16–24, at 19; Samuel R. Williamson Jr. and Steven L. Rearden, *The Origins of US Nuclear Strategy, 1945–1953* (New York: St. Martin's Press, 1993), 162–68.

51. Williamson and Rearden, *Origins*, 104–5, 124; Steven T. Ross and David Alan Rosenberg, eds., *America's Plans for War Against the Soviet Union, 1945–1950*, vol. 13, *Evaluating the Air Offensive: the WSEG I Study* (New York: Garland, 1990), 158–93; Meilinger, *Early Years of SAC*, 270–82.

52. Williamson and Rearden, *Origins*, 105–7, 111–37; Charles E. Egan, "Symington on Retiring, Finds Air Force Fighting Value Cut," *New York Times*, April 25, 1950.

53. See table 14.4; Borowski, *Hollow Threat*, 191; Meilinger, *Early Years of SAC*, 315.

54. The one identified strategic target that was not attacked was judged too close to the Soviet border to be safely bombed. Meilinger, *Early Years of SAC*, 224–30, at 225; Office of Air Force History, *Steadfast and Courageous: FEAF Bomber Command and the Air War in Korea, 1950–1953* (Washington, DC: Office of Air Force History, 2000), 14–19.

55. From the start, US pilots suspected that the MiG-15s were flown by Soviets because of their skill; this was later confirmed. Meilinger, *Early Years of SAC*, 227, 242–44, at 227; Office of Air Force History, *Steadfast and Courageous*, 43–47.

56. Meilinger, *Early Years of SAC*, 242–44; Office of Air Force History, *Steadfast and Courageous*, 43–47; Korean War Armistice Agreement, July 27, 1953, http://news.findlaw.com /cnn/docs/korea/kwarmagro72753.html.

57. Meilinger, *Early Years of SAC*, 246–47; Office of Air Force History, *Steadfast and Courageous*, 56.

58. Meilinger, *Early Years of SAC*, 283–302; Williamson and Rearden, *Origins*, 189–95.

59. Meilinger, *Early Years of SAC*, 232–35; Richard Hewlett and Francis Duncan, *Atomic Shield, 1947–1952* (Washington, DC: Atomic Energy Commission, 1972), 537–38; Kozak, *Curtis LeMay*, 281, 301; Coffey, *Iron Eagle*, 303–5.

60. Meilinger, *Early Years of SAC*, 236–38; Hewlett and Duncan, *Atomic Shield*, 538–39; Coffey, *Iron Eagle*, 305.

61. Williamson and Rearden, *Origins*, 165–68; Meilinger, *Early Years of SAC*, 304–11.

62. Meilinger, *Early Years of SAC*, 311–17, at 314.

15. IGOR KURCHATOV DEVELOPS SOVIET NUCLEAR WEAPONS

1. Quoted by Steven J. Zaloga, *Target America: The Soviet Union and the Strategic Arms Race, 1945–1964* (Novato, CA: Presidio Press, 1993), 11.

2. David Holloway, *Stalin and the Bomb: The Soviet Union and Atomic Energy, 1939–1956* (New Haven, CT: Yale University Press, 1994), 11–12; Igor N. Golovin, *I. V. Kurchatov: A Socialist-Realist Biography of the Soviet Nuclear Scientist* (Bloomington, IN: Selbstverlag Press, 1968), 12–14.

3. Holloway, *Stalin and the Bomb*, 12–15, at 14; Golovin, *Kurchatov*, 13–16.

4. Margaret Gowing, *Britain and Atomic Energy, 1939–1945* (London: Macmillan, 1964), 17–20; Golovin, *Kurchatov*, 21–26; Holloway, *Stalin and the Bomb*, 34–39.

5. Holloway, *Stalin and the Bomb*, 16–24, 26–28, 41–46.

6. Golovin, *Kurchatov*, 21–31; Holloway, *Stalin and the Bomb*, 35, 47–48, at 47 and 48.

7. Holloway, *Stalin and the Bomb*, 49–67; Golovin, *Kurchatov*, 31–34; William L. Laurence, "Vast Power Source in Atomic Energy Opened by Science," *New York Times*, May 5, 1940; Zaloga, *Target America*, 7–8.

8. Golovin, *Kurchatov*, 32–34; Holloway, *Stalin and the Bomb*, 54–56, 70–75, 98.

9. Gerhard L. Weinberg, *A World At Arms: A Global History of World War II* (New York: Cambridge University Press, 1994), 264–69; John Erickson, *The Road to Stalingrad: Stalin's War with Germany*, vol. 1 (New York: Harper & Row, 1975), 13–292 passim; John Erickson, "Threat Identification and Strategic Appraisal by the Soviet Union, 1930–1941," in *Knowing One's Enemies: Intelligence Assessment Before the Two World Wars*, ed. Ernest R. May (Princeton, NJ: Princeton University Press, 1984), 409–23; Holloway, *Stalin and the Bomb*, 72–74.

10. Golovin, *Kurchatov*, 34–38; Holloway, *Stalin and the Bomb*, 72–75.

11. Holloway, *Stalin and the Bomb*, 76–79; Golovin, *Kurchatov*, 30–40.

12. Gowing, *Britain and Atomic Energy*, 45–89, 97–132, 167–77; Richard G. Hewlett and Oscar E. Anderson Jr., *The New World: A History of the United States Atomic Energy Commission*, vol. 1, *1939–1946* (Berkeley: University of California Press, 1990), 29–49, 71–75; Holloway, *Stalin and the Bomb*, 79–81.

13. Christopher Andrew and Oleg Gordievsky, *KGB: The Inside Story of Its Foreign Operations from Lenin to Gorbachev* (New York: HarperCollins, 1990), 216–17, 293–94, 311–20; Robert C. Williams, *Klaus Fuchs: Atom Spy* (Cambridge, MA.: Harvard University Press, 1987), 35–91; Holloway, *Stalin and the Bomb*, 79–83.

14. Campbell Craig and Sergey Radchenko, *The Atomic Bomb and the Origins of the Cold War* (New Haven, CT: Yale University Press, 2008), 47–48; Golovin, *Kurchatov*, 39–40; Holloway, *Stalin and the Bomb*, 83–86; Zaloga, *Target America*, 10–13.

15. Holloway, *Stalin and the Bomb*, 86–88, at 88; Golovin, *Kurchatov*, 40; Craig and Radchenko, *Atomic Bomb*, 49. One scholar argues that Pervukhin at Beria's initiative was involved in the decision process earlier; see Zaloga, *Target America*, 11–15.

16. Holloway, *Stalin and the Bomb*, 70; Richard Rhodes, *Dark Sun: The Making of the Hydrogen Bomb* (New York: Simon & Schuster, 1995), 63–65; Zaloga, *Target America*, 15.

17. Golovin, *Kurchatov*, 40–41, at 41.

18. Golovin, *Kurchatov*, 28–29; Holloway, *Stalin and the Bomb*, 40.

19. Rhodes, *Dark Sun*, 28–32; Holloway, *Stalin and the Bomb*, 35–38.

20. Holloway, *Stalin and the Bomb*, 38–39, 97–99, at 39; Rhodes, *Dark Sun*, 29–31.

21. Holloway, *Stalin and the Bomb*, 38–41, at 40; Rhodes, *Dark Sun*, 32–39.

22. Holloway, *Stalin and the Bomb*, 90–91, at 91; Rhodes, *Dark Sun*, 70–71.

23. Rhodes, *Dark Sun*, 71–77; Holloway, *Stalin and the Bomb*, 91–95, at 9.

24. Amy Knight, *Beria: Stalin's First Lieutenant* (Princeton, NJ: Princeton University Press, 1993), 139; Holloway, *Stalin and the Bomb*, 96–97, 141, 182; Rhodes, *Dark Sun*, 265–77.

25. Holloway, *Stalin and the Bomb*, 89, 99, 499, at 89 and 99; Rhodes, *Dark Sun*, 314.

26. Holloway, *Stalin and the Bomb*, 87, 97, 447, at 87; Rhodes, *Dark Sun*, 63–64, 69.

27. Craig and Radchenko, *Atomic Bomb*, 52–53; Holloway, *Stalin and the Bomb*, 102–3, 114–15, at 102 and 103; Rhodes, *Dark Sun*, 163.

28. Holloway, *Stalin and the Bomb*, 115; Craig and Radchenko, *Atomic Bomb*, 49–50, 60–61; Rhodes, *Dark Sun*, 54, 74.

29. Golovin, *Kurchatov*, 42–46; Holloway, *Stalin and the Bomb*, 97–100, 105–6; Rhodes, *Dark Sun*, 77–79.

30. Holloway, *Stalin and the Bomb*, 68, 98–99; Golovin, *Kurchatov*, 46–47; Rhodes, *Dark Sun*, 79, 148.

31. Holloway, *Stalin and the Bomb*, 91–94, 97, 100–101, 395; Rhodes, *Dark Sun*, 38, 70–73, 80–81, 146; Golovin, *Kurchatov*, 47–48. During the war years, the Soviet Union imported between 4,000 and 6,000 tons of graphite a year from the United States to supplement the production of its own three plants.

32. Holloway, *Stalin and the Bomb*, 60–64, 100–103; Rhodes, *Dark Sun*, 146–48.

33. Holloway, *Stalin and the Bomb*, 108–12; Rhodes, *Dark Sun*, 160–62, at 162.

34. Holloway, *Stalin and the Bomb*, 114–15, at 115; Rhodes, *Dark Sun*, 163–64, 173–74; Williams, *Klaus Fuchs*, 78–80.

35. Craig and Radchenko, *Atomic Bomb*, 90–94; W. Averell Harriman and Elie Abel, *Special Envoy to Churchill and Stalin, 1941–1946* (New York: Random House, 1975), 317–19, 335–61, 426–31, 444–58; Vojtech Mastny, *Russia's Road to the Cold War: Diplomacy,*

Warfare, and the Politics of Communism, 1941–1945 (New York: Columbia University Press, 1979), 253–66; Holloway, *Stalin and the Bomb*, 116–17.

36. Craig and Radchenko, *Atomic Bomb*, 94–97; Holloway, *Stalin and the Bomb*, 125–32; Rhodes, *Dark Sun*, 176–78.

37. Holloway, *Stalin and the Bomb*, 129–35, at 129 and 132; Craig and Radchenko, *Atomic Bomb*, 95–96, 106–9; Rhodes, *Dark Sun*, 179; Golovin, *Kurchatov*, 49–52.

38. Avraamii P. Zaveniagin, in addition to being a deputy to Vannikov on the atomic project, also served under Beria as deputy commissar of internal affairs from 1941 to 1950 with the rank of colonel-general in the NKVD. Holloway, *Stalin and the Bomb*, 109–11, 136–37, 141, 453, at 141; Golovin, *Kurchatov*, 50–51.

39. Holloway, *Stalin and the* Bomb, 135–38; Rhodes, *Dark Sun*, 187–95, 217–21. In a series of exchanges with Beria and Stalin, Peter Kapitsa boldly challenged the decision to copy the American design instead of developing a Soviet solution, and he strongly criticized Beria's management of the project and his ignorance of basic physics. For this risky behavior, Stalin some months later removed Kapitsa from all official positions and had him placed under house arrest for eight years. But he prevented Beria from imprisoning and almost certainly killing the impetuous physicist. On these clashes, see Holloway, *Stalin and the Bomb*, 138–44; and Rhodes, *Dark Sun*, 196–97.

40. Holloway, *Stalin and the Bomb*, 144–49; Rhodes, *Dark Sun*, 213–14, 222–23.

41. Rhodes, *Dark Sun*, 257.

42. Holloway, *Stalin and the Bomb*, 172–80; Golovin, *Kurchatov*, 50; Rhodes, *Dark Sun*, 214. The only available estimates of the total manpower required by the atomic bomb program come from a 1950 CIA report. It contends that up to 460,000 people were engaged with most in mining and construction, about 30,000 in production, and 8,000 in research. Holloway finds these figures "plausible, and certainly of the right order of magnitude." See Holloway, *Stalin and the Bomb*, 172.

43. Rhodes, *Dark Sun*, 215–22; Holloway, *Stalin and the Bomb*, 173.

44. Rhodes, *Dark Sun*, 265–72, at 271; Golovin, *Kurchatov*, 52–54; Holloway, *Stalin and the Bomb*, 180–82.

45. Rhodes, *Dark Sun*, 270–75, at 275; Golovin, *Kurchatov*, 54–55; Holloway, *Stalin and the Bomb*, 181–82.

46. Igor N. Golovin and Yuri N. Smirnov, *It Began in Zamoskvorechie* (Moscow: Kurchatov Institute, 1989), quoted by Rhodes, *Dark Sun*, 275, 277; Holloway, *Stalin and the Bomb*, 182.

47. Kramish was a physicist who had worked on the Manhattan Project and later on the hydrogen bomb, and he had served with the Atomic Energy Commission as its liaison with the CIA. The book was written at the RAND Corporation and drew heavily on his connections with the intelligence community. See Arnold Kramish, *Atomic Energy in the Soviet Union* (Stanford, CA: Stanford University Press, 1959), 108–29; and Jascha Hoffman, "Arnold Kramish, Expert on Nuclear Intelligence, Dies at 87," *New York Times*, July 15, 2010.

48. John Earl Haynes, Harvey Klehr, and Alexander Vassiliev, *Spies: The Rise and Fall of the KGB in America* (New Haven, CT: Yale University Press, 2009), 65–67, 561n 50; Rhodes,

Dark Sun, 267–75. Holloway, *Stalin and the Bomb*, 182, essentially dismisses the espionage argument in comparing the F-1 with Enrico Fermi's original reactor design of December 1942 rather than the later Hanford 305 design. He attributes the high number of similarities to the desire of two top physicists to build a reactor quickly from graphite and uranium and adds that the Smyth Report contained a detailed description of the 1942 Fermi design.

49. Holloway, *Stalin and the Bomb*, 183–84.

50. Rhodes, *Dark Sun*, 214, 314–15; Golovin, *Kurchatov*, 58–59; Holloway, *Stalin and the Bomb*, 184–85.

51. L. D. Riabeva, ed., *Atomnyi proekt SSSR: dokumenty i materialy* [The atomic project of the Soviet Union: documents and materials], 7 vols. (Moscow: Nauka, Fizmatlit, 1999), book 3, 757–59; Holloway, *Stalin and the Bomb*, 185–87; Golovin, *Kurchatov*, 59–62; Rhodes, *Dark Sun*, 314–16, 331–32.

52. Golovin, *Kurchatov*, 62; Rhodes, *Dark Sun*, 332.

53. Holloway, *Stalin and the Bomb*, 187–89; Rhodes, *Dark Sun*, 351–53.

54. Rhodes, *Dark Sun*, 242–43, 332–36; Holloway, *Stalin and the Bomb*, 189–92.

55. Holloway, *Stalin and the Bomb*, 196–200; Rhodes, *Dark Sun*, 352–53.

56. Holloway, *Stalin and the Bomb*, 172, 192–95; Rhodes, *Dark Sun*, 349–51.

57. Holloway, *Stalin and the Bomb*, 197–200.

58. Holloway, *Stalin and the Bomb*, 203; Rhodes, *Dark Sun*, 352.

59. Holloway, *Stalin and the Bomb*, 200; Rhodes, *Dark Sun*, 352.

60. Golovin, *Kurchatov*, 63; Holloway, *Stalin and the Bomb*, 200–201, at 201; Rhodes, *Dark Sun*, 352–53.

61. Holloway, *Stalin and the Bomb*, 201–2, at 202; Rhodes, *Dark Sun*, 285–89.

62. Golovin makes no mention of the agitation against Western concepts in physics; nor does he explain why Kurchatov chose to join the party at this time. Golovin, *Kurchatov*, 62; Holloway, *Stalin and the Bomb*, 202–3, 206–8.

63. Holloway, *Stalin and the Bomb*, 208–13, at 211 and 213.

64. Rhodes, *Dark Sun*, 364–65; Holloway, *Stalin and the Bomb*, 213–14; Golovin, *Kurchatov*, 63–64.

65. Holloway, *Stalin and the Bomb*, 214–15; Rhodes, *Dark Sun*, 365.

66. Rhodes, *Dark Sun*, 364–66, at 366; Holloway, *Stalin and the Bomb*, 215–16; Golovin, *Kurchatov*, 63–64.

67. Rhodes, *Dark Sun*, 366–67, at 366 and 367; Holloway, *Stalin and the Bomb*, 216.

68. Holloway, *Stalin and the Bomb*, 214, 217–18, at 217; Rhodes, *Dark Sun*, 367–68.

69. Holloway, *Stalin and the Bomb*, 218–19, at 218; Rhodes, *Dark Sun*, 368.

70. Riabeva, *Atomnyi proekt*, book 7, 556–57; N. S. Simonov, *Voenno-promyshlenni kompleks SSSR v 1920–1950 gody: Tempy ekonomicheskogo rosta, struktura, organizatsiia proizvodstva i upravleniie* [The Soviet military-industrial complex from 1920 to 1950: Economic growth, structure, production, and management] (Moscow: Rosspen, 1996), 242; CIA, "Memorandum: Military Expenditures and National Income of the USSR," December 26, 1950, www.foia.cia.gov/sites/default/files/document_conversions/89801/DOC_0000969834.pdf; Holloway, *Stalin and the Bomb*, 220–21.

71. Holloway, *Stalin and the Bomb*, 222–23, 417n127.

72. Riabeva, *Atomnyi proekt*, book 7, 546–49, 572, 585; Zaloga, *Target America*, 94–106; Holloway, *Stalin and the Bomb*, 219, 303–9, 312–17; Rhodes, *Dark Sun*, 523–25.

73. Riabeva, *Atomnyi proekt*, book 5, 346–48; book 7, 552.

74. Riabeva, *Atomnyi proekt*, book 5, 342; NIE, "The Soviet Atomic Energy Program to Mid-1957," NIE 11-3A-54, February 16, 1954, in *Selected Estimates on the Soviet Union, 1950–1959*, ed. Scott A. Koch (Washington, DC: Center for the Study of Intelligence of the Central Intelligence Agency, 1993), 13–17.

75. Rhodes, *Dark Sun*, 482–512, 541–42, 579–80; Holloway, *Stalin and the Bomb*, 305–17; Golovin, *Kurchatov*, 64–67.

76. Holloway, *Stalin and the Bomb*, 224–27, 231–37, 242–50; Zaloga, *Target America*, 34–35, 118–38.

77. Holloway, *Stalin and the Bomb*, 237–42, at 242.

78. Ibid.

16. WALTER BEDELL SMITH REFORMS AND EXPANDS THE CIA

1. G. John Ikenberry, *After Victory: Institutions, Strategic Restraint, and the Rebuilding of Order After Major Wars* (Princeton, NJ: Princeton University Press, 2001), 163–214; G. John Ikenberry, "Political Structures and Postwar Settlements," in *New European Orders, 1919 and 1991*, ed. Samuel F. Wells Jr. and Paula Bailey Smith (Washington, DC: Woodrow Wilson Center Press, 1996), 1–17.

2. Ludwell Lee Montague, *General Walter Bedell Smith as Director of Central Intelligence, October 1950–February 1953* (University Park: Pennsylvania State University Press, 1992) (hereafter, *Smith as DCI*), 1–17.

3. Truman to secretaries of state, war, and navy, January 22, 1946, *Foreign Relations, 1945–1950: Emergence of the Intelligence Establishment* (Washington, DC: US Government Printing Office, 1996), 178–79; Montague, *Smith as DCI*, 25–26; Michael Warner and J. Kenneth McDonald, *US Intelligence Community Reform Studies since 1947* (Washington, DC: Center for the Study of Intelligence of Central Intelligence Agency, 2005), 3–5.

4. Montague, *Smith as DCI*, 27–30.

5. Montague, *Smith as DCI*, 34–35.

6. Montague, *Smith as DCI*, 9–14, 35–43; Warner and McDonald, *Intelligence Community Reform*, 8–9.

7. Warner and McDonald, *Intelligence Community Reform*, 8–10, at 9–10.

8. Warner and McDonald, *Intelligence Community Reform*, 10–11, at 10 and 11; Montague, *Smith as DCI*, 43–44.

9. Montague, *Smith as DCI*, 46–47.

10. Montague, *Smith as DCI*, 47–50, at 47; Warner and McDonald, *Intelligence Community Reform*, 11.

11. Tim Weiner, *Legacy of Ashes: The History of the CIA* (New York: Doubleday, 2007), 3–26, at 3; Montague, *Smith as DCI*, 40–50.

12. The new covert action program was initially called the Office of Special Projects, but its name was soon changed to the Office of Policy Coordination. Evan Thomas, *The Very Best Men: The Daring Early Years of the CIA* (New York: Simon & Schuster, 1996), 28–30, 354–55; Weiner, *Legacy of Ashes*, 22–29; Kennan, memorandum on the inauguration of political warfare, May 4, 1948, NSC Report 10/2, June 18, 1948, *Foreign Relations, 1945–1950: Intelligence*, 668–72, 713–15; W. R. Smyser, *From Yalta to Berlin: The Cold War Struggle Over Berlin* (New York: St. Martin's Press, 1999), 73–75.

13. Smyser, *From Yalta to Berlin*, 75–78; Weiner, *Legacy of Ashes*, 19–21, 28–31; Thomas, *Very Best Men*, 24–26.

14. Weiner, *Legacy of Ashes*, 28–31; Frank Wisner, memoranda of talks on counterpart funds and operations with senior Marshall Plan representatives in Paris and with John McCloy in Bonn, November 16, 1948–June 1, 1949, *Foreign Relations, 1945–1950: Intelligence*, 732–36; Michael J. Hogan, *The Marshall Plan: America, Britain, and the Reconstruction of Western Europe, 1947–1952* (New York: Cambridge University Press, 1987), 85–86, 152–55; Herman Van der Wee, *Prosperity and Upheaval: The World Economy, 1945–1980* (Berkeley: University of California Press, 1986), 43–47; Thomas, *Very Best Men*, 40–41, 87–88.

15. Thomas, *Very Best* Men, 15–19, 33–42; Weiner, *Legacy of Ashes*, 30–34.

16. Weiner, *Legacy of Ashes*, 33–36; Thomas, *Very Best Men*, 33–39; Burton Hersh, *The Old Boys: The American Elite and the Origins of the CIA* (New York: Charles Scribner's Sons, 1992), 253–66.

17. Weiner, *Legacy of Ashes*, 40.

18. Weiner, *Legacy of Ashes*, 41–42, 540–41; Thomas, *Very Best Men*, 35–36; Hersh, *Old Boys*, 266–71.

19. Weiner, *Legacy of Ashes*, 43–47, at 45; Thomas, *Very Best Men*, 27–39; Hersh, *Old Boys*, 269–81.

20. This compromise of signals intelligence on Soviet communications with Asia was later characterized in an NSA history as "perhaps the most significant intelligence loss in US history." This incident led to the creation two years later of the NSA. Weiner, *Legacy of Ashes*, 41–51, at 51; Thomas, *Very Best Men*, 50–51, at 51.

21. D. K. R. Crosswell, *Beetle: The Life of General Walter Bedell Smith* (Lexington: University Press of Kentucky, 2012), 109–13, at 109 and 112.

22. Crosswell, *Beetle*, 113–18.

23. Crosswell, *Beetle*, 115–19.

24. Crosswell, *Beetle*, 117–18.

25. Crosswell, *Beetle*, 121–42, 157.

26. Crosswell, *Beetle*, 143–62.

27. Crosswell, *Beetle*, 163–200, at 165, 169, 172, and 189.

28. Crosswell, *Beetle*, 200–206; Forrest C. Pogue, *George C. Marshall: Ordeal and Hope, 1939–1942* (New York: Viking Press, 1966), 7–8.

29. Crosswell, *Beetle*, 206–14

30. Crosswell, *Beetle*, 209–10, at 209.

31. Crosswell, *Beetle,*, 211–28, at 211, 224, and 226.

32. Crosswell, *Beetle*, 227–34, at 234; Pogue, *Marshall: Ordeal and Hope*, 261–63.

33. Crosswell, *Beetle*, 233–40; Pogue, *Marshall: Ordeal and Hope*, 264–88.

34. Crosswell, *Beetle*, 238–55, 272, at 244 and 255.

35. Crosswell, *Beetle*, 257–92.

36. Crosswell, *Beetle*, 3–5, 314–18, at 5 and 318; Forrest C. Pogue, *The Supreme Command: The United States Army in World War II, the European Theater of Operations* (Washington, DC: Office of the Chief of Military History, 1954), 33–35, 62–65; Montague, *Smith as DCI*, 9.

37. Crosswell, *Beetle*, 287–312, 318–30.

38. Crosswell, *Beetle*, 330–433 passim.

39. Crosswell, *Beetle*, 450–67.

40. Crosswell, *Beetle*, 454–55, 469–78; for a full discussion of the frenzied Italian maneuvers, see Elena Agarossi, *A Nation Collapses: The Italian Surrender of September 1943* (Cambridge: Cambridge University Press, 2000).

41. Crosswell, *Beetle*, 478–82.

42. Crosswell, *Beetle*, 482–87, at 483.

43. Crosswell, *Beetle*, 487–93, at 488.

44. Crosswell, *Beetle*, 493–95, at 493; for the Darlan deal and its repercussions, see ibid., 334–52.

45. Churchill, visiting the White House after the Quebec Conference, was not taken aback by the Italian betrayal, exclaiming to Roosevelt: "That's what you would expect from those Dagoes." Crosswell, *Beetle*, 497–547, at 504.

46. SHAEF is the acronym for Supreme Headquarters, Allied Expeditionary Force. Ibid., 551–81, at 581.

47. Ibid., 583–626.

48. Ibid., 626–828 passim, 838–47.

49. Ibid., 682–92, 830–38, 847–58; Alex Danchev and Daniel Todman, eds., *War Diaries, 1939–1945: Field Marshal Lord Alanbrooke* (Berkeley: University of California Press, 2001), 401–11, 441–43, 462–66, 473–76, 481–88, 628–30; Alistair Horne, with David Montgomery, *Monty: The Lonely Leader, 1944–1945* (New York: HarperCollins, 1994), 298–321.

50. Crosswell, *Beetle*, 854–61; Danchev and Todman, *War Diaries: Alanbrooke*, 441–43, 651–52.

51. Crosswell, *Beetle*, 861–64, at 861; Danchev and Todman, *War Diaries: Alanbrooke*, 652–55, at 653.

52. Crosswell, *Beetle*, 915–18; Walter Bedell Smith, *Eisenhower's Six Great Decisions: Europe, 1944–1945* (London: Longmans, Green, 1956), 200–204; Horne, *Monty*, 335–38.

53. Smith, *Eisenhower's Six Great Decisions*, 204–5; Crosswell, *Beetle*, 918–19.

54. Smith, *Eisenhower's Six Great* Decisions, 205–6; Crosswell, *Beetle*, 919–24, at 924.

55. Montague, *Smith as DCI*, 5–6; Crosswell, *Beetle*, 9–17.

56. One sentence in Kennan's "long telegram" has a remarkably contemporary resonance: "The very disrespect of Russians for objective truth—indeed, their disbelief in its existence—leads them to view all stated facts as instruments for furtherance of one

ulterior purpose or another." Kennan to Byrnes, February 22, 1946, *Foreign Relations, 1946*, vol. 6, 701. Crosswell, *Beetle*, 17–21, at 18; Kennan to Byrnes, February 22, 1946, Smith to Byrnes, April 5, 1946, *Foreign Relations, 1946*, vol. 6, 696–709, 732–36, at 734; Walter Bedell Smith, *My Three Years in Moscow* (Philadelphia: J. B. Lippincott, 1950), 49–54.

57. The Federal Republic of Germany was established from the three Western occupation zones on May 23, 1949, two weeks after the Soviets lifted the blockade of Berlin. Crosswell, *Beetle*, 21–28; Montague, *Smith as DCI*, 6–7.

58. Smith, *My Three Years in Moscow*, 55–84, at 55 and 62–63; Crosswell, *Beetle*, 28–30; Stephen Kotkin, *Stalin: Waiting for Hitler, 1929–1941* (New York: Penguin Press, 2017), 9–33.

59. Smith, *My Three Years in Moscow*, 307–34, at 307, 333, and 334.

60. Crosswell, *Beetle*, 30–31, at 31; Montague, *Smith as DCI*, 54–56.

61. Montague, *Smith as DCI*, 9–12, 56–57.

62. Montague, *Smith as DCI*, 56.

63. Houston, memorandum for the record, August 29, 1950, *Foreign Relations, 1950–1955, The Intelligence Community* (Washington, DC: US Government Printing Office, 2007), 29–32; Montague, *Smith as DCI*, 60–62.

64. The resistance of the departmental intelligence agencies to accepting leadership from the DCI and cooperating with the CIA was a typical bureaucratic reaction to attempts to centralize previously autonomous units. The state and navy departments had gained significant intelligence capability and influence during World War I, and the army and air force developed later. But all the departmental intelligence agencies felt that their budgets and missions were threatened by the creation of the CIA. It required several serious intelligence failures and the unanticipated war in Korea to force the necessary changes. Montague, *Smith as DCI*, 58–64, 120–23; Crosswell, *Beetle*, 33–35.

65. The IAC was composed of the heads of intelligence in the state, army, navy, and air force departments, the joint staff, AEC, and the FBI. Montague, *Smith as DCI*, 64–66, at 65; Walter B. Smith, memorandum for the president, October 12, 1950, Michael Warner, ed., *The CIA under Harry Truman* (Washington, DC: Central Intelligence Agency, 1994), 349–72, at 354.

66. Minutes of a meeting of the Intelligence Advisory Committee, October 20, 1950, *Foreign Relations, 1950–1955, Intelligence*, 47–52, at 48, 49, 50, and 51; Montague, *Smith as DCI*, 66–69, at 66.

67. Montague, *Smith as DCI*, 69–74.

68. Weiner, *Legacy of Ashes*, 49.

69. Montague, *Smith as DCI*, 200–201; Peter Grose, *Gentleman Spy: The Life of Allen Dulles* (Boston: Houghton Mifflin, 1994), 308.

70. Montague, *Smith as DCI*, 79–91; Hersh, *Old Boys*, 287–88; Crosswell, *Beetle*, 33–34; Warner, *CIA under Truman*, xlvi; Christopher Andrew, *For the President's Eyes Only: Secret Intelligence and the American Presidency from Washington to Bush* (New York: Harper Perennial, 1996), 192.

71. Montague, *Smith as DCI*, 92–95; Crosswell, *Beetle*, 35–36; Hersh, *Old Boys*, 288–89.

72. Montague, *Smith as DCI*, 95–100; Hersh, *Old Boys*, 289–91.

73. Montague, *Smith as DCI*, 100–102, at 102.
74. Smith, memorandum to the NSC, April 23, 1952, *Foreign Relations, 1950–1955, Intelligence*, 250–51.
75. Ibid., 252–53, at 253.
76. Ibid., 254.
77. Crosswell, *Beetle*, 692–93; Montague, *Smith as DCI*, 203–27, at 204.
78. Montague, *Smith as DCI*, 204–5.
79. Smith, memorandum to the NSC, May 8, 1951, NSC Report 10/5, "Scope and Pace of Covert Operations," October 23, 1951, *Foreign Relations, 1950–1955: Intelligence*, 141–48, 206–8; Montague, *Smith as DCI*, 205–11; Grose, *Gentleman Spy*, 308–10.
80. This reorganization also created a cable secretariat in the office of the DCI and had the communications and training offices report directly to the DCI. Montague, *Smith as DCI*, 217–27, at 227; Smith, memorandum on the "Organization of the Clandestine Services," July 15, 1952, Warner, *CIA under Truman*, 465–67; Thomas Powers, *The Man Who Kept the Secrets: Richard Helms & the CIA* (New York: Alfred A. Knopf, 1979), 48–51.
81. Harry Rositzke, *The CIA's Secret Operations: Espionage, Counterespionage, and Covert Action* (New York: Reader's Digest Press, 1977), 148–54; Powers, *Man Who Kept the Secrets*, 28–33; Grose, *Gentleman Spy*, 300–302.
82. Weiner, *Legacy of Ashes*, 53.
83. Rositzke, *CIA's Secret Operations*, 167–71; Weiner, *Legacy of Ashes*, 43–46; Grose, *Gentleman Spy*, 311, 315–17.
84. Rositzke, *CIA's Secret Operations*, 166–73; John Prados, *Presidents' Secret Wars: CIA and Pentagon Covert Operations Since World War II* (New York: William Morrow, 1986), 45–52; Weiner, *Legacy of Ashes*, 45–47, 67–68; Grose, *Gentleman Spy*, 354–56.
85. After a delay of some months, MI6 employed Philby again as a contract agent in Beirut under cover as a journalist. When further evidence of his work for the KGB came from a Soviet defector and a leak to the press by FBI director J. Edgar Hoover revealed some of the details of his treason, Philby defected to Moscow in January 1963. Ben Macintyre, *A Spy Among Friends: Kim Philby and the Great Betrayal* (New York: Broadway Books, 2014), 163–64, 256–75; Crosswell, *Beetle*, 38–41.
86. Weiner, *Legacy of Ashes*, 53–57; Andrew, *For the President's Eyes Only*, 193–94.
87. Hersh, *Old Boys*, 297–98; Weiner, *Legacy of Ashes*, 64–66.
88. Weiner, *Legacy of Ashes*, 66–67; Montague, *Smith as DCI*, 213; Grose, *Gentleman Spy*, 328–29; Hersh, *Old Boys*, 298.
89. Montague, *Smith as DCI*, 35; Prados, *Presidents' Secret Wars*, 67–68; Weiner, *Legacy of Ashes*, 54–55, at 55.
90. Weiner, *Legacy of Ashes*, 56; Prados, *Presidents' Secret Wars*, 68–69.
91. Weiner, *Legacy of Ashes*, 56–57, at 57; John Limond Hart, *The CIA's Russians* (Annapolis, MD: Naval Institute Press, 2003), 8–9, at 8 and 9.
92. Weiner, *Legacy of Ashes*, 58, quoting Kellis to Eisenhower, May 24, 1954.
93. Ibid., 59–60, at 60; Prados, *Presidents' Secret Wars*, 67–72.
94. Nicholas Dujmovic, "Two CIA Prisoners in China, 1952–1973," *Studies in Intelligence* 50, no. 4 (2004); Weiner, *Legacy of Ashes*, 60, 551–53.

95. Weiner, *Legacy of Ashes*, 60–61, 553–54, at 61; Crosswell, *Beetle*, 38; Hersh, *Old Boys*, 300; Prados, *Presidents' Secret Wars*, 73–77.

96. Andrew, *For the President's Eyes Only*, 194–96, at 194.

97. Andrew, *For the President's Eyes Only*, 196–97.

98. Weiner, *Legacy of Ashes*, 62. Frank Wisner survived Smith's attacks, but at a high cost. He drank heavily, became erratic in behavior, lapsed into mental illness, and committed suicide in 1965 at the age of fifty-six. See Hersh, *Old Boys*, 298–316; Weiner, *Legacy of Ashes*, 262–63.

99. Grose, *Gentleman Spy*, 327; Andrew, *For the President's Eyes Only*, 191–92.

17. KOREA TRANSFORMS THE COLD WAR

1. Charles E. Bohlen, *Witness to History, 1929–1969* (New York: W. W. Norton, 1973), 305–4.

2. Truman diary entry, December 9, 1950, PSF, Truman Library.

SELECTED BIBLIOGRAPHY

Acheson, Dean. *Present at the Creation: My Years in the State Department*. New York: W. W. Norton, 1969.

Air Force History, Office of. *Steadfast and Courageous: FEAF Bomber Command and the Air War in Korea, 1950–1953*. Washington, DC: Office of Air Force History, 2000.

Andrew, Christopher. *For the President's Eyes Only: Secret Intelligence and the American Presidency from Washington to Bush*. New York: Harper Perennial, 1996.

Andrew, Christopher, and Oleg Gordievsky. *KGB: The Inside Story of Its Foreign Operations from Lenin to Gorbachev*. New York: HarperCollins, 1990.

Andrew, Christopher, and Vasili Mitrokhin. *The Sword and the Shield: The Mitrokhin Archive and the Secret History of the KGB*. New York: Basic Books, 1999.

Armstrong, Charles K. *The North Korean Revolution, 1945–1950*. Ithaca, NY: Cornell University Press, 2003.

Bajanov, Evgeniy P., and Natalia Bajanova. "The Korean Conflict, 1950–1953: The Most Mysterious War of the 20th Century—Based on Secret Soviet Archives." Unpublished typescript, n.d., copy in archives of North Korea International Documentation Project, Woodrow Wilson International Center for Scholars.

Beisner, Robert L. *Dean Acheson: A Life in the Cold War*. New York: Oxford University Press, 2006.

Blair, Clay. *The Forgotten War: America in Korea, 1950–1953*. Annapolis, MD: Naval Institute Press, 2003.

——. *Ridgway's Paratroopers: The American Airborne in World War II*. New York: Dial Press, 1985.

Bohlen, Charles E. *Witness to History, 1929–1969*. New York: W. W. Norton, 1973.

Borowski, Harry R. *A Hollow Threat: Strategic Air Power and Containment Before Korea*. Westport, CT: Greenwood Press, 1982.

Chang, Jung, and Jon Halliday. *Mao: The Unknown Story*. New York: Alfred A. Knopf, 2005.

Caridi, Ronald J. *The Korean War and American Politics: The Republican Party as a Case Study.* Philadelphia: University of Pennsylvania Press, 1968.

Chen Jian. *China's Road to the Korean War: The Making of the Sino-American Confrontation.* New York: Columbia University Press, 1994.

Condit, Doris M. *The Test of War, 1950–1953: History of the Office of the Secretary of Defense,* vol. II. Washington, DC: Historical Office of the Office of the Secretary of Defense, 1988.

Congressional Quarterly. *Congress and the Nation, 1945–1963.* Washington, DC: Congressional Quarterly, 1965.

Chuev, Felix. *Molotov Remembers: Inside Kremlin Politics—Conversations with Felix Chuev.* Chicago: Ivan R. Dee, 1993.

Coffey, Thomas M. *Iron Eagle: The Turbulent Life of General Curtis LeMay.* New York: Crown, 1986.

Craig, Campbell, and Sergey Radchenko. *The Atomic Bomb and the Origins of the Cold War.* New Haven, CT: Yale University Press, 2008.

Crosswell, D. K. R. *Beetle: The Life of General Walter Bedell Smith.* Lexington: University Press of Kentucky, 2012.

Cumings, Bruce. *The Korean War: A History.* New York: Modern Library, 2010.

——. *The Origins of the Korean War,* vol. I, *Liberation and the Emergence of Separate Regimes, 1945–1947.* Princeton, NJ: Princeton University Press, 1981.

——. *The Origins of the Korean War,* vol. II, *The Roaring of the Cataract, 1947–1950.* Princeton, NJ: Princeton University Press, 1990.

Dallek, Robert. *Franklin D. Roosevelt and American Foreign Policy, 1932–1945.* New York: Oxford University Press, 1979.

——. *The Lost Peace: Leadership in a Time of Horror and Hope, 1945–1953.* New York: Harper-Collins, 2010.

Danchev, Alex, and Daniel Todman, eds. *War Diaries, 1939–1945: Field Marshal Lord Alanbrooke.* Berkeley: University of California Press, 2001.

Djilas, Milovan. *Conversations with Stalin.* New York: Harcourt, Brace & World, 1962.

Donovan, Robert. *Conflict and Crisis: The Presidency of Harry S Truman, 1945–1950.* New York: W. W. Norton, 1977.

——. *Tumultuous Years: The Presidency of Harry S Truman, 1949–1953.* New York: W. W. Norton, 1982.

Duffy, Paul, and Andrei Kandalov. *Tupolev: The Man And His Aircraft.* Warrendale, PA: SAE, 1996.

Duke, Simon W., and Wolfgang Krieger, eds. *US Military Forces in Europe: The Early Years, 1945–1970.* Boulder, CO: Westview Press, 1993.

Erickson, John. *The Road to Stalingrad: Stalin's War with Germany,* vol. 1. New York: Harper & Row, 1975.

Freedman, Lawrence. *The Evolution of Nuclear Strategy.* New York: St. Martin's Press, 1981.

Fried, Richard M. *Men Against McCarthy.* New York: Columbia University Press, 1976.

——. *Nightmare in Red: The McCarthy Era.* New York: Oxford University Press, 1990.

Futrell, Robert Frank. *Ideas, Concepts, Doctrine: A History of Basic Thinking in the United States Air Force, 1907–1964.* Maxwell Air Force Base, AL: Air University Press, 1974.

Gaddis, John Lewis. *George F. Kennan: An American Life.* New York: Penguin Press, 2011.

Gallop, George H. *The Gallop Poll: Public Opinion, 1935–1971.* 3 vols. New York: Random House, 1972.

Gao Wenqian. *Zhou Enlai: The Last Perfect Revolutionary.* New York: PublicAffairs, 2007.

Golovin, Igor N. *I. V. Kurchatov: A Socialist-Realist Biography of the Soviet Nuclear Scientist.* Bloomington, IN: Selbstverlag Press, 1968.

Goncharov, Sergei N., John W. Lewis, and Xue Litai. *Uncertain Partners: Stalin, Mao, and the Korean War.* Stanford, CA: Stanford University Press, 1993.

Gordon, Yefim, and Peter Davison. *Tupolev: Tu-95 Bear.* North Branch, MN: Specialty Press, 2006.

Gordon, Yefim, and Vladimir Rigmant. *OKB Tupolev: A History of the Design Bureau and Its Aircraft.* Hinckley, UK: Midland Publishing, 2005.

Gorlizki, Yoram, and Oleg Khlevniuk. *Cold Peace: Stalin and the Soviet Ruling Circle, 1945–1953.* New York: Oxford University Press, 2004.

Goulden, Joseph C. *Korea: The Untold Story of the War.* New York: Times Books, 1982.

Gowing, Margaret. *Britain and Atomic Energy, 1939–1945.* London: Macmillan, 1964.

Griffith, Robert. *The Politics of Fear: Joseph R. McCarthy and the Senate.* Amherst: University of Massachusetts Press, 1987.

Grose, Peter. *Gentleman Spy: The Life of Allen Dulles.* Boston: Houghton Mifflin, 1994.

Hackett, Clifford P., ed. *Monnet and the Americans: The Father of a United Europe and His US Supporters.* Washington, DC: Jean Monnet Council, 1995.

Hamby, Alonzo L. *Man of the People: A Life of Harry S. Truman.* New York: Oxford University Press, 1995.

Hart, John Limond. *The CIA's Russians.* Annapolis, MD: Naval Institute Press, 2003.

Hasegawa, Tsuyoshi, ed. *The Cold War in Asia, 1945–1991.* Washington, DC, and Stanford, CA: Woodrow Wilson Center Press and Stanford University Press, 2011.

Hastings, Max. *Armageddon: The Battle for Germany, 1944–1945.* New York: Alfred A. Knopf, 2004.

——. *The Korean War.* New York: Simon & Schuster, 1987.

Haynes, John Earl, Harvey Klehr, and Alexander Vassiliev. *Spies: The Rise and Fall of the KGB in America.* New Haven, CT: Yale University Press, 2009.

Heinl, Robert Debs, Jr. *Victory at High Tide: The Inchon-Seoul Campaign.* Washington, DC: Naval and Aviation Publishing Company of America, 1979.

Herman, Arthur. *Joseph McCarthy: Reexamining the Life and Legacy of America's Most Hated Senator.* New York: Free Press, 1999.

Hersh, Burton. *The Old Boys: The American Elite and the Origins of the CIA.* New York: Charles Scribner's Sons, 1992.

Hewlett, Richard, and Francis Duncan. *Atomic Shield, 1947–1952.* Washington, DC: Atomic Energy Commission, 1972.

Hogan, Michael J. *The Marshall Plan: America, Britain, and the Reconstruction of Western Europe, 1947–1952.* New York: Cambridge University Press, 1987.

Holloway, David. *Stalin and the Bomb: The Soviet Union and Atomic Energy.* New Haven, CT: Yale University Press, 1994.

Horne, Alistair, with David Montgomery. *Monty: The Lonely Leader, 1944–1945.* New York: HarperCollins, 1994.

Iakubovich, N. V., and V. N. Lavrov. *Samolety V. M. Miasishcheva* [The airplanes of V. M. Mia-sishchev]. Moscow: Rusavia, 1999.

Ikenberry, G. John. *After Victory: Institutions, Strategic Restraint, and the Rebuilding of Order After Major Wars*. Princeton, NJ: Princeton University Press, 2001.

Isaacson, Walter, and Evan Thomas. *The Wise Men: Six Friends and the World They Made*. New York: Simon & Schuster, 2013.

Jager, Sheila Miyoshi. *Brothers at War: The Unending Conflict in Korea*. New York: W. W. Norton, 2013.

James, D. Clayton. *The Years of MacArthur: Triumph and Disaster, 1945–1964*, vol. III. Boston: Houghton Mifflin, 1985.

Kaplan, Fred. *The Wizards of Armageddon*. New York: Simon & Schuster, 1983.

Kennan, George F. *Memoirs, 1925–1950*, vol. I. Boston: Little, Brown, 1967.

——. *Memoirs, 1950–1963*, vol. II. Boston: Little, Brown, 1972.

Kerber, L. L., and Von Hardesty. *Stalin's Aviation Gulag: A Memoir of Andrei Tupolev and the Purge Era*. Washington, DC: Smithsonian Institution Press, 1996.

Khan, Sulmaan Wasif. *Haunted by Chaos: China's Grand Strategy from Mao Zedong to Xi Jinping*. Cambridge, MA: Harvard University Press, 2018.

Khrushchev, Nikita S. *Khrushchev Remembers*. Boston: Little, Brown, 1970.

Kissinger, Henry. *On China*. New York: Penguin Press, 2011.

Knight, Amy. *Beria: Stalin's First Lieutenant*. Princeton, NJ: Princeton University Press, 1993.

Koch, Scott A., ed. *Selected Estimates on the Soviet Union, 1950–1959*. Washington, DC: Center for the Study of Intelligence of the Central Intelligence Agency, 1993.

Koen, Ross Y. *The China Lobby in American Politics*. New York: Harper & Row, 1974.

Kolodziej, Edward J. *The Uncommon Defense and Congress, 1945–1963*. Columbus: Ohio State University Press, 1966.

Kotkin, Stephen. *Stalin: Waiting for Hitler, 1929–1941*. New York: Penguin Press, 2017.

Kozak, Warren. *Curtis LeMay: Strategist and Tactician*. Washington, DC: Regnery History, 2014.

Lankov, Andrei. *From Stalin to Kim Il-sung: The Formation of North Korea, 1945–1960*. New Brunswick, NJ: Rutgers University Press, 2002.

Leffler, Melvyn P. *A Preponderance of Power: National Security, the Truman Administration, and the Cold War*. Stanford, CA: Stanford University Press, 1992.

LeMay, Curtis, with MacKinlay Kantor. *Mission with LeMay: My Story*. Garden City, NY: Doubleday, 1965.

MacFarquhar, Roderick, and John K. Fairbank, eds. *The People's Republic of China, Part I: The Emergence of Revolutionary China, 1949–1965—Volume 14, The Cambridge History of China*. Cambridge: Cambridge University Press, 1987)

Macintyre, Ben. *A Spy Among Friends: Kim Philby and the Great Betrayal*. New York: Broadway Books, 2014.

McLellan, David S. *Dean Acheson: The State Department Years*. New York: Dodd, Mead, 1976.

Mao Zedong. *Selected Works of Mao Tse-Tung*, vol. V. Beijing: Foreign Languages Press, 1977.

Meilinger, Phillip S. *The Formation and Early Years of the Strategic Air Command, 1946–1957: Why the SAC Was Formed.* Lewiston, NY: Edwin Mellen Press, 2013.

Mikoian, Anastas Ivanovich. *Tak Bylo: Razmyshleniia o minuvshem.* Moscow: Vagrius, 1999.

Millett, Allan R. *The War for Korea, 1950–1951: They Came From the North.* Lawrence: University Press of Kansas, 2010.

Mitchell, George C. *Matthew B. Ridgway: Soldier, Statesman, Scholar, Citizen.* Mechanicsburg, PA: Stackpole, 2002.

Montague, Ludwell Lee. *General Walter Bedell Smith as Director of Central Intelligence, October 1950–February 1953.* University Park: Pennsylvania State University Press, 1992.

Moroz, S. *Dal'nie bombardirovschiki M-4 i 3M* [Long-range bombers M4 and 3M]. Moscow: Exprint, 2005.

Nitze, Paul H. *From Hiroshima to Glasnost: At the Center of Decision—A Memoir.* New York: Grove Weidenfeld, 1989).

Oshinsky, David M. *A Conspiracy So Immense: The World of Joe McCarthy.* New York: Oxford University Press, 2005.

Ostapenko, Yu. A. *Tovarishch ministr: Povest' o rukovoditele aviatsionnoi promyshlennosti SSSR P. V. Dement'eve* [Comrade Minister: A narrative about P. V. Dement'eve, the head of the aviation industry in the USSR]. Moscow: Aerosphere, 2006.

Overy, Richard. *The Bombers and the Bombed: Allied Air War Over Germany, 1940–1945.* New York: Penguin Press, 2015.

Paige, Glenn D. *The Korean Decision [June 24–30, 1950].* New York: Free Press, 1968.

Patterson, James T. *Mr. Republican: A Biography of Robert A. Taft.* Boston: Houghton Mifflin, 1972.

Pogue, Forrest C. *George C. Marshall: Education of a General, 1880–1939.* New York: Viking Press, 1963.

——. *George C. Marshall: Ordeal and Hope, 1939–1942.* New York: Viking Press, 1966.

——. *George C. Marshall: Statesman, 1945–1959.* New York: Viking Press, 1987.

Pollard, Robert A. *Economic Security and the Origins of the Cold War, 1945–1950.* New York: Columbia University Press, 1985.

Pantsov, Alexander V., and Steven I. Levine. *Mao: The Real Story.* New York: Simon & Schuster, 2012.

Powers, Thomas. *The Man Who Kept the Secrets: Richard Helms and the CIA.* New York: Alfred A. Knopf, 1979.

Prados, John. *Presidents' Secret Wars: CIA and Pentagon Covert Operations Since World War II.* New York: William Morrow, 1986.

Rearden, Steven L. *The Evolution of American Strategic Doctrine: Paul H. Nitze and the Soviet Challenge.* Boulder, CO: Westview Press, 1984.

——. *The Formative Years, 1947–1950: History of the Office of the Secretary of Defense,* vol. I. Washington, DC: Historical Office of the Office of the Secretary of Defense, 1984.

Riabeva, L. D., ed. *Atomnyi proekt SSSR: Dokumenty i materialy* [The Atomic project of the Soviet Union: Documents and materials]. 7 vols. Moscow: Nauka, Fizmatlit, 1999.

Rhodes, Richard. *Dark Sun: The Making of the Hydrogen Bomb.* New York: Simon & Schuster, 1995.

Ridgway, Matthew B. *Soldier: The Memoirs of Matthew B. Ridgway.* Westport, CT: Greenwood Press, 1974.

Rigmant, V. *Samolety OKB A. N. Tupolev* [The aircraft of A. N. Tupolev's design bureau]. Moscow: Rusavia, 2001.

Rioux, Jean-Pierre. *The Fourth Republic, 1944–1958.* Cambridge: Cambridge University Press, 1987.

Rosenberg, David Alan. "The Origins of Overkill: Nuclear Weapons and American Strategy, 1945–1960." *International Security* 7 (Spring 1983).

Rositzke, Harry. *The CIA's Secret Operations: Espionage, Counterespionage, and Covert Action.* New York: Reader's Digest Press, 1977.

Ross, Steven T. *American War Plans, 1945–1950.* New York: Garland, 1988).

Rovere, Richard. *Senator Joe McCarthy.* Berkeley: University of California Press, 1959.

Schnabel, James F. *Policy and Direction: The First Year—The United States Army in the Korean War.* Washington, DC: Office of the Chief of Military History, US Army, 1972.

Schnabel, James F., and Robert J. Watson. *The Korean War, History of the Joint Chiefs of Staff: The Joint Chiefs of Staff and National Policy,* vol. III (2 parts). Washington, DC: Office of Joint History of the Office of the Chairman of the Joint Chiefs of Staff, 1998.

Schwartz, Thomas A. *America's Germany: John J. McCloy and the Federal Republic of Germany.* Cambridge, MA: Harvard University Press, 1991.

Settle, Frank A. *General George C. Marshall and the Atomic Bomb.* Santa Barbara, CA: Praeger, 2016.

Shen Zhihua. *Mao, Stalin and the Korean War: Trilateral Communist Relations in the 1950s.* New York: Routledge, 2012.

Shen Zhuhua, and Danhui Li. *After Leaning to One Side: China and Its Allies in the Cold War.* Washington, DC, and Stanford, CA: Woodrow Wilson Center Press and Stanford University Press, 2011.

Shen Zhihua, and Yafeng Xia. *Mao and the Sino-Soviet Partnership, 1945–1959: A New History.* Lanham, MD: Lexington Books, 2015.

——. *A Misunderstood Friendship: Mao Zedong, Kim Il-sung, and Sino-North Korean Relations, 1949–1976.* New York: Columbia University Press, 2018.

Sides, Hampton. *On Desperate Ground: The Marines at the Reservoir, the Korean War's Greatest Battle.* New York: Doubleday, 2018.

Simonov, N. S. *Voenno-promyshlenni kompleks SSSR v 1920–1950 gody: Tempy ekonomicheskogo rosta, struktura, organizatsiia proizvodstva i upravlenie* [The Soviet military-industrial complex from 1920 to 1950: Economic growth, structure, production, and management]. Moscow: Rosspen, 1996.

Smith, Walter Bedell. *Eisenhower's Six Great Decisions: Europe: 1944–1945.* London: Longmans, Green, 1956.

——. *My Three Years in Moscow.* Philadelphia: J. B. Lippincott, 1950.

Smyser, W. R. *From Yalta to Berlin: The Cold War Struggle Over Germany.* New York: St. Martin's Press, 1999.

Snow, Edgar. *Red Star over China.* London: Victor Gollancz, 1937.

Suh, Dae-Sook. *Kim Il Sung: The North Korean Leader.* New York: Columbia University Press, 1988.

Taubman, William. *Khrushchev: The Man and His Era.* New York: W. W. Norton, 2003.

——. *Stalin's American Policy: From Entente to Détente to Cold War.* New York; W. W. Norton, 1982.

Thomas, Evan. *The Very Best Men: The Daring Early Years of the CIA.* New York: Simon & Schuster, 1996.

Thompson, Nicholas. *The Hawk and the Dove: Paul Nitze, George Kennan, and the History of the Cold War.* New York: Henry Holt, 2009.

Tillman, Barrett. *LeMay.* New York: Palgrave Macmillan, 2009.

Troianovskii, Oleg. *Cherez gody i rasstoianiia: Istoriia odnoi sem'i.* Moscow: Vagrius, 1997.

Ulam, Adam B. *Stalin: The Man and His Era.* New York: Viking Press, 1974.

US Department of State. *Foreign Relations of the United States.* Various volumes. Washington, DC: US Government Printing Office, 1968–84.

Van der Wee, Herman. *Prosperity and Upheaval: The World Economy, 1945–1980.* Berkeley: University of California Press, 1986.

Wada, Haruki. *Hanguk Chonjaeng* [The Korean War]. Korean translation of Japanese edition. Seoul: Changbi, 1999.

——. *North Joseon.* Paju, South Korea: Dolbaegae, 2002.

Wall, Irwin M. *The United States and the Making of Postwar France, 1945–1954.* Cambridge: Cambridge University Press, 1991.

Warner, Michael, ed. *The CIA under Harry Truman.* Washington, DC: Central Intelligence Agency, 1994.

Warner, Michael, and J. Kenneth McDonald. *US Intelligence Community Reform since 1947.* Washington, DC: Center for the Study of Intelligence of Central Intelligence Agency, 2005.

Weinberg, Gerhard L. *A World at Arms: A Global History of World War II.* New York: Cambridge University Press, 1994.

Weiner, Tim. *Legacy of Ashes: The History of the CIA.* New York: Doubleday, 2007.

Weinstein, Allen. *Perjury: The Hiss-Chambers Case.* New York: Random House, 1997.

Wells, Samuel F., Jr. "Sounding the Tocsin: NSC 68 and the Soviet Threat." *International Security* 4 (Fall 1979): 116–58.

Wells, Sherrill Brown. *Jean Monnet: Unconventional Statesman.* Boulder, CO: Lynne Rienner, 2011.

Westad, Odd Arne. ed. *Brothers in Arms: The Rise and Fall of the Sino-Soviet Alliance, 1945–1963.* Washington, DC, and Stanford, CA: Woodrow Wilson Center Press and Stanford University Press, 1998.

——. *Decisive Encounters: The Chinese Civil War, 1946–1950.* Stanford, CA: Stanford University Press, 2003.

Williams, Robert C. *Klaus Fuchs: Atom Spy.* Cambridge, MA: Harvard University Press, 1987.

Williamson, Samuel R., Jr., and Steven L. Rearden. *The Origins of US Nuclear Strategy, 1945–1953.* New York: St. Martin's Press, 1993.

Zaloga, Steven J. *The Kremlin's Nuclear Sword: The Rise and Fall of Russia's Strategic Nuclear Forces, 1945–2000.* Washington, DC: Smithsonian Institution Press, 2002.

——. *Target America: The Soviet Union and the Strategic Arms Race, 1945–1964*. Novato, CA: Presidio Press, 1993.

Zhang, Shu Guang. *Mao's Military Romanticism: China and the Korean War, 1950–1953*. Lawrence: University Press of Kansas, 1995.

Zubok, Vladislav, and Constantine Pleshakov. *Inside the Kremlin's Cold War: From Stalin to Khrushchev*. Cambridge, MA: Harvard University Press, 1996.

INDEX

Italicized page numbers refer to photographs; figures, notes, and tables are indicated by f, n, and t following the page numbers.